Information Visualization

PERCEPTION FOR DESIGN

Fourth Edition

Colin Ware

ELSEVIER

Morgan Kaufmann is an imprint of Elsevier
50 Hampshire Street, 5th Floor, Cambridge, MA 02139, United States

Library of Congress Control Number: 2019955462

ISBN: 978-0-12-812875-6

Content Strategist: Stephen Merken
Content Development Manager: Rebecca Gruliow
Content Development Specialist: Beth LoGiudice
Publishing Services Manager: Deepthi Unni
Project Manager: Janish Paul

Typeset by TNQ Technologies

Printed in the United States of America

Last digit is the print number: 10 9 8 7 6 5 4 3

Contents

Preface

Cognitive neuroscience has made rapid progress in the last few years. When this book first appeared in the year 2000, there was no unified model of how we think visually. In the intervening years, the theory of *predictive cognition* has appeared and it provides a new and much more solid foundation for the later chapters of this edition. The brain is now regarded as first and foremost as a prediction engine. For example, theories of how we predict the future and remember the past are now unified. To recall the past we construct a likely scenario for what might have happened using a few recalled fragments together with relevant aspects of our cognitive model of the world, we do not simply pull it out of a memory like a video replay; predicting the future uses the same mechanisms except that we construct a likely future scenario based on a knowledge of the present and the same cognitive model of the world. We remember in order to predict the future and that the neural mechanisms are the same. In addition, the idea that cognition occurs in a distributed fashion, combining brain function with cognitive tools, such as visualizations, is now mainstream. We are all cognitive cyborgs. The later chapters of *Information Visualization: Perception for Design* have been rewritten, reorganized, and extended to reflect this new understanding. Chapter 10 is about interaction, Chapter 11 is about the visual thinking process, and Chapter 12 is about the design of efficient thinking tools.

In addition to these major changes, the book has been revised and updated throughout to take recent research into account. In many cases the changes are small, the replacement of a figure or a brief description of a recent study. In other places, whole sections, such as one on narrative, have undergone major rewrites to take incorporate current thinking on the subject.

Now let me tell you how this book came about. In 1973, after I had completed my master's degree in the psychology of vision, I was frustrated with the overly focused academic way of studying perception. Inspired by the legacy of freedom that seemed to be in the air in the late 1960s and early 1970s, I decided to become an artist and explore perception in a very different way. But after three years with only very small success, I returned, chastened, to the academic fold, though with a broader outlook, a great respect for artists, and a growing interest in the relationship between the way we present information and the way we see. After obtaining a doctorate in the psychology of perception at the University of Toronto, I still did not know what to do next. I moved into computer science, via the University of Waterloo and another degree, and have been working on data visualization, in one way or another, ever since. In a way, this book is a direct result of my ongoing attempt to reconcile the scientific study of perception with the need to convey meaningful information. It is about art in the sense that "form should follow function," and it is about science because the science of perception can tell us what kinds of patterns are most readily perceived.

Why should we be interested in visualization? Because the human visual system is a pattern seeker of enormous power and subtlety. The eye and the visual cortex of the brain form a massively parallel processor that provides the highest bandwidth channel into human cognitive centers. At higher levels of processing, perception and cognition are closely interrelated, which is the reason why the words "understanding" and "seeing" are synonymous. However, the visual system has its own rules. We can easily see patterns presented in certain ways, but if they are presented in other ways they become invisible. Thus, for example, the word *goggle*, shown in the accompanying figure, is much more visible in the version shown at the bottom than in the one at the top. This is despite the fact that identical parts of the letters are visible in each case and in the lower figure there is more irrelevant "noise" than in the upper figure. The rule that applies here, apparently, is that when the missing pieces are interpreted as foreground objects then continuity between the background letter fragments is easier to infer. The more general point is that when data is presented in certain ways the patterns can be readily perceived. If we can understand how perception works, our knowledge can be translated into guidelines for displaying information. Following perception-based rules, we can present our data in such a way that the important and informative patterns stand out. If we disobey these rules, our data will be incomprehensible or misleading.

This is a book about what the science of perception can tell us about visualization. There is a gold mine of information about how we see to be found in more than a century of work by vision researchers. The purpose of this book is to extract from that large body of research literature those design principles that apply to displaying information effectively.

Visualization can be approached in many ways. It can be studied in the art school tradition of graphic design. It can be studied within computer graphics as an area concerned with the algorithms needed to display data. It can be studied as part of semiotics, the constructivist approach to symbol systems. These are valid approaches, but a scientific approach based on perception uniquely promises design rules that transcend the vagaries of design fashion, being based on the relatively stable structure of the human visual system.

The study of perception by psychologists and neuroscientists has advanced enormously over the past three decades, and it is possible to say a great deal about how we see that is relevant to data visualization. Unfortunately, much of this information is stored in highly specialized journals and usually couched in language that is accessible only to the research scientist. The research literature concerning human perception is voluminous. Several hundred new papers are published every month, and a surprising number of them have some application in information display. This information can be extremely useful in helping us design better displays, both by avoiding mistakes and by coming up with original solutions. *Information Visualization: Perception for Design* is intended to make this science and its applications available to the nonspecialist. It should be of interest to anyone concerned with displaying data effectively. It is designed with a number of audiences in mind: multimedia designers specializing in visualization, researchers in both industry and academia, and anyone who has a deep interest in effective information display. The book presents extensive technical information about various visual acuities, thresholds, and other basic properties of human vision. It also contains, where possible, specific guidelines and recommendations.

The book is organized according to bottom-up perceptual principles. The first chapter provides a general conceptual framework and the theoretical context for a vision-science-based approach. The next four chapters discuss what can be considered to be the low-level perceptual elements of vision, color, texture, motion, and elements of form. These primitives of vision tell us about the design of attention-grabbing features and the best ways of coding data so that one object will be distinct from another. The later chapters move on to discussing what it takes to perceive patterns in data: first two-dimensional pattern perception and later three-dimensional space perception. Visualization design, data space navigation, interaction techniques, and visual problem solving are all discussed.

Here is a road map to the book: In general, the pattern for each chapter is first to describe some aspect of human vision and then to apply this information to some problem in visualization. The first chapters provide a foundation of knowledge on which the later chapters are built. Nevertheless, it is perfectly reasonable to randomly access the book to learn about specific topics. When it is needed, missing background information can be obtained by consulting the index.

Chapter 1: Foundations for an Applied Science of Data Visualization A conceptual framework for visualization design is based on human perception. The nature of claims about sensory representations is articulated, with special attention paid to the work of perception theorist J.J. Gibson. This analysis is used to define the differences between a design-based approach and an approach based on the science of perception. A classification of abstract data classes is provided as the basis for mapping data to visual representations.

Chapter 2: The Environment, Optics, Resolution, and the Display This chapter deals with the basic inputs to perception. It begins with the physics of light and the way light interacts with objects in the environment. Central concepts include the structure of light as it arrives at a viewpoint and the information carried by that light array about surfaces and objects available for interaction. This chapter goes on to discuss the basics of visual optics and issues such as how much detail we can resolve. Human acuity measurements are described and applied to display design.

The applications discussed include design of 3D environments, how many pixels are needed for visual display systems and how fast they should be updated, requirements for virtual reality display systems, how much detail can be displayed using graphics and text, and detection of faint targets.

Chapter 3: Lightness, Brightness, Contrast, and Constancy The visual system does not measure the amount of light in the environment; instead, it measures *changes* in light and color. How the brain uses this information to discover properties of the surfaces of objects in the environment is presented. This is related to issues in data coding and setting up display systems.

The applications discussed include integrating the display into a viewing environment, minimal conditions under which targets will be detected, methods for creating gray-scales to code data, and errors that occur because of contrast effects.

Chapter 4: Color This chapter introduces the science of color vision, starting with receptors and trichromacy theory. Color measurement systems and color standards are presented. The standard equations for the CIE standard and the *CIELUV* uniform color space are given. Opponent process theory is introduced and related to the way data should be displayed using luminance and chrominance.

The applications discussed include color measurement and specification, color selection interfaces, color coding symbols, colormapping scientific data, color reproduction, and color for multidimensional discrete data.

Chapter 5: Visual Salience: Finding and Reading Data Glyphs A "searchlight" model of visual attention is introduced to describe the way eye movements are used to sweep for information. The bulk of the chapter is taken up with a description of the massively parallel processes whereby the visual image is broken into elements of color, form, and motion. Preattentive processing theory is applied to critical issues of making one data object distinct from another. Methods for coding data so it can be perceptually integrated or separated are discussed.

The applications discussed include display for rapid comprehension, information coding, the use of texture for data coding, the design of symbology, and multidimensional discrete data display.

Chapter 6: Static and Moving Patterns This chapter looks at the process whereby the brain segments the world into regions and finds links, structure, and prototypical objects. These are converted into a set of design guidelines for information display.

The applications discussed include display of data so that patterns can be perceived, information layout, charts, node-link diagrams, and layered displays.

Chapter 7: Space Perception Increasingly, information display is being done in 3D virtual spaces as opposed to 2D screen-based layouts. The different kinds of spatial cues and the ways we perceive them are introduced. The latter half of the chapter is taken up with a set of spatial tasks and the perceptual issues associated with each.

The applications discussed include 3D information displays, stereo displays, the choice of 2D versus 3D visualization, 3D graph viewing, and virtual environments.

Chapter 8: Visual Objects and Data Objects Both image-based and 3D structure-based theories of object perception are reviewed. The concept of the object display is introduced as a method for using visual objects to organize information.

The applications discussed include presenting image data, using 3D structures to organize information, and the object display.

Chapter 9: Images, Narrative, and Gestures for Explanation Visual information and verbal information are processed in different ways and by different parts of the brain. Each has its own strengths and often both should be combined in a presentation. This chapter addresses when visual and verbal presentation should be used and how the two kinds of information should be linked. Also how visual narratives should be constructed.

The applications discussed include integrating images and words, visual storytelling, visual programming languages, and effective diagrams.

Chapter 10: Interacting with Visualizations Major interaction cycles are defined. Within this framework, low-level data manipulation, dynamic control over data views, and navigation through data spaces are discussed in turn.

The applications discussed include using visualization to discover patterns in data.

Chapter 11: Thinking with Visualizations This chapter begins by outlining the cognitive system involved in thinking with visualizations. These are processes that occur partly in a computer and partly in the visual brain of the user. The output of the computer is a series of visual images that are processed through the visual system of the user. The output of the user is a set of epistemic actions, such as clicking on an object or moving a slider, which result in the visualization being modified in some way by the computer.

The applications discussed include problem solving with visualization, design of interactive systems, and creativity.

Chapter 12: Designing Cognitively Efficient Visualizations A design methodology for producing cognitively efficient visualizations is introduced. The method involves seven steps (1) A high-level cognitive task description; (2) A data inventory; (3) Cognitive task refinement; (4) Identification of appropriate visualization types; (5) Applying visual thinking design patterns (VTDPs); (6) Prototype development; and (7) Evaluation and design refinement. Most of the chapter is devoted to a set of VTPDs. These are descriptions of interactive visualization methods that have demonstrated value, together with a description of perceptual and cognitive issues relating to their use and guidelines for applicability. Design patterns provide a method for taking into account perceptual and cognitive issues in designing interaction especially with respect to key bottlenecks in the visual thinking process, such as limited visual working memory capacity. They also provide a way of reasoning about semiotic issues in perceptual terms via the concept of the visual query.

These are exciting times for visualization design. The computer technology used to produce visualizations has reached a stage at which sophisticated interactive views of data can be produced on laptop and tablet computers and even phones. Newspapers such as *The New York Times* include interactive visualizations in their online editions. The trend toward more and more visual information is accelerating, and there is an explosion of new visualization techniques being invented to help us cope with our need to analyze huge and complex bodies of information. This creative phase will not last for long. With the dawn of a new technology, there is often only a short burst of creative design before the forces of standardization make what is new into what is conventional. Undoubtedly, many of the visualization techniques that are now emerging will become routine tools in the near future. Even badly designed things can become industry standards. Designing for perception and cognition can help us avoid such mistakes. If we can harness the knowledge that has accumulated regarding how we think visually, we can make more efficient cognitive tools for reasoning about data.

I wish to thank the many people who have helped me with this book. The people who most influenced the way I think about perception and visualization are Donald Mitchell, John Kennedy, and William Cowan. I have gained enormously by working with Larry Mayer in developing new tools to map the oceans, as well as with colleagues many, in particular, Kelly Booth, Dave Wells, Scott Mackenzie, Jennifer Dijkstra, John Kelley, and David Wiley. Working with scientists and engineers who have data and interesting visualization problems is what make the discipline of data visualization worthwhile. It has also been my good fortune to work with many talented graduate students and research assistants on visualization-related projects: Daniel Jessome, Richard Guitard, Timothy Lethbridge, Sean Riley, Serge Limoges, David Fowler, Stephen Osborne, Dale Chapman, Pat Cavanaugh, Ravin Balakrishnan, Mark Paton, Monica Sardesai, Cyril Gobrecht, Justine Hickey, Yanchao Li, Kathy Lowther, Li Wang, Greg Parker, Daniel Fleet, Jun Yang, Graham Sweet, Roland Arsenault, Natalie Webber, Poorang Irani, Jordan Lutes, Irina Padioukova, Glenn Franck, Lyn Bartram, Matthew Plumlee, Pete Mitchell, and Dan Pineo. Many of the ideas presented here have been refined through their efforts.

Peter Pirolli, Leo Frishberg, Doug Gillan, Nahum Gershon, Ron Rensink, Dave Gray, and Jarke van Wijk made valuable suggestions that helped me improve the manuscript. I also wish to thank the editorial staff at Morgan Kaufmann: Diane Cerra, Belinda Breyer, and Heather Scherer. Since Morgan Kaufman has been acquired by Elsevier, Nate McFadden and Beth LoGiudice have assisted in the procedures leading to publication. Finally, my wife, Dianne Ramey, read every word four times (!), made it readable, and kept me going.

Figure P.1 The word *goggle* is easier to read when the overlapping bars are visible. (*Redrawn from Nakayama, Shimono, and Silverman (1989).*)

About the Author

Colin Ware takes the "visual" in visualization very seriously. He has advanced degrees in both computer science (MMath, Waterloo) and the psychology of perception (Ph.D., Toronto). He has published over 160 articles in scientific and technical journals and at leading conferences, many of which relate to the use of color, texture, motion, and 3D in information visualization. In addition, Professor Ware also builds useful visualization software systems. He has been involved in developing 3D interactive visualization systems for ocean mapping for over 20 years and Fledermaus, a commercial product for visualization of ocean data, came originally from prototypes developed by him and his students. Current projects involve software to interpret data from tagged whales and visualizing ocean currents as well as optimizing colormaps. He is Director of the Data Visualization Research Lab in the Center for Coastal and Ocean Mapping at the University of New Hampshire.

CHAPTER ONE

Foundations for an Applied
Science of Data Visualization

In his book *The End of Science*, science writer John Horgan (1997) argued that science is finished except for the mopping up of details. He made a good case where physics is concerned. In that discipline, the remaining deep problems may involve generating so much energy as to require the harnessing of entire stars. Similarly, biology has its foundations in DNA and genetics and is now faced with the infinite but often tedious complexity of mapping genes into proteins through intricate pathways. What Horgan failed to recognize is that cognitive science has fundamental problems that are still to be solved. In particular, the mechanisms of the construction and storage of knowledge remain open questions. He implicitly adopted the physics-centric view of science, which holds that physics is the queen of sciences and in descending order come chemistry, then biology, with psychology barely acknowledged as a science at all. In this pantheon, sociology is regarded as somewhere on a par with astrology. This attitude is shortsighted. Chemistry builds on physics, enabling our understanding of materials; biology builds on chemistry, enabling us to understand the much greater complexity of living organisms; and psychology builds on neurophysiology, enabling us to understand the processes of cognition. At each level is a separate discipline greater in complexity and level of difficulty than those beneath. It is difficult to conceive of a value scale for which the mechanisms of thought are not of fundamentally greater interest and importance than the interaction of subatomic particles. Those who dismiss psychology as a pseudoscience have not been paying attention. Over the past few decades, enormous strides have been made in identifying the brain structures and cognitive mechanisms that have enabled humans to create the huge body of knowledge that now exists. But we need to go one step further and recognize that a person

Information Visualization. https://doi.org/10.1016/B978-0-12-812875-6.00001-3

working with the aid of thinking tools is much more cognitively powerful than that person alone with his or her thoughts. This has been true for a long time. Artifacts such as paper and pens, as well as techniques such as writing and drawing, have been cognitive tools for millennia.

As Hutchins (1995) so effectively pointed out, thinking is not something that goes on entirely, or even mostly, inside people's heads. Little intellectual work is accomplished with our eyes and ears closed. Most cognition is done as a kind of interaction with cognitive tools, pencils and paper, calculators, and, increasingly, computer-based intellectual supports and information systems. Neither is cognition mostly accomplished alone with a computer. It occurs as a process in systems containing many people and many cognitive tools. Since the beginning of science, diagrams, mathematical notations, and writing have been essential tools of the scientist. Now we have powerful interactive analytic tools, such as MATLAB, Tableau, and S-PLUS, together with databases. The entire fields of genomics and proteomics are built on computer storage and analytic tools. The social apparatus of the school system, the university, the academic journal, and the conference are obviously designed to support cognitive activity.

Cognition in engineering, banking, business, and the arts is similarly carried out through distributed cognitive systems. In each case, "thinking" occurs through interaction between individuals, using cognitive tools and operating within social networks. Hence, cognitive systems theory is a much broader discipline than psychology. This is emerging as the most interesting, difficult, and complex, yet fundamentally the most important, of sciences.

Visualizations are an increasingly important part of cognitive systems. Visual displays provide the highest bandwidth channel from the computer to the human. Indeed, we acquire more information through vision than through all of the other senses combined. The 20 billion or so neurons of the brain devoted to analyzing visual information provide a pattern-finding mechanism that is a fundamental component in much of our cognitive activity. Improving cognitive systems often means optimizing the search for data and making it easier to see important patterns. An individual working with a computer-based visual thinking tool is a cognitive system where the critical components are, on one side, the human visual system, a flexible pattern finder coupled with an adaptive decision-making cognitive mechanism, and, on the other side, the computational power and vast information resources of a computer coupled to the World Wide Web. Data analysis programs are themselves the encapsulation, in executable form, of the thinking process of many individuals who have already solved parts of the analytic problem. Interactive visualization is the interface between the two sides. Improving this interface can substantially improve the performance of the entire system.

Until recently, the term *visualization* meant constructing a visual image in the mind (Little, Fowler, & Coulson, 1972). It has now come to mean something more like a graphical representation of data or concepts. Thus, from being an internal construct of the mind, a visualization has become an external artifact supporting decision-making. The way visualizations can function as cognitive tools is the subject of this book.

Figure 1.1 Passamoquoddy Bay visualization. *(Data courtesy of the Canadian Hydrographic Service.)*

One of the greatest benefits of data visualization is the sheer quantity of information that can be rapidly interpreted if it is presented well. Fig. 1.1 shows a visualization derived from a multibeam echo sounder scanning part of Passamaquoddy Bay, between Maine in the United States and New Brunswick in Canada, where the tides are the highest in the world. Approximately one million measurements were made. Traditionally, this kind of data is presented in the form of a nautical chart with contours and spot soundings; however, when the data is converted to a height field and displayed using standard computer graphics techniques, many things become visible that were previously invisible on the chart. A pattern of features called *pockmarks* can immediately be seen, and it is easy to see how they form lines. Also visible are various problems with the data. The linear ripples (not aligned with the pockmarks) are errors in the data because the roll of the ship that took the measurements was not properly taken into account.

The Passamaquoddy Bay image highlights a number of the advantages of visualization:

- Visualization provides an ability to comprehend huge amounts of data. The important information from more than a million measurements is immediately available.

- Visualization allows the perception of emergent properties that were not anticipated. In this visualization, the fact that the pockmarks appear in lines is immediately evident. The perception of a pattern can often be the basis of a new insight. In this case, the pockmarks align with the direction of geological faults, suggesting a cause. They may be due to the release of gas.

- Visualization often enables problems with the data to become immediately apparent. A visualization commonly reveals things not only about the data itself but also about the way it is collected. With an appropriate visualization, errors and artifacts in the data often jump out at you. For this reason, visualizations can be invaluable in quality control.

- Visualization facilitates understanding of both large-scale and small-scale features of the data. It can be especially valuable in allowing the perception of patterns linking local features.

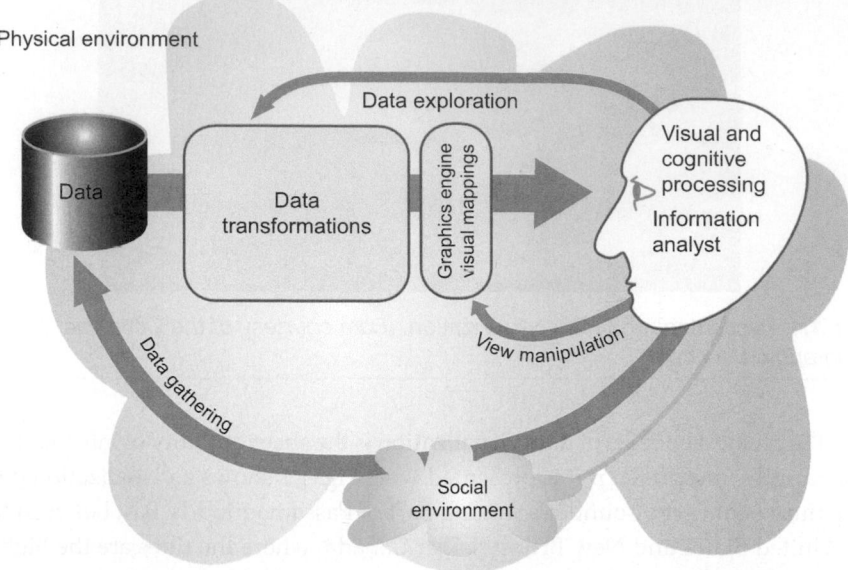

Figure 1.2 The visualization process.

- Visualization facilitates hypothesis formation. For example, the visualization in Fig. 1.1 led to questions about the how the pockmarks might have formed and motivated a research paper concerning the geological significance of the features (Gray, Mayer, & Hughes Clarke, 1997).

Visualization Stages

The process of data visualization includes four basic stages, combined in a number of feedback loops. These are illustrated in Fig. 1.2. The four stages consist of the following:

- The collection and storage of data.

- A preprocessing stage designed to transform the data into something that is easier to manipulate. Usually there is some form of data reduction to reveal selected aspects. Data exploration is the process of changing the subset that is currently being viewed.

- Mapping from the selected data to a visual representation, which is accomplished through computer algorithms that produce an image on the screen. User input can transform the mappings, highlight subsets, or transform the view. Generally this is done on the user's own computer.

- The human perceptual and cognitive system (the perceiver).

The longest feedback loop involves gathering data. A data seeker, such as a scientist or a stock-market analyst, may choose to gather more data to follow up on an interesting lead. Another loop controls the computational preprocessing that takes place prior to visualization. The analyst may feel that if the data is subjected to a certain transformation prior to visualization, it can be persuaded to give up its meaning. Sometimes the process is a search through a very large volume of data to find an important nugget. Finally, the visualization process itself may be highly interactive; for example, in three-dimensional (3D) data visualization, the scientist may "fly" to a different vantage point to better understand the emerging structures. Alternatively, a computer mouse may be used interactively to select the parameter ranges that are most interesting.

Both the physical environment and the social environment are involved in the data-gathering loop. The physical environment is a source of data, while the social environment determines in subtle and complex ways what is collected and how it is interpreted. In this book, the emphasis is on data, perception, and the various tasks to which visualization may be applied. In general, algorithms are discussed only insofar as they are related to perception. The computer is treated, with some reservations, as a universal tool for producing interactive graphics. This means that once we figure out the best way to visualize data for a particular task, we assume that we can construct algorithms to create the appropriate images.

The critical question is how best to transform the data into something that people can understand for optimal decision-making. Before plunging into a detailed analysis of human perception and how it applies in practice, however, we must establish the conceptual basis for the endeavor. The purpose of this discussion is to stake out a theoretical framework wherein claims about visualizations being "visually efficient" or "natural" can be pinned down in the form of testable predictions.

Experimental Semiotics Based on Perception

This book is about the applied science of visualization. It is based on the idea that the value of a good visualization is that it lets us see patterns in data and therefore the science of pattern perception can provide a basis for design decisions, but the claim that visualization can be based on science may be disputed. Let us look at the alternative view. Some scholars argue that visualization is best understood as a kind of learned language and not as a science at all. In essence, their argument is the following. Visualization is about diagrams and how they can convey meaning. Diagrams are made up of symbols, and symbols are based on social interaction. The meaning of a symbol is normally understood to be created by convention, which is established in the course of person-to-person communication. Diagrams are arbitrary and are effective in much the same way as the written words on this page are effective—we must learn the conventions of the language, and the better we learn them the clearer that language will be. Thus, one diagram may ultimately be as good as another; it is just a matter of learning the code, and the laws of perception are largely irrelevant. This view has strong philosophical proponents from the classical field of semiotics. Although it is not the position adopted here, the debate can help us define where vision research can assist us in designing better visualizations and where we would be wise to consult a graphic designer trained in an art college.

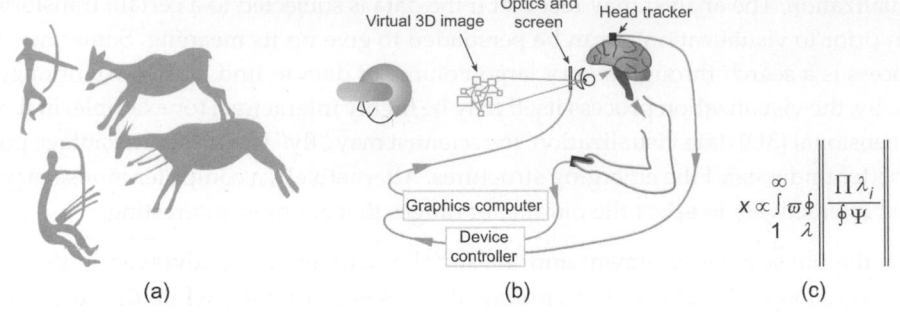

Figure 1.3 Three graphics. Each could be said to be a visualization.

Semiotics of Graphics

The study of symbols and how they convey meaning is called *semiotics*. This discipline was originated in the United States by C. S. Peirce and later developed in Europe by the French philosopher and linguist de Saussure (1959). Semiotics has been dominated mostly by philosophers and by those who construct arguments based on example rather than on formal experiment. In his great masterwork, *Semiology of Graphics*, Bertin (1983) attempted to classify all graphic marks in terms of how they could express data. For the most part, this work is based on his own judgment, although it is a highly trained and sensitive judgment. There are few references to theories of perception or scientific studies.

It is often claimed that visual languages are easy to learn and use, but what do we mean by the term *visual language*? Clearly not the writing on this page. Reading and writing take years of education to master and it can take almost as long to master some diagrams. Fig. 1.3 shows three examples of languages that have some claim to being visual. The first example of visual language is based on a cave painting. We can readily interpret human figures and infer that the people are using bows and arrows to hunt deer. The second example is a schematic diagram showing the interaction between a person and a computer in a virtual environment system; the brain in the diagram is a simplified picture, but it is a part of the anatomy that few have directly perceived. The arrows show data flows and are arbitrary conventions, as are the printed words.

The third example is the expression of a mathematical equation that is utterly obscure to all but the initiated. These examples clearly show that some visual languages are easier to "read" than others. But why? Perhaps it is simply that we have more experience with the kind of pictorial image shown in the cave painting and less with the mathematical notation. Perhaps the concepts expressed in the cave painting are more familiar than those in the equation.

The most profound threat to the idea that there can be a scientific basis for visualization design originates with Saussure. He defined a principle of arbitrariness as applying to the relationship between the symbol and the thing that is signified. Saussure was also a founding member of a group of structuralist philosophers and anthropologists who, although they disagreed on many fundamental issues, were unified in their general insistence that truth is relative to its social context. Meaning in one culture may be nonsense in another. A trash can as a visual symbol for deletion is meaningful only to those who know how trash cans are used. Thinkers such as Levi-Strauss, Barthes, and Lacan have condemned the cultural imperialism and intellectual arrogance implicit in applying our intellects to characterizing other cultures as "primitive." As a result, they have developed the theory that all meaning is relative to the culture. Indeed, meaning is created by society. They claim that we can interpret another culture only in the context of our own culture and using the tools of our own language. Languages are conventional means of communication in which the meanings of symbols are established through custom. Their point is that no one representation is "better" than another. All representations have value. All are meaningful to those who understand them and agree to their meanings. Because it seems entirely reasonable to consider visualizations as communications, their arguments strike at the root of the idea that there can be an applied science of visualization with the goal of establishing specific guidelines for better representations. We reject this view and instead argue that it is possible to have a new semiotics based not on philosophical claims for symbols being arbitrary, but instead on scientific evidence.

Are Pictures Arbitrary?

The question of whether pictures and diagrams are purely conventional or are perceptual symbols with special properties has been the subject of considerable scientific investigation. A good place to begin reviewing the evidence is the perception of pictures. There has been a debate over the past century between those who claim that pictures are every bit as arbitrary as words and those who believe that there may be a measure of similarity between pictures and the things that they represent. This debate is crucial to the theory presented here; if even "realistic" pictures do not embody a sensory language, it will be impossible to make claims that certain diagrams and other visualizations are better designed perceptually.

The nominalist philosopher, Goodman (1968), has delivered some of the more forceful attacks on the notion of similarity in pictures:

> *Realistic representation, in brief, depends not upon imitation or illusion or information but upon inculcation. Almost any picture may represent almost anything; that is, given picture and object there is usually a system of representation—a plan of correlation— under which the picture represents the object.*

For Goodman, realistic representation is a matter of convention; it "depends on how stereotyped the model of representation is, how commonplace the labels and their uses have become." Bieusheuvel (1947) expressed the same opinion: "The picture, particularly one printed on paper, is a highly conventional symbol, which the child reared in Western culture has learned to interpret." These statements, taken at face value, invalidate any meaningful basis for saying that a certain visualization is fundamentally better or more natural than another, for if even a realistic picture must be learned this would mean that all graphical representations of data are equally valid in that their conventions must be learned. If we accept this position, the best approach to designing visual languages would be to establish graphical conventions early and stick to them. It would not matter what the conventions were, only that we adhered to them in order to reduce the labor of learning new conventions.

In support of the nominalist argument, a number of anthropologists have reported expressions of puzzlement from people who encounter pictures for the first time. "A Bush Negro woman turned a photograph this way and that, in attempting to make sense out of the shadings of gray on the piece of paper she held" (Herskovits, 1948). The evidence related to whether or not we must learn to see pictures has been carefully reviewed and analyzed by Kennedy (1974). He rejected the strong position that pictures and other visual representations are entirely arbitrary. In the case of the reported puzzlement of people who are seeing pictures for the first time, Kennedy argued that these people are amazed by the technology rather than unable to interpret the picture. After all, a photograph is a remarkable artifact. What curious person would not turn it over to see if, perhaps, the reverse side contains some additional interesting information?

Here are two of the many studies that contradict the nominalist position and suggest that people can interpret pictures without training. Deregowski (1968) reported studies of adults and children in a remote area of Zambia who had very little graphic art. Despite this, these people could easily match photographs of toy animals with the actual toys. In an extraordinary but very different kind of experiment, Hochberg and Brooks (1962) raised their daughter nearly to the age of two in a house with no pictures. She was never read to from a picture book, and there were no pictures on the walls in the house. Although her parents could not completely block the child's exposure to pictures on trips outside the house, they were careful never to indicate a picture and tell the child that it was a representation of something. Thus, she had no social input telling her that pictures had any kind of meaning. When the child was finally tested she had a reasonably large vocabulary, and she was asked to identify objects in line drawings and in black-and-white photographs. Despite her lack of instruction in the interpretation of pictures, she was almost always correct in her answers, indicating that a basic understanding of pictures is not a learned skill.

Nevertheless, the issue of how pictures, especially line drawings, are able to unambiguously represent things is still not fully understood. Clearly, a portrait is a pattern of marks on a page; in a physical sense, it is utterly unlike the flesh-and-blood person it depicts. The most probable explanation is that, at some stage in visual processing, the pictorial outline of an object and the object itself excite similar neural processes (Pearson, Hanna, & Martinez, 1990). This view is made plausible by the ample evidence that one of the most important products of early visual processing is the extraction of linear features in the visual array. These may be either the visual boundaries of objects or the lines in a line drawing. The nature of these mechanisms is discussed further in Chapter 6.

Figure 1.4 Two graphical methods for showing the same set of relationships between entities.

When we turn to diagrams and nonpictorial visualizations, it is clear that convention must play a greater role. Fig. 1.3(b) is not remotely "like" any scene in the real world under any system of measurement. Nevertheless, we can argue that many elements in it are constructed in ways that for perceptual reasons make the diagram easy to interpret. The lines that connect the various components, for example, are a notation that is easy to read, because the visual cortex of the brain contains mechanisms specifically designed to seek out continuous contours. Other possible graphical notations for showing connectivity would be far less effective. Fig. 1.4 shows two different conventions for demonstrating relationships between entities. The connecting lines on the left are much more effective than the symbols on the right.

Sensory versus Arbitrary Symbols

In this book, the word *sensory* is used to refer to symbols and aspects of visualizations that derive their expressive power from their ability to use the perceptual processing power of the brain without learning. The word *arbitrary* is used to define aspects of representation that must be learned, because the representations have no perceptual basis. For example, the written word *dog* bears no perceptual relationship to any actual animal. Probably very few graphical languages consist of entirely arbitrary conventions, and probably none is entirely sensory; however, the sensory-versus-arbitrary distinction is important. If well designed, sensory representations are effective because they are well matched to the first stages of neural processing. They tend to be stable across individuals, cultures, and time. A circle represents a bounded region for everyone. Conversely, arbitrary conventions derive their power from culture and are therefore dependent on the particular cultural milieu of an individual.

The theory that a visual representation can be good or poor depending on how well it fits with visual processing is ultimately based on the idea that the human visual system has evolved as a specialized instrument to perceive the physical world. It rejects the idea that the visual system can adapt to any universe. It was once widely held that the brain at birth was an undifferentiated neural net, capable of configuring itself to perceive in any world, no matter how strange. According to this theory, if a newborn human infant were to be born into a world with entirely different rules for the propagation of light, that infant would nevertheless learn to see. Partly, this view came from the fact that all cortical brain tissue looks more or less the same, a uniform pinkish

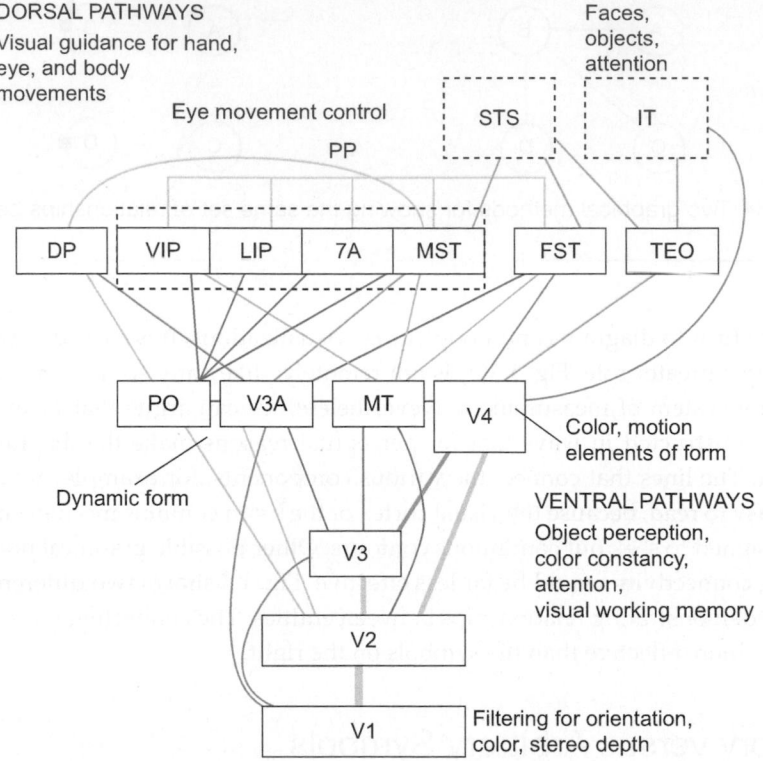

Figure 1.5 The major visual pathways of the Macaque monkey. This diagram is included to illustrate the structural complexity of the visual system and because a number of these areas are referenced in different sections of this book. V1 to V4, visual areas 1 to 4; *PO*, parietooccipital area; *MT*, middle temporal area; *IT*, inferotemporal cortex. *(Redrawn from Distler et al. (1993))*

gray, so it was thought to be functionally undifferentiated. This tabula rasa view has been overthrown as neurologists have come to understand that the brain has a great many specialized regions. Fig. 1.5 shows the major neural pathways between different parts of the brain involved in visual processing (Distler, Boussaoud, Desmone, & Ungerleider, 1993). Although much of the functionality remains unclear, this diagram represents an amazing achievement and summarizes the work of dozens of researchers. These structures are present in both higher primates and humans. The brain is clearly not an undifferentiated mass; it is more like a collection of highly specialized parallel processing machines with high-bandwidth interconnections. The entire system evolved to extract information from the world in which we live, not from some other environment with entirely different physical properties.

Certain basic elements are necessary for the visual system to develop normally; for example, cats reared in a world consisting only of vertical stripes develop distorted visual cortices, with an unusual preponderance of vertical-edge detectors. Nevertheless, the basic elements for the development of normal vision are present in all but the most abnormal circumstances. The interaction of the growing nervous system with everyday reality leads to a more or less standard visual system. This should not surprise us; the everyday world has ubiquitous properties that are common to all environments. All earthly environments consist of objects with well-defined surfaces, surface textures, surface colors, and a variety of shapes. Objects exhibit temporal persistence—they do not randomly appear and vanish, except when there are specific causes. At a more fundamental level, light travels in straight lines and reflects off surfaces in certain ways. The law of gravity continues to operate. Given these ubiquitous properties of the everyday world, the evidence suggests that we all develop essentially the same visual systems, irrespective of cultural milieu.

Monkeys and even cats have visual structures very similar to those of humans; for example, although Fig. 1.5 is based on the visual pathways of the Macaque monkey, a number of lines of evidence show that the same structures exist in humans. First, the same areas can be identified anatomically in humans and animals. Second, specific patterns of blindness occur that point to the same areas having the same functions in humans and animals; for example, if the brain is injured in area V4, patients suffer from achromatopsia (Milner & Goodale, 1995; Zeki, 1992). These patients perceive only shades of gray, and they cannot recall colors from times before the lesion was formed. Color processing occurs in the same region of the monkey cortex. Third, new research imaging technologies, such as positron emission tomography (PET) and functional magnetic resonance imaging (fMRI), show that in response to colored or moving patterns the same areas are active in people as in the Macaque monkey (Beardsley, 1997; Zeki, 1992). The key implication of this is that, because we all have the same visual system, it is likely that we all see in the same way, at least as a first approximation. Hence, the same visual designs will be effective for all of us.

Sensory aspects of visualizations derive their expressive power from being well designed to stimulate the visual sensory system. In contrast, arbitrary, conventional aspects of visualizations derive their power from how well they are learned. Sensory and arbitrary representations differ radically in the ways they should be studied. In the former case, we can apply the full rigor of the experimental techniques developed by sensory neuroscience, while in the latter case visualizations and visual symbols can best be studied with the very different interpretive methodology, derived from the structuralist social sciences. With sensory representations, we can also make claims that transcend cultural and racial boundaries. Claims based on a generalized perceptual processing system will apply to all humans, with obvious exceptions such as color blindness.

This distinction between the sensory and social aspects of the symbols used in visualization also has practical consequences for research methodology. It is not worth expending a huge effort carrying out intricate and highly focused experiments to study something that is only this year's fashion; however, if we can develop generalizations that apply to large classes of visual representations, and for a long time, the effort is worthwhile. If we accept the distinction between sensory and arbitrary codes,

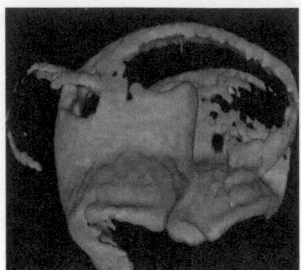

Figure 1.6 The expanding wavefront of a chemical reaction is visualized (Cross et al., 1997). Even though this process is alien to most of us, the shape of the structure is readily perceived.

we nevertheless must recognize that most visualizations are hybrids. In the obvious case, they contain both pictures and words, but in many cases the sensory and arbitrary aspects of a representation are much more difficult to tease apart. There is an intricate interweaving of learned conventions and hardwired processing. The distinction is not as clean as we would like, but there are ways of distinguishing the different kinds of codes.

Properties of Sensory Representation

The following paragraphs summarize some of the important properties of sensory representations:

> *Understanding without training.* A sensory code is one for which the meaning is perceived without additional training. Usually, all that is necessary is for the audience to understand that some communication is intended. For example, it is immediately clear that the image in Fig. 1.6 has an unusual spiral structure. Even though this visual represents a physical process that cannot actually be seen, the detailed shape can be understood because it has been expressed using an artificial shading technique to make it look like a 3D solid object. Our visual systems are built to perceive the shapes of 3D surfaces.

> *Resistance to alternative denotation.* Many sensory phenomena, such as the illusions shown in Fig. 1.7, persist despite the knowledge that they are illusory. We can tell someone that the lines are the same length, but they will still seem to that person as different. When such illusions occur in diagrams, they are likely to be misleading. What is important to the present argument, though, is that some aspects of perception will be taken as facts that we contradict at our peril; for example, using connecting lines to denote that two objects are *not* (conceptually) connected would be a very bad idea, as it would contradict a deep perceptual metaphor.

> *Sensory immediacy.* The processing of certain kinds of sensory information is hardwired and fast. We can represent information in certain ways that are

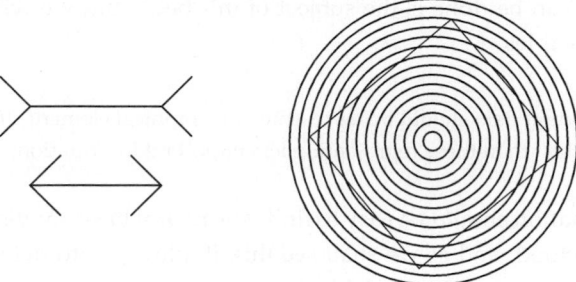

Figure 1.7 In the Muller-Lyer illusion on the left, the horizontal line in the upper figure appears longer than the one below. On the right, the rectangle appears distorted into a pincushion shape.

Figure 1.8 Five regions of texture. Some areas are easier to distinguish from others. *(Adapted from Beck (1966).)*

neurally processed in parallel. This point is illustrated in Fig. 1.8, which shows five different textured regions. The two regions on the left are very difficult to separate; the upright Ts and inverted Ts appear to be a single patch. The region of oblique Ts is easy to differentiate from the neighboring region of inverted Ts. The circles are the easiest to distinguish (Beck, 1966). The way in which the visual system divides the visual world into regions is called *segmentation*. The evidence suggests that this is a function of early rapid-processing systems. (Chapter 5 presents a theory of texture discrimination.)

Cross-cultural validity. A sensory code will, in general, be understood across cultural boundaries. These may be national boundaries or the boundaries between different user groups. Instances in which a sensory code is misunderstood occur when some group has dictated that a sensory code be used arbitrarily in contradiction to the natural interpretation. In this case, the natural response to a particular pattern will, in fact, be wrong.

The foregoing analysis leads us to our first guideline.

[G1.1] Design graphic representations of data by taking into account human sensory capabilities in such a way that important data elements and data patterns can be quickly perceived.

Exactly how this can be done is the subject of this book, but we will begin with two fundamental principles.

> **[G1.2]** Important data should be represented by graphical elements that are more visually distinct than those representing less important information.

Important information should be easy to find. The neural basis for visual search is now quite well understood, and as we shall see this, it allows us to determine with some precision which items are more findable than others.

> **[G1.3]** Greater numerical quantities should be represented by more distinct graphical elements.

This can be accomplished, for example, by making those elements, larger, more vividly colored, or more strongly textured. The basis for this claim is that even nonvisual thought as embodied in spoken and written language is grounded in sensory metaphors (Pinker, 2007).

Notice that guidelines G1.2 and G1.3 propose using the same kind of coding (visual distinctness) for different purposes, and this can lead to design conflicts. Also, sometimes a large quantity of something may not be especially important. Indeed, if we are running out of a critical asset (such as petroleum in the gas tank), we will want whatever represents this small quantity to be visually distinct. Ultimately, deciding how to use visual coding principles is a design issue. In any complex design problem, the optimal perceptually based coding solution may not be possible for each individual piece of information because some graphic resource (e.g., a bright color) may have already been used. It is only possible to provide perceptually based design guidelines for relatively simple situations. Where requirements are complex, it is the designer's task to make the right choices and use graphic resources wisely. The solution in the gas tank problem, for example, can be something additional and very visually salient—a blinking light—to indicate the shortage of gas.

Testing Claims About Sensory Representations

Entirely different methodologies are appropriate to the study of representations of the sensory and arbitrary types. In general, the study of sensory representations can employ the scientific methods of vision researchers and biologists. The study of arbitrary conventional representations is best done using the techniques of the social sciences, such as sociology and anthropology; philosophers and cultural critics have much to contribute. Appendix C provides a brief summary of the research methodologies that apply to the study of sensory representations. All are based on the concept of the controlled experiment. For more detailed information on techniques used in vision research and human-factors engineering, see Palmer (1999) and Wickens (1992).

Representations That Are Arbitrary

One way of looking at the sensory-versus-arbitrary distinction is in terms of the time the two modes have taken to develop. Sensory codes are the products of the millions of years it has taken for our visual systems to evolve. The development of arbitrary conventional representations (such as number systems) occurred over the past thousands of years, but many more have had only a few decades of development. High-performance interactive computer graphics have greatly enhanced our capability to create new codes. We can now control motion and color with flexibility and precision. For this reason, we are currently witnessing an explosive growth in the invention of new graphic codes.

Arbitrary codes are by definition socially constructed. The word *dog* is meaningful because we all agree on its meaning and we teach our children the meaning. The word *carrot* would do just as well, except we have already agreed on a different meaning for that word. In this sense, words are arbitrary; they could be swapped and it would make no difference, as long as they are used consistently from the first time we encounter them. Arbitrary visual codes are often adopted when groups of scientists and engineers construct diagramming conventions for new problems that arise. Examples include circuit diagrams used in electronics, diagrams used to represent molecules in chemistry, and the unified modeling language used in software engineering. Of course, many designers will intuitively use perceptually valid forms in the codes, but many aspects of these diagrams are entirely conventional. Arbitrary codes have the following characteristics:

Hard to learn. It takes a child hundreds of hours to learn to read and write, even if the child has already acquired spoken language. The graphic codes of the alphabet and their rules of combination must be laboriously learned. The Chinese character set is reputed to be even harder to work with than the Roman.

Easy to forget. Arbitrary conventional information that is not overlearned can easily be forgotten. It is also the case that arbitrary codes can interfere with each other. In contrast, sensory codes cannot be forgotten.

Embedded in culture and applications. Different cultures have created their own distinctive symbol sets. An Asian student in my laboratory was working on an application to visualize changes in computer software. She chose to represent deleted entities with the color green and new entities with red. I suggested to her that red is normally used for a warning, while green symbolizes renewal, so perhaps the reverse coding would be more appropriate. She protested, explaining that green symbolizes death in China, while red symbolizes luck and good fortune.

Many graphical symbols are transient and tied to a local culture or application. Think of the graffiti of street culture or the hundreds of new graphical icons that are being created on the Internet. These tend to convey meaning with little or no syntax to bind the symbols into a formal structure. On the other hand, in some cases, arbitrary

Figure 1.9 Two methods for representing the first five digits. The code given below is easier to learn but is not easily extended.

representations can be almost universal and have elaborate grammars associated with their use. The Arabic numerals shown in Fig. 1.9 are used widely throughout the world. Even if a more perceptually valid code could be constructed, the effort would be wasted. The designer of a new symbology for Air Force or Navy charts must live within the confines of existing symbols because of the huge amount of effort invested in the standards. We have many standardized visualization techniques that work well and are solidly embedded in work practices, and attempts to change them would be foolish. In many applications, good design is standardized design.

Conventional symbol systems persist because they have become embedded in ways in which we think about problems. For many geologists, the topographic contour map is the ideal way to understand relevant features of the Earth's surface. They often resist shaded computer graphics representations, even though these appear to be much more intuitively understandable to most people. Contour maps are embedded in cartographic culture and training.

> **Formally powerful.** Arbitrary graphical notations can be constructed that embody formally defined, powerful languages. Mathematicians have created hundreds of graphical languages to express and communicate their concepts. The expressive power of mathematics to convey abstract concepts in a formal, rigorous way is unparalleled; however, the languages of mathematics are extremely difficult to learn (at least for most people). Clearly, the fact that something is expressed in a visual code does not mean that it is easy to understand.

The foregoing analysis leads to our fourth guideline.

[G1.4] Graphical symbol systems should be standardized within and across applications.

It is important, however, that they first be designed to be perceptually efficient.

The Study of Arbitrary Conventional Symbols

The appropriate methodology for studying arbitrary symbols is very different from that used to study sensory symbols. The tightly focused, narrow questions addressed by psychophysics are wholly inappropriate to investigating visualization in a cultural context. A more appropriate methodology for the researcher of arbitrary symbols may derive from the work of anthropologists such as Geertz (1973), who advocated "thick description." This approach is based on careful observation, immersion in culture, and an effort to keep "the analysis of social forms closely tied … to concrete social events and occasions." Also borrowing from the social sciences, Carroll and coworkers developed an approach to understanding complex user interfaces that they call *artifact analysis* (Carroll, 1989). In this approach, user interfaces (and presumably visualization techniques) are best viewed as artifacts and studied much as an anthropologist studies cultural artifacts of a religious or practical nature. Formal experiments are out of the question in such circumstances, and if they were actually carried out, they would undoubtedly change the very symbols being studied. Unfortunately for researchers, sensory and arbitrary aspects of symbols are closely intertwined in many representations, and although they have been presented here as distinct categories the boundary between them is very fuzzy. There is no doubt that culture influences cognition; it is also true that the more we know, the more we perceive. Pure instances of sensory or arbitrary coding may not exist, but this does not mean that the analysis is invalid. It simply means that for any given example we must be careful to determine which aspects of the visual coding belong in each category.

In general, our scientific understanding of how visualizations work is still in its infancy. There is much about visualization and visual communication that is more craft than science. For the visualization designer, training in art and design is at least as useful as training in perceptual psychology. For those who wish to do good design, the study of design by example is generally most appropriate, but the science of perception can provide a scientific basis for design rules, and it can suggest entirely new design ideas and methods for displaying data that have not been tried before.

Gibson's Affordance Theory

The great perception theorist J. J. Gibson brought about radical changes in how we think about perception with his theories of ecological optics, affordances, and direct perception. Aspects of each of these theoretical concepts are discussed throughout this book. We begin with affordance theory (Gibson, 1979).

Gibson argued that we perceive in order to operate on the environment. Perception is designed for action. Gibson called the perceivable possibilities for action *affordances*, and a cornerstone of his theory is that affordances are perceived in a *direct* and immediate way. They are not *inferred* from sensory clues. This theory is clearly attractive from the perspective of visualization, because the goal of most visualization is decision-making. Thinking about perception in terms of action is likely to be much more useful than thinking about how two adjacent spots of light influence each other's appearance (which is the typical approach of classical psychophysicists). Much of Gibson's work was in direct opposition to the approach of theorists who reasoned that we must deal with perception from the bottom-up, as with geometry. The pre-Gibsonian theorists tended to have an atomistic view of the world. They thought we should first understand how single points of light were sensed, and then we could work on understanding how pairs of lights interacted. Gradually, building layers of theory from the bottom-up, we would eventually gain understanding of how people

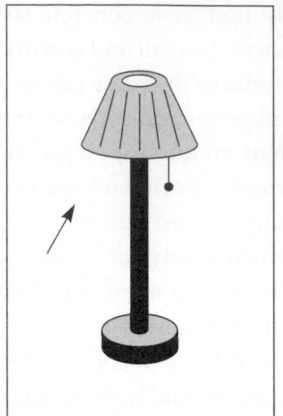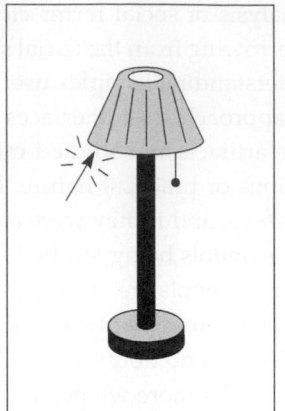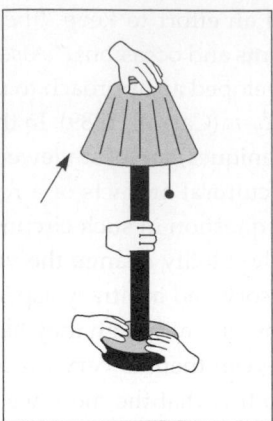

Figure 1.10 Cartoon cues are used to illustrate what interactions are possible. *(From Houde (1992). Reproduced with permission.)*

perceive the vibrant, dynamic visual world in which we live. Gibson took a radically different, top-down approach. He claimed that we do not perceive points of light; rather, we perceive possibilities for action. We perceive surfaces for walking, handles for pulling, space for navigating, tools for manipulating, and so on.

In general, our whole evolution has been geared toward perceiving useful possibilities for action. In an experiment that supports this view, Warren (1984) showed that subjects were capable of accurate judgments of the "climbability" of staircases. These judgments depended on their own leg lengths. Gibson's affordance theory is tied to a theory of direct perception. He claimed that we perceive affordances of the environment directly and immediately, not indirectly by piecing together evidence from our senses.

Translating the affordance concept into the interface domain, we might construct the following principle: A good interface has affordances that make the user's task easy; for example, if we have a task of moving an object in 3D space, it should have clear handles to use in rotating and lifting the object. Fig. 1.10 shows a design for a 3D object manipulation interface from Houde (1992). When an object is selected, "handles" appear that allow the object to be lifted or rotated. The function of these handles is made more explicit by illustrations of gripping hands that show the affordances.

Gibson's theory, however, presents problems if it is taken literally. According to Gibson, affordances are physical properties of the environment that we directly perceive. Many theorists, unlike Gibson, think of perception as a very active process. They show that the brain continuously predicts properties of the environment based on the available sensory evidence, and continuously updates and tests these predictions. Gibson rejected this view in favor of the idea that our visual system is tuned to perceiving the visual world and that we perceive it accurately except under extraordinary circumstances. He preferred to concentrate on the visual system as a whole and not to break perceptual processing down into components and operations. He used the term *resonating* to describe the way the visual system responds to properties of the environment. This view has been remarkably influential and has radically changed the way vision researchers think about perception; nevertheless, few would accept it today in its pure form.

There are three problems with Gibson's direct perception approach in developing theories of how visualizations work. The first problem is that even if perception of the environment is direct, it is clear that visualization of data through computer graphics is very indirect. Typically, there are many layers of processing between the data and its representation. In some cases, the source of the data may be microscopic or otherwise invisible. The source of the data may be quite abstract, such as company statistics in a stock-market database. Direct perception is not a meaningful concept in these cases.

Second, there are no clear physical affordances in any graphical user interface. To say that a screen button "affords" pressing in the same way as a flat surface affords walking is to stretch the theory beyond reasonable limits. In the first place, it is not even clear that a real-world button affords pressing. In another culture, these little bumps might be perceived as rather dull architectural decorations. Clearly, the use of buttons is arbitrary; we must learn that buttons, when pressed, do interesting things in the real world. Perception and action are linked in even more indirect ways when we use a computer; for instance, we must learn that a picture of a button can be "pressed" using a mouse, a cursor, or yet another button. This is far from being direct interaction with the physical world.

Third, Gibson's rejection of visual mechanisms is a problem. To take but one example, much that we know about color is based on years of experimentation, analysis, and modeling of the perceptual mechanisms. Color television and many other display technologies are based on an understanding of these mechanisms. To reject the importance of understanding visual mechanisms would be to reject most of vision research as irrelevant. This entire book is based on the premise that an understanding of perceptual mechanisms is basic to providing visualization designers with sound design principles. The modern theory of predictive perception is the basis for the final two chapters.

Despite these reservations, Gibson's theories influence much of this book. The concept of affordances, loosely construed, can be extremely useful from a design perspective. The idea suggests that we build interfaces that beg to be operated in appropriate and useful ways. We should make virtual handles for turning, virtual buttons for pressing. If components are designed to work together, this should be made perceptually evident, perhaps by creating shaped sockets that afford the attachment of one object to another. This is the kind of design approach advocated by Norman in his famous book, *The Psychology of Everyday Things* (1988). Nevertheless, on-screen widgets present affordances only in an indirect sense. They borrow their power from our ability to represent pictorially, or otherwise, the affordances of the everyday world. Therefore, we can be inspired by affordance theory to produce good designs, but we cannot expect much help from that theory in building an applied science of visualization.

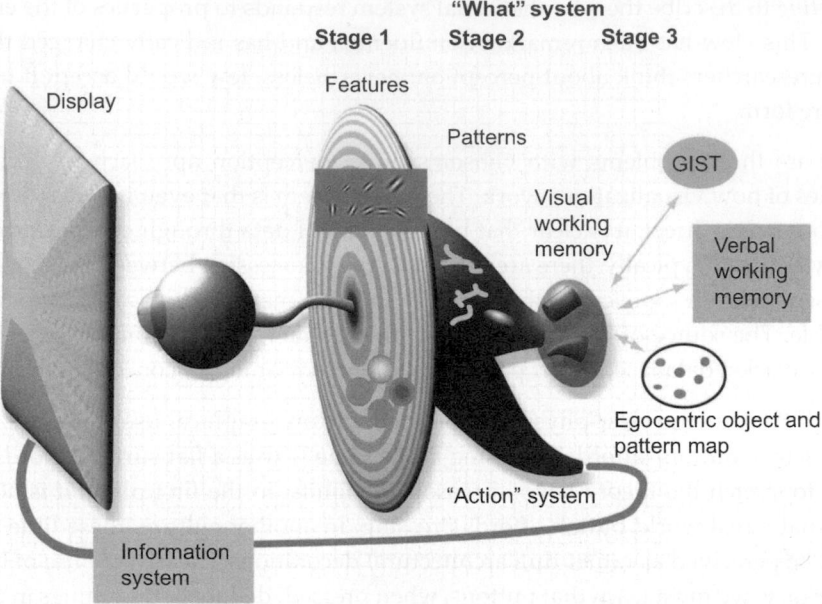

Figure 1.11 A three-stage model of visual information processing.

A Model of Perceptual Processing

In this section, we introduce a simplified information processing model of human visual perception. As Fig. 1.5 shows, there are many subsystems in vision, and we should always be wary of overgeneralization. Still, an overall conceptual framework is useful in providing a starting point for more detailed analysis. Fig. 1.11 gives a broad schematic overview of a three-stage model of perception. In Stage 1, information is processed in parallel to extract basic features of the environment. In Stage 2, active processes of pattern perception pull out structures and segment the visual scene into regions of different color, texture, and motion patterns. In Stage 3, the information is reduced to only a few objects held in visual working memory by active mechanisms of attention to form the basis of visual thinking.

Stage 1. Parallel Processing to Extract Low-Level Properties of the Visual Scene

Visual information is first processed by large arrays of neurons in the eye and in the primary visual cortex at the back of the brain. Individual neurons are selectively tuned to certain kinds of information, such as the orientation of edges or the color of a patch of light. In Stage 1 processing, billions of neurons work in parallel, extracting features from every part of the visual field simultaneously. Treisman (1985) described the result as a set of feature maps. This parallel processing proceeds whether we like it or not and is largely independent of what we choose to attend to (although not where we look). It is also rapid. If we want people to understand information quickly, we should present it in such a way that it can be easily detected by these large, fast computational systems in the brain. Important characteristics of Stage 1 processing include the following:

- Rapid parallel processing

- Extraction of features, orientation, color, texture, and movement patterns

- Transitory nature of information, which is briefly held in an iconic store

- Bottom-up, data-driven processing

- Retuning of the feature extraction mechanisms, based on visual task requirements

- Serving as the basis for signaling the visual salience of elements in displays

Stage 2. Pattern Perception

At the second stage of visual analysis, rapid active processes divide the visual field into regions and simple patterns, such as continuous contours, regions of the same color, and regions of the same texture. Patterns of motion are also very important, although the use of motion as an information code is relatively neglected in visualization. The pattern-finding stage of visual processing is extremely flexible, influenced both by the massive amount of information available from Stage 1 parallel processing and by the top-down action of attention driven by visual queries. Marr (1982) called this stage of processing the *2-1/2D sketch*. Rensink (2002) called it a *proto-object flux* to emphasize its dynamic nature. Important characteristics of Stage 2 processing include the following:

- Slower serial processing

- Top-down attention being critical to the formation of objects and patterns pulled out from the feature maps

- A small number (one to three) patterns becoming "bound" and held for a second or two under top-down attentional processes

- Different pathways for object recognition and visually guided hand motion (the perception and action channels)

There is a major fork in the pattern-processing pathway, with one branch leading to object perception and the other branch leading to parts of the brain involved in the control of actions. This is the basis for the two-visual-system theory: one system for locomotion and action, called the *action system*, and another for object identification, called the *what system*. A detailed and convincing account of it can be found in Milner and Goodale (1995).

Stage 3. Visual Cognition

At higher levels, what we perceive is more a property of what we are doing and what problems we are trying to solve than what is actually coming in through our eyes.

In order to use an external visualization, we construct a sequence of visual queries that are answered through visual search strategies. At this level, only a few objects can be held at a time in visual working memory; they are constructed from the available patterns that may provide answers to the visual query and from information stored in long-term memory related to the task. For example, if we use a road map to look for a route, the visual query will trigger a search for connected red contours (representing major highways) between two visual symbols (representing cities).

Describing the visual system as a set of processing stages implies that visual information flows only from Stage 1 through Stage 2 to Stage 3. When a *new* image flashes on the screen in front of our eyes, or we make an eye movement to a part of the world we have not seen before, this is the only way information can flow. But, immediately following the upflow of information there is a top-down signal that consolidates and enhances what is happening at earlier stages. The entire system is being constantly tuned from top to bottom based on mental predictions and on what will be most useful to us. Furthermore, where we direct our eyes on the next fixation is dependent on our current visual query and what we have just taken in.

The generic name for this is *attention*. Attention is a multifaceted pervasive set of processes involving the entire visual system. Even the Stage 1 feature maps are subject to attention being tuned to be more sensitive to what we need to find. The Stage 2 patterns are the very essence of attention, and where our brains direct our eyes to move determines what will become the focus of our attention in the next instant. Eye movements are literally acts of reallocation of attention.

One of the more radical ideas in this book is that the effects of attention can be propagated outside of the brain into the world through cleverly designed interactive visualizations that cause information we are interested in to be highlighted on the screen.

Beyond the visual processing stages shown in Fig. 1.11 are interfaces to other subsystems. The visual object identification process interfaces with the verbal linguistic subsystems of the brain so that words can be connected to images. The action system interfaces with the motor systems that control muscle movements.

The three-stage model of perception is the basis for the organization of the first seven chapters of this book. We work our way up from early to late stages of processing. Later chapters are more concerned with the system as a whole and the way visual thinking occurs as a process. The later chapters also discuss the interfaces between perceptual and other cognitive processes, such as those involved in language and decision-making.

Costs and Benefits of Visualization

The ultimate goal of interactive visualization design is to optimize applications so that they help us perform cognitive work more efficiently. Optimizing a system requires that we have at least some conception of value. We use visualizations because they help us solve problems faster or better, or they let us learn something new, and these activities usually have monetary value. The following analysis is based in part on an economic model of the value of visualizations carried out by Jarke van Wijk (2006), but it differs in some important respects. Where van Wijk took *knowledge gain* to be the value of visualization we shall use the broader concept of *cognitive work*, as visualization can help us with many routine tasks: Executing trades on the stock market, cooking with a recipe, and working a cash register all involve cognitive work, part of which may be achieved through a form of visual thinking. The cash register in a fast-food restaurant has many specialized buttons relating to distinct combinations of fried potatoes, drinks, and different types of sandwiches. With the right layout and graphic design, a worker will process orders more rapidly with less training. At the other end of the spectrum is a major scientific discovery arising through the use of a visualization tool. In either case, the cognitive work has monetary value. This is not to deny that sometimes we pursue knowledge for its own sake and that it can be extremely difficult to place a value on a particular insight. But, if we are to compare the costs of producing a visual thinking tool with the value of using it, then we must use the same units on both sides of the equation and money is the obvious token of value. Because it is so difficult to quantify the value of knowledge, a highly detailed analysis is pointless—why add variables that we cannot quantify? Nevertheless, there are useful insights to be gained from first-order approximations.

A visualization can be viewed from two important perspectives: the perspective of the developer and the perspective of the user.

The basic user costs are:

> *(The time to learn to use the visualization * the value of the user's time) +*
> *(the time spent carrying out the work * the value of the user's time)*

The user benefits are:

> *The cognitive work done * the value of the work*

There are some straightforward implications of this.

> **[G1.5]** Where two or more tools can perform the same task, choose the one that allows for the most valuable work to be done per unit time.

This rather obvious guideline is the basis for much of the content of this book, because in many cases we will be considering alternative visual representations of the same data for the same purpose. Efficient visualizations allow people to find important patterns faster and thereby perform work in less time.

> **[G1.6]** Consider adopting novel design solutions only when the estimated payoff is substantially greater than the cost of learning to use them.

Learning to interpret a novel data representation or a novel mode of interaction can require a significant effort. It is often not worth learning a new tool, especially if the number of times it will be used is uncertain.

People use a variety of different thinking tools that are inconsistent with one another in the sense that operations must be carried out with different commands and the same data types are represented using different visual symbols. There is a cognitive cost to this, both in learning and continuous use.

> **[G1.7]** Unless the benefit of a novel design outweighs the cost of inconsistency, adopt tools that are consistent with other commonly used tools.

This guideline can be extremely frustrating for the designer of innovative solutions. It often means that something that seems to be clearly and measurably superior when viewed in isolation is in fact not useful overall.

Now look at the developer side of the ledger.

The basic developer costs are:

> *The cost to design and implement a cognitive tool + the cost to market + the cost to manufacture + the cost to service*

The developer benefits are

> *(The number of units sold * the price per unit) + the revenue from maintenance contracts*

With computer software, manufacturing costs are essentially zero and the cost to service is typically covered by maintenance. Profit can be approximated as follows:

> *Profit = (Units sold * price) − (cost to create + cost to market)*

Significant revenue can come by selling a lot of cheap things or selling a few expensive ones. Examples of high-volume visualizations are the weather maps used by millions of people everyday. Examples of customized, high-value visualizations are the tools used to control spacecraft. Because tool developers are interested in profiting from their efforts, the amount of design effort should be related to the anticipated payoff.

> **[G1.8]** Effort spent on developing tools should be in proportion to the profits they are expected to generate. This means that small-market custom solutions should be developed only for high-value cognitive work.

It must be recognized that this simple profit model often does not apply because many people who generate visualizations are academics not motivated by profit or even by the goal of increasing the efficiency of cognitive work. To the academic, for the most part, value is not based on monetary return; instead, it is based on published ideas. Published academic papers result in job tenure, increased recognition, and ultimately greater salary. Although this suggests an ultimate financial motive, novelty and a certain level of sophistication are more important requirements for getting a paper published, as opposed to whether a method is actually superior. The academic approach often results in methods that are not valuable, but sometimes it results in inventions that a more commercial approach would never discover.

Types of Data

If the goal of visualization research is to transform data into a perceptually efficient visual format, and if we are to make statements with some generality, we must be able to say something about the types of data that can exist for us to visualize. It is useful, but less than satisfying, to be able to say that color coding is good for stock-market symbols but texture coding is good for geological maps. It is far more useful to be able to define broader categories of information, such as continuous quantity maps (scalar fields), continuous flow fields (vector maps), and category data, and then to make general statements such as "Color coding is good for category information" and "Motion coding is good for highlighting selected data." If we can give perceptual reasons for these generalities, we have an applied science of visualization.

Unfortunately, the classification of data is a big issue. It is closely related to the classification of knowledge, and it is with great trepidation that we approach the subject. What follows is an informal classification of data classes using a number of concepts that we will find helpful in later chapters. We make no claims that this classification is especially profound or all encompassing.

Bertin (1977) suggested that there are two fundamental forms of data: data values and data structures. A similar idea is to divide data into entities and relationships (often called *relations*). Entities are the objects we wish to visualize; relations define the structures and patterns that relate entities to one another. Sometimes the relationships are provided explicitly; sometimes discovering relationships is the very purpose of visualization. We can also talk about the attributes of an entity or a relationship; for example, an apple can have color as one of its attributes. The concepts of entity, relationship, and attribute have a long history in database design and have been adopted more recently in systems modeling; however, we shall extend these concepts beyond the kinds of data that are traditionally stored in a relational database. In visualization, it is necessary to deal with entities that are more complex, and we are also interested in seeing complex structured relationships—data structures—not captured by the entity relationship model.

Entities

Entities are generally the objects of interest. People can be entities; hurricanes can be entities. Both fish and fishponds can be entities. A group of things can be considered a single entity if it is convenient—for example, a school of fish. Even an abstract philosophical concept can be an entity.

Relationships

Relationships form the structures that relate entities. There can be many kinds of relationships. A wheel has a "part-of" relationship to a car. One employee of a firm may have a supervisory relationship to another employee. Relationships can be structural and physical, as in defining the way a house is made of its many component parts, or they can be conceptual, as in defining the relationship between a store and its customers. Relationships can be causal, as when one event causes another, and they can be purely temporal, defining an interval between two events.

Attributes of Entities or Relationships

Both entities and relationships can have attributes. In general, something should be called an attribute (as opposed to an entity itself) when it is a property of some entity and cannot be thought of independently. Thus, the color of an apple is an attribute of the apple. The temperature of water is an attribute of the water. Duration is an attribute of a journey. Defining what should be an entity and what should be an attribute is not always straightforward. The salary of an employee, for example, could be thought of as an attribute of the employee, but we can also think of an amount of money as an entity unto itself, in which case we would have to define a relationship between the employee entity and the sum-of-money entity.

Data Dimensions: 1D, 2D, 3D, ...

An attribute of an entity can have multiple dimensions. We can have a single scalar quantity, such as the weight of a person. We can have a vector quantity, such as the direction in which that person is traveling. Tensors are higher-order quantities that describe both direction and shear forces, such as occur in materials that are being stressed. We can have a field of scalars, vectors, or tensors. The gravitational field of the Earth is a three-dimensional attribute of the Earth. In fact, it is a three-dimensional vector field attribute. If we are interested only in the strength of gravity at the Earth's surface, it is a two-dimensional scalar attribute. Often, the term *map* is used to describe this kind of field; thus, we talk about a gravity map or a temperature map.

Types of Numbers

It is often desirable to describe data visualization methods in light of the quality of attributes they are capable of conveying. A useful way to consider the quality of data is the taxonomy of number scales defined by the statistician Stevens (1946). According to Stevens, there are four levels of measurement: nominal, ordinal, interval, and ratio scales:

> *Nominal.* This is the labeling function. Fruit can be classified into apples, oranges, bananas, and so on. There is no sense in which the fruit can be placed in an ordered sequence. Sometimes numbers are used in this way; for example, the number on the front of a bus generally has a purely nominal value. It identifies the route on which the bus travels.

Ordinal. The ordinal category encompasses numbers used for ordering things in a sequence. It is possible to say that a certain item comes before or after another item. The position of an item in a queue or list is an ordinal quality. When we ask people to rank some group of things (films, political candidates, computers) in order of preference, we are requiring them to create an ordinal scale.

Interval. When we have an interval scale of measurement, it becomes possible to derive the gap between data values. The time of departure and the time of arrival of an aircraft are defined on an interval scale.

Ratio. With a ratio scale, we have the full expressive power of a real number. We can make statements such as "Object A is twice as large as object B." The mass of an object is defined on a ratio scale. Money is defined on a ratio scale. The use of a ratio scale implies a zero value used as a reference.

In practice, only three of Stevens's levels of measurement are widely used, and these in somewhat different form. The typical basic data classes most often considered in visualization have been greatly influenced by the demands of computer programming. They are the following:

Category data. This is like Stevens's nominal class.

Integer data. This is like his ordinal class in that it is discrete and ordered.

Real-number data. This combines the properties of interval and ratio scales.

Uncertainty

In science and engineering it is common to attach an uncertainty attribute either to raw data or to derived data. Estimating uncertainty is a major part of engineering practice, and showing uncertainty in a visualization is important, although difficult to achieve. The problem is that once data is represented as a visual object, it attains a kind of literal concrete quality that makes the think it is accurate.

Operations Considered as Data

An entity-relationship model can be used to describe most kinds of data; however, it does not capture the operations that may be performed on entities and relationships. We tend to think of operations as somehow different from the data itself, neither entities nor relationships nor attributes. The following are a few common operations:

- Mathematical operations on numbers—multiplication, division, a log transform, and so on

- Merging two lists to create a longer list

- Inverting a value to create its opposite

- Bringing an entity or relationship into existence (such as the mean of a set of numbers)

- Deleting an entity or relationship (a marriage breaks up)

- Transforming an entity in some way (the chrysalis turns into a butterfly)

- Forming a new object out of other objects (a pie is baked from apples and pastry)

- Splitting a single entity into its component parts (a machine is disassembled)

In some cases, these operations can themselves form a kind of data that we may wish to capture. Chemistry contains a huge catalog of the compounds that result when certain operations are applied to combinations of other compounds. These operations may form part of the data that is stored. Certain operations are easy to visualize; for example, the merging of two entities can easily be represented by showing two visual objects that combine (visually merge) into a single entity. Other operations are not at all easy to represent in any visualization; for example, the detailed logical structure of a computer program may be better represented using a written code that has its basis in natural language than using any kind of diagram. What should and should not be visualized is a major topic in Chapter 9.

Operations and procedures often present a particularly difficult challenge for visualization. It is difficult to express operations effectively in a static diagram, and this is especially a problem in the creation of visual languages. On the other hand, the use of animation opens up the possibility of expressing at least certain operations in an immediately accessible visual manner. We shall deal with the issue of animation and visual languages in Chapter 9.

Metadata

Metadata is data about data—who collected it, what transformations it has been subjected to, what is its uncertainty. When we are striving to understand data, certain products are sure to emerge as we proceed. We may discover correlations between variables or clusters of data values. We may postulate certain underlying mechanisms that are not immediately visible. The result is that theoretical entities come into being. Atoms, photons, black holes, and all the basic constructs of physics are like this. As more evidence accumulates, the theoretical entities seem more and more real, but they are nonetheless only observable in the most indirect ways. Metadata can be of any kind. It can consist of new entities, such as identified classes of objects, or new relationships, such as postulated interactions between different entities, or new rules. We may impose complex structural relationships on the data, such as tree structures or directed acyclic graphs, or we may find that they already exist in the data.

The visualization of metadata presents the same kinds of challenges as the visualization of nonmetadata, as metadata consists ultimately of entities and relationships and of different kinds of numbers from nominal to real, and metadata may have a complex structure. Graphically representing metadata can be very challenging because it inevitably adds complexity, but the problems of representation are essentially the same. For this reason, metadata visualization is not discussed as a separate topic in this book.

Conclusion

Visualization applies vision research to practical problems of data analysis in much the same way as engineering applies physics to practical problems of building factories. Just as engineering has influenced physicists to become more concerned with areas such as semiconductor technology, so we may hope that the development of an applied science of data visualization can encourage vision researchers to intensify their efforts in addressing such problems as 3D space and task-oriented perception. There is considerable practical benefit in understanding these things because of the perceptual and cognitive efficiencies that come with well-designed analytic tools. As the importance of visualization grows, so do the benefits of a scientific approach, but there is no time left to lose. New symbol systems are being developed constantly to meet the needs of a society increasingly dependent on data. Once developed, they may stay with us for a very long time, so we should try to get them right.

We have introduced a key distinction between the ideas of sensory and arbitrary conventional symbols. This is a difficult and sometimes artificial distinction. Nonetheless, the distinction is essential. Were there no basic model of visual processing to support the idea of a good data representation, all visual representations would be arbitrary, and ultimately the problem of visualization would come down to establishing consistent notations.

In opposition to the view that consistency is the only important criterion, this book takes the view that all humans have more or less the same visual system. This visual system has evolved over tens of millions of years to enable creatures to perceive and act within the natural environment. Although very flexible, the visual system is tuned to receiving data presented in certain ways, but not in others. If we can understand how the mechanism works, we can produce better displays and better thinking tools.

CHAPTER TWO

The Environment, Optics, Resolution, and the Display

We can think of the world itself as an information display. Each object by its shape suggests uses, such as a tool or construction material, or it may be seen as an obstacle to be avoided. Every intricate surface reveals the properties of the material from which it is made. Creatures signal their intentions inadvertently or deliberately through movement. There are almost infinite levels of detail in nature, and we must be responsive to both small and large things, but in different ways: Large things, such as logs, may be seats or tables; smaller things, such as hand-sized rocks, can be used as tools; still smaller things, such as grains of sand, are useful by the handful. In an evolutionary sense, our visual system is designed to extract useful information from the environment and lessons from this can lead to the design of better visualizations.

The visual display of a computer is only a single rectangular planar surface, divided into a regular grid of small colored dots. It is astonishing how successful it is as an information display, given how little it resembles the world we live in. This chapter concerns the lessons we can learn about information display by appreciating the environment in broad terms and how the same kind of information can be picked up from a flat screen. It begins with a discussion of the most general properties of the visual environment and then considers the lens and receptor system of the eye as the principal instrument of vision. Later, the basic abilities of the eye are applied in an analysis of problems inherent in creating optimal display devices.

This level of analysis bears on a number of display problems. If we want to make virtual objects seem real, how should we simulate the interaction of light with their surfaces? What is the optimal display device and how do current display devices measure

Information Visualization. https://doi.org/10.1016/B978-0-12-812875-6.00002-5

up? How much detail can we see? How faint a target can we see? How good is the lens system of the human eye? This is a foundation chapter, introducing much of the basic vocabulary of vision research.

The Environment

A strategy for designing a visualization is to transform the data so that it appears like a common environment—a kind of data landscape. We should then be able to transfer skills obtained in interpreting the real environment to understanding our data. This is not to say that we should represent data by means of synthetic trees, flowers, and undulating lawns—that would be quaint and ludicrous. It seems less ludicrous to create synthetic offices, with desks, filing cabinets, phones, books, and Rolodexes, and this has been done in a number of computer interfaces. But, still, the space efficiency of these designs is poor; better methods exist, and understanding the properties of the environment is important for a more basic reason than simple imitation.

When trying to understand perception, it is always useful to think about what perception is for. The theory of evolution tells us that the visual system must have survival value and adopting this perspective allows us to understand visual mechanisms in the broader context of useful skills, such as navigation, food seeking (which is an optimization problem like information seeking), and tool use (which depends on object-shape perception).

What follows is a short tour of the visual environment, beginning with light.

Visible Light

Perception is about understanding patterns of light. Visible light constitutes a very small part of the electromagnetic spectrum, as is shown in Figure 2.1. Some animals, such as snakes, can see in the infrared, while certain insects can see in the ultraviolet. Humans can perceive light only in the range of 400–700 nm (In vision research, wavelength is generally expressed in units of 10^{-9} m, called *nanometers*). At wavelengths shorter than 400 nm are ultraviolet light and X-rays. At wavelengths longer than 700 nm are infrared light, microwaves, and radio waves.

Ecological Optics

The most useful broad framework for describing the visual environment is given by *ecological optics*, a discipline developed by J. J. Gibson. Gibson radically changed the way we think about perception of the visual world. Instead of concentrating on the image on the retina, as did other vision researchers, Gibson emphasized perception of surfaces in the environment. The following quotations strikingly illustrate how he broke with a traditional approach to space perception that was grounded in the classical geometry of points, lines, and planes (Gibson, 1979):

> *A surface is substantial; a plane is not. A surface is textured; a plane is not. A surface is never perfectly transparent; a plane is. A surface can be seen; a plane can only be visualized.*

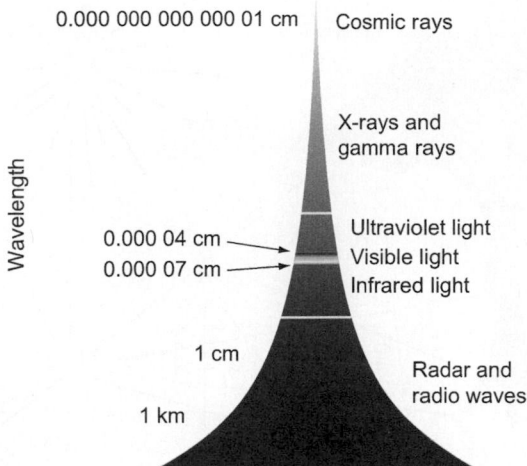

Figure 2.1 The visible light spectrum is a tiny part of a much larger spectrum of electromagnetic radiation.

A fiber is an elongated object of small diameter, such as a wire or thread. A fiber should not be confused with a geometrical line.

In surface geometry the junction of two flat surfaces is either an edge or a corner; in abstract geometry the intersection of two planes is a line.

Much of human visual processing becomes more understandable if we assume that a key function of the visual system is to extract properties of surfaces. As our primary interface with objects, surfaces are essential to understanding the potential for interaction and manipulation in the environment that Gibson called *affordances* (discussed in Chapter 1).

A second key concept in Gibson's ecological optics is the ambient optical array (Gibson, 1986). To understand the ambient optical array, consider what happens to light entering the environment from some source such as the sun. It is absorbed, reflected, refracted, and diffracted as it interacts with various objects such as stones, grass, trees, and water. The environment, considered in this way, is a hugely complex matrix with photons traveling in all directions, consisting of different mixtures of wavelengths and polarized in various ways. This complexity is impossible to simulate; however, from any particular stationary point in the environment, critical information is contained in the structure of the light arriving at that point. This vast simplification is what Gibson called the *ambient optical array*. This array encompasses all the rays arriving at a particular point as they are structured in both space and time. Figure 2.2 is intended to capture the flavor of the concept.

Much of the effort of computer graphics can be characterized as an attempt to model the ambient optical array. Because the interactions of light with surfaces are vastly complex, it is not possible to directly model entire environments, but

Figure 2.2 *Ambient optical array* is a term that describes the spherical array of light arriving from all directions at some designated point in the environment. Simulating the colors of the subset of rays that would pass through a glass rectangle is one of the main goals of computer graphics.

the ambient array provides the basis for simplifications such as those used in ray tracing so that approximations can be computed. If we can capture the structure of a bundle of rays passing through a glass rectangle on their way to the stationary point, we have something that we may be able to reproduce on a screen (see Figure 2.2).

Optical Flow

The ambient optical array is dynamic, changing over time both as the viewpoint moves and as objects move. As we advance into a static environment, a characteristic visual flow field develops. Figure 2.3 illustrates the visual field expanding outward as a result of forward motion. There is evidence that the visual system contains processes to interpret such flow patterns and that they are important in understanding how animals (including humans) navigate through space, avoid obstacles, and generally perceive the layout of objects in the world. The flow pattern in Figure 2.3 is only a very simple case; if we follow something with our eyes while we move forward, the pattern becomes more complex. The perceptual mechanisms to interpret flow patterns must therefore be sophisticated. The key point here is that visual images of the world are dynamic, so that the perception of motion patterns may be as important as the perception of the static world, albeit less well understood. Chapter 7 deals with motion perception in the context of space perception and three-dimensional (3D) information display.

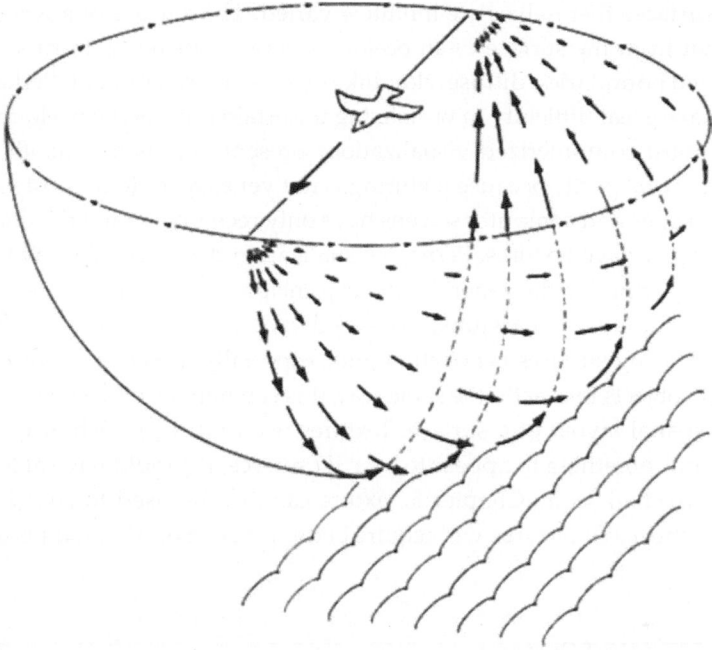

Figure 2.3 An expanding flow pattern of visual information is created as an observer moves while gazing in a forward direction. *(From Gibson (1979). Reproduced with permission.)*

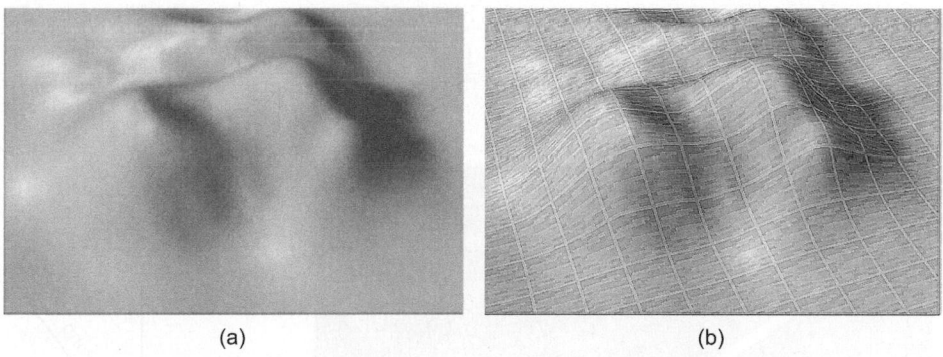

(a)	(b)

Figure 2.4 An undulating surface with (a) and without (b) surface texture.

Textured Surfaces and Texture Gradients

Gibson pointed out that surface texture is one of the fundamental visual properties of an object. In visual terms, a surface is merely an unformed patch of light unless it is textured. Texture is critical to perception in a number of ways. The texture of an object helps us see where an object is and what shape it has. On a larger scale, the texture of the ground plane on which we walk, run, and crawl is important in judging distances and other aspects of space. Figure 2.4 shows that the texture of the ground plane produces a characteristic texture gradient that is important in space perception.

Of course, surfaces themselves are infinitely varied. The surface of a wooden table is very different from the surface of an ocelot. Generally speaking, most surfaces have clearly defined boundaries; diffuse, cloudlike objects are exceptional. Perhaps because of this, we have great difficulty in visualizing uncertain data as fuzzy clouds of points. At present, most computerized visualizations present objects as smooth and untextured. This may be partly because texturing is not yet easy to do in most visualization software packages and computer screens have only recently gained the fine resolution to display unobtrusive textures. Perhaps visualization designers have avoided texturing surfaces by applying the general esthetic principle that we should avoid irrelevant decoration in displays—"chart junk," to use Edward Tufte's memorable phrase (Tufte, 1983), but texturing surfaces is not chart junk, especially in 3D visualizations. Even if we texture all objects in exactly the same way, this can help us perceive the orientation, shape, and spatial layout of a surface. Textures need not be garish or obtrusive, but when we want something to appear to be a 3D surface, it should have at least a subtle texture. As we shall see in Chapter 6, texture can also be used to code information, but using unobtrusive textures will require better pixel resolution than is available on most displays.

The Paint Model of Surfaces

Surfaces in nature are endlessly varied and complex. Microtextures give irregular patterns of reflection, so the amount and color of reflected light can vary with both the illumination angle and the viewing angle. However, there is a simple model that approximates many common materials. This model can be understood by considering a glossy paint. The paint has pigment particles embedded in a more or less clear medium, as shown in Figure 2.5. Some of the light is reflected from the surface of the

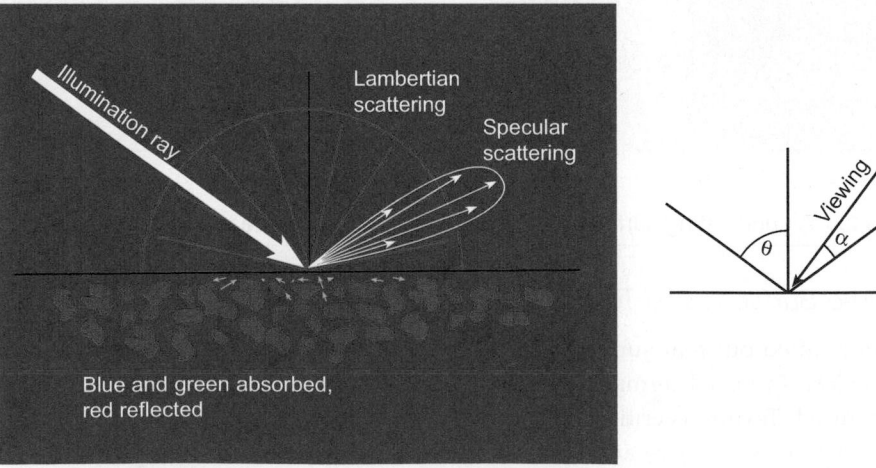

Figure 2.5 This simplified model of light interacting with surfaces is used in most computer graphics. Specular reflection is light that is reflected directly from the surface without penetrating into the underlying pigment layer.

glossy medium and is unchanged in color. Most of the light penetrates the medium and is selectively absorbed by the pigment particles, altering its color. According to this model, there are three important direct interactions of light with surfaces, as described in the following paragraphs. An additional fourth property is related to the fact that parts of objects cast shadows, revealing more information about their shapes (see Figure 2.6).

- *Lambertian shading.* With most materials, light penetrates the surface and interacts with the pigment in the medium. This light is selectively absorbed and reflected depending on the color of the pigment, and some of it is scattered back through the surface out into the environment. If we have a perfectly matte surface, how bright the surface appears depends only on the cosine of the angle between the incident light and the surface normal. This is called the *Lambertian model*, and although few real-world materials have exactly this property it is computationally very simple. A patch of a Lambertian surface can be viewed from any angle and the surface color will seem the same. Figure 2.6(a) shows a surface with only Lambertian shading. Lambertian shading is the simplest method for representing surface shape from shading. It can also be highly effective.

- *Specular shading.* The light that is reflected directly from a surface is called *specular.* This is what we see as the highlights on glossy objects. Specular reflection obeys the optical principle of mirror reflection: The angle of reflection equals the angle of incidence. It is possible to simulate high-gloss, semigloss, or eggshell finishes by causing the specular light to spread out somewhat, simulating different degrees of roughness at a microscopic level. Specular light reflected from a surface retains the color of the illuminant; it is not affected by the color of the underlying pigment. Hence, we see white highlights gleaming from the surface of a red automobile. Specular reflection depends on the viewpoint, unlike Lambertian reflection; both the viewing direction and the positions of the light sources affect the locations where highlights appear. Figure 2.6(b) shows a surface with both Lambertian and specular shading.

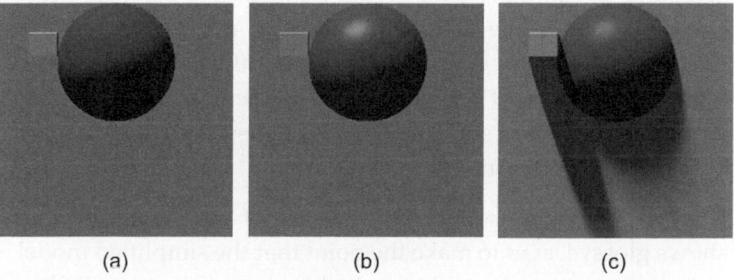

(a)   (b)   (c)

Figure 2.6 (a) Lambertian shading only. (b) Lambertian shading with specular and ambient shading. (c) Lambertian shading with specular, ambient, and cast shadows.

- *Ambient shading.* Ambient light is the light that illuminates a surface from everywhere in the environment, except for the actual light sources. In reality, ambient light is as complex as the scene itself; however, in computer graphics, ambient light is often grossly simplified by treating it as a constant, which is like assuming that an object is situated in a uniformly gray room. The radiosity technique (Cohen & Greenberg, 1985) properly models the complexity of ambient light, but it is rarely used for visualization. One of the consequences of modeling ambient light as a constant is that no shape from shading information is available in areas of cast shadow. In Figure 2.6(b) and (c), ambient light is simulated by the assumption that a constant amount of light is reflected from all points on the surface. Ambient light is reflected both specularly and nonspecularly.

- *Cast shadows.* An object can cast shadows either on itself or on other objects. As shown in Figure 2.6(c), cast shadows can greatly influence the perceived height of an object.

The mathematical expression for the amount of light reflected, *r*, toward a particular viewpoint, according to this simplified model, is as follows:

$$r = \boldsymbol{a} + \boldsymbol{b} \, \cos(\theta) + \boldsymbol{c} \, \cos^{k}(\alpha) \tag{2.1}$$

where θ is the angle between the incident ray and the surface normal, α is the angle between the reflected ray and the view vector, and $\boldsymbol{a}$, $\boldsymbol{b}$, and $\boldsymbol{c}$ represent the relative amounts of ambient, Lambertian, and specular light, respectively. The exponent k is used to control the degree of glossiness. A high value of k, such as 50, models a very shiny surface, whereas a lower value, such as 6, results in a semigloss appearance. Note that this is a simplified treatment, providing only the crudest approximation of the way light interacts with surfaces, but nevertheless it is so effective in creating real-looking scenes that it is widely used in computer graphics with only a small modification to simulate color. It is sufficient for most visualization purposes. This surface/light interaction model and others are covered extensively by computer graphics texts concerned with realistic image synthesis. More information can be found in Shirley and Marschner (2009) or any other standard computer graphics text.

What is interesting is that these simplifying assumptions may, in effect, be embedded in our visual systems. The brain may assume a model similar to this when we estimate the shape of a surface defined by shading information. In some cases, using more sophisticated modeling of light in the environment is actually detrimental to our understanding of the shapes of surfaces. Chapter 7 discusses the way we perceive this shape from shading information.

Figures 2.7 and 2.8 illustrate some consequences of the simplified lighting model. Figure 2.7 shows glossy leaves to make the point that the simplified model is representative of at least some nonsynthetic objects. In this picture, the specular highlights from the shiny surface are white because the illuminant is white. The nonspecular light from the leaf pigmentation is green. As a tool in data visualization, specular reflection is

Figure 2.7 Note how the highlights are the color of the illuminant on glossy leaves.

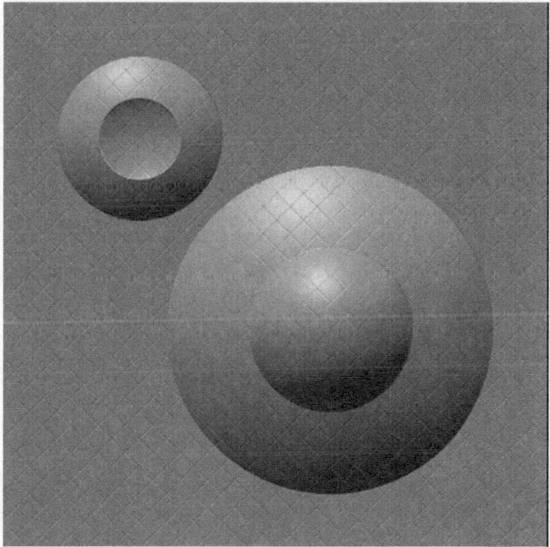

Figure 2.8 Specular light can reveal fine details of surface structure, depending on the viewpoint.

useful in visualization of fine surface features, such as scratches on glass. The effect is illustrated in Figure 2.8, in which the grid lines are most distinct in the region of specular reflection. Specular highlights can be similarly useful in revealing subtle differences in surface microroughness. The nonspecular Lambertian reflection is more effective in giving an overall impression of the shape of the surface.

The different kinds of information contained in the different lighting models suggest the following three guidelines:

[G2.1] Use Lambertian shading to reveal the shapes of smooth surfaces.

[G2.2] Use specular shading to reveal fine surface details. Make it possible to move the light source or rotate the object so that specular light is reflected from regions of critical interest.

[G2.3] Consider using cast shadows to reveal large-scale spatial relationships. Shadows should be created only where the connection between the shadow and the casting object is clear and where the value of the additional information outweighs the information that it obscured.

Another source of spatial information can come from the amount of ambient light that reaches into the interstices of an object. This is called *ambient occlusion* because in the depths of hollows some of the ambient light is occluded by other parts of the object. Tarini, Cignoni, and Claudio Montani (2006) used ambient occlusion to help reveal the shape of a complex molecule (Figure 2.9).

[G2.4] Consider applying ambient occlusion in the lighting model to support two-dimensional (2D) shape perception for objects that otherwise supply no shape-from-shading information.

To summarize this brief introduction to the visual environment, we have seen that much of what is useful to organisms is related to objects, to their layout in space, and to the properties of their surfaces. As Gibson so effectively argued, in understanding how surfaces are perceived, we must understand how light becomes structured when it arrives at the eye. We have covered two important kinds of structuring. One is the structure that is present in the ambient array of light that arrives at a viewpoint. This

Figure 2.9 In the molecule on the left, only individual atoms are shaded. In the molecule on the right, the amount of ambient light reaching the inner parts of the molecule is reduced due to occlusion by the outer atoms.

structure has both static pattern components and dynamic pattern flows as we move through the world. The second is the more detailed structuring of light that results from the interaction of light with surfaces. In data the goal is to use rendering techniques that best convey the important information, not to obtain photorealistic realism.

The Eye

We now consider the instrument of sight. The human eye, like a camera, contains a variable focus lens, an aperture (the pupil), and a sensor array (the retina). Figure 2.10 illustrates these parts. The lens focuses a small, inverted picture of the world onto the retina. The iris performs the function of a variable aperture, helping the eye to adjust to different lighting conditions. Some people find it difficult to understand how we can see the world properly when the image is upside down. The right way to think about this is to adopt a computational perspective. We do not perceive what is on the retina; instead, a percept is formed through a complex chain of neural computations. A control computer does not care which way is up, and inversion of the image is the least of the brain's computational problems.

We should not take the eye/camera analogy too far. If seeing were like photography, you would only have to copy the image on the back of the eye to produce a perfect likeness of a friend; anyone could be a great portrait painter. Yet, artists spend years studying

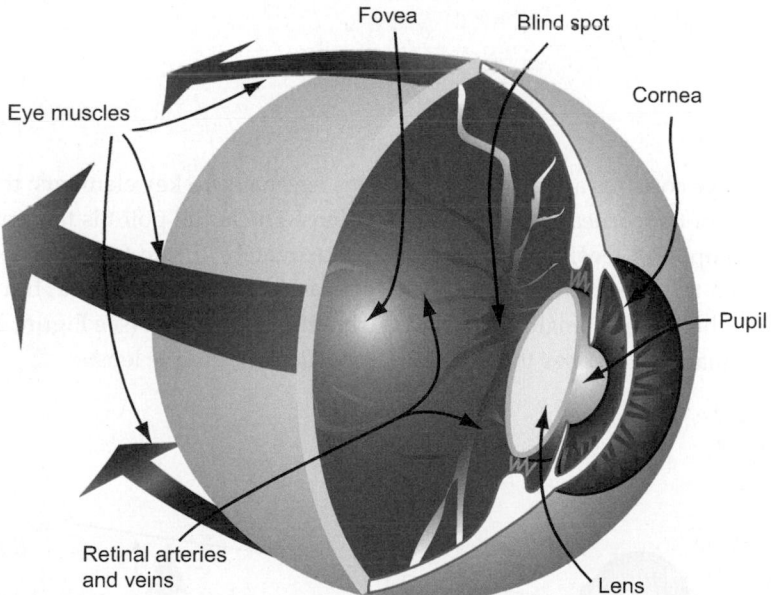

Figure 2.10 The human eye. Important features include the fovea, where vision is sharpest; the pupil, a round aperture through which light enters the eye; the two principal optical elements, the lens and the cornea; and the large eye muscles that control eye movements. This blind spot is caused by the absence of receptors where the retinal arteries enter the eyeball.

perspective geometry and anatomy and constantly practice their skills. It took thousands of years, culminating in the golden age of Greek art, for artists to develop the skills to draw natural figures, properly shaded and foreshortened. Following this, the skill was largely lost again until the Renaissance, in the 15th century. Yet, in the image on the back of the eye, everything is in perfect proportion and in perspective. Clearly, we do not "see" what is on the retina. The locus of conscious perception is farther up the chain of processing, and at this later stage most of the simple properties of the retinal image have been lost.

Visual Angle Defined

Visual angle is a key concept in defining the properties of the eye and early vision. As Figure 2.11 illustrates, a visual angle is the angle subtended by an object at the eye of an observer. Visual angles are generally defined in degrees, minutes, and seconds of arc. (A minute is 1/60 degree and a second is 1/60 minute). As a useful approximation, a thumbnail held at arm's length subtends about 1 degree of visual angle. Another useful fact is that a 1-cm object viewed at 57 cm has a visual angle of approximately 1 degree, and 57 cm is a reasonable approximation for the distance at which we view a computer monitor. To calculate visual angle, use this equation:

$$\tan\left(\frac{\theta}{2}\right) = \frac{h}{2d} \tag{2.2}$$

$$\theta = 2 \ \arctan\left(\frac{h}{2d}\right) \tag{2.3}$$

Lens

The human eye contains a compound lens. This lens has two key elements: the curved front surface of the cornea and the crystalline lens. The nodal point is the optical center of the compound lens; it is positioned approximately 17 mm from the retina. The distance from the eye to an object is usually measured from the cornea, but in terms of optics it is better to estimate the distance from the nodal point (see Figure 2.11). The following equation describes the imaging properties of a simple lens:

$$\frac{1}{f} = \frac{1}{d} + \frac{1}{r} \tag{2.4}$$

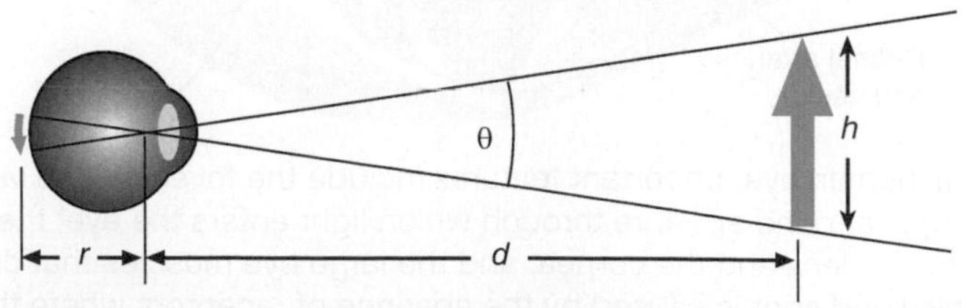

Figure 2.11 The visual angle of an object is measured from the optical center of the eye.

where f is the focal length of the lens, d is the distance to the object that is imaged, and r is the distance to the image that is formed. If the units are meters, the *power* of a lens is given by the reciprocal of the focal length $(1/f)$ in units of *diopters*. Thus, a 1-diopter lens has a focal length of 1 m. The 17-mm focal length of the human lens system corresponds to a power of 59 diopters. To get this from Equation (2.3), consider viewing an object at infinity $(d = \infty)$.

To a first approximation, the power of a compound lens can be computed by adding the powers of the components. We obtain the focal length of a two-part compound lens by using the following equation:

$$\frac{1}{f_3} = \frac{1}{f_1} + \frac{1}{f_2}$$

(2.5)

where f_3 is the result of combining lenses f_1 and f_2.

In the compound lens of the human eye, most of this power, about 40 diopters, comes from the front surface of the cornea; the remainder comes from the variable-focus lens. When the ciliary muscle that surrounds the lens contracts, the lens assumes a more convex and more powerful shape, and nearby objects come into focus. Young children have very flexible lenses, capable of adjusting over a range of 12 diopters or more, which means that they can focus on an object as close as 8 cm. However, the eye becomes less flexible with age, at roughly the rate of 2 diopters per decade, so that by the age of 60 the lens is almost completely rigid (Sun et al., 1988), hence the need for reading glasses at about the age of 48, when only a few diopters of accommodation are left.

The *depth of focus* of a lens is the range over which objects are in focus when the eye is adjusted for a particular distance. The depth of focus of the human eye varies with the size of the pupil (Smith & Atchison, 1997), but assuming a 3-mm pupil and a human eye focused at infinity, objects between about 3 m and infinity are in focus. Depth of focus can usefully be described in terms of the power change that takes place without the image becoming significantly blurred. This is about 1/3 diopter for a 3-mm pupil.

Assuming the 1/3-diopter depth of focus value and an eye focused at distance d (in meters), objects in the range:

$$\left[\frac{3d}{d+3}, \frac{-3d}{d-3} \right]$$

(2.6)

will be in focus. To illustrate, for an observer focusing at 50 cm, roughly the normal monitor viewing distance, an object can be about 7 cm in front of the screen or 10 cm behind the screen before it appears to be out of focus. In virtual reality displays, it is common to use lenses that set the screen at a virtual focal distance of 2 m. This means that in the range 1.2–6.0 m it is not necessary to worry about simulating depth of focus effects, something that is difficult and computationally expensive to do. In any case, the large pixels in current virtual reality displays prevent us from modeling image blur to anywhere near this resolution.

Table 2.1 gives the range that is in focus for a number of viewing distances, given a 3-mm pupil. For more detailed modeling of depth of focus as it varies with pupil diameter, consult Smith and Atchison (1997).

Optics and Augmented Reality Systems

Augmented reality systems superimpose computer graphics imagery on the real world. This enables data to be visualized *in situ,* so that, for example, medical data visualizations appear at the appropriate place in a living person. For this blending of real and virtual imagery to be achieved, the viewpoint of the observer must be accurately known and the objects' positions and shapes in the local environment must also be stored in the controlling computer. With this information, it is a straightforward application of standard computer graphics techniques to draw 3D images that are superimposed on the real-world images. Getting the perspective right is easy; the difficult problems to solve include accurately measuring the observer's eye position, which is essential to precise registration, and designing optical systems that are light, undistorted and portable.

Figure 2.12 illustrates an experimental augmented reality system in which a surgeon sees a brain tumor highlighted within the brain during surgical planning or to guide

Table 2.1 Depth of Focus at Various Viewing Distances

Viewing Distance	Near	Far
50 cm	43 cm	60 cm
1 m	75 cm	1.5 m
2 m	1.2 m	6.0 m
3 m	1.5 m	Infinity

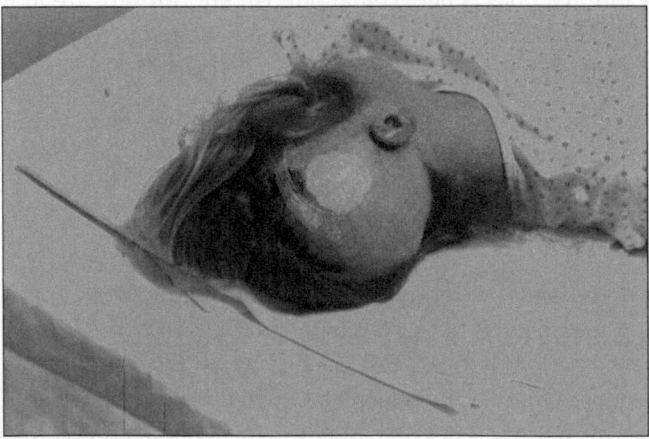

Figure 2.12 Augmented reality has been used experimentally in the medical field. Here, an image of a tumor is superimposed on a patient's head. *(From Grimson et al. (1999). Image-guided surgery. Scientific American, 280(6), 54-61.)*

a biopsy needle (Grimson et al., 1999). Given how difficult it is for the surgeon to accomplish this task, such a development would have very large benefits. Other applications for augmented displays include aircraft maintenance, where the mechanic sees instructions and structural diagrams superimposed on the actual machinery; tactical military displays, in which the pilot or tank driver sees indicators of friendly or hostile targets superimposed on a view of the landscape; and shopping, where information about a potential purchase appears next to the item. In each case, visual data is superimposed on real objects to supplement the information available to the user and enable better or more rapid decision-making. This data may take the form of written text labels or sophisticated symbology.

In many augmented reality systems, a device called a beam splitter is used to superimpose computer graphics imagery on the environment. The splitter is actually used not to split but to combine the images coming from the real world with those presented on a small computer monitor. The result is like a double-exposed photograph. A typical beam splitter allows approximately half the light to pass through and half the light to be reflected. Figure 2.13 illustrates the essential optical components of this type of display.

Because the optics are typically fixed, in augmented reality systems there is only one depth at which both the computer-generated imagery and the real-world imagery are in focus. This can be both good and bad. If real-world and virtual-world scenes are both in focus, it will be easier to perceive them simultaneously. If this is desirable, care should be taken to set the focal plane of the virtual imagery at the typical depth of the real imagery. It is sometimes desirable, however, that the computer imagery remains perceptually distinct from the real-world image; for example, a transparent layer of text from an instruction manual might be presented on a see-through display (Feiner, MacIntyre, Haupt, & Solomon, 1993). If the focal distances are different, the user can choose to focus either on the text or on the imagery and in this way selectively attend to one or the other.

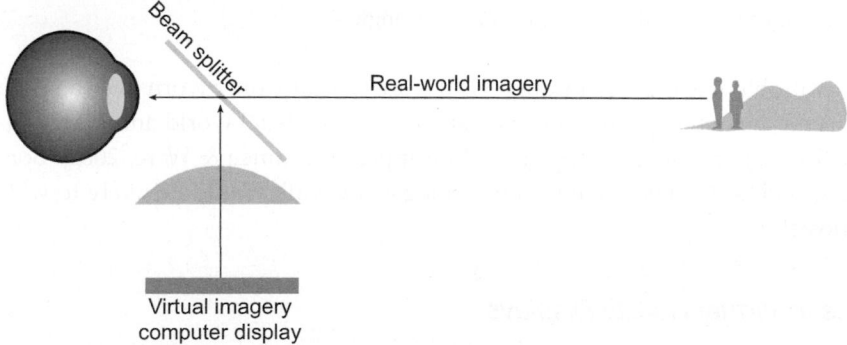

Figure 2.13 In augmented=reality displays, computer graphics imagery is superimposed on the real-world environment using a beam splitter. The effect is like a transparent overlay on the environment. The focal distance of the computer imagery depends on the power of the lenses used.

[G2.5] In augmented reality systems, an augmenting image linked to an external object should be at the same focal distance.

[G2.6] In augmented reality systems, when augmenting imagery does not need to be linked to external objects, the focal distance of the augmenting imagery should be closer, which will reduce visual interference. This will not work for older users who have little or no ability to change the focus of their eyes.

There is evidence that focus can cause problems with distance estimation in aircraft heads-up displays (HUDs). In these displays, the virtual image is set at optical infinity, because only distant objects are normally seen through a cockpit screen. Despite this, experiments have shown that observers tend to focus at a distance closer than infinity with HUDs, and this can cause overestimation of distances to objects in the environment (Roscoe, 1991). This may be a serious problem; according to Roscoe, it has been at least partially responsible for large numbers (one per month) of generally fatal "controlled flight into the terrain" accidents in the US Air Force.

There are a number of other optical and perceptual problems with head-mounted displays (HMDs). The complex optics of progressive eyeglass lenses is not compatible with HMD optics. With progressive glasses, the optical power varies from top to bottom of the lens. Also, people normally use coordinated movements of both the eyes *and the head* to conduct visual searches of the environment, and HMDs do not allow for redirection of the gaze with head movements. Ordinarily, when the angular movement of the eyes to the side is large, head movements actually begin first. Peli (1999) suggests that looking sideways more than 10 degrees off the centerline is very uncomfortable to maintain. With an HMD the image moves with the head, so compensatory head movements will fail to eliminate the discomfort.

[G2.7] When using a head-mounted display to read text, make the width of the text area no more that 18 degrees of visual angle.

Another problem is that see-through HMDs are typically only worn over one eye, and the effect of binocular rivalry means that parts of the visual world and HMD imagery are likely to spontaneously appear and disappear (Laramee & Ware, 2002). Someone wearing such a display while walking along a sidewalk would be likely to walk into lampposts!

Optics in Virtual Reality Displays

Virtual reality (VR) displays block out the real world, unlike the see-through augmented reality displays discussed previously. The VR system designer need only be concerned with computer-generated imagery. It is still highly desirable, however, that correct depth of focus information be presented to the user. Ideally, objects on which the user fixates should be in sharp focus, while objects farther away or nearer should be blurred to the appropriate extents. Focus is important in helping us to differentiate objects that we wish to attend to from other objects in the environment. Most computer graphics is based on the assumption of rays passing through a point pupil, as in a pin-hole camera, but in fact the pupil is a few millimeters in diameter and as a result rays of light arrive from objects in the environment from slightly different angles. This cannot be simulated with a single flat screen, but a new technology, called a *light field display* is emerging to solve the problem. The principle of a light field display is to recreate how light arrives at the retina from objects in the environment depending on the focal length of the lens of the eye. Perhaps the simplest way of achieving this is through the use of multiple screens at different focal planes that are optically combined to create more than one focal distance. The advantage of such a display is that as the eye refocuses, objects at the appropriate depth appear sharper or out of focus in a natural manner. The example system illustrated in Figure 2.14 has two screens for each eye, and the result is a blend of the two focal depths, but more screens would provide even better depth of field information (Huang, Chen, & Wetzstein, 2015). An alternative method to providing depth of focus information is to use a microlens array in front of a single very high-resolution display (Burke and Brickson, 2013).

Chromatic Aberration

The human eye is not corrected for chromatic aberration. Chromatic aberration means that different wavelengths of light are focused at different distances within the eye. Short-wavelength blue light is refracted more than long-wavelength red light. A typical monitor has a blue phosphor peak wavelength at about 480 nm and a red peak at about 640 nm, and a lens with a power of 1.5 diopters is needed to make blue and red focus at the same depth. This is the kind of blur that causes people to reach for their reading glasses. If we focus on a patch of light produced by the red phosphor, an adjacent blue patch will be significantly out of focus. Because of chromatic aberration, it is inadvisable to make fine patterns that use undiluted blue phosphor on a black background. Pure blue text on a black background can be almost unreadable, especially if there is white or red text nearby to attract the focusing mechanism. The addition of even a small amount of red and green will alleviate the problem, because these colors will provide luminance edges to perceptually define the color boundary.

The chromatic aberration of the eye can give rise to strong illusory depth effects (Jackson, MacDonald, & Freeman, 1994), although the actual mechanism remains unknown. This is illustrated in Figure 2.15, where both blue text and red text are superimposed on a black background. For about 60% of observers, the red appears closer, but 30% see the reverse, and the remaining 10% see the colors lying in the same plane. It is common to take advantage of this in slide presentations by making the background a deep blue, which makes white or red lettering appear to stand out for most people.

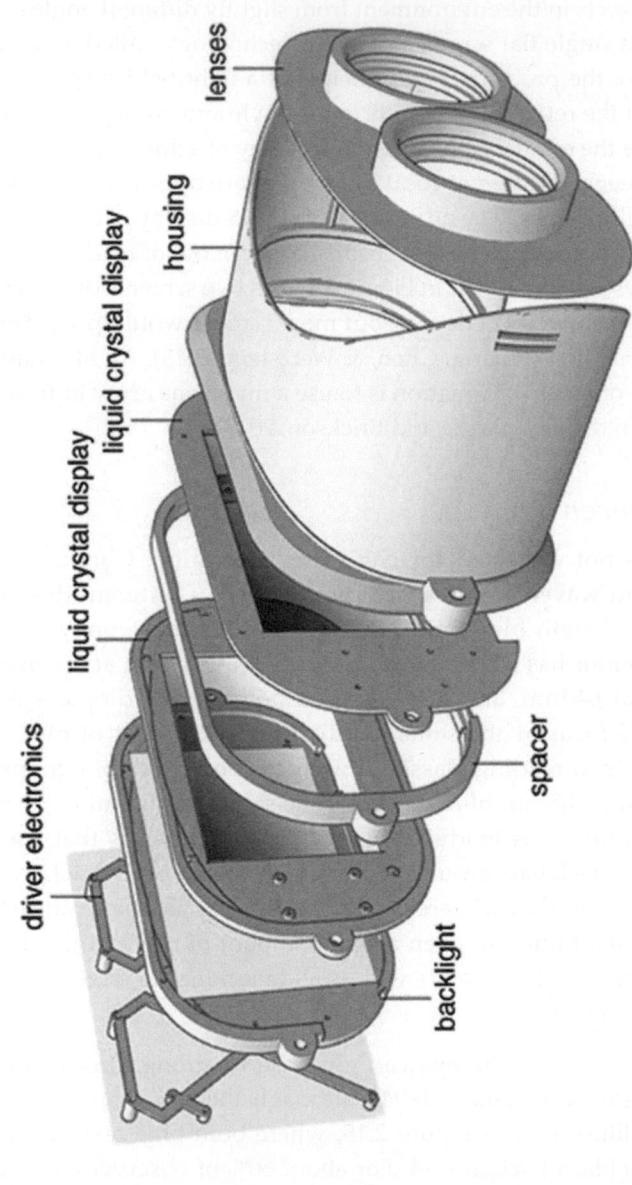

Figure 2.14 The light field display is a solution to the problem of proding correct depth-of-focus in a virtual-reality (VR) display. In the system illustrated here, two screens provide two different focal planes. The images are optically combined. *(From Huang, et al. (2015). Reproduced with permission.)*

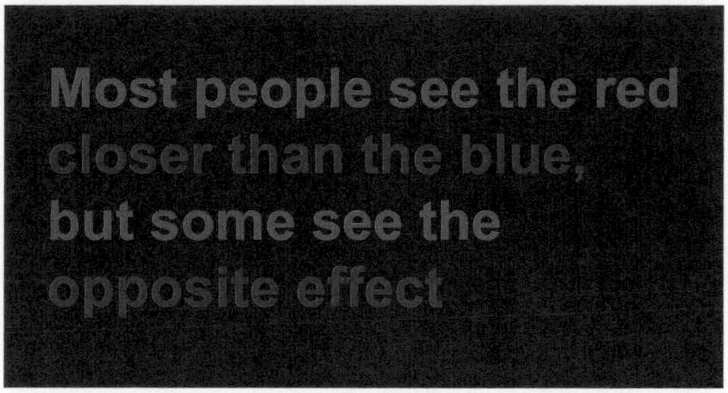

Figure 2.15 Chromostereopsis. For most people, red seems nearer than blue on a black background.

Receptors

The lens focuses an image on a mosaic of photoreceptor cells that line the back of the eye in a layer called the *retina*. There are two types of such cells: rods, which are extremely sensitive at low light levels, and cones, which are sensitive under normal working light levels. There are about 100 million rods and only 6 million cones. Rods are optimized for night vision and contribute far less to normal daytime vision than cones. The input from rods is pooled over large areas, with thousands of rods contributing to the signal that passes up through a single fiber in the optic nerve. Rods are so sensitive that they are overloaded in daylight and effectively shut down; therefore, most vision researchers ignore their very slight contribution to normal daylight vision.

The fovea is a small area in the center of the retina that is densely packed only with cones, and it is here that vision is sharpest. Cones at the fovea are packed about 20–30 seconds of arc apart (180 per degree). There are more than 100,000 cones packed into this central small area, subtending a visual angle of 1.5–2 degrees. Although it is usual to speak of the fovea as a 2-degree field, the greatest resolution of detail is obtained only in the central 1/2 degrees of this region. Remember that 1 degree is about the size of your thumbnail held at arm's length. Figure 2.16 is an image of the receptor mosaic in the fovea. The receptors are arranged in an irregular but roughly hexagonal pattern.

Simple Acuities

Visual acuities are measurements of our ability to see detail. Acuities are important in display technologies because they give us an idea of the ultimate limits on the information densities that we can perceive. Some of the basic acuities are summarized in Figure 2.17.

Most of the acuity measurements in Figure 2.17 suggest that we can resolve things, such as the presence of two distinct lines, down to about 1 minute of arc. This is in rough agreement with the spacing of receptors in the center of the fovea. For us to

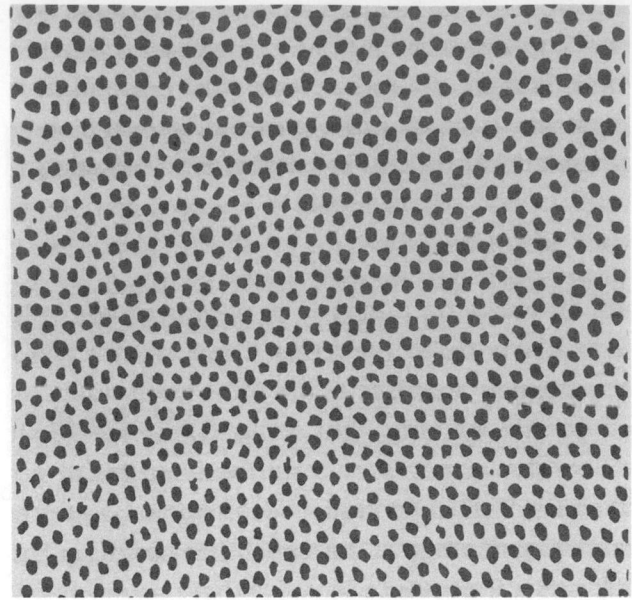

Figure 2.16 The receptor mosaic in the fovea.

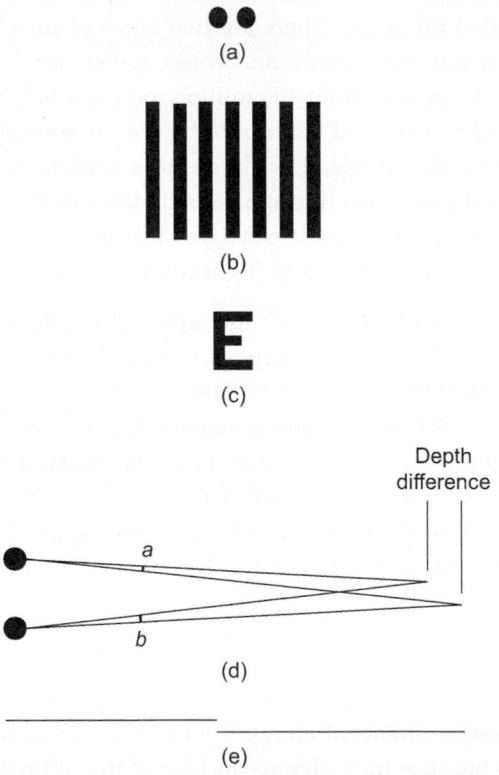

Figure 2.17 The basic acuities. (a) Point acuity (1 minute of arc): The ability to resolve two distinct point targets. (b) Grating acuity (1 to 2 minutes of arc): The ability to distinguish a pattern of bright and dark bars from a uniform gray patch. (c) Letter acuity (5 minutes of arc): The ability to resolve letters. The Snellen eye chart is a standard way of measuring this ability. 20/20 vision means that a 5-minute letter can be seen 90% of the time. (d) Stereo acuity (10 seconds of arc): The ability to resolve depth. The acuity is measured as the difference between two angles (*a* and *b*). (e) Vernier acuity (10 seconds of arc): The ability to see if two line segments are collinear.

see that two lines are distinct, the blank space between them should lie on a receptor; therefore, we should only be able to perceive lines separated by roughly twice the receptor spacing. However, there are a number of *superacuities*; vernier acuity and stereo acuity are two examples. A superacuity is the ability to perceive visual properties of the world to a greater precision than could be achieved based on a simple receptor model. Superacuities can be achieved only because postreceptor mechanisms are capable of integrating the input from many receptors to obtain better than single-receptor resolution. A good example of this is vernier acuity, the ability to judge the colinearity of two fine line segments. This can be done with amazing accuracy to better than 10 seconds of arc. To give an idea of just how accurate this is, a normal computer monitor has about 40 pixels (picture elements) per centimeter. We can perform vernier acuity tasks that are accurate to about 1/10 of a pixel.

Neural postprocessing can efficiently combine input from two eyes. Campbell and Green (1965) found that binocular viewing improves acuity by 7% as compared with monocular viewing. They also found a $\sqrt{2}$ improvement in contrast sensitivity. This latter finding is remarkable because it supports the theory that the brain is able to perfectly pool information from the two eyes, despite the three or four synaptic connections that lie between the receptors and the first point at which the information from the two eyes can be combined. Interestingly, Campbell and Green's findings suggest that we should be able to use the ability of the eye to integrate information over space and time to allow perception of higher resolution information than is actually available on our display device. One technique for achieving higher than device resolution is antialiasing, which is discussed later in this chapter. There is also an intriguing possibility that the temporal integration capability of the human eye could be used to advantage. This is why a sequence of video frames seems of substantially higher quality than any single frame.

Acuity Distribution and the Visual Field

If we look directly ahead and hold our arms straight out to either side, then we can just see both hands when we wiggle our fingers. This tells us that both eyes together provide a visual field of a bit more than 180°. The fact that we cannot see our fingers until they move also tells us that motion sensitivity in the periphery is better than static sensitivity. Figure 2.18 illustrates the visual field and shows the roughly triangular region of binocular overlap within which both eyes receive input. The reason that there is not more overlap is that the nose blocks the view. Visual acuity is distributed over this field in a very nonuniform manner. As shown in Figure 2.19, acuity outside of the fovea drops rapidly, so that we can only resolve about one-tenth the detail at 10 degrees from the fovea.

Normal acuity measures are one-dimensional; they measure our ability to resolve two points or two parallel lines as a function of the distance between them. But, if we consider the total number of points that can be perceived per unit area, this measure falls according to an inverse square law. We can actually only see one hundredth the

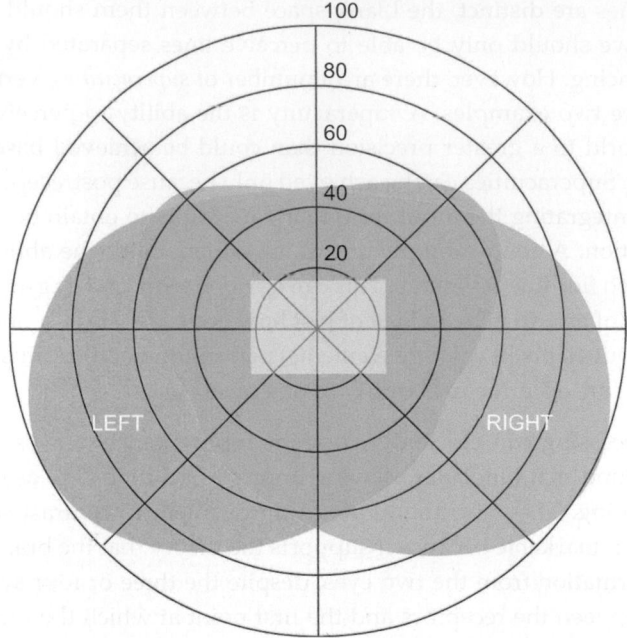

Figure 2.18 The visual field of view for a person gazing straight ahead. The irregular boundaries of the left and right fields are caused by facial features such as the nose and eyebrow ridges. The central blue–green area shows the region of binocular overlap. The larger rectangle at the center is the area covered by a monitor at a typical viewing distance. The smaller rectangle represents a smart phone. It provides visual information to less than half a percent of the visual field.

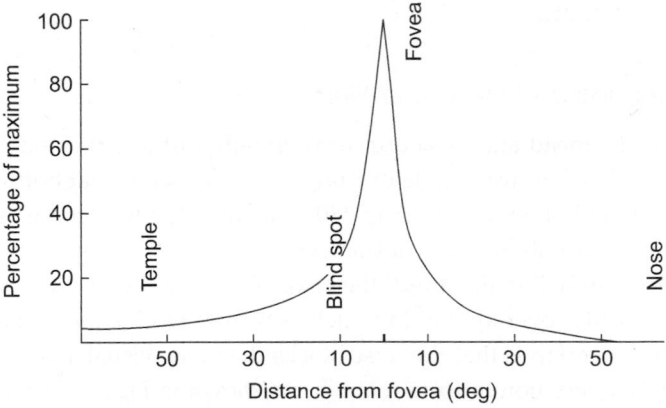

Figure 2.19 The acuity of the eye falls off rapidly with distance from the fovea.

number of points in an area at 10 degrees of eccentricity from the fovea. To put it another way, in the middle of the visual field, at the fovea, we can resolve about 100 points on the head of a pin. At the edge of the visual field, we can only discriminate objects the size of a fist.

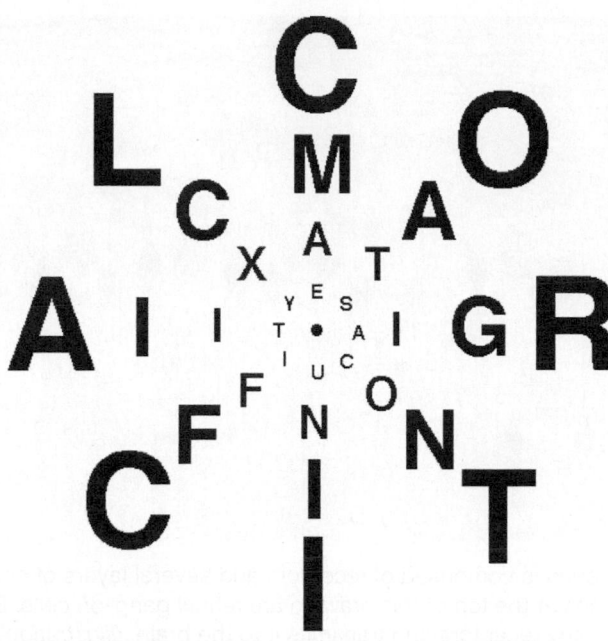

Figure 2.20 An eye chart developed by Anstis (1974). Each character is about five times the smallest perceivable size when the center is fixated. This is the case for any viewing distance. (*Courtesy of Stuart Anstis (Anstis, 1974)*)

The variation in acuity has been vividly expressed in an eye chart developed by Anstis (1974). The chart is shown in Figure 2.20. If you look at the center of the chart, each of the characters is equally distinct. To make this chart, Anstis took measurements of the smallest letter that could be seen at many angles of eccentricity from the fovea. In this version, each letter is about 5 times the smallest resolvable size for people with 20/20 vision. Anstis found that the size of the smallest distinct characters could be approximated by the simple function:

$$Character\ Size = 0{:}0.046e \tag{2.7}$$

where e is the eccentricity from the fovea measured in degrees of visual angle.

This variation in acuity with eccentricity comes from something called *cortical magnification*. Visual area 1 (V1) is the primary cortical reception area for signals from the eye. Fully half of the neurons in V1 are devoted to processing signals from the central 10 degrees of vision, representing only about 3% of the visual field.

Brain Pixels and the Optimal Screen

Because space in the brain is carved up very differently than the uniform pixels of a computer screen, we need a new term to talk about the image units used by the brain to process space. Let's call them *brain pixels*. Although there are many areas in the brain with nonuniform image maps, retinal ganglion cells best capture the brain pixel idea.

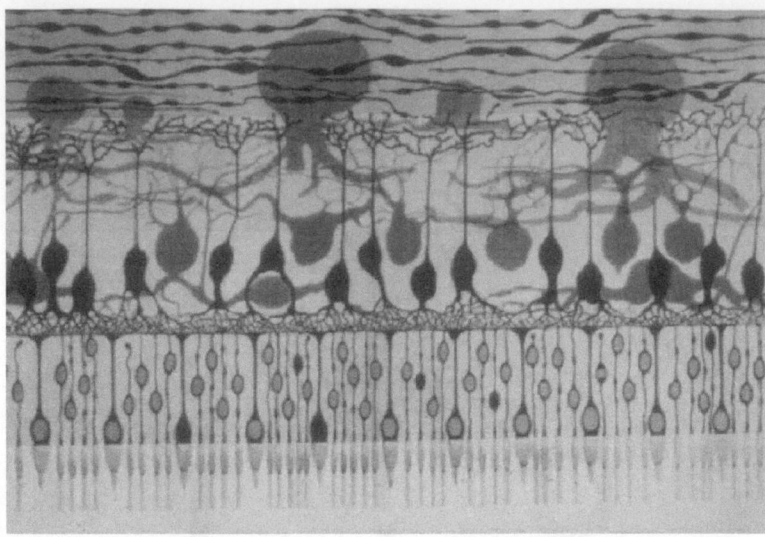

Figure 2.21 The retina is comprised of receptors and several layers of neurons. The big octopus-like neurons at the top of this drawing are retinal ganglion cells. Each integrates information from many receptors and transmits it to the brain. *(Illustration by Ferruccio Tartufieri (1887).)*

Retinal ganglion cells are neurons that send information from the eyeball up the optic nerve to the cortex. Each one pools information from many rod and cone receptors, as illustrated in Figure 2.21. In the fovea, a single ganglion cell may be devoted to a single cone, whereas in the far periphery each ganglion cell receives information from thousands of rods and cones. Each neuron has one nerve fiber called an *axon*, which carries the signal from each ganglion cell, and there are about a million axons in each optic nerve. The visual area that feeds into a ganglion cell is called its *receptive field*. Drasdo (1977) found that retinal ganglion cell size could be approximated by the function:

$$Receptive\ Field\ Size = 0.006(e+1.0) \tag{2.8}$$

where e is the eccentricity from the fovea measured in degrees of visual angle. Note that Equation (2.8) is very similar to Anstis' Equation (2.7) when we take into account that many brain pixels are needed to resolve something as complex as a letter of the alphabet. Assuming that a 7×7 matrix of brain pixels is needed to represent a character brings the two functions into close agreement.

In light of the extreme variation in the sizes of brain pixels, we can talk about the visual efficiency of a display screen by asking what screen size provides the best match of screen pixels to brain pixels. What happens when we look at the very wide-angle screen provided by some head-mounted virtual reality displays? Are we getting more information into the brain, or less? What happens when we look at the small screen of a personal digital assistant or even a wristwatch size screen? One way to answer these questions is to model how many brain pixels are stimulated by different screens having different sizes but the same number of pixels. To make the

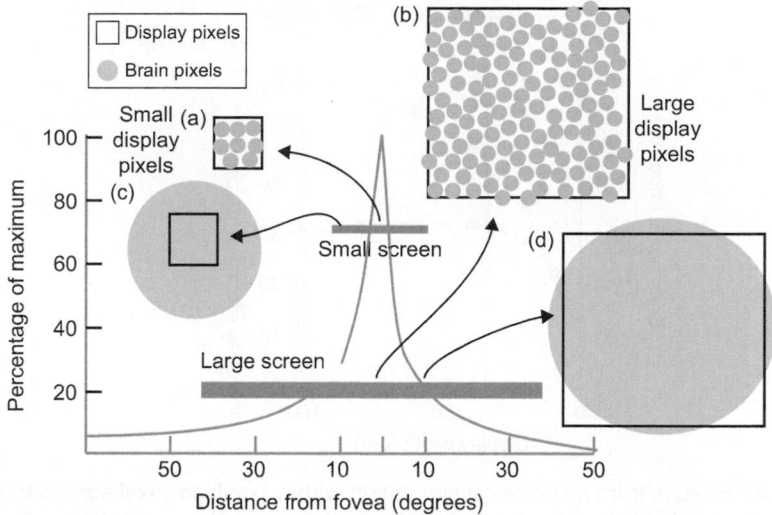

Figure 2.22 Differently sized screens having the same number of pixels have different areas of visual inefficiency. (a) With the small screen, there are 10 brain pixels per screen pixel at the center of the fovea. (b) With the large screen, the situation is worse, as there are 100 brain pixels per screen pixel at the center of the fovea. (c) At the edge of the small screen display, pixels are smaller than brain pixels. (d) At 10 degrees of eccentricity, with the big screen there is an approximate match between screen pixels and brain pixels.

---

comparison fair, we should keep the viewing distance constant. The two types of inefficiency that occur when we view flat displays are illustrated in Figure 2.22. At the fovea, there are many brain pixels for each screen pixel. To have higher resolution screens would definitely help foveal vision; however, off to the side, the situation is reversed, as there are many more screen pixels than brain pixels. We are, in a sense, wasting information, because the brain cannot appreciate the detail and we could easily get away with fewer pixels. In modeling the visual efficiency of different screen sizes, we can compute the *total number of brain pixels (TBP)* stimulated by the display simply by adding up all of the retinal ganglion cells stimulated by a display image.

We can also compute the number of *uniquely stimulated brain pixels (USBP)*. Many brain pixels get the same signal when we look at a low-resolution screen and are therefore redundant, providing no extra information. Therefore, to count uniquely stimulated brain pixels, we use the following formula:

$$USBP = TBP - redundant\ brain\ pixels \tag{2.9}$$

To obtain a measure of how efficiently a display is being used, we take the ratio of USBP to *screen pixels (SP)*. This measure is called *display efficiency (DE)*.

$$DE = USBP/SP \tag{2.10}$$

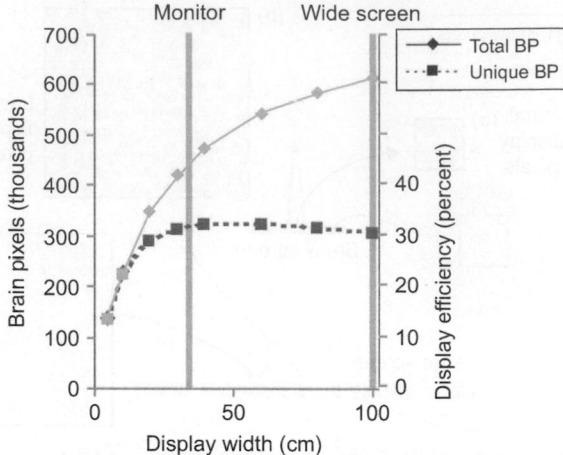

Figure 2.23 Results from a numerical simulation with a 1-million-pixel screen to show how many brain pixels are stimulated as a display increases in size. Display efficiency (right-hand scale) gives the percentage of screen pixels that uniquely influence the visual system (unique brain pixels) and only applies to the lower curve.

Note that if there were a perfect match, with one screen pixel for every brain pixel, we would have a display efficiency of 1.0, or 100%, but this is never the case because screen pixels are uniformly distributed and brain pixels are not.

Finally, we might be interested in the ratio between USBP and the brain pixels covered by a display. This measure of *visual efficiency (VE)* tells us the proportion of brain pixels in the screen area that are getting unique information.

$$VE = USBP/TBP \qquad (2.11)$$

Figure 2.23 illustrates a numerical simulation of what happens to TBP and USBP as we change the size of the screen. It is based on Drasdo's (1977) model and assumes one million square pixels in a 1000 × 1000 array at a constant viewing distance of 50 cm. It takes into account that pixels near the edge of a large screen are both farther away and viewed obliquely—and are therefore visually smaller than pixels in the center. In fact, their visual area declines by $\cos^2(\theta)$, where θ is the angle of eccentricity. For illustrative purposes, the display widths equivalent to a conventional monitor and a single wall of a Cave Automatic Virtual Environment (CAVE) display are shown (Cruz-Neira, Sandin, DeFanti, Kenyon, & Hart, 1992). A CAVE is a virtual reality display where the participant stands in the center of a cube, each wall of which is a display screen. In Figure 2.23, the sizes have been normalized to a standard viewing distance by using equivalent visual angles. Thus, a CAVE wall of 2 m at a viewing distance of 1 m is equivalent to a 1 m display at 50 cm, given that both have the same number of pixels.

The simulation of the one million–pixel display reveals a number of interesting things. For a start, even though a conventional monitor covers only about 5%–10% of our visual field when viewed normally, it stimulates almost 50% of our brain pixels. This means that even if we could have very high-resolution large screens, we would not be getting very much more information into the brain. Figure 2.23 shows that USBPs peak at a width close to the normal monitor viewing with a display efficiency of 30%, and decline somewhat as the screen gets larger. If we consider that our visual field is a precious resource and there are other things besides computer graphics that we may wish to see, this confirms that computer screens are currently about the right size for most tasks. A modern smart phone has pixels that approximate a one-to-one match with brain pixels at the center of the fovea. Remarkably, given that they only fill a half of 1% of the visual field, they still stimulate about a quarter of our brain pixels.

There is an argument that the center of the visual field is even more important for many tasks than its huge brain pixel concentration would suggest. A natural way of seeking information (discussed in Chapter 11) is to use eye movements to bring the information to the center of the visual field where we see the best. The *parafovea* may be optimal for pattern perception; it is an area that is about 6° in diameter, centered on the fovea. Most charts and diagrams in this book are presented to be roughly parafoveal size. The periphery is undoubtedly important in situation awareness and alerting, but when visual pattern finding for decision-making is required, the relatively small parafoveal region is the most critical.

The StarCAVE (DeFanti et al., 2009) is, at the time of this writing, perhaps the highest resolution completely immersive display currently available. It is a five-sided room with curved walls on which a total of 68 million pixels are projected, 34 million for each eye. Compare this with a top of the line monitor with 15 million pixels, at the time this of writing, or a high-quality smart phone display at about two million pixels.

The StarCAVE and its four-walled CAVE predecessors are the only displays that can fill the visual field of the eye. This arguably makes it very good for simulating the feel of an architectural space or for other simulator applications where a sense of presence is important. *Presence* is a term used by those who strive for virtual realism and is used to describe the degree to which virtual objects and spaces seem real.

But presence is not usually important in data visualization, and when we wish to understand the structure of a cell or the shape of a molecule, being inside of it does not help. We need to stand back. To best see the structure of a cell it should fill the parafovea, not the entire visual field, and ideally the most important information will fall on the fovea.

The brain's way of getting new information is to make rapid eye movements of about 5 degrees on average. In a StarCAVE, when we make such an eye movement we get only another 10% of our brain pixels stimulated in our parafoveal region because of its low resolution. With a high-resolution monitor at normal viewing distances, an eye movement generates at least an additional 60% of new information within the parafovea. Ultimately, what matters is the time and mental effort required to get new information. The final chapters of this book deal with this in detail. But, for now, it is worth

Figure 2.24 A sine wave grating.

saying that interactive methods combined with moderately sized high-resolution screens are likely to be much more efficient than low-resolution immersive screens. They also use much less of the working environment of the user and are not as costly.

> **[G2.8]** Use a high-resolution display with a moderate viewing angle (e.g., 40 degrees) for data analysis. This applies both to individual data analysis when the screen can be on a desktop and close to the user and to collaborative data analysis when the screen must be larger and farther away.

> **[G2.9]** Use wrap-around screens to obtain a sensation of "presence" in a virtual space. This is useful in vehicle simulations and some entertainment systems.

Spatial Contrast Sensitivity Function

The rather simple pattern shown in Figure 2.24 has become one of the most useful tools in measuring basic properties of the human visual system. This pattern is called a *sine wave grating* because its brightness varies sinusoidally in one direction. There are five ways in which this pattern can be varied:

1. Spatial frequency (the number of bars of the grating per degree of visual angle)

2. Orientation

3. Contrast (the amplitude of the sine wave)

4. Phase angle (the lateral displacement of the pattern)

5. Visual area covered by the grating pattern

The grating luminance is defined by the following equation:

$$L = 0.5 + \frac{a}{2}\sin\left(\frac{2\pi x}{\omega} + \frac{\phi}{\omega}\right)$$

(2.12)

where *a* is the contrast (amplitude), ω is the wavelength, ϕ is the phase angle, and *x* is the position on the screen. *L* denotes the resulting output light level in the range [0, 1], assuming that the monitor is linear (see the discussion of gamma correction in Chapter 3).

Figure 2.25 This grating pattern changes spatial frequency from the left to the right and varies in contrast in a vertical direction. The highest spatial frequency you can resolve depends on the distance from which you view the pattern.

One way to use a sine wave grating is to measure the sensitivity of the eye/brain system to the lowest contrast that can be detected and to see how this varies with spatial frequency. Contrast is defined by:

$$C = \frac{L_{max} - L_{min}}{L_{max} + L_{min}} \tag{2.14}$$

where L_{max} is the peak luminance, L_{min} is the minimum luminance, and C is the contrast. The result is called a *spatial modulation sensitivity function*.

Figure 2.25 is a pattern designed to allow you to directly see the high-frequency falloff in the sensitivity of your own visual system. It is a sinusoidally modulated pattern of stripes that varies from left to right in terms of spatial frequency and from top to bottom in terms of contrast. If you view this from 2 m, you can see how your sensitivity to high-frequency patterns is reduced. When it is close, you can also see a low-frequency falloff.

The human spatial contrast sensitivity function varies dramatically with spatial frequency, falling off at both high and low values. We are most sensitive to patterns of bright and dark bars occurring at about two or three cycles per degree. Figure 2.26 shows typical functions for three different age groups. Sensitivity falls off to zero for fine gratings of about 60 cycles per degree for younger people. As we age, we become less and less sensitive to higher spatial frequencies (Owlsley, Sekuler, & Siemensne, 1983). It is not just that the finest detail we can resolve declines with age. We actually become less sensitive to any pattern components above one cycle per degree.

One of the practical implications of the low-frequency falloff in sensitivity is that many projectors are very nonuniform, yet this goes unremarked. A typical projector display will vary by 30% or more over the screen (it is usually brightest in the center), even if it is displaying a supposedly uniform field; but because we are insensitive to this very

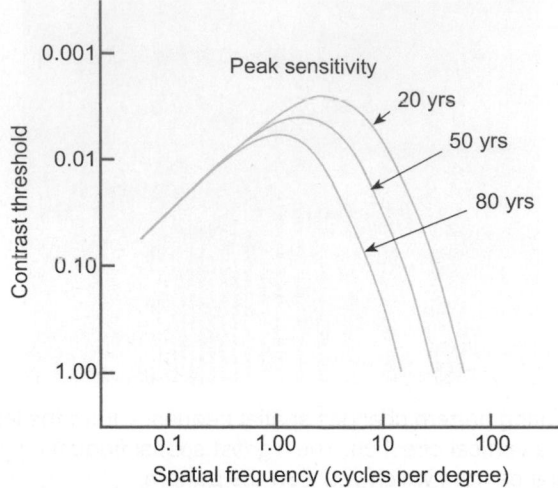

Figure 2.26 Contrast sensitivity varies with spatial frequency as shown in this log-log scale plot. The function is illustrated for three age groups. As we age, our sensitivity to higher spatial frequencies is reduced. *(Redrawn from Owlsley et al. (1983).)*

gradual (low-frequency) variation, we fail to notice the poor quality. The falloff in low spatial frequency sensitivity may also hinder our perception of large spatial patterns as they are presented in large field displays.

Most tests of visual acuity, such as letter or point acuity, are really tests of high-frequency resolution, but this may not always be the most useful thing to measure. In tests of pilots, it has been shown that low-frequency contrast sensitivity is actually more important than simple acuity in measuring their performance in flight simulators (Ginsburg, Evans, Sekuler, & Harp, 1982).

Visual images on the retina vary in time as well as in space. We can measure the temporal sensitivity of the visual system in much the same way that we measure the spatial sensitivity. This involves taking a pattern, such as that shown in Figure 2.24 and causing it to oscillate in contrast from high to low and back again over time. This temporal oscillation in contrast is normally done using a sinusoidal function. When this technique is used, both the spatial and the temporal sensitivity of human vision can be mapped out. Once this is done, it becomes evident that spatial frequency sensitivity and temporal frequency sensitivity are interdependent.

Figure 2.27 shows the contrast threshold for a flickering grating as a function of its temporal frequency and its spatial frequency (Kelly, 1979). This shows that optimal sensitivity is obtained for a grating flickering at between 2 and 10 cycles per second (Hz). It is interesting to note that the low-frequency falloff in sensitivity is much less when a pattern is flickering at between 5 and 10 Hz. If we were only interested in being able to detect the presence of blurry patterns in data, making those components of the image flicker at 7 or 8 Hz would be the best way to present them. There are many other

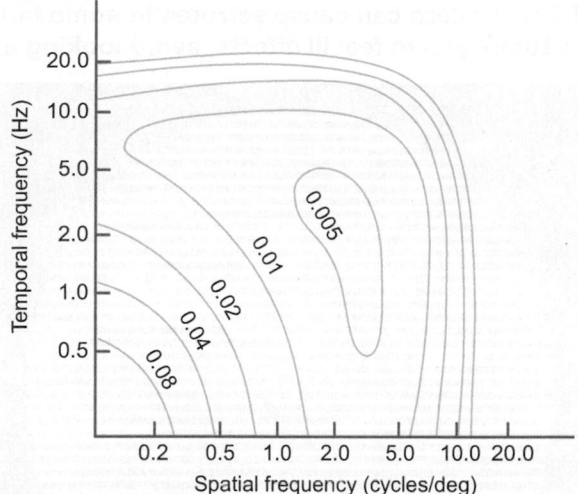

Figure 2.27 Contour map of the human spatiotemporal threshold surface. Each contour represents the contrast at which a particular combination of spatial and temporal frequencies can be detected. *(Redrawn from Kelly (1979).)*

reasons, however, why this is not a good idea; in particular, it would undoubtedly be extremely irritating. The limit of human sensitivity to flicker is about 50 Hz, which is why computer monitors and lightbulbs flicker at higher rates.

When the spatial and temporal frequency analysis of the visual system is extended to color, we find that chromatic spatial sensitivity is much lower, especially for rapidly changing patterns. In Chapter 4, the spatial and temporal characteristics of color vision are compared to those of the black-and-white vision we have been discussing.

Visual Stress

On December 17, 1997, a Japanese television network canceled broadcasts of an action-packed cartoon because its brightly flashing scenes caused convulsions, and even vomiting of blood, in more than 700 children. The primary cause was determined to be the repetitive flashing lights produced by the computer-generated graphics. The harmful effects were exacerbated by the tendency of children to sit very close to the screen. Vivid, repetitive, large field flashes are known to be extremely stressful to some people.

The disorder known as *pattern-induced epilepsy* has been reported and investigated for decades. Some of the earliest reported cases were caused by the flicker from helicopter rotor blades; this resulted in prescreening of pilots for the disorder. In an extensive study of the phenomenon, Wilkins (1995) concluded that a particular combination of spatial and temporal frequencies is especially potent: Striped patterns of about three cycles per degree and flicker rates of about 20 Hz are most likely to induce seizures in susceptible individuals. Figure 2.28 illustrates a static pattern likely to cause visual

**Warning! This pattern can cause seizures in some individuals.
If it causes you to feel ill effects, avoid looking at it.**

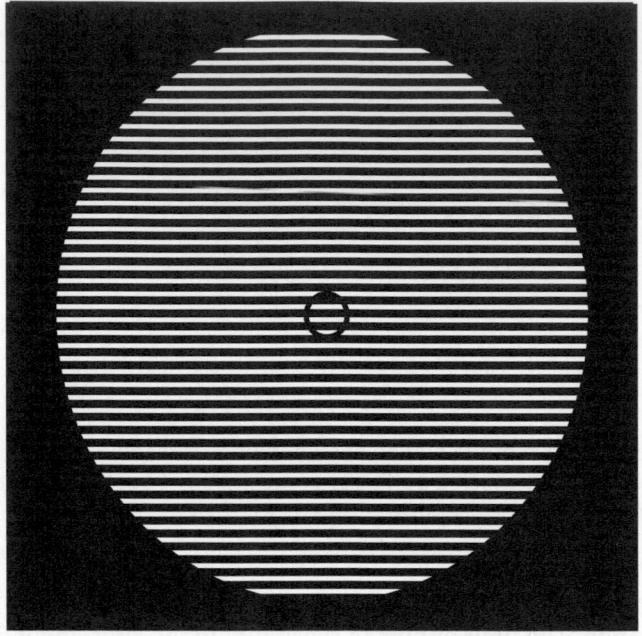

Figure 2.28 A pattern that is designed to be visually stressful. If it is viewed from 40 cm, the spacing of the stripes is about three cycles per degree.

stress. The ill effects also increase with the overall size of the pattern. Visual stress, however, may not be confined to individuals with a particular disorder. Wilkins argued that striped patterns can cause visual stress in most people. He gave normal text as an example of a pattern that may cause problems because it is laid out in horizontal stripes and suggested that certain fonts may be worse than others.

[G2.10] Avoid using high-contrast grating patterns in visual displays. In particular, avoid using high-contrast grating patterns that flicker or any pattern flickering at rates between 5 and 50 Hz.

The Optimal Display

The cone receptors at the center of the eye are spaced at roughly 20–30 seconds of arc, meaning that 180 pixels per cm should be adequate for almost all visualizations (assuming a display held at 56 cm from the eye). At the time of writing this is available on quality smart phones and tablets. Some computer monitors come close.

If 180 pixels per cm is sufficient, we must ask why manufacturers produce laser printers capable of 1200 dots per inch (460 dots per centimeter) or more. There are three

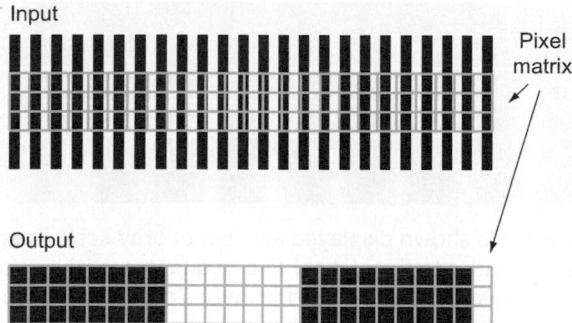

Figure 2.29 A striped pattern is sampled by pixels. The output is shown below.

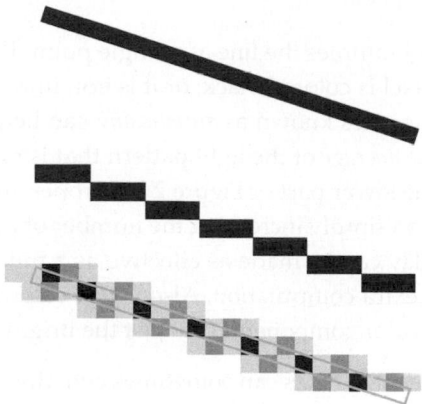

Figure 2.30 Aliasing artifacts with antialiasing as a solution.

reasons: aliasing, gray levels, and superacuities. The first two reasons are essentially technical, not perceptual, but they are worth discussing because they have significant implications in perception. The problems are significant for most display devices, not just for printers.

Aliasing

Aliasing effects occur when a regular pattern is sampled by another regular pattern at a different spatial frequency. Figure 2.29 illustrates what happens when a pattern of black-and-white stripes is sampled by an array of pixels whose spacing is slightly greater than the wavelength. We assume that the pattern of input stripes is sampled at the center of each pixel. The resulting pattern has a much wider spacing. Aliasing can cause all kinds of unwanted effects. Patterns that should be invisible because they are beyond the resolving power of the human eye can become all too visible. Patterns that are unrelated to the original data can occur in Moiré fringes. This is surely the reason why the retinal mosaic of receptor cells is not regular except in small patches (Figure 2.16). Another aliasing effect is illustrated in Figure 2.30. The line shown in the top part of the figure becomes a staircase pattern when it is drawn using large pixels. The

Figure 2.31 A sine wave is shown displayed as a set of gray scale images under various sampling schemes (all relative to the original sine frequency). In the upper set the signal is reconstructed using uniform values extended across each sample. In the lower set reconstruction is done using linear interpolation.

problem is that each pixel samples the line at a single point. Either that point is on the line, in which case the pixel is colored black, or it is not, in which case the pixel is colored white. A set of techniques known as *antialiasing* can help with this. Antialiasing consists of computing the *average* of the light pattern that is represented by each pixel. The result is shown in the lower part of Figure 2.30. Proper antialiasing can be a more cost-effective solution than simply increasing the number of pixels in the display. With it, a low-resolution display can be made as effective as a much higher resolution display, but it does require extra computation. Also, a full-color image requires properly antialiasing of the three-color components, not just the brightness levels.

In data visualization, aliasing effects can sometimes actually be useful; for example, it is much easier to judge whether a line is perfectly horizontal on the screen with aliasing than without it (Figure 2.31). Because of our ability to see very small line displacements (vernier acuity), aliasing makes small misalignments completely obvious. The spatial frequency amplification illustrated in Figure 2.29 can be used as a deliberate technique to magnify certain kinds of regular patterns to make invisibly fine variations visible (Post et al., 1997). It is used in optics to judge the sphericity of mirrors and lenses.

Mathematical analysis of aliasing is based on a fundamental theorem of signal transmission called the Nyquist limit (Gonzalez & Woods, 1993). It is often (wrongly) stated that the consequence of the Nyquist limit is that a signal can be reconstructed from its samples if the samples are obtained at a frequency at least twice the highest frequency contained in the source. However this is only correct for the frequency, not the amplitude, and only for infinitely long signal trains.

Figure 2.31 shows a pure sine wave, represented as a gray-scale image and the same data represented with sampling at 2.05, 3.05, 4.05, 5.05, and 6.05 times the spatial frequency of the original. To get a reasonable representation clearly requires sampling at a frequency considerably greater than the Nyquist limit.

[G2.11] To provide a reasonable representation of features sample at least 5 times the highest spatial frequency needed to perceive those features.

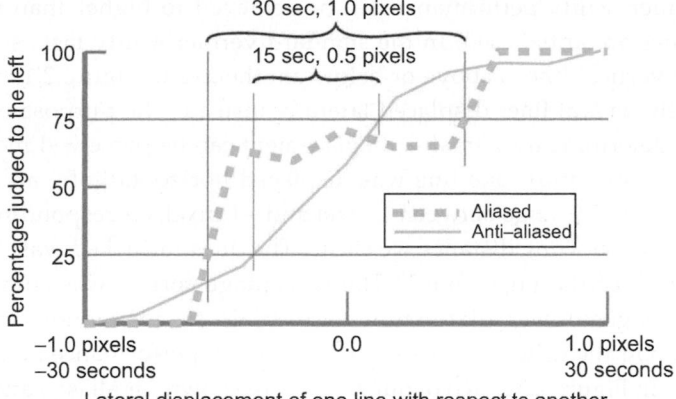

Figure 2.32 Results from an experiment showing that vernier acuity can be improved by antialiasing. The threshold is defined as half the horizontal difference between the 25% threshold and the 75% threshold.

Number of Dots

The main reason why we need 1200 dots per inch on a laser printer is that the dots of a laser printer are either black or white; to represent gray, many dots must be used. Essentially, one pixel is made up of many dots. Thus, for example, a 16 × 16 matrix of dots can be used to generate 257 levels of gray because from 0 to 256 of the dots can be colored black. In practice, square patches are not used, because these cause aliasing problems. To correct aliasing effects, randomness is used in distributing the dots, and errors are propagated from one patch to neighboring patches. Most graphics textbooks provide an introduction to these techniques (e.g., Foley, van Dam, Feiner, & Hughes, 1990). The fact that grays are made from patterns of black-and-white dots means that the resolution of a laser printer actually is 1200 dots per inch only for black-and-white patterns. For gray patterns, the resolution is at least 10 times lower.

> **[G2.12]** Antialias visualizations wherever possible, especially where regular patterns, fine textures, or narrow lines are being displayed.

Superacuities and Displays

Superacuities provide a reason why we might wish to have very high-resolution monitors. As discussed earlier, superacuities occur because the human visual system can integrate information from a number of retinal receptors to give better than receptor resolution; for example, in vernier acuity, better than 10 arc-second resolution is achievable. However, in my laboratory, we have obtained experimental evidence that antialiasing can result in superacuity performance on vernier acuity tasks. This involves making judgments to see differences in the alignment of fine lines that are actually smaller than individual pixels. Figure 2.32 shows data from an experiment that my research assistant, Tim Millar, and I carried out to determine whether vernier acuity performance can be achieved to higher than pixel resolution if the lines are antialiased. In the standard vernier acuity task, subjects judge whether one vertical line is above or below another, as in Figure 2.17(d), although we did it with vertical lines displaced laterally instead. The purpose of the experiment was to determine how small a displacement can be perceived more than 50% of the time. In our study, one line was displaced horizontally by an amount that varied randomly in a range between 1 pixel and −1 pixel, corresponding to ±30 seconds of arc at the viewing distance we chose. The question asked was, "Is the lower line to the right of the upper line?" The percentage correct was computed based on the answers given over a large number of trials. By convention, vernier acuity is defined as half the difference between 25% correct performance and 75% correct performance. In Figure 2.32, two of our results are shown for aliased and antialiased lines. The actual threshold is half of each range on the x-axis. Thus, Figure 2.32 shows a 15 second vernier acuity threshold (30 seconds × 0.5) for aliased lines and a 7.5 second threshold (15 seconds × 0.5) for antialiased lines. This data shows that, given proper antialiasing, superacuity performance to better than pixel resolution can be achieved.

Temporal Requirements of the Perfect Display

Just as we can evaluate the spatial requirements for a perfect monitor, so can we evaluate the temporal requirements. The limit of resolution that most of us can perceive is about 50-Hz flicker; hence, the 50- to 75-Hz refresh rate of the typical monitor would seem to be adequate. However, temporal aliasing artifacts are common in computer graphics and movies. The "reversing wagon wheel" effect is the one most often noticed (the wheel of a wagon in a western movie appears to rotate in the wrong direction). Temporal aliasing effects are especially pronounced when the image update rate is low, and it is common in data visualization systems to have animated images that are updated only about 10 times per second even though the screen is refreshed at 60 Hz or better. An obvious result is the breaking up of a moving object into a series of discrete objects. If the data contains a repetitive temporal pattern, aliasing and sampling effects can occur that are the analogs of the spatial aliasing effects. Sometimes a single object can appear to be multiple objects. To correct these problems, temporal antialiasing can be employed. Part of a moving image may pass through several pixels over the course of a single animation frame. The correct antialiasing solution is to color each pixel according to the percentage contributions of all the different objects as they pass through it for the duration of the animation frame. Thus, if the refresh rate is 60 Hz, a program must calculate the *average* color for each pixel that is affected by the moving pattern for each 1/60-second interval. This technique is often called *motion blur*. It can be computationally expensive in practice and is rarely done except in the case of high-quality animations created for the movie industry. As computers become faster, we can expect antialiasing to be more widely used in data visualization, because there is no doubt that aliasing effects can be visually disturbing and occasionally misleading.

Conclusion

In comparison with the richness of the visual world, the computer screen is simple indeed. It is remarkable that we can achieve so much with such a limited device. In the world, we perceive subtly textured, visually rich surfaces, differentiated by shading, depth of focus effects, and texture gradients. The computer screen merely produces a two-dimensional array of colors. Gibson's concept of the ambient optical array, introduced at the beginning of this chapter, provides a context for understanding the success of this device, despite its shortcomings. Given a particular direction and a viewing angle of 20° or so, a computer monitor is capable of reproducing many (but not all) of those aspects of the ambient array that are most important to perception. As discussed in Chapter 4, this is especially true in the realm of color, where a mere three colors are used to effectively reproduce much of the gamut to which humans are sensitive. Spatial information, in the form of texture gradients and other spatial cues, is also reproducible to some extent on a monitor; however, there are problems in the reproduction of fine texture. The actual pixel pattern may provide a texture that visually competes with the texture designed for display. As discussed in Chapter 5, this represents a serious shortcoming when we wish to use texture as a display option.

A typical monitor only stimulates perhaps 5%–10% of the visual field at normal viewing distances, as shown in Figure 2.18. This is not as serious a shortcoming as it might seem, because the central field of view is heavily overweighted in human visual processing. In fact, looking at the center of a monitor screen from a normal viewing distance stimulates considerably more than 50% of the visual processing mechanisms in the brain. Even a smart phone with a high-resolution screen will stimulate at least 25% of the visual system and this is the most important 25% in terms of pattern processing.

If we wish to create artificial virtual reality displays as a method for presenting visual data, current displays have serious problems. One of these is their lack of ability to provide focal depth of focus information. In the real world, the eye must refocus on objects at different distances. Because this is not the case for computer graphics presented on the screen, it can confuse our spatial processing systems. This problem will be discussed further in Chapter 7 under the heading "The Vergence–Focus Problem."

Fortunately, the most important pattern perception mechanisms for data visualization operate in two dimensions, not three. The value of VR approaches has yet to be demonstrated for data visualization although the naïve assumption that interactive 3D must be better has caused much squandering of money and resources. The good news is that we can achieve almost everything that is important without recourse to radical new technologies. Also, the gains in screen resolution that have occurred have real value. The best monitors are now approaching the limits of resolution of the human eye.

CHAPTER THREE

Lightness, Brightness, Contrast, and Constancy

It would be dull to live in a gray world, but we would actually get along just fine 99% of the time. Technically, we can divide color space into one luminance (gray scale) dimension and two chromatic dimensions. It is the luminance dimension that is most basic to perception. Understanding it can help us answer practical questions: How do we map data to a gray scale? How much information can we display per unit area? How much data can we display per unit time? Can gray scales be misleading? (The answer is "yes.")

To understand the applications of gray scales, we need to address other more fundamental questions: How bright is a patch of light? What is white? What is black? What is a middle gray? These are simple-sounding questions, but the answers are complex and lead us to many of the basic mechanisms of perception. The fact that we have light-sensing receptors in our eyes might seem like a good starting point, but individual receptor signals tell us very little. The nerves that transmit information from the eyes to the brain transmit nothing about the amount of light falling on the retina. Instead, they signal the *relative* amount of light: how a particular patch of light differs from a neighboring patch, or how a particular patch of light has changed in the past instant. Neurons processing visual information in the early stages of the retina and primary visual cortex do not behave like light meters; they act as *change* meters.

The signaling of differences is not special to lightness and brightness; it is a general characteristic of early stage sensory processing, and we will come across it again and again throughout this book. The implications are fundamental to the way we perceive information. The fact that differences, not absolute values, are transmitted to

Information Visualization. https://doi.org/10.1016/B978-0-12-812875-6.00003-7

the brain accounts for contrast illusions that can cause substantial errors in the way data are "read" from a visualization. The signaling of differences also means that the perception of lightness is nonlinear and this has implications for the gray scale coding of information. But, to belabor the occasional inaccuracies of perception does not do justice to millions of years of evolution. The fact that the early stages of vision are nonlinear does not mean that all perception is inaccurate. On the contrary, we can usually make quite sophisticated judgments about the lightness of *surfaces* in our environments. This chapter shows how simple, early visual mechanisms can help our brains do sophisticated things, such as perceive the surface colors of objects correctly no matter what the illumination level.

This chapter is also the first part of a presentation of color vision. Luminance can be regarded as but one of three color dimensions, albeit the most important one. Discussing this dimension in isolation gives us an opportunity to examine many of the basic concepts of color with a simpler model. (This is expanded in Chapter 4 into a full three color–channel model.) We start by introducing properties of neurons including the concept of the *visual receptive field*, together with a number of display distortion effects that can be explained by simple neural models. The bulk of this chapter is taken up with a discussion of the concepts of luminance, lightness, and brightness and the implications of these for data display.

The practical lessons of this chapter are related to the way data values can be mapped to gray values using gray scale coding. The kinds of perceptual errors that can occur owing to simultaneous contrast are discussed at length. More fundamentally, the reasons why the visual system makes these errors provide a general lesson. The nervous system works by computing difference signals at almost every level. The lesson is that visualization is not good for representing precise absolute numerical values, but rather for displaying patterns of differences or changes over time, to which the eye and brain are extremely sensitive.

Neurons, Receptive Fields, and Brightness Illusions

Neurons are the basic circuits of information processing in the brain. In some respects, they are like transistors, only much more complex. Like the digital circuits of a computer, neurons respond with discrete pulses of electricity. But, unlike transistors, neurons are connected to hundreds and sometimes thousands of other neurons. Much of our knowledge about the behavior of neurons comes from single-cell recording techniques where a tiny microelectrode is inserted into a cell in the brain of a live animal and the cell's electrical activity is monitored as various patterns are displayed in front of its eyes. This research revealed that most neurons are constantly active, emitting pulses of electricity through connections with other cells. Depending on the visual pattern shown to the animal, the rate of firing can be increased or decreased as the neuron is excited or inhibited. Neuroscientists often set up amplifiers and loudspeakers in their laboratories so that they can hear the activity of cells that are being probed. The sound is like the clicking of a Geiger counter, becoming rapid when the cell is excited and slowing when it is inhibited.

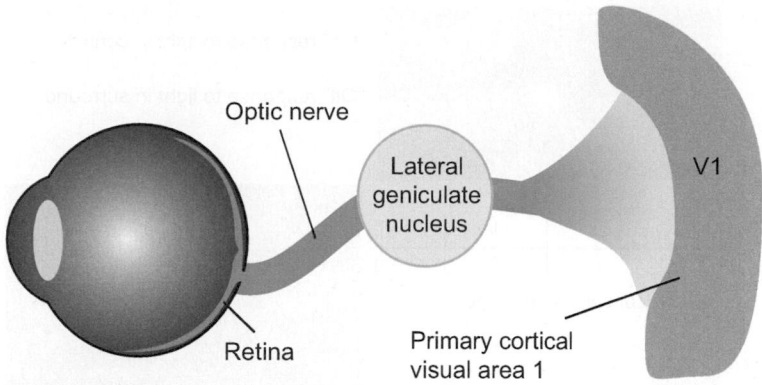

Figure 3.1 Signals from the retina are transmitted along the optic nerve to the lateral geniculate nucleus. From there, they are distributed to a number of areas, but mostly to visual area 1 of the cortex, located at the back of the head.

There is considerable neural processing of information in the eye itself. Several layers of cells in the eye culminate in retinal ganglion cells. These ganglion cells send information through the optic nerve via a way station, called the *lateral geniculate nucleus*, onto the primary visual processing areas at the back of the brain, as shown in Fig. 3.1.

The *receptive field* of a cell is the visual area over which a cell responds to light. This means that patterns of light falling on the retina influence the way the neuron responds, even though it may be many synapses removed from receptors. Retinal ganglion cells are organized with circular receptive fields and they can be either on-center or off-center. The activity of an on-center cell is illustrated in Fig. 3.2. When this kind of cell is stimulated in the center of its receptive field, it emits pulses at a greater rate. When the cell is stimulated outside of the center of its field, it emits pulses at a lower than normal rate and is said to be inhibited. Fig. 3.2 also shows the output of an array of such neurons being stimulated by a bright edge. The output of this system is an enhanced response on the bright side of the edge and a depressed response on the dark side of the edge, with an intermediate response to the uniform areas on either side. The cell fires more on the bright side because there is less light in the inhibitory region; it is less inhibited.

A widely used mathematical description of the concentric receptive field is the difference of Gaussians model (often called the DoG function):

$$f(x) = \alpha_1 e^{-\left(\frac{x}{w_1}\right)^2} - \alpha_2 e^{\left(\frac{x}{w_2}\right)^2}$$

3.1

In this model, the firing rate of the cell is the difference between two Gaussians. One Gaussian represents the center and the other represents the surround, as illustrated in Fig. 3.3. The variable x represents the distance from the center of the field, w_1 defines the width of the center, and w_2 defines the width of the surround. The amount of

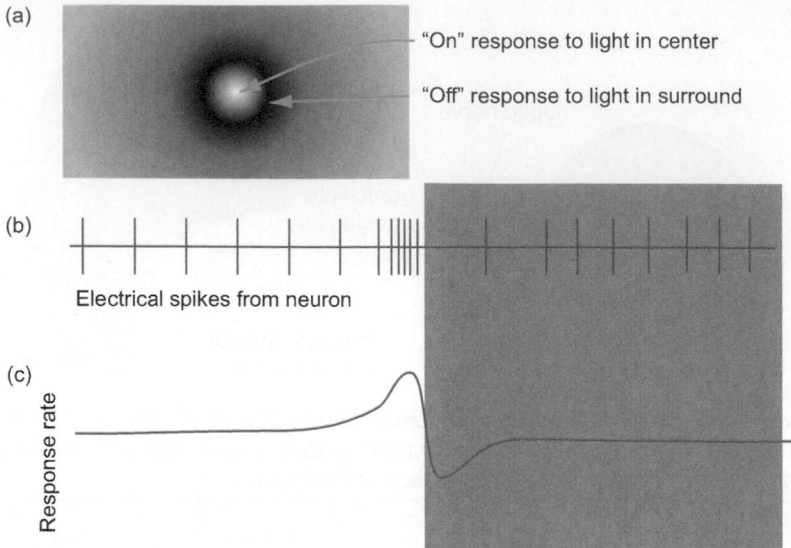

Figure 3.2 (a) The receptive field structure of an on-center simple lateral geniculate cell. (b) As the cell passes over from a light region to a dark region, the rate of neural firing increases just to the bright side of the edge and decreases on the dark side. (c) A smoothed plot of the cell activity level.

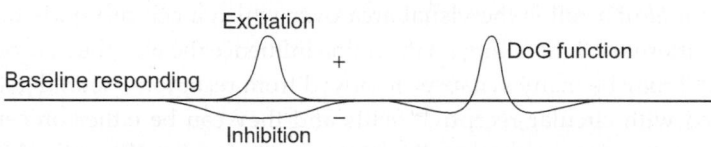

Figure 3.3 Difference of Gaussians (DoG) model of a receptive field.

excitation or inhibition is given by the amplitude parameters α_1 and α_2. The DoG function and the concentric receptive field are an example of lateral inhibition in action. Stimulation of receptors at the edge of the field *laterally inhibits* the response at the center.

We can easily calculate how a DoG type of receptor responds to various patterns. We can either think of the pattern passing over the receptive field of the cell or think of the output of a whole array of DoG cells arranged in a line across the pattern. When we use a computer to simulate either operation, we discover that the DoG receptive field can be used to explain a variety of brightness contrast effects.

In the Hermann grid illusion, shown in Fig. 3.4, black spots appear at the intersections of the bright lines. The explanation is that there is more inhibition at the spaces between two squares, so they seem brighter than the regions at the intersections.

 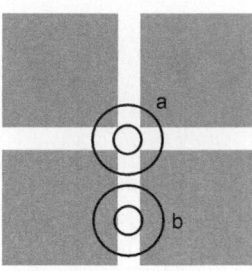

Figure 3.4 Hermann grid illusion. The black spots that are seen at the intersections of the lines are thought to result from the fact that there is more inhibition from the light in the periphery of the receptive field at position (a) than at position (b).

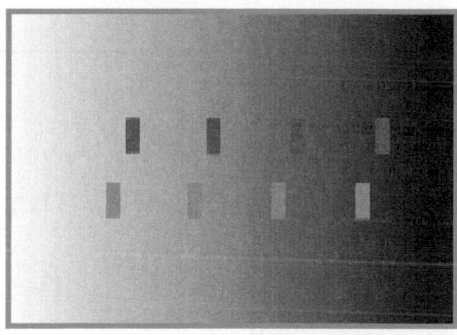

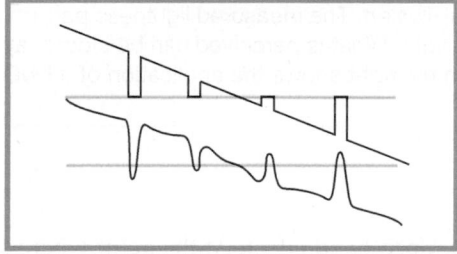

Figure 3.5 Illustration of simultaneous brightness contrast. The upper row contains rectangles of an identical gray. The lower rectangles are a lighter gray, also identical. The graph below illustrates the effect of a DoG filter applied to this pattern.

Simultaneous Brightness Contrast

The term *simultaneous brightness contrast* is used to explain the general effect whereby a gray patch placed on a dark background looks lighter than the same gray patch on a light background. Fig. 3.5 illustrates this effect and the way it is predicted by the DoG model of concentric opponent receptive fields.

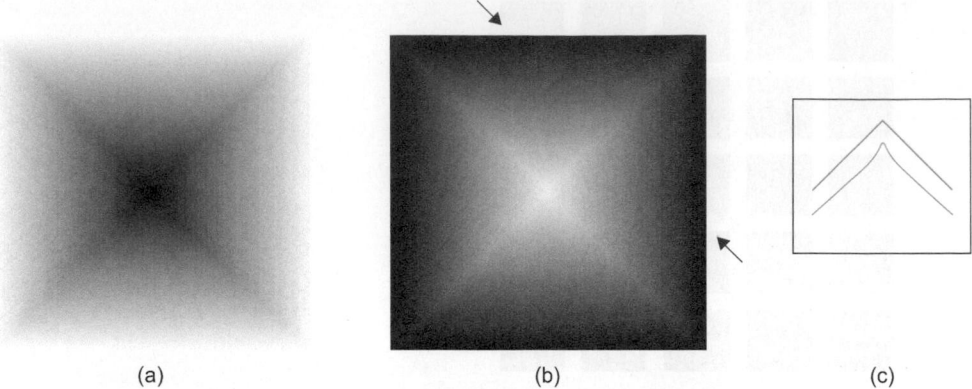

(a)   (b)   (c)

Figure 3.6 Illustration of Mach banding. (a, b) Dark and bright Mach bands are evident at the boundaries between the internal triangles. (c) The red curve shows the actual brightness profile between the two arrows. The blue curve shows how the application of a DoG filter models the bright bands that are seen.

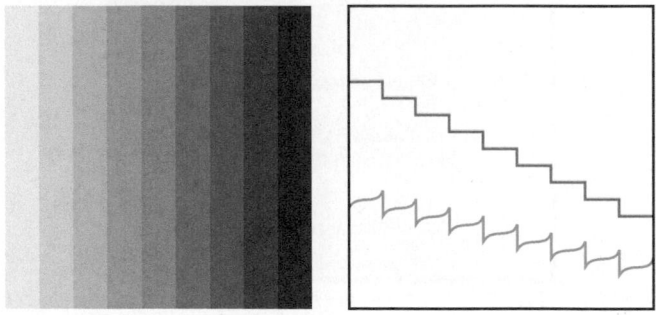

Figure 3.7 The Chevreul illusion. The measured lightness pattern is shown by the staircase pattern on the right. What is perceived can be closely approximated by a DoG model. The lower plot on the right shows the application of a DoG filter to the staircase pattern shown above.

Mach Bands

Fig. 3.6 demonstrates a Mach band effect. At the point where a uniform area meets a luminance ramp, a bright band is seen. In general, Mach bands appear where there is an abrupt change in the first derivative of a brightness profile. The lower plot on the right shows how this is simulated by a DoG model.

The Chevreul Illusion

When a sequence of gray bands is generated as shown in Fig. 3.7, the bands appear darker at one edge than the other, even though they are uniform. The diagram to the right in Fig. 3.7 shows that this visual illusion can be simulated by the application of a DoG model of the neural receptive field.

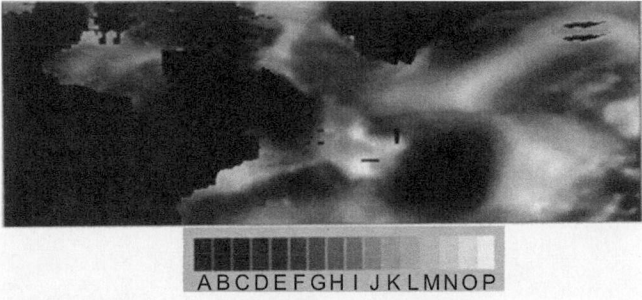

Figure 3.8 A gravity map of the North Atlantic Ocean. Large errors occur when gray-scale maps are read using a key. *(From Ware (1988). Reproduced with permission.)*

Simultaneous Contrast and Errors in Reading Maps

Simultaneous contrast effects can result in large errors of judgment when reading quantitative (value) information displayed using a gray scale (Cleveland & McGill, 1983); for example, Fig. 3.8 shows a gravity map of part of the North Atlantic Ocean where the local strength of the gravitational field is encoded in shades of gray. In an experiment to measure the effects of contrast on data encoded in this way, we found substantial errors averaging 20% of the entire scale (Ware, 1988). The contrast in this case comes from the background of the gray scale itself and the regions surrounding any designated sampling point. Better schemes for displaying scalar maps using color in addition to lightness scaling are discussed in Chapter 4.

> **[G3.1]** Avoid using gray scale as a method for representing more than a few (two to four) numerical values.

Contrast Effects and Artifacts in Computer Graphics

One of the consequences of Mach bands, and of contrast effects in general, is that they tend to highlight the deficiencies in the common shading algorithms used in computer graphics. Smooth surfaces are often displayed using polygons, both for simplicity and to speed the computer graphics rendering process, the fewer the polygons the faster the object can be drawn. This leads to visual artifacts because of the way the visual system enhances the boundaries at the edges of polygons. Fig. 3.9 shows three different shading methods applied to a sphere that has been constructed from four-sided polygons.

> *Uniform shading.* The light reflected from each polygonal facet is computed by taking into account the incident illumination and the orientation of the surface with respect to the light. The entire facet is then filled uniformly with the resulting color. Scanning across an object modeled in this way reveals stepwise changes in color. The steps are exaggerated, producing the Chevreul illusion.

Figure 3.9 Three different shading methods used in computer graphics. Flat shading on the left is subject to the Chevreul illusion. Gouraud shading in the center results in Mach banding. Phong shading, on the right, produces something that looks smooth even though it is based on the same number of facets.

> *Gouraud shading.* A shading value is calculated not for the facets but for the edges between the facets. This is done by averaging the surface normals at the boundaries where facets meet. As each facet is painted during the rendering process, the color is linearly interpolated between the facet boundaries. Scanning across the object, we see linear changes in color across polygons, with abrupt transitions in gradient where the facets meet. Mach banding occurs at these facet boundaries, enhancing the discontinuities.

> *Phong shading.* As with Gouraud shading, surface normals are calculated at the facet boundaries; however, in this case, the surface normal is interpolated between the edges. The result is smooth changes in lightness with no appreciable Mach banding.

Edge Enhancement

Lateral inhibition can be considered the first stage of an edge detection process that signals the positions and contrasts of edges in the environment. One of the consequences is that pseudoedges can be created; two areas that physically have the same lightness can be made to look different by having an edge between them that shades off gradually to the two sides (Fig. 3.10). The brain does perceptual interpolation so that the entire central region appears lighter than surrounding regions. This is called the *Cornsweet effect*, after the researcher who first described it (Cornsweet, 1970).

Cornsweet style contours have a clear inside and outside, unlike regular lines. In some visualizations, what is inside and outside a bounded region can become unclear, especially if the boundary is convoluted. Fig. 3.11 demonstrates that Cornsweet contours can solve the problem. Alternative methods for defining complex regions are color or texture fills.

Luminance profile

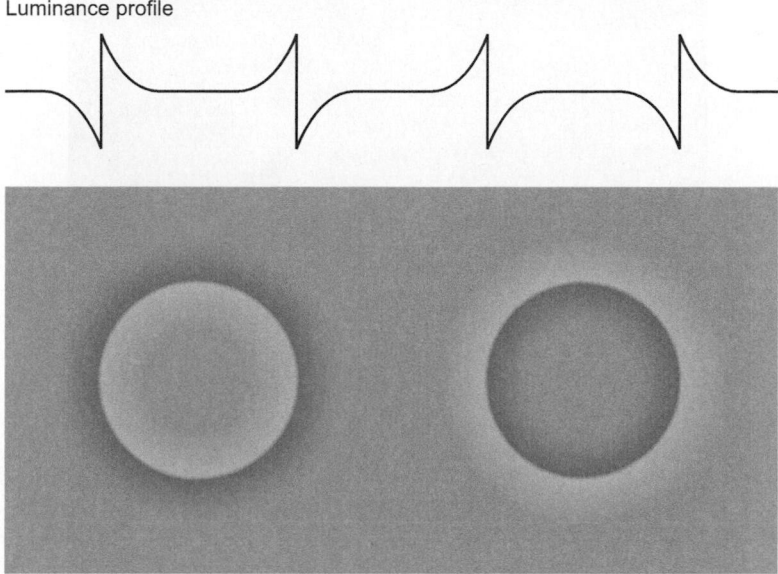

Figure 3.10 The Cornsweet effect. The curve above shows a horizontal luminance profile across the image below. The areas in the centers of the circles tend to look lighter than the surrounding area, even though they are actually the same shade. This provides evidence that the brain constructs surface color based largely on edge contrast information.

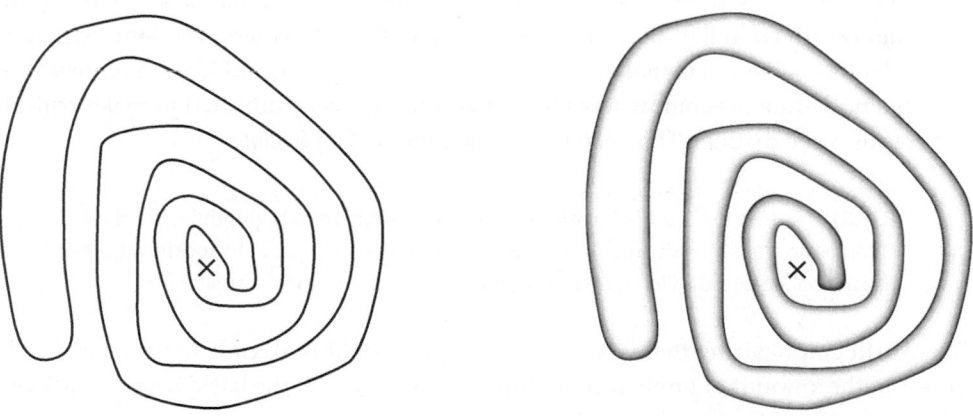

Figure 3.11 It is difficult to see if the X is inside or outside of the bounded region. Using a Cornsweet contour makes it possible to see the solution much more rapidly.

Figure 3.12 Seurat deliberately enhanced edge contrast to make his figures stand out.

[G3.2] Consider using Cornsweet contours instead of simple lines to define convoluted bounded regions.

The enhancement of edges is also an important part of some artists' techniques. It is a way to make objects more clearly distinct, given the limited dynamic range of paint. The example given in Fig. 3.12 is from Seurat's painting of bathers. The same idea can be used in visualization to make areas of interest stand out. Fig. 3.13(b) is a representation of a node-link diagram where the background has been adjusted to make critical subgraphs more distinct. This method is sometimes called *haloing*.

[G3.3] Consider using adjustments in luminance contrast as a highlighting method. It can be applied by reducing the contrast of unimportant items or by locally adjusting the background to increase the luminance contrast of critical areas.

It is worth emphasizing that it is not the amount of light that leads to visual distinctness, but the amount of luminance contrast that occurs with the background. Black on white is as distinctive as white on black.

Luminance, Brightness, Lightness, and Gamma

Contrast effects may cause annoying problems in the presentation of data, but a deeper analysis shows that they can also be used to reveal the mechanisms underlying normal perception. How the contrast mechanism works to enable us to perceive our environment

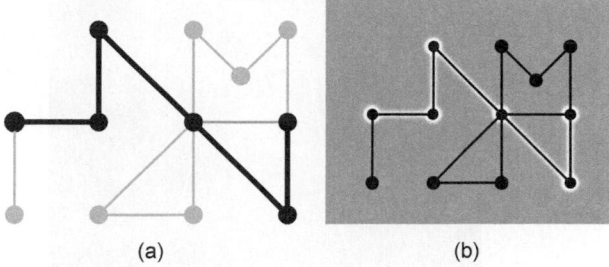

Figure 3.13 Two methods for highlighting a node-link diagram. (a) The contrast is reduced for the less important parts of the network. (b) The background contrast is increased using haloing to emphasize important parts.

accurately, under all but unusual circumstances, is the main subject of the discussion that follows. The severe illusory contrast effects in computer displays are mostly a consequence of the impoverished nature of those displays, not of any inadequacy of the visual system.

It should now be evident that the perceived brightness of a particular patch of light has almost nothing to do with the amount of light coming from that patch as we might measure it with a photometer. Thus, what might seem like a simple question—"How bright is that patch of light?"—is not at all straightforward. To understand some of the issues involved we start with an ecological perspective, then consider perceptual mechanisms, and finally discuss applications in visualization.

Constancies

In order to survive, we need to be able to manipulate objects in the environment and determine their properties. Generally, information about the quantity of illumination is of very little use to us. Illumination is a prerequisite for sight, but otherwise we do not need to know whether the light we are seeing by is dim because it is late on a cloudy day or brilliant because of the noonday sun. What we do need to know about are objects—food, tools, plants, animals, other people, and so on—and we can find out a lot about objects from their surface properties. In particular, we can obtain knowledge of the spectral reflectance characteristics of objects—what we call their *color* and *lightness*. The human vision system evolved to extract information about surface properties of objects, often at the expense of losing information about the quality and quantity of light entering the eye. This phenomenon, the fact that we experience colored surfaces and not colored light, is called *color constancy*. When we are talking about the apparent overall reflectance of a surface, it is called *lightness constancy*. Three terms are commonly used to describe the general concept of quantity of light: *luminance*, *brightness*, and *lightness*. The following brief definitions precede more extensive descriptions:

> *Luminance* is the easiest to define; it refers to the *measured amount of light* coming from some region of space. It is measured in units such as candelas per square meter. Of the three terms, only luminance refers to something that can be physically measured. The other two terms refer to psychological variables.

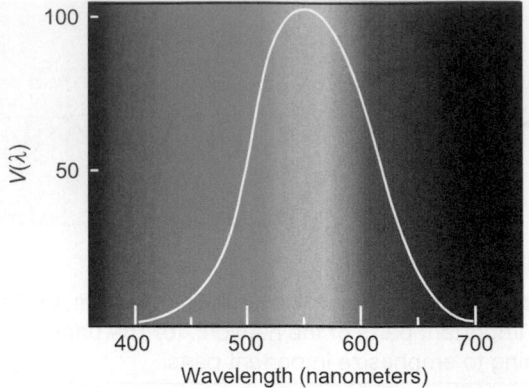

Figure 3.14 The CIE $V(\lambda)$ function representing the relative sensitivity of the human eye to light of different wavelengths.

Brightness generally refers to the *perceived amount of light* coming from a source. In the following discussion, it is used to refer only to things that are perceived as self-luminous. Sometimes people talk about bright colors, but *vivid* or *saturated* are better terms.

Lightness generally refers to the *perceived reflectance of a surface*. A white surface is light. A black surface is dark. The shade of paint is another concept of lightness.

Luminance

Luminance is not a perceptual quantity at all. It is a physical measure used to define an amount of light in the visible region of the electromagnetic spectrum. Unlike lightness and brightness, luminance can be read out directly from a scientific measuring instrument. Luminance is a measurement of light energy weighted by the spectral sensitivity function of the human visual system.

We are about 100 times less sensitive to light at 450 nm than we are to light at 510 nm, and it is clearly important to take this difference into account when we are measuring light levels with human observers in mind. The human spectral sensitivity function is illustrated in Fig. 3.14 and given at 10-nm intervals in Table 3.1. This function is called the $V(\lambda)$ function, where λ represents wavelength. It is an international standard maintained by the *Commission Internationale de l'Éclairage* (CIE). The $V(\lambda)$ function represents the spectral sensitivity curve of a standard human observer. To find the luminance of a light, we integrate the light energy distribution, $E(\lambda)$, with the CIE estimate of the human sensitivity function, $V(\lambda)$.

$$L = \int_{400}^{700} V_\lambda E_\lambda \delta\lambda \tag{3.2}$$

When multiplied by the appropriate constant, the result is luminance, L, in units of candelas per square meter. Note that a great many technical issues must be considered when we

Table 3.1 V(λ) *Function*

λ(nm)	Sensitivity	λ(nm)	Sensitivity	λ(nm)	Sensitivity
400	.0004	510	.5030	620	.3810
410	.0012	520	.7100	630	.2650
420	.0040	530	.8620	640	.1750
430	.0116	540	.9540	650	.1070
440	.0230	550	.9950	660	.0610
450	.0380	560	.9950	670	.0320
460	.0600	570	.9520	680	.0170
470	.0910	580	.8700	690	.0082
480	.1390	590	.7570	700	.0041
490	.4652	600	.6310	710	.0010
500	.3230	610	.5030	720	.0005

Note: Luminance sensitivity as it varies with wavelength.

are measuring light, such as the configuration of the measuring instrument and the sample. Wyszecki and Stiles (1982) wrote an excellent reference. It is directly relevant to data display that the blue pixel color of a monitor has a peak at about 450 nm. Table 3.1 shows that at this wavelength human sensitivity is only 4% of the maximum in the green range. In Chapter 2, we noted that the chromatic aberration of the human eye means that a monitor's blue light is typically out of focus. The fact that we are also insensitive to this part of the spectrum is another reason why representing text and other detailed information using the pure blue of a monitor is not a good idea, particularly against a black background.

The $V(\lambda)$ function is extremely useful because it provides a close match to the combined sensitivities of the individual cone receptor sensitivity functions. It is reasonable to think of the $V(\lambda)$ function as measuring the luminance efficiency of the first stage of an extended process that ultimately allows us to perceive useful information such as surface lightness and the shapes of surfaces. Technically, it defines how the sensitivity of the so-called *luminance channel* varies with wavelength.

The luminance channel is an important theoretical concept in vision research; it is held to be the basis for most pattern perception, depth perception, and motion perception. In Chapter 4, the properties of the luminance channel are discussed in more detail in comparison to the color processing *chrominance* channels.

Displaying Details

As the spatial modulation sensitivity function shows (see Figure 2.26 in Chapter 2), the finer the detail, the greater the contrast required.

[G3.4] Use a minimum 3:1 luminance contrast ratio between a pattern and its background whenever information is represented using fine detail, such as texture variation, small-scale patterns, or text.

This rule has been generalized from the International Standards Organization (ISO) guideline applying to text (ISO 9241, Part 3), but it is only a minimum; the ISO goes on to recommend that a 10:1 ratio is optimal for text, and the same can be said of any display of detail. Of course, this severely restricts the range of colors that can be used, but if the detail is critical this cannot be helped.

Brightness

The term *brightness* usually refers to the perceived amount of light coming from self-luminous sources. It relates to the perception of the brightness of indicator lights in an otherwise darkened display—for example, nighttime instrument displays in the cockpits of aircraft and on the darkened bridges of ships. Perceived brightness is a very nonlinear function of the amount of light emitted by a lamp. Stevens (1961) popularized a technique known as *magnitude estimation* to provide a way of measuring the perceptual impact of simple sensations. In magnitude estimation, subjects are given a stimulus, such as a patch of light viewed in isolation. They are told to assign this stimulus a standard value—for example, 10—to denote its brightness. Subsequently, they are shown other patches of light, also in isolation, and asked to assign them values relative to the standard that they have set. If a patch seems twice as bright as the reference sample, it is assigned the number 20; if it seems half as bright, it is assigned the number 5, and so on. Applying this technique, Stevens discovered that a wide range of sensations could be described by a simple power law:

$$S = aI^n \qquad (3.3)$$

This law states that perceived sensation S is proportional to the stimulus intensity I raised to a power n. The power law has been found to apply to many types of sensations, including loudness, smell, taste, heaviness, force, and touch. The power law applies to the perceived brightness of lights viewed in the dark.

$$Perceived\ Brightness = Luminance^n \qquad (3.4)$$

However, the value of n depends on the size of the patch of light. For circular patches of light subtending 5 degrees of visual angle, n is 0.333, whereas for point sources of light n is close to 0.5.

These findings are really only applicable to lights viewed in relative isolation in the dark. Although they have some practical relevance to the design of control panels to be viewed in dark rooms, many other factors must be taken into account in more complex displays. Before we go on to consider these perceptual issues, it is useful to know something about the way computer monitors are designed.

Monitor Gamma

Most visualizations are produced on monitor screens. Anyone who is serious about producing such a thing as a gray scale with perceptually equal steps, or color

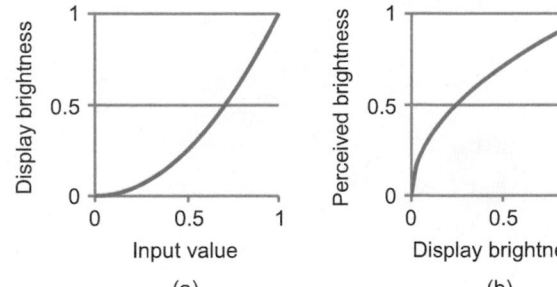
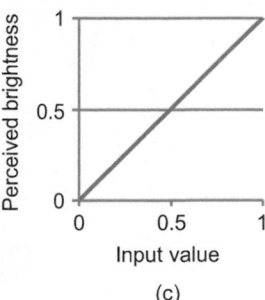

(a)   (b)   (c)

Figure 3.15 (a) On a computer display, the brightness increases faster than the input value. (b) Perceived brightness of a display varies in the opposite way. (c) The two effects cancel out.

reproductions in general, must come to grips with the properties of computer monitors. The relationship of physical luminance to the input signal on a cathode ray tube (CRT) monitor was approximated by a gamma function:

$$L = V^\gamma \tag{3.5}$$

where V is the voltage driving one of the electron guns in the monitor, L is the luminance, and γ is an empirical constant that varies widely from monitor to monitor (values can range from 1.4 to 3.0).

This monitor nonlinearity was not accidental; it was created by early television engineers to make the most of the available signal bandwidth. They made television screens nonlinear precisely because the human visual system is nonlinear in the opposite direction, as Stevens had observed. For example, a gamma value of 2.0 will exactly cancel a brightness power function exponent of 0.5, resulting in a display that produces a linear relationship between voltage and perceived brightness. Fig. 3.15 illustrates this point. Apple CRT monitors had a gamma of about 1.8 whereas PCs had a gamma of about 2.2. In the present world of LCD and OLED displays, the analog gamma has given way to the digital sRGB standard. Part of this is a function which is close to a gamma of 2.2. The exact details are given in Appendix A.

Adaptation, Contrast, and Lightness Constancy

A major task of the visual system is to extract information about the lightness and color of objects despite a great variation in illumination and viewing conditions. It cannot be emphasized enough that luminance is completely unrelated to perceived lightness or brightness. If we lay out a piece of white paper in full sunlight on a bright day and point a photometer at it, we may easily measure a value of 1000 cd for reflected light per square meter. A typical "black" surface reflects about 10% of the available light, a black would reflect about 100 cd per square meter. If we now take our photometer into a typical office and point it at a white piece of paper, we will probably measure a value of about 50 cd per square meter. Thus, a black object on a bright day in a beach

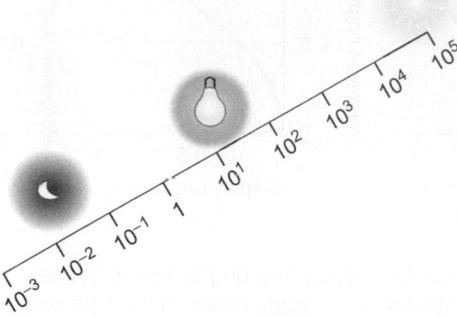

Figure 3.16 The eye/brain system is capable of functioning over a huge range of light levels. The amount of light available on a bright day at the beach is 10,000 times greater than the light available in a dimly lit room.

environment may reflect to the eye much more light than white paper in an office. Even in the same environment, white paper lying under the boardwalk may reflect less light (be darker) than black paper lying in the sun. Nevertheless, we can distinguish black from white from gray (achieve lightness constancy) with ease.

Fig. 3.16 illustrates the range of light levels we encounter, from bright sunlight to starlight. A normal interior will have an artificial illumination level of approximately 50 lux. (Lux is a measure of incident illumination that incorporates the $V(\gamma)$ function.) On a bright day in summer, the light level can easily be 50,000 lux. Except for the brief period of adaptation that occurs when we come indoors on a bright day, we are almost totally oblivious to this huge variation. Remarkably, our visual systems can achieve lightness constancy over virtually this entire range; in bright sunlight or moonlight, we can tell whether a surface is black, white, or gray.

The first-stage mechanism of lightness constancy is *adaptation*. The second stage of level invariance is *lateral inhibition*. Both mechanisms help the visual system to factor out the effects of the amount and color of the illumination.

The role of adaptation in lightness constancy is straightforward. The changing sensitivity of the receptors and neurons in the eye helps factor out the overall level of illumination. One mechanism is the bleaching of photopigment in the receptors themselves. At high light levels, more photopigment is bleached and the receptors become less sensitive. At low light levels, photopigment is regenerated and the eyes regain their sensitivity. This regeneration can take some time, which is why we are briefly blinded when coming into a darkened room out of bright sunlight. It can take up to half an hour to develop maximum sensitivity to very dim light, such as moonlight. In addition to the change in receptor sensitivity, the iris of the eye opens and closes. This modulates the amount of light entering the pupil but is a much less significant factor than the change in receptor sensitivity. In general, adaptation allows the visual system to adjust overall sensitivity to the ambient light level.

Figure 3.17 These two pieces of paper are illuminated by a desk lamp just to the right of the picture. This makes the amount of light reflected from the gray paper about the same as the light reflected from the white paper.

Contrast and Constancy

Contrast mechanisms, such as the concentric opponent receptive fields discussed previously, help us achieve constancy by signaling differences in light levels, especially at the edges of objects. Consider the simple desktop environment illustrated in Fig. 3.17. A desk lamp, just to the right of the picture, has created nonuniform illumination over a wooden desk that has two pieces of paper lying on it. The piece nearer the lamp is a medium gray. Because it is receiving more light, it reflects about the same amount of light as the white paper, which is farther from the light. In the original environment, it is easy for people to tell which piece of paper is gray and which is white. Simultaneous contrast can help to explain this. Because the white paper is lighter relative to its background than the gray paper is relative to its background, the same mechanism that caused contrast in Fig. 3.5 is responsible for enabling an accurate judgment to be made in this example. The illumination profile across the desk and the pieces of paper is similar to that illustrated in Fig. 3.5, except that, in this case, contrast does not result in an illusion; instead, it helps us to achieve lightness constancy.

Contrast on Paper and on Screen

There is a subtlety here that is worth exploring. Paper reproductions of contrast and constancy effects are often less convincing than these effects are in the laboratory. Looking at Fig. 3.17, the reader may well be excused for being less than convinced. The two pieces of paper may not look very different, but try the experiment with your own desk lamp and paper. Two holes punched in a piece of opaque cardboard can be used as a mask, enabling you to compare the brightness of the gray and white pieces of paper. Under these real-world viewing conditions, it is usually impossible to perceive the true relative luminance; instead, the surface lightness is perceived. But, take a photograph of the scene, like Fig. 3.17, and the effect is less strong. It would be even weaker with a poorly printed gray image. Why is this? The answer lies in the dual nature of pictures. The photograph itself has a surface, and to some extent we perceive the actual gray levels of the photographic pigment, as opposed to the gray levels of what is depicted. The poorer the reproduction, the more we see the actual color printed on the paper. A related effect occurs with depth perception and perspective pictures; to some extent we can see both the surface flatness and the three-dimensional (3D) layout of a depicted environment.

Contrast illusions are generally much worse in computer displays. On most screens there is no fine texture, except for the uniform pattern of pixels. Moreover, the screen is self-luminous, which may also confound our lightness constancy mechanisms. Scientists studying simultaneous contrast in the laboratory generally use perfectly uniform texture-less fields and obtain extreme contrast effects—after all, under these circumstances, the only information is the differences between patches of light. Computer-generated virtual reality images lie somewhere between real-world surfaces and the artificial featureless patches of light used in the laboratory in allowing the accurate perception of lightness.

How lightness is judged will depend on exactly how images are designed and presented. On the one hand, a monitor can be set up in a dark room and made to display featureless gray patches of light; in this case, simple contrast effects will dominate. However, if the monitor is used to simulate a very realistic 3D model of the environment, surface lightness constancies can be obtained, depending on the degree of realism, the quality of the display, and the overall setup. To obtain true virtual reality, the screen surface should disappear; to this end, some head-mounted displays contain diffusing screens that blur out the pixels and the dot matrix of the screen.

Perception of Surface Lightness

Although both adaptation and contrast can be seen as mechanisms that act in the service of lightness constancy, they are not sufficient. Ultimately, the solution to this perceptual problem can involve every level of perception. Three additional factors seem especially important. The first is that the brain must somehow take the direction of illumination and surface orientation into account in lightness judgments. A flat white surface turned away from the light will reflect less light than one turned toward the light. Fig. 3.18 illustrates two surfaces being viewed, one turned away from the light and one turned toward it. Under these circumstances, people can still make reasonably accurate lightness judgments, showing that our brains can take into account both the direction of illumination and the spatial layout (Gilchrist, 1980).

The second important factor is that the brain seems to use the lightest object in the scene as a kind of reference white to determine the gray values of all other objects (Cataliotti & Gilchrist, 1995). This is discussed in the following section in the context of lightness scaling formulas, but first we must briefly mention the role of glossy highlights, something that is clearly important, though poorly understood.

Figure 3.18 When making surface lightness judgments, the brain can take into account the fact that a surface turned away from the light receives less light than a surface turned toward the light.

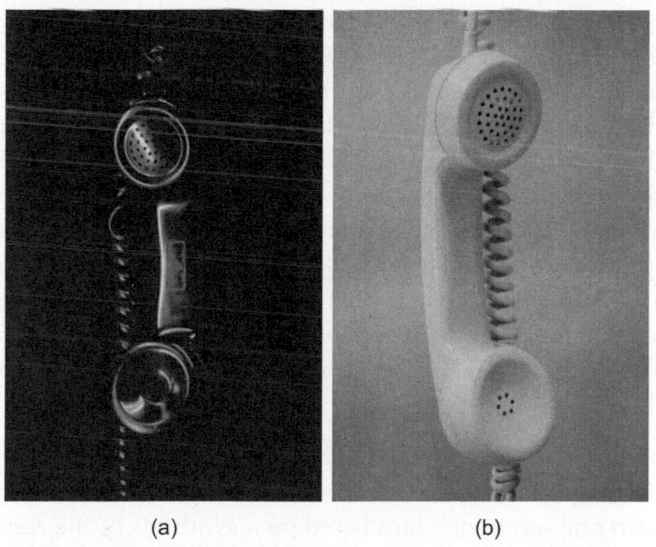

(a)   (b)

Figure 3.19 These two photographs show a scene in which everything is black (a) and another where everything is white (b).

The ratio of specular and nonspecular reflection can be important under certain circumstances. Fig. 3.19 contains a picture of a world where everything is black and next to it a picture of a world in which everything is white. If we imagine these images as slides projected in a darkened room, it is obvious that every point on the black image is brighter than the surroundings in the room. How can we perceive something to be black when it is a bright image? In this case, the most important factor differentiating black from white is the ratio between the specular and the nonspecular reflected light. In the all-black world, the ratio between specular and nonspecular is much larger than in the all-white world.

Lightness Differences and the Gray Scale

Suppose that we wish to display map information using a gray scale. We might, for example, wish to illustrate the variability in population density within a geographical region or to produce a gravity map as shown in Fig. 3.8. Ideally, for this kind of application, we would like a gray scale such that equal differences in data values are displayed as perceptually equally spaced gray steps (an interval scale). Such a scale is called a *uniform gray scale*. As we discussed earlier the gray scale is probably not the best way of coding this kind of information because of contrast effects (chromatic scales are generally better), but the problem does merit some attention because it allows us to discuss some fundamental and quite general issues related to perceptual scales.

Leaving aside contrast effects, the perception of brightness differences depends on whether lightness differences in a scene are small or large. At one extreme, we can consider the smallest difference that can be distinguished between 2 gray values. In this case, one of the fundamental laws of psychophysics applies. This is called *Weber's law*, after the 19th-century physicist Max Weber (Wyszecki & Stiles, 1982). Weber's law states that if we have a background with luminance L and superimpose on it a patch that is a little bit brighter ($L + \delta L$), then the value of δ that makes this small increment just visible is independent of the overall luminance. Thus, $\delta L / L$ is constant. Typically, under optimal viewing conditions, we can detect the brighter patch if δ is greater than about 0.005. In other words, we can just detect about a 0.5% change in brightness. Most computer graphics is done with just 256 Gy levels (8 bits), and this is not quite sufficient to create a smooth gray sequence that varies in brightness by a factor of 100 from the darkest to the lightest with undetectable steps. Weber's law applies only to small differences. When large differences between gray samples are judged, many other factors become significant.

A typical experimental procedure used to study large differences involves asking subjects to select a gray value midway between two other values. The CIE has produced a uniform gray-scale standard based on a synthesis of the results from large numbers of experiments of this kind. This formula includes the concept of a reference white, although many other factors are still neglected. The following pair of equations approximates the relationship between relative luminance and perceived lightness.

$$if \, ^{Y}/_{Y_n} > 0.08856$$

$$L^* = 116 \left(Y/Y_n \right)^{1/3} - 16$$

else

$$L^* = 903.296 \left(\frac{Y}{Y_n} \right) \tag{3.6}$$

where Y is the luminance of the color being judged and Y_n is the luminance of a reference white in the environment, normally the surface that reflects most light to the eye. The result, L^*, is a value in an approximately uniform gray scale. Equal measured differences on this scale approximate equal perceptual differences. Generally it is reasonable to assume that $Y/Y_n > 0.08$, because even the black inks and fabrics reflect a few percent incident illumination. This standard is used by the paint and lighting industries to specify such things as color tolerances. Eq. (3.6) is part of the CIELUV uniform color space standard, which is described more fully in Chapter 4.

Uniform lightness and color scales can only provide rough approximations. Because the perception of lightness is changed radically by many factors that are not taken into account by formulas such as Eq. (3.6)—perceived illumination, specular reflection from glossy surfaces, and local contrast effects—the goal of obtaining a perfect gray scale is not attainable. Such formulas should be taken as no more than useful approximations.

Contrast Crispening

Another perceptual factor that distorts gray values is called *contrast crispening* (see Wyszecki & Stiles, 1982). Generally, differences are perceived as larger when samples are similar to the background color. Fig. 3.20 shows a set of identical gray scales on a range of different gray backgrounds. Notice how the scales appear to divide perceptually at the value of the background. The term *crispening* refers to the way more subtle

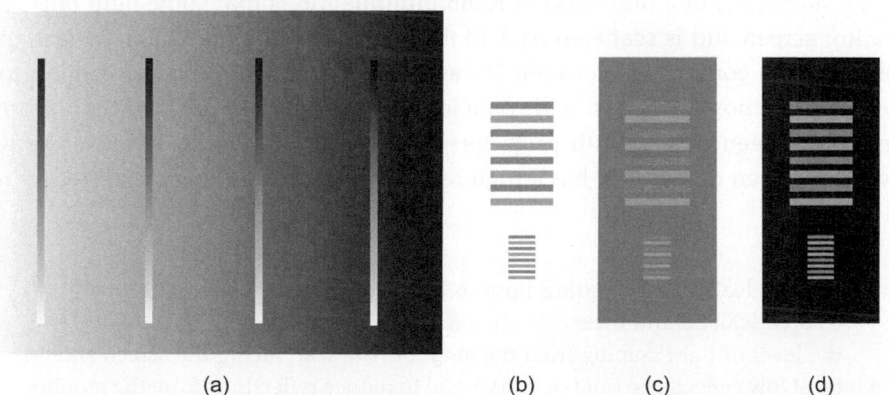

(a) (b) (c) (d)

Figure 3.20 (a) All the gray strips are the same. Perceived differences between gray-scale values are enhanced where the values are close to the background gray value, an effect known as crispening. (b, c, d) The differences in the grays of the gray lattice are more evident (c) than with either the white (b) or the black (d) backgrounds, another example of crispening.

gray values can be distinguished at the point of crossover. Crispening is not taken into account by uniform gray-scale formulas.

> **[G3.5]** If subtle gray-level gradations within the bounds of a small object are important, create low-luminance contrast between the object and its background.

Monitor Illumination and Monitor Surrounds

In some visualization applications, the accurate perception of surface lightness and color is critical. One example is the use of a computer monitor to display wallpaper or fabric samples for customer selection. It is also important for graphic designers that colors be accurately perceived. To accomplish this, not only is it necessary to calibrate the monitor so that it actually displays the specified color range, but other factors affecting the state of adaptation of the user's eyes must also be taken into account. The color and the brightness of the surround of the monitor can be very important in determining how screen objects appear. The adaptation effect produced by room lighting can be equally important.

How should the lighting surrounding a monitor be set up? A monitor used for visual displays engages only the central part of the visual field, so the overall state of adaptation of the eye is maintained at least as much by the ambient room illumination. This means that the amount of light reflected from the walls of the room and other surfaces should not be too dissimilar to the amount of light coming from the screen, especially if the screen is small. There are other reasons for maintaining a reasonably high level of illumination in a viewing room, such as the ability to take notes and see other people. When people spend lots of time in dimly lit work environments, it can cause depression and reduced job satisfaction (Rosenthal, 1993); however, a side effect of a high level of room illumination is that some light falls on the monitor screen and is scattered back to the eye, degrading the image. In fact, under normal office conditions, between 5% and 20% of the illumination coming to the eye from the monitor screen will come indirectly from the room light, not from the luminous screen pixels. With projectors the situation is worse, because the white projector screen necessarily has a high reflectance, meaning that it will reflect room illumination.

> **[G3.6]** Ideally, when setting up a monitor for viewing data, a light neutral-colored wall behind the screen should reflect an amount of light comparable to the level of light coming from the monitor. The wall facing the screen should be of low reflectance (mid- to dark gray) to reduce reflections from the monitor screen. Lights should be placed so that they do not reflect from the monitor screen.

[G3.7] When setting up a room for a projection system, ensure that minimal room light falls on the projector screen. This can be done by means of baffles to shield the screen from direct illumination. Low-reflectance (mid- to dark gray) walls are also desirable, as the walls will scatter light, some of which inevitably reaches the screen.

Fig. 3.21 shows a monitor display with a shadow lying across its face. Although this is a rather extreme example, the effects are clear. Overall contrast is reduced where the room light falls on the display.

Modern LCD and OLED displays have much blacker blacks than earlier CRTs (they reflect less of the ambient room lighting). Nevertheless, they still typically reflect about 1.5%–2.0% of the ambient light and this can be significant. Fig. 3.22 shown what happens when graphics input color values (on the range 0–1) is first transformed according

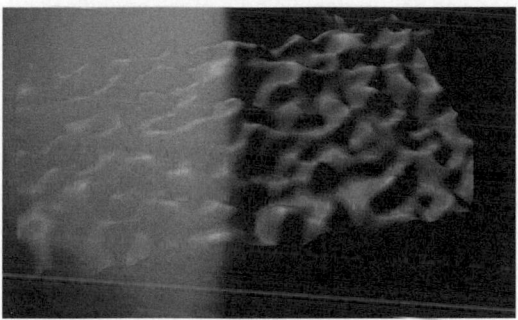

Figure 3.21 A monitor with a shadow falling across the left-hand side.

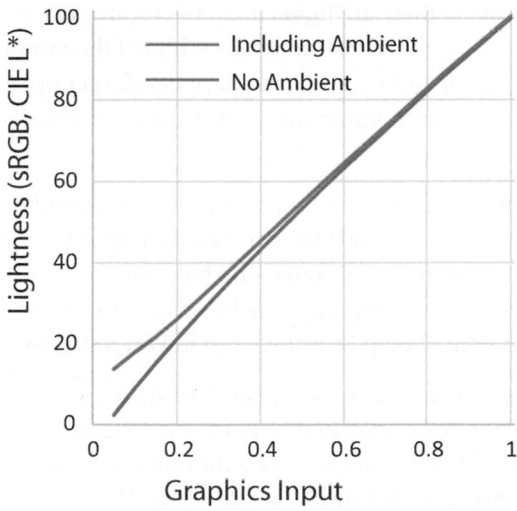

Figure 3.22 The blue curve shows how monitor gun voltage is transformed into lightness, according to the CIE model. Adding 1.5% of ambient light results in the red curve which is actually more linear.

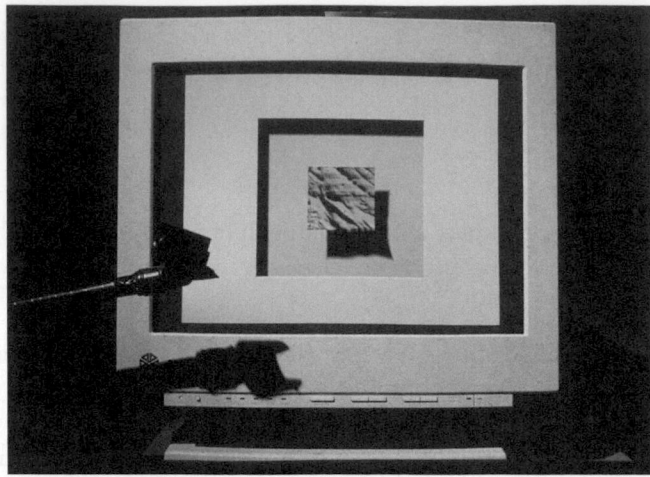

Figure 3.23 A projector was set up containing a mask specifically designed so that no light actually fell on the portion of the monitor screen containing the image. In this way, the illumination in the virtual environment displayed on the monitor was made to closely match the room illumination falling on the monitor frame and stand.

to the sRGB standard, and then transformed according to CIE L* calculation. The result is closer to a straight-line relationship between estimated perceived lightness (L*) when an ambient constant amounting to 1.5% of the reference white is added to the monitor output. In short, if we assume that users are working in offices with the lights on, we can produce excellent linear gray scales (assuming that the CIE standard is a good model) without applying any corrections to the RGB inputs.

If you cover part of your monitor screen with a sheet of white paper, under normal working conditions (when there are lights on in the room), you will probably find that the white of the paper is very different from the white of the monitor screen. The paper may look relatively blue or yellow, and it may appear darker or lighter. There are often large discrepancies between monitor colors and colors of objects in the surrounding environment.

For the creation of an environment where computer-generated colors are comparable to colors in a room, the room should have a standard light level and illuminant color. The monitor should be carefully calibrated and balanced so that the white of the monitor matches that of a sheet of white paper held up beside the screen. In addition, only a minimal amount of light should be allowed to fall on the monitor screen.

Fig. 3.23 shows a computer display setup so that the lighting in the virtual environment shown on the monitor is matched with the lighting in the real environment surrounding the monitor. This was achieved by illuminating the region surrounding the monitor with a projector that contains a special mask. This mask was custom designed so that light was cast on the monitor casing and the desktop surrounding the computer, but no light at all fell on the part of the screen containing the picture. In addition, the direction and color of the light in the virtual environment were adjusted to exactly match the light from the projector. Simulated cast shadows were also created to match the cast shadows from the projector. Using this setup, it is possible to create a virtual environment whose simulated colors and other material properties can be directly compared to the colors and material properties of objects in the room. (This work was done by Justin Hickey and the author.)

Conclusion

As a general observation, the use of gray-scale colors is not a particularly good method for categorically coding data (nominal scale). Contrast effects reduce accuracy, and the luminance channel of the visual system is fundamental to so much of perception (shape perception, in particular) that it is a waste of perceptual resources to use gray-scale encoding. Nevertheless, it is important to understand the problems of brightness and lightness perception because they point to issues that are fundamental to all perceptual systems. One of these basic problems is how perception works effectively in visual environments where the light level can vary by six orders of magnitude. The solution, arrived at over the course of evolution, is a system that essentially ignores the level of illumination. This may seem like an exaggeration—after all, we can certainly tell the difference between bright sunlight and dim room illumination—but we are barely aware of a change of light level on the order of a factor of 2. For example, in a room lit with a two-bulb fixture, it often goes unnoticed that one bulb has burned out, as long as the bulbs are hidden within a diffusing surround.

A fundamental point made in this chapter is the *relative* nature of low-level visual processing. As a general rule, nerve cells situated early in the visual pathway do not respond to absolute signals. Rather, they respond to differences in both space and time. At later stages in the visual system, more stable percepts such as the perception of surface lightness can emerge, but this is only because of sophisticated image analysis that takes into account such factors as the position of the light, cast shadows, and orientation of the object. The relative nature of lightness perception sometimes causes errors, but these errors are due mostly to a simplified graphical environment that confounds the brain's attempt to achieve surface lightness constancy. The mechanism that causes contrast errors is also the reason why we can perceive subtle changes in data values and can pick out patterns despite changes in the background light level.

Luminance contrast is an especially important consideration for choosing backgrounds and surrounds for a visualization. The way a background is chosen depends on what is important. If the outline shapes of objects are critical, the background should be chosen for maximum luminance contrast with foreground objects. If it is important to see subtle gradations in gray level, the crispening effect suggests that choosing a background in the midrange of gray levels will help us to see more of the important details.

Luminance is but one dimension of color space. In Chapter 4, this one-dimensional model is expanded to a three-dimensional color perception model. The luminance channel, however, is special. We could not get by without luminance perception, but we can certainly get by without color perception. This is demonstrated by the historic success of black-and-white movies and television. Later chapters describe how information encoded in the luminance channel is fundamental to perception of fine detail, discrimination of the shapes of objects through shading, stereoscopic depth perception, motion perception, and many aspects of pattern perception.

CHAPTER FOUR

Color

In the summer of 1997, I designed an experiment to measure human ability to trace paths between connected parts in a three-dimensional diagram. Then, as is my normal practice, I ran a pilot study in order to see whether the experiment was well constructed. By ill luck, the first person tested was a research assistant who worked in my lab. He had far more difficulty with the task than anticipated– so much so that I put the experiment back on the drawing board to reconsider, without trying any more pilot subjects. Some months later, my assistant told me he had just had an eye test and the optometrist had determined that he was color blind. This explained the problems with the experiment. Although it was not about color perception, I had marked the targets red in my experiment. He therefore had had great difficulty in finding them, which rendered the rest of the task meaningless. The remarkable aspect of this story is that my assistant had gone through 21 years of his life without knowing that he was blind to many color differences. This is not uncommon, and it strongly suggests that color vision cannot be all that important to everyday life. In fact, color vision is irrelevant to much of normal vision. It does not help us determine the layout of objects in space, how they are moving, or what their shapes are. It is not much of an overstatement to say that color vision is largely superfluous in modern life; nevertheless, color is extremely useful in data visualization.

Color vision does have a critical function, which is hardly surprising because this sophisticated ability must surely provide some evolutionary advantage. Color helps us break camouflage. Some things differ visually from their surroundings only by their color. An especially important example is illustrated in Fig. 4.1. If we have color vision,

Figure 4.1 Finding the cherries is much easier with color vision.

we can easily see the cherries hidden in the leaves. If we do not, this becomes much harder. Color also tells us much that is useful about the material properties of objects. This is crucial in judging the condition of our food. Is this fruit ripe or not? Is this meat fresh or putrid? What kind of mushroom is this? It is also useful if we are making tools. What kind of stone is this? Clearly, these can be life-or-death decisions. In modern hunter-gatherer societies, men are the hunters and women are the gatherers. This may have been true for long periods of human evolution, which could explain why it is mostly men who are color blind. If they had been gatherers, they would have been more than likely to eat poison berries—a selective disadvantage. In the modern age of supermarkets, these skills are much less valuable; this is perhaps why color vision deficiencies so often go unnoticed.

The role that color plays ecologically suggests ways that it can be used in information display. It is useful to think of color as an attribute of an object rather than as its primary characteristic. It is excellent for labeling and categorization, but poor for displaying shape, detail, or spatial layout. These points are elaborated in this chapter. We begin with an introduction to the basic theory of color vision to provide a foundation for the applications. The latter half of the chapter consists of a set of four visualization problems requiring the effective use of color; these have to do with color selection interfaces, color labeling, pseudocolor sequences for mapping, color reproduction and color for multidimensional discrete data. Each has its own special set of requirements. Some readers may wish to skip directly to the applications, sampling the more technical introduction only as needed.

Trichromacy Theory

The most important fact about color vision is that we have three distinct color receptors in our retinas, called *cones*, that are active at normal light levels—hence *trichromacy*. We also have rods, sensitive at low light levels, but they are so overstimulated in all but the dimmest light that their influence on color perception can be ignored. Thus, in order to understand color vision, we need to only consider the cones. There are also instances where women have four cone types, but only in very rare cases are their brains wired to take advantage of the extra capability and see more colors (Jordan, Deeb, Bosten, & Mollon, 2010). The fact that for most of us there are only three receptors is the reason

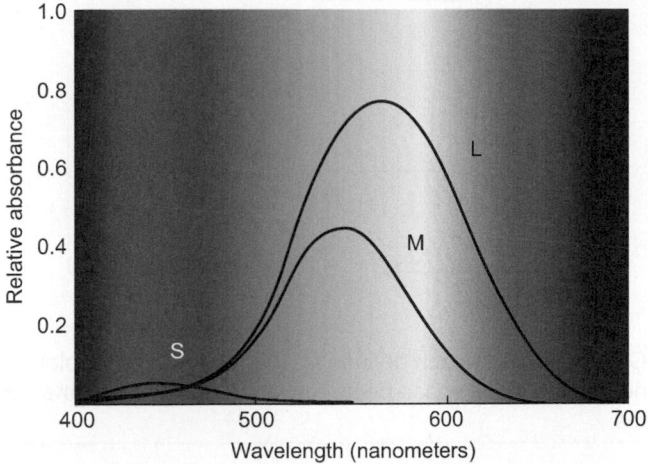

Figure 4.2 Cone sensitivity functions. The colors are only rough approximations to spectrum hues. *Abbreviations*: S, short-wavelength cone sensitivity; M, medium-wavelength cone sensitivity; L, long-wavelength cone sensitivity.

for the basic three-dimensionality of human color vision. The term *color space* means an arrangement of colors in a three-dimensional space. In this chapter a number of color spaces designed for different purposes are discussed. Complex transformations are sometimes required to convert from one color space to another, but the color spaces are all three dimensional, and this three-dimensionality derives ultimately from the three cone types. This is the reason why there are three different colors of liquid crystal in a television screen—red, green, and blue—and this is the reason why we learn in school that there are three primary paint colors—red, yellow, and blue. It is also the reason why printers have a minimum of three colored inks for color printing—cyan, magenta, and yellow. Engineers should be grateful that humans have only three color receptors. Some birds, such as chickens, have as many as 12 different kinds of color-sensitive cells. A television set for chickens would require 12 types of differently colored pixels!

Fig. 4.2 shows the human cone sensitivity functions. The plots show how light of different wavelengths is absorbed by the three different receptor types (S, M, and L). It is evident that two of the functions, L and M, which peak at 540 and 580 nm, respectively, overlap considerably; the third, S, is much more distinct, with peak sensitivity at 450 nm. The short-wavelength S receptor absorbs light in the blue part of the spectrum and is much less sensitive, which is another reason (besides chromatic aberration, discussed in Chapter 2) why we should not show detailed information such as text in pure blue on a black background.

Because only three different receptor types are involved in color vision, it is possible to match a particular patch of colored light with a mixture of just three colored lights, usually called *primaries*. It does not matter that the target patch may have a completely different spectral composition. The only thing that matters is that the matching primaries are balanced to produce the same response from the cone receptors as the patch of

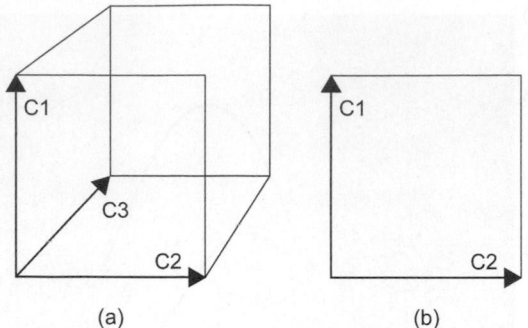

Figure 4.3 (a) Cone response space defined by the response to a colored light of each of the three cone types. (b) The space becomes two dimensional in the case of common color deficiencies.

light to be matched. Fig. 4.3(a) illustrates the three-dimensional space formed by the responses of the three cones.

Color Blindness

An unfortunate result of using color for information coding is the creation of a new class of people with a disability. Color blindness already disqualifies applicants for some jobs, such as telephone line maintenance workers, because of the myriad colored wires, and pilots, because of the need to distinguish color-coded lights. About 10% of the male population and about 1% of the female population have some form of color vision deficiency. The most common deficiencies are explained by lack of either the long-wavelength-sensitive cones (protanopia) or the medium-wavelength-sensitive cones (deuteranopia). Both protanopia and deuteranopia result in an inability to distinguish red and green, meaning that the cherries in Fig. 4.1 are difficult for people with these deficiencies to see. One way to describe color vision deficiency is by pointing out that the three-dimensional color space of normal color vision collapses to a two-dimensional space, as shown in Fig. 4.3(b).

Color Measurement

The fact that we can match any color with a mixture of no more than three primary lights is the basis of colorimetry and an understanding of this technical field is essential for anyone who wishes to specify colors precisely for reproduction.

We can describe a color by the following equation:

$$C \equiv rR + gG + bB \tag{4.1}$$

where C is the color to be matched; R, G, and B are the primary light sources to be used to create a match; and r, g, and b represent the amounts of each primary light. The $\equiv$ symbol is used to denote a perceptual match; that is, the sample and the mixture of the red, green, and blue (rR, gG, bB) primaries look identical. Fig. 4.4 illustrates

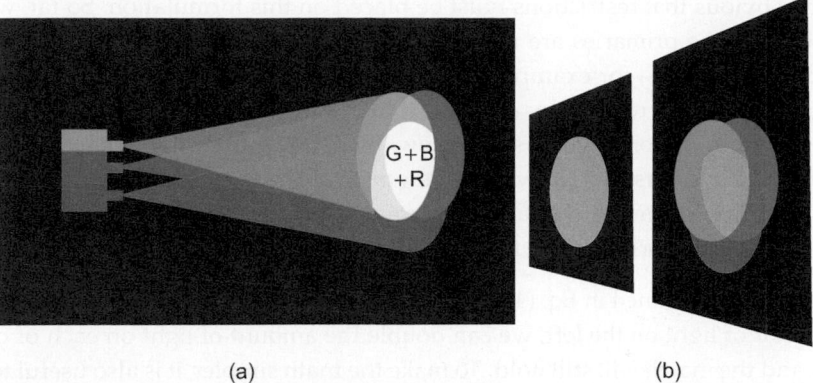

(a)   (b)

Figure 4.4 A color-matching setup. (a) When the light from three projectors is combined the results are as shown. Yellow light is a mixture of red and green. Purple light is a mixture of red and blue. Cyan light is a mixture of blue and green. White light is a mixture of red, green, and blue. (b) Any other color can be matched by adjusting the proportions of red, green, and blue lights.

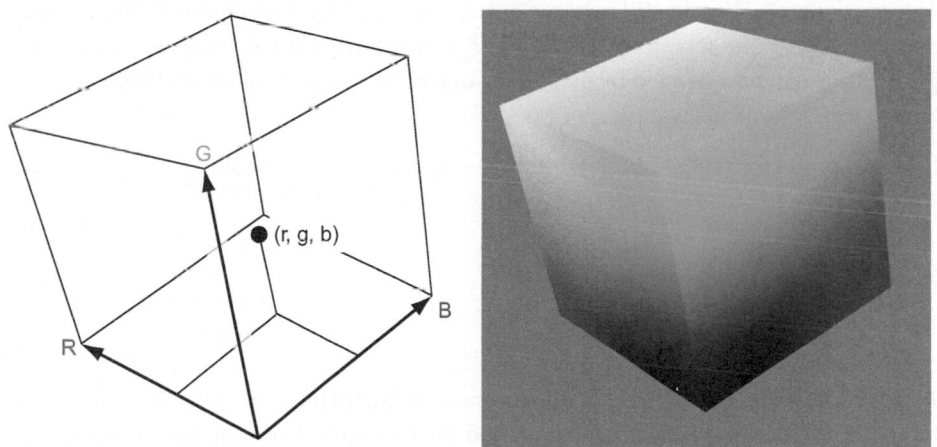

Figure 4.5 The three-dimensional space formed by three primary lights. Any internal color can be created by varying the amount of light produced by each of the primaries.

the concept. Three projectors are set up with overlapping beams. In the figure, the beams only partially overlap so that the mixing effect can be illustrated, but in a color-matching experiment they would overlap perfectly. To match the lilac-colored sample, the projectors are adjusted so that a large amount of light comes from the red and blue projectors and a smaller amount of light comes from the green projector.

The *RGB* primaries form the coordinates of a color space, as illustrated in Fig. 4.5. If these primaries are physically formed by the phosphor colors of a color monitor, this space defines the *gamut* of the monitor. In general, a gamut is the set of all colors that can be produced by a device or sensed by a receptor system.

It seems obvious that restrictions must be placed on this formulation. So far, we have assumed that the primaries are red, green, and blue, but what if we were to choose other primary lights—for example, yellow, blue, and purple? We have stated no rule saying they must be red, green, and blue. How could we possibly reproduce a patch of red light out of combinations of yellow, blue, and purple lights? In fact, we can only reproduce colors that lie within the *gamut* of the three primaries. Yellow, blue, and purple would simply have a smaller gamut, meaning that if we used them then a smaller range of colors could be reproduced.

The relationship defined in Eq. (4.1) is a linear relationship; consequently, if we double the amount of light on the left, we can double the amount of light on each of our primaries and the match will still hold. To make the math simpler, it is also useful to allow the concept of negative light. Thus, we may allow expressions such as

$$C \equiv -rR + gG + bB \tag{4.2}$$

Although this concept may nonsensical, because negative light does not exist in nature, it is, in fact, practically useful in the following situation. Suppose we have a colored light that cannot be matched because it is outside the gamut of our three primary sources. We can still achieve a match by adding part of one of the primaries to our sample. If the test samples and the *RGB* primaries are all projected as shown in Fig. 4.4, this can be achieved by swiveling one of the projectors around and adding its light to the light of the sample.

If the red projector were redirected in this way, we would have had

$$C + rR \equiv gG + bB \tag{4.3}$$

which can be rewritten as

$$C \equiv rR + gG + bB \tag{4.4}$$

Once we allow the concept of negative values for the primaries, it becomes possible to state that any colored light can be matched by a weighted sum of *any* three primaries as long as each is distinctive in cone space. The primaries do not even have to match an actual color, and in fact the most widely used color standard is based on nonphysical primaries, as we shall see.

Change of Primaries

Primaries are arbitrary from the point of view of color mixture—there is no special red, green, or blue light that must be used. Fundamental to colorimetry is the ability to change from one set of primaries to another. This gives us freedom to choose any set of primaries we want. We can choose as primaries the liquid crystal hues of a monitor, three differently colored lasers, or some hypothetical set of lamps. We can even choose to base our primaries on the sensitivities of the human cone receptors. Given a standard way of specifying colors (using a standard set of primaries); we can use a transformation to create that same color on any number of different output devices. This transformation is described in Appendix A.

We now have the foundations of a color measurement and specification system. To illustrate how color specification works, it is useful to think about how it might be done with real lamps, before moving toward more abstract concepts. Red, green, and blue lamps could be manufactured to precise specifications and set up in an instrument so that the amounts of red, green, and blue light falling on a standard white surface could be set by adjusting three calibrated dials, one for each lamp. Identical instruments, each containing sets of colored lamps, would be sent around the world to color experts. Then, to give a precise color specification to someone with the standard instrument, we would simply need to make a color match by adjusting the dials and sending that person the dial settings. The recipient could then adjust his or her own standard lamps to reproduce the color.

Of course, although this approach is theoretically sound, it is not very practical. Standard primary lamps would be very difficult to maintain and calibrate and they would be very expensive. But, we can apply the principle by creating a set of *abstract* primary lamps defined on the basis of the human receptor characteristics. This is how color specification systems work.

One of the basic concepts in any color standard is that of the standard observer. This is a hypothetical person whose color sensitivity functions are held to be typical of all humans. The idea assumes that everyone has the same receptor functions. In fact, although humans do not display exactly the same sensitivities to different colors, with the exception of the color deficiencies, they come close. Most serious color specification is done using the *Commission Internationale de l'Eclairage* (CIE) system of color standards. These are based on standard observer measurements that were made prior to 1931. Color measuring instruments contain glass filters that are derived from the specifications of the human standard observer. One advantage is that glass filters are more stable than lamps.

The CIE system uses a set of abstract observer sensitivity functions called *tristimulus values*; these can be thought of as a set of abstract receptors and they are labeled XYZ. They are transformations of actual measured sensitivities, chosen for their mathematical properties. One important feature of the system is that the Y tristimulus value is the same as luminance. More details of the way the system is derived are given in Appendix B.

Fig. 4.6 illustrates the color volume created by the XYZ tristimulus functions of the CIE system. The colors that can actually be perceived are represented as a gray volume entirely contained within the positive space defined by the axes. The colors that can be created by a set of three colored lights, such as the red, green, and blue monitor phosphors, are defined by the pyramid-shaped volume within the RGB axes, as shown. This is the *monitor gamut*. The X, Y, and Z axes are the CIE primaries, and they are outside the gamut of physically realizable colors.

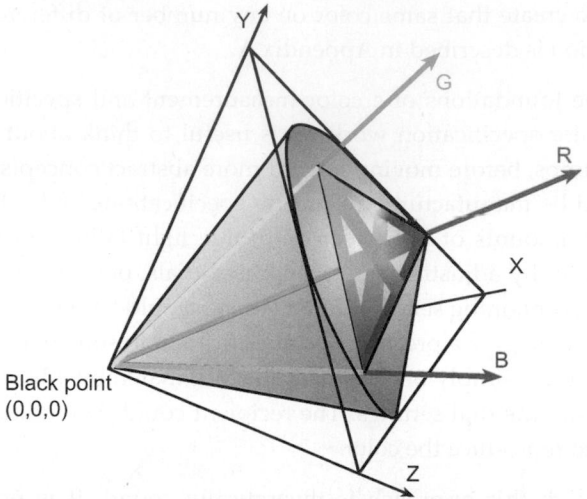

Figure 4.6 The *X*, *Y*, and *Z* axes represent the CIE standard virtual primaries. Within the positive space defined by the axes, the gamut of perceivable colors is represented as a gray solid. The colors that can be created by means of the red, green, and blue monitor primaries are defined by the pyramid enclosed by the *R*, *G*, and *B* lines.

The CIE tristimulus system based on the standard observer is by far the most widely used standard for measuring colored light. For this reason, it should always be used when precise color specification is required. Because a monitor is a light-emitting device with three primaries, it is relatively straightforward to calibrate a monitor in terms of the CIE coordinates. If a color generated on one monitor, such as a cathode ray tube (CRT), is to be reproduced on another, such as a liquid crystal display, the best procedure is first to convert the colors into the CIE tristimulus values and then to convert them into the primary space of the second monitor.

The specification of surface colors is far more difficult than the specification of lights, because an illuminant must be taken into account and because, unlike lights, pigment colors are not additive. The color that results from mixing paints is difficult to predict because of the complex way that light interacts with pigment. A treatment of surface color measurement is beyond the scope of this book, although later we will deal with perceptual issues related to color reproduction.

Chromaticity Coordinates

The three-dimensional abstract space represented by the *XYZ* coordinates is useful for specifying colors, but it is difficult to understand. As discussed in Chapter 3, there are good reasons for treating lightness, or luminance, information as special. In everyday speech, we often refer to the color of something and its lightness as different and independent properties. Thus, it is useful to have a measure that defines the hue and vividness of a color while ignoring the amount of light. *Chromaticity coordinates* have exactly this property through normalizing with respect to the amount of light.

To transform tristimulus values to chromaticity coordinates, use

$$x = X/(X + Y + Z)$$
$$y = Y/(X + Y + Z)$$
$$z = Z/(X + Y + Z)$$

(4.5)

Because $x + y + z = 1$, it is sufficient to use x and y values only. It is common to specify a color by its luminance (Y) and its x *and* y chromaticity coordinates (x, y, Y). The inverse transformation from x, y, Y to tristimulus values is

$$X = Yx/y$$
$$Y = Y$$
$$Z = (1 - x - y)\, Y/y$$

(4.6)

Fig. 4.7 shows a CIE x *and* y chromaticity diagram and graphically illustrates some of the colorimetric concepts associated with it. Some of the useful and interesting properties of the chromaticity diagram include the following:

1. If two colored lights are represented by two points in a chromaticity diagram, the color of a mixture of those two lights will always lie on a straight line between those two points.

2. Any set of three lights specifies a triangle in the chromaticity diagram. Its corners are given by the chromaticity coordinates of the three lights. Any color within that triangle can be created with a suitable mixture of the three lights. Fig. 4.7 illustrates this with typical monitor *RGB* primaries.

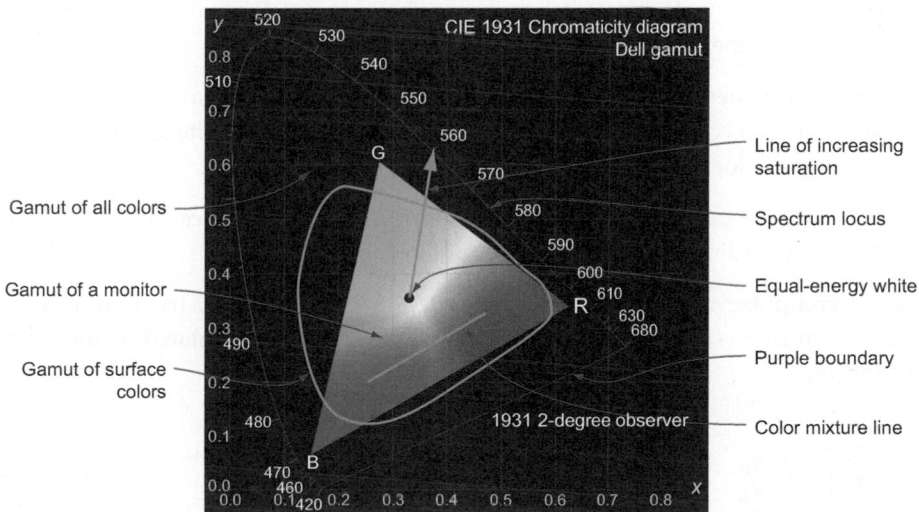

Figure 4.7 CIE chromaticity diagram with various interesting features added. The colored triangle represents the gamut of a computer monitor. Colors as shown are only approximate.

3. The *spectrum locus* is the set of chromaticity coordinates of pure monochromatic (single-wavelength) lights. All realizable colors fall within the spectrum locus.

4. The *purple boundary* is the straight line connecting the chromaticity coordinates of the longest visible wavelength of red light (about 700 nm) to the chromaticity coordinates of the shortest visible wavelength of blue (about 400 nm).

5. The chromaticity coordinates of equal-energy white (light having an equal mixture of all wavelengths) are 0.333, 0.333. But, when a white light is specified for some application, what is generally required is one of the CIE standard illuminants. The CIE specifies a number that corresponds to different phases of daylight; of these, the most commonly used is D65. D65 was made to be a careful approximation of daylight with an overcast sky. It also happens to be very close to the mix of light that results when both direct sunlight and light from the rest of the sky fall on a horizontal surface. D65 also corresponds to a black-body radiator at 6500 degrees Kelvin. D65 has chromaticity coordinates $x = 0.313, y = 0.329$. Another CIE standard illuminant corresponds to the light produced by a typical incandescent tungsten source. This is illuminant A (chromaticity coordinates $x = 0.448, y = 0.407$), and it is considerably more yellow than normal daylight.

6. Saturation is a measure of the purity of a hue. It is often used informally to refer to vividness. But colors can have high saturation even if they are very dark and do not appear vivid. A technical scientific term for perceived vividness is *chroma*. This is one of the most confusing terms in color science since chroma simply means "color" in Greek and as we have seen "chromaticity" means any variation in the color plane.

7. The complementary wavelength of a color is produced by drawing a line between that color and white and extrapolating to the opposite spectrum locus. Adding a color and its complementary color produces white.

There is a widely used standard for the color of monitor primaries called *sRGB*. The chromaticity coordinates for sRGB are set out in Table 4.1.

When a computer display is used to generate a color, the CIE tristimulus values formed from some set of red, green, and blue settings can be calculated by the following formula:

$$
\begin{bmatrix} X \\ Y \\ Z \end{bmatrix} = \begin{bmatrix} \dfrac{x_R}{y_R} & \dfrac{x_G}{y_G} & \dfrac{x_B}{y_B} \\ 1 & 1 & 1 \\ \dfrac{z_R}{y_R} & \dfrac{z_G}{y_G} & \dfrac{z_B}{y_B} \end{bmatrix} \begin{bmatrix} Y_R \\ Y_G \\ Y_B \end{bmatrix}
$$

(4.7)

Table 4.1 *Chromaticity Coordinates for the sRGB Standard*

	Red	Green	Blue
x	0.64	0.30	0.15
y	0.33	0.60	0.06

where (x_R, y_R, z_R), (x_G, y_G, z_G), and (x_B, y_B, z_B) are the chromaticity coordinates of the particular monitor primaries and Y_R, Y_G, and Y_B are the actual luminance values produced from each phosphor for the particular color being converted. Notice that for a particular monitor, the transformation matrix will be constant; only the Y vector will change.

To generate a particular color on a monitor that has been defined by CIE tristimulus values, it is only necessary to invert the matrix and create an appropriate voltage to each of the red, green, and blue electron guns of the monitor. Naturally, to determine the actual value that must be specified, it is necessary to calibrate the monitor's red, green, and blue outputs in terms of luminance and apply gamma correction, as described in Chapter 3. Once this is done, the monitor can be treated as a linear color creation device with a particular set of primaries, depending on its phosphors. For more on monitor calibration, see Cowan (1983). It is also possible to purchase self-calibrating monitors adequate for all but the most demanding applications.

Color Differences and Uniform Color Spaces

Sometimes it is useful to have a color space in which equal perceptual distances are equal distances in the space. Here are three applications:

- **Specification of color tolerances.** When a manufacturer wishes to order a colored part from a supplier, such as a plastic molding for an automobile, it is necessary to specify the color tolerance within which the part will be accepted. It only makes sense for this tolerance to be based on human perception, because ultimately it is people who decide whether the door trim matches the upholstery.

- **Specification of color codes.** If we need a set of colors to code data as symbols in a visualization, we would normally like those colors to be clearly distinct so that they will not be confused. Uniform color spaces provide a way of ensuring this.

- **Pseudocolor sequences for maps.** Many scientific maps use sequences of colors to represent ordered data values. This technique, called *pseudocoloring*, is widely used in astronomy, physics, medical imaging, and geophysics. A uniform color space can theoretically be used to create perceptually equal steps in a sequence of colors, although as we shall see, the ones designed for the paint industry to do a poor job.

The CIE XYZ color space is very far from being perceptually uniform; however, in 1978, the CIE produced a set of recommendations on the use of two uniform color spaces that are transformations of the *XYZ* color space. These are called the *CIELAB* and the *CIELUV* uniform color spaces. The reason why there are two color spaces, rather than one, has to do with the fact that different industries, such as the paint industry, had already adopted one standard or the other. Also, the two standards have somewhat different properties that make them useful for different tasks. Only the *CIELUV* formula is described here. It is generally held to be better for specifying large color differences; however, one measurement made using the *CIELAB* color difference formula is worth noting. Using *CIELAB*, Hill, Roger, and Vorhagen (1997) estimated that there are between two and six million discriminable colors available within the gamut of a color monitor.

The *CIELUV* equations are as follows:

$$L^* = 116(Y/Y_n)^{1/3} - 16$$
$$u^* = 13L^*(u' - u'_n)$$
$$v^* = 13L^*(v' - v'_n) \tag{4.8}$$

where

$$u' = \frac{4X}{X + 15Y + 3Z} \quad u'_n = \frac{4X}{X_n + 15Y_n + 3Z_n}$$
$$v' = \frac{9Y}{X + 15Y + 3Z} \quad v'_n = \frac{4X}{X_n + 15Y_n + 3Z_n} \tag{4.9}$$

u' and v' are a projective transformation of the x, y chromaticity diagram, designed to produce a perceptually more uniform color space. X_n, Y_n, and Z_n are the tristimulus values of a reference white. To measure the difference between colors, ΔE^*_{uv}, the following formula is used:

$$\Delta E^*_{uv} = \sqrt{\left(\Delta L^*\right)^2 + \left(\Delta u^*\right)^2 + \left(\Delta v^*\right)^2} \tag{4.10}$$

The *CIELUV* system retains many of the useful properties of the *XYZ* tristimulus values and the x, y chromaticity coordinates.

The u^* and v^* diagram is shown in Fig. 4.8. Its official name is the *CIE 1976 Uniform Chromaticity Scale diagram*, or UCS diagram. Because u^* and v^* is a projective transformation, it retains the useful property that blends of two colors will lie on a line between the u^* and v^* chromaticity coordinates. (It is worth noting that this is not a property of the *CIELAB* uniform color space.)

The u^* and v^* values change the scale of u^* and v^* with respect to the distance from black to white defined by the sample lightness, L^* (recall from Chapter 3 that L^* requires Y_n, a reference white in the application environment). The reason for this is straightforward — the darker the colors, the fewer we can see. At the limit, there is only one color, black. A value of 1 for ΔE^*_{uv} is an approximation to a *just noticeable difference* (JND).

More accurate uniform color spaces, such as CIEDE2000 (Luo, Cui, & Rigg, 2001), have more recently been developed. However, they are much more complex and are also generally unsuited to problems of data visualization because they are designed

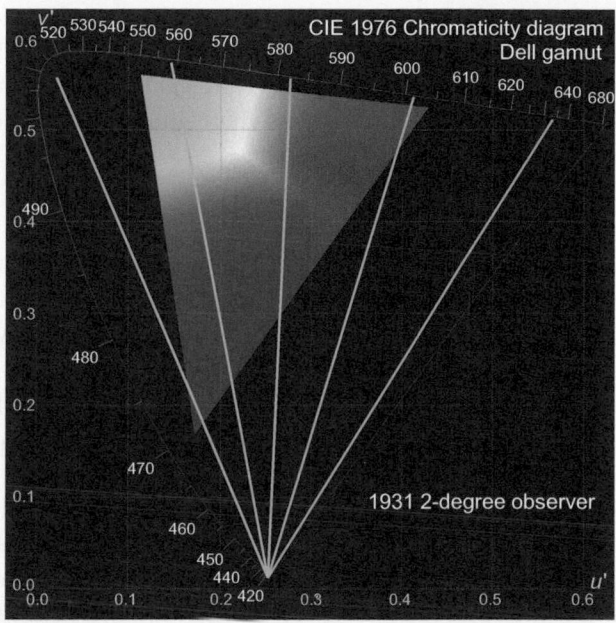

Figure 4.8 CIE *Lu*v** UCS diagram. The lines radiating from the lower part of the diagram are called *tritanopic confusion lines*. Colors that differ along these lines can still be distinguished by the great majority of color-blind individuals.

Figure 4.9 (a) Large samples of saturated colors. (b) Large samples of the same colors less saturated. (c) Small samples of the same saturated colors. (d) Small samples of the less saturated colors.

only for large patches of color. Uniform color spaces can only do so much. Factors such as simultaneous contrast, adaptation, and shading effects can radically alter color appearances and hence alter the shape of color space.

Most importantly, we are much more sensitive to differences between large patches of color than small patches and color uniform colors spaces were designed for large patch discrimination but most symbols used in visualization are quite small. When the patches are small, the perceived differences are smaller, and this is especially true in the yellow-blue direction. Ultimately, with very small samples, small field tritanopia occurs; this is the inability to distinguish colors that are different in the yellow-blue direction. Fig. 4.9 shows two examples of large patches of color on a white background and the same set of colors in smaller patches. In the larger patches, the low-saturation colors are easy to distinguish. To support the needs of data visualization and the perception of small symbols and patterns, modifications of the standard uniform color spaces have been developed (Stone et al., 2014; Ware et al., 2017). These are discussed later in the applications section of this chapter where guidelines will be provided.

Opponent Process Theory

Late in the 19th century, German psychologist Ewald Hering proposed the theory that there are six elementary colors and that these colors are arranged perceptually as opponent pairs along three axes: black-white, red-green, and yellow-blue (Hering, 1920). In recent years, this principle has become a cornerstone of modern color theory, supported by a variety of experimental evidence (for a review, see Hurvich, 1981). Modern opponent process theory has a well-established physiological basis: Input from the cones is processed into three distinct channels immediately after the receptors. The luminance channel (black-white) is based on input from all the cones. The red-green channel is based on the difference of long- and middle-wavelength cone signals. The yellow-blue channel is based on the difference between the short-wavelength cones and the sum of the other two. These basic connections are illustrated in Fig. 4.10. There are many lines of scientific evidence for the opponent process theory. These are worth examining, because they provide useful insights.

Naming

Opponent color theory predicts that certain color names should not occur in combination. We often describe colors using combinations of color terms, such as *yellowish green* or *greenish blue*. The theory predicts that people will never use *reddish green* or *yellowish blue* because these colors are polar opposites in the opponent color theory (Hurvich, 1981). Experiments have confirmed this.

Cross-Cultural Naming

In a remarkable study of more than 100 languages from many diverse cultures, anthropologists Berlin and Kay (1969) showed that primary color terms are remarkably

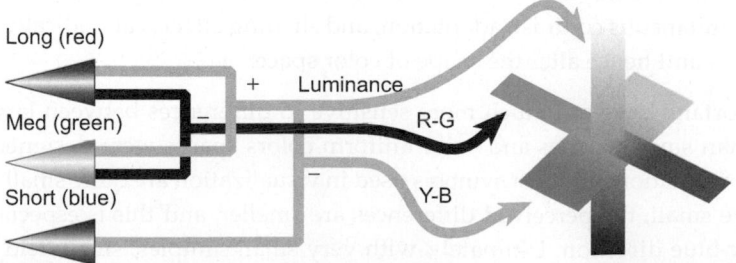

Figure 4.10 In the color opponent process model, cone signals are transformed into black-white (luminance), red-green, and yellow-blue channels.

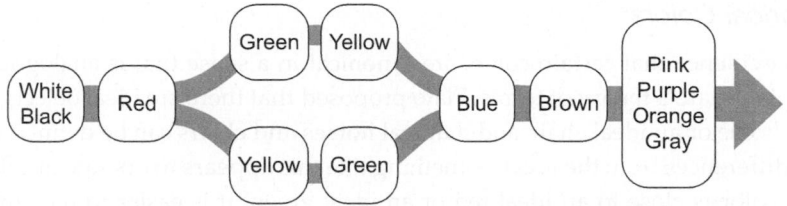

Figure 4.11 This is the order of appearance of color names in languages around the world, according to the research of Berlin and Kay (1969). The order is fixed, with the exception that sometimes yellow is present before green and sometimes the reverse is the case.

consistent across cultures (Fig. 4.11). In languages with only two basic color words, these are always black and white; if a third color is present, it is always red; the fourth and fifth are either yellow and then green, or green and then yellow; the sixth is always blue; the seventh is brown, followed by pink, purple, orange, and gray in no particular order. The key point here is that the first six terms define the primary axes of an opponent color model. This provides strong evidence that the neural basis for these names is innate; otherwise, we might expect to find cultures where lime green or turquoise is a basic color term. The cross-cultural evidence strongly supports the idea that certain colors—specifically, red, green, yellow, and blue—are far more valuable in coding data than others.

Unique Hues

There is something special about yellow. If subjects are given control over a device that changes the spectral hue of a patch of light and are told to adjust it until the result is a pure yellow, neither reddish nor greenish, they do so with remarkable accuracy. In fact, they are typically accurate within 2nm (Hurvich, 1981).

Interestingly, there is good evidence for two unique greens. Most people set a pure green at about 514 nm, but about one third of the population sees pure green at about 525 nm (Richards, 1967). This may be why some people argue about the color turquoise; some people consider it to be a variety of green, whereas others consider it to be a kind of blue.

It is also significant that unique hues do not change a great deal when the overall luminance level is changed (Hurvich, 1981). This supports the idea that chromatic perception and luminance perception really are independent.

Neurophysiology

Neurophysiological studies have isolated classes of cells in the primary visual cortexes of monkeys that have exactly the properties of opponency required by the opponent process theory. Red-green and yellow-blue opponent cells exist, and other configurations do not appear to exist (de Valois & de Valois, 1975).

Categorical Colors

There is evidence that certain colors are canonical in a sense that is analogous to the philosopher Plato's theory of forms. Plato proposed that there are ideal objects, such as an ideal horse or an ideal chair, and that real horses and chairs can be defined in terms of their differences from the ideal. Something like this appears to operate in color naming. If a color is close to an ideal red or an ideal green, it is easier to remember and name. Colors that are in between, such as blue gray or lime green, are not as easy to remember.

A recent online survey solicited color names from 10,000 English speaking participants. (The Dolores Lab experiment; https://datahub.io/dataset/colournames). The results were analyzed by Chuang, Stone, and Hanrahan (2008) and part of their analysis is given in Fig. 4.12. In this figure the size of the rectangles indicates how consistently particular colors were named. There are clear patches representing reds, greens, yellows, blues, browns, grays, etc. that match the color names of Berlin and Kay. Between these patches are smaller rectangles, indicating that people lack consistent names for these colors. Although these results are broadly in support of opponent color theory, they cannot be fully explained by it. A study by Sayim, Jameson, Alvarado, and Szeszel (2005) strongly suggests that there are at least two distinct representations of color in the brain—one is perceptual and derives from neurophysiology that is more-or-less common to all humans while the other is semantic and based partly on language and cultural conventions and partly on underlying neurophysiology.

Properties of Color Channels

From the perspective of data visualization, the different properties of the color channels have profound implications for the use of color. The most significant differences are between the two chromatic channels and the luminance channel, although the two color channels also differ from each other.

To display data on the luminance channel *alone* is easy; it is stimulated by patterns that vary only from black to white through shades of gray. But, with careful calibration (which must be customized to individual subjects), patterns can be constructed that vary only for the red-green or the yellow-blue channel. A key quality of such a pattern is that its component colors must not differ in luminance. This is called an *isoluminant* or *equiluminous* pattern. In this way, the different properties of the color channels can be explored and compared with the luminance channel capacity.

Spatial Sensitivity

The red-green and yellow-blue chromatic channels are each capable of far less detail than the black-white channel (Mullen, 1985; Poirson & Wandell, 1996). Fig. 4.13 illustrates spatial sensitivity curves for red-green, yellow-blue and luminance channels. As can be seen, the red-green and yellow-blue spatial sensitivities fall off much faster than the luminance sensitivity. This reinforces a point already made: luminance variation is

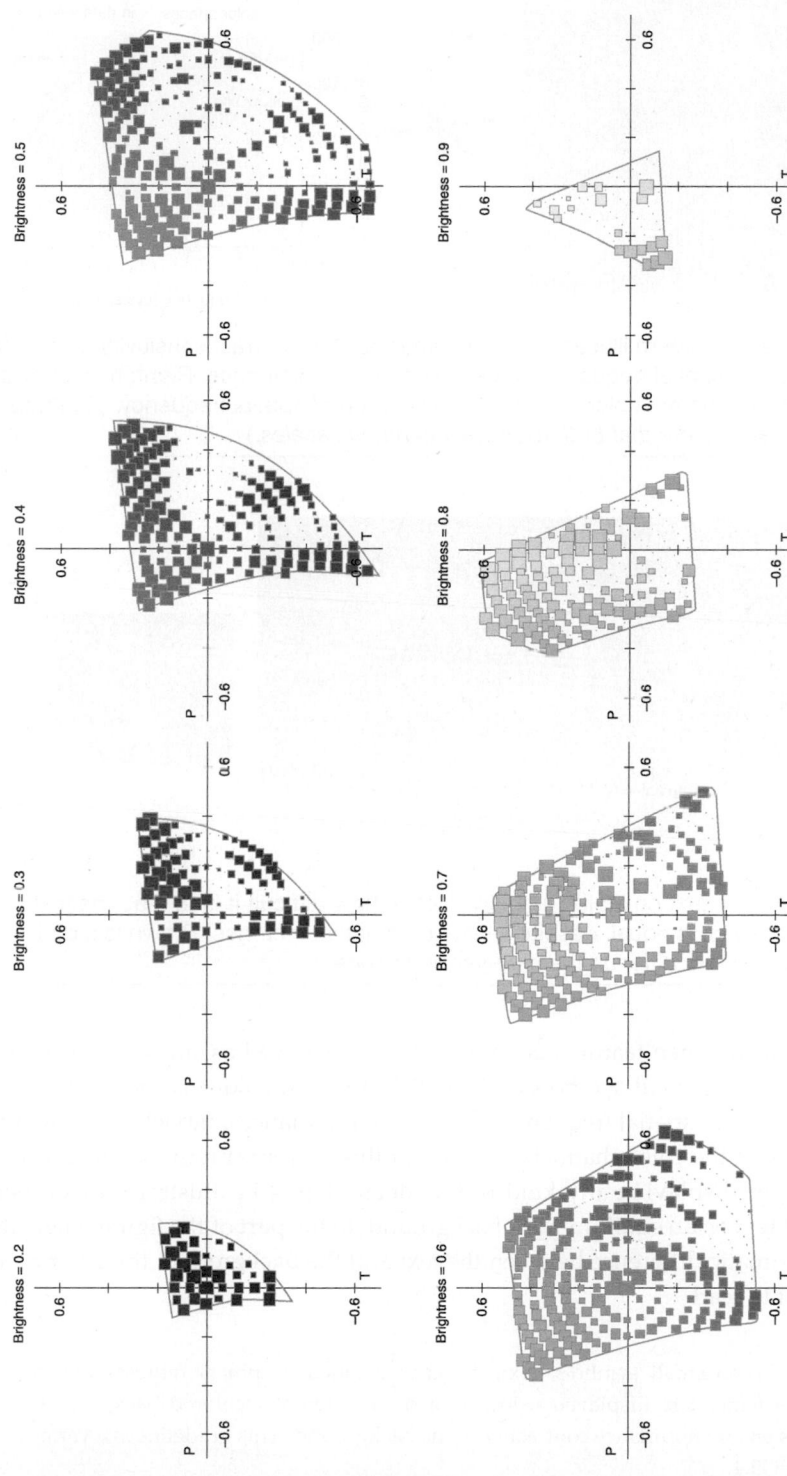

Figure 4.12 Colors on equiluminous slices across color space. The size of squares shows how consistently named the colors were. *(Adapted from Chuang et al. (2008) with permission.)*

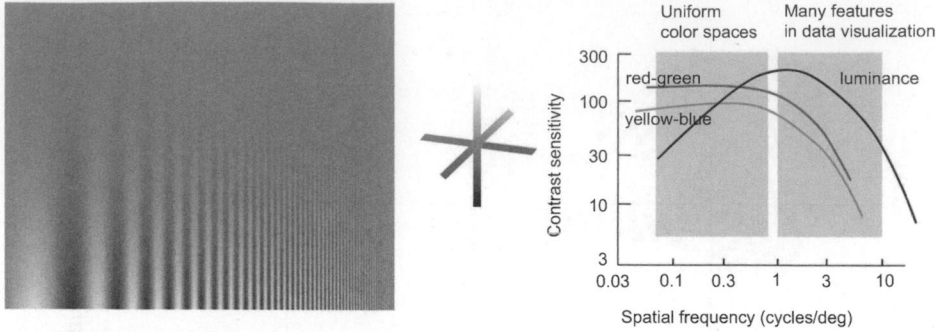

Figure 4.13 Left: a pattern illustrating how human spatial contrast sensitivity falls off for both high and low spatial frequency patterns defined by luminance. Right: human pattern sensitivity for the different color channels as a function of spatial frequency. (*Adapted from Mullen (1985). Note that both axes are logarithmic scales.*)

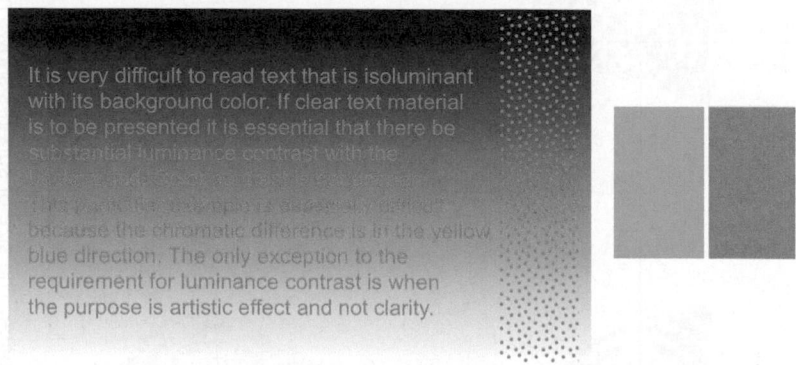

Figure 4.14 Brown text on a blue gradient. Notice how difficult it is to read the text where the luminance is equal, despite a large chromatic difference. Brown is a dark yellow so these colors differ on the blue-yellow channel.

absolutely critical when features in data are to be displayed as small patterns. When we are considering small symbols and small features in color-mapped data, we are dealing with higher spatial frequencies where the luminance channel has many times the sensitivity of the color channels. Because of this, purely chromatic differences are not suitable for displaying any kind of fine detail. Fig. 4.14 illustrates this problem with colored text on an equiluminous background. In the part of the figure where there is only a chromatic difference between the text and the background, the text becomes very difficult to read.

[G4.1] When small symbols, text, or other detailed graphical representations of information are displayed using color on a differently colored background, always ensure luminance contrast with the background. This guideline is a variation of G3.4.

Stereoscopic Depth

It appears to be impossible, or at least very difficult, to see stereoscopic depth in stereo pairs that differ only in terms of the color channels (Gregory, 1977; Lu & Fender, 1972). This is because stereoscopic depth perception is based primarily on information from the luminance channel.

> [G4.2] Ensure adequate luminance contrast in order to define features important for perceiving stereoscopic depth.

Motion Sensitivity

If a pattern is created that is equiluminous with its background and contains only chromatic differences, and that pattern is set in motion, something strange occurs. The moving pattern appears to move much more slowly than a black against white pattern moving at the same speed (Anstis & Cavanaugh, 1983). Motion perception appears to be primarily based on information from the luminance channel.

> [G4.3] Ensure adequate luminance contrast in order to define features important for perceiving moving targets.

Form

We are very good at perceiving the shapes of surfaces based on their shading; however, when the shading is transformed from a luminance gradient into a purely chromatic gradient, the impression of surface shape is much reduced. Perception of shape and form appears to be processed mainly through the luminance channel (Gregory, 1977).

> [G4.4] When applying shading to define the shape of a curved surface, use adequate luminance (as opposed to chromatic) variation. This is a supplement to G2.1.

Even though small shapes should not be defined by purely chromatic boundaries, this does not apply to large shapes, such as the R in Fig. 4.15, which can be seen clearly. Nevertheless, the shape will be more clearly perceived if a luminance difference border is added, however thin. This also helps distinguish the color of the shape.

> [G4.5] If large areas are defined using nearly equiluminous colors, consider using thin border lines with large luminance differences (from the colors of the areas) to help define the shapes.

To summarize this set of properties, the red-green and yellow-blue channels are inferior to the luminance channel in almost every respect. The implications for data display are clear. Purely chromatic differences should never be used for displaying object shape, object motion, or detailed information such as text. From this perspective, color

Figure 4.15 Even large shapes are seen more clearly if a luminance contrast boundary is provided.

would seem almost irrelevant and certainly a secondary method for information display; nevertheless, when it comes to coding information, using color to display data categories is usually the best choice. To see why, we need to look beyond the basic processes that we have been considering thus far.

Color Appearance

Color (as opposed to luminance) processing, it would appear, does not help us to understand the shape and layout of objects in the environment. Color does not help the hunter aim an arrow accurately. Color does not help us see shape from shading and thereby shape a lump of clay or bread dough. Color does not help us use stereoscopic depth to guide our hands when we reach out to grasp something. But color is useful to the gatherer of food. Fruits and berries are often distinguished by their color.

Color creates a kind of visual attribute of objects: this is a red berry; that is a yellow door. Color names are used as adjectives because colors are perceived as attributes of objects. This suggests a most important role for color in visualization, namely the coding of information. Visual objects can represent complex data entities and colors can naturally code attributes of those objects. The goal of color processing in the visual system is to discount the effects of illumination and let us see the surface colors of objects. For a general model of color appearance, taking various factors such as contrast into account, consider CIECAM02 (Moroney et al., 2002).

Screen Surrounds

The *XYZ* tristimulus values of a patch of light physically define a color, but they do not tell us how it will appear. Depending on the surrounding colors in the environment and a whole host of spatial and temporal factors, the same physical color can look very different. If it is desirable that color appearance be preserved, it is important to pay close attention to surrounding conditions. In a monitor-based display, a large patch of standardized reference white will help ensure that color appearance is preserved. When colors are reproduced on paper, viewing them under a standard lamp will help preserve their appearance. In the paint and fabric industries, where color appearance is critical, standard viewing booths are used. These booths contain standard illumination systems that can be set to approximate daylight or a standard indoor illuminant, such as a warm tungsten light bulb or cold LED lamp.

Color Constancy

The mechanisms of surface lightness constancy, discussed at some length in Chapter 3, generalize to trichromatic color perception. Both chromatic adaptation and chromatic contrast occur and play a role in color constancy. Differential adaptation in the cone receptors helps us to discount the color of the illumination in the environment. When there is colored illumination, different classes of cone receptors undergo independent changes in sensitivity; thus, when the illumination contains a lot of blue light, the short-wavelength cones become relatively less sensitive than the others. The effect of this is to shift the neutral point at which the three receptor types are in equilibrium, such that more blue light must be reflected from a surface for it to seem white. This discounting of the illumination, of course, is exactly what is necessary for color constancy. A piece of everyday evidence that adaptation is effective is the fact that not many people were aware of how much yellower old-style tungsten room lighting was compared to daylight. The consequence for adaptation is that we cannot see absolute colors, and when colored symbols appear on differently colored backgrounds their apparent hue will be altered.

Color Contrast

Chromatic contrast occurs in a way that is similar to the lightness contrast effects discussed and illustrated in Chapter 3. Fig. 4.16 shows a color contrast illusion. It has been

Figure 4.16 A color contrast illusion. The ellipses are all the same color but seem pinker on the right and bluer on the left. The longer you look, the greater the differences will appear.

shown that contrast effects can distort readings from color-coded maps (Cleveland & McGill, 1983; Ware, 1988). Contrast effects can be theoretically accounted for by activity in the color opponent channels (Ware & Cowan, 1982). However, as with lightness contrast, the ultimate purpose of the contrast-causing mechanism is to help us see surface colors accurately by revealing differences between colored patches and background regions.

From the point of view of the monitor engineer and the user of color displays, the fact that colors are perceived relative to their overall context has the happy consequence of making the eye relatively insensitive to poor color balance. Try comparing an image on a computer screen with that same image printed. Individual colors will undoubtedly be very different, but the overall impression and the information conveyed will be mostly preserved. This is because relative color is much more important than absolute color.

Saturation and Chroma

When describing color appearance in everyday language, people use many terms in rather imprecise ways. Besides using color names such as *lime green, mauve, brown, baby blue,* and so on, people also use adjectives such as *vivid, bright,* and *intense* to describe colors that seem especially pure. Because these terms are used so variably, artists and scientists use the technical term *saturation* to denote how pure or vivid colors seem to the viewer. A high-saturation color is pure, and a low-saturation color is close to black, white, or gray. However, dark colors such as dark orange (which appears brown) and dark green are seen as less vivid even though they may be equally saturated. The technical term from color science *chroma* refers to the perceived vividness of colors. As mentioned earlier it is a badly coined term because it can be confused with chromaticity (all color variation) and it comes from a Greek term which simply means "color". For these reasons, saturation is more often used informally. Fig. 4.17(a) illustrates the chroma concept. For mid-lightness colors saturation and chroma mean much the same thing.

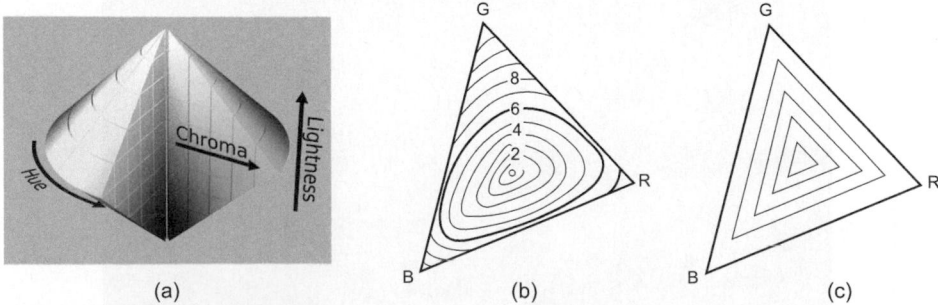

Figure 4.17 (a) The concepts of hue lightness and chroma. (b) The triangle represents the gamut of colors obtained using a computer monitor plotted in CIE chromaticity coordinates. The contours show perceptually determined equal-chroma contours. (c) Equal-saturation contours created using the HSV color space, also plotted in chromaticity coordinates.

Equal-chroma contours have been derived from psychophysical experiments (Wyszecki & Stiles, 1982). Fig. 4.17(b) shows a plot of equal-saturation values in a CIE chromaticity diagram. These contours, derived from studies of human perception, show that it is possible to obtain much more highly saturated red, green, and blue colors on a monitor than yellow, cyan, or purple values. Fig. 4.17(c) shows equal-saturation contours (not derived from perception) in the popular hue, saturation, and value (HSV) transformation commonly used in computer graphics (Smith, 1978). Comparing the two diagrams, it is striking that two colors having equal HSV saturations will not have even close to equal perceptual saturation. In particular, pure red, pure green, and pure blue on a monitor will be more perceptually saturated than pure cyan, magenta, or yellow. To obtain a set of perceptually equally saturated colors we would have to restrict our color gamut to contour 6 in Fig. 4.17(b), but this would mean giving up a large amount of useful RGB color space, including the most vivid colors, so this is usually inadvisable.

Using the general principle that stronger visual effects should be used to show greater quantities (G1.3), we can establish a guideline for the use of chroma in color coding. Because there are few discriminable steps in chroma, and because of contrast effects that may occur if the background is variable, only a few chroma levels can be reliably judged.

[G4.6] If using color chroma to encode numerical quantity, use greater chroma to represent greater numerical quantities. Avoid using a chroma sequence to encode more than four values.

Brown

Brown is one of the most mysterious colors. Brown is dark yellow. Whereas people talk about a light green or a dark green, a light blue or a dark blue, they do not talk about dark yellow. When colors in the vicinity of yellow and orange are darkened, they turn to shades of olive green and brown. Unlike red, blue, and green, brown requires that there be a reference white somewhere in the vicinity for it to be perceived. Brown appears qualitatively different from orange or yellow.

There is no such thing as an isolated brown light in a dark room, but when a yellow or yellowish orange is presented with a bright white surround, brown appears. The relevance to visualization is that, if color sets are being devised for the purposes of color coding—for example, a set of blues, a set of reds, a set of greens and a set of yellows—in the case of yellows, brown may not be recognized as a set member.

Applications of Color in Visualization

So far, this chapter has been mainly a presentation of the basic theory underlying color vision and color measurement. Now we shift the emphasis to applications of color, for which new theory will be introduced only as needed. We will examine four different application areas: color selection interfaces, color labeling, color sequences for map coding, and color reproduction. Each of these presents a different set of problems, and each benefit from an analysis in terms of the human perception of color. We will use these applications to develop guidelines and continue to develop theory.

Application 1: Color Specification Interfaces and Color Spaces

In data visualization software, drawing applications, and CAD systems, it is often essential to let users choose their own colors. There are a number of approaches to this user interface problem. The user can be given a set of controls to specify a point in a three-dimensional color space, a set of color names to choose from, or a palette of predefined color samples.

Color Spaces for Choosing Colors

The simplest color interface to implement on a computer involves giving someone controls to adjust the amounts of red, green, and blue light that combine to make a patch of color on a monitor. The controls can take the form of sliders, or the user can simply type in three numbers. This provides access, in a straightforward way, to any point within the RGB color cube shown in Fig. 4.5; however, although it is simple, many people find this kind of control confusing. For example, most people do not know that to get yellow you must additively combine red and green light. Many of the most widely used color interfaces in computer graphics are based on the hue, saturation, and value (HSV) color space (Smith, 1978). This is a simple transformation from HSV coordinates to *RGB* monitor coordinates. *Hue*, in Smith's scheme, represents an approximation to the visible spectrum by interpolating in sequence from red to yellow (= red + green) to green to cyan (= green + blue) to blue to purple (= blue + red) and back to red. *Saturation* is the distance from neutral monitor values, on the white-gray-black axis, to the purest hue possible given the limits of monitor primaries. Fig. 4.18 shows how hue and saturation can be laid out in two dimensions, with hue on one axis and saturation on the other, based on the HSV transformation of monitor primaries. As Fig. 4.17(c) shows, HSV creates only the crudest approximation to perceptually equal *croma* contours. *Value* is the name given to the black-white axis. Some color specification interfaces based on HSV allow the user to control hue, saturation, and value variables with three sliders.

Because color research has shown the luminance channel to be very different from the chromatic (red-green, yellow-blue) channels, it is a good idea to separate a luminance (or lightness) dimension from the chromatic dimensions in a color specification interface. In addition, because the chromatic channels are perceived integrally, it is usually best to lay out the various hue and saturation choices on a plane, but not as shown in Fig. 4.18, as this devotes far too much space to neutral colors and does not reflect the perceptual structure of color space derived from the color opponent channels. Fig. 4.19 provides a selection of much better layouts. All are compromises among

Figure 4.18 This plot shows hue and saturation, based on Smith (1978) transformation of the monitor primaries.

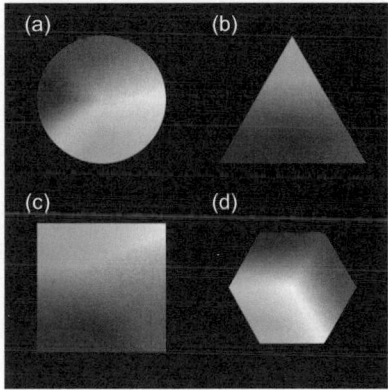

Figure 4.19 A sampling of four different geometric color layouts, each of them embodying the idea of a chromatic plane. (a) Circle. (b) Triangle. (c) Square. (d) Hexagon.

the constraints of colors produced by computer monitors, the desire to produce a neat geometric space, and the goal of producing a perceptually meaningful representation of a color plane orthogonal to the luminance channel.

[G4.7] In an interface for specifying colors, consider laying out the red-green and yellow-blue channel information on a plane. Use a separate control for specifying the dark-light dimension.

A common interface method is to provide a single slider control for the black-white dimension and to lay out the two opponent color dimensions on a chromatic plane. The idea of laying out colors on a plane has a long history; for example, a color circle is a feature of a color textbook created for artists by Rood (1897). With the invention of computer graphics, it has become far simpler to create and control colors, and many ways of laying out colors are now available.

Fig. 4.19(a) shows a color circle with red, green, yellow, and blue defining opposing axes. Many such color circles have been devised over the past century. They differ mainly in the spacing of colors around the periphery.

Fig. 4.19(b) shows a color triangle with the monitor primaries, red, green, and blue, at the corners. This color layout is convenient because it has the property that mixtures of two colors will lie on a line between them (assuming proper calibration); however, because of linear interpolation, only a very weak yellow occurs between the red and green corners (50% red, 50% green). The strongest yellow on a monitor comes from having both red and yellow at full strength.

Fig. 4.19(c) shows a color square with the opponent color primaries, red-green and yellow-blue, at opposite corners (Ware & Cowan, 1990).

Fig. 4.19(d) shows a color hexagon with the colors red, yellow, green, cyan, blue, and magenta at the corners. This represents a plane through the single-hexcone color model (Smith, 1978). The hexagon representation has the advantage that it gives both the monitor primaries (red, green, and blue) and the print primaries (cyan, magenta, and yellow) prominent positions around the circumference.

To create a color interface using one of these color planes, it is necessary to allow the user to pick a sample from the color plane and adjust its lightness with a luminance slider or some other control. In some interfaces, when the luminance slider is moved, the entire plane of colors becomes lighter and darker according to the currently selected level. For those interested in implementing color interfaces, algorithms for a number of color geometries can be found in Foley, van Dam, Feiner, and Hughes (1990). The reader may be wondering why uniform color spaces are not used to create more uniformly distributed colors, but generally this is not done, presumably because of the odd shapes that result for the color plane. The circles, squares, and hexagons shown in Fig. 4.19 sacrifice perceptual uniformity for a better use of screen space.

Another valuable addition to a color design interface is a method for showing a color sample on differently colored backgrounds. This allows the designer to understand how contrast effects can affect the appearance of particular color samples.

[G4.8] In an interface for designing visualization color schemes, consider providing a method for showing colors against different backgrounds.

The problem of the best color selection interface is by no means resolved. Experimental studies have failed to show that one way of controlling color is substantially better than another (Douglas & Kirkpatrick, 1996; Schwarz, Cowan, & Beatty, 1987). Douglas and Kirkpatrick, however, have provided evidence that good feedback about the location of the color being adjusted in color space can help in the process.

Color Naming and Color Sample Systems

The facts that there are so few widely agreed upon color names and that color memory is so poor suggest that choosing colors by name will not be useful except for the simplest applications. People agree on red, green, yellow, blue, black, and white as labels, but not much more; nevertheless, it is possible to remember a rather large number of color names and use them accurately under controlled conditions. Displays in paint stores generally have a standard illuminant and standard background for sample strips containing several hundred samples. Under these circumstances, the specialist can remember and use as many as 1000 color names, but many of the names are idiosyncratic; the colors corresponding to *taupe, fiesta red*, and *primrose* are imprecisely defined for most of us.

The Natural Color System (NCS), a standardized color naming system, has been developed based on Hering's opponent color theory (1920). NCS was developed in Sweden and is widely used in England and other European countries. In NCS, colors are characterized by the amounts of redness, greenness, yellowness, blueness, blackness, and whiteness that they contain. As shown in Fig. 4.20, red, green, yellow, and blue lie at the ends of two orthogonal axes. Intervening "pure" colors lie on the circle circumference, and these are given numbers by sharing out 100 arbitrary units; thus, a yellowish orange might be given the value Y70R30, meaning 70 parts yellow and 30 parts red. Colors are also given independent values on a black-white axis by allocating a blackness value between 0 and 100. A third color attribute, intensity (roughly corresponding to chroma), describes the distance from the grayscale axis. In NCS, for example, the color *spring nymph* becomes 0030-G80Y20, which expands to blackness 00, intensity 30, green 80, and yellow 20 (Jackson, MacDonald, & Freeman, 1994). The NCS system combines some of the advantages of a color geometry with a reasonably intuitive and precise naming system.

NCS is sometimes used in defining sets of physical painted samples used in the paint and design industries. In North America, competing systems such as Pantone

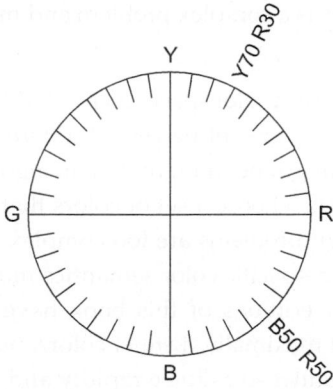

Figure 4.20 The Natural Color System (NCS) circle, defined midway between black and white. Two example color names are shown in addition to the "pure" opponent color primaries. yellow and blue dots.

and Munsell are widely used. The Pantone system is widely used in the printing industry. The Munsell system provides a set of standard color chips designed to represent equal perceptual spacing in a three-dimensional mesh; these provide a physical embodiment of a uniform color space. (Munsell color chips and viewing booths are available commercially, as are Pantone products.) The NCS, Pantone, and Munsell systems were originally designed to be used with carefully printed paper samples providing the reference colors, but computer-based interfaces to these systems have been developed as part of illustration and design packages (Rhodes & Luo, 1996).

Color Palettes

When the user requires only a small set of standardized colors, providing a color palette is a good solution to the color selection problem. Often, color selection palettes are laid out in a regular order according to one of the color geometries defined previously. It is useful to provide a facility for the user to develop a personal palette. This allows for consistency in color style across a number of visualization displays.

[G4.9] To support the use of easy-to-remember and consistent color codes, consider providing color palettes for designers.

Application 2: Color for Labeling (Nominal Codes)

Suppose we require a visualization where colored symbols represent companies from different industrial sectors—red for manufacturing, green for finance, blue for retail, and so on. The technical name for this kind of labeling is nominal information coding. A nominal code does not have to be orderable; it simply must be remembered and recognized, or matched to an identifying label in a legend. Color can be extremely effective for this kind of coding because colors tend to be perceived categorically. But designing a good set of labels is a complex problem and many aspects of color perception are relevant.

Sufficient Distinctness. A uniform color space, such as CIELUV, CIELAB or CIEDE2000, can be used to determine the degree of perceived difference between two colors that are placed close together. It might be thought that an algorithm based on one of these spaces could be used to simply choose a set of colors that are most widely separated, but most color scheme design problems are too complex for this; background colors, symbol sizes, and application-specific color semantics must all be taken into account. Many researchers and prior editions of this book have suggested that the proper approach is to create a set of maximally distinct colors, but in fact it is only necessary that colors be sufficiently distinct so as to be rapidly and unambiguously matched to a legend.

We are far more sensitive to differences between large patches of color than small patches of color. Work by Stone et al. (2014) has shown how the CIELAB uniform

Figure 4.21 Large area colors, such as may be used for background maps can be very low saturation and still be discriminated. The four colors above are part of a Tableau palette for large regions.

Figure 4.22 The Tableau 10 set of colors for coloring symbols. For accurate representation see the Tableau Website (screen colors are never exactly reproduced on paper).

color space can be adapted to provide guidance on sufficient color distinctness, taking symbol size into account. Their method involves underweighting the *a* (red-green) and *b* (yellow-blue) terms in CIELAB when computing differences between pairs of colors for small symbols. In general, the larger the area that is color coded the more easily colors can be distinguished, so when large areas of color coding are used (for example, with map regions), the colors should be of low chroma (saturation) and differ only slightly from one another. Small marks that are color coded should have strong, highly saturated colors for maximum discrimination. This enables small, vivid color-coded targets to be perceived against background regions. Fig. 4.21 shows a sample of colors designed to code large areas on background maps. Fig. 4.22 shows a set of colors designed to code small symbols. The Tableau10 is a set of 10 colors used in Tableau data visualization software. These colors are quite distinct, even when used for small symbols and lines, but are by no means the most distinctive colors that can be generated. For an evaluation of the Tableau 10 and some other carefully designed color sets, see Gramazio et al. (2017).

Luminance Contrast with Background. In many displays, color-coded objects can be expected to appear on a variety of backgrounds. Simultaneous contrast with background colors can dramatically alter color appearance, making one color look like another. This is one reason why it is advisable to have only a small set of color codes. A method for reducing contrast effects is to place a thin white or black border around the color-coded object. We should never display codes using purely chromatic differences with the background. There should be a significant luminance difference in addition to the color difference. Fig. 4.23 illustrates this principle with a variety of colors against a variety of backgrounds.

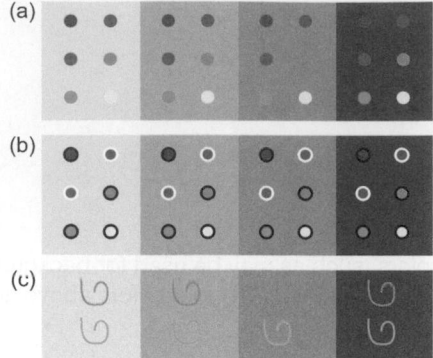

Figure 4.23 (a) Note that at least one member of the set of six symbols lacks distinctness against each background. (b) Adding a luminance contrast border ensures distinctness against all backgrounds. (c) Showing color-coded lines can be especially problematic.

The following are basic guidelines to be used in creating discriminable symbols.

[G4.10] Use more higher chroma (more vivid) colors when color coding small symbols.

[G4.11] Ensure sufficient distinctness for clear discrimination of symbols in a symbol set. Do not aim for maximal distinctness.

[G4.12] Use low-chroma colors to color code large areas. Generally, light colors will be best because there is more room in color space in the high-lightness region than in the low-lightness region.

[G4.13] When color coding large background areas to be overlaid with small symbols, consider using all low chroma, high-value (pastel) colors for the background, together with high-chroma darker colors for the overlaid symbols.

[G4.14] For small color-coded symbols, ensure luminance contrast with the background as well as large chromatic differences with the background.

[G4.15] If colored symbols may be nearly isoluminant against parts of the background, add a border having a highly contrasting luminance value to the color, for example, black around a yellow symbol or white around a dark blue symbol.

Fig. 4.24 illustrates guideline 4.13. High-chroma dark symbols are overlaid on a background consisting of light, low-chroma colors. The reverse looks terrible.

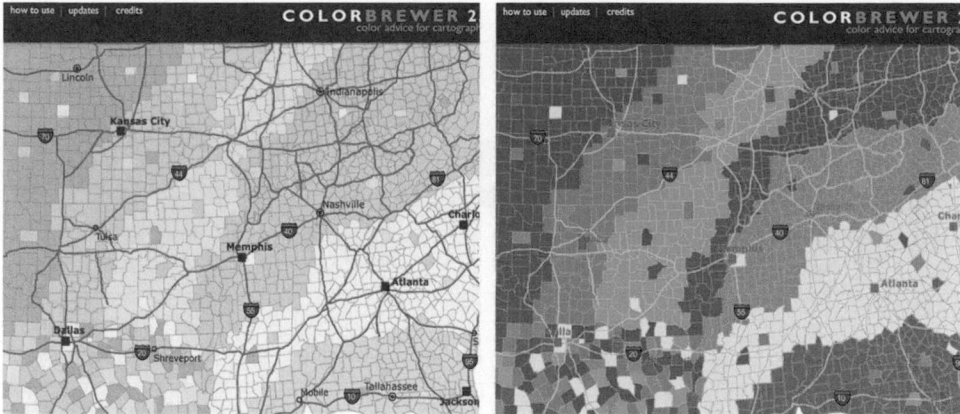

Figure 4.24 On the left is a map using low-chroma light colors for the area coding and high-saturation dark colors for the town and city symbols and linear features. On the right, a much worse solution shows high-chroma coding for areas and low-chroma symbols and linear features. Maps were generated using ColorBrewer2 (http://colorbrewer2.org).

Nameability and Categorization. As discussed earlier in this chapter (see Fig. 2.12) some colors are far more nameable and memorable than others. It is not a coincidence that the colors in the Berlin and Key set of nameable colors are used in Tableau 10. It is also the case that colors near to boundaries between color categories are likely to be mislabeled.

[G4.16] Consider using nameable colors such as red, green, yellow, blue, brown, pink purple, and gray for color coded symbols.

Color Semantics. Sometimes the meaning of colors must be taken into account when color coding symbols. Some common naming conventions are green = {go, safety, profit, vegetation}; red = {hot, anger, danger, financial loss}; blue = {cold, water, melancholy, calm}. It is important to keep in mind, however, that these conventions do not necessarily cross-cultural borders. In China, for example, red means life and good fortune, and green sometimes means death. Combinations of colors can also have affective qualities. Bartram, Patra, and Stone (2017) found that certain palettes were reliable rated at calm, serious, playful or trustworthy. These are illustrated in Fig. 4.25.

Color Blindness. Because there is a substantial color-blind population, it may be desirable to use colors that can be distinguished even by people who are color blind. Recall that the majority of color-blind people cannot distinguish colors that differ in a red-green direction. Almost everyone can distinguish colors that vary in a yellow-blue direction, as shown in Fig. 4.8. Colors separated along the radial lines can be discriminated by most color-blind individuals. Unfortunately, this drastically reduces the design choices that are available, especially since the yellow-blue color channel has the lowest capacity to resolve features.

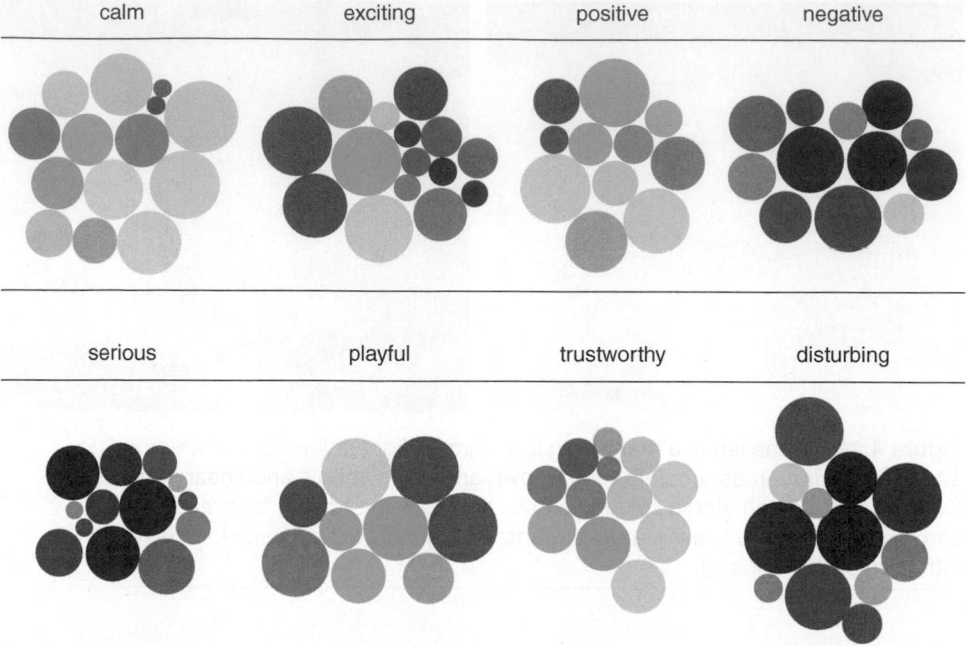

| calm | exciting | positive | negative |
| serious | playful | trustworthy | disturbing |

Figure 4.25 Different color sets with various affective qualities. (*From Bartram et al. (2017).*)

[G4.17] To create a set of symbol colors that can be distinguished by most color-blind individuals, ensure variation in the yellow-blue direction.

Number: Although color coding is an excellent way to display category information, only a small number of color codes can be rapidly perceived. Estimates vary between about 5 and 10 codes (e.g., Healey, 1996). Healey (1996) only used colors of the same luminance, although there is no need for this. With luminance variation, a somewhat larger color set can be achieved (Szafir et al., 2014).

[G4.18] Do not use more than 10 colors for coding symbols if reliable identification is required, especially if the symbols are to be used against a variety of backgrounds.

COLOR FAMILIES: Sometimes it is useful to group color codes into families. This can be done by using hue as a primary attribute denoting family membership, with secondary values mapped to a combination of saturation and lightness. Fig. 4.26 illustrates some examples. Generally, we cannot expect to get away with more than three different color steps in each family. The canonical red, green, and blue hues make good categories for defining families. Ideally, family members vary in both saturation and lightness.

Color used in highlighting: The goal of highlighting is to make some small subset of a display clearly distinct from the rest. The same principles apply to the highlighting of

Figure 4.26 Color families can sometimes be used for distinguishing items within a broader category. These are most distinctive is the colors are made to vary in both saturation and lightness.

(a) Higlighting text by changing the characters must be done
using high saturation colors that contrast with the background.

(b)

```
import java.applet.Applet;
import java.awt.Graphics;
import java.awt.Color;

    public class ColorText extends Applet
{
        public void init()
    {
                red = 100;
                green = 255;
                blue = 20;
    }

        public void paint (Graphics g)
    {
                Gr.setColor(new Color(red, green, blue));

                Gr.drawString("ColoredText". 30,50);
    }

        private int red;
        private int green;
        private int blue;

}
```

Figure 4.27 Two different methods for highlighting black text. (a) Change text itself using a relatively dark, high-saturation color. (b) Change text background using low-saturation light colors. Both maintain luminance contrast.

text or other features in a display. Fig. 4.27 illustrates two alternative text highlighting methods for use with black on white text. In one, the font is altered from black to colored. When this method is used, it is critical to maintain luminance contrast with the background; high-saturation dark colors must be used to maintain text legibility. The second method is to change the background. In this method, low-saturation light colors should be used. The same principles apply for other small symbols.

> **[G4.19]** When highlighting text by changing the color of the font, it is important to maintain luminance contrast with the background. With a white background, high-saturation dark colors should be used to change the font color.

[G4.20] When highlighting text by changing the background color, low-saturation light colors should be **used** if the text is black on white. The exception is yellow, because it is can be both light and have high saturation.

Application 3: Pseudocolor Sequences for Data Maps

Somewhere in almost every newspaper and on every weather website is a map where regions are colored differently to show the forecast temperatures. Red is used to show hot weather, blue is used to show cold weather, and other colors are arranged in between, often using the colors of the rainbow, blue-cyan-green-yellow-orange-red.

Pseudocoloring is the technique of representing continuously varying map values using a sequence of colors. The result is sometimes called a *choropleth* map. Pseudocoloring is used widely for astronomical radiation charts, medical imaging, and many other scientific applications. Geographers use a well-defined color sequence to display height above sea level—lowlands are always colored green, which evokes vegetation, and the scale continues upward, through brown, to white at the peaks of mountains.

The most common coding scheme used in data visualization is a color sequence that approximates the physical spectrum, like that shown in Fig. 4.28. Although this sequence is frequently used in physics and other disciplines and has some useful properties, it is not a perceptual sequence. This can be demonstrated by the following test. Give someone a series of gray paint chips and ask them to place them in order. They will happily comply with either a dark-to-light ordering or a light-to-dark ordering. Give the same person paint chips with the colors red, green, yellow, and blue and ask them to place them in order, and the result will be varied. For most people, the request will not seem particularly meaningful. They may even use an alphabetical ordering. This demonstrates that the whole spectrum is not perceptually ordered, although short sections of it are. For example, sections from red to yellow, yellow to green, and

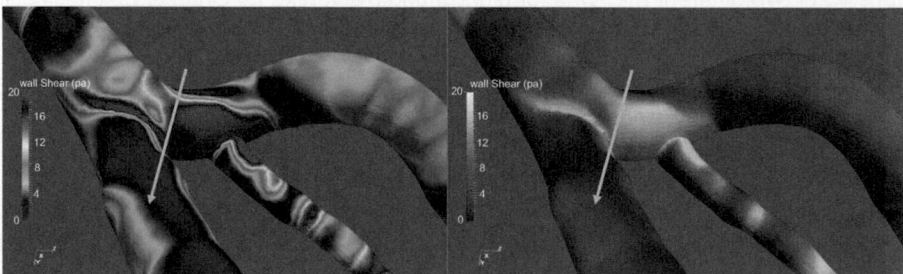

Figure 4.28 Low shear stress is correlated with atheroschlerosis. On the left the ubiquitous rainbow colormap is applied to shear stress data in branching arteries. Most people looking at this would associate the red area as problematic. This is wrong. Also, the various distinctive bands seen in the image actually have no meaning. The image on the right presents a much clearer picture. Red areas have problems, the darker the color, the worse the condition. (*Image from Ian Campbell, reproduced with permission.*)

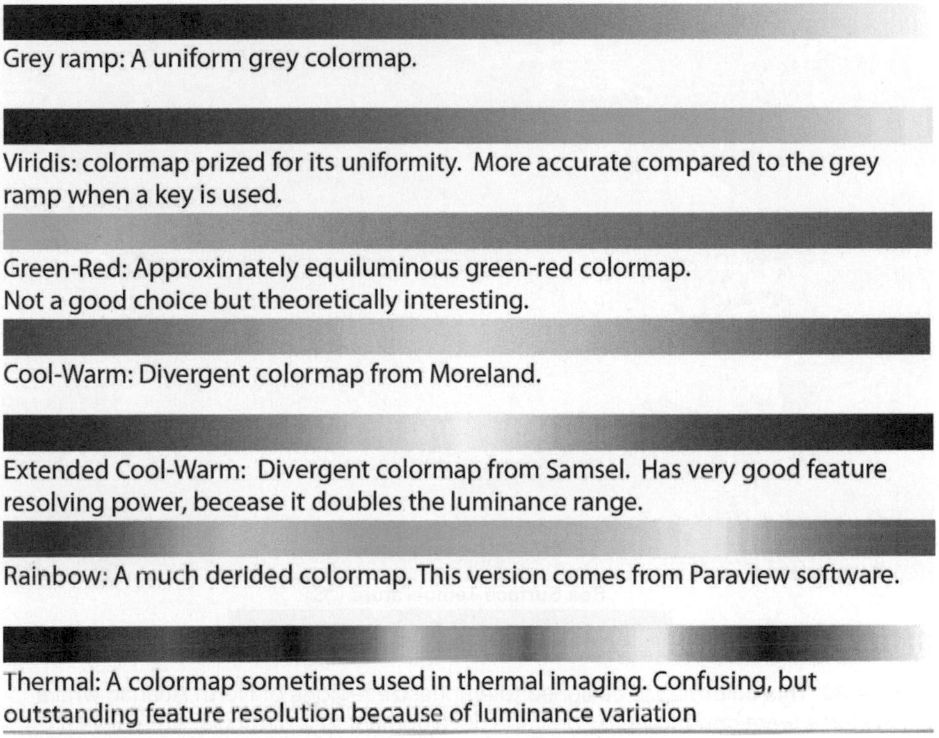

Grey ramp: A uniform grey colormap.

Viridis: colormap prized for its uniformity. More accurate compared to the grey ramp when a key is used.

Green-Red: Approximately equiluminous green-red colormap. Not a good choice but theoretically interesting.

Cool-Warm: Divergent colormap from Moreland.

Extended Cool-Warm: Divergent colormap from Samsel. Has very good feature resolving power, becease it doubles the luminance range.

Rainbow: A much derided colormap. This version comes from Paraview software.

Thermal: A colormap sometimes used in thermal imaging. Confusing, but outstanding feature resolution because of luminance variation

Figure 4.29 A set of seven colormaps discussed in the text.

green to blue all vary monotonically (they continuously increase or decrease) on both the red-green and yellow-blue channels. Fig. 4.28 illustrates some of the bad qualities of a rainbow colormap. It represents the data with bewildering stripes, and provides no sense of what is important.

Fig. 4.29 shows seven different colormaps. Many of them are in common use, but which ones are best and for what purposes? We will consider the problem in the light of *four basic* tasks for which pseudocolored maps are used, relevant perceptual theory and experimental results. *The basic tasks are as follows:*

Task 1: Resolve features: Feature resolution refers to our ability to perceive that a feature is present and colormaps vary enormously in terms of this property. This is a basic quality, because if a feature cannot be seen, it obviously cannot be interpreted.

Task 2: Identify patterns: It is impossible to know all of the different pattern-related tasks because the number of patterns that may be of interest to scientists is potentially infinite. But there are simple and somewhat generic pattern tasks that are common in scientific analysis, such as identifying highs and lows, telling positive from negative features, and comparing gradients. More complex tasks can include locating saddle points, elongated features, chains of similar features and many other patterns that only domain scientists will appreciate as important.

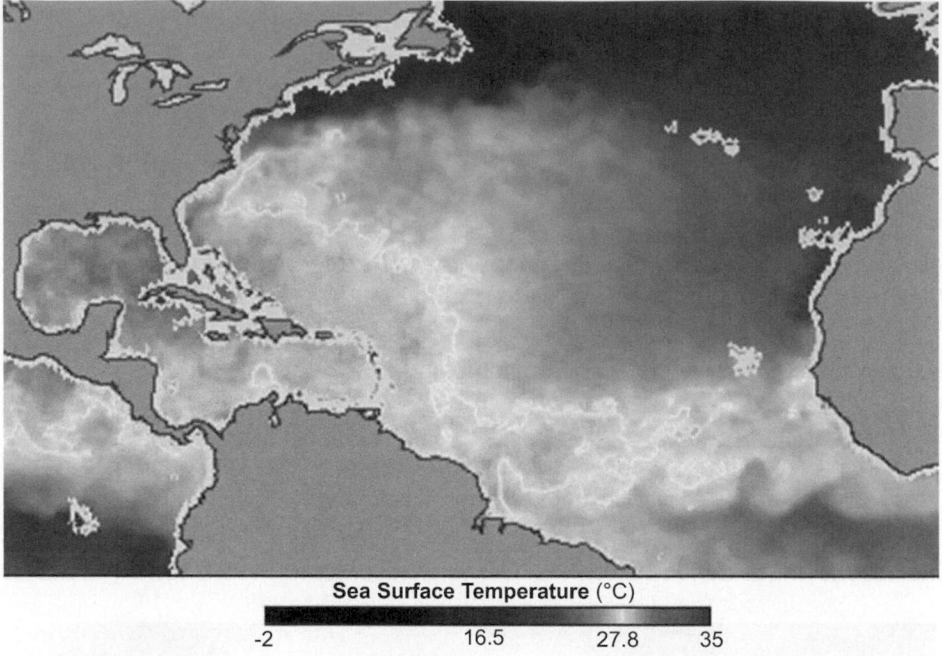

Sea Surface Temperature (°C)

-2   16.5   27.8   35

Figure 4.30 This colormap is designed to emphasize regions of North Atlantic where temperatures were conducive to hurricane development at a particular time of year. (*Courtesy of NOAA.*)

Task 3: Reading values from a key: In most cases color-mapped data is accompanied by a key which relates colors to data values. A simple use case is looking at a weather map to determine the forecast maximum temperature at a particular location. Usually visualization is about perceiving patterns, but sometimes we just want to know how hot it will be.

Task 4: Classifying regions: Sometimes colormaps are designed to highlight particular regions of interest, while reducing the visual salience of others. A particularly simple form of classification is binary, we may be concerned if temperatures are hotter or colder than normal. In a global map of average temperatures, it is common to show data above and below a long-term average, using red for hotter than average and blue for colder than average. Another example occurs where there is a defined threshold for some phenomenon. Fig. 4.30 shows the ocean surface temperature for the North Atlantic using shades of yellow and orange to highlight areas conducive to the genesis of hurricanes (temperatures above 27°C).

Now we turn our attention to the perceptual properties of colormaps which bear on these tasks. There are three main categories. The resolving power of a colormap and its uniformity, its perceptual monontonicity, especially in luminance, and how readily the colors in the sequence are categorized.

Uniformity and Resolving Power

Feature resolution is basic to pattern perception; if a feature cannot be seen, it cannot be interpreted. Fig. 4.31 shows a pattern designed to illustrate how the feature resolving power of colormaps varies along the color sequence. It has oblique sinusoidal features added to a simple data ramp. These features increase in contrast exponentially from the top to the bottom. The point at the top of each column of features where it can no longer be perceived indicates the feature resolving power of that part of the colormap. The same data underlies both the left and right images; the only thing that has changed is the colormap. As can be seen, the rainbow colormap is extremely non-uniform in its resolving power. It is very bad in the middle (the feature bars appear to extend only a short distance upwards) but good at the left and right ends (the bars extend much higher). In contrast, notice that with the Viridis colormap all the bars appear to fade out at the same height showing that the colormap is indeed uniform for the task.

A uniform colormap is usually defined as one that has equal perceptual steps throughout its range. Most researchers have used uniform color space models as a way of achieving uniformity (e.g., Robertson & O'Callaghan, 1988). Unfortunately, as we have already discovered with symbols the standard uniform color spaces do not provide a good basis for modeling feature resolution for any but the very largest patterns. The problem is that even for moderately small features we are far less sensitive to red-green and yellow-blue chromatic differences than we are for luminance differences, compared to what is predicted by CIELAB, CIELUV, CIEDE2000, or other spaces.

Fig. 4.32 shows feature resolving power curves for the seven different colormaps shown in Fig. 4.29. These were measured using patterns similar to those shown in Fig. 4.31 (Ware, 2017). A number of points are immediately clear:

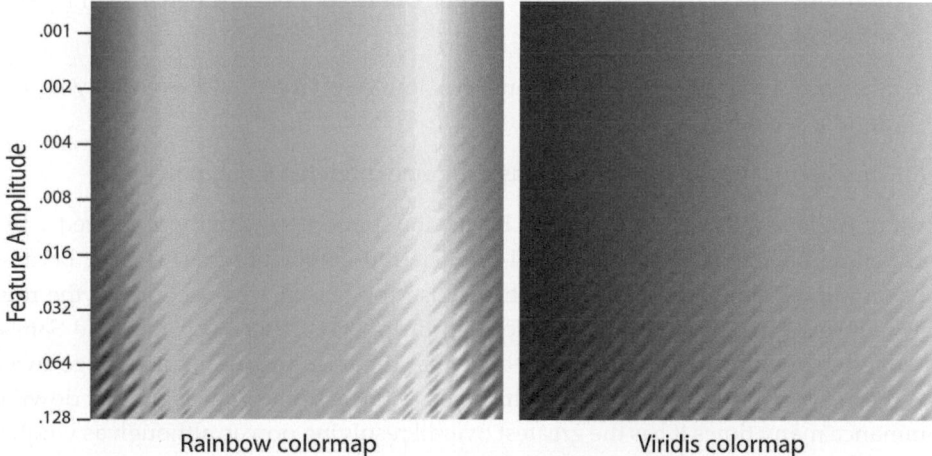

Rainbow colormap   Viridis colormap

Figure 4.31 A test pattern is designed to reveal the feature resolving power of different colormaps. The rainbow on the left is extremely nonuniform whereas Viridis, on the right is very uniform.

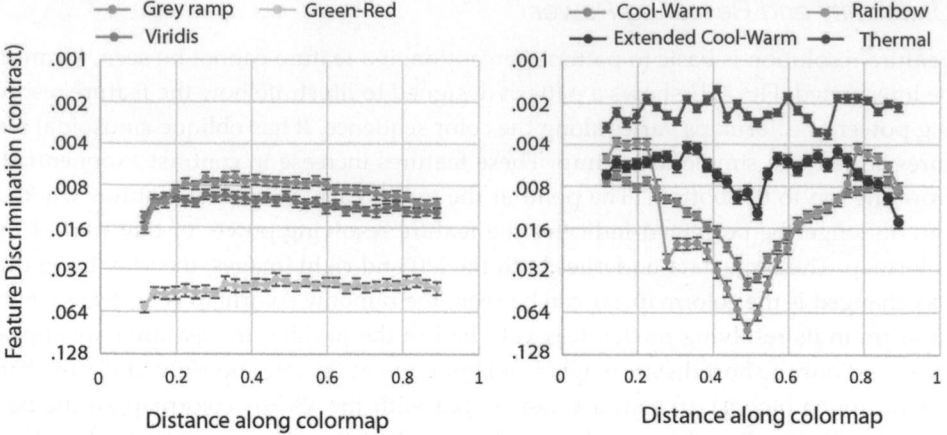

Figure 4.32 Measured feature discrimination curves for the seven colormaps. The x-axis give the amount of contrast in the data required for a feature to by just perceived. These measurements were made with spatial patterns having approximately three cycles/ degree of visual angle, in the range where red-green and yellow-blue patterns have little resolving power.

1) In addition to its other flaws, the rainbow colormap is extremely nonuniform. Indeed, this particular version has about 20 times less feature discrimination power in its central section compared to the ends.

2) Colormaps such as Viridis and the grayscale are far more uniform in their discrimination power compared to the rainbow colormap.

3) The red-green colormap is quite uniform but has very low resolving power.

4) The Samsel ECW colormap shown in the lower center has very good overall resolving power except at the very center, but even there it is better than most other colormaps.

5) The cool-warm colormap (Moreland) has low resolving power especially in its middle section.

6) The thermal imaging colormap has extremely high resolving power.

Most of these results can be explained by the low pattern sensitivity of the red-green and yellow-blue color channels (Fig. 4.13). The red-green colormap is poor because it has minimal luminance variation. This is also the reason why sections of the rainbow colormap and the cool-warm colormap do poorly. The reason why the Samsel extended cool-warm colormap does well is that it covers the luminance range twice. The thermal imaging colormap takes this logic to the extreme, it goes up and down in luminance many times it has the greatest overall resolving power, although as we shall see it can result in very confusing images.

One might think that most useful information is encoded in the lower spatial frequencies, but this is not so. It is a basic fact of signal theory that higher spatial frequencies carry more far information than lower frequencies. The CIELAB uniform color space can be modified to properly model the discrimination power of different colormaps simply by reducing the weights of the red-green and yellow-blue channels when computing color differences.

Recent work has shown that a uniform color space (CIELAB) can provide good estimates of the resolving power of different colormaps if the contribution of the red-green and yellow-blue channels are greatly underweighted (Ware et al., 2017). For patterns above spatial frequencies of one cycle/degree and above, the weights had to be reduced to 15% of their normal values.

> **[G4.21]** To create a colormap with good feature resolving power, ensure changes in luminance throughout its extent. If extreme resolving power is needed, the colormap can transit from dark to light and back several times (although this can cause problems in interpretation).

Overall Feature Resolving Power

Overall feature resolving power is the aggregate ability to resolve features along the length of the color sequence. Given an appropriate uniform color space, the overall resolving power is simply the length of the trajectory of the colormap in that space (Bujack). With appropriate adjustments, any colormap can be made uniform, by adjusting the spacing of the color points along that trajectory.

Perceptual Monotonicity, Luminance, and Form Perception

Perceptual monotonicity is the presence of a clear order to a color sequence. The most important ordering is in terms of luminance. Because the luminance channel helps us see forms, a grayscale sequence should allow us to see forms much better than pure color sequences (no luminance variation), and experimental studies have confirmed that grayscale maps are much better for form perception (Kindlmann, Reinhard, & Creem, 2004; Rogowitz & Treinish, 1996; Ware, 1988). In spite of this, a survey of papers containing pseudocolored maps found that more than 50% used an approximation to the physical spectrum—a rainbow as a color sequence (Borland & Taylor, 2007). The same paper argued that the rainbow sequence "hinders this task [of effectively conveying information] by confusing, obscuring and actively misleading."

We can have ordering on any direction in color space. Fig. 4.33 illustrates the importance of perceptual monotonicity for form perception. In this figure the artificial data has a simple linear ramp increasing from left to right. Sets of ripple patterns are superimposed on this. Observed that these patterns appear consistently with Veridis. They are also consistent with the green to red colormap, but seem much fainter. With the double ended colormap, they are bright on the left but inconsistently dark on the right. With the thermal imaging colormap the result is confusing, the features are very clear but it would be very difficult to tell if the ripples are raised or depressed at any point.

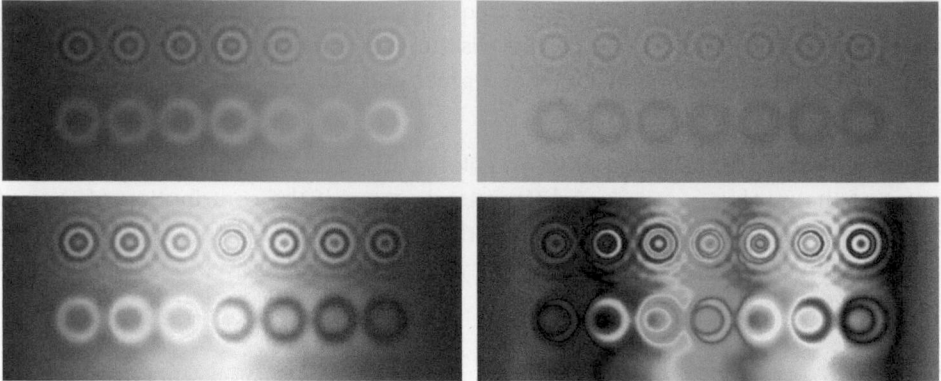

Figure 4.33 In this figure, artificial data has a background ramp increasing from left to right. Superimposed on this are ripple patterns. Notice how with the top two colormaps the ripples are seen consistently. With the bottom two they are not.

> **[G4.22]** For consistent form of perception create a colormap that varies monotonically in luminance from one end to the other.

Contrast and Accuracy. Simultaneous contrast effects can cause large errors when reading a map value using a color key. This is especially true for sequences that vary in luminance or saturation, but not in hue (Ware, 1988). Color sequences that vary in hue can be read more accurately. Note that these do not eliminate luminance contrast effects, but the contrast effects tend to cancel out.

Categorization: In some cases colormaps are used to make different regions appear visually distinct (Fig. 4.30). The issues in color categorization are the same as those described previously concerning colors used as labels. It is not necessary to repeat them here. But when color is used for categorization, a flexible color assignment tool is needed (Samsel). In this case, perceptual smoothness and uniformity are not the goals of colormap design, instead the purpose is to create distinctive regions in the data map.

Spiral Colormaps

Some authors have recommended that, for clarity, color sequences should constitute a straight line through a perceptual color space, such as *CIELUV* or *CIELAB* (Robertson & O'Callaghan, 1988; Levkowitz & Herman, 1992). A better choice may be to design a sequence that cycles through a variety of hues, each lighter than the previous one. Sometimes this is called a *spiral color sequence*, because it can be thought of as spiraling upward in color space. Such a sequence can combine the advantages of monotonicity in luminance, so as to show form and detail, as well as reduce contrast-induced errors and enable accurate readings from a color key (Ware, 1988; Levkowitz & Herman, 1992; Kindelmann et al., 2004).

[G4.23] If it is important to perceive forms correctly and also read values from a key, cycle through a variety of hues while trending upward or downward in luminance.

Interval Pseudocolor Sequences

An interval sequence is one in which each unit step of the sequence represents an equal change in magnitude of the characteristic being displayed across the whole range of the sequence. In terms of color, this suggests using a uniform color space in which equal perceptual steps correspond to equal metric steps (Robertson & O'Callaghan, 1988). Using a contour map, not a color sequence, is the traditional way to display an interval sequence. Isovalue contour maps show the pattern of equal heights or other physical attributes with great precision, but using them to understand the overall shape of a terrain or an energy field takes considerable skill and experience. To support unskilled map readers, contours can be usefully combined with pseudocoloring, as shown in Fig. 4.34(a). Even better may be a stepped pseudocolor sequence as shown in Fig. 4.34(b).

Representing Zero with Colormaps

A ratio sequence is an interval sequence that has a true zero and all that this implies: the ratio of amounts is important; it should be possible to see that one value may be twice as large as another. Expressing this in a color sequence is a tall order. No known visualization technique is capable of accurately conveying ratios with any precision; however, a sequence can be designed that effectively expresses a zero point and numbers above

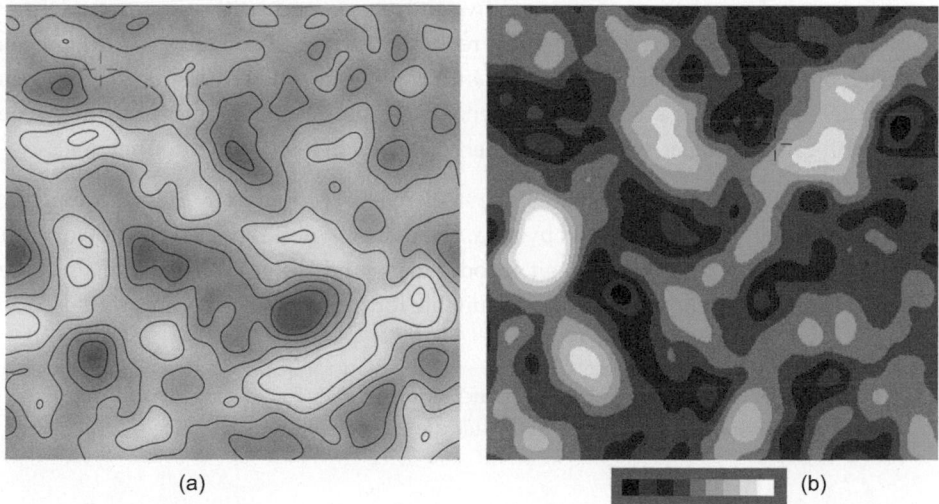

(a)   (b)

Figure 4.34 (a) Contours can show equal intervals in the data although numerical labels must be added for most applications. (b) A sequence of colors in discrete steps may be more reliably read using a key than a smoothly blended sequence.

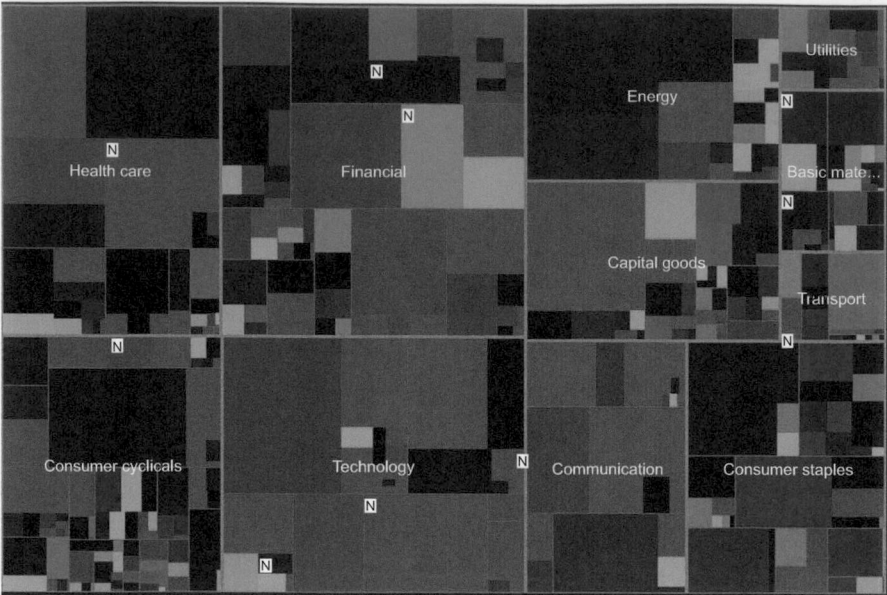

Figure 4.35 A color sequence with black representing zero. Increasing positive values are shown by increasing amounts of red. Increasing negative values are shown by increasing amounts of green. The map itself is a form of treemap (*Johnson & Shneiderman, 1991*). (*Courtesy of SmartMoney.com.*)

and below zero. Brewer (1996a, 1996b) called such sequences *diverging sequences*, whereas Spence and Efendov (2001) called them *bipolar sequences*. Such sequences typically use a neutral value on one or more opponent channels to represent zero, and diverging colors (on one or more channels) to represent positive and negative quantities. For example, gray may be used to represent zero, increasing redness to represent positive quantities, and increasing blueness to represent negative quantities. In a target detection study, Spence and Efendov (2001) found that a red-green sequence was most effective, confirming the greater information-carrying capacity of this channel compared to the yellow-blue channel.

The example in Fig. 4.35 shows a map of the stock market provided by SmartMoney.com. Market capitalization is represented by area, luminance encodes the magnitude of value change in the past year, and red-green encodes gains and losses. The website also gives users the option of a yellow-blue coding, suitable for most color-blind individuals.

> **[G4.24]** To represent zero values construct a double ended colormap, with a neutral color, such as white or black in the middle.

Sequences for the Color Blind

Some color sequences will not be perceived by people who suffer from the common forms of color blindness: protanopia and deuteranopia. Both cause an inability to discriminate red from green. Sequences that vary mainly on a black-to-white scale or on a yellow-to-blue dimension (this includes green to blue and red to blue) will still be clear to color-blind people. Two sequences that will be acceptable to these individuals are shown in Fig. 4.27(e, f). Meyer and Greenberg (1988) provided a detailed analysis of color sequences designed for common forms of color blindness.

Bivariate Color Sequences

Because color is three dimensional, it is possible to display two or even three dimensions using pseudocoloring (Trumbo, 1981). Indeed, this is commonly done in the case of satellite images, in which invisible parts of the spectrum are mapped to the red, green, and blue monitor primaries.

Although this mapping is simple to implement and corresponds to capabilities of the display device (which usually has red, green, and blue phosphors); such a scheme does not map the data values to perceptual channels. In general, it is better to map data dimensions to perceptual color dimensions. For example:

Variable one → hue

Variable two → chroma

or

Variable one → hue

Variable two → lightness

Fig. 4.36 gives an example of a bivariate color sequence from Brewer (1996a, 1996b) that maps one variable to yellow-blue variation and the other to a combination of light-dark variation and chroma variation. It suffers from the usual problem that the low-chroma colors are difficult to distinguish.

As a word of caution, it should be noted that bivariate colormaps are notoriously difficult to read. Wainer and Francolini (1980) carried out an empirical evaluation of a color sequence designed for U.S. census data and found that it was essentially unintelligible. One approach to a solution is to apply a uniform color space, and Robertson and O'Callaghan (1986) discussed how to do this. But, distinctness may not lead to something that is interpretable. We do not seem to be able to read different color dimensions in a way that is highly separable.

Pseudocoloring is not the only way to display a two-dimensional scalar field. Generally, when the goal is to display two variables on the same map, it may be better to use visual texture, height difference, or another channel for one variable and color for the other, in this way mapping data dimensions to more perceptually separable dimensions. Mapping the scalar field to artificial height and shading the resulting surface with an artificial light source using standard computer graphics techniques is another alternative. These methods are discussed later in the book.

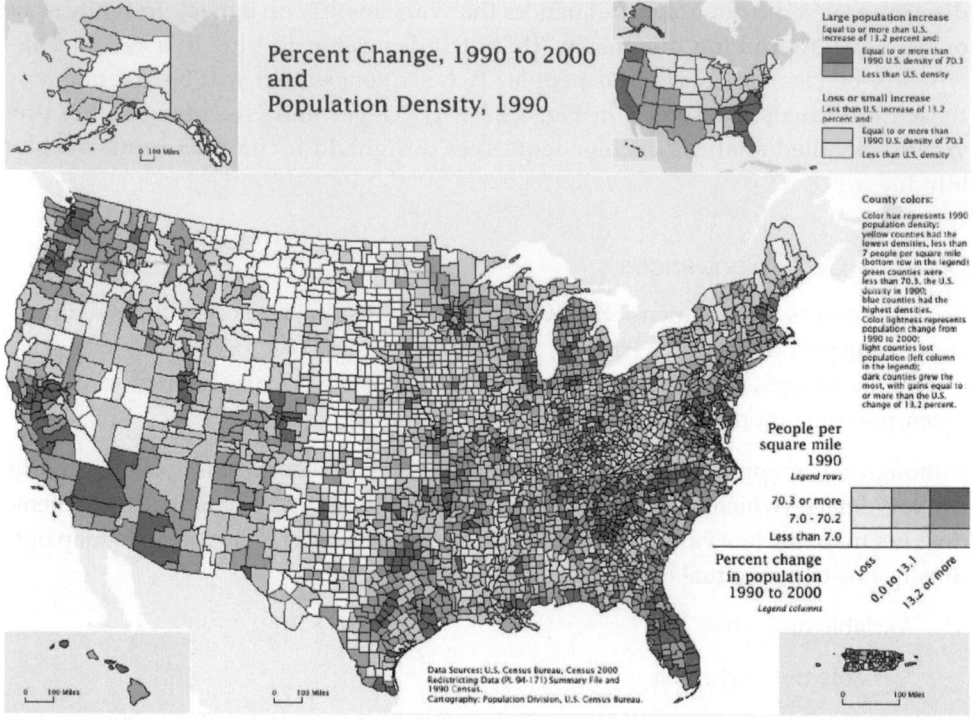

Figure 4.36 A bivariate coloring scheme using chroma and lightness for one variable and yellow-green-blue hue variation for the other. (*Courtesy of Cindy Brewer.*)

Many considerations go into making a color sequence that displays quantities without significant distortions, and this makes it unlikely that any predefined set of colors will exactly suit a particular data set and visualization goal. To show both overall form and detail and to provide the ability to read values from a key, it is often desirable to emphasize certain features in the data by deliberately using a nonuniform sequence; assigning more variation in color to a particular data range will lead to its visual emphasis and better discrimination of those values. Generally, the best way to achieve an effective color sequence is to place a good color editing tool in the hands of someone who understands both the data display requirement and the perceptual issues of color sequence construction (Guitard & Ware, 1990).

Application 4: Color Reproduction

The problem of color reproduction is essentially one of transferring color appearances from one display device, such as a computer monitor, to another device, such as a sheet of paper. The colors that can be reproduced on a sheet of paper depend on such factors as the color and intensity of the illumination. Northern daylight is much bluer than direct sunlight or tungsten light, which are both quite yellow, and is prized by artists for this reason. Halogen light is more balanced. Also, monitor colors can be reproduced only within the range of printing inks; therefore, it is neither possible nor meaningful to reproduce colors directly using a standard measurement system such as the CIE *XYZ* tristimulus values.

As we have discussed, the visual system is built to perceive relationships between colors rather than absolute values. For this reason, the solution to the color reproduction problem lies in preserving the color relationships as much as possible, not the absolute values. It is also important to preserve the white point in some way, because of the role of white as a reference in judging other colors.

Stone, Cowan, and Beatty (1988) described a process of gamut mapping designed to preserve color appearance in a transformation between one device and another. The set of all colors that can be produced by a device is called the *gamut* of that device. The gamut of a monitor is larger than that of a color printer (roughly the gamut of surface colors shown in Fig. 4.7). Stone et al. described the following set of heuristic principles to create good mapping from one device to another:

1. The gray axis of the image should be preserved. What is perceived as white on a monitor should become whatever color is perceived as white on paper.

2. Maximum luminance contrast (black to white) is desirable.

3. Few colors should lie outside the destination gamut.

4. Hue and saturation shifts should be minimized.

5. An overall increase of color saturation is preferable to a decrease.

Fig. 4.37 illustrates, in two dimensions, what is in fact a three-dimensional set of geometric transformations designed to accomplish the principles of gamut mapping. In this example, the process is a transformation from a monitor image to a paper hard copy, but the same principles and methods apply to transformations between other devices.

- **Calibration.** The first step is to calibrate the monitor and the printing device in a common reference system. Both can be characterized in terms of CIE tristimulus values. The calibration of the color printer must assume a particular illuminant.

- **Range scaling.** To equate the luminance range of the source and destination images, the monitor gamut is scaled about the black point until the white of the monitor has the same luminance as the white of the paper on the target printer.

- **Rotation.** What we perceive as neutral white on the monitor and on the printed paper can be very different, depending on the illumination. In general, in a printed image, the white is defined by the color of the paper. Monitor white is usually defined by the color that results when the red, green, and blue monitor primaries are set to their maximum values. To equate the monitor white with the paper white, the monitor gamut is rotated so as to make the white axes colinear.

- **Saturation scaling.** Because colors can be achieved on a monitor that cannot be reproduced on paper, the monitor gamut is scaled radially with respect to the

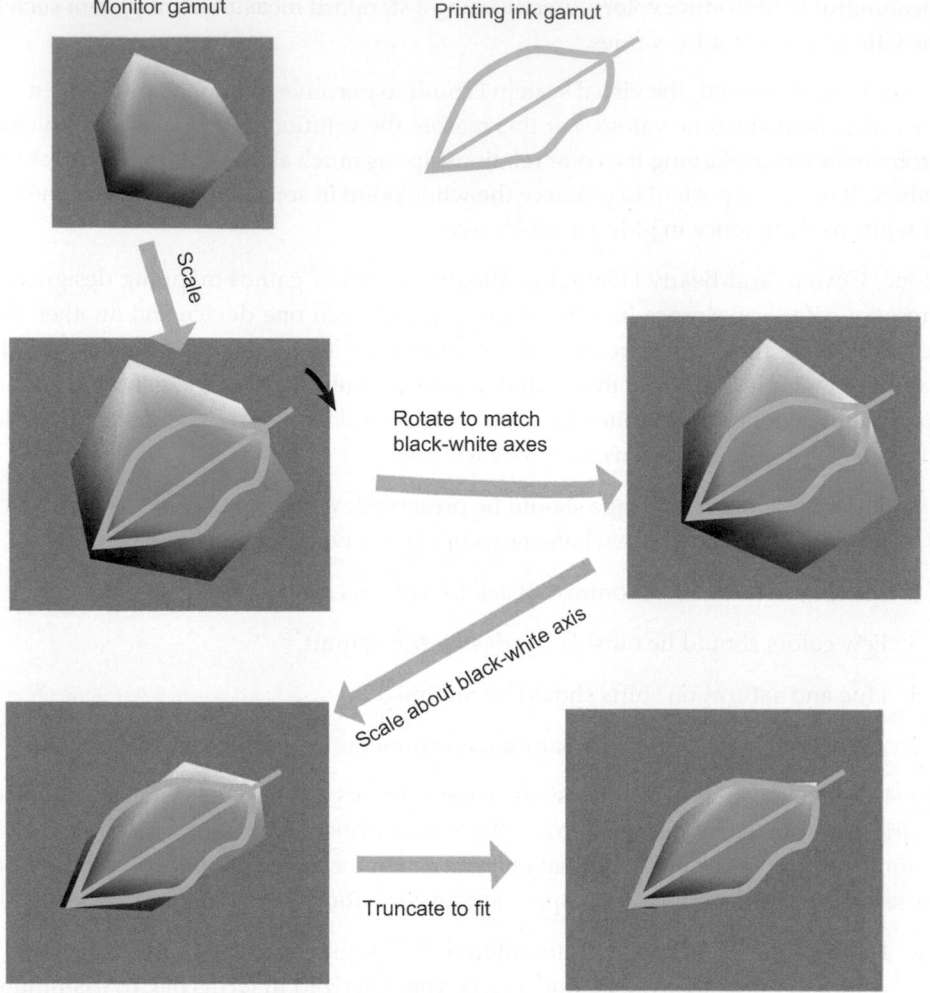

Monitor gamut

Printing ink gamut

Scale

Rotate to match
black-white axes

Scale about black-white axis

Truncate to fit

Figure 4.37 Illustration of the basic geometric operations in gamut mapping between two devices, as defined by Stone et al. (1988).

black-white axis to bring the monitor gamut within the range of the printing gamut. It may be preferable to leave a few colors outside the range of the target device and simply truncate them to the nearest color on the printing-ink gamut boundary.

For a number of reasons, it may not always be possible to apply these rules automatically. Different images may have different scaling requirements; some may consist of pastel colors that should not be made too vivid, whereas others may have vivid colors that must be truncated.

The approach adopted by Stone et al. (1988) is to design a set of tools that support these transformations, making it easy for an educated technician to produce a good result; however, this elaborate process is not feasible with off-the-shelf printers and routine color printing. In these cases, the printer drivers will contain heuristics designed to produce generally satisfactory results. They will contain assumptions about such things as the gamma value of the monitor displaying the original image and methods for dealing with oversaturated colors. Sometimes, the heuristics embedded in devices can lead to problems. In our laboratory, we usually find it necessary to start a visualization process with somewhat muted colors to avoid oversaturated colors on videotape or in paper reproduction.

Another issue that is important in color reproduction is the ability of the output device to display smooth color changes. Neural lateral inhibition within the visual system tends to amplify small artificial boundaries in smooth gradients of color as Mach bands. This sensitivity makes it difficult to display smoothly shaded images without artifacts. Because most output devices cannot reproduce the 16 million colors that can be created with a monitor, considerable effort has gone into techniques for generating a pattern of color dots to create the overall impression of a smooth color change. Making the dots look random is important to avoid aliasing artifacts (discussed in Chapter 2). Unless care is taken, artifacts of color reproduction can produce spurious patterns in scientific images.

Conclusion

There has been more research on the use of color in visualization than any other perceptual issue. Nevertheless, the important lessons are relatively few, and mostly they can be derived from opponent process theory. There are two chromatic channels (red-green and yellow-blue) and a luminance channel. Because of the low spatial resolution of the chromatic channels, small symbols should have high-saturation colors. Because of chromatic contrast in the opponent channels, we can only expect to have a few color symbols reliably identifiable. Contrast effects also make it desirable that larger regions should be less strongly colored in general.

It is impossible to keep a discussion of color entirely segregated in one chapter. Color affects every aspect of visualization and is mentioned in many other chapters, especially Chapter 5, which places color in the context of other methods for coding information.

CHAPTER FIVE

Visual Salience: Finding and Reading Data Glyphs

Suppose there is a crisis at a large bank because an employee, George, has lost billions on risky stock trades. We need to identify the vice president who is responsible for George's activities, and we have at our disposal an organization chart showing the management hierarchy of the company. This problem can be solved through a straightforward visual thinking process. First, conduct a visual search for the box representing George, then visually trace upward, following the chain of lines and boxes up to the level of vice president.

Another example: Suppose we are looking at the floor plan of a museum building and we wish to find a coffee shop. We locate the symbol for coffee shop on the key at the side of the floor plan, and then we carry out a visual search to find that symbol on the plan. A second more complex visual thinking process will be needed to find a route from where we are currently to the location of our coffee.

In both of these examples, a core activity can be described in terms of a two-step process:

> **Step 1.** A visual query is formulated in the mind of the person, relating to the problem to be solved.

> **Step 2.** A visual search of the display is carried out to find patterns that resolve the query.

The visual query can have many different forms, but it always involves reformulating part of the problem so that the solution can be found through a visual pattern

Information Visualization. https://doi.org/10.1016/B978-0-12-812875-6.00005-0

search. The visual pattern to be found can range from a symbol of a particular shape or color to an arbitrary complex or subtle visual pattern. In all cases, understanding what makes a pattern easy to find is critical in determining how efficiently the query will be executed, and what makes for efficient search is the central theme of this and the next chapters. In explaining this we will be putting flesh on the bare bones of the first two guidelines of this book set out in Chapter 1 and restated here to save the need to look back. [G1.1] *Design graphic representations of data by taking into account human sensory capabilities in such a way that important data elements and data patterns can be quickly perceived.* [G1.2] *Important data should be represented by graphical elements that are more visually distinct than those representing less important information.*

In understanding how visual queries are resolved we gain a deeper understanding of how best to design two of the most common things used in data visualization—namely, graphical *symbols* and *glyphs*. A graphical *symbol* is a *graphical object that represents an entity*. An example is the coffee shop symbol on the map. If this were to look like a coffee cup it would be an *iconic* symbol. Other examples are the noniconic triangles and squares used to represent data points in statistical graphs. Designing symbols for efficient search involves making each symbol visually distinct. Methods for achieving this are covered in this chapter.

Whereas symbols have a purely nominal function, *glyphs* also represent quantitative values. A *glyph* is a *graphical object designed to represent some entity and convey one or numerical attributes of that entity*. For information about stocks on the stock exchange, the color of a glyph can be used to show the price-to-earnings ratio, the size of the glyph can display the growth trend, and the shape of the glyph can represent the type of company—square for technology stocks, round for resources, and so on. A well-designed glyph is one that, in addition to being easily found, supports rapid and accurate resolution of visual queries regarding the ordinal, interval, or ratio quantities that are expressed.

Visual search is one of the basic things the visual system is designed for, and it involves the entire visual system. A large part of search is the way the eyes are moved around the scene to pick up information, but as we shall see it also involves the retuning of every visual part of the brain to meet the needs of the query task. There is a kind of mental inner scan, within a fixation, where a few visual patterns are tested for query-resolving properties. We will start with some basic facts about eye movements and then go on to discuss the factors that make something a target of an eye movement, before returning to the overall process.

Eye Movements

Moving our eyes causes different parts of the visual environment to be imaged on the high-resolution fovea where we can see in detail. Eye movements are frequent. For example, as you read this page, your eye is making between two and five jerky movements, called *saccades*, per second, and each of these movements can be thought of as a basic act of visual search.

There are three important types of eye movements:

1. **Saccadic movements.** In a visual search task, the eye moves rapidly from fixation to fixation. The fixation period is generally between 200 and 400 msec; the saccadic movement takes between 20 and 180 msec and depends on the angle moved. For eye movements of more than 20°, head movements follow, and this can take half a second or more (Hallett, 1986; Barfield, Hendrix, Bjorneseth, Kaczmarek, & Lotens, 1995; Rayner, 1998). The typical length of a saccade for someone scanning a scene is about 5 degrees of visual angle. The typical length of a saccade when reading is 2 degrees (Land & Tatler, 2009). The typical length of the saccade that people make when using visualizations depends on the design and the size of the display, but we can expect it to be in the range of 2–5 degrees for a well-designed display. As a general principle, visual search will be considerably more efficient for more compact displays because eye movements will be shorter and faster.

> **[G5.1]** To minimize the cost of visual searches, make visualization displays as compact as possible, compatible with visual clarity. For efficiency, information nodes should be arranged so that the average saccade is 5 degrees or less.

2. **Smooth-pursuit movements.** When an object is moving smoothly in the visual field, the eye has the ability to lock onto it and track it. This is called a *smooth-pursuit* eye movement. This ability also enables us to make head and body movements while maintaining fixation on an object of interest.

3. **Convergent movements (also called vergence movements).** When an object moves toward us, our eyes converge. When it moves away, they diverge. Convergent movements can be either saccadic or smooth.

Saccadic eye movements are said to be *ballistic*. This means that once the brain decides to switch attention and make an eye movement, the muscle signals for accelerating and decelerating the eye are preprogrammed; the movement cannot be adjusted in midsaccade. During a saccadic eye movement, we are less sensitive to visual input. This is called *saccadic suppression* (Riggs, Merton, & Mortion, 1974). The implication is that certain kinds of events can easily be missed if they occur while we happen to be moving our eyes. This is important when we consider the problem of alerting a computer operator to an event.

Another implication of saccadic suppression is that the brain is usually processing a rapid sequence of discrete images. Our capacity to do this is increasingly being exploited in television advertising, in which more than one cut per second of video has become commonplace. More generally, the staccato nature of seeing means that what we can see *at a single glance* is tremendously important.

Accommodation

When the eye moves to a new target at a different distance from the observer, it must refocus, or accommodate, so that the new target is clearly imaged on the retina. An accommodation response typically takes about 200 msec. As we age, however, the ability to accommodate declines and refocusing the eyes must be accomplished by changing eyeglasses or, for users of bifocals or progressive lenses, by moving the head so that a different lens is between the pupil and the object being fixated. Another solution is to use laser surgery to make one eye have a near focus and the other a far focus. In this case, change of focus is accomplished by switching attention from one eye's input to the other. This is a skill that must be learned.

The Eye Movement Control Loop

Seeing can be thought of as a never-ending series of cognitive acts, each of which has the same structure: make an eye movement, pick up some information, interpret that information, and plan the next eye movement. Short term cognitive goals are updated continuously as new information is acquired. Fig. 5.1 summarizes the major components of this process. As a first step, search queries are constructed to help with whatever task is at hand, and these typically consist of the cognitive construction of a simple pattern to be found. The next step is a visual search for that pattern.

But, how can the brain prepare for an eye movement without already knowing what is at the target location? How do we know where to look next? According to the theory of Wolfe and Gancarz (1996), a heuristic strategy is employed. First, a set of feature maps of the entire visual field is produced in a parallel processing operation mostly done in the V1 area of the primary visual cortex. Each feature map is devoted to a particular kind of feature, for example, vertical contours, blobs of a particular size, or a

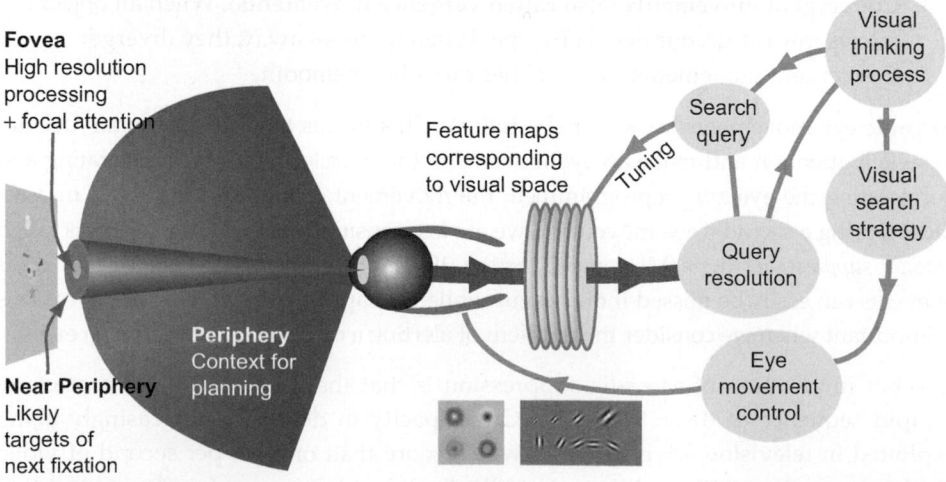

Figure 5.1 The visual search process.

particular color. Each map is weighted according to the current task. If we are scanning a crowd to look for someone we know who has a yellow raincoat, the feature maps will emphasize yellow blobs. Next, eye movements are executed in sequence, visiting the strongest possible target area (as defined by the feature maps) first and proceeding to the next strongest. Eye movements are also weighted according to the distance from the current focus along with other strategic factors.

Three things determine what is easily findable:

1. *A priori* **salience.** Some patterns excite more neural activity in the feature maps than others.

2. **Top-down salience modification.** Depending on what we are looking for, top-down mechanisms retune the feature maps to increase their sensitivity to certain features; for example, we may wish to find a mostly vertical elongated symbol. The vertical orientation feature map will gain enhanced sensitivity.

3. **Scene gist.** This has less to do with feature maps and more to do with experience. It is something that is discussed in Chapter 11 in the context of eye movement control strategies. The important point for now is that the brain very rapidly recognizes the type of scene that is being viewed (store interior, open landscape, city street), allowing it to activate visual search strategies appropriate to a visual scene (Oliva, Torralba, Castelhano, & Henderson, 2003). If a type of visualization is well known, then the eye movement strategies will be automatically primed for activation. This is part of the skill we develop in repeatedly using a particular style of visualization.

In this chapter we examine the low-level perceptual mechanisms relating to ease of search and these occur mostly in the primary visual cortex (V1 and V2). The lessons of scene gist and the overall strategy can be found in later chapters when we discuss the skills of visual thinking.

V1, Channels, and Tuned Receptors

After preliminary processing in the retina of the eye, visual information passes up the optic nerve through a neural junction at the lateral geniculate nucleus (LGN) and through several stages of processing in the cortex. The first areas in the cortex to receive visual inputs are called, simply, *visual area 1* (V1) and *visual area 2* (V2). Most of the output from area one goes on to area 2, and together these two regions make up more than 40% of vision processing (Lennie, 1998). There is plenty of neural processing power, as several billion neurons in V1 and V2 are devoted to analyzing the signals from only two million nerve fibers coming from the optic nerves of two eyes. This makes possible the massively parallel simultaneous processing of the entire visual field for incoming signals for color, motion, texture, and the elements of form. It is here that the elementary vocabularies of both vision and data display are defined.

By the time it gets to the LGN, the signal has already been decomposed by the concentric receptive fields discussed in the previous chapter that convert the signal into red-green, yellow-blue, and dark-light differences. These signals are then passed on to V1 where slightly more complex patterns are processed.

Fig. 5.2 is derived from Livingston and Hubel's diagram (1988) that summarizes both the neural architecture and the features processed in V1 and V2. A key concept in understanding this diagram is the tuned receptive field. In Chapter 3, we saw how single cell recordings of cells in the retina and the LGN reveal cells with distinctive concentric receptive fields. Such cells are said to be tuned to a particular pattern of a white spot surrounded by black or a black spot surrounded by white. In general, a tuned filter is a device that responds strongly to a certain kind of pattern and responds much less, or not at all, to other patterns. In the primary visual cortex, some cells respond only to elongated blobs with a particular position and orientation, others respond most strongly to blobs of a particular position moving in a particular direction at a particular velocity, and still others respond selectively to color.

There are cells in V1 and V2 that are differentially tuned to each of the following properties:

- The local elements of form: orientation and size (with luminance).

- Color (two types of signals) via the opponent processing channel mechanisms discussed in Chapter 4.

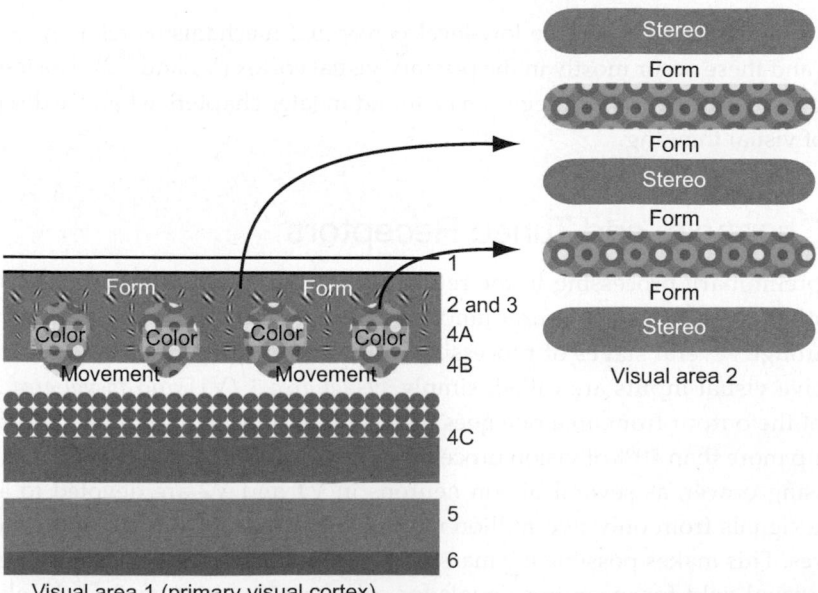

Figure 5.2 Architecture of the primary visual cortex. (*Redrawn from Livingston and Hubel (1988).*)

- Elements of local stereoscopic depth.

- Elements of local motion.

Visual areas V1 and V2 process these features as a set of spatial "maps". The features are processed in parallel so that every part of visual space is simultaneously broken down in terms of its visual properties. These maps are highly distorted, however, because the fovea is given far more space in the cortex than in regions in the periphery of vision. In cortical regions devoted to the fovea, receptive fields are much smaller. It is a system in which, for each point in visual space, neurons are tuned for many different orientations, many different kinds of color information, many different directions and velocities of motion, and many different stereoscopic depths.

Notice that here we have been talking about V1 as containing a single map of the visual field, but in fact it contains a set of semiindependent feature maps, all spatially coregistered.

Visual Channel Theory

The different kinds of information that are processed in V1 and V2 can be thought of as making up a set of visual "channels" (leaving aside stereoscopic depth processing for now); Fig. 5.3 shows the basic channel architecture. At the highest level, information is processed via either the visual or auditory channel. The visual branch is subdivided into the elements of form, color, and motion. Each of these is further subdivided. We have already dealt with color channels in Chapter 4, but it is important to reemphasize the special role of the luminance processing. The luminance channel underlies perception of the elements of form (shape), texture, and motion, whereas the red-green and yellow-blue channels do not carry shape, texture, or motion information, or at least they do so only weakly.

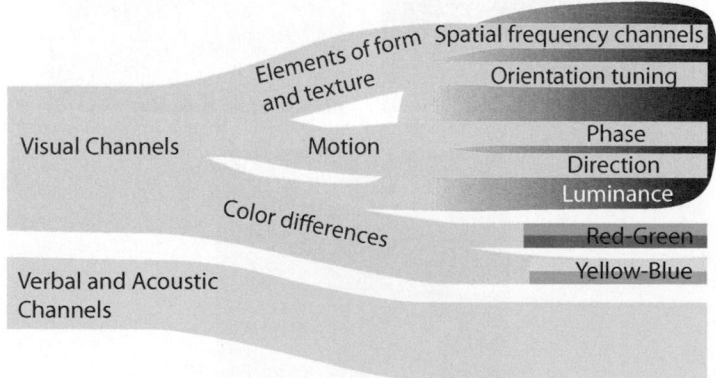

Figure 5.3 An overview of the basic visual channels. At the highest level we distinguish between visual and acoustic information. Visual information is further divided into the elements of form and texture, motion, and color. These channels can be further subdivided as shown.

The importance of channels from the design perspective is that information on different channels is easy to separate visually—by means of an act of attention we can choose to focus on information in one channel or another; whereas information on the same channel is easy to fuse, but difficult to separate. There is also less interference between information displayed on separate channels.

> **[G5.2]** Use different visual channels to display aspects of data that are conceptually distinct.

The Elements of Form and Texture

A number of electrophysiological and psychophysical experiments show that V1 and V2 contain large arrays of neurons that filter for orientation and size information at each point in the visual field, although with much higher resolution near the fovea. This information is the basis for both shape perception (via contour perception and other high-level mechanisms) and texture perception. These neurons have both a preferred orientation and a preferred size (they are said to have orientation and spatial tuning). They are either weakly color coded or not color coded, responding to luminance patterns only.

A simple mathematical model used widely to describe the receptive field properties of these neurons is the Gabor function (Barlow, 1972; Daugman, 1984). The Gabor function has two components as illustrated in Fig. 5.4: a cosine wave and a Gaussian envelope. Multiply them together, and the result is a function that responds strongly to bars

Figure 5.4 Gabor model of a V1 receptive field. Multiply the cosine wave grating on the upper left figure by the Gaussian envelope in the upper right figure to get the two-dimensional Gabor function shown on the bottom figure. The result is an excitatory center flanked by two inhibitory bars.

and edges of a particular orientation and not at all to edges of a bar or edges at right angles to that orientation. Roughly, this can be thought of as a kind of fuzzy bar detector. It has a clear orientation, and it has an excitatory center, flanked by inhibitory bars. The opposite kind of neuron also exists, with an inhibitory center and an excitatory surround, as well as other variants.

Mathematically, a Gabor function has the following form (simplified for ease of explanation):

$$R = C \, \cos\left(\frac{Ox}{S}\right) \exp\left(-\frac{x^2+y^2}{S}\right)$$

(5.1)

The C parameter gives the amplitude or contrast value, S gives the overall size of the Gabor function by adjusting both the wavelength of the cosine grating and the rate of decay of the Gaussian envelope, and O is a rotation matrix that orients the cosine wave. Other parameters can be added to position the function at a particular location in space and adjust the ratio of the Gaussian size to the sine wavelength; however, orientation, size, and contrast are most significant in modeling human visual processing.

In an influential paper, Barlow (1972) developed a set of principles that have become influential in guiding our understanding of human perception. The second of these, called the "second dogma," provides an interesting theoretical background to the Gabor model. In the second dogma, Barlow asserted that the visual system is simultaneously optimized in both the spatial-location and spatial-frequency domains. Gabor detectors optimally preserve a combination of spatial information (the location of the information in visual space) and oriented-frequency information. A single Gabor detector can be thought of as being tuned to a little packet of orientation and size information that can be positioned anywhere in space. Daugman (1984) showed mathematically that Gabor detectors satisfy the requirements of the Barlow dogma.

Many things about low-level perception can be explained by this model. Gabor-type detectors are used in theories of the detection of contours at the boundaries of objects (form perception), the detection of regions that have different visual textures, stereoscopic vision, and motion perception. The Gabor-type detector yields a basic set of properties out of which all more complex patterns are built. This stage of visual processing also determines some of the basic rules that make patterns distinctive at all subsequent levels of processing.

One thing that Gabor functions do is process parts of the image in terms of different spatial frequencies (see Chapter 2), and this has led to the concept of *spatial frequency channels*. These are subchannels of the form channel that encodes texture and the elements of shape. The half width of the spatial tuning curve is approximately a period change (in the sinusoid) of a factor of 3, and the total number of spatial frequency channels is about 4. Wilson and Bergen (1979) determined these values using a masking technique, which essentially determines the extent to which one type of information interferes with another. The resulting estimation of spatial frequency channels is illustrated in Fig. 5.5. It is useful to think of spatial frequency channels as subchannels of the broader shape channel.

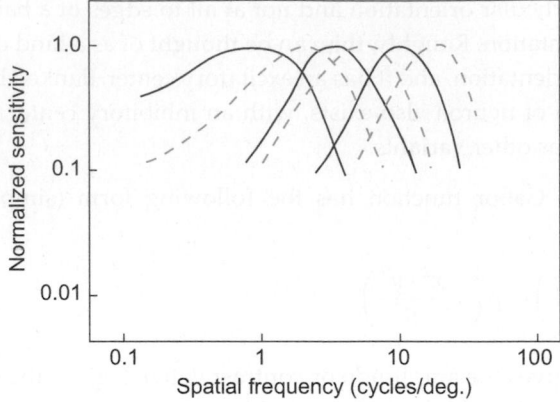

Figure 5.5 Wilson and Bergen (1979) spatial channels.

A single Gabor-type neuron is also broadly tuned with respect to orientation. Orientation tuning-in appears to be about 30 degrees (Blake & Holopigan, 1985); therefore, objects that differ from one another by more than 30 degrees in orientation will be more easily distinguished. Orientation can also be considered as a subchannel of form.

Probably none of the perceptual channels we shall discuss is fully independent; nevertheless, it is certainly the case that some kinds of information are processed in ways that are more independent than others. A channel that is independent from another is said to be orthogonal to it. Here, the concept is applied to the spatial information carried by Gabor detectors.

Because all information passes through spatial frequency channels, it is important to keep different kinds of information as separate as possible in terms of their frequency components and orientations.

Fig. 5.6 shows the letters of the alphabet on top of a random visual noise pattern that has a range of spatial frequencies from low to high (Solomon & Pelli, 1994). The letters are difficult to perceive where the background has spatial frequency components similar to the letters. This is an example of visual interference between spatial frequency subchannels.

A Differencing Mechanism for Fine Discrimination

The very broad spatial and orientation tuning of Gabor-type detectors implies that we should not be able to discriminate small-sized orientation differences, yet this is clearly not the case. When people get enough time, they can resolve far smaller differences than they can with brief exposures. Given time, the resolvable size difference for a Gabor pattern is a size change of about 9% (Caelli & Bevan, 1983). The resolvable orientation difference is about 5 degrees (Caelli & Bevan, 1983). These resolutions are much smaller than the channel-tuning functions would predict. Neural differencing mechanisms can account for the higher resolution. The explanation for finer discriminations is *differencing mechanisms*, higher-level processes that sharpen up the

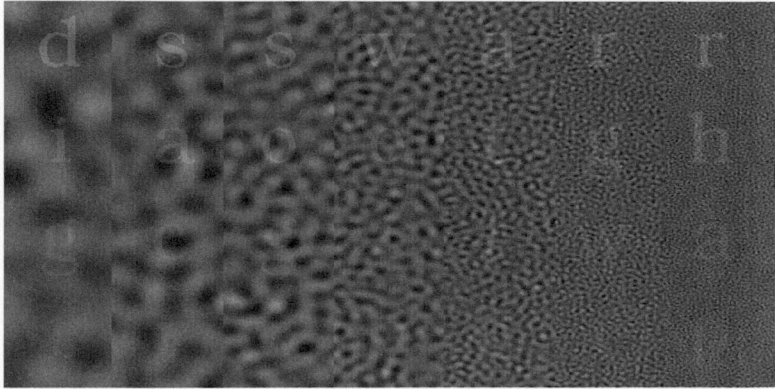

Figure 5.6 The letters are harder to see where they lie on top of visual noise that has spatial frequency components similar to the letters. (*From Solomon and Pelli (1994), Reproduced with permission.*)

output from individual receptors. The mechanism is based on inhibition. If a neuron has an excitatory input from one neuron and an inhibitory input from another with a slightly different tuning, the resulting difference signal is much more sensitive to spatial tuning than either of the original signals. This kind of sharpening is common in neural systems; it appears in color systems, edge detection, and size comparisons. Fig. 5.7 illustrates the concept. Neurons A and B both have rather broadly tuned and somewhat overlapping response functions to some input pattern. Neuron C has an excitatory input from A and an inhibitory input from B. The result is that C is highly sensitive to differences between A and B at the crossover point.

The differencing mechanism explains why the visual system is exquisitely sensitive to differences, but not to absolute values. It also explains contrast effects because if one of the signals is rendered less sensitive, through lateral inhibition, the crossover point moves, but such fine discriminations are processed more slowly than the basic low-level responses. So, for rapid target finding, it is important that targets be distinct in orientation by 30 degrees or more and in size by a factor of two.

Feature Maps, Channels, and Lessons for Visual Search

To summarize to this point, because different kinds of visual properties are processed separately they can be thought of as forming a set of feature maps, roughly at the V1 level. These maps cover the entire visual field, and there are many of them, each based on a different kind of feature. There is a map for redness, a map for greenness, a map for vertical orientation, a map for horizontal orientation, a map for vertical motion, horizontal motion, and so on.

When we are looking for something, a target set of feature properties is defined made up of the kinds of features that are found in feature maps (Eckstein, Beutter, Pham, Shimozaki, & Stone, 2007). Eye movements are directed to feature map regions that best match the target properties. Fig. 5.8 illustrates the idea. On the left is a set of

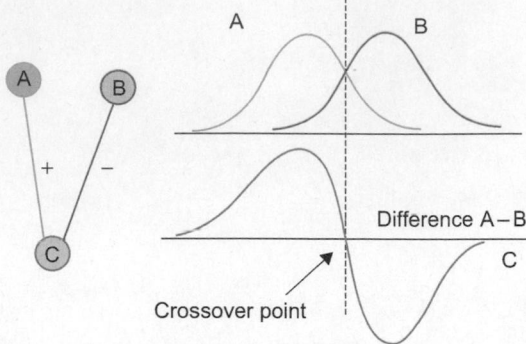

Figure 5.7 Differences between signals from neurons A and B are created by an excitatory and an inhibitory connection to neuron C.

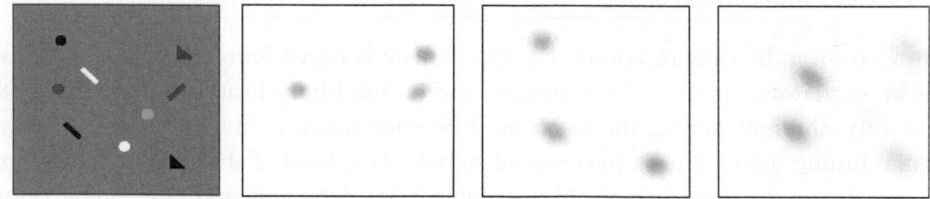

Figure 5.8 The symbols shown on the left are processed via a set of feature maps and the result directs eye movements.

symbols. On the right is how this image appears in a few of the feature maps. A search for red objects yields three candidate targets, and a search for black objects yields three different targets. A search for a left-slanted shape yields two strong and two weak targets. The oblique edges of the triangular symbols produce the weak signals, and these will somewhat distract in a search for the left-oriented bars.

Based on what we have learned so far, we can derive a number of lessons that can be applied to symbol set design. Low-level feature properties are critical.

> **[G5.3]** For maximum visibility make symbols distinct from each other in terms of their spatial frequency components, their orientation components, and color.

> **[G5.4]** For maximum visibility make symbols distinct from background patterns in terms of their spatial frequency components, their orientation components, and color.

Fig. 5.9 illustrates guideline G5.3 and G5.4 with a number of examples of scatterplots. The ones on the left use symbol shapes that are typical in many plotting packages. The squares and circles are not very distinct because the differences are encoded in high spatial frequencies (see Figure 2.25 in Chapter 2, which shows how spatial sensitivity

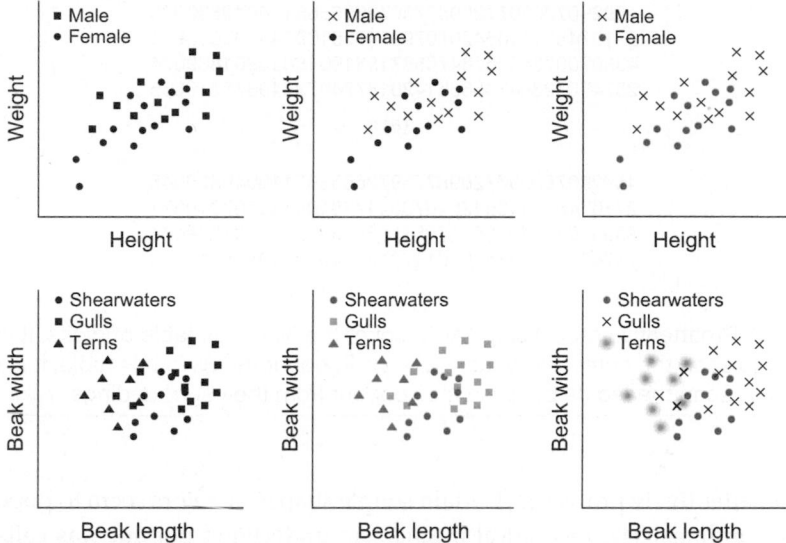

Figure 5.9 Feature channels can be used to make symbols more distinct from one another. The graphs on the right use redundant color coding in addition to more distinctive shapes.

declines with high spatial frequencies). If the symbols were made larger they would be more distinct. The other examples in the center and the right have much more distinctive spatial subchannel components.

Another way of thinking about low-level processing mechanisms is to consider them as defining a *feature space*. This space has as many dimensions as there are types of features; for example, four size dimensions, six orientation dimensions, two chromatic channel dimensions, and an unknown number of motion dimensions. Increasing the separation between symbols in the feature space will increase their distinctness.

Preattentive Processing and Ease of Search

Neuroscience can only tell us so much about what makes shapes distinctive, because although the field is advancing rapidly the level of effort required for each discovery is huge. Inevitably, neuroscience theory lags behind results from direct experiments using psychophysical methods with human observers. Psychophysics is the study of human responses to physically defined stimuli. There have been many experiments in which human observers are asked if a particular shape appears in a pattern of other shapes that are flashed briefly in front of their eyes. These studies have led to the concept of *preattentive processing* that is central to how we understand visual distinctiveness (Treisman, 1985).

Preattentive processing is best introduced with an example. To count the 3s in the table of digits shown in Fig. 5.10(a), it is necessary to scan all the numbers sequentially. To count the 3s in Fig. 5.10(b), it is only necessary to scan the red digits. This is because

4592907805977209877597265566511004 9836645
2710746214465420707901473810974389 7010971
4390709734926684785871581904863090 1889074
2574707235474566614201877407284987 5310665

(a)

4592907805977209877597265566511004 9836645
2710746214465420707901473810974389 7010971
4390709734926684785871581904863090 1889074
2574707235474566614201877407284987 5310665

(b)

Figure 5.10 Preattentive processing. (a) To count the 3s in this table of digits, it is necessary to scan the numbers sequentially. (b) To count the 3s in this table, it is only necessary to scan the red 3s because they popout from their surroundings.

color is preattentively processed. Certain simple shapes or colors seem to popout from their surroundings. The theoretical mechanism underlying popout was called *preattentive processing* because early researchers thought that it must occur prior to conscious attention, although a more modern view is that attention is integral, and we shall return to this point. In essence, preattentive processing determines what visual objects are offered up to our attention and easy to find in the next fixation (Findlay & Gilchrist, 2005), so prior attention is part of the phenomenon. Still, although the term is misleading, we shall continue to use it because of its widespread adoption. In any case, the phenomena described by the term are very real and of critical importance.

A typical experiment conducted to find out whether some pattern is preattentively distinct involves measuring the response time to find a target among a set of other symbols called *distractors*—for example, finding the 3s in a set of other numbers. If processing is preattentive, the time taken to find the target should be equally fast no matter how many distracting nontargets there are. So, if time to find the target is plotted against number of distractors, the result should be a horizontal line. Fig. 5.11 illustrates a typical pattern of results. The circles illustrate data from a visual target that is preattentively different from the distractors. The time taken to detect whether there is a red digit in the array of digits shown in Fig. 5.10 is independent of the number of black digits. The Xs in Fig. 5.11 show the results from processing a feature that is *not* preattentively distinct. In this case, time to respond *increases* with number of distractors suggesting sequential processing. The gradient of the slope yields the rate at which items are processed by the visual system in milliseconds per item. The results of this kind of experiment are not always as perfectly clear cut as Fig. 5.11 would suggest. Sometimes there is a small, but still measurable, slope in the case of a feature that is thought to be preattentive. As a rule of thumb, anything that is processed at a rate faster than 10 msec per item is considered to be preattentive. Typical processing rates for nonpreattentive targets are 40 msec per item and more (Treisman & Gormican, 1988).

Why is this important? In displaying information, it is often useful to be able to show things "at a glance." If you want people to be able to instantaneously identify some

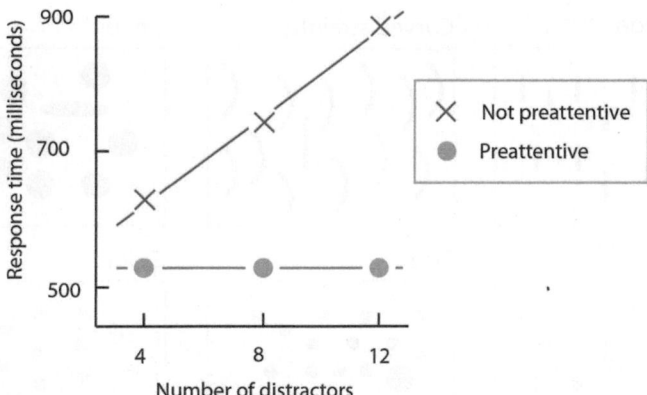

Figure 5.11 Typical results from a pattern of preattentive processing. The circles show time to perceive an object that is preattentively distinct from its surroundings. In this case, time to process is independent of the number of irrelevant objects (distractors). The Xs show how time to process nonpreattentively distinct targets increases with the number of distractors.

mark on a map as being of type A, it should be differentiated from all other marks in a preattentive way. There have been literally hundreds of experiments to test whether various kinds of features are processed preattentively. Fig. 5.12 illustrates a few of the results. Orientation, size, basic shape, convexity, concavity, and an added box around an object are all preattentively processed. However, the junction of two lines is not preattentively processed; neither is the parallelism of pairs of lines, so it is more difficult to find the targets in the last two boxes in Fig. 5.12.

There is a risk of misinterpreting the findings of psychophysical studies and proposing a new kind of detector for every distinct shape. To take a single example, curved lines can be preattentively distinguished from straight lines. Despite this, it may be a mistake to think that there are curved line detectors in early vision. It may simply be the case that cells responsive to long, straight line segments will not be strongly excited by the curved lines. Of course, it may actually be that early vision curvature detectors do exist; it is just that the evidence must be carefully weighed. It is not a good idea to propose a new class of detector for everything that exhibits the popout effect. The scientific principle of finding the most parsimonious explanation, known as Occam's razor, applies here.

It is also important to note that not all preattentive effects are equally strong. There are degrees of popout. In general the strongest effects are based on color, orientation, size, contrast, and motion or blinking, corresponding to the findings of neuropsychology. Effects such as line curvature tend to be weaker. Also, there are degrees of difference. Large color differences have more popout than small ones. Some popout effects occur with no instruction and are difficult to miss, such as the red 3s in Fig. 5.11 and blinking points, but other patterns labeled preattentive require considerable attention for them to be seen. So the term *preattentive* should not be taken too literally because prior attention must be given to prime the relevant properties using the tuning mechanisms we have already discussed.

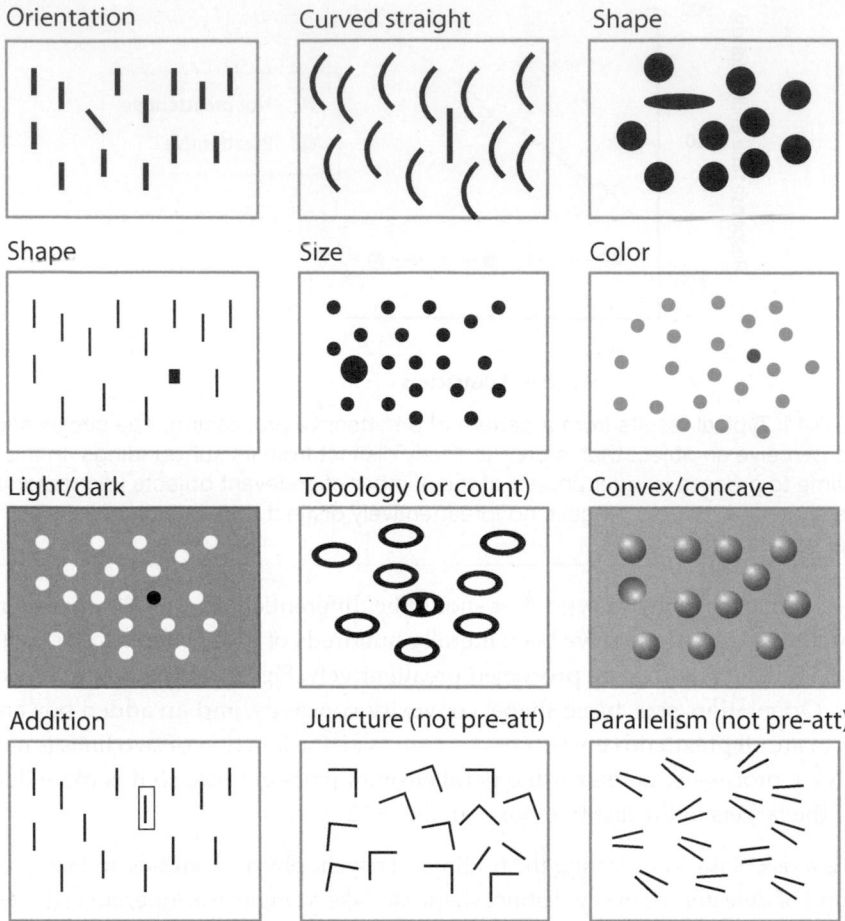

Figure 5.12 Most of the preattentive examples given here can be accounted for by the processing characteristics of neurons in the primary visual cortex.

A more modern view of preattentive processing is that these are the properties that can guide the deployment of attention (Wolfe & Horowitz, 2004). In other words, these are the properties that our brains can use to decide what to look at next. They determine the ease with which something can be found. Wolfe and Horowitz reviewed the enormous literature on preattentive processing and came up with five categories, relating to how well visual attributes can guide visual search. The top three categories are reproduced in Table 5.1. What they classify as "undoubted attributes" are the same as the primary channels shown in Fig. 5.3. The other classes of attributes should be regarded as a less reliable basis for highlighting. However, bear in mind that these attributes are not all or nothing. A small color difference will be less distinctive than a large curvature, even though color is a stronger cue overall.

[G5.5] Use strong preattentive cues before weak ones where ease of search is critical.

Table 5.1 *Different Classes of Attributes That can Guide Visual Search*

Undoubted Attributes	Probable Attributes	Possible Attributes
Color	Luminance onset (flicker)	Lighting direction (shading)
Motion	Luminance polarity	Glossiness (luster)
Orientation	Vernier offset	Expansion
Size	Stereoscopic depth	Number
	Pictorial depth cues	Aspect ratio
	Shape	
	Line termination	
	Closure	
	Curvature	
	Topological status	

Adapted from Wolfe and Horowitz (2004).

Attention and Expectations

A problem with most research into attention, according to a book by Arien Mack and Irvin Rock (1998), is that almost all perception experiments (except their own) demand attention in the very design. The authors have a point. Typically, a subject is paid to sit down and pay close attention to a display screen and to respond by pressing a key when some specified event occurs. This is not everyday life. Usually we pay very little attention to what goes on around us. To understand better how we see when we are not primed for an experiment, Mack and Rock conducted a laborious set of experiments that only required one observation from each experiment. They asked subjects to look at a cross for a fraction of a second and report when one of the arms changed length. So far, this is like most other perception studies, but the real test came when they flashed up something near the cross that the subjects had *not* been told to expect. Subjects rarely saw this unexpected pattern, even though it was very close to the cross they were attending to in the display. Mack and Rock could only do this experiment once per subject, because as soon as subjects were asked if they had seen the new pattern they would have started looking for "unexpected" patterns. Hundreds of subjects had to be used, but the results were worth it; they tell us how much we are likely to see when we are looking for something else. The answer is, not much.

The fact that most subjects did not see a wide range of unexpected targets tells us that humans do not perceive much unless we have a need to find something and a vague idea of what that something looks like. In most systems, brief, unexpected events will be missed. Mack and Rock initially claimed from their results that there is no perception without attention; however, because they found that subjects generally noticed larger objects, they were forced to abandon this extreme position.

The question of which visual dimensions are preattentively stronger and therefore more salient cannot be answered in a simple way, because it always depends on the strength of the particular feature and the context. For example, Callaghan (1989) compared color to orientation as a preattentive cue. The results showed that the preattentiveness of the color depended on the saturation (vividness) and size of the color patch, as well as the degree of difference from surrounding colors. So it is not just a question of color versus orientation, but exactly how the color differs from other colors in the set. Similarly, the preattentiveness of line orientation depends on the length of the line, the degree to which it differs from surrounding lines, and the contrast of the line pattern with the background. Fig. 5.13 shows how an oblique line stands out from a set of vertical lines. When the same oblique line is in a set of lines of various orientations it is much more difficult to see, even though the difference in orientation between the target and the distractor set is just as large or larger. One thing that is clear from this example is that preattentive symbols become less distinct as the variety of distractors increases. It is easy to spot a single hawk in a sky full of pigeons, mostly because it has a different motion pattern, but if the sky contains a greater variety of birds, the hawk will be more difficult to see.

Studies have shown that two factors are important in determining whether something stands out preattentively: the degree of difference of the target from the nontargets and the degree of difference of the nontargets from each other (Duncan & Humphreys, 1989; Quinlan & Humphreys, 1987). For example, yellow highlighting of text works well if yellow is the only color in the display besides black and white, but if there are many colors the highlighting will be less effective.

> [G5.6] For maximum popout, a symbol should be the only object in a display that is distinctive on a particular feature channel; for example, it might be the only item that is colored in a display where everything else is black and white.

Highlighting and Asymmetries

Another issue relating to making targets distinctive comes from research that has revealed *asymmetries* in some preattentive factors; for example, *adding* marks to highlight a symbol is generally better than taking them away (Treisman & Gormican, 1988). If all of the symbols in a set except for a target object have an added mark, the target will be less distinctive. It is better to highlight a word by underlining it than to

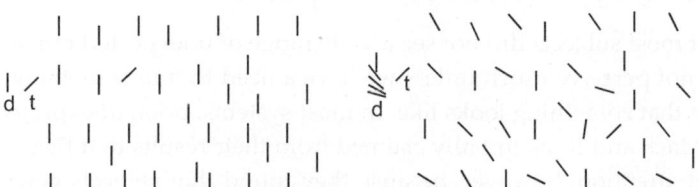

Figure 5.13 On the left, the right-slanted bar pops out; on the right, it does not. Yet, most of the distractors on the right have an orientation that is more different from the target orientation than the distracters on the left.

underline all the words in a paragraph except for the target word. Another asymmetry is the finding that a big target is easier to see surrounded by small targets than a small target surrounded by big targets. Several examples are given in Fig. 5.14.

[G5.7] Use positively asymmetric preattentive cues for highlighting.

When a visual design is complex, employing color, texture, shape, and the highlighting problem becomes more difficult. If all of the fonts in a display have the same size, for example, an increase in size can be used for highlighting.

[G5.8] For highlighting, use whatever feature dimension is used least in other parts of the design.

Modern computer graphics permit the use of motion for highlighting. This can be very effective when there is little other motion in the display (Bartram & Ware, 2002; Ware & Bobrow, 2004); however, making things move may be too strong a cue for many applications, although quite subtle motion can be effective.

[G5.9] When color and shape channels are already fully utilized, consider using motion or blink highlighting. Make the motion or blinking as subtle as possible, consistent with rapid visual search.

A relatively new idea for highlighting is the use of blur. Kosara, Miksch, and Hauser (2002) suggested blurring everything else in the display to make certain information stand out. They call the technique *semantic depth of field*, because it applies the depth-of-focus effects that can be found in photography to the display of data according to semantic content. As Fig. 5.14 illustrates, blur works well, although again there is an obvious potential drawback to the technique. By blurring, the designer runs the risk of making important information illegible, as it is usually not possible to reliably predict the interests of the viewer.

Coding with Combinations of Features

So far we have been concentrating on using a single visual channel to make symbols distinct, or to highlight; often, though, we may wish to make objects distinctive using

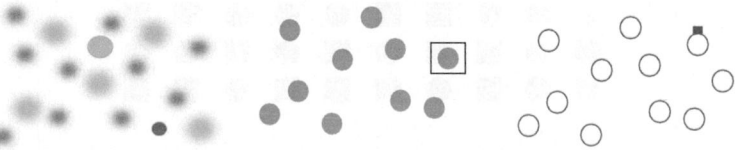

Figure 5.14 A number of highlighting methods that use positive asymmetric preattentive cues: sharpness, added surrounding feature, added shape.

two or more channels. There are two issues here. The first is using redundant coding for extra distinctiveness. The second is, what can we expect if we use more complex patterns in symbol design?

Coding with Redundant Properties

We can choose to make something distinct on a single feature dimension, such as color, or we can choose to make it distinct on several dimensions, such as color, size, and orientation. This is called *redundant coding*. It means that someone can search based on any or all of the properties. The degree to which search is improved by redundant coding is a complex issue; sometimes the benefit is a simple addition and sometimes it is less than additive. It depends on what visual properties are being employed and the background. Nevertheless, there is almost always a benefit to redundant coding (Egeth & Pachella, 1969; Eriksen & Hake, 1955). Fig. 5.9 gives examples of redundant coding of symbols in scatterplots.

[G5.10] To make symbols in a set maximally distinctive, use redundant coding wherever possible; for example, make symbols differ in both shape and color.

What Is Not Easily Findable: Conjunctions of Features

So far we have been discussing what can easily be found, but what kinds of things are difficult to spot? The answer is that, even if visual patterns get just a little bit more complex, a search can change from being almost instantaneous to something requiring much longer serial processing. What happens, for example, if we wish to search for a red square, not just something that is red or something that is square? Fig. 5.15 illustrates a conjunction search task in which the targets are three red squares. It turns out that this kind of search is slow if the surrounding objects are squares (but not red ones) and other red shapes. We are forced to do a serial search of *either* the red shapes or the square objects. This is called a *conjunction* search, because it involves searching for the

Figure 5.15 Searching for the red squares is slow because they are identified by a conjunction of shape and color.

specific conjunction of redness *and* shape attributes (Treisman & Gelade, 1980). This is very different from redundant coding, where parallel search can be carried out on one *or* the other. Conjunction searches are generally not preattentive, although there are a few very interesting exceptions that we will get to shortly.

The fact that conjunction searches are slow has broad implications. It means, among other things, that we cannot learn to rapidly find more complex patterns. Even though we may have hundreds or thousands of hours of experience with a particular symbol set, searching for conjunctions of properties is still slow, although a modest speedup is possible (Treisman, Vieira, & Hayes, 1992).

[G5.11] If symbols are to be preattentively distinct, avoid designs that rely on conjunctions of basic graphical properties.

Highlighting Two Data Dimensions: Conjunctions That Can Be Seen

Although early research suggested that conjunction searches were never preattentive, it has emerged that there are a number of preattentive dimension pairs that do allow for conjunctive search. Interestingly, these exceptions are all related to space perception. Searches can be preattentive when there is a conjunction of spatially coded information and a second attribute, such as color or shape. The spatial information can be a position on the *XY* plane, stereoscopic depth, shape from shading, or motion.

Spatial grouping on the *XY* plane. Treisman and Gormican (1988) argued that preattentive search can be guided by the identification of spatial clusters. This led to the discovery that the conjunction of space and color can be searched preattentively. In Fig. 5.16(a), we cannot conjunctively search for green ellipses, but in Fig. 5.16(b), we can rapidly search the conjunction of lower cluster and green target.

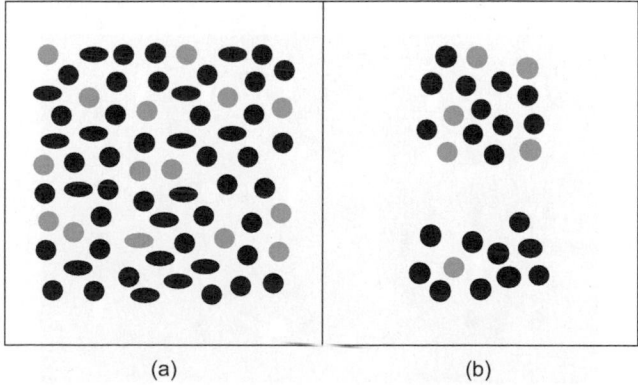

(a)   (b)

Figure 5.16 (a) With the conjunction of shape and color, search is slow. (b) If we search the lower group for the green object, the search is fast. This is also a conjunction.

Stereoscopic depth. Nakayama and Silverman (1986) showed that the conjunction of stereoscopic depth and color, or of stereoscopic depth and movement, can be preattentively processed.

Luminance polarity and shape. Theeuwes and Kooi (1994) showed that luminance polarity with targets lighter and darker than a gray background can support a preattentive conjunction search. In Fig. 5.17, the white circles can be searched in parallel (a conjunction of whiteness and shape).

Convexity, concavity, and color. D'Zmura et al. (1997) showed that the conjunction of perceived convexity and color can be preattentively processed. In this case, the convexity is perceived through shape-from-shading information.

Motion. Driver, McLeod, and Dienes (1992) determined that motion and target shape can be preattentively scanned conjunctively. Thus, if the whole set of targets is moving, we do not need to look for nonmoving targets. We can preattentively find, for example, the red moving target. This may be very useful in producing highlighting techniques that allow for a preattentive search within the set of highlighted items (Bartram & Ware, 2002; Ware & Bobrow, 2004).

An application in which preattentive spatial conjunction may be useful is found in geographic information systems (GISs). In these systems, data is often characterized as a set of layers—for example, a layer representing the surface topography, a layer representing minerals, and a layer representing ownership patterns. Such layers may be differentiated by means of motion or stereoscopic depth cues.

[G5.12] When it is important to highlight two distinct attributes of a set of entities, consider coding one using motion or spatial grouping and the other using a property such as color or shape.

Ware and Bobrow (2005) used a conjunction coding method in an interactive network visualization application. To make it possible to trace paths in a visually impenetrable

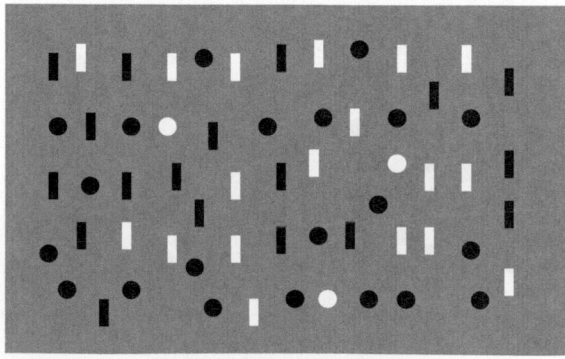

Figure 5.17 The white circles are a conjunction of shape and luminance polarity; nevertheless, they can be found preattentively.

mass of hundreds of nodes and links, we added a feature whereby when someone touched a node, a subnetwork of closely linked nodes and edges jiggled by a small amount (motion coding). This made the subnetwork stand out strongly from the background information. Previously found subnetworks were highlighted in a more conventional way using color coding. We found that it was easy for people to focus either on the recently selected subnetwork or on the previously selected subnetwork or on a sub-subnetwork that was both recently and previously selected (a conjunction).

Integral and Separable Dimensions: Glyph Design

Another body of theory that is relevant to glyph design is the theory of *integral and separable dimensions*, developed by Garner (1974). The kind of multidimensional coding that occurs in the use of glyphs raises questions about the perceptual independence of the display dimensions. In many ways, the lessons are the same as from channel theory (visual dimensions are much the same as channels), but Garner's theory provides a useful alternative description. We will use it to discuss approaches to glyph design.

Sometimes we need a symbol to do more than simply stand for something. Sometimes it is useful if symbols can convey how large, hot, or wet something is. Fig. 5.18 shows an example in which the size of each circle represents the population of a country, and the color represents the geographic region to which that country belongs. In this case, color functions as a nominal coding, whereas size represents a quantity, a ratio coding. Symbols that represent quantity are called *glyphs*. To create a glyph, one or more quantitative data attributes are mapped in a systematic way to the different graphical properties of an object.

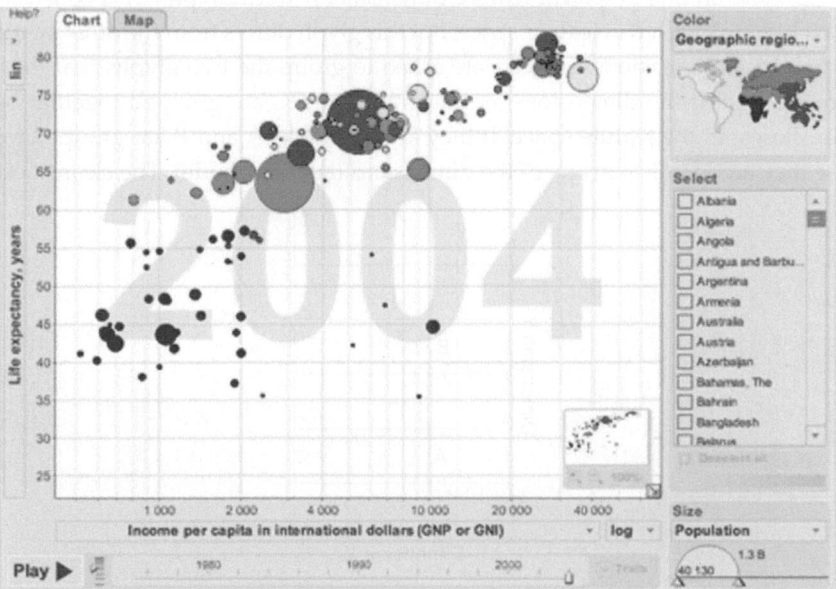

Figure 5.18 In this visualization, the color of each circle represents a geographic region and the size of the circle represents population. (*From www.gapminder.org.*)

Garner's theory helps us answer questions such as, "Will the color-coding scheme interfere with our perception of glyph size and therefore distort perceived population level?" or "What if we use both color and size to represent a single variable—will this make the information clearer?" The concept of integral versus separable visual dimensions tells us when one display attribute (e.g., color) will be perceived independently from another (e.g., size).

With *integral display dimensions,* two or more attributes of a visual object are perceived holistically and not independently. An example is a rectangular shape, perceived as a holistic combination of the rectangle's width and height. Another is the combination of green light and red light; this is seen holistically as yellow light, and it is difficult to respond independently to the red and green components.

With *separable dimensions,* people tend to make separate judgments about each graphical dimension. This is sometimes called *analytic processing.* Thus, if the display dimensions are the diameter of a ball and the color of a ball, they will be processed relatively independently. It is easy to respond independently to ball size and ball color. Integral and separable dimensions have been determined experimentally in a number of ways.

Three experimental paradigms are discussed here. All are related to interactions between pairs of graphical qualities, such as size and color. Very little work has been done on interactions among three or more graphical qualities.

Restricted Classification Tasks

In a restricted classification task, an observer is shown sets of three glyphs that are constructed according to the diagram shown in Fig. 5.19. Two of the glyphs (A and B) are made the same on one graphical feature dimension. A third glyph (C) is constructed so that it is closer to glyph B in feature space, but this glyph differs from the other two in both of the graphical dimensions. Subjects are asked to group the two glyphs that they think go together best. If the dimensions are integral, B and C are grouped together because they are closest in the feature space. If they are separable, A and B are grouped together because they are identical in one of the dimensions (analytic mode). The clearest example

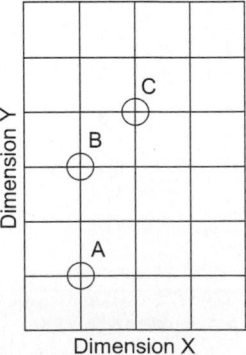

Figure 5.19 It is useful to think in terms of two display dimensions when considering the integral-separable concept. One dimension might be color, while another might be some aspect of shape.

of integral dimensions is color space dimensions. If dimension X is the red-green dimension and dimension Y is the yellow-blue dimension of color space, subjects tend to classify objects (roughly) according to the Euclidean distance between the colors (defined according to one of the uniform color spaces discussed in Chapter 4). Note that this is a simplification as the evidence of color categories (also discussed in Chapter 4) shows.

The width and height of an ellipse create an integral perception of shape. Thus, in Fig. 5.20(a, top) the ellipses appear to be more similar to each other than to the circle, even though the width of the circle matches the width of the first ellipse. If the two dimensions are separable, subjects act in a more analytic manner and react to the fact that two of the objects are actually identical on one of the dimensions. Shape and color are separable. Thus, in Fig. 5.20(a, below) either the green shapes or the two elliptical shapes will be categorized together. With separable dimensions, it is easy to attend to one dimension or the other and sorting on a single dimension will be quicker.

Speeded Classification Tasks

Speeded classification tasks tell us how glyphs can visually interfere with each other. In a speeded classification task, subjects are asked to quickly classify visual patterns according to only one of the visual attributes of a glyph. The other visual attribute can be set up in two different ways; it can be given random values (interference condition), or it can be coded in the same way as the first dimension (redundant coding). If the data dimensions are integral, substantial interference occurs in the first case. With redundant coding, classification is generally speeded for integral dimensions. With separable codes, the results are different. There is little interference from the irrelevant graphical dimension, but there is also little advantage in terms of speeded classification when redundant coding is used. Of course, in some cases, using redundant separable codes may still be desirable; for example, if both color and shape are used for information coding, color-blind individuals will still have access to the information. Fig. 5.21 gives examples of the kinds of patterns that are used in integral-separable dimension experiments, illustrating these points.

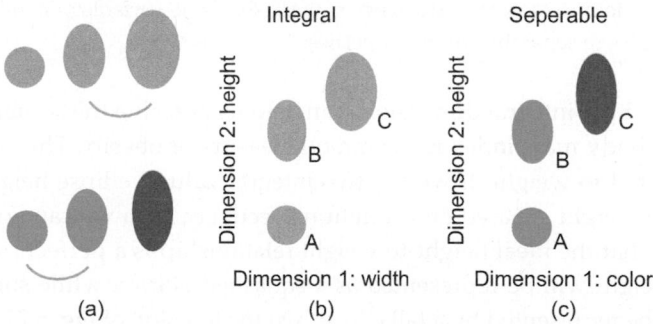

Figure 5.20 (a) The width and height of an ellipse are perceived integrally, so the ellipses are seen as more similar to each other (because they have the same shape) than the pair having the same width. The color and height of a shape are perceived separably, so the two green shapes are seen as most similar. (b, c) Space plots of the two examples.

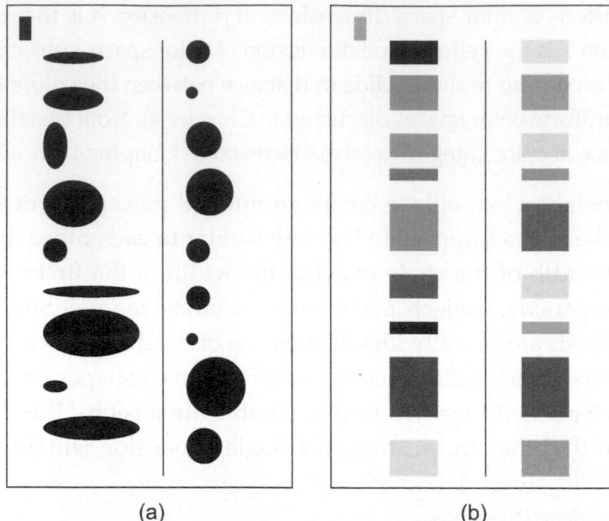

(a)   (b)

Figure 5.21 Sets of patterns for a speeded classification task. In both cases, (a) and (b), participants are required to respond positively to only those glyphs that have the same *height* as the bar in the upper corner. The interference condition is on the left in both (a) and (b). (a, left) The variable widths interfere with classification based on height. (b, left) The variable color does not interfere with classification based on height. (a, right) Redundant size coding speeds classification. (b, right) Redundant color and size coding does not speed classification.

The lessons to be learned from integral-separable dimension experiments are easy to apply in cases in which each data entity has only two attributes.

> **[G5.13]** If it is important for people to respond *holistically* to a combination of two variables in a set of glyphs, map the variables to integral glyph properties.

> **[G5.14]** If it is important for people to respond *analytically* to a combination of variables, making separate judgments on the basis of one variable or another, map the variables to separable glyph properties.

Fig. 5.22 shows how integral dimensions can help us perceive the combination of two variables. The body mass index is a common measure of obesity. This index is a ratio of height squared to weight. If we use two integral values, ellipse height and ellipse width, to show height squared and weight respectively, then we can arrange the plot in such a way that the ideal height-to-weight relationship is a perfect circle. Someone who is overweight will be represented as a squashed ellipse, while someone who is very thin will be represented by a tall ellipse. On the left side of Fig. 5.22, we can see at a glance who is overweight and who is underweight.

The right-hand side of Fig. 5.22 shows the same data represented using two separable variables: red-green variation for weight and vertical size for height. This is a poor choice, as it is very difficult to see who is overweight and who is underweight.

Figure 5.22 Height and weight data from 400 elderly Dutch people is displayed. On the left, height squared is mapped to the height of each ellipse and the weight is mapped to the width. On the right, weight is mapped to color and the width is held constant (red is more, green is less).

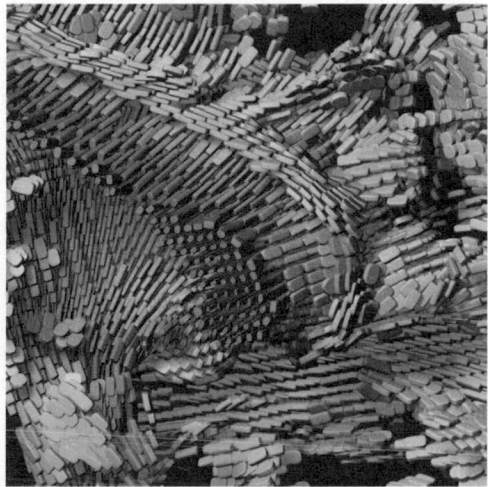

Figure 5.23 This map of a tensor field from Kindlmann and Westin (2006) has some variables mapped to the color of the lozenge-like glyphs and some variables mapped to their shape and orientation.

We can also apply the lessons of integral and separable dimensions to data glyphs designed to represent many variables. Fig. 5.23 shows a field of data glyphs from Kindlmann and Westin (2006) in which three variables are mapped to color and many more are mapped to the shape of the glyphs. Detailed knowledge of the application would be required to decide if this is a good representation, but this is not our concern here. The point of showing it is to illustrate how the color-mapped variables tend to be seen integrally and independently (separably) from the shape variables, which also tend to be viewed holistically, making up the lozenge shapes.

Integral-Separable Dimension Pairs

The preceding analysis presented in integral and separable dimensions as if they were qualitatively distinct. This overstates the case; a continuum of integrality-separability more accurately represents the facts. Even between the most separable dimension pairs, there is always some interference between different data values presented using the different channels. Likewise, the most integral dimension pairs can be regarded analytically to some extent. We can, for example, perceive the degree of redness and the degree of yellowness of a color—for example, orange or pink. Indeed, the original experimental evidence for opponent color channels was based on analytic judgments of exactly this type (Hurvich, 1981).

Fig. 5.24 provides a list of display dimension pairs arranged on an integral-separable continuum. At the top are the most integral dimensions. At the bottom are the most separable dimensions. Some display dimensions are not represented in Fig. 5.24 because of very little evidence. For example, one method of separating values is to use stereoscopic depth. It seems likely that stereoscopic depth is quite separable from other dimensions, especially if only two depth layers are involved.

As a theoretical concept, the notion of integral and separable dimensions is undoubtedly simplistic; it lacks mechanism and fails to account for a large number of exceptions and asymmetries that have been discovered experimentally. Also, it says essentially the same thing as channel theory, and channel theory has a firm neuropsychological basis. The beauty of the integral-separable distinction lies in its simplicity as a design guideline.

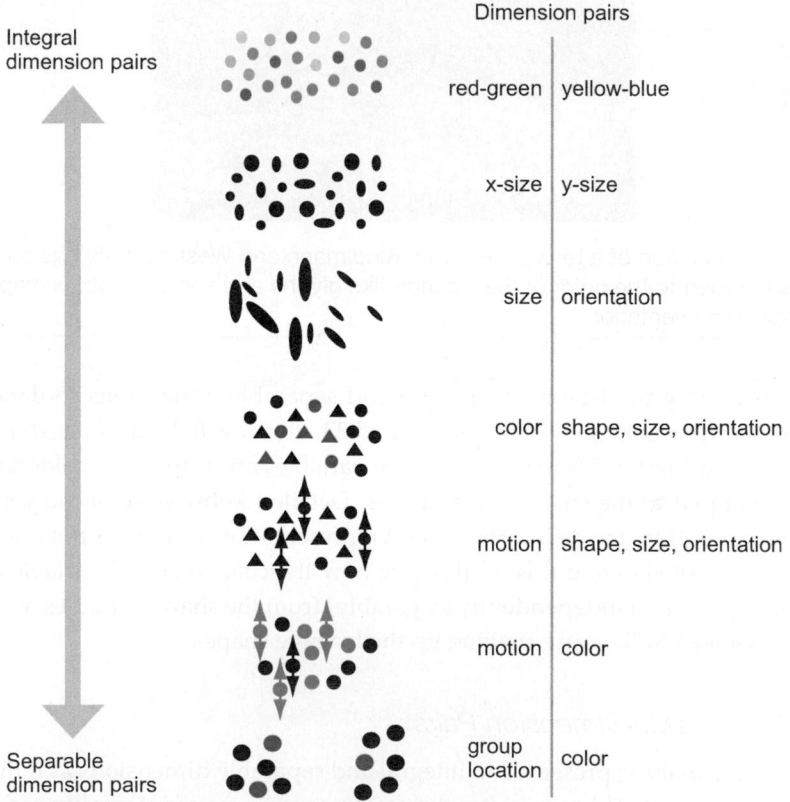

Figure 5.24 Examples of glyphs coded according to two display attributes. At the top are more integral coding pairs. At the bottom are more separable coding pairs.

Representing Quantity

Any visual attribute, such as symbol size, color, or even movement can be used to represent quantity. Fig. 5.25 summarizes the variables that are commonly used. Some authors have produced detailed rankings of visual attributes for quantity representation (e.g., Cleveland & McGill, 1984; MacKinlay, 1986) but for the most part this is problematic. Whether texture density, or color saturation leads to greater accuracy depends on the exact range and nature of the textures and the colors being compared. In addition, a very small position range will be less effective than a large texture density range. Nevertheless, it is clear that linear size and linear position have *the potential* for greater accuracy than color saturation. So it is best to consider visual variables as

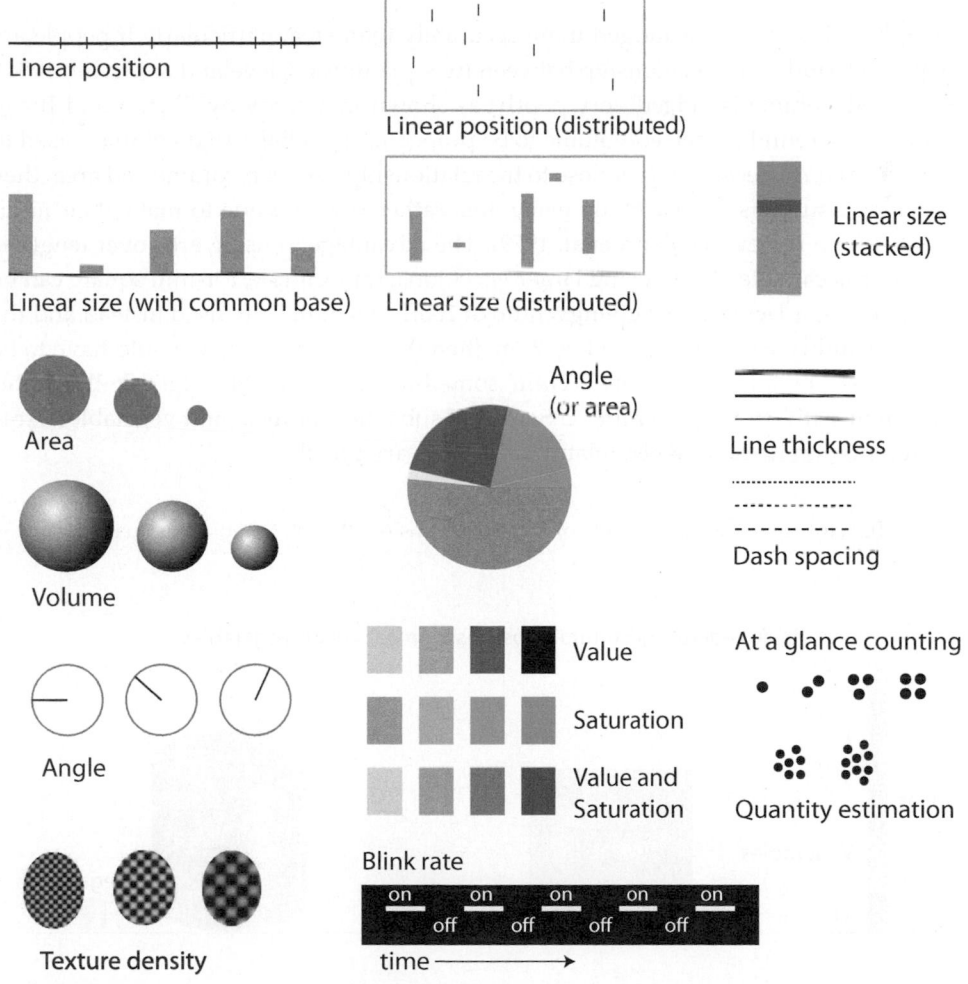

Figure 5.25 Some to the ways of encoding quantity. Length and position generally lead to the greatest accuracy, with alternatives such as color, area, and texture density resulting is less accuracy.

belonging to two broad classes with respect to equivalent: Position and length and all the rest, including area, angle, hue, saturation and texture density. In all cases, the details matter, colors are not all equally good because they vary in saturation (See Chapter 4). Textures can be very diverse and there are many ways in which density can be adjusted, so saying that color is better or worse than texture is meaningless.

> **[G5.15]** Ideally, use glyph length or height or position to represent quantity. If these possibilities are exhausted, use other available graphical attributes depending on the task requirement and natural semantic coding relating to the application.

Length, Area, and Volume

Length will generally be judged more accurately than area, particularly if people are required to judge the relationship between two quantities (Cleveland & McGill, 1984). Perceived volume is judged very poorly, as shown in a study by Ekman and Junge (1961), who found perceived volume to be proportional to the actual volume raised to a power of 0.75. Because this is close to the relationship between volume and area, they concluded subjects were actually using area rather than volume to make their judgments (For a review see Baird et al. 1979). The advantage to using area over length is that area is capable of conveying larger variations; for example, a 1-mm square can be compared to a 1-cm square, giving a ratio of 100:1. If length were used instead and the larger quantity were represented by 2 cm, then the smaller quantity would have to be represented by a length of only 0.2 mm, something barely visible. Fig. 5.26 illustrates this point with data representing U.S. federal subsidies for meat and vegetables. Area representation is useful when relative amounts vary greatly.

> **[G5.16]** Never use the volume of a three-dimensional glyph to represent quantity.

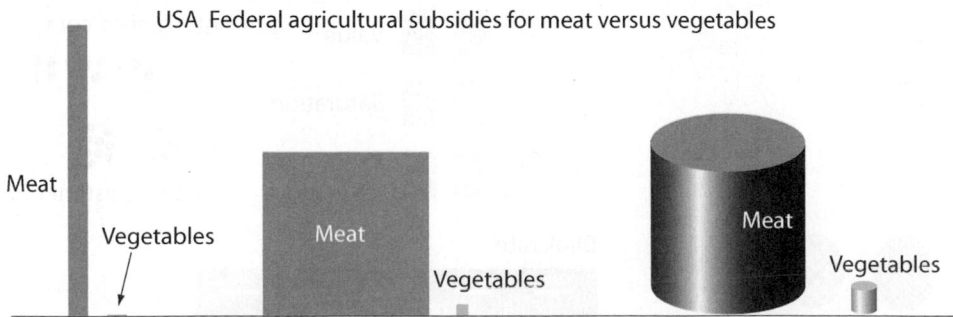

Figure 5.26 The same information is shown using length, area, and volume. Research shows that the quantities shown in the volume display on the right will be mostly judged according to the relative area of the images, not according to volume, resulting in large errors.

One particular kind of visualization that has received considerable attention regarding its accuracy is the pie chart. Although one influential study by McDonald-Ross (1977) argued that pie charts are less accurate than bar charts other studies have disputed this (e.g., Spence and Lewandowsky, 1999) especially for percentage judgments. Small pie charts are commonly used on maps and for this purpose they are likely to be as good as small bar charts. When pie charts are used to represent actual quantities, rather than percentages, they will be less accurate than, for example, stacked bar charts because area judgments are not as accurate as length judgments. Also, at larger sizes, bar charts can have y-axis scales and horizontal rules that increase their accuracy whereas scales are not easily added to a pie chart making them inferior when a scale is required.

One method for obtaining greater accuracy in quantity representation is to use groupings of discrete iconic symbols to represent quantities called Isotypes (Neurath, 1936). For example, a grid of small soldier icons might represent war casualties; each soldier icon might represent 1000 casualties.

A more abstract version of this idea is to divide up linear, area, and volume glyphs into discrete parts. Fig. 5.27 illustrates the concept. A study by Mihtsentu and Ware (2015) showed that this method could greatly increase the accuracy with which area and volume glyphs could be read, eliminating the nonlinearities discussed previously.

Subitizing

People, and even some animals, are able to count small numbers of objects "at a glance," and *subitizing* is the term used for this rapid, apparently effortless counting process (Gallistel & Gelman, 1992). When there are more than a subitizable number of items, the number must be estimated, or counted which is a slow process. Grouping may also help with rapid estimation. Beckwith and Restle (1966) found that estimation of the number of object grouped in rows and columns was more accurate than estimation of randomly scattered objects.

Monotonicity

Some visual qualities increase continuously, such as size, brightness, or height above the ground, and are said to be *monotonic*. Some visual qualities are not monotonic.

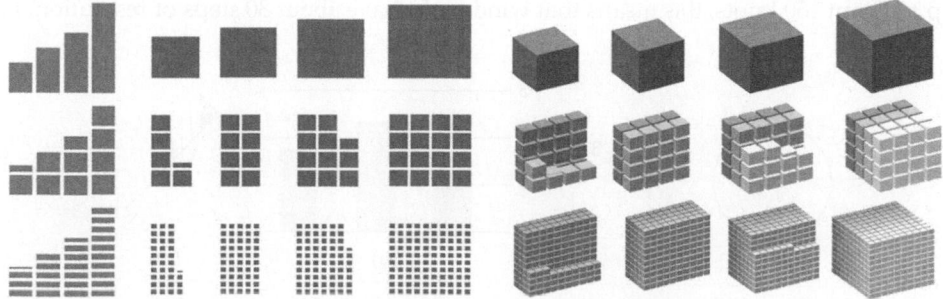

Figure 5.27 Greater accuracy can be obtained if area and volume glyphs are broken into discrete parts. However, if this is done, they cannot be made small.

Orientation is one. It is meaningless to say that one orientation is greater or less than another. The same is true of the phase angle between two oscillating objects. As the phase difference is increased, the objects first appear to move in opposite directions, but as the phase difference continues to increase, they appear to move together again. Phase is cyclic, just as line orientation is cyclic. Hue also lacks a natural order.

Monotonic display variables naturally express relations, such as greater than or less than, if they have a quality that we associate with increasing value. For example, in a three-dimensional data space, the up direction is defined by gravity, and using up to represent a greater quantity of some variable will be readily interpreted, but the left and right directions do not have as clear a value. In the west, we read left to right but this is learned. Other languages, such as Arabic, have right-to-left ordering.

Representing Absolute Quantities

Sometimes rapid access to exact quantities is important. There are a number of solutions. One is simply to add numbers to a glyph, or a numerical scale; see Fig. 5.28(a and b). But, unless it is done carefully, the numbers will add visual noise, obscuring important patterns in data. To solve this, numbers can appear with a mouse-over. Numerical scales are essential on many types of chart such as bar charts and time series graphs. Adding faint horizontal or vertical rules will also increase accuracy and should be standard practice. It is strange that many studies of the accuracy of bar graphs have failed to provide such lines, making them largely irrelevant.

> [G5.17] Provide faint, unobtrusive horizontal and/or vertical lines on charts to improve the accuracy with which they can be read.

A second solution is to create a glyph that uses its shape to convey numerical values. The best known example of this is the wind barb, which is shown in Fig. 5.28(c). A wind barb is a glyph widely used in meteorology; it is a kind of hybrid of perceptual features and symbolic features. The shaft of the barb represents the direction of the wind. The "feathers" of the barb encode wind speed, so that someone familiar with the code can read off the wind speed to an accuracy of 5 knots. Given that surface wind speeds range up to about 150 knots, this means that wind barbs have about 30 steps of resolution, far

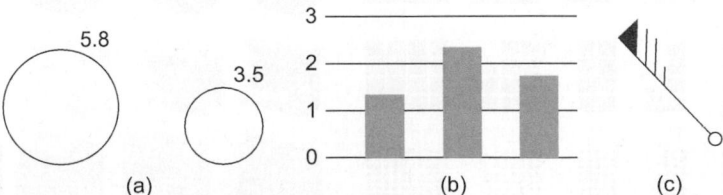

Figure 5.28 Three different ways that more exact numerical values can be read from a diagram. Bar and line graphs should be given faint horizontal lines extending the scale into the background of the chart.

better than any simple variation in size or color. The wind barb, however, has perceptual problems. The barb feathers greatly interfere with the perception of wind direction and because of this wind barbs are very poor at showing patterns in the winds.

Multidimensional Discrete Data: Uniform Representation versus Multiple Channels

This is a good place to step back and look at the general problem of multivariate discrete data display in light of the concepts that have been presented here and in previous chapters. It is worth restating this problem. We are provided with a set of entities, each of which has values on a number of attribute dimensions. For example, we might have 1000 beetles, each measured on 30 anatomical characteristics, or 500 stocks, each described by 20 financial variables. The reason for displaying such data graphically is often data exploration—to find meaning in the diversity. In the case of the beetles, the meaning might be related to their ecological niche. In the case of the stocks, the meaning is likely to lie in opportunities for profit. In either case, we are likely to be interested in patterns in the data, such as clusters of beetles that share similar attribute values.

If we decide to use a glyph display, each entity becomes a graphical object and data attributes are mapped to graphical attributes of each glyph. The problem is one of mapping data dimensions to the graphical attributes of the glyph. The work on pre-attentive processing, early visual processing, and integral and separable dimensions suggests that a rather limited set of visual attributes is available to us if we want to understand the values rapidly. Table 5.2 lists the most useful low-level graphical attributes that can be applied to glyph design, with a few summary comments about the number of dimensions available.

Many of these display dimensions are not independent of one another. To display texture, we must use at least one color dimension (luminance) to make the texture visible. Blink coding will certainly interfere with motion coding. Overall, we will probably be fortunate to display eight types of dimensional data clearly, using color, shape, spatial position, and motion to create the most differentiated set possible.

There is also the issue of how many resolvable steps are available in each dimension. The number here is also small. When we require rapid preattentive processing, only a handful of colors are available. The number of orientation steps that we can easily distinguish is probably about four. The number of size steps that we can easily distinguish is no more than four, and the values for the other data dimensions are also in the single-digit range. It is reasonable, therefore, to propose that we can represent about 2 bits of information for each of the eight graphical dimensions. If the dimensions were truly independent, this would yield 16 displayable bits per glyph (64,000 values). Unfortunately, conjunctions are generally not preattentive. If we allow no conjunction searching, we are left with four alternatives on each of eight dimensions, yielding only 32 rapidly distinguishable alternatives, a far smaller number. Anyone who has tried to design a set of easily distinguishable glyphs will recognize this number to be more plausible.

Table 5.2 *Graphical Attributes That may be Useful in Glyph Design.*

Visual Variable	Dimensionality	Comment
Spatial position	Two dimensions: X, Y	The Z dimension is not included because it is much harder to resolve than the other two.
Color	Three dimensions: Defined by color-opponent theory	Luminance contrast is needed to specify all other graphical attributes.
Size	Two dimensions: X, Y	The dimensions of shape that can be rapidly processed are unknown; however, the number is certainly small.
Orientation	One dimension	Using orientation depends on the glyph having an elongated shape
Surface texture	Three dimensions: orientation, size, and contrast	Surface texture is not independent of shape or orientation; uses one color dimension.
Motion coding	Approximately two to three dimensions; more research is needed, but phase is critical	
Blink coding	One dimension	Motion and blink coding are highly interdependent.

There is also the issue of the semantics associated with design choices, such as whether to use color or size to represent a particular attribute. Temperature, for example, has a natural mapping to color because of the association of redness with greater heat and blueness to lesser heat. Using the size of a glyph to represent temperature would normally be a poor design choice; however, there is a natural mapping between an increase in the amount of some variable and vertical size, or height above a baseline (Pinker, 2007). Orientation information, such as the direction of flow in a vector field is best represented by the orientation of a glyph—if a glyph representation is chosen, using color to represent orientation would normally be a poor design choice.

[G5.18] In general, the use of heterogeneous display channels is best combined with meaningful mappings between data semantics and graphical features of a set of glyphs.

Stars and Whiskers

Sometimes no natural mappings to channels exist and what is needed is a more symmetric mapping of data dimensions to the visual properties of a glyph. In this case, bar charts and *star and whisker glyphs* can be considered.

In the whisker glyph, each data value is represented by a line segment radiating out from a central point, as shown in Fig. 5.29(a). The length of the line segment denotes the value of

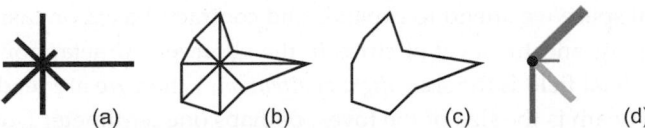

Figure 5.29 (a) Whisker glyph. (b) Star glyph. (c) Polygon glyph. (d) Whisker glyph with only four variables and varying line width and color designed to work in dense displays.

the corresponding data attribute. A variant of the whisker glyph is the star plot (Chambers, Cleveland, Kleiner, & Tukey, 1983) This is the same as the whisker plot but with the ends of the lines connected, as in Fig. 5.29(b). Another variant is the polygon glyph which removes the internal lines altogether (Fig. 5.29(c)). Experimental studies by Fuchs, Isenberg, Bezerianos, Fischer, and Bertini (2014) suggest that the whisker variant is the best for shape matching tasks. It is possible to show a large number of variables with whisker or star glyphs, but this does not mean that the results will be intelligible. If there are a large number of whisker glyphs in a display, there will be visual interference between all contours having a similar orientation, with the star glyph being the worst in this regard. The external polygon contains many more lines without adding extra information. If a large number of these kinds of glyphs are to be displayed in a scatterplot, a small number of whiskers is recommended—four is probably the maximum to minimize interference between similarly oriented contours. It may also be useful to change other attributes of glyph segments by altering the line width and color as well as the length of the line; see Fig. 5.29(c).

A more common alternative to star and whisker plots is small bar charts, such as miniature versions of Fig. 5.28(b). These have the advantage that orientation does not have to be taken into account in judging the represented quantities, and the bars can be color coded to make it easier to distinguish the variables. Comparisons between bar charts and whisker or star glyphs have produce mixed results without either being the clear winner (Fuchs, Isenberg, Bezerianos, & Keim, 2017).

When the data has many dimensions, a much better tool for its analysis is the parallel coordinates plot discussed in later chapters. This uses interactivity to minimize interference between dimensions.

The Searchlight Metaphor and Cortical Magnification

We now return to the topic of visual search with which we began this chapter. Consider the eyeball as an information-gathering searchlight, sweeping the visual world under the guidance of the cognitive centers that control our attention. Information is acquired in bursts, a snapshot for each fixation. More complex, nonpreattentive objects are scanned in series, one after another, at about the rate of 40 items per second. This means that we can typically parse somewhere between three and six items before the eye jumps to another fixation.

Useful Field of View

The attention process is concentrated around the fovea, where vision is most detailed; however, we can to some extent redirect attention to objects away from the fovea. The region of visual space we attend to expands and contracts based on task, the information in the display, and the level of stress in the observer. A metaphor for the fovea-centered attentional field is the *searchlight of attention*. When we are reading fine print, the searchlight beam is the size of the fovea, perhaps one centimeter from the point of fixation. If we are looking at a larger pattern, the searchlight beam expands. A concept called the *useful field of view* (UFOV) has been developed to define the size of the region from which we can quickly take in information. The UFOV varies greatly, depending on the task and the information being displayed. Experiments using displays densely populated with targets reveal small UFOVs, from 1 to 4 degrees of visual angle (Wickens, 1992). Drury and Clement (1978), however, have shown that for low target densities (less than one per degree of visual angle) the UFOV can be as large as 15 degrees. Roughly, the UFOV varies with target density to maintain a constant number of targets in the attended region. With greater target density, the UFOV becomes smaller and attention is more narrowly focused; with a low target density, a larger area can be attended.

Tunnel Vision, Stress, and Cognitive Load

A phenomenon known as *tunnel vision* has been associated with operators working under extreme stress. In tunnel vision, the UFOV is narrowed so that only the most important information, normally at the center of the field of view, is processed. This phenomenon has been specifically associated with various kinds of nonfunctional behaviors that occur during decision making in disaster situations. The effect can be demonstrated quite simply. Williams (1985) compared performance on a task that required intense concentration (high foveal load) to one that was simpler. The high-load task involved naming a letter drawn from six alternatives; the low-load task involved naming a letter drawn from two alternatives. They found a dramatic drop in detection rate for objects in the periphery of the visual field (down from 75% correct to 36% correct) as the task load increased. The Williams data shows that we should not think of tunnel vision strictly as a response to disaster. It may generally be the case that as cognitive load goes up, the UFOV shrinks.

> [G5.19] When designing user interrupts, peripheral alerting cues must be made stronger if the cognitive load is expected to be high.

The Role of Motion in Attracting Attention

A study by Peterson and Dugas (1972) suggests that the UFOV function can be far larger for detection of moving targets than for detection of static targets. They showed that subjects can respond in less than 1 s to targets 20 degrees from the line of sight, if the targets are moving. If static targets are used, performance falls off rapidly beyond about 4 degrees from fixation (see Fig. 5.30). This implies a UFOV of at least 40 degrees for the moving-targets task.

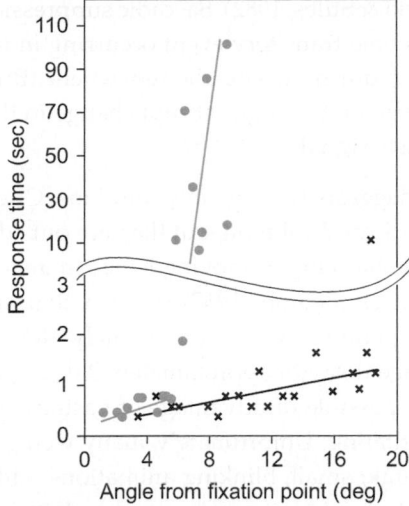

Figure 5.30 Results of a study by Peterson and Dugas (1972). The task was to detect small symbols representing aircraft in a simulation display. The circles show the response times from the appearances of static targets. The crosses show response times from the appearances of moving targets. Note the two different scales.

Motion as a User Interrupt

As we conduct more of our work in front of computer screens, there is an increasing need for signals that can attract a user's attention. Often someone is busy with a primary task, perhaps filling out forms or composing e-mail, while at the same time events may occur on other parts of the display that require attention. These *user interrupts* can alert us to an incoming message from a valued customer or a signal from a computer agent that has been out searching the Internet for information on the latest flu virus.

There are four basic visual requirements for a user interrupt:

1. A signal should be easily perceived, even if it is outside of the area of immediate focal attention.

2. If the user wishes to ignore the signal and attend to another task, the signal should continue to act as a reminder.

3. The signal should not be so irritating that it makes the computer unpleasant to use.

4. It should be possible to endow the signal with various levels of urgency.

Essentially, the problem is how to attract the user's attention to information outside the central parafoveal region of vision (approximately the central 6 degrees). For a number of reasons, the options are limited. We have a low ability to detect small targets in the periphery of the visual field. Peripheral vision is color blind, which rules out color signals (Wyszecki & Stiles, 1982). Saccadic suppression (blindness during eye movements) means that some transitory event occurring in the periphery will generally be missed if it occurs during a saccadic movement (Burr & Ross, 1982). Taken together, these facts suggest that a single, abrupt change in the appearance of an icon is unlikely to be an effective signal.

The set of requirements suggests two possible solutions. One is to use auditory cues. In certain cases, these are a good solution, but they are outside the scope of this book. Another solution is to use blinking or moving icons. In a study involving shipboard alarm systems, Goldstein and Lamb (1967) showed that subjects were capable of distinguishing five flash patterns with approximately 98% reliability and that they responded with an average delay of approximately 2.0 seconds. Anecdotal evidence, however, indicates that a possible disadvantage of flashing lights or blinking cursors is that users find them irritating. Unfortunately, many web page designers generate a kind of animated chart junk; small, blinking animations with no functional purpose are often used to jazz up a page. Moving icons may be a better solution. Moving targets are detected more easily in the periphery than static targets (Peterson & Dugas, 1972). In a series of dual-task experiments, Bartram, Ware, and Calvert (2003) had subjects carry out a primary task, either text editing or playing Tetris or solitaire, while simultaneously monitoring for a change in an icon at the side of the display in the periphery of the visual field. The results showed that having an icon move was far more effective in attracting a user's attention than having it change color or shape. The advantage increased as the signal was farther from the focus of attention in the primary task. Another advantage of moving or blinking signals is that they can persistently attract attention, unlike a change in an icon, such as the raising of a mailbox flag, which fades rapidly from attention. Also, although rapid motions are annoying, slower motions need not be and they can still support a low level of awareness (Ware, Bonner, Knight, & Cater, 1992).

Interestingly, more recent work has suggested that it may not be motion per se that attracts attention, but the appearance of a new object in the visual field (Enns, Austin, Di Lollo, Rauchenberger, & Yantis, 2001; Hillstrom & Yantis, 1994). This seems right; after all, we are not constantly distracted in an environment of swaying trees or people moving about on a dance floor. It also makes ecological sense; when early man was outside a cave, intently chipping a lump of flint into a hand axe, or when early woman was gathering roots out on the grasslands, awareness of emerging objects in the periphery of vision would have had clear survival value. Such a movement might have signaled an imminent attack. Of course, the evolutionary advantage goes back much further than this. Monitoring the periphery of vision for moving predators or prey would provide a survival advantage for most animals. Thus, the most effective reminder might be an object that moves into view, disappears, and then reappears every so often. In a study that measured the eye movements made while viewing multimedia presentations, Faraday and Sutcliffe (1997) found that the onset of motion of an object generally produced a shift of attention to that object.

Conclusion

This chapter has provided an introduction to the early stages of vision, in which billions of neurons act in parallel to extract elementary aspects of form, color, texture, motion, and stereoscopic depth. The fact that this processing is done for each point of the visual field means that objects differentiated in terms of these simple low-level features popout and can be easily found. These low-level filters are not unbiased; they are tuned by the effects of top-down attention. This means that to a great extent what we need to see as well as what we expect to see will have a large influence on what we actually see.

For glyphs to be seen rapidly, they must stand out clearly from all other objects in their near vicinity on at least one coding dimension. In a display of large symbols, a small symbol will stand out. In a display of blue, green, and gray symbols, a red symbol will stand out. Because only simple basic visual properties guide visual search, glyphs and symbols that are distinctive in terms of more complex combinations of features cannot be easily found.

The lessons from this chapter have to do with fundamental tradeoffs in design choices about whether to use color, shape, texture, or motion to display a particular set of variables. These basic properties provide a set of channels that can be used to code information.

There is more visual interference within channels. The basic rule is that, in terms of low-level properties, "like" interferes with "like." If we have a set of small symbols on a textured background, a texture with a grain size similar to that of the symbols will make them difficult to see.

There is more separability between channels. If we wish to be able to read data values from different data dimensions, each of these values should be mapped to a different display channel. Mapping one variable to color and another to glyph orientation will make them independently readable. If we map one variable to height and another to width, they will be read more holistically. If we have a set of symbols that are difficult to see because they are on a textured background, they can be made to stand out by using another coding channel; having the symbols oscillate will also make them distinct. The way to differentiate variables readily is to employ more perceptual channels. Unfortunately, although this solves one problem, it creates another. We have to decide which variable to map to color, to shape, and to texture, and we have to worry about which mappings will be most intuitive for the intended audience. These are difficult design decisions.

CHAPTER SIX

Static and Moving Patterns

Data analysis is about finding patterns that were previously unknown or that depart from the norm. The stock market analyst looks for any pattern of variables that may predict a future change in price or earnings. The marketing analyst is interested in perceiving trends and patterns in a customer database. The scientist searches for patterns that may confirm or refute a hypothesis. When we look for patterns, we are making visual queries. Sometimes the queries are vague; we are on the lookout for a variety of structures in the data or any exception to a general rule. Sometimes they are precise, as when we look for a positive trend in a graph.

The visual brain is a powerful pattern-finding engine; indeed, this is the fundamental reason why visualization techniques are becoming important. There is no other way of presenting information so that structures, groups, and trends can be discovered among hundreds of data values. If we can transform data into the appropriate visual representation, its structure may be revealed, but what is the best mapping from data to display? What does it take for us to see a group? How can two-dimensional (2D) space be divided into perceptually distinct regions? Under what conditions are two patterns recognized as similar? What constitutes a visual connection between objects? These are some of the perceptual questions addressed in this chapter. The answers are central to visualization, because most data displays are two dimensional and pattern perception deals with the extraction of structure from 2D space. Consider again our three-stage model of perception (illustrated in Fig. 6.1). At the early stages of feature abstraction, the visual image is analyzed in terms of primitive elements of form, motion, color, and stereoscopic depth. At the middle 2D pattern-perception stage,

Information Visualization. https://doi.org/10.1016/B978-0-12-812875-6.00006-2

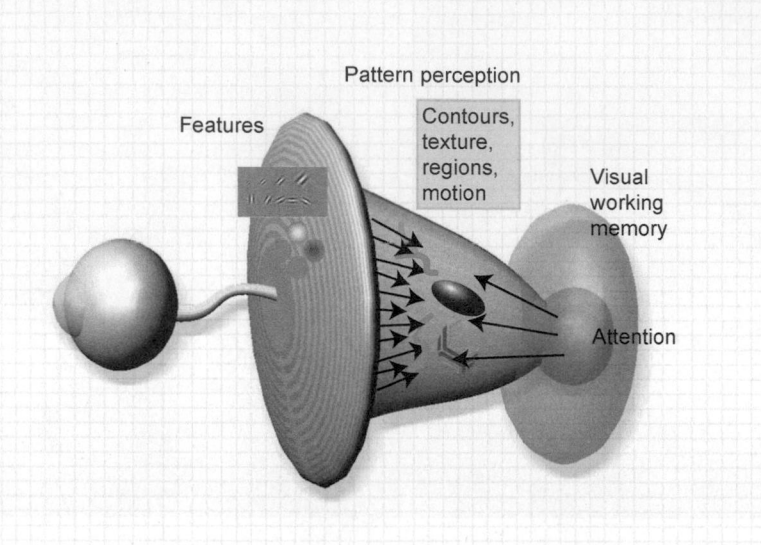

Figure 6.1 Pattern perception occurs in a middle ground where bottom-up feature processing meets the requirements of top-down active attention.

active processes driven by top-down visual queries cause contours to be formed, distinct regions to be segmented, and connections to be made. At the top level, objects and scenes are discovered, using information about the connections between component parts, shape-from-shading information, and so on.

Pattern perception is the flexible middle ground where objects are extracted from patterns of features. Active processes of attention reach down into the pattern space to keep track of those objects and to analyze them for particular tasks; the essentially bottom-up processing of features from simple to complex meets the top-down processes of cognitive perception. Rensink (2000) called the middle ground a proto-object flux. According to Ullman (1984), active processes under top-down control, called visual routines, pull out only a small number of patterns at any given instant.

Pattern perception is a set of mostly 2D processes occurring between feature analysis and full object perception, although aspects of three-dimensional space perception, such as stereoscopic depth and structure from motion, can be considered particular kinds of pattern perception, the most powerful mechanisms are devoted to parsing 2D space. Finally, objects and significant patterns are pulled out by attentional processes to meet the needs of the visual query constructed for the currently active cognitive task.

There are radical differences in the kinds of processing that occur at the different stages. In the early stages, massively parallel processing of the entire image occurs. This drives perception from the bottom up, but object and pattern recognition is driven from the top down through active attention, meeting the requirements of visual thinking. At the highest level, only one to five objects (or simple patterns) are held in visual working memory from one fixation to the next, as we make comparisons and conduct visual searches to meet the demands of visual queries.

Our knowledge of pattern perception can be distilled into abstract design principles which state how to organize data so that important structures will be perceived. If we can map information structures to readily perceived patterns, then those structures will be more easily interpreted.

Gestalt Laws

The first serious attempts to understand pattern perception were undertaken by a group of German psychologists who, in 1912, founded what is known as the Gestalt school of psychology. The group consisted principally of Max Westheimer, Kurt Koffka, and Wolfgang Kohler (see Koffka, 1935, for an original text). The word *Gestalt* simply means "pattern" in German. The work of the Gestalt psychologists is still valued today because they provided a clear description of many basic perceptual phenomena in the form of a set of Gestalt "laws" of pattern perception. These are robust rules that describe the way we see patterns in visual displays, and although the neural mechanisms proposed by these researchers to explain the laws have not withstood the test of time, the laws themselves have proved to be of enduring value. The Gestalt laws easily translate into a set of design principles for information displays. Eight Gestalt laws are discussed here: proximity, similarity, connectedness, continuity, symmetry, closure, relative size, and common fate (the last concerns motion perception and appears later in the chapter).

Proximity

Spatial proximity is a powerful perceptual organizing principle and one of the most useful in design. Things that are close together are perceptually grouped together. Fig. 6.2 shows two arrays of dots that illustrate the proximity principle. Only a small change in spacing causes us to change what is perceived from a set of rows, inFig. 6.2(a), to a set of columns, in Fig. 6.2(b). In Fig. 6.2(c), the existence of two groups is perceptually inescapable. But proximity is not the only factor in predicting perceived groups. In Fig. 6.3, the dot labeled x is perceived to be part of cluster a rather than cluster b, even though it is as close to the other points in cluster b as they are to each other. Slocum (1983) called this the *spatial concentration* principle; we perceptually group regions of similar element density. The application of the proximity law in display design is straightforward.

[G6.1] Place symbols and glyphs representing related information close together.

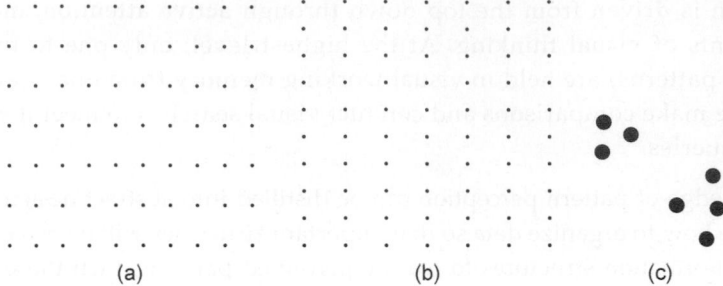

Figure 6.2 Spatial proximity is a powerful cue for perceptual organization. A matrix of dots is perceived as rows on the left (a) and columns on the right (b). In (c) we perceive two groups of dots because of proximity relationships.

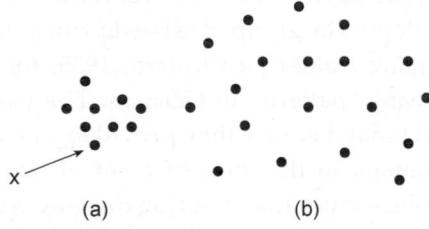

Figure 6.3 The principle of spatial concentration. The dot labeled x is perceived as part of cluster a rather than cluster b.

In addition to the perceptual organization benefit, there is also a perceptual efficiency to using proximity. Because we more readily pick up information close to the fovea, less time and effort will be spent in neural processing and eye movements if related information is spatially grouped.

Similarity

The shapes of individual pattern elements can also determine how they are grouped. Similar elements tend to be grouped together. In Fig. 6.4(a and b) the similarity of the elements causes us to see rows more clearly. Acknowledging that similarity is important begs the question of what determines visual similarity. Both channel theory and the concepts of integral and separable dimensions (discussed in the previous chapter) can help with design decisions. Two different ways of visually separating row and column information are shown in Fig. 6.4(c) and (d). In Fig. 6.4(c), integral color and grayscale coding is used. In Fig. 6.4(d), green is used to delineate rows and texture is used to delineate columns. Color and texture are separate channels, and the result is a pattern that can be more readily visually segmented either by rows or by columns. This technique can be useful if we are designing so that users can easily attend to either one pattern or the other.

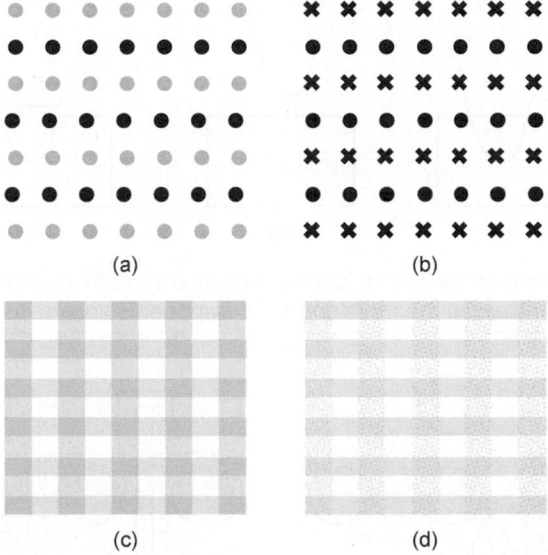

(a) (b)

(c) (d)

Figure 6.4 (a, b) According to the Gestalt psychologists, similarity between the elements in alternate rows causes the row percept to dominate. (c) Integral dimensions are used to delineate rows and columns. (d) When separable dimensions (color and texture) are used, it is easier to attend separately to either the rows or the columns.

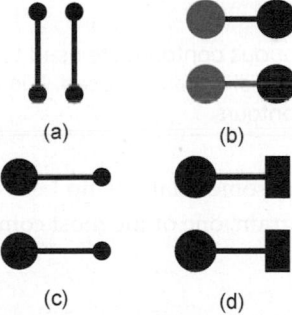

(a) (b)

(c) (d)

Figure 6.5 Connectedness is a powerful grouping principle that is stronger than (a) proximity, (b) color, (c) size, or (d) shape.

[G6.2] When designing a grid layout of a data set, consider coding rows and/ or columns using low-level visual channel properties, such as color and texture.

Connectedness

Palmer and Rock (1994) argued that connectedness is a fundamental Gestalt organizing principle that the Gestalt psychologists overlooked. The demonstrations in Fig. 6.5 show that connectedness can be a more powerful grouping principle than proximity, color, size, or shape. Connecting different graphical objects by lines is a very powerful

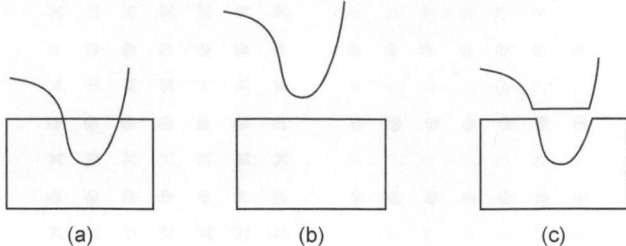

(a)   (b)   (c)

Figure 6.6 The pattern on the left (a) is perceived as a smoothly curved line overlapping a rectangle (b) rather than as the more angular components shown in (c).

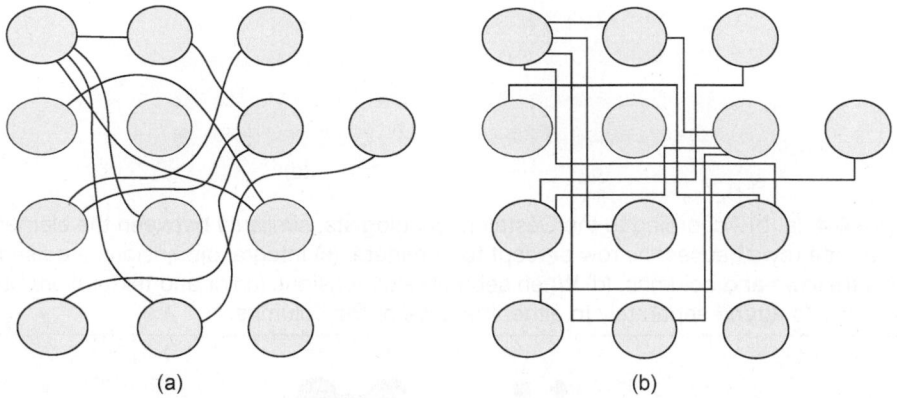

(a)   (b)

Figure 6.7 In (a), smooth continuous contours are used to connect nodes in the diagram; in (b), lines with abrupt changes in direction are used. It is much easier to perceive connections with the smooth contours.

way of expressing that there is some relationship between them. Indeed, this is fundamental to the node-link diagram, one of the most common methods of representing relationships between concepts.

> [G6.3] To show relationships between entities, consider linking graphical representations of data objects using lines or ribbons of color.

Continuity

The Gestalt principle of continuity states that we are more likely to construct visual entities out of visual elements that are smooth and continuous, rather than ones that contain abrupt changes in direction. (See Fig. 6.6.). The principle of good continuity can be applied to the problem of drawing diagrams consisting of networks of nodes and the links between them. It should be easier to identify the sources and destinations of connecting lines if they are smooth and continuous. This point is illustrated in Fig. 6.7. A graph drawing method known as a confluent diagram (Bach, Riche, Hurter, Marriott, & Dwyer, 2017) combines link bundling with the principle of continuity to make paths between nodes clear and unambiguous (Fig. 6.8 illustrates).

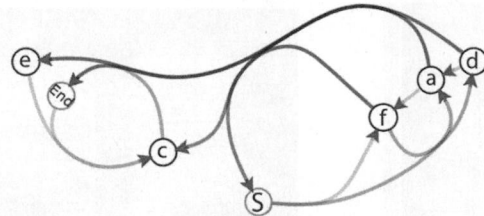

Figure 6.8 Confluent diagram from Bach et al., 2017. Smooth continuity makes it clear that there is no direct path from S to c even though they are connected by short lines. In contrast there are clearly direct paths from d to e and d to c. (*From Bach et al., 2017.*)

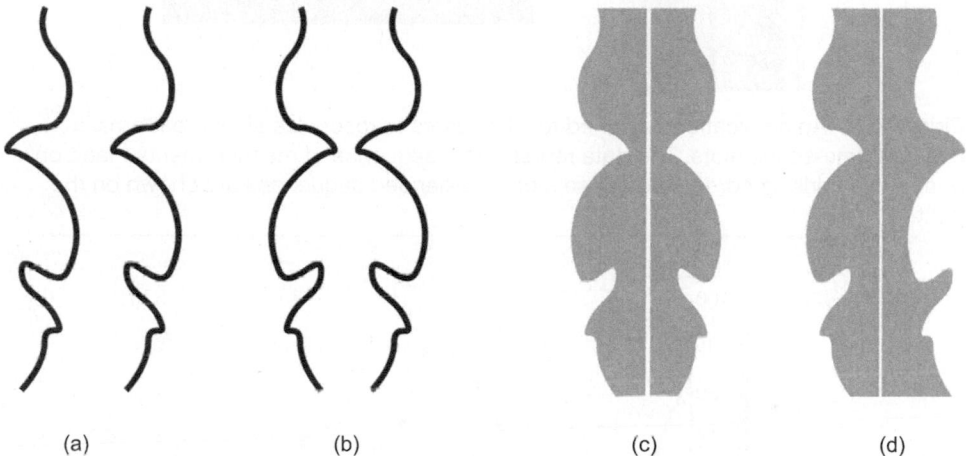

(a) (b) (c) (d)

Figure 6.9 (a) The pattern on the left consists of two identical parallel contours. (b) Mirror symmetry provides more of a sense of a whole figure. In (d) the edge parallel symmetry and reversed edge polarity make it more difficult to see the symmetry respect to (c).

Symmetry

Symmetry can provide a powerful organizing principle. The pairs of lines shown in Fig. 6.9(b) are perceived more strongly as forming a visual whole than the lines with parallel symmetry (Fig. 6.9a). Also, when edges instead of lines are used, symmetry is more difficult to perceive if the polarity is reversed on the edges (Fig. 6.9(c)). A possible application of symmetry is in tasks in which data analysts are looking for similarities between two different sets of time-series data. It may be easier to perceive similarities if these time series are arranged using vertical symmetry, as shown in Fig. 6.10, rather than using the more conventional parallel plots.

To take advantage of symmetry the important patterns must be small. Research by Dakin and Herbert (1998) suggests that we are most sensitive to symmetrical patterns that are small, less than 1 degree in width and 2 degrees in height, and centered around the fovea. The display on the right in Fig. 6.10 is somewhat too large to be optimal

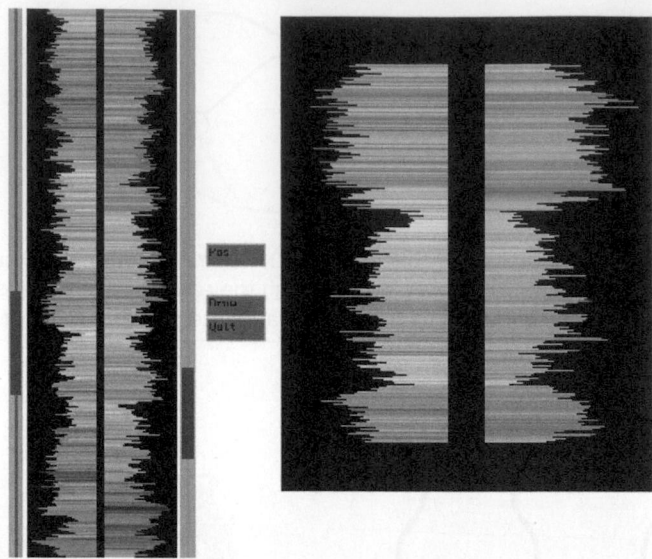

Figure 6.10 An application designed to allow users to recognize similar patterns in different time-series plots. The data represents a sequence of measurements made on deep ocean drilling cores. Two subsets of the extended sequences are shown on the right.

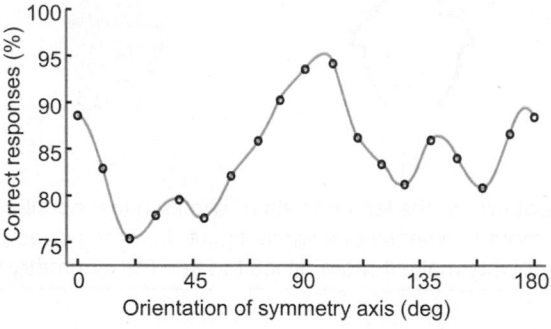

Figure 6.11 Results from Wenderoth (1994) illustrating the detection rates for symmetric patterns embedded in noise as a function of orientation.

from this point of view. Also, symmetrical patterns are more readily perceived around a vertical or horizontal axis than around an oblique axis, Fig. 6.11 as summarized in results from a study by Wenderoth (1994) using symmetrical patterns hidden within background noise. The detection rates were much higher for patterns with a vertical axis of symmetry and worst for oblique axes.

The bias toward seeing patterns with a vertical axis of symmetry is illustrated in a different way in Fig. 6.12(a and b); however, this bias can be altered with a frame of reference provided by a larger-scale pattern, as shown in Fig. 6.12(c) and (d). See Beck, Pinsk, and Kastner (2005).

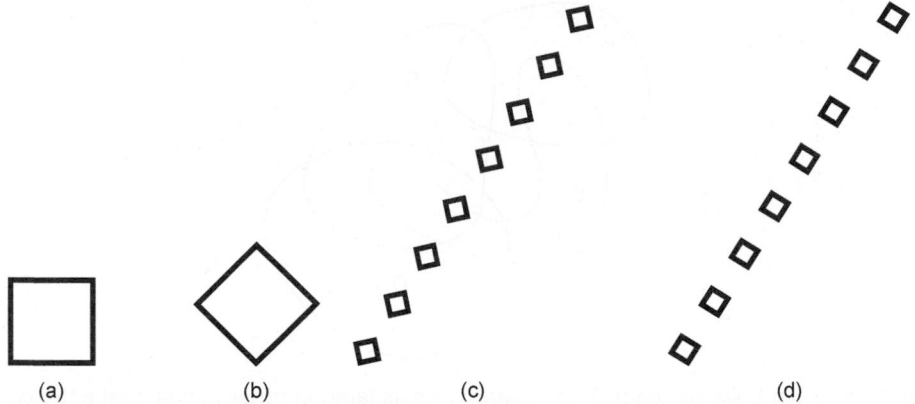

Figure 6.12 Because symmetries about vertical and horizontal axes are more readily perceived, (a) is seen as a square and (b) is seen as diamond. (c, d) A larger pattern can provide a frame of reference that defines the axes of symmetry; (c) is seen as a line of diamonds and (d) as a line of squares.

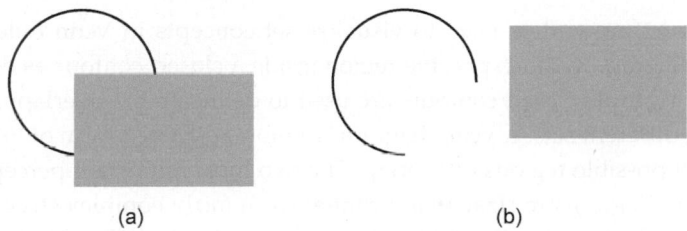

Figure 6.13 The Gestalt principle of closure holds that neural mechanisms operate to find perceptual solutions involving closed contours. In (a), we see a circle behind a rectangle, not a broken ring as in (b).

> **[G6.4]** Consider using symmetry to make pattern comparisons easier, but be sure that the patterns to be compared are small in terms of visual angle (<1 degree horizontally and <2 degrees vertically). Symmetrical relations should be arranged with a vertical axis unless some framing pattern is used.

Closure and Common Region

A closed contour tends to be seen as an object. The Gestalt psychologists argued that there is a perceptual tendency to close contours that have gaps in them. This can help explain why we see Fig. 6.13(a) as a complete circle and a rectangle rather than as a circle with a gap in it as in Fig. 6.13(b).

Wherever a closed contour is seen, there is a very strong perceptual tendency to divide regions of space into "inside" or "outside" the contour. A region enclosed by a contour becomes a *common region* in the terminology of Palmer (1992), who showed common region to be a much stronger organizing principle than simple proximity.

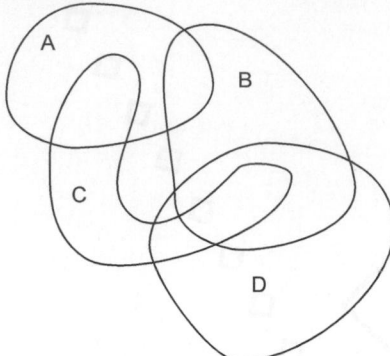

Figure 6.14 An Euler diagram. This diagram tells us (among other things) that entities can simultaneously be members of sets A and C but not of A, B, and C. Also, anything that is a member of both B and C is also a member of D. These rather difficult concepts are clearly expressed and understood by means of closed contours.

Closed contours are widely used to visualize set concepts in Venn-Euler diagrams. In an Euler diagram, we interpret the region inside a closed contour as defining a set of elements. Multiple closed contours are used to delineate the overlapping relationships among different sets. A Venn diagram is a more restricted form of Euler diagram containing all possible regions of overlap. The two most important perceptual factors in this kind of diagram are closure and continuity. A fairly complex structure of overlapping sets is illustrated in Fig. 6.14, using an Euler diagram. This kind of diagram is almost always used in teaching introductory set theory, and this in itself is evidence for its effectiveness. Students easily understand the diagrams, and they can transfer this understanding to the more difficult formal notation (Stenning & Oberlander, 1994).

When the boundary of a contour-defined region becomes complex, what is inside or outside may become unclear. In such cases, using color, texture, or Cornsweet contours (discussed in Chapter 3) will be more effective (Fig. 6.15). Although simple contours are generally used in Euler diagrams to show set membership, we can effectively define more complex sets of overlapping regions by using color and texture in addition to simple contours (Fig. 6.16). Fig. 6.17 shows an example from Collins et al. (2009) where both transparent color and contour are used to define extremely convoluted boundaries for three overlapping sets.

[G6.5] Consider putting related information inside a closed contour. A line is adequate for regions having a simple shape. Color or texture can be used to define regions that have more complex shapes.

[G6.6] To define multiple overlapping regions, consider using a combination of line contour, color, texture, and Cornsweet contours.

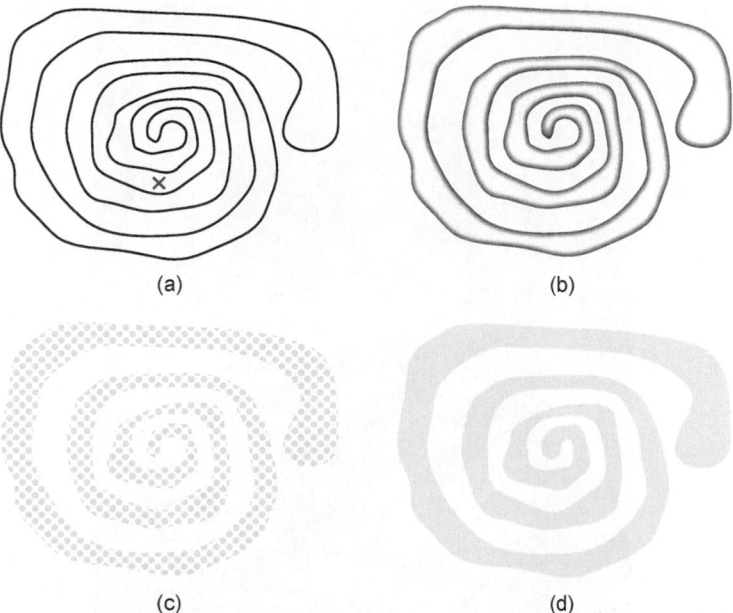

Figure 6.15 When the shape of the region is complex, a simple contour (shown in the upper left) is inadequate. (a) It is not easy to see if the x is inside or outside of the enclosed region. Common region can be defined less ambiguously by means of (b) a Cornsweet (1970) edge, (c) texture, or (d) color.

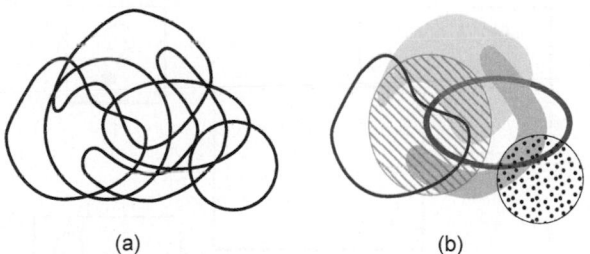

Figure 6.16 An Euler diagram enhanced using texture and color can convey a more complex set of relations than a conventional Euler diagram using only closed contours.

Both closure and closed contours are critical in segmenting the monitor screen in windows-based interfaces. The rectangular overlapping boxes provide a strong segmentation cue, dividing the display into different regions. In addition, rectangular frames provide frames of reference: The position of every object within the frame tends to be judged relative to the enclosing frame (see Fig. 6.18).

Figure and Ground

Gestalt psychologists were also interested in what they called *figure-ground* effects. A *figure* is something object-like that is perceived as being in the foreground. The *ground*

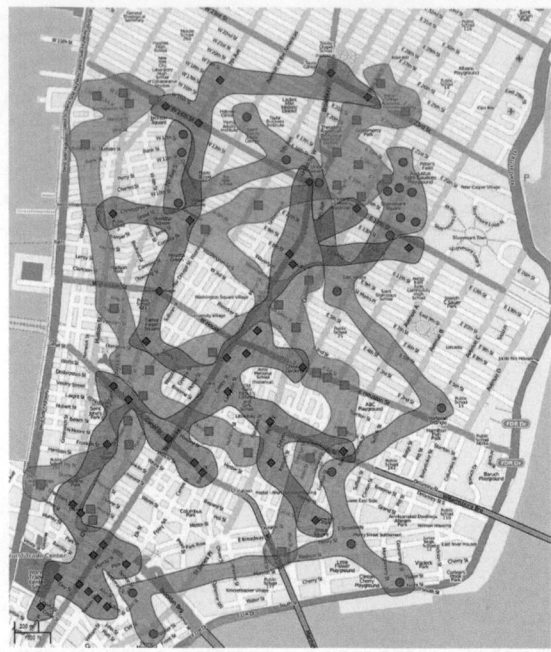

Figure 6.17 Both contour- and color-defined regions have been added to make clear the distribution of hotels (orange), subway stations (brown), and medical clinics (purple). (*From Collins et al. (2009). Reproduced with permission.*)

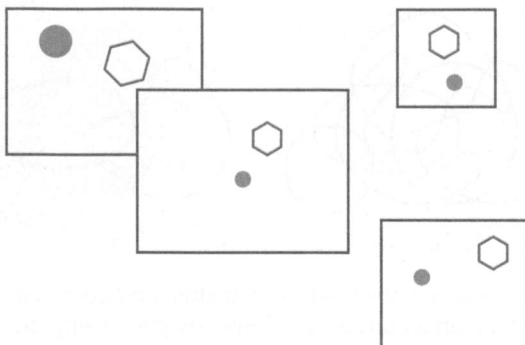

Figure 6.18 Closed rectangular contours strongly segment the visual field. They also provide reference frames. The positions and sizes of the enclosed shapes are, to some extent, interpreted with respect to the surrounding frame.

is whatever lies behind the figure. In general, smaller components of a pattern tend to be perceived as objects. In Fig. 6.19(a), a black propeller is seen on a white background, as opposed to the white areas being perceived as objects.

The perception of figure as opposed to ground can be thought of as part of the fundamental perceptual act of identifying objects. All of the Gestalt laws contribute to creating a figure, along with other factors that the Gestalt psychologists did not consider,

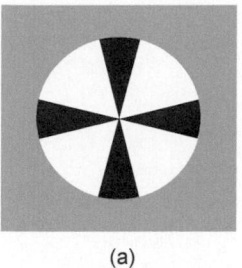 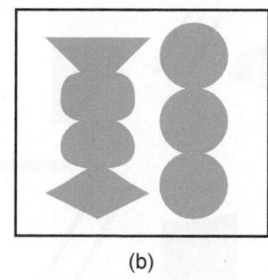 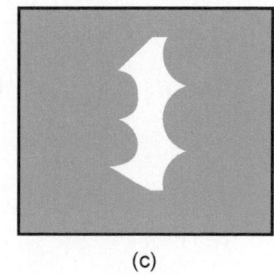

(a)   (b)   (c)

Figure 6.19 (a) The black areas are smaller and therefore more likely to be perceived as an object. It is also easier to perceive patterns that are oriented horizontally and vertically as objects. (b) The green areas are seen as figures because of several Gestalt factors, including size and closed form. The area between the green shapes in (c) is generally not seen as a figure.

Figure 6.20 Rubin's Vase. The cues for figure and ground are roughly equally balanced, resulting in a bistable percept of either two faces or a vase.

such as texture segmentation. Closed contour, symmetry, and the surrounding white area all contribute to the perception of the two shapes in Fig. 6.19(b) as figures, as opposed to cut-out holes. However, by changing the surroundings, as shown in Fig. 6.19(c), the irregular shape that was perceived as a gap in Fig. 6.19(b) can be made to become the figure.

> **[G6.7]** Use a combination of closure, common region, and layout to ensure that data entities are represented by graphical patterns that will be perceived as figures, not ground.

Fig. 6.20 shows the classic Rubin's Vase figure, in which it is possible to perceive either two faces, nose to nose, or a green vase centered in the display. The fact that the two percepts tend to alternate illustrates how competing active processes are involved in constructing figures from the pattern; however, the two percepts are driven by very different mechanisms. The vase percept is supported mostly by symmetry and being a closed region. Conversely, the faces percept is mostly driven by prior knowledge, not gestalt factors. It is only because of the great importance of faces that they are so readily seen. The result is a competition between high-level and mid-level processes.

Figure 6.21 Most people see a faint illusory contour surrounding a blobby shape at the center of this figure.

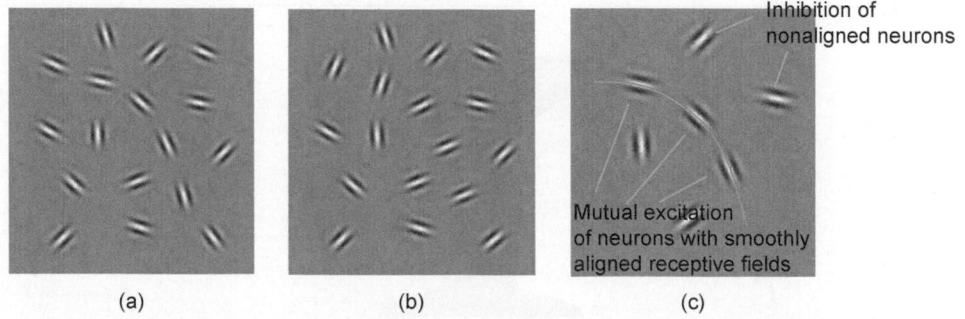

(a)   (b)   (c)

Figure 6.22 An illustration of the experiments conducted by Field et al. (1993). If the elements are aligned as shown in (a) so that a smooth curve can be drawn through some of them, a curve is seen. If the elements are at right angles, no curve is seen (b). This effect is explained by mutual excitation of neurons (c). (*Data from Field et al. (1993).*)

More on Contours

We now return to the topic of contours to discuss what recent research tells us about how they are processed in the brain. Contours are continuous, elongated boundaries between regions of a visual image, and the brain is exquisitely sensitive to their presence. A contour can be defined by a line, by a boundary between regions of different color, by stereoscopic depth, by motion patterns, or by the edge of a region of a particular texture. Contours can even be perceived where there are none. Fig. 6.21 illustrates an illusory contour; a ghostly boundary of a blobby shape is seen even where none is physically present (see Kanizsa, 1976). Because the process that leads to the identification of contours is seen as fundamental to object perception, contour detection has received considerable attention from vision researchers, and contours of various types are critical to many aspects of visualization.

A set of experiments by Field, Hayes, and Hess (1993) proved to be a landmark in placing the Gestalt notion of continuity on a firmer scientific basis. In these experiments, subjects had to detect the presence of a continuous path in a field of 256 randomly oriented Gabor patches (see Chapter 5 for a discussion of Gabor functions). The setup is illustrated schematically in Fig. 6.22. The results showed that subjects were very

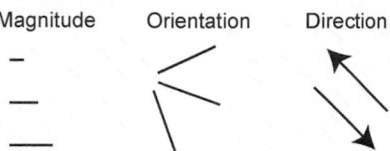

Figure 6.23 The components of a vector.

good at perceiving a smooth path through a sequence of patches. As one might expect, continuity between Gabor patches oriented in straight lines was the easiest to perceive. More interesting, even quite wiggly paths were readily seen if the Gabor elements were aligned as shown in Fig. 6.22(a). The theory underlying contour perception is that there is mutual reinforcement between neurons that have receptive fields that are smoothly aligned; there is inhibition between neurons with nonaligned receptive fields. The result is a kind of winner-take-all effect. Stronger contours beat out weaker contours.

Higher order neurophysiological mechanisms of contour perception are not well understood. One result, however, is intriguing. Gray, Konig, Engel, and Singer (1989) found that cells with collinear receptive fields tend to fire in synchrony. Thus, we do not need to propose higher order feature detectors, responding to more and more complex curves, to understand the neural encoding of contour information. Instead, it may be that groups of cells firing in synchrony is the way that the brain holds related pattern elements in mind. Theorists have suggested a fast enabling link, a kind of rapid feedback system, to achieve the firing of cells in synchrony (Singer & Gray, 1995). The theory of synchronous firing binding contours is still controversial; however, there is agreement that *some* neural mechanism enhances the response of neurons that lie along a smoothly connected edge (Grossberg & Williamson, 2001; Li, 1998).

Representing Vector Fields: Perceiving Orientation and Direction

The basic problem of representing a vector can be broken down into three components: the representation of vector magnitude, the representation of orientation, and the representation of direction with respect to a particular orientation. Fig. 6.23 illustrates this point. Some techniques display one or two components, but not all three; for example, wind speed (magnitude) can be shown as a scalar field by means of color coding.

There are direct applications of the Field et al. (1993) theory of contour perception in displaying vector field data. A common technique is to create a regular grid of oriented elements, such as the one shown in Fig. 6.24(a). The theory suggests that head-to-tail alignment should make it easier to see the flow patterns (Ware, 2008). When the line segments are displaced so that smooth contours can be drawn between them, the flow pattern is much easier to see, as shown in Fig. 6.24(c).

Instead of the commonly used grid of small arrows, one obvious and effective way of representing vector fields is through the use of continuous contours; a number of

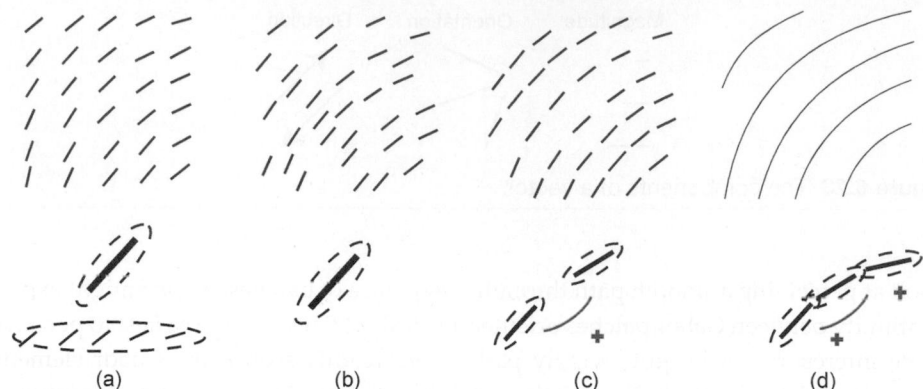

(a)   (b)   (c)   (d)

Figure 6.24 The results of Field et al. (1993) suggest that vector fields should be easier to perceive if smooth contours can be drawn through elements representing the flow. (a) A gridded pattern will weakly stimulate neurons with oriented receptive fields but also cause the perception of false contours from the rows and columns. (b) Line segments in a jittered grid will not create false contours. (c) If contour segments are aligned, mutual reinforcement will occur. (d) The strongest response will occur with continuous contours. (*Data from Field et al. (1993).*)

Figure 6.25 Streamlines can be an effective way to represent vector field or flow data. But here the direction is ambiguous and the magnitude is not shown. (*From Turk & Banks, 1996; with permission.*)

effective algorithms exist for this purpose. Fig. 6.25 shows an example from Turk and Banks (1996). This effectively illustrates the orientation of the vector field, although it is ambiguous in the sense that for a given contour there can be two directions of flow. In addition, Fig. 6.25 does not show magnitude.

Comparing 2D Flow Visualization Techniques

Laidlaw et al. (2001) carried out an experimental comparison of the six different flow visualization methods, illustrated in Fig. 6.26: (a) arrows on a regular grid; (b) arrows

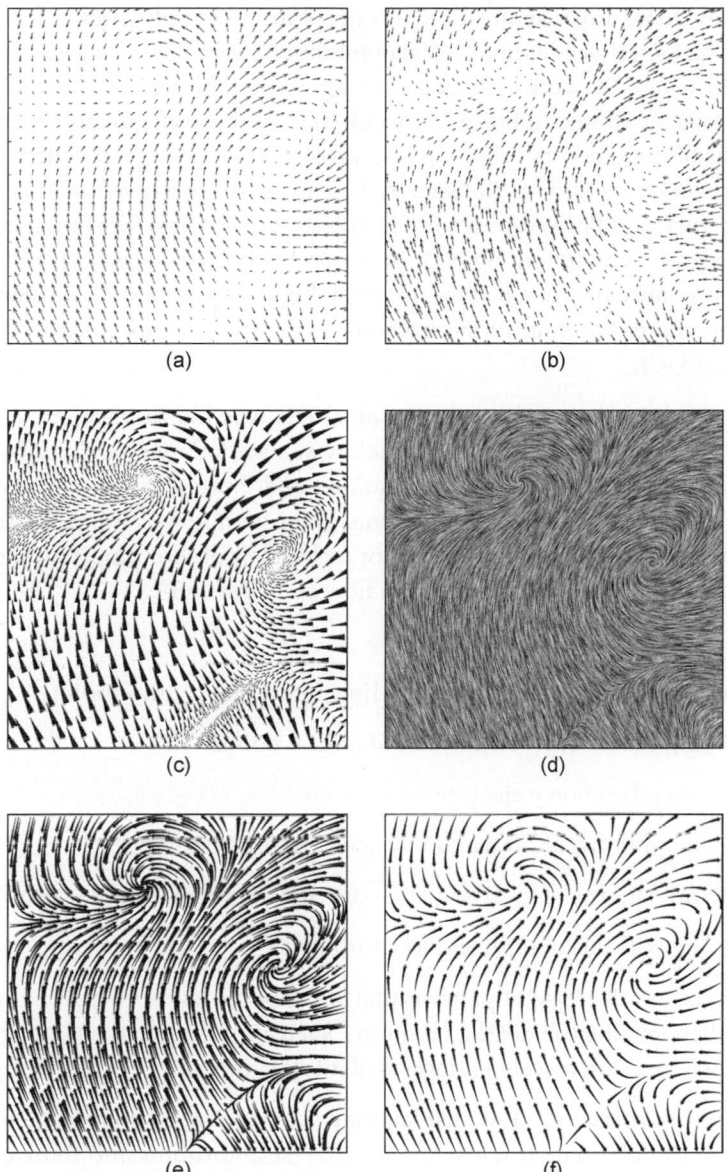

Figure 6.26 Six different flow visualization techniques (a–f) evaluated by Laidlaw et al. (2001). (*From Laidlaw et al. (2001). Reproduced with permission.*)

on a jittered grid to reduce perceptual aliasing effects; (c) triangle icons, with icon size proportional to field strength and density inversely related to icon size (Kirby, Marmanis, & Laidlaw, 1999); (d) line integral convolution (Cabral & Leedom, 1993); (e) large-head arrows along a streamline using a regular grid (Turk & Banks, 1996); and (f) large-head arrows along streamlines using a constant spacing algorithm (Turk & Banks, 1996).

In order to evaluate any visualization, it is necessary to specify a set of tasks. Laidlaw et al. (2001) had subjects identify critical points as one task. These are points in a vector or flow field where the vectors have zero magnitude. The results showed the arrow-based methods illustrated in Fig. 6.26(a) and (b) to be the least effective for identifying the locations of these points. A second task involved perceiving advection trajectories. An *advection trajectory* is the path taken by a particle dropped in a flow. The streamline methods of Turk and Banks, shown in Fig. 6.26(f), proved best for showing advection. The line integral convolution method, shown in Fig. 6.26(d), was by far the worst for advection, probably because it does not unambiguously identify direction. It is also worth pointing out that three of the methods do not show vector magnitude at all; see Fig. 6.26(d and e, f).

Although the study done by Laidlaw et al. (2001) was the first serious comparative evaluation of the effectiveness of vector field visualization methods, it is by no means exhaustive. There are alternative visualizations, and those shown have many possible variations: longer and shorter line segments, color variations, and so on. In addition, the tasks studied by Laidlaw et al. did not include all of the important visualization tasks that are likely to be carried out with flow visualizations.

Here is a more complete list:

- Judging the speed, orientation, and direction at an arbitrary point
- Identifying the location and nature of critical points
- Judging an advection trajectory
- Perceiving patterns of high and low speed (or magnitude)
- Perceiving patterns of high and low vorticity (sometimes called *curl*)
- Perceiving patterns of high and low turbulence

Both the kinds and the scale of patterns that are important will vary from one application to another; small-scale detailed patterns, such as eddies, will be important to one researcher, whereas large-scale patterns will interest another.

The problem of optimizing flow display may not be quite so complex and multifaceted as it would first seem. If we ignore the diverse algorithms and think of the problem in purely visual terms, then the various display methods illustrated in Fig. 6.26 have many characteristics in common. They all consist principally of contours oriented in the flow direction, although these contours have different characteristics in terms of length, width, and shape. The shaft of an arrow is a short contour. The line integral convolution method illustrated in Fig. 6.26(d) produces a very different-looking, blurry result; however, something similar could be computed using blurred contours. Contours that vary in shape and gray value along their lengths could be expressed with two or three parameters. The different degrees of randomness in the placement of contours could be parameterized; thus, we might consider the various 2D flow visualization methods as part of a family of related methods—different kinds

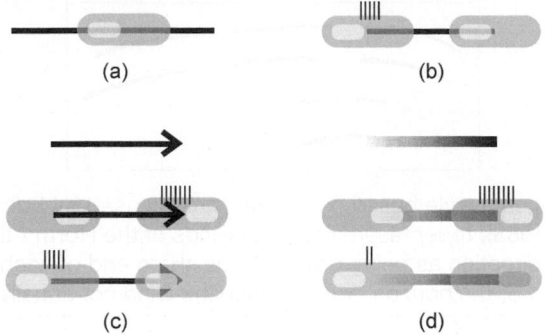

Figure 6.27 (a) An end-stopped cell (shown as a green blob) will not respond when a line passes through it. (b) It responds only when the line terminates in the cell from a particular direction. (c) This asymmetry of response will weakly differentiate the heads of arrows from their tails. (d) It will more strongly differentiate the ends of a broad line with a gradient along its length. The little bars represent neuron firing rates.

of flow-oriented contours. Considered in this way, the display problem becomes one of optimizing the various parameters that control how vector magnitude, orientation, and direction are mapped to contour in the display.

Showing Direction

In order to show direction, something must be added to a contour to give it asymmetry along its path. A neural mechanism that can account for the perception of asymmetric endings of contours is called the *end-stopped cell*. Many V1 neurons respond strongly to a contour that ends in the receptive field of the cell, but only coming from one direction (Heider, Meskanaite, and Peterhaus, 2000). The more asymmetry there is in the way contour segments terminate, the greater the asymmetry in neural response, so this can provide a mechanism for detection of flow direction (Ware, 2008). Fig. 6.27 illustrates this concept.

Conventional arrowheads are one way of providing directional asymmetry, as in Fig. 6.27(c), but the asymmetric signal is relatively weak. Arrowheads also produce visual clutter because the contours from which they are constructed are not tangential to the vector direction.

An interesting way to resolve the flow direction ambiguity is provided in a 17th-century vector field map of North Atlantic wind patterns by Edmund Halley (discussed in Tufte, 1983). Halley's elegant pen strokes, illustrated in Fig. 6.28, are shaped like long, narrow airfoils oriented to the flow, with the wind direction given by the blunt end. Halley also arranges his strokes along streamlines. These can produce a stronger asymmetric signal than an arrowhead. We verified experimentally that strokes like Halley's are unambiguously interpreted with regard to direction (Fowler & Ware, 1989).

Fowler and Ware (1989) developed a new method for creating an unambiguous sense of vector field direction that involves varying the gray level along the length of a

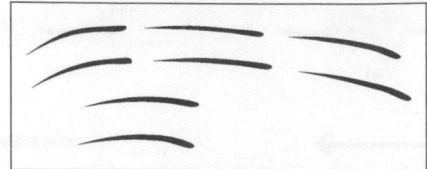

Figure 6.28 Drawing in a style based on the pen strokes used by Edmond Halley (1696), discussed in Tufte (1983), to represent the trade winds of the North Atlantic. Halley described the wind direction as being given by "the sharp end of each little stroak pointing out that part of the horizon, from whence the wind continually comes."

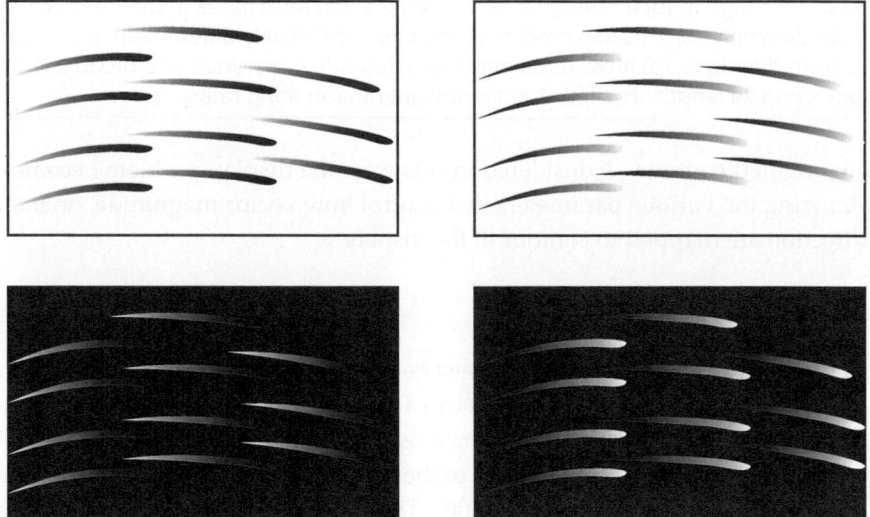

Figure 6.29 Vector direction can be unambiguously given by means of lightness change along the particle trace, relative to the background. This gives the greatest asymmetry between the different ends of each trace.

stroke. This is illustrated in Fig. 6.29. If one end of the stroke is given the background gray level, the stroke direction is perceived to be in the direction of change away from the background gray level. In our experiments, the impression of direction produced by lightness change completely dominated that given by shape. This is what the end-stopped cell theory predicts—the greater the asymmetry between the two ends of each contour, the more clearly the direction will be seen. Unfortunately, the perception of orientation may be somewhat weakened. The problem is to get both a strong directional response and a strong orientation response.

We can distill the above discussion into two guidelines.

[**G6.8**] For vector field visualizations, use contours tangential to streamlines to reveal the orientation component.

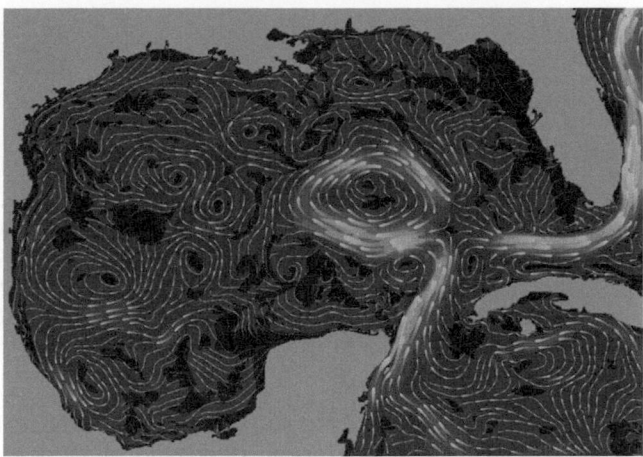

Figure 6.30 The surface currents in the Gulf of Mexico from the AMSEAS model. Head-to-tail elements are used, with each element having a more distinct head than tail. Speed is given by width, length, and background color.

> **[G6.9]** To represent flow direction in a vector field visualization, use streamlets with heads that are more distinct than tails, based on luminance contrast. A *stream-let* is a glyph that is elongated along a streamline and which induces a strong response in neurons sensitive to orientations tangential to the flow.

To reveal the magnitude component of a vector field, we can fall back on the basic principle of using something that produces a stronger neural signal to represent fast flow or a stronger field. Fig. 6.30 gives an example that follows both guidelines G6.8 and G6.9, and in addition uses longer and wider graphical elements to show regions of stronger flow (Mitchell, Ware, and Kelley, 2009).

> **[G6.10]** For vector field visualizations, use more distinct graphical elements to show greater field strength or speed. They can be wider, longer, more contrasting, or faster moving.

Showing Speed

Often speed is the most important property of a vector field and this is usually displayed as a background scalar field using the color mapping methods described in the Chapter 4. Alternatively, speed is mapped to arrow length and sometimes arrow width. This also applies to curved glyphs arranged along streamlines. In some cases the arrows themselves are colored. The tradeoffs have also been covered in the previous chapter. However, it is worth stating that using a variable such as length or width to show speed will be useful in a qualitative sense but is unlikely to result in accuracy. A carefully designed color sequence will be a better solution if accurate perception of speed is important.

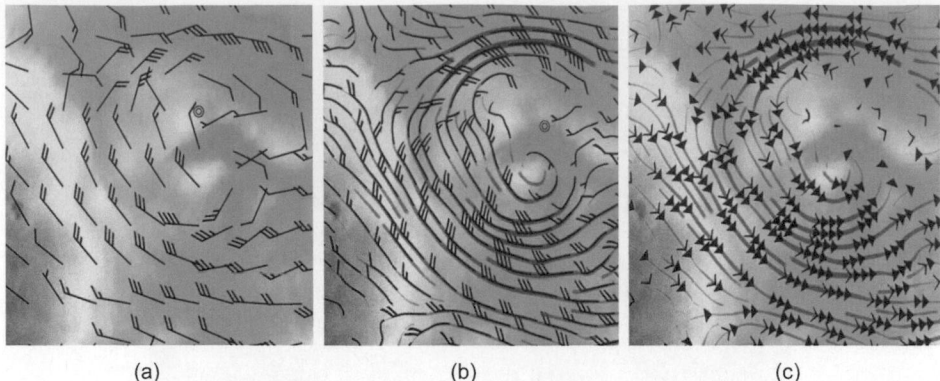

(a)   (b)   (c)

Figure 6.31 (a) The wind barb glyph is commonly used by meteorologists to show wind speed from weather model data. (b) If barbs are arranged along streamlines pattern perception is improved. (a) An even better solution is to use a symmetrical speed coding scheme along streamlines. (*From Pilar & Ware, 2013.*)

There is a method, widely used in meteorology, for showing wind speeds that merits discussion here. This is the wind barb and it was briefly mentioned in the previous chapter. Wind barbs were designed to represent point locations representing weather stations where the wind speed and direction was measured by means of an anemometer. Unfortunately, they have also come to be used in the representation of wind patterns based on computer models and for this purpose they are inadequate. Fig. 6.31 shows the traditional wind barb and better alternatives which use the same concept in the coding of speed, but which enable the wind patterns to be seen more clearly (Pilar & Ware, 2013).

Animated 2D Flow Visualization

There is increasing evidence that the best way of representing 2D flow patterns is though animated streamlets (Ware, Bolan, Miller, Rogers, & Ahrens, 2016). Animation has several advantages over static representations. It shows direction very clearly and is the best way of enabling, for example, rapid discrimination of clockwise from counterclockwise rotation. In addition if animated streamlets can be made partially transparent, they provide a good basis for the tuning of peripheral attention, taking advantage of the motion channel. This means that a viewer can choose to *see though* an animated layer, focusing attention on static background information with minimal visual interference between static elements and animated elements. Alternatively the viewer can focus attention on the animated layer. Where animation falls short is in the representation of speed; animation allows for the qualitative differentiation of fast areas from slow areas, but is poor in terms of accuracy. Solutions include color coding the streamlets (Fig. 6.32). But the color of transparent animated streamlets may be difficult to perceive against colored backgrounds.

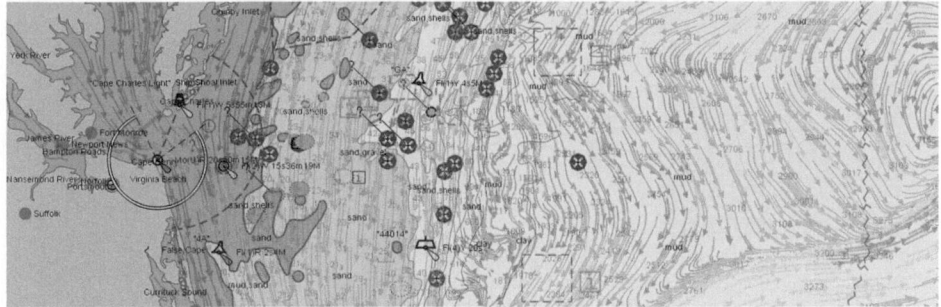

Figure 6.32 Animated streamlines are superimposed on a nautical chart display. The animation and the transparency make it possible to see through the animated layer and perceive the background chart information with minimal interference.

Texture: Theory and Data Mapping

Texture can provide a whole set of subchannels for displaying information. Like color, we can use texture as a nominal code, displaying different categories of information, or as a method for representing quantity over a spatial map, using texture to provide ordinal or interval coding.

Texture segmentation is the name given to the process whereby the brain divides the visual world into regions based on texture. The Gabor model of V1 receptive fields, introduced in Chapter 5, is a key component of most theories of what makes a texture distinctive (Bovik, Clark, and Geisler, 1990; Malik and Perona, 1990; Turner, 1986). These theories of texture segmentation rely on the same set of feature maps that were introduced in Chapter 5 to account for rapid search of individual targets, so it will come as no surprise that the rules of texture segmentation are very similar to the rules for individual target salience. Indeed, the boundary between having many glyphs and having a texture is poorly defined, and texture can be thought of as a densely populated field of small glyphs.

The Malik and Perona (1990) type of segmentation model is illustrated in Fig. 6.33. It has three main stages. In the first stage, feature maps of Gabor filters respond strongly to regions of texture where particular spatial frequencies and orientations predominate. In the next stage, the output from this early stage is low-pass filtered. This creates regions, each having the same general characteristics. At the final stage, boundaries are identified between regions with strongly dissimilar characteristics. This model predicts that we will divide visual space into regions according to the predominant spatial frequency and orientation information. A region with large orientation and size differences will be the most differentiated. Also, regions can be differentiated based on texture contrast. A low-contrast texture will be differentiated from a high-contrast texture with the same orientation and size components.

Fig. 6.34 illustrates the Gabor segmentation theory applied to the classic perceptual conundrum. Why are the Ts and Ls difficult to distinguish? And why are they easy to distinguish when the Ts are rotated? The Gabor model accurately predicts what we see.

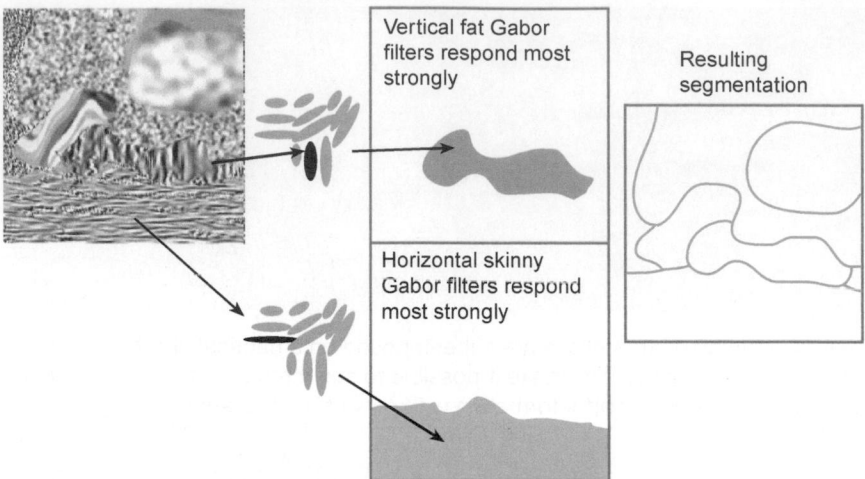

Figure 6.33 A texture segmentation model. Two-dimensional feature maps of Gabor detectors filter every part of the image for all possible orientations and sizes. Extended areas that excite similar classes of detectors form perceived regions of the image.

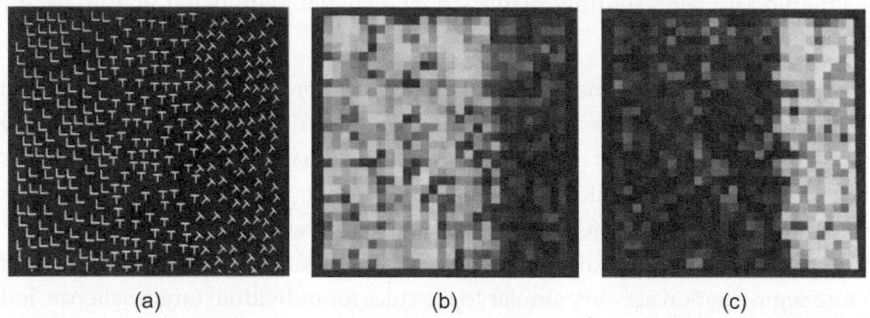

(a) (b) (c)

Figure 6.34 (a) The Ts and Ls in the left and middle are difficult to visually separate, but the region of rotated Ts on the right is easier to spot. (b) The output of a feature map consisting of vertical Gabors. (c) The output of a feature map consisting of oblique Gabors. (*From Turner (1986). Reproduced with permission.*)

Tradeoffs in Information Density: an Uncertainty Principle

Daugman (1985) showed that a fundamental uncertainty principle is related to the perception of position, orientation, and size. Given a fixed number of detectors, resolution of size can be traded for resolution of orientation or position. We have shown that same principle applies to the synthesis of texture for data display when we have a data field with a high degree of spatial variation (Ware & Knight, 1995). A gain in the ability to display orientation information precisely inevitably comes at the expense of precision in displaying information through size. If size is used as a display parameter, larger elements mean that less detail can be shown.

Fig. 6.35 illustrates this tradeoff, with a set of textures created with Gabor functions, although the same point applies to other primitives. Recall that a Gabor is the product

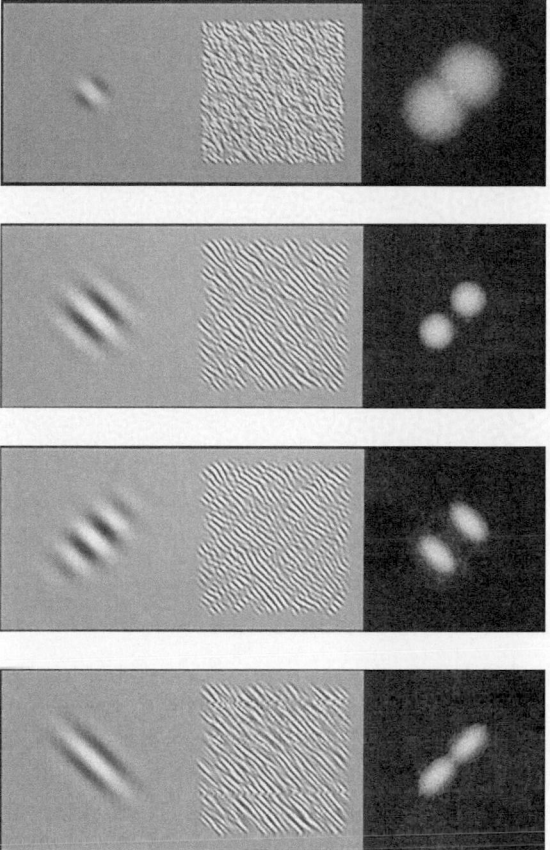

Figure 6.35 In the left-hand column are different Gabors constructed with the same sinusoidal component but with different Gaussian multipliers. The center panels show textures constructed by reducing the Gabor size by a factor of five and summing a large number using a random process. The right-hand panels show 2D Fourier transforms of the textures.

of a Gaussian envelope with a sine wave. In this figure, the textures are created by summing together a large number of randomly scattered Gabors. By changing the shape and size of the Gaussian multiplier function with the same sinusoidal grating, the tradeoff can be directly observed. When the Gaussian is large, the spatial frequency is specified quite precisely, as shown by the small image in the Fourier transform. When the Gaussian is small, position is well specified but spatial frequency is not, as shown by the large image in the Fourier transform. The lower two rows of Fig. 6.35 show how the Gaussian envelope can be stretched to specify either the spatial frequency or the orientation more precisely. The implication here is that there are fundamental limits and tradeoffs related to the ways texture can be used for information display.

[G6.11] Consider using texture to represent continuous map variables. This is likely to be most effective where the data varies smoothly and where surface shape features are substantially larger than texture element spacing.

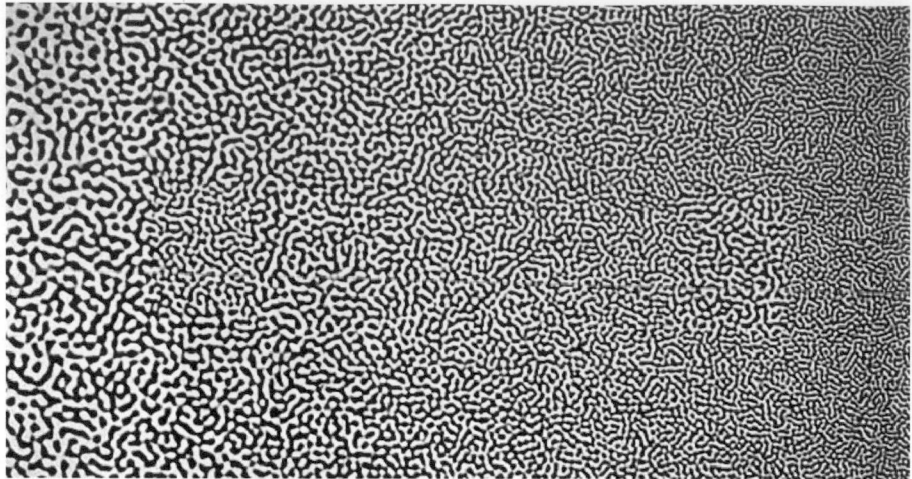

Figure 6.36 Texture contrast effect. The two patches to the left of center and the right of center have the same texture granularity, but texture contrast makes them appear different.

Primary Perceptual Dimensions of Texture

A completely general Gabor model has parameters related to orientation, spatial frequency, phase, contrast, and the size and shape of the Gaussian envelope. However, in human neural receptive fields, the Gaussian and cosine components tend to be coupled so that low-frequency cosine components have large Gaussians and high-frequency cosine components have small Gaussians (Caelli & Moraglia, 1985). This allows us to propose a simple three-parameter model for the perception and generation of texture.

Orientation O: The orientation of the cosine component

Scale S: The size—$1/(spatial frequency)$ component

Contrast C: An amplitude or contrast component

Texture Contrast Effects

Textures can appear distorted because of contrast effects, just like the luminance contrast illusions that were described in Chapter 3. A given texture on a coarsely textured background will appear finer than the same texture on a finely textured background. This phenomenon is illustrated in Fig. 6.36. The effect is predicted by higher order inhibitory connections. It will cause errors in reading data mapped to texture element size. In addition, texture orientation can cause contrast illusions in orientation, and this, too, may cause misperception of data (see Fig. 6.37).

Other Dimensions of Visual Texture

Although there is considerable evidence to suggest that orientation, size, and contrast are the three dominant dimensions of visual texture, it is clear that the world of

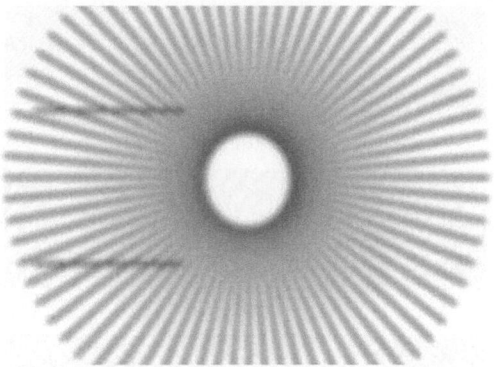

Figure 6.37 The radial texture causes the two parallel lines to the left to appear tilted.

texture is much richer than this. The dimensionality of visual texture is very high, as a visual examination of the world around us attests. Think of the textures of wood, brick, stone, fur, leather, and other natural materials. One of the important additional texture dimensions is certainly randomness (Liu & Picard, 1994). Textures that are regular have a very different quality from random ones.

Nominal Texture Codes

The most common use of texture in information display is as a nominal coding device. Geologists, for example, commonly use texture, in addition to color, in order to differentiate many different types of rock and soil. The orientation tuning of V1 neurons indicates that glyph element orientations should be separated by at least 30 degrees for a texture field of glyphs to be distinct from an adjacent texture field (Blake & Holopigan, 1985), and, because oriented elements will be confused with identical elements rotated through 180 degrees, fewer than six orientations can be rapidly distinguished.

Fig. 6.38 shows examples of textures actually constructed using Gabor functions, randomly placed. In Fig. 6.38(a), only orientation is changed among different regions of the display, and although the word TEXTURE appears distinct from its background, it is weak. The difference appears much stronger when both the spatial frequency and the orientation differ between the figure and the background, as in Fig. 6.38(b). The third way that textures can be made easy to distinguish is by changing the contrast, as illustrated in Fig. 6.38(c).

Of course, textures can be constructed in much more conventional ways, using stripes and dots, like the examples shown in Fig. 6.39, but, still, the main key to rapid segmentation will be the spatial frequency components. This figure shows the 2D Fourier transforms of the images. The theory we have been discussing suggests that the more displayed information differs in spatial frequency and in orientation, the more distinct that information will be. The psychophysical evidence suggests that for textured regions to be visually distinct the dominant spatial frequencies should differ by at least a factor of 3, and the dominant orientations should differ by more than 30 degrees, all other factors (such as color) being equal.

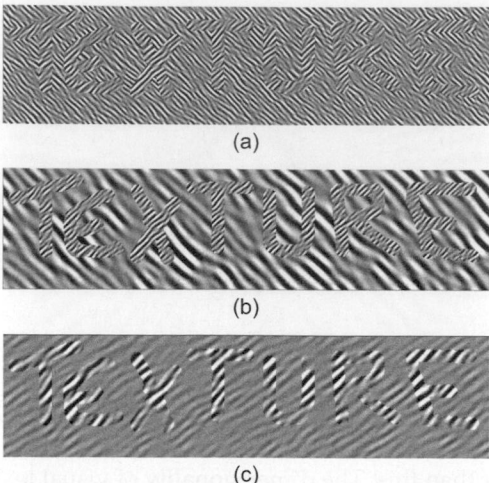

(a)

(b)

(c)

Figure 6.38 The word TEXTURE is legible only because of texture differences between the letters and the background; overall luminance is held constant. (a) Only texture orientation defines the letters. (b) Orientation and size differ. (c) Texture contrast differs.

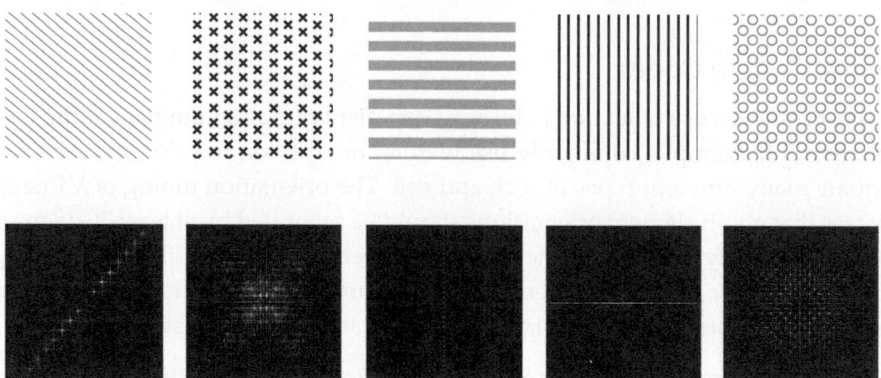

Figure 6.39 (Top row) A set of highly distinguishable textured squares, each of which differs from the others in terms of multiple spatial frequency characteristics. (Bottom row) The 2D Fourier transforms of the same textures.

> **[G6.12]** In order to make a set of nominal coding textures distinctive, make them differ as much as possible in terms of dominant spatial frequency and orientation components. As a secondary factor, make texture elements vary in the randomness of their spacing.

The simple spatial frequency model of texture discrimination suggests that the number of textures that can be rapidly distinguished will be in the range of 12–24. The lower number is what we get from the product of three sizes and four orientations. When other factors, such as randomness, are taken into account, the number can be significantly larger. When we consider that in Chapter 4 we concluded that the

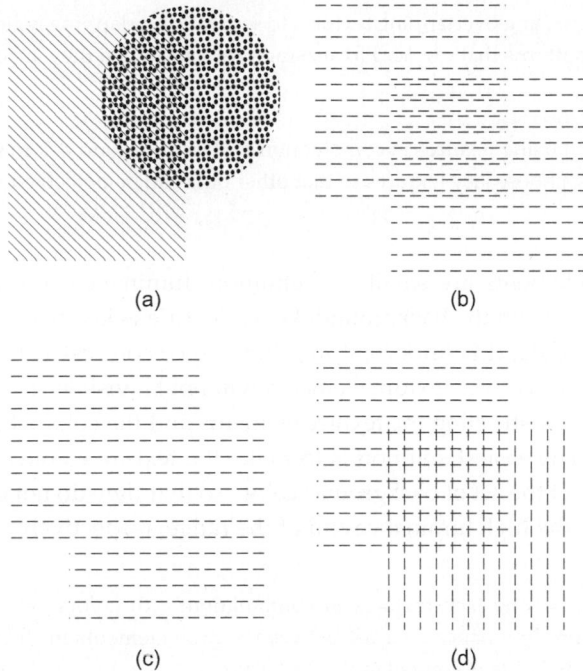

(a)   (b)

(c)   (d)

Figure 6.40 Watanabe and Cavanaugh (1996) called the texture equivalency of transparency *laciness*. This figure is based on their work.

number of rapidly distinctive color codes is fewer than 12, the use of texture clearly adds greatly to the possibility of distinctive nominal codes for areas. In addition, we can consider texture to provide a distinct channel from color, and this means that overlapping regions can be coded, as illustrated in Fig. 6.16.

Laciness

A way to represent layers of data is to show each layer as a see-through texture or screen pattern (Fig. 6.40). Watanabe and Cavanaugh (1996) explored the conditions under which people perceive two distinct overlapping layers, as opposed to a single fused composite texture. They called the effect *laciness*. In Fig. 6.40(a) and (b), two different overlapping shapes are clearly seen, but in Fig. 6.40(c), only a single textured patch is perceived. In Fig. 6.40(d), the percept is bistable. Sometimes it looks like two overlapping squares containing patterns of "—" elements, and sometimes a central square containing a pattern of "+" elements seems to stand out as a distinct region.

In general, when we present layered data, we can expect the basic rules of perceptual interference, discussed in Chapter 5, to apply. Similar patterns interfere with one another. The problem with Fig. 6.40(c) is one of aliasing. Graphical patterns that are similar in terms of color, spatial frequency, motion, and so on tend to interfere more (and fuse more) with one another than do those with dissimilar components.

[G6.13] When using overlapping textures to separate overlapping regions in a display, avoid patterns that can lead to aliasing problems when they are combined.

[G6.14] When using textures in combination with background colors for overlapping regions, choose lacy textures so that other data can be perceived through the gaps.

Because texture elements are small by definition, luminance contrast is needed to make them distinct from the background. When texture is layered transparently over other color-coded data, it is important that luminance contrast with the background coding exists; otherwise, the texture elements will not be visible. This constrains both the colors used in constructing the texture elements and the colors that can be used in the background. The easiest solution is to make the texture elements either black or white and to restrict the set of background colors so that they do not occupy either the low luminance or the high luminance end of the range, respectively.

[G6.15] When using lacy textures in combination with colors for overlapping regions, ensure luminance contrast between texture elements in the foreground and color-coded data presented in the background.

Using Textures for Univariate and Multivariate Map Displays

Texture can be used to display continuous scalar map information, such as temperature or pressure. The most common ways of doing this are to map a scalar variable to texture element size, spacing, or orientation. Fig. 6.41 illustrates a simple texture variation using texture element size. No more than three or four steps can be reliably discriminated with such a scheme because texture elements must typically be quite

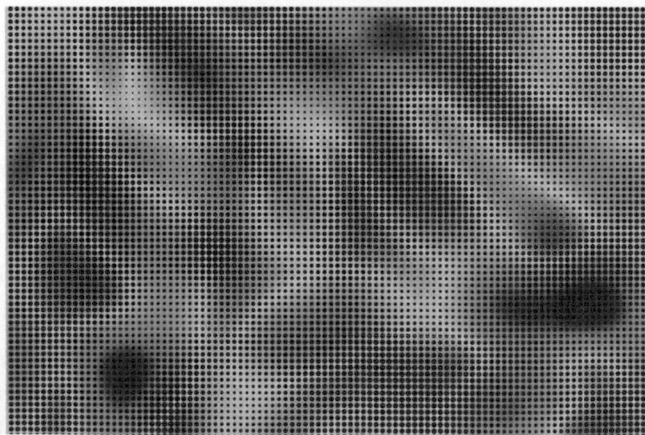

Figure 6.41 A bivariate map. One of the variables is mapped to a color sequence. The other is mapped to texture element size.

small to maintain a reasonable information density, and this limits spatial channel bandwidth. Also, simultaneous contrast acting on the perceived size or orientation of texture elements can cause errors of judgment.

> **[G6.16]** Use simple texture parameters, such as element size or element density, only when fewer than five ordinal steps must be reliably distinguished.

What are the prospects for encoding more than one scalar value using texture? Weigle et al. (2000) developed a technique called *oriented sliver textures* specifically designed to take advantage of the parallel processing of orientation information. Each variable in a multivariate map was mapped to a 2D array of slivers where all the slivers had the same orientation. Differently oriented 2D sliver arrays were produced for each variable. The values of each scalar map were shown by controlling the amount of contrast between the sliver and the background. Combining all of the sliver fields produced the visualization illustrated in Fig. 6.42. The right-hand part of this figure shows the combination of the eight variables illustrated in the thumbnail patterns shown on the left. Weigle et al. conducted a study showing that if slivers were oriented at least 15 degrees from surrounding regions they stood out clearly; however, the experiment was only carried out with a single sliver at each location (unlike in Fig. 6.42), making the task easier. To judge the effectiveness of the sliver plot for yourself, try looking for each of the thumbnail patterns in the larger combined plot. The fact that many of the patterns cannot easily be seen strongly suggests that the technique is not effective for so many variables. Also, tuning of orientation-sensitive cells suggests that slivers should be at least 30 degrees apart to be rapidly readable.

Another attempt to map multiple variables to texture is illustrated in Fig. 6.43. In addition to glyph color, which shows temperature, texture element orientation shows the orientation and direction of the wind. Wind speed is shown using glyph area coverage. Atmospheric pressure is shown in the number of elements per unit area. This example is based on a design by Healey, Kocherlakota, Rao, Mehta, and St. Amant (2008). The reader is invited to try to see how many pressure levels are displayed (there are three) and where the highest winds are. Clearly, this is not an adequate solution for displaying forecast temperatures, pressures within a few millibars, or wind speeds within a few knots.

A third example of high-dimensional data display comes from Laidlaw and his collaborators (Laidlaw et al., 1998) (Fig. 6.44). It was created using a very different design strategy. Rather than attempting to create a simple general technique (like slivers), the data display mapping was handcrafted in a collaboration between the scientist and the designer. Fig. 6.44 shows a cross-section of a mouse spinal column. The data has seven values at each location in the image. The image is built up in layers comprised of image intensity; sampling rate, which determines the grid; elliptical shapes, which show the in-plane component of principal diffusion and anisotropy; and texture on the ellipses, which shows absolute diffusion rate. Without specific knowledge of mouse physiology it is impossible to judge the success of this example. Nevertheless, it provides a

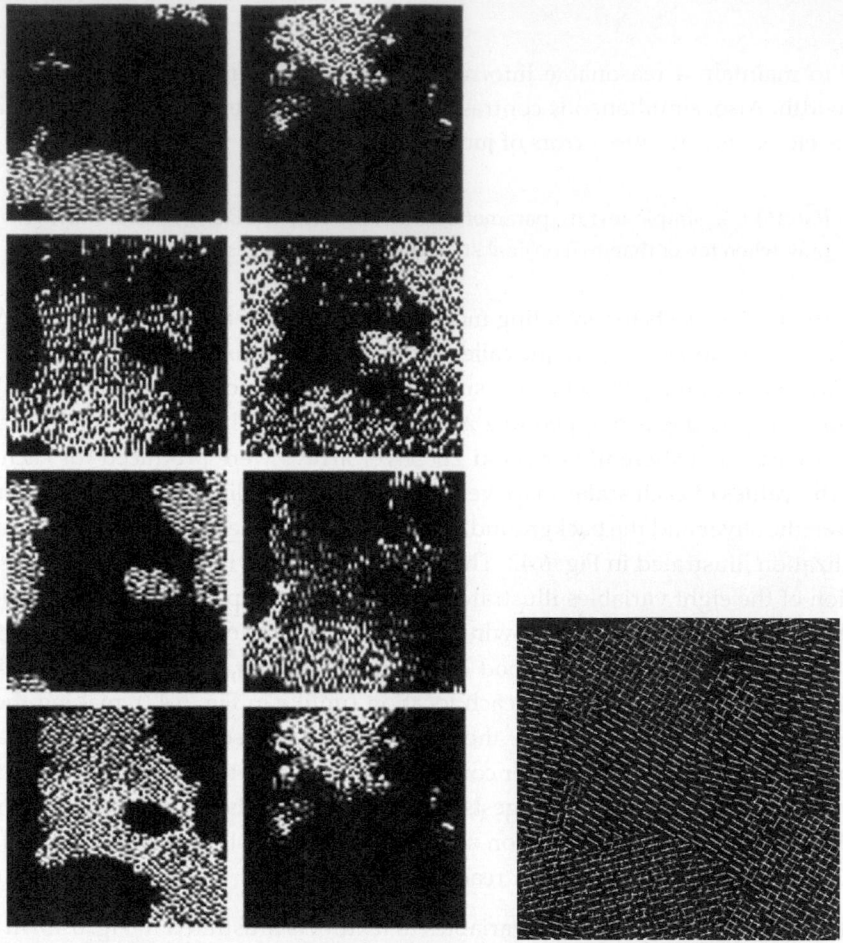

Figure 6.42 The sliver plot of Weigle et al. (2000). Each of the variables shown in the thumbnail patterns in the left part of the figure is mapped to a differently oriented sliver pattern in the combined plot. (*Courtesy of Chris Weigle.*)

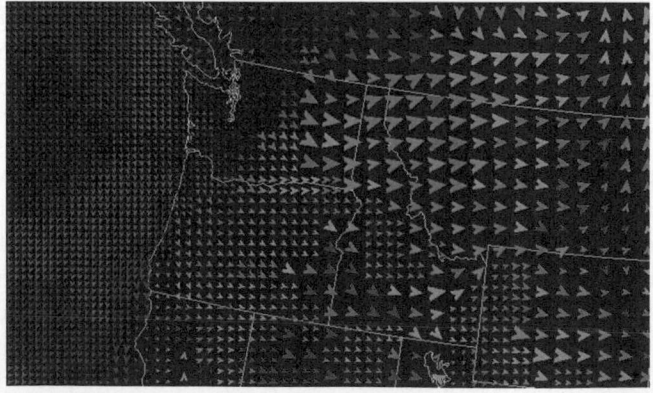

Figure 6.43 Weather patterns over the northwest continental United States. Wind orientation and direction are mapped to glyph rotation angle. Wind speed is mapped to glyph area coverage. Atmospheric pressure is mapped to density. Temperature is mapped to color.

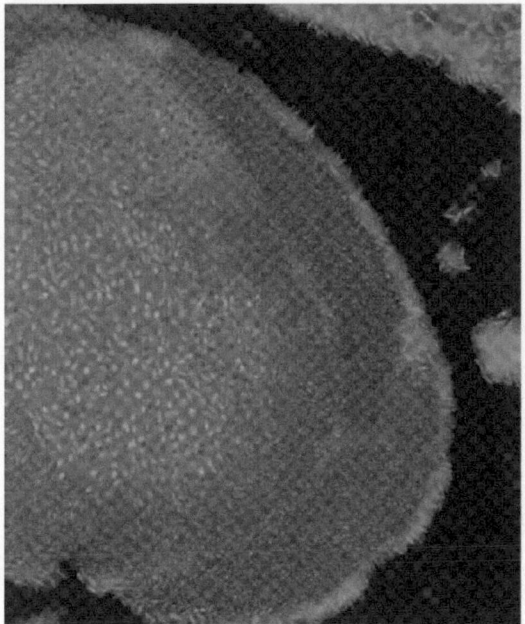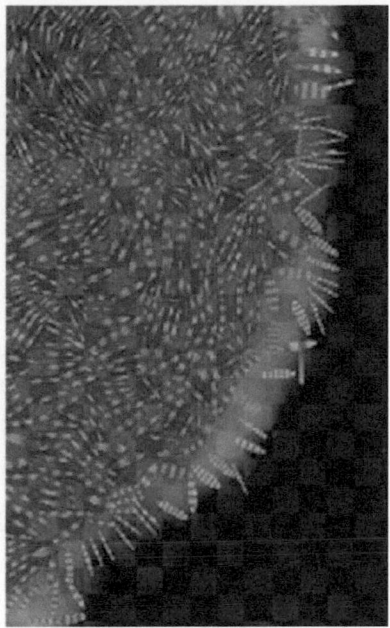

Figure 6.44 Cross-section of a mouse spinal column. Seven variables are shown at each location. Part of the image is enlarged on the right. See text for description. (*Courtesy of David Laidlaw.*)

vivid commentary on the tradeoffs involved in trying to display high-dimensional multivariate maps. In this figure, for example, each of the elliptical glyphs is textured to display an additional variable; however, the texture striations are at right angles to the ellipse major axes, and this camouflages the glyphs, making their orientation more difficult to see. The use of texture will inevitably tend to camouflage glyph shape; if the textures are oriented, the problem will be worse. In general, the more similar the spatial frequencies of the different pattern components, the more likely they are to disrupt one another visually.

None of the preceding three examples (Figs. 6.41–6.44) reveals much detail. There is a good reason for this; we only have one luminance channel, and luminance variation is the only way of displaying detailed information. If we choose to use texture (or any kind of glyph field), we inevitably sacrifice the ability to show detail, because to be clear each glyph element must be displayed using luminance contrast. Larger glyphs mean that less detail can be shown.

Texture is most likely to be valuable if two scalar variables are to be displayed. In this case, we can take advantage of the fact that color and texture provide reasonably separable channels. Although, to be visible, texture necessarily consumes at least some luminance channel bandwidth. For the two-variable problem, mapping one variable to texture and another to a carefully designed color sequence can provide a reliable solution.

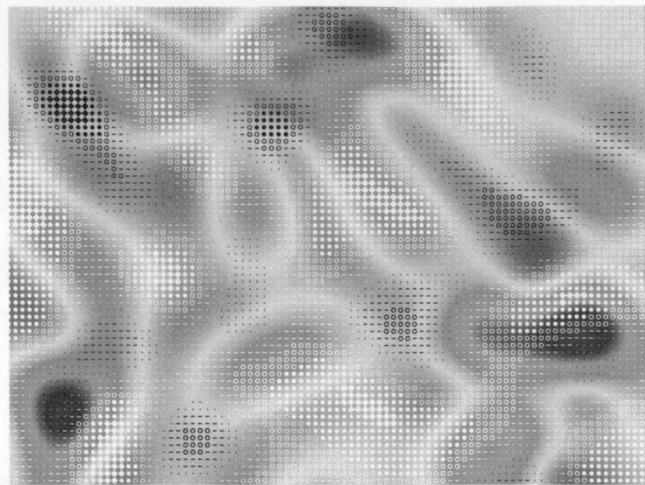

Figure 6.45 A carefully designed 10-step sequence of textures shows one variable, and a color sequence shows a second.

[G6.17] To display a bivariate scalar field, consider mapping one variable to color and a second variable to variations in texture.

Quantitative Texture Sequences

As we have observed, simultaneous contrast causes problems when using textures just as it does with color. Because the eye judges relative sizes and other properties, large errors can result and only a few steps of absolute resolution are available. But, for many visualization problems, people wish to be able to read quantitative values from a map in addition to seeing overall patterns. The displays of atmospheric pressure and temperature are two examples. Bertin (1983) suggested using a series of textures to show quantitative values. I further developed the idea of using a carefully calibrated sequence of texture elements, each of which is monotonically lighter or darker than the previous, in order to show both quantity and form in a data set (Ware, 2009). Fig. 6.45 shows an example of a 10-step sequence of texture overlaid on a map of color variation. Fig. 6.46 shows a more complex example that has 14 texture steps visible, showing atmospheric pressure. This example actually uses three different perceptual channels. Motion is used for wind speed and direction, quantitative texture sequences are used for pressure, and a color sequence is used for temperature.

[G6.18] To design textures so that quantitative values can be reliably judged, use a sequence of textures that are both visually ordered (for example, by element size or density) and designed so that each member of the sequence is distinct from the previous one in some low-level property.

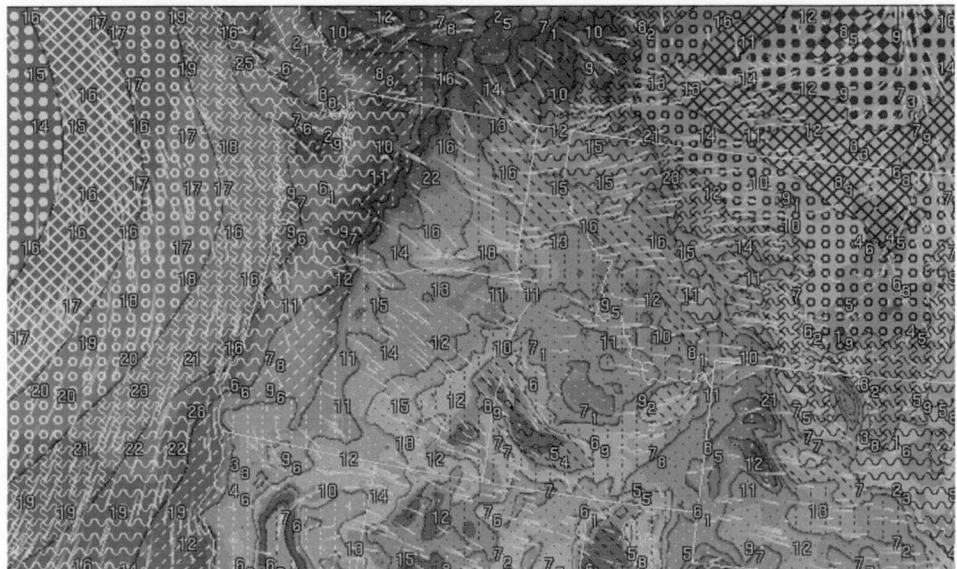

Figure 6.46 In this weather map, temperature is mapped to color. Pressure is mapped to a sequence of 14 textures. Wind orientation and direction are given using *animated* streaklets, and wind speed is displayed using the animation speed as well as numbers.

Perception of Transparency with Uniform Colors

In many visualization problems, it is desirable to present data in a layered form. This is especially common in geographic information systems (GISs). So that the contents of different layers are simultaneously visible, a useful technique is to present one layer of data transparently over another; however, there are many perceptual pitfalls in doing this. The contents of the different layers will always interfere with each other to some extent, and sometimes the two layers will fuse perceptually so that it is impossible to determine to which layer a given object belongs.

In simple displays, as in Fig. 6.47(a), the two main determinants of perceived transparency are good continuity (Beck & Ivry, 1988) and the ratio of colors or gray values in the different pattern elements. A reasonably robust rule for transparency to be perceived is $x\,y < z$ or $x > y > z$ or $y < z < w$ or $y > z > w$, where x, y, z, and w refer to gray values arranged in the pattern shown in Fig. 6.47(b) (Masin, 1997). Readers who are interested in perceptual rules of transparency should consult Metelli (1974).

One possible application of transparency in user interfaces is to make pop-up menus transparent so that they do not interfere with information located behind them. Harrison and Vincente (1996) investigated the interference between background patterns and foreground transparent menus. They found that it took longer to read from the menu with text or wireframe drawings in the background than with continuously shaded images in the background. This is exactly what would be expected from an interference model. Because a continuously shaded image lacks the high spatial frequency detail of a wireframe image or text, there will be less interference between the two.

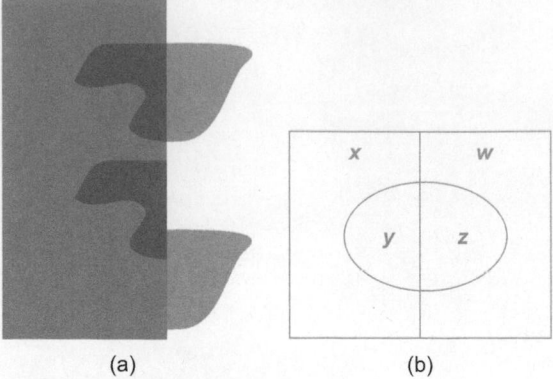

(a)   (b)

Figure 6.47 In (a) transparency depends both on the color relationships and on good continuity. (b) See text for transparency rules.

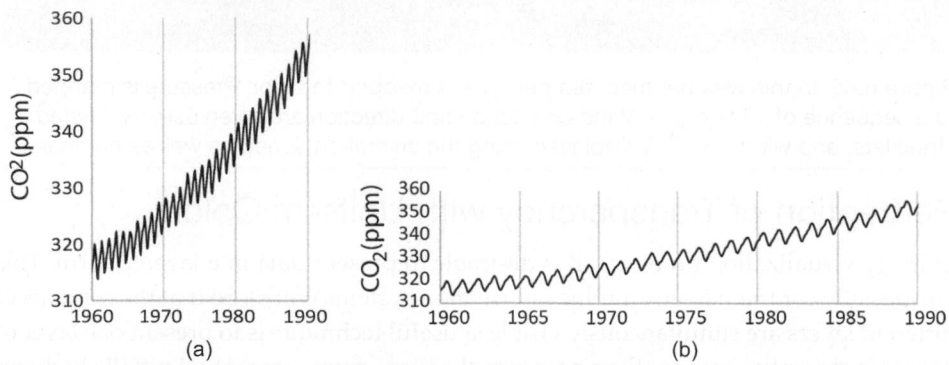

(a)   (b)

Figure 6.48 The optimal slope for feature discrimination in a line plot is 45 degree. By adjusting the plot aspect ratio different features can be made clearer. This is illustrated here with a plot of the increase of CO2 over time (the Keeling curve). (a) The shape of the overall trend is emphasized. (b) The shape of the annual rise and fall is emphasized. This example is adapted from data in Heer and Agrawala (2006).

Perceiving Patterns in Continuous Line Charts

One of the most common types of visualizations is a plot wherein a continuous line is used to represent the variation of one continuous variable with respect to another. Probable the most common example is the time-series plot with time shown progressing from left to right on the x-axis and where a wiggly line shows how a particular variable changes with respect to time. The method is used to show stock market trends, mathematical functions, and engineering performance data. The example shown in Fig. 6.48 is the Keeling curve; it shows the amount of atmospheric carbon dioxide measured at the summit of Mount Moana Loa plotted against time. This example is adapted from Heer and Agrawala (2006). Previously, Cleaveland (1993) had noted that an average line orientation of 45 degree will maximize slope discrimination in a

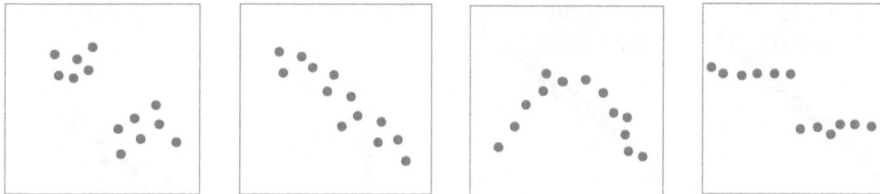

Figure 6.49 The scatterplot is an essential tool when looking for pattern in discrete data having two quantitative attributes.

continuous line plot. Heer and Agrawala used the Keeling data to illustrate this, pointing out that in 6.48a the shape of the overall trend is clearer, whereas in 6.48b the shape the annual variation is clearer. For example, the infection point, just prior to 1970 is clear in 6.48a whereas in 6.48b it is easy to see that CO_2 declines faster than it rises in the annual cycle.

Perceiving Patterns in Multidimensional Discrete Data

One of the most interesting but difficult challenges for data visualization is to support the exploratory data analysis of discrete multidimensional data. Visualization can be a powerful tool in data mining, in which the goal is often a kind of general search for relationships and data trends. For example, marketing experts often collect large amounts of data about individuals in potential target populations. The variables that are collected might include age, income, educational level, employment category, tendency to purchase chocolate, and so on. Each of the measured variables can be thought of as a data dimension. If the marketer can identify clusters of values in this multi-dimensional data set related to the likelihood of purchasing different products, this can result in better targeted, more effective advertising. The task of finding particular market segments is one of finding distinct clusters in the multidimensional space that is formed by many variables.

Sometimes a scientist or a data analyst approaches data with no particular theory to test. The goal is to explore the data for meaningful and useful information in masses of mostly meaningless numbers. Plotting techniques have long been tools of the data explorer. In essence, the process is to plot the data, look for a pattern, and interpret the findings, so the critical step in the discovery process is an act of perception.

The four scatterplots in Fig. 6.49 illustrate very different kinds of data relationships. In the first, there are two distinct clusters, perhaps suggesting distinct subpopulations of biological organisms. In the second, there is a clear negative linear relationship between two measured variables. In the third, there is a curvilinear, inverted U-shaped relationship. In the fourth, there is an abrupt discontinuity. Each of these patterns will lead to a very different hypothesis about underlying causal relationships between the variables. If any of the relationships were previously unknown, the researcher would be rewarded with a discovery. It would be very difficult to see the patterns by scrutinizing

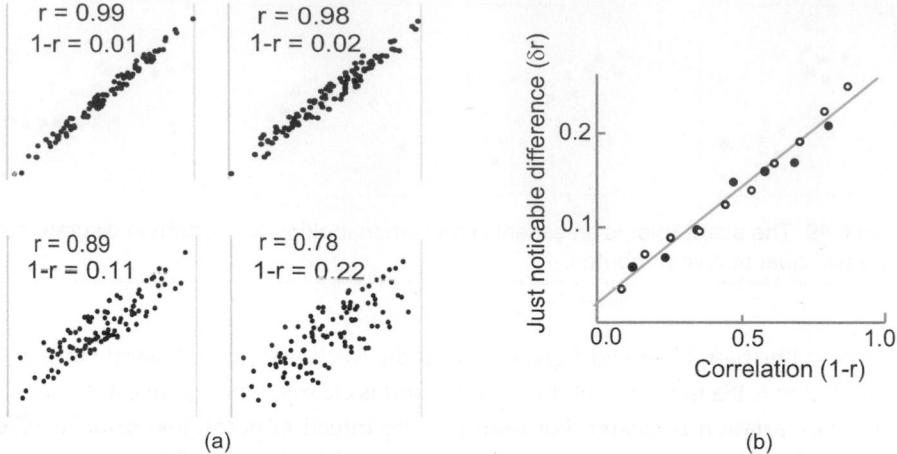

Figure 6.50 (a) Two pairs of scatterplots are compared. In the top pair the r values differ by 0.01. In the lower pair they differ by 10 times as much. Yet to a first approximation our ability to perceive these differences is roughly the same. (b) Data from a study by Rensink and Baldridge is redrawn to illustrate the point that we tend to perceive correlations in terms of 1-r. This corresponds to the amount of variation *not accounted for* by a straight-line fit.

tables of numbers. The power of a visualization method comes from enabling people to see patterns in noisy data or, in other words, letting them see meaningful signals in noise.

Of course, there is an infinite variety of different meaningful patterns that may be found in data, and what is a signal in one context may be noise in another. But there are two particular kinds of patterns that are very commonly of interest: *correlations* and *clusters*. Examples are shown in the first two boxes of Fig. 6.49.

Correlations are usually expressed numerically in terms of a metric called r^2. This is the amount of data (technically the variance) accounted for by a straight-line fit through the cloud of data points in a linear regression. However work by Rensink and Baldridge (2010) shows that what we perceive is much more closely related the amount of correlation *not accounted for* by a straight line. Fig. 6.50 is adapted from Rensink and Baldridge (2010 Fig. 5) and it shows that to first approximation, the threshold for perceiving a difference between two correlations is related to 1-r. The interested reader should see their paper for a more exact formulation.

Conventional scatterplots are probably the best solution when each data point has two attributes. The problem gets more difficult when more than two numerical attributes are involved. For four attributes, it is common to add glyph size and color (Fig. 6.51). Limoges, Ware, and Knight (1989) investigated glyph size, gray value, and the *phase* of oscillatory motion as a way of displaying correlations and found that subjects were most sensitive to phase differences. Nevertheless, the use of color and/or point size is well established as a method for representing three or four dimensional discrete data in scatterplots.

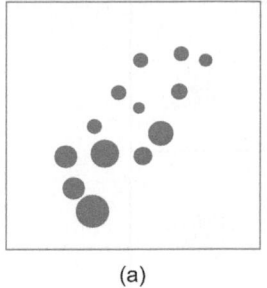 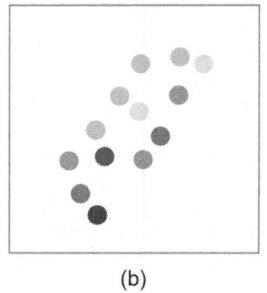 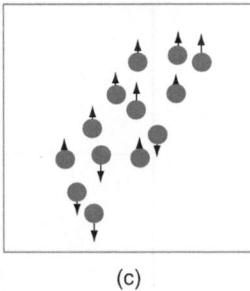

(a)   (b)   (c)

Figure 6.51 Three-dimensional discrete data. The third dimension is given by (a) point size, (b) gray value, and (c) phase of oscillatory point motion.

What do we do about data with more than three dimensions? One solution for higher dimensional discrete data display is the *scatterplot matrix* (Chambers, Cleveland, Kleiner, & Tukey, 1983). A scatterplot matrix is a set of 2D scatterplots that shows all pairwise combinations of variables. An example, from Li, Martens, and van Wijk (2010), is shown in Fig. 6.52. Although a scatterplot matrix can often be useful, it suffers from a disadvantage in that it is very difficult to see higher dimensional data patterns that can be understood only when three or more data dimensions are simultaneously taken into account.

A second solution is the *parallel coordinates* plot (Inselberg & Dimsdale, 1990). In a parallel coordinates plot, each attribute dimension is represented by a vertical line, as shown in Fig. 6.52(b) and Fig. 6.53. The data points become lines that connect the various attribute values.

One of the problems with the parallel coordinates plot is that the patterns that are seen depend on the way the axes are ordered with respect to one another. For this reason, most implementations of parallel coordinates allow the axes to be reordered.

In a study of subjects' ability to see clusters in multidimensional discrete data using parallel coordinate's plots, Holten and van Wijk (2010) found that a version with embedded scatterplots was the clear winner, both in terms of correctness and speed of response. This leads one to suspect that a scatterplot matrix would have performed best without the parallel coordinates.

Even when axis reordering is supported in parallel coordinates, studies show that scatterplots are much better at showing correlations (Li et al., 2010; Dimara et al., 2017).

It is important to recognize, though, that parallel coordinates plots are intended to be used with an interactive technique called *brushing*. With brushing, a range on one of the axes is selected, causing the polylines passing through that range to become highlighted in some way. This makes the method become part of an exploratory process, where the instantaneous view may be less important; however, brushing can also be applied to a scatterplot matrix so this is not a unique advantage. Fig. 6.54 illustrates selective brushing with both parallel coordinates and a scatterplot matrix (Fig. 2 from Dimara et al., 2017).

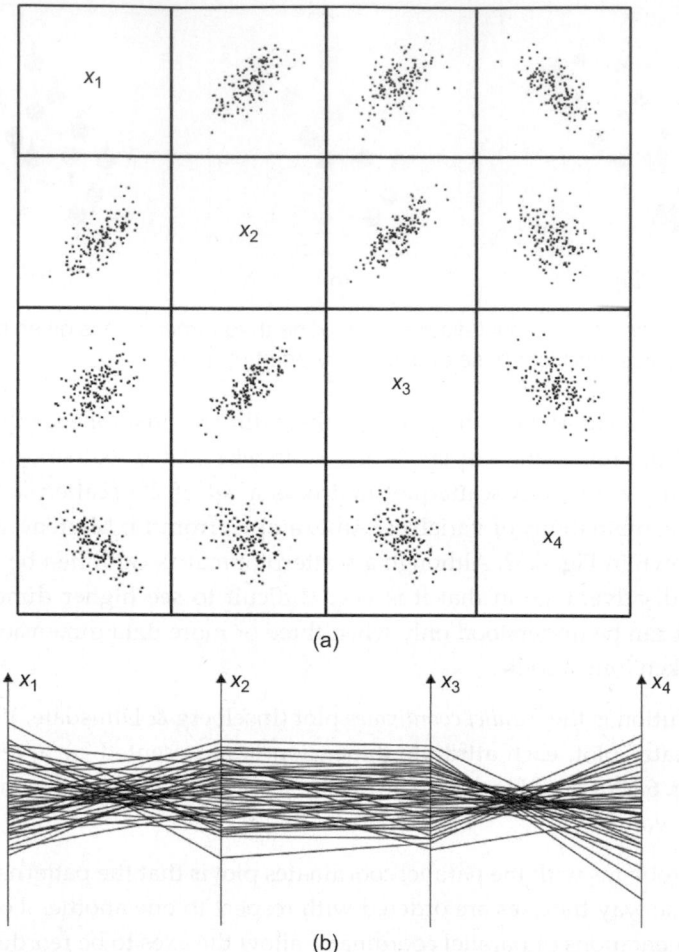

(a)

(b)

Figure 6.52 (a) Four-dimensional discrete data displayed using a scatterplot matrix (b) The same data displayed using a parallel coordinates plot. (*From Li et al. (2010). Reproduced with permission.*)

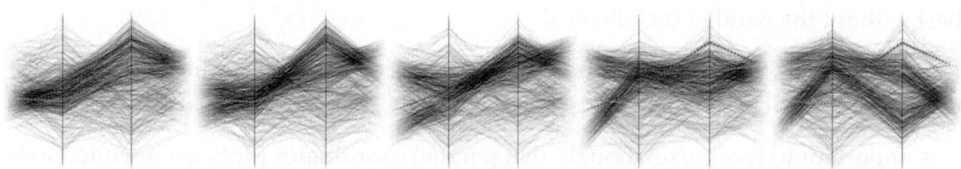

Figure 6.53 Parallel coordinates plot with permuted axes. (*From Holten and van Wijk (2010). Reproduced with permission.*)

[G6.19] To display discrete data with many dimension, consider using a scatterplot matrix.

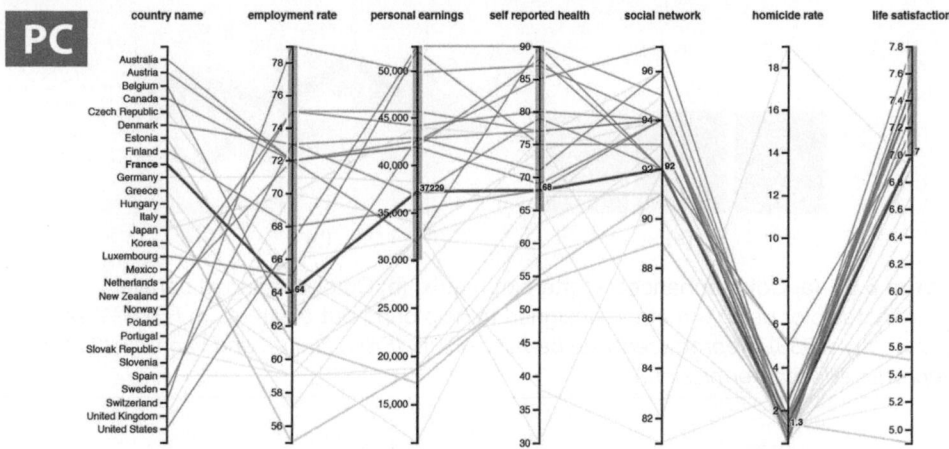

Figure 6.54 Examples of a problem represented in (a) parallel coordinates and (b) a matrix of pairwise scatterplots. A subset of the data points has been highlighted by means of brushing in both cases. (*From Dimara et al. 2017. Reproduced with permission.*)

Most studies have only compared parallel tasks for perception of basic patterns but the whole point of these visualization techniques is to support decision-making where many variables are involved. In a study of a decision-making task where participants had to choose between vacation packages on the basis of such variables as hotel quality, price, and historic interest, Dimara et al., (2017) found no statistically significant differences between parallel coordinates and scatterplot matrices, but there were more negative comments complaining that parallel coordinates were difficult to understand. Also, a third technique, based on interactive table views turned out to be the overall winner on the complex task, although not for simpler tasks such as perception of correlations. We will discuss table-based approaches in Chapter 10.

Color mapping can be used to extend the number of displayable data dimensions to five in a single scatterplot, as shown in Fig. 6.55(a). Ware and Beatty (1988) developed a simple scheme for doing this. The technique is to create a scatterplot in which each point is a colored patch rather than a black point on a white background. Up to five data variables can be mapped and displayed as follows:

Variable 1 → x-axis position

Variable 2 → y-axis position

Variable 3 → amount of red

Variable 4 → amount of green

Variable 5 → amount of blue

In an evaluation of cluster perception in this kind of display, Ware and Beatty (1988) concluded that color display dimensions could be as effective as spatial

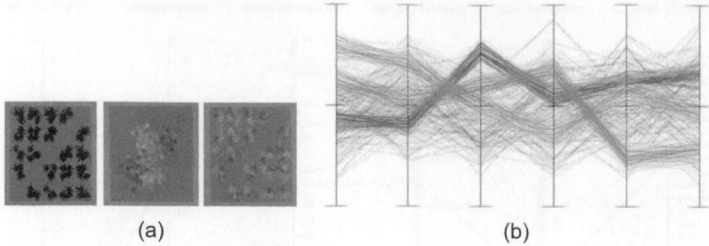

Figure 6.55 (a) Color-enhanced scatterplot matrix. (b) Color-enhanced parallel coordinates plot using a method designed to help bring out clusters. (a) *From Ware and Beatty (1988). Reproduced with permission.* (b) *(From Holten and van Wijk (2010). Reproduced with permission.)*

dimensions in allowing the visual system to perceive clusters. For this task, at least, the technique produced an effective five-dimensional window into the data space, but there are drawbacks to this kind of color-mapped scatterplot. Although identifying clusters and other patterns can be easy, interpreting them can be difficult. A cluster may appear greenish because it is low on the red variable or high on the green variable. It can be difficult to distinguish the two. The use of color can help us to identify the presence of multidimensional clusters and trends, but once the presence of these trends has been determined, other methods are needed to analyze them.

Color can also be used to enhance parallel coordinates plots as well as scatterplots. Fig. 6.55(b) shows an example from Holten and van Wijk, using a coloring method designed specifically to enhance the perception of clusters.

Overall, the empirical results suggest that patterns are more readily perceived using a scatterplot matrix than using parallel coordinates.

> **[G6.20]** To display discrete data with more than four dimensions, consider using a color-enhanced scatterplot matrix in combination with brushing.

Pattern Perception and Deep Learning

The human object pattern processing chain is illustrated in Fig. 6.56a. At each level of processing, more complex patterns are responded to over larger areas of visual space. Also, the further up the chain we go, the more the task demands dictate what is pulled out via the mechanisms of attention.

In human infants low-level brain regions, such as V1 and V2, mature before higher level regions and successively more complex stages mature in sequence. Mimicking this bottom-up process was one of the key insights that lead to the revolutionary advance in artificial intelligence known as deep learning (LeCun et al., 2015). Deep learning has been taking the AI world by storm, and because of it computers are becoming better than humans at all kinds of pattern recognition tasks. Before this insight was

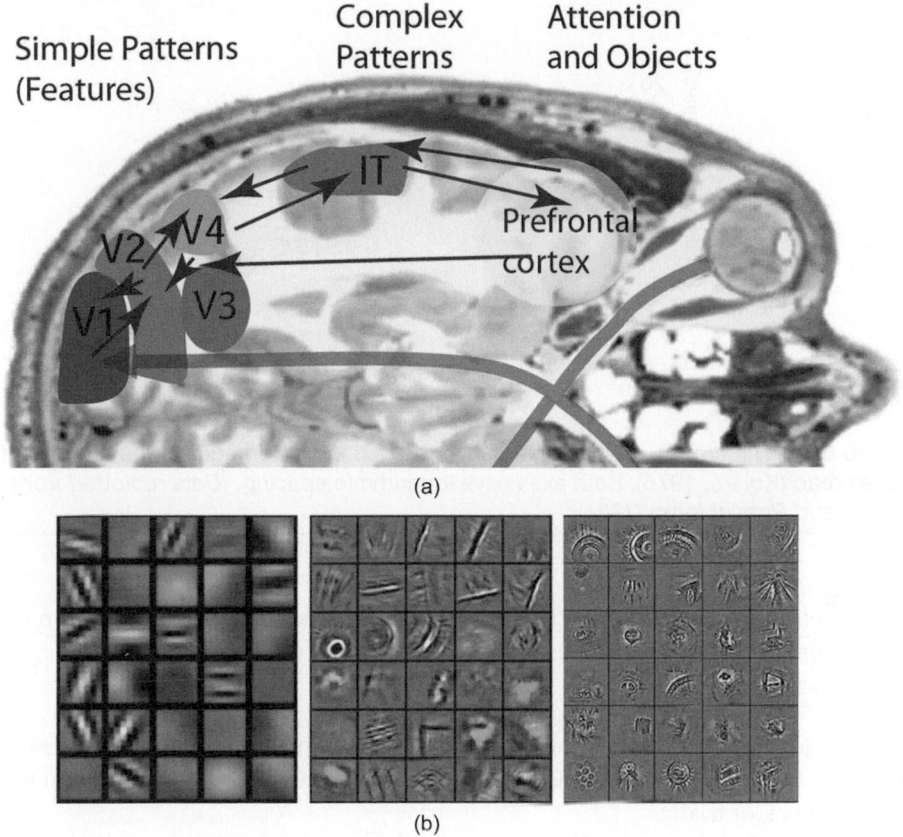

(a)

(b)

Figure 6.56 (a) Human pattern processing occurs in a series of brain regions in which increasingly complex patterns are responded to. (b) The low-level features from the environment discovered by machine learning algorithms are strikingly similar to those found in primate brains Examples of three levels of feature detector from an artificial "deep learning" neural net are shown. (*Adapted from Zeiler and Fergus (2014).*)

gained, multi-layer artificial neural nets quickly became unstable, but artificial neural nets made to mimic the biological bottom-up consolidation process resulted in much more accurate and manageable networks.

It is striking that when artificial neural nets are trained with thousands of images, the low-level features that emerge are very similar to the features that have been discovered by painstaking studies of the primate visual cortex (see Fig. 6.56b from Zeiler & Fergus, 2014). It may be strange to use machine learning patterns to illustrate the processes of human vision, but at higher levels of primate vision the patterns that are responded to are largely unknown, because of the difficulty of testing for a near infinite number of patterns. However, both theory and some results suggest that human vision pattern perception has similar progression of pattern complexity. Pattern learning is driven from the top down as well as the bottom up. Top-down processes reinforce and consolidate basic patterns that lead to useful higher level patterns, throughout life they refine and tune the mechanisms at lower levels.

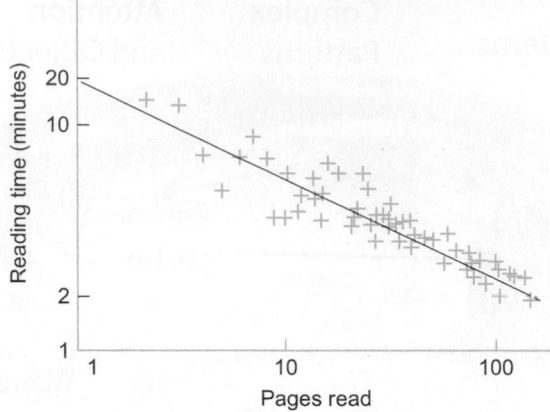

Figure 6.57 The time to read a page of inverted text is plotted against the number of pages read (Kolers, 1975). Both axes have logarithmic spacing. (*Data replotted from Newell and Rosenbloom (1981).*)

A function called *the power law of practice* provides a mathematical description of how rapidly patterns can be learned.

$$\log(T_n) = C - \alpha \log(n) \tag{6.1}$$

This law states that the log of the time to respond on the nth trial (T_n) is inversely proportional to the log of the number of trials. The constant C is the time taken on the first trial (or block of trials).

The power law of practice is usually applied to manual skill learning, but it has also been shown to apply to the perception of complex patterns. Kolers (1975) found that the power law applied to the task of learning to read inverted text. His results are illustrated in Fig. 6.57. Initially, it took subjects about 15 minutes to read a single inverted page, but when over 100 pages had been read, the time was reduced to 2 minutes. Although Fig. 6.57 shows a straight-line relationship between practice and learning, this is only because of the logarithmic transformation of the data. The relationship is actually very nonlinear. Consider a hypothetical task where people improve by 30% from the first day's practice to the second day. Doubling the amount of practice has resulted in a 30% gain. According to the power law, someone with 10 years of experience at the same task will require a further 10 years to improve by 30%. In other words, practice yields decreasing gains over time.

If pattern perception is fundamental to extraction of meaning from visualizations, then an important question arises: How we learn to see patterns better? Artists talk about seeing things that the rest of us cannot see, and ace detectives presumably spot visual clues that are invisible to the beat officer. The results of many studies generally suggest that it is difficult to learn to see *simple basic* patterns better. There have been some studies of pattern learning where almost no learning occurred; an often cited example is the visual search for the simple conjunction of features such as color and shape (Treisman & Gelade, 1980). Other studies, however, have found that learning does occur for certain types of patterns (Logan, 1994).

A plausible way of reconciling the differences in results is that pattern learning occurs for simple, basic patterns processed early in the visual system and early in life, but not for complex, unfamiliar patterns processed late in the visual system and later in life. By age 20 we have had millions of hours of exposure to simple pattern when the brain is most flexible. When we learn new complex patterns, for example, learning to discriminate anomalous cancer cells, learning will initially be very rapid, especially if we have had no prior experience with cell classification. New connections must be established higher up in the pattern discrimination hierarchy. Also, the learning of complex patterns involves interactions between many brain areas involved in determining the meaning of those patterns, not just a tuning of a neural layer (Dosher and Lu, 2017). These changes take place early in the learning curve (defined by the power law) and so performance may improve by a factor of two or more in the first hour or training. But after years of experience, further gains will be small or nonexistent.

One of the main implications of perceptual learning was already stated in a guideline that was given in Chapter 1: [G1.4]. Graphical symbol systems should be standardized within and across applications. This can be restated in terms of patterns.

> **[G6.21]** In order to minimize the amount of learning needed to understand a visualization, make every effort to standardize the mapping of data to visual patterns within and across applications.

Priming

In addition to long term pattern learning skills, there are also *priming* effects that are much more transient. Whether these constitute learning is still the subject of debate. Priming refers to the phenomenon that, once a particular pattern has been recognized, it will be much easier to identify in the next few minutes or even hours, and sometimes days. This is usually thought of as a kind of heightened receptivity within the visual system, but some theorists consider it to be visual learning. In either case, once a neural pathway has been activated, its future activation becomes facilitated. For a modern theory of perceptual priming based on neural mechanisms, see Huber and O'Reilly (2003).

What are the implications of these findings for visualization? One is that people can learn pattern-detection skills, although the ease of gaining these skills will depend on the specific nature of the patterns involved. Experts do indeed have special expertise. The radiologist interpreting an X-ray, the meteorologist interpreting radar, and the statistician interpreting a scatterplot will each bring a differently tuned visual system to bear on his or her particular problem. People who work with visualizations must learn the skill of seeing particular kinds of patterns in data that relate to analytic tasks, for example, finding a cancerous growth. In terms of making visualizations that contain easily identified patterns, one strategy is to rely on pattern-finding skills that are common to everyone. These can be based on low-level perceptual capabilities, such

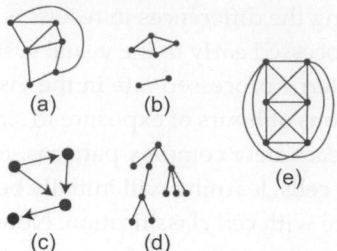

Figure 6.58 Node-link diagrams, technically called *graphs*: (a) A graph. (b) A graph with two connected components. (c) A directed graph. (d) A tree structure graph. (e) A nonplanar graph; it cannot be laid out on a plane without links crossing.

as seeing the connections between objects linked by lines. We can also rely on skill transfer. If we know that our users are cartographers, already good at reading terrain contour maps, we can display other information, such as energy fields, in the form of contour maps. The evidence from priming studies suggests that when we want people to see particular patterns, even familiar ones, it is a good idea to show them a few examples ahead of time.

The Visual Grammar of Node-link Diagrams

Diagrams are always hybrids of the conventional and the perceptual. Diagrams contain conventional elements, such as abstract labeling codes, that are difficult to learn but formally powerful. They also contain information that is coded according to perceptual rules, such as Gestalt principles. Arbitrary mappings may be useful, as in the case of mathematical notation, but a good diagram takes advantage of basic perceptual mechanisms that have evolved to perceive structure in the environment. By presenting examples, the following sections describe the visual grammar of two different kinds of diagrams: node-link diagrams and the layered maps used in GISs.

For a mathematician, a graph is a structure consisting of nodes and edges (links between the nodes). See Fig. 6.58 for examples. There is a specialized academic field called *graph drawing* dedicated to making graphs that are pleasantly laid out and easy to read. In graph drawing, layout algorithms are optimized according to aesthetic rules, such as the minimization of link crossings, displaying symmetry of structure, and minimizing bends in links (Di Battista, Eades, Tamassia, & Tollis, 1998). Path bendiness and the number of link crossings have both been shown empirically to degrade performance on the task of finding the shortest path between two nodes (Ware, Purchase, Colpoys, & McGill, 2002). For the most part, however, there has been little attempt either to systematically apply our knowledge of pattern perception to problems in graph drawing or to use empirical methods to determine that graphs laid out according to aesthetic principles are, in fact, easier to understand.

In the following paragraphs, we broaden the concept of a graph to consider a very large class of diagrams that we will call, generically, *node-link diagrams*. The essential

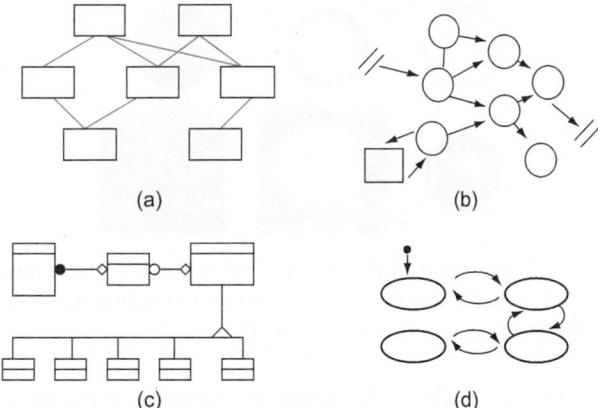

(a) (b)

(c) (d)

Figure 6.59 Four different kinds of node-link diagrams used in software engineering: (a) A code module diagram. (b) A data-flow diagram. (c) An object modeling diagram. (d) A state-transition diagram. Each of these diagrams would normally contain text labels on the nodes and the arcs.

characteristic of these diagrams is that they consist of *nodes*, representing various kinds of entities, and *links*, representing relationships between the entities. Dozens of different diagrams have this basic form, including software structure diagrams, data-flow diagrams, organization charts, and software modeling diagrams. Fig. 6.59 provides four examples commonly used in software engineering. The set of abstractions common to node-link diagrams is so close to ubiquitous that it can be called a *visual grammar*. Entities are almost always shown using outline boxes, circles, or small symbols. The connecting lines generally represent different kinds of relationships, transitions, or communication paths between nodes.

The various reasons why we may be justified in referring to these graphical codes as *perceptual* are distributed throughout this book, but are addressed mostly in this chapter and Chapter 5. The fundamental argument is that closed contours are basic in defining visual objects. Thus, although a circular line may be only a mark drawn on paper, at some level in the visual system it is *object-like*. Similarly, two objects can be connected by a line, and this visual connection has the ability to represent any of a number of relationships. The likely explanation for why nodes represent entities so well and linking lines represent relationships so well is that there are deep metaphors, based on sensory perception of the world, that provide a scaffolding for even our most abstract concepts (Lakoff & Johnson, 1980; Pinker, 2007).

Although lines get their expressive power from neural mechanisms designed to interpret objects, they are fundamentally ambiguous. Kennedy (1974) elucidated several ways in which contours (lines) can represent aspects of the environment. Some of them are illustrated in Fig. 6.60. A circle can represent a ring, a flat disk, a ball, a hole, or the boundary between two objects (a disk in a hole). This nicely illustrates the mixture of perception and convention that is common to diagrams. Our visual systems are capable of interpreting a line contour in any of these ways. In real-world scenes,

Figure 6.60 The line circle shown at the top left can represent many kinds of objects: a wire ring, a disk, a ball, a cut-out hole, or the boundary between regions of different color. More importantly, it can represent abstract concepts relating to objects.

additional information is available to clarify ambiguous contours. In a diagram, the contour may remain perceptually ambiguous, and some convention may be necessary to remove the ambiguity. In one kind of diagram, a circle may represent an abstract entity; in a second, it may represent a hole; in a third, it may represent the boundary of a geographic region. The diagram convention, the context, and the Gestalt factors tell us which interpretation is correct, but contours are not subject to an infinite number of interpretations. Their power comes from the small set of general meanings that they support through deep perceptual analogies.

Generally, though, the Gestalt figure-ground rules tell us that small, closed regions are likely to be seen as figures, or in other words, as object-like. Looking ahead to the next chapter, we find theories suggesting that attributes such as color, shape, and size are mostly perceived as secondary attributes of objects.

[G6.22] When developing glyphs, use small, closed shapes to represent data entities, and use the color, shape, and size of those shapes to represent attributes of those entities.

Fig. 6.60 provides a number of examples illustrating this guideline.

A general data model that uses a form of node-link diagram is the entity-relationship model. It is widely used in computer science and business modeling (Chen, 1976). In entity-relationship modeling, entities can be objects and parts of objects, or more abstract things such as parts of organizations. Relationships are the various kinds of connections that can exist between entities (notice the metaphor in the use of the word *connection*). For example, an entity representing a wheel will have a part-of relationship to an entity representing an automobile. A person may have a customer relationship to a store. Both entities and relationships can have attributes. Thus, a particular customer might be a preferred customer. An attribute of an organization might be the number of its employees. There are standard diagrams for use in entity-relationship modeling, but we are not concerned with these here. We are more interested in the different ways diagrams can be constructed to represent entities, relationships, and attributes in an easily perceived manner.

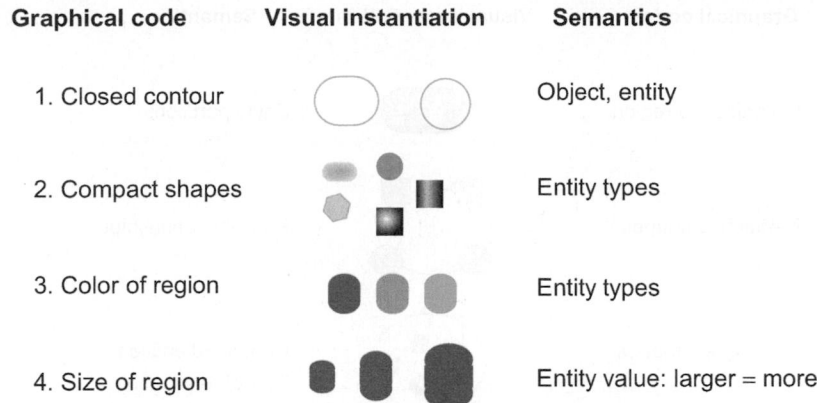

Graphical code	Visual instantiation	Semantics
1. Closed contour		Object, entity
2. Compact shapes		Entity types
3. Color of region		Entity types
4. Size of region		Entity value: larger = more

Figure 6.61 The basic visual grammar of entity representations for node-link diagrams.

The vast majority of node-link diagrams currently in use are very simple. For the most part, these diagrams use identical rectangular or circular nodes and constant width lines, like those shown in Fig. 6.60. Although such generic diagrams are very effective in conveying patterns of structural relationships among entities, they are often poor at showing the types of entities and the types of relationships. Attributes, when they are shown, are often provided in the form of text labels attached to the boxes and lines, although occasionally dashed lines and other variations are used to denote types. As Figs. 6.61 and 6.62 suggest, a great variety of graphical styles can be used to enrich diagrams and express attributes of both entities and relationships.

The visual metaphors embedded in language, in words such as *connection, linkage, attachment*, or *part-of* suggest ways of graphically encoding relationships between entities. According to Pinker (2007), such metaphors are not embellishments to language, but reflect the basic structure of thought.

> **[G6.23]** Use connecting lines, enclosure, grouping, and attachment to represent relationships between entities. The shape, color, thickness of lines, and enclosures can represent the types of relationships.

Fig. 6.62 shows examples of graphical methods for defining relationships. Most of these methods are only useful for symmetric relationships, but in fact most relationships between entities are not symmetrical. One entity *controls* another in some way, or is *used by* another, or is *part of* another. A graph that shows asymmetric relationships is called *directed*, and a standardized convention that shows the asymmetry is a line with an arrowhead at one end. In a recent study, Holten and van Wijk (2009) showed that a better alternative exists, as illustrated in Fig. 6.63. The version using the tapered lines made it significantly easier to trace relationships compared to the use of conventional arrows. A theory that explains why this may be superior is based on a concept of attention spreading along contours (Houtkamp, Spekreijse, & Roelfsema, 2003). From a given node, activation should tend to spread more readily along lines that start out thick than lines that start out thin.

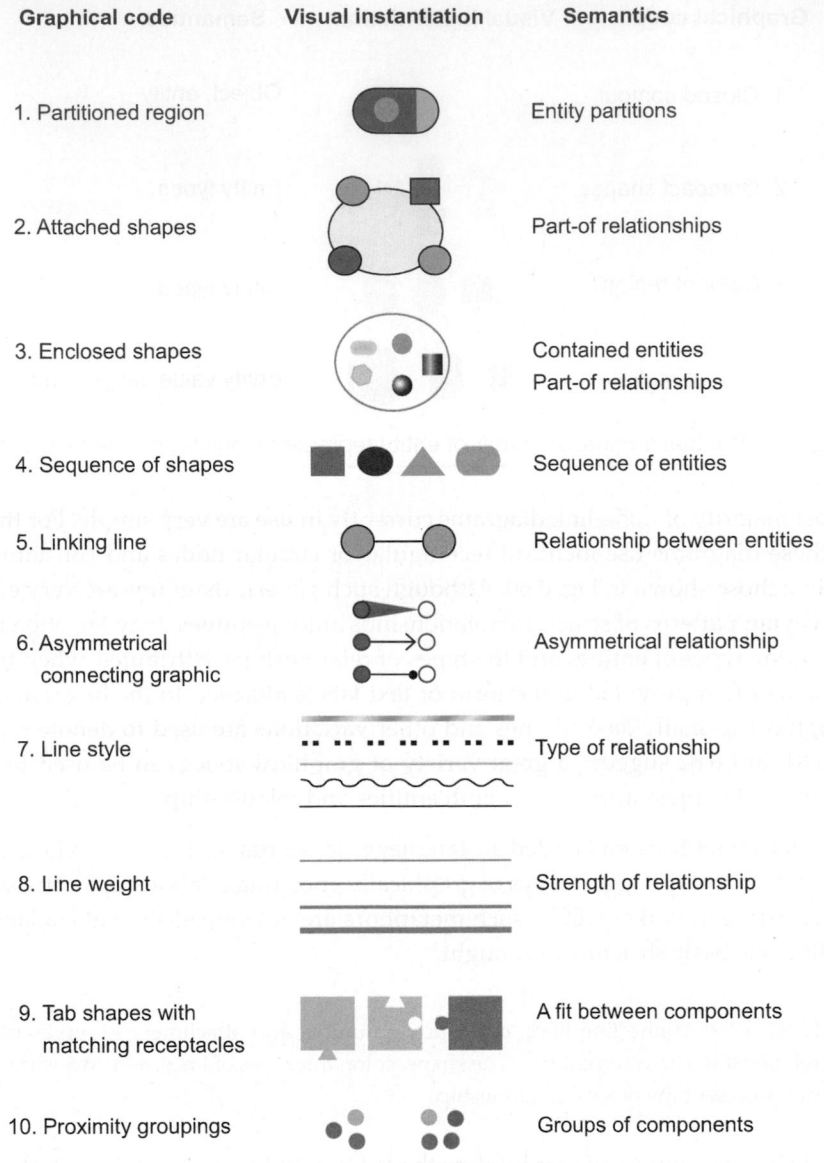

Graphical code	Visual instantiation	Semantics
1. Partitioned region		Entity partitions
2. Attached shapes		Part-of relationships
3. Enclosed shapes		Contained entities Part-of relationships
4. Sequence of shapes		Sequence of entities
5. Linking line		Relationship between entities
6. Asymmetrical connecting graphic		Asymmetrical relationship
7. Line style		Type of relationship
8. Line weight		Strength of relationship
9. Tab shapes with matching receptacles		A fit between components
10. Proximity groupings		Groups of components

Figure 6.62 The visual grammar of relationship representations.

[G6.24] As an alternative to arrows to represent directed relationships in diagrams, consider using tapered lines with the broadest end at the source node.

The Visual Grammar of Maps

A second visual grammar can be found in the way maps are designed and interpreted. As with node-link diagrams, we rely on strong visual metaphors, although in this case

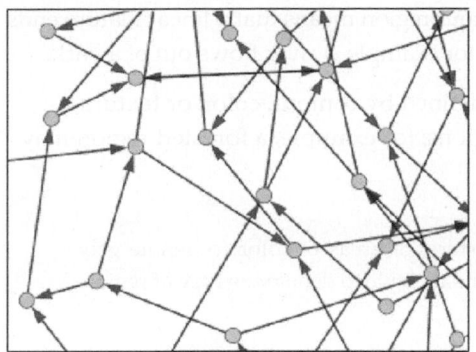

Figure 6.63 Two methods for representing directed relationships in a diagram. Research suggests that the one on the right can be interpreted more rapidly. (*From Holten and van Wijk (2009). Reproduced with permission.*)

they are used to reason about geographical space. The terms *enclosure*, *path*, *region*, *overlap*, and *connection* all have visual expressions. Only three basic kinds of graphical marks are common to most maps: areas, line features, and small symbols (Mark & Franck, 1996). Fig. 6.63 elaborates the basic grammar of maps and shows how areas, lines, or small symbols can work in isolation and in combination.

1, 2, 3. Geographical areas are usually denoted by closed contours, tinted areas, or textured areas. Often all three methods can be used—for example, lines to represent county boundaries, color coding to represent climate, and texture to represent vegetation.

4. Geographical linear features represent either boundaries or elongated geographical regions. The difference between geographical areas and linear features is sometimes related to scale. On a small scale, a river will be represented by a thin line of constant width; on a larger scale, it can become an extended geographical area.

5. Dots or other small symbols are used to represent point features, although whether or not something is a point feature depends on the scale. On a large scale, an entire city may be represented by a single dot; on a small scale, a dot might be used to show the locations of churches, schools, or tourist attractions.

6. A dot on a line means that the entity denoted by the point feature is on, or attached to, the entity denoted by the linear feature; for example, a city is "on" a river.

7. A dot within a closed contour means that the entity denoted by the point feature lies within the boundaries of the area feature; for example, a town is within a province.

8. A line crossing a closed contour region means that a linear feature crosses an area feature; for example, a road passes through a county.

9. A line that ends in a closed-contour region means that a linear feature ends or starts within an area feature; for example, a river flows out of a park.

10. Overlapping contour regions defined by contour, color, or texture denote overlapping spatial regions; for example, a forested region may overlap a county boundary.

[G6.25] Use closed contours, areas of texture, or areas of color to denote geographic regions. Use color, texture, or boundary style to denote the type of region.

[G6.26] Use lines to represent paths and linear geographic features. Use line color and style to represent the type of linear feature.

[G6.27] Use small, closed shapes to represent point entities, such as cities, that appear small on a map. Use color, shape, and size to represent attributes of these entities.

Maps need not be used only for geographical information. Johnson and Shneiderman (1991) developed a visualization technique they called a *treemap*, for displaying information about the tree data structures commonly used in computer science. Fig. 6.64 shows an example of a tree data structure presented in treemap form and in a conventional node-link diagram.

The original treemap was based on the following algorithm. First, the rectangle is divided with a vertical partition according to the number of branches from the base of the tree. Next, each subrectangle is similarly divided, but with horizontal partitions. This process is repeated to the leaves of the tree. The area of each leaf on the tree corresponds to the amount of information that is stored there.

The great advantage of the treemap over conventional tree views is that the amount of information on each branch of the tree can be easily visualized. Because the method is space-filling, it can show quite large trees containing thousands of branches. The disadvantage is that the nonleaf nodes are not shown and the hierarchical structure is not as clear as it is in a more conventional tree drawing. Of course, there are many hybrid designs where, for example, a node-link representation is used and the size of the node points represents some quantity.

[G6.28] Consider using a treemap to display tree structured data where it is only necessary to display the leaf nodes and where it is important to display a quantity associated with each leaf node.

[G6.29] Consider using a node-link representation of a tree where the hierarchical structure is important, where internal (nonleaf) nodes are important, and where quantitative attributes of nodes are less important.

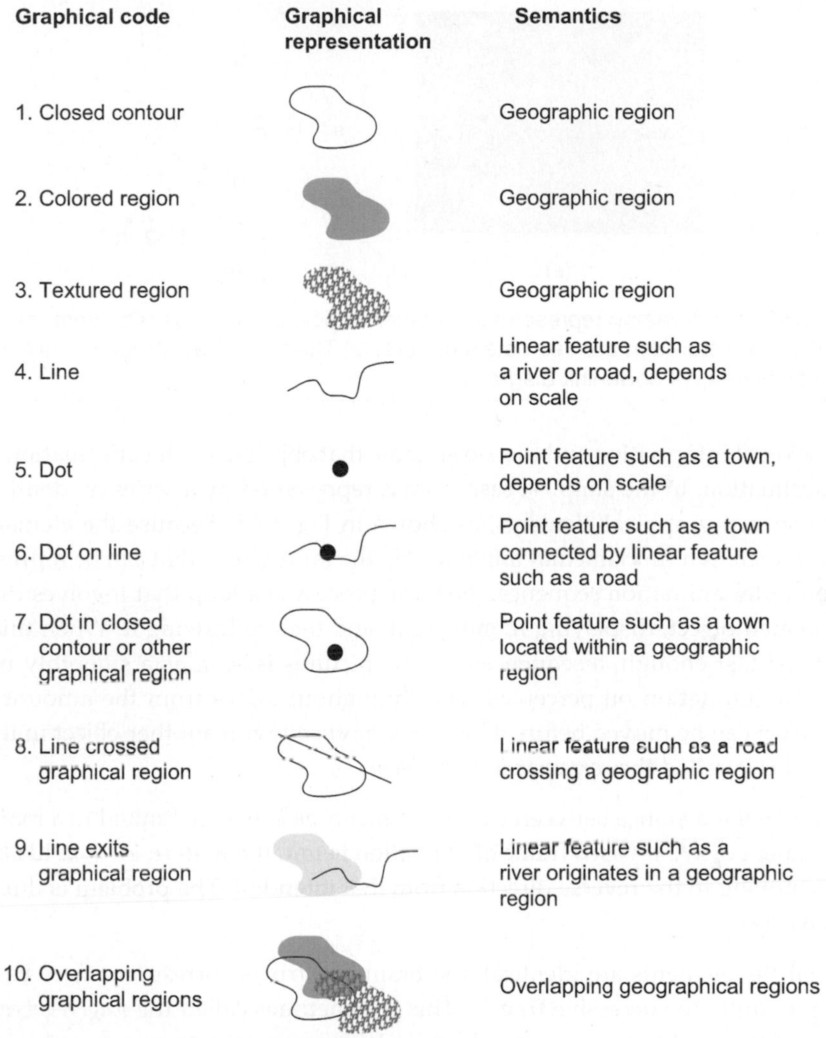

Graphical code	Graphical representation	Semantics
1. Closed contour		Geographic region
2. Colored region		Geographic region
3. Textured region		Geographic region
4. Line		Linear feature such as a river or road, depends on scale
5. Dot		Point feature such as a town, depends on scale
6. Dot on line		Point feature such as a town connected by linear feature such as a road
7. Dot in closed contour or other graphical region		Point feature such as a town located within a geographic region
8. Line crossed graphical region		Linear feature such as a road crossing a geographic region
9. Line exits graphical region		Linear feature such as a river originates in a geographic region
10. Overlapping graphical regions		Overlapping geographical regions

Figure 6.64 The basic visual grammar of map elements.

Patterns in Motion

To this point, we have mainly discussed the use of static patterns to represent data, even though the data is sometimes dynamic. We can use motion as a display technique to represent data that is either static or dynamic. The perception of dynamic patterns is not understood as well as the perception of static patterns, but we are very sensitive to patterns in motion, and if we can learn to use motion effectively it may be a good way to display certain aspects of data. In this section we are only concerned with using motion as a visual coding method, not with animation used for story telling. We will get to that in later chapters.

We start by considering the problem of how to represent data communications with computer animation. One way of doing this is to use a graphical object to represent

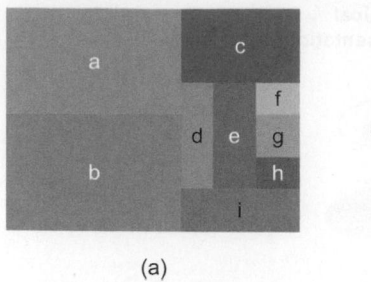 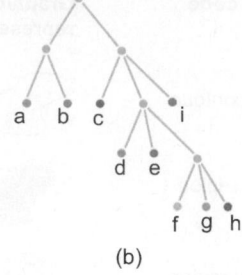

(a)   (b)

Figure 6.65 (a) A treemap representation of hierarchical data. Areas represent the amount of data stored in the tree data structure. (b) The same tree structure, represented using a conventional node-link diagram.

each packet of information and then to animate that object from the information source to its destination. In the simplest case, data is represented by a series of identical and equally spaced graphical elements, as shown in Fig. 6.65. Because the elements are identical, there is a fundamental limitation on the throughput that can be represented. In a computer animation sequence, the basic process is a loop that involves drawing the animated object, displaying it, moving it, and then redrawing it. When this cycle is repeated fast enough, a sequence of static pictures is seen as a smoothly moving image. The limitation on perceived data throughput arises from the amount that a given object can be moved before it becomes confused with another object in the next frame—this is called the *correspondence problem.*

If we define the distance between pattern elements as λ, we are limited to a maximum displacement of $\lambda/2$ on each frame of animation before the pattern is more likely to be seen as moving in the reverse direction from that intended. The problem is illustrated in Fig. 6.65(a).

When all the elements are identical, the brain constructs correspondences based on object proximity in successive frames. This is sometimes called the *wagon-wheel effect,* because of the tendency of wagon wheels in Western movies to appear to be rotating in the wrong direction. Experiments by Fleet (1998) suggest that the maximum change per frame of animation for motion to be seen reliably in a particular direction is about $\lambda/3$ for the basic representation shown in Fig. 6.65(a). Given an animation frame rate of 60 frames per second, this establishes an upper bound of 20 messages per second that can be represented.

There are many ways in which the correspondence limitation can be overcome by giving the graphical elements a different shape, orientation, or color. Two possibilities are illustrated in Fig. 6.65(b) and (c). In one, the gray values of the elements are varied from message to message; in the other, the shapes of the elements are varied. Research with element shapes suggests that correspondence of shape is more important than correspondence of color in determining perceived motion (Caelli, Manning, & Finlay, 1993). In a series of experiments that examined a variety of enhanced representations like those illustrated in Fig. 6.65(b) and (c), Fleet (1998) found that the average phase shift per animation frame could be increased to 3λ before correspondence was lost. Given an animation frame rate of 60 frames per second, this translates to an upper bound of 180 messages per second that can be represented using animation.

Of course, when the goal is to visualize high traffic rates, there is no point in representing individual messages in detail. Most digital communications systems transfer millions of data packets per second. What is important at high data rates is an impression of data volumes, the direction of traffic flow, and large-scale patterns of activity.

Form and Contour in Motion

A number of studies have shown that people can see *relative* motion with great sensitivity. For example, contours and region boundaries can be perceived with precision in fields of random dots if defined by differential motion alone (Regan, 1989; Regan & Hamstra, 1991). Human sensitivity to such motion patterns rivals our sensitivity to static patterns; this suggests that motion is an underutilized method for displaying patterns in data. For purposes of data display, we can treat motion as an attribute of a visual object, much as we consider size, color, and position to be object attributes. We evaluated the use of simple sinusoidal motion in enabling people to perceive correlations between variables (Limoges et al., 1989). We enhanced a conventional scatterplot representation by allowing the points to oscillate sinusoidally, either horizontally or vertically (or both), about a center point. An experiment was conducted to discover whether the frequency, phase, or amplitude of point motion was the most easily "read." The task was to distinguish a high correlation between variables from a low one. A comparison was made with more conventional graphical techniques, including using point size, gray value, and x,y position in a conventional scatterplot. The results showed that data mapped to phase was perceived best; in fact, it was as effective as most of the more conventional techniques, such as the use of point size or gray value. In informal studies, we also showed that motion appears to be effective in revealing clusters of distinct data points in a multidimensional data space (see Fig. 6.66). Related data shows up as clouds of points moving together in elliptical paths, and these can be easily differentiated from other clouds of points.

Moving Frames

Perceived motion is highly dependent on its context. A rectangular frame provides a very strong contextual cue for motion perception, as shown in Fig. 6.67(a). It is so strong that if a bright frame is made to move around a bright static dot in an otherwise completely dark environment, it is often the static dot that appears to move (Wallach, 1959). Johansson (1975) has demonstrated a number of grouping phenomena that show that the brain has a strong tendency to group moving objects in a hierarchical fashion. One of the effects he investigated is illustrated in Fig. 6.67(b) and (c). In this example, three dots are set in motion. The two outer dots move in synchrony in a horizontal direction. The third dot, located between the other two, also moves in synchrony but in an oblique direction; however, the central dot is not perceived as moving

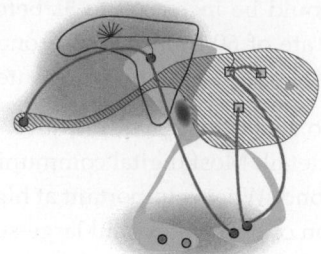

Figure 6.66 (a) If motion is represented using a regular sequence of identical and equally spaced elements, there is a strict limit on the throughput that can be perceived. (b, c) This limit can be extended by varying the sizes and shapes of the graphical elements.

Figure 6.67 An illustration of the elliptical motion paths that result when variables are mapped to the relative phase angles of oscillating dots. The result is similar elliptical motion paths for points that are similar. In this example, two distinct groups of oscillating dots are clearly perceived.

along an oblique path as shown in Fig. 6.67(b). Instead, what is perceived is illustrated in Fig. 6.67(c). An overall horizontal motion of the entire group of dots is seen; within this group, the central dot also appears to move vertically.

Computer animation is often used in a straightforward way to display dynamic phenomena, such as a particle flow through a vector field. In these applications, the main goal from a perceptual point of view is to bring the motion into the range of human sensitivities. The issue is the same for viewing high-speed or single-frame movie photography. The motions of flowers blooming or bullets passing through objects are speeded up and slowed down, respectively, so that we can perceive the dynamics of the phenomena. Humans are most sensitive to motion ranging from 0.5 to 4 cm per second for objects viewed at normal screen distances (Dzhafarov, Sekuler, & Allik, 1993).

> **[G6.30]** When animation is used in a visualization, aim for motion in the range of 0.5–4 degrees/second of visual angle.

The use of motion to help us distinguish patterns in abstract data is at present only a research topic, albeit a very promising one. One application of the research results is the use of frames to examine dynamic flow-field animations. Frames can be used as an

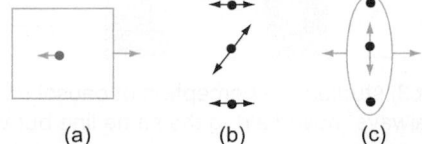

(a)   (b)   (c)

Figure 6.68 (a) When a stationary dot is placed within a moving frame in a dark room, it is the dot that is perceived to move in the absence of other cues. (b) When dots are set in synchronized motion, they form a frame within which individual motion is seen. (c) The entire group of dots is seen to move horizontally, and the central dot moves vertically within the group.

effective device for highlighting local relative motion. If we wish to highlight the local relative motion of a group of particles moving through a fluid, a rectangular frame that moves along with the group will create a reference area within which local motion patterns can emerge.

Another way in which motion patterns are important is in helping us perceive visual space and rigid three-dimensional shapes. This topic is covered in Chapter 8 in the context of the other mechanisms of space perception.

Expressive Motion

Using moving patterns to represent motion on communication channels, or in vector fields, is a rather obvious use of motion for information display, but there are other, more subtle uses. There appears to be a vocabulary of expressive motion comparable in richness and variety to the vocabulary of static patterns explored by the Gestalt psychologists. In the following sections, some of the more provocative results are discussed, together with their implications for data visualization.

Perception of Causality

When we see a billiard ball strike another and set the second ball in motion, we perceive that the motion of the first ball *causes* the motion of the second, according to the work of Michotte (translated 1963). Michotte's book, *The Perception of Causality*, is a compendium of dozens of experiments, each showing how variations in the basic parameters of velocity and event timing can radically alter what is perceived. He conducted detailed studies of the perception of interactions between two patches of light and came to the conclusion that the perception of causality can be as direct and immediate as the perception of simple form. In a typical experiment, illustrated in Fig. 6.68, one rectangular patch of light moved from left to right until it just touched a second patch of light and then stopped. At this point, the second patch of light would start to move. This was before the advent of computer graphics, and Michotte conducted his experiments with an apparatus that used little mirrors and beams of light. Depending on the temporal relationships between the moving light events and their relative velocities, observers reported different kinds of causal relationships, variously described as "launching," "entraining," or "triggering."

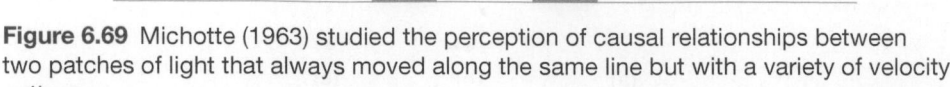

Figure 6.69 Michotte (1963) studied the perception of causal relationships between two patches of light that always moved along the same line but with a variety of velocity patterns.

Precise timing is required to achieve perceived causality. Michotte found that, for the effect he called *launching* to be perceived, the second object had to move within 70 ms of contact; after this interval, subjects still perceived the first object as setting the second object in motion, but the phenomenon was qualitatively different. He called it *delayed launching*. Beyond about 160 ms, there was no longer an impression that one event caused the other; instead, the movements of the two objects were perceived as separate. Fig. 6.69 shows some of his results. For causality to be perceived, visual events must be synchronized within at least one-sixth of a second. Given that virtual-reality animation often occurs at only about 10 frames per second, events should be frame accurate for clear causality to be perceived.

If an object makes contact with another and the second object moves off at a much greater velocity, a phenomenon that Michotte called *triggering* is perceived. The first object does not seem to cause the second object to move by imparting its own energy; rather, it appears that contact triggers *propelled* motion in the second object.

More recent developmental work by Leslie and Keeble (1987) has shown that infants at only 27 weeks of age can perceive causal relations such as launching. This would appear to support the contention that such percepts are in some sense basic to perception.

The significance of Michotte's work for data visualization is that it provides a way to increase the expressive range beyond what is possible with static diagrams. In a static visualization, the visual vocabulary for representing relationships is quite limited. To show that one visual object is related to another, we can draw lines between them, we can color or texture groups of objects, or we can use some kind of simple shape coding. The only way to show a causal link between two objects is by using some kind of conventional code, such as a labeled arrow; however, such codes owe their meaning more to our ability to understand conventional coded language symbols than to anything essentially perceptual. Arrows are used to show many kinds of directed relationships, not just causal ones. This point about the differences between language-based codes and perceptual codes is elaborated in Chapter 9. What Michotte's work gives us is the ability to significantly enrich the vocabulary of things that can be immediately and directly represented in a diagram, although it would be premature to recommend this as a specific guideline.

Perception of Animated Motion

In addition to the fact that we can perceive causality using simple animation, there is evidence that we are highly sensitive to motion that has a biological origin. In a series

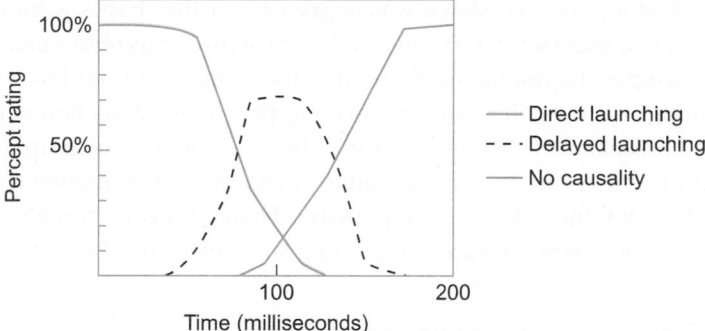

Figure 6.70 When one object comes into contact with another and the second moves off, the first motion may be seen to cause the second if the right temporal relationships exist. The graph shows how different kinds of phenomena are perceived, depending on the delay between the arrival of one object and the departure of the other. (*From Michotte (1963). Reproduced with permission.*)

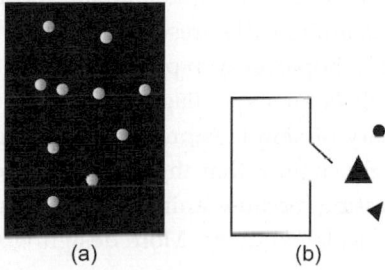

(a) (b)

Figure 6.71 (a) In Johansson's (1973) experiments, a pattern of moving dots was produced by making a movie of actors with lights attached to parts of their bodies. (b) Heider and Simmel (1944) made a movie of simple geometric shapes moving through complex paths. Viewers of both kinds of displays attribute anthropomorphic characteristics to what they see.

of now classic studies, Gunnar Johansson attached lights to the limb joints of actors (Johansson, 1973). He then produced moving pictures of the actors carrying out certain activities, such as walking and dancing. These pictures were made so that only the points of light were visible, and, in any given still frame, all that was perceived was a rather random-seeming collection of dots, as shown in Fig. 6.70(a). But, once the dots were animated, viewers were immediately conscious of the fact that they were watching human motion. In addition, they could identify the genders of the actors and the tasks they were performing. Some of these identifications could be made after exposures lasting only a small fraction of a second.

Another experiment pointing to our ability to recognize form from motion was a study by Heider and Simmel (1944). In this study, an animated movie was produced incorporating the motion of two triangles and a circle, as shown in Fig. 6.71(b). People viewing this movie readily attributed human characteristics to the shapes; they would say, for example, that a particular shape was angry or that the shapes were chasing one another. Moreover, these interpretations were consistent across observers. Because the figures were simple shapes, the implication is that patterns of motion were conveying the meaning. Other studies support this interpretation. Rimé, Boulanger, Laubin, Richants, and Stroobants (1985) did a cross-cultural evaluation of simple animations using European, American, and African subjects and found that motion could express such concepts as kindness, fear, and aggression. There was considerable similarity in these interpretations across cultures, suggesting some measure of universality.

Enriching Diagrams with Simple Animation

The research findings of Michotte, Johansson, Heider, Simmel, and others suggest that the use of simple motion can powerfully express certain kinds of relationships in data. Animation of abstract shapes can significantly extend the vocabulary of things that can be conveyed naturally beyond what is possible with a static diagram. The fact that motion does not require the support of complex depictive representations (of animals or people) for movement to be perceived as animate means that simplified motion techniques may be useful in multimedia presentations. The kinds of animated critters that are starting to crawl and hop over web pages are often unnecessary and distracting. Just as elegance is a virtue in static diagrams, so is it a virtue in diagrams that use animation. A vocabulary of simple expressive animation requires development, but research results strongly suggest that this will be a productive and worthwhile endeavor. The issue is pressing, because animation tools are becoming more widely available for information display systems. More design work and more research are needed.

The Processes of Pattern Finding

We conclude this chapter with some remarks on the process within which the pattern-finding machinery of the brain operates. When we look at something that is well known to us, what we perceive is largely a product of information stored in our brains. For the most part we see what we know, but the discovery of novel patterns is very different, since the brain does not have the same memory resources to build meaning.

Ullman (1984) proposed that low-level processes run in the brain to pull out abstract patterns, and, in this chapter, we have seen research suggesting how these may operate in terms of extended contours, and we have suggested that similar mechanisms exist for regions of common texture or color. A key point about Ullman's theory is that only a small number of pattern operators can run simultaneously. We can only mentally trace a very small number of contours, probably fewer than five at the same time, if they are simple, and only one that is slightly more complex. The same goes for regions defined by texture or color. The theory of attentional shrouds proposes that there are mechanisms whereby regions of different texture compete for attention (Bhatt, Carpenter, & Grossberg, 2007). How attention is allocated depends both on how salient the regions are and the top-down influence of visual queries derived from the cognitive task of the moment. The actual number of simple patterns that can be held in attention is tied to the limits of visual working memory, only three or four patterns. In Chapter 11, we will see how this is a key bottleneck in visual cognition.

In data exploration, cognitive task demands lead to the formation of visual queries. Understanding the visual queries required for a cognitive task to be executed means discovering the task relevant patterns in data and this is the key to critical analysis and design. Understanding the problems to be solved using a visualization and the task relevant patterns that must be perceived is the key to the graphical aspects of good design. The designer's job is to make a design such that all task relevant patterns are easily perceived, with a minimum of cognitive effort, and distractions are minimized. Understanding visual queries is also the key to the critical analysis of existing visualization solutions. They can be used to deconstruct a design to determine where it succeeds and where it falls short.

CHAPTER SEVEN

Space Perception

We live in a three-dimensional world (actually, four dimensions if time is included). In the short history of visualization research, most graphical display methods have required that data be plotted on sheets of paper, but computers have evolved to the point that this is no longer necessary. Now we can create the illusion of three-dimensional (3D) space behind the monitor screen, changing over time if we wish. The big question is why should we do this? There are clear advantages to conventional two-dimensional (2D) techniques, such as the bar chart and the scatterplot. The most powerful pattern-finding mechanisms of the brain work in 2D, not 3D. Designers already know how to draw diagrams and represent data effectively in two dimensions, and the results can easily be included in books and reports. Of course, one compelling reason for an interest in 3D space perception is the explosive advance in 3D computer graphics. Because it is so inexpensive to display data in an interactive 3D virtual space, people are doing it—often for the wrong reasons. It is inevitable that there is now an abundance of ill-conceived 3D design, just as the advent of desktop publishing brought poor use of typography and the advent of cheap color brought ineffective and often garish use of color. Through an understanding of space perception, we hope to reduce the amount of poor 3D design and clarify those instances in which 3D representation is really useful.

The first half of this chapter presents an overview of the different factors, called *depth cues*, involved in the perception of 3D space. This will provide the foundation for the second half, which is about how these cues can be effectively applied in design. The way we use spatial information depends greatly on the task at hand. Docking one

Information Visualization. https://doi.org/10.1016/B978-0-12-812875-6.00007-4

object with another or trying to trace a path in a tangled web of imaged blood vessels require different ways of seeing. The second half gives a task-based analysis of the ways in which different cues are used in performing seven different tasks, ranging from tracing paths in 3D networks to judging the morphology of surfaces to appreciating an aesthetic impression of spaciousness.

Depth Cue Theory

The visual world provides many different sources of information about 3D space. These sources are usually called *depth cues*, and a large body of research is related to the way the visual system processes depth cue information to provide an accurate perception of space. Following is a list of the more important depth cues. They are divided into categories according to whether they can be reproduced in a static picture (monocular static) or a moving picture (monocular dynamic) or require two eyes (binocular).

Monocular static (pictorial)

- Linear perspective
- Texture gradient from perspective
- Size gradient from perspective
- Occlusion
- Depth of focus
- Shape from shading
- Vertical position
- Relative size to familiar objects
- Cast shadows

Monocular dynamic (moving picture)

- Structure from motion (kinetic depth, motion parallax)

Monocular nonpictorial

- Depth-from-eye accommodation

Binocular

- Eye convergence
- Stereoscopic depth

More attention is devoted to stereoscopic depth perception than to the other depth cues, not because it is the most important—it is not—but because it is relatively complex and because it is difficult to use effectively.

Perspective Cues

Fig. 7.1 shows how perspective geometry can be described for a particular viewpoint and a picture plane. The position of each feature on the picture plane is determined by extending a ray from the viewpoint to that feature in the environment. If the resulting picture is subsequently scaled up or down, the correct viewpoint is specified by similar triangles, as shown. If the eye is placed at the specified point with respect to the picture, the result is a correct perspective view of the scene. A number of the depth cues are direct results of the geometry of perspective. These are illustrated in Figs. 7.2 and 7.3.

- Parallel lines converge to a point.

- Objects at a distance appear smaller on the picture plane than do nearby objects. Objects of known size may have a very powerful role in determining the perceived size of adjacent unknown objects. An image of a person placed in a picture of otherwise abstract objects gives a scale to the entire scene.

- Uniformly textured surfaces result in texture gradients in which the texture elements become smaller with distance.

In terms of the total amount of information available from an information display, there is no evidence that a perspective picture lets us see *more* than a nonperspective image. A study by Cockburn and McKenzie (2001) showed that perspective cues added no advantage to a version of the data mountain display of Robertson et al. (1998). The version shown in Fig. 7.4(b) was just as effective as the one in Fig. 7.4(a); however, both of

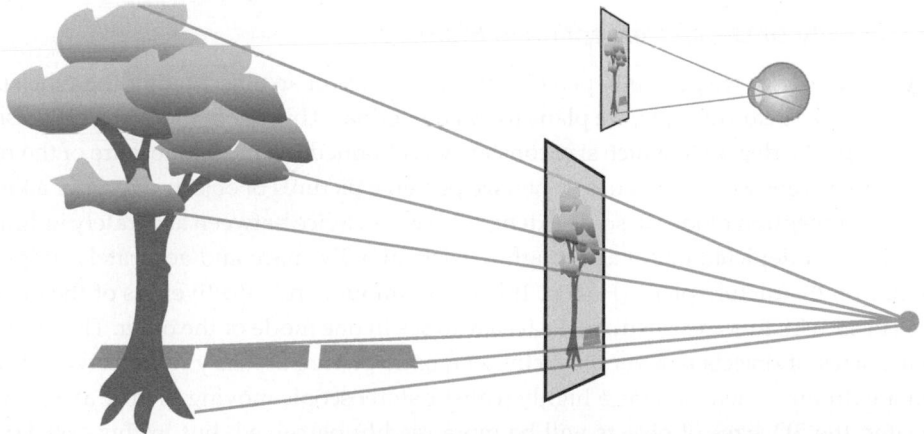

Figure 7.1 The geometry of linear perspective is obtained by sending a ray from each point in the environment through a picture window to a single fixed point. To obtain a perfect perspective picture, each point on the picture window is colored according to the light that emanates from the corresponding region of the environment. The result is that objects vary in size on the picture plane in inverse proportion to their distance from the fixed point. If an image is created according to this principle, the correct viewpoint is determined by similar triangles, as shown in the upper right.

Figure 7.2 Perspective cues arising from perspective geometry include the convergence of lines and the fact that more distant objects become smaller on the picture plane.

Figure 7.3 A texture gradient is produced when a uniformly textured surface is projected onto the picture plane.

these versions make extensive use of other depth cues, namely occlusion and height on the picture plane, so the comparison was not really between 2D and 3D but between slightly 3D and slightly more 3D.

The Duality of Depth Perception in Pictures

In the real world, we generally perceive the actual size of an object rather than the size at which it appears on a picture plane (or on the retina). This phenomenon is called *size constancy*. The degree to which size constancy is obtained is a useful measure of the relative effectiveness of depth cues. When we perceive pictures of objects, we enter a kind of dual perception mode. To some extent, we have a choice between accurately judging the size of a depicted object as though it exists in a 3D space and accurately judging its size on the picture plane (Hagen, 1974). The amount and effectiveness of the depth cues used will, to some extent, make it easy to see in one mode or the other. The picture plane sizes of objects in a very sketchy schematic picture are easy to perceive. At the other extreme, when viewing a highly realistic stereoscopic moving picture at a movie theater, the 3D sizes of objects will be more readily perceived, but in this case large errors will be made in estimating picture plane sizes. Fig. 7.5 shows how perspective cues can affect the perceived size of two objects that have identical sizes on the picture plane. This has implications if accurate size judgments are required in a visualization.

[G7.1] If accurate size judgments are required for abstract 3D shapes viewed in a computer-generated 3D scene, provide the best possible set of depth cues.

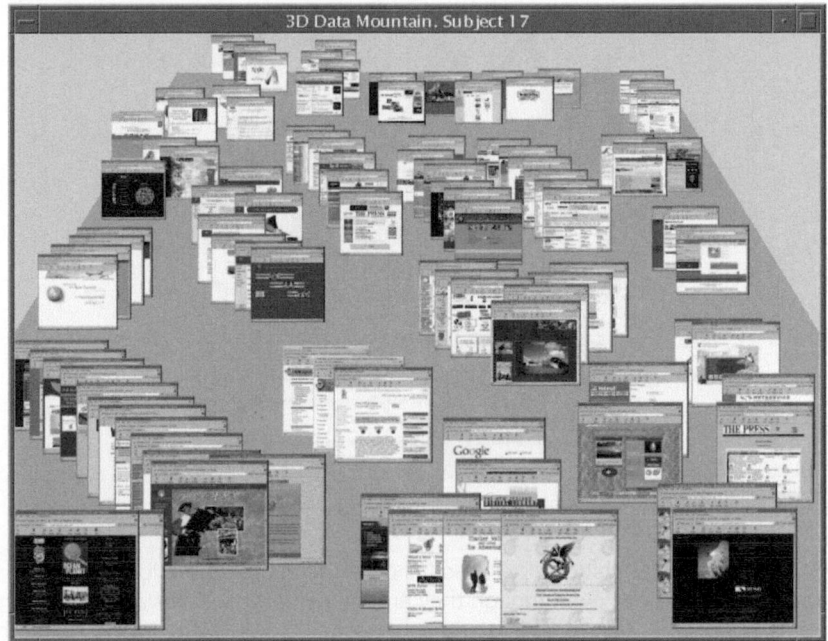

(a)

(b)

Figure 7.4 (a) Variation on the Robertson et al. (1998) Data Mountain display. (b) Same as (a) but without perspective. *((a)Courtesy of Andy Cockburn.)*

Figure 7.5 Because of the strong perspective cues the figure above looks much bigger than the one below, even though they are the same size. This would be even more pronounced with greater realism and stereoscopic cues. In the image plane the two figures are identical. *(From* http://www.sapdesignguild.org/contact.asp. *(With permission).)*

Pictures Seen from the Wrong Viewpoint

Most pictures are not viewed from their correct centers of perspective. In a movie theater, only one person can occupy this optimal viewpoint (determined by viewpoint position, the focal length of the original camera, and the scale of the final picture). When a picture is viewed from somewhere other than the center of perspective, the laws of geometry suggest that significant distortions should occur; for example, the angle between objects differing in distance will be perceived incorrectly. Work by Banks, Cooper, and Piazza (2014) suggests that people prefer to look at images from the correct viewing distance. For computer graphics renderings of data, this means that the aspect ratio of the view frustum used in rendering should match the aspect ratio formed by the distance of an observer from the display screen and the width of image on the screen. This means that, ideally, an image of a 3D data visualization should not be simply shrunk if it is to be displayed small on a monitor screen or a small phone screen, rather it should be rendered with very different viewing parameters. The frustum aspect ratio (d/w) should be larger and the viewing angle correspondingly smaller. This is equivalent to the use of a long-focal-length lens in photography.

[G7.2] If it is known in advance that an image of 3D data is to be viewed on a large screen or a small screen, adjust the parameters of the viewing frustum accordingly when rendering. The viewing angle of the frustum used in rendering the virtual scene should approximate the viewing angle of the displayed image.

.Images of 3D data may also be viewed off-axis. Fig. 7.6 illustrates this. When the mesh shown in Fig. 7.6 is projected on a screen with a geometry based on viewpoint labeled *a*, but actually viewed from position *b*, it should be perceived to stretch along the line of sight as shown. However, although people report seeing some distortion at the start of looking at *moving* pictures from the wrong viewpoint, they become unaware of the distortion after a few minutes. Kubovy (1986) calls this the *robustness of linear perspective*. Apparently, the human visual system overrides some aspects of perspective in constructing the 3D world that we perceive.

One of the mechanisms that can account for this lack of perceived distortion may be a built-in perceptual assumption that objects in the world are rigid. Suppose that the mesh in Fig. 7.7 is smoothly rotated around a vertical axis and projected assuming the correct viewpoint, but viewed from an incorrect viewpoint. It should appear as a nonrigid, elastic body, but perceptual processing is constrained by a rigidity assumption, and this causes us to see a stable, nonelastic 3D object.

Under extreme conditions, some distortion is still seen with off-axis viewing of moving pictures. Hagen and Elliott (1976) showed that this residual distortion is reduced if the projective geometry is made more parallel. This can be done by simulating long-focal-length lenses, which may be a useful technique if displays are intended for off-axis viewing.

[G7.3] To minimize perceived distortions from off-axis viewing of 3D data spaces, avoid extremely wide viewing angles when defining perspective views. As a rule of thumb, keep the horizontal viewing angle below 30 degrees.

Fish-Tank Virtual Reality

Various technologies exist that can track a user's head position with respect to a computer screen and thereby estimate the position of the eye(s). With this information, a 3D scene can be computed and viewed so the perspective is "correct" at all times

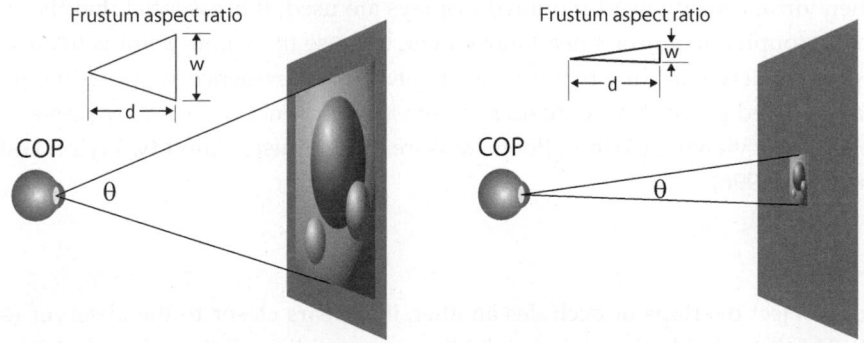

Figure 7.6 When a computer-generated perspective image of data is shown on a small screen the aspect ratio of the viewing frustum should be adjusted.

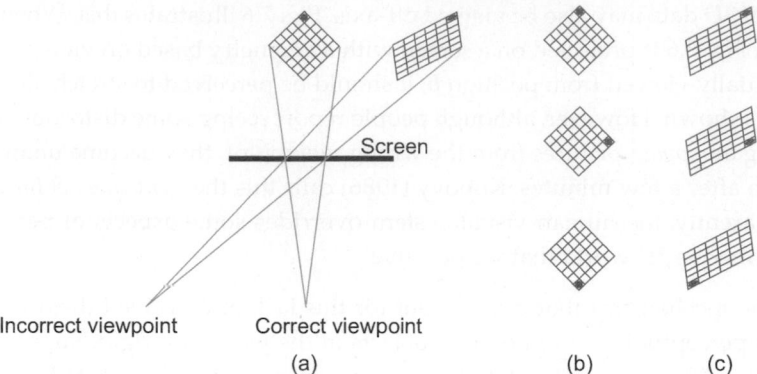

Incorrect viewpoint   Correct viewpoint

(a)   (b)   (c)

Figure 7.7 (a) When a perspective picture is seen from the wrong viewpoint, simple geometry predicts that large distortions should be seen. In fact, they are not seen or, when seen, are minimal. (b) A rotating object seen from the incorrect viewpoint appears undistorted. (c) Were the mental calculation based on simple geometry, it should appear to warp as shown in the top-to-bottom sequence.

by adjusting the viewpoint parameters in the computer graphics software (Deering, 1992). I called this setup *fish-tank virtual reality* to contrast it with the immersive virtual reality that is obtained with head-mounted displays (Ware, Arthur, & Booth, 1993). It is like having a small, bounded, fish-tank-sized artificial environment with which to work. There are two reasons why this might be desirable, despite the fact that incorrect perspective viewing of a picture seems generally unimportant. The first reason is that, as an observer changes position, the perspective image will change accordingly, resulting in motion parallax. Motion parallax is itself a depth cue, as discussed later in the structure-from-motion section. The second reason is that in some virtual-reality systems it is possible to place the subject's hand in the same space as the virtual computer graphics imagery. Fig. 7.8 shows an apparatus that uses a half-silvered mirror to combine computer graphics imagery with a view of the user's own hand. To get the registration between the hand and virtual objects correct, the eye position must be tracked and the perspective computed accordingly.

When virtual-reality head-mounted displays are used, it is essential that the perspective be coupled to a user's head movement, because the whole point is to allow users to change viewpoint in a natural way. Experimental evidence supports the idea that head-coupled perspective enhances the sense of presence in virtual spaces more than stereoscopic viewing (Arthur, Booth, & Ware, 1993; Pausch, Snoddy, Taylor, Watson, & Haseltine, 1996).

Occlusion

If one object overlaps or occludes another, it appears closer to the observer (see Fig. 7.9). This is probably the strongest depth cue, overriding all the others, but it provides only binary information. An object is either behind or in front of another; no information is given about the distance between them. A kind of partial occlusion occurs when

Figure 7.8 A user is attempting to trace 3D blood vessels in an interface that puts his hands in the same space as the virtual computer graphics imagery. *(From Serra, Hern, Choon, and Poston (1997). Reproduced with permission.)*

Figure 7.9 The figures depicted on the left can be seen as having the same size but different distances. On the right, the occlusion depth cue ensures that we see the upper figure as at the same depth or closer than the left figure. It therefore appears smaller.

one object is transparent or translucent. In this case, there is a color difference between the parts of an object that lie behind the transparent plane and the parts that are in front of it.

Occlusion can be useful in design; for example, the tabbed cards illustrated in Fig. 7.10(a) use occlusion to provide rank-order information, in addition to rapid access to individual cards. Although modern graphical user interfaces (GUIs) are usually described as being 2D, they are actually 3D in a nontrivial way. Overlapping windows rely on our understanding of occlusion to be effective; see Fig. 7.10(b).

Shape From Shading

Continuous surfaces are common in 3D visualization, and the shape of their bumps, ridges, and indentations can contain important information. Examples include digital

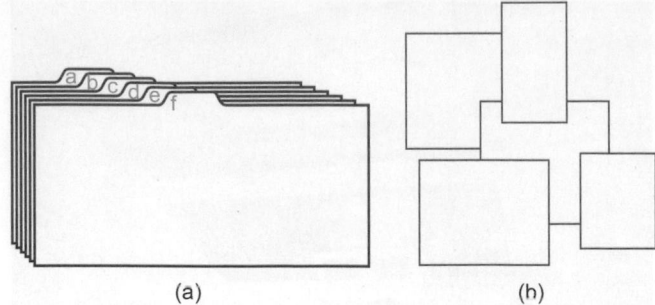

(a)   (h)

Figure 7.10 (a) Careful use of occlusion enables small tabs to provide access to larger objects. (b) Window interfaces use occlusion.

elevation maps representing the topography of the land or the ocean floor; maps of physical properties of the environment, such as pressure and temperature; and maps representing mathematical functions that are only distantly related to the raw data. These kinds of data objects are variously called *2D scalar fields*, *univariate maps*, or *2D manifolds*. The two traditional methods for displaying scalar field information are the contour map, which originated in cartography, and the pseudocolor map, discussed in Chapter 4. Here we consider using the spatial cues that let us perceive curved surfaces in the world, mainly shape from shading and conformal texture.

Shading Models

The basic shading model used in computer graphics to represent the interaction of light with surfaces has already been discussed in Chapter 2. It has four basic components, as follows:

1. **Lambertian shading**—Light reflected from a surface equally in all directions
2. **Specular shading**—Highlights reflected from a glossy surface
3. **Ambient shading**—Light coming from the surrounding environment
4. **Cast shadows**—Shadows cast by an object, either on itself or on other objects

Fig. 7.11 illustrates the shading model, complete with cast shadows, applied to a digital elevation map of San Francisco Bay. As can be seen, even this simple lighting model is capable of producing a dramatic image of surface topography. A key question in choosing a shading model for data visualization is not its degree of realism but how well it reveals the surface shape. There is some evidence that more sophisticated lighting may actually be harmful in representing surfaces.

Experiments by Ramachandran (1988) suggest that the brain assumes a single light source from above in determining whether a particular shaded area is a bump or a hollow (see Fig. 7.12). The kinds of complex shadows that result from multiple light sources and radiosity modeling may be visually confusing rather than helpful. As discussed in Chapter 2 (Fig. 2.8), specular highlights can be extremely useful in revealing

Figure 7.11 A shaded representation of the floor of San Francisco Bay, shown as if the water had been drained out of it. *(Data courtesy of James Gardner, U.S. Geological Survey. Image constructed using IVS Fledermaus software.)*

Figure 7.12 The brain generally assumes that lighting comes from above. The bumps in this image become hollows when the picture is turned upside down, and vice versa.

fine surface details, as when a light is used to show scratches on glass. At other times, highlights will obscure patterns of surface color. Also, discussed and illustrated in Chapter 2 (Fig. 2.9), the technique of ambient occlusion reduces the amount of simulated ambient light reaching recessed parts of objects (Tarini, Cignoni, & Claudio Montani, 2006). It may be preferable to the use of cast shadows in certain circumstances. Overall, the choice of lighting cues as aids to visualization cannot be captured with simple guidelines. It is a design problem that can only be addressed by carefully considering which parts of a 3D data object should be made clear, the shapes of those parts and the surrounding spatial context.

A clever use of shape from shading is shown in Fig. 7.13. van Wijk and Telea (2001) developed a method that allows for the perception of surface shape using shape-from-shading information. In addition, they added ridges that also allow for contours to be perceived.

Shading information can also be useful in emphasizing the affordances of display widgets such as buttons and sliders, even in displays that are very flat. Fig. 7.14 illustrates a slider enhanced with shading. This technique is widely used in today's graphical user interfaces.

Cushion Maps

The treemap visualization technique was introduced in Chapter 6 and illustrated in Fig. 6.65 (Johnson & Shneiderman, 1991). As discussed, a problem with treemaps is that they do not convey tree structure well, although they are extremely good at

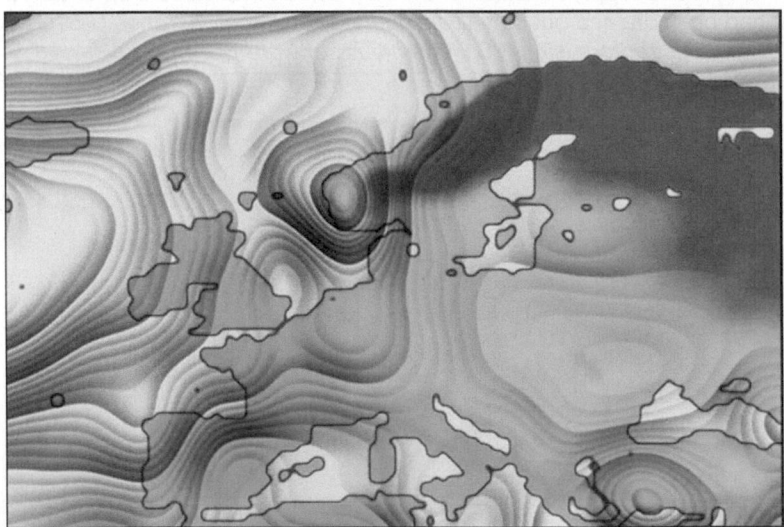

Figure 7.13 In this image, the average precipitation over Europe for January has been converted to a smoothed surface using the method of van Wijk and Telea (2001). The shape of this surface is revealed through shape-from-shading information. *(Courtesy of J van Wijk; van Wijk and Telea, 2001.)*

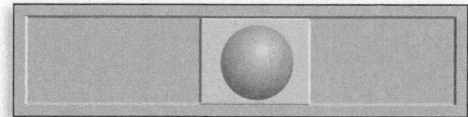

Figure 7.14 Even with mostly 2D interfaces, subtle shading can make sliders and other widgets look like objects that can be manipulated.

showing the sizes and groupings of the leaf nodes. An interesting solution devised by van Wijk and van de Wetering (1999) makes use of shading. They called it a *cushion map*. To create it, the hierarchical shading model is applied to a treemap in such a way that areas representing large branches are given an overall shading, and regions representing smaller branches are given their own shading within the overall shading. This is repeated down to the leaf nodes, which have the smallest scale shading. An example is shown in Fig. 7.15 showing a computer file system. As can be seen, the hierarchical structure of the system is more visible than it would be in an unshaded treemap.

Surface Texture

Surfaces in nature are generally textured. Gibson (1986) took the position that surface texture is an essential property of a surface. A nontextured surface, he said, is merely a patch of light. The way in which textures wrap around surfaces can provide valuable information about surface shape.

Without texture, it is usually impossible to distinguish one transparent curved surface from another transparent curved surface lying beneath it. Fig. 7.16 shows an illustration from Interrante, Fuchs, and Pizer (1997) containing experimental see-through textures designed to reveal one curved surface lying above another. The concept of laciness, discussed in Chapter 6, is relevant here, because it tells us something about how to make layers visually distinct and thereby clearly show separate surfaces, one beneath another.

There are many ways to make oriented textures conform to a surface. Texture lines can be constructed to follow the fall line (down slope), to be horizontal contours, to be at right angles to maximum curvature direction, or to be orthogonal to the line of site of a viewer, to present just a few examples.

Kim, Hagh-Shenas, and Interrante (2003) investigated combinations of first and second principal directions of curvature contours, as illustrated in Fig. 7.17 (the principal curvature direction is the direction of maximum curvature). All of the textured surfaces were artificially lit using standard computer graphics shading algorithms. Subjects made smaller errors in surface orientation judgments when two contour directions were used to form a mesh, as shown in Fig. 7.17(a). Nevertheless, this study and Norman, Todd, and Phillips (1995) found that errors *averaged* 20 degrees. This is surprisingly large and suggests that further gains are possible.

Figure 7.15 The cushion map is a variation of a treemap that uses shape-from-shading information to reveal hierarchical structure. *(Courtesy of Jack van Wijke.)*

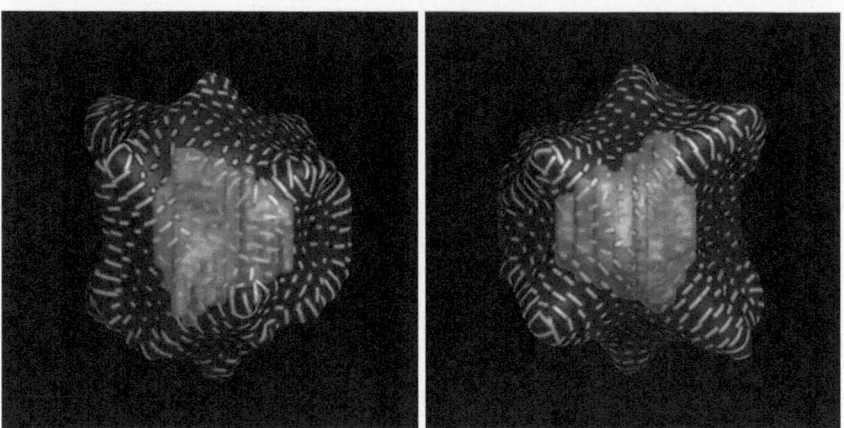

Figure 7.16 Textures designed to reveal surface shape so another surface can be seen beneath. *(From Interrante et al. (1997). Reproduced with permission.)*

A simpler way of a revealing the shape of a surface through texture is to drape a regular grid mesh over it (Bair, House, & Ware, 2009; Sweet & Ware, 2004). See Fig. 7.18. More studies are needed to do direct comparisons between the various conformal texture generation methods, but cross-paper comparisons suggest that simple draped meshes yield smaller errors than the fall line or principal curvature textures, as Bair et al. (2009) measured mean errors of less than 12 degrees using grids. In addition, if grids are constructed with a standard cell size they provide useful scale information. Another interesting result is that perspective views result in smaller errors than plan views.

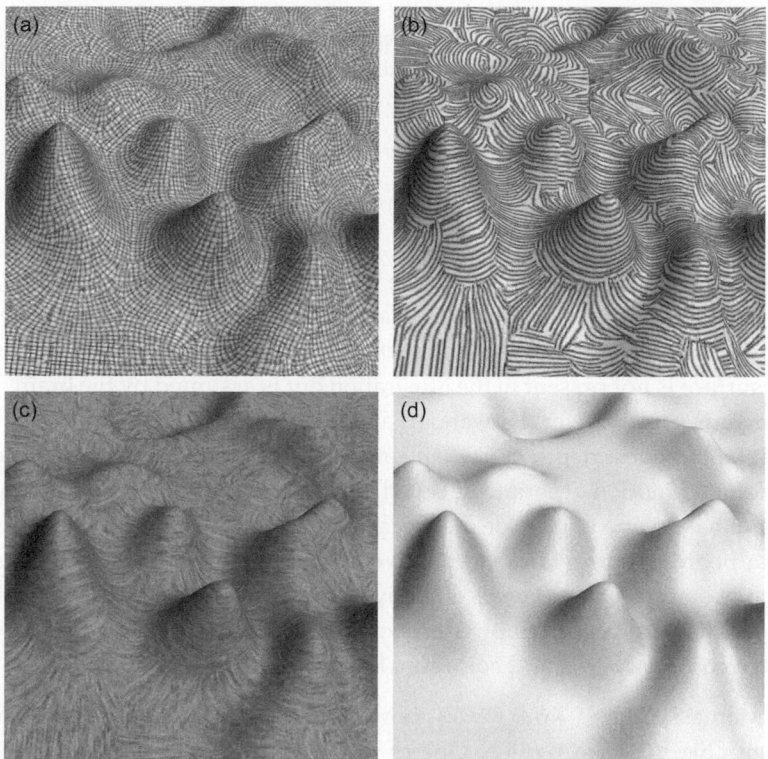

Figure 7.17 Surface-revealing texture patterns. (a) Two-directional texture pattern following first and second principal directions. (b) One-directional texture pattern following first principal curvature direction. (c) One-directional, line-integral convolutions texture following first principal curvature direction. (d) No texture. *(From Kim et al. (2003). Reproduced with permission.)*

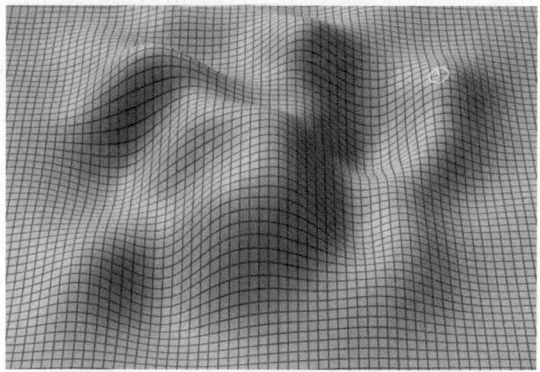

Figure 7.18 Simple draped grids can help reveal surface shape.

[G7.4] In 3D visualizations of height field data, consider using draped grids to enhance surface shape information. This is likely to be most useful where the data varies smoothly so surface shape features are substantially larger than grid squares.

Cast Shadows

Cast shadows are a very potent cue to the height of an object above a plane, as illustrated in Fig. 7.19. They can function as a kind of indirect depth cue—the shadow locates the object with respect to some surface in the environment. In the case of Fig. 7.19, this surface is not present in the illustration but is assumed by the brain. In a multifactor experiment, Wanger, Ferwander, and Greenberg (1992) found that shadows provided the strongest depth cue when compared to texture, projection type, frames of reference, and motion. It should be noted, however, that they used an oblique checkerboard as a base plane to provide the actual distance information, so strictly speaking the checkerboard was providing the depth cue. Cast shadows function best as a cue to height above surface when there is a relatively small distance between the object and the surface. They can be especially effective in showing when an object is very close to the point of contact (Madison, Thompson, Kersen, Shirley, & Smits, 2001).

Kersten, Mamassian, and Knill (1997) showed that cast shadows are especially powerful when objects are in motion. One of their demonstrations is illustrated in Fig. 7.20(b). In this case, the apparent trajectory of a ball moving in 3D space is caused to change dramatically depending on the path of the object's shadow. The image of the ball actually travels in a straight line, but the ball appears to bounce because of the way the shadow moves. In this study, shadow motion was shown to be a stronger depth cue than change in size with perspective.

It has been shown that shadows can be correctly interpreted without being realistic. Kersten, Mamassian, Knill, and Bulthoff (1996) found no effect of shadow quality in their results; however, one of the principal cues in distinguishing shadows from

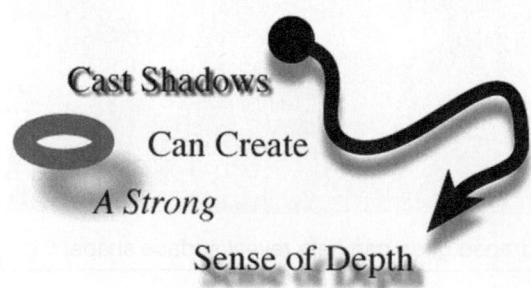

Figure 7.19 Cast shadows can be useful in making data appear to stand above an opaque plane.

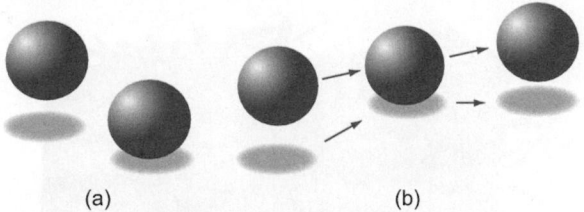

(a)   (b)

Figure 7.20 (a) Shadows can provide a strong cue for the relative height of objects above a plane. (b) The effect is even stronger with motion. The ball actually appears to bounce when the ball and shadows are animated to follow the trajectories shown by the arrows.

nonshadows in the environment is the lack of sharpness in shadow edges. Fuzzy-edged shadows are likely to lead to less confusing images.

Cast shadows are useful in distinguishing information that is layered a small distance above a planar surface, as illustrated in Fig. 7.19. In this case, they are functioning as a depth cue. This technique can be applied to layered map displays of the type used in geographical information systems (GISs).

In complex environments, however, where objects are arranged throughout 3D space, cast shadows can be confusing rather than helpful, because it may not be possible to determine perceptually which object is casting a particular shadow.

[G7.5] In 3D data visualizations, consider using cast shadows to tie objects to a surface that defines depth. The surface should provide strong depth cues, such as a grid texture. Only use cast shadows to aid in depth perception where the surface is simple and where the objects casting the shadow are close to it.

Ambient Occlusion

Fig. 7.21 shows an image of blood vessels rendered using a variant on ambient occlusion (Díaz, Ropinski, Navazo, Gobbetti, & Vázquez, 2017) to evaluate the value of different shading cues for depth judgments in a stereoscopic display. The researchers found that depth judgments were better with this display than when no shading was applied. *However, simple Phong shading also improved performance and there was no significant* difference between the rendering methods.

Distance Based on Familiar Size

Many objects that we see have a known size and this can be used to help us judge distance. Fig. 7.22 illustrates this. The German shepherd dog and the chair are objects known to be of roughly comparable size; therefore, we see them as at the same distance in the composition on the left. A different interpretation is available on the right, where the size and vertical position depth cues are consistent with the result that the dog is seen as more distant than the chair.

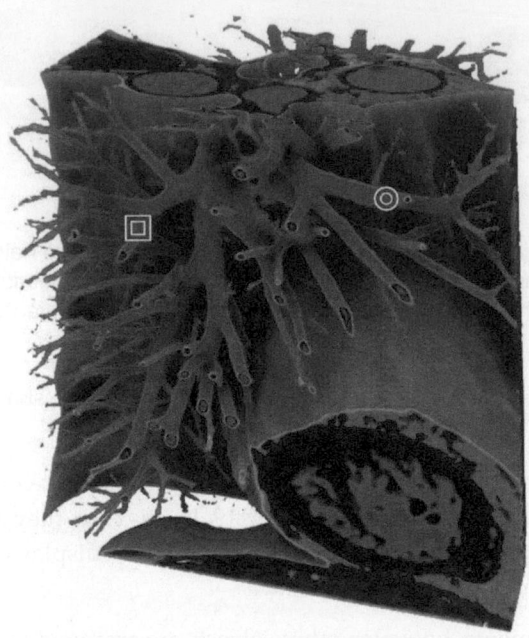

Figure 7.21 An image of blood vessels shaded using ambient occlusion. *(From Díaz et al., 2017. With permission.)*

Figure 7.22 On the left, we see a picture of a dog and a chair, arranged rather arbitrarily but appearing to be the same distance from the viewer. On the right, the known sizes of dog and chair are consistent with another interpretation, that of a coherent 3D scene with the dog at a greater distance.

Depth of Focus

When we look around, our eyes change focus to bring the images of fixated objects into sharp focus on the fovea. As a result, the images of both nearby and more distant objects become blurred, making blur an ambiguous depth cue. In an image with some objects that are sharp and others that are blurred, all the sharp objects tend to be seen at a single distance, and the blurred objects tend to be seen at a different distance, either closer or farther away. Focus effects are important in separating foreground objects from background objects, as shown in Fig. 7.23. Perhaps because of its role as a depth cue, simulating depth of focus is an excellent way to highlight information by blurring everything except that which is critical. Of course, this only makes sense if the critical information can be reliably predicted.

The effect of depth of focus can be properly computed only if the object of fixation can be predicted. In normal vision, our attention shifts and our eyes refocus dynamically depending on the distance of the object fixated. Chapter 2 describes a system designed to change focus information based on a measured point of fixation in a virtual environment. An alternative is a holographic display which structures the light field in a way that mimics the natural environment and therefore provides accurate depth-of-focus information.

Eye Accommodation

The eye changes focus so that an attended object forms a sharp image on the retina. If the brain could measure the eye's accommodation this might be a depth cue. But, because we are only capable of focusing to an accuracy of half a diopter, theoretically, accommodation can provide only limited information about the distance to objects closer than 2 m (Hochberg, 1971). In fact, accommodation does not appear to be used to judge distance directly but may be used indirectly in computing the sizes of nearby objects (Wallach & Floor, 1971).

Structure from motion

When an object is in motion or when we ourselves move through the environment, the result is a dynamically changing pattern of light on the retina. Structure-from-motion information is generally divided into two different classes: motion parallax and kinetic depth effect. An example of motion parallax occurs when we look sideways out of a car or train window. Things nearby appear to be moving very rapidly, whereas objects close to the horizon appear to move gradually. Overall, there is a velocity gradient, as illustrated in Fig. 7.24(a).

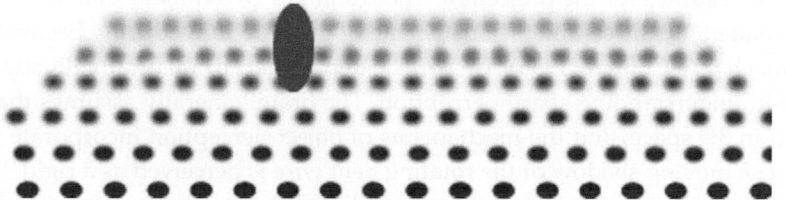

Figure 7.23 The eye adjusts to bring objects of interest into sharp focus. As a result, objects that are closer or more distant become blurred.

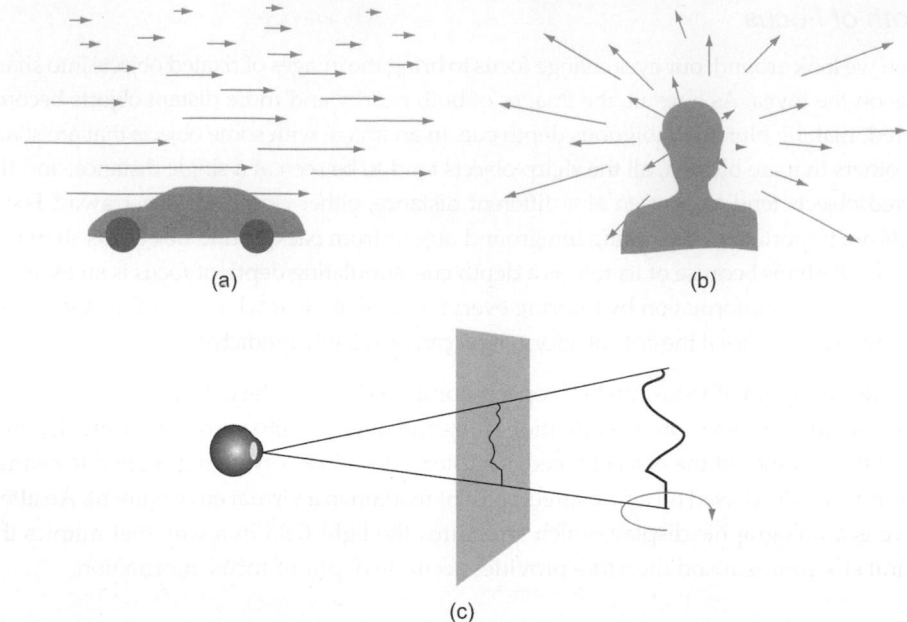

Figure 7.24 Three different kinds of structure-from-motion information. (a) The velocity gradient that results when the viewer is looking sideways out of a moving vehicle. (b) The velocity field that results when the viewer is moving forward through the environment. (c) The kinetic depth information that results when a rotating rigid object is projected onto a screen.

When we move forward through a cluttered environment, the result is a very different expanding pattern of motion, like that shown in Fig. 7.24(b). Wann et al. (1995) showed that subjects were able to control their headings with an accuracy of 1–2 degrees when they were given feedback from a wide-screen field of dots through which they had to steer. There is also evidence for specialized neural mechanisms sensitive to the time to contact with a visual surface that is being approached. This is inversely proportional to the rate of optical expansion of the pattern of surface features (Lee & Young, 1985), a variable called *tau*.

The kinetic depth effect can be demonstrated with a wire bent into a complex 3D shape and projected onto a screen, as shown in Fig. 7.24(c). Casting the shadow of the wire will suffice for the projection. The result is a two-dimensional line, but if the wire is rotated, the three-dimensional shape of the wire immediately becomes apparent (Wallach & O'Connell, 1953). The kinetic depth effect dramatically illustrates a key concept in understanding space perception. The brain generally assumes that objects are rigid in 3D space, and the mechanisms of object perception incorporate this constraint. The moving shadow of the rotating bent wire is perceived as a rigid 3D object, not as a wiggling 2D line. It is easy to simulate this in a computer graphics system by creating an irregular line, rotating it about a vertical axis, and displaying it using standard graphics techniques. Visualizations where many small discrete objects are arranged in space as well as 3D node-link structures can become much clearer with kinetic depth. Structure from motion is one reason for the effectiveness of fly-through animated movies that take an observer through a data space.

An obvious problem when using kinetic depth in data visualization is that people often wish to contemplate a structure from a particular viewpoint; rotating it causes the viewpoint to be continuously changed. This can be mitigated by having the scene rotate about a vertical axis. If the rotation is oscillatory, then the viewpoint can be approximately preserved.

> **[G7.6]** To help users understand depth relationships in 3D data visualizations, consider using structure from motion by rotating the scene around the center of interest. This is especially useful when objects are unattached to other parts of the scene.

Eye Convergence

When we fixate an object with both eyes, the eyes converge to a degree dictated by the distance of the object. This *vergence* angle is illustrated in Fig. 7.25. Given the two line-of-sight vectors, it is a matter of simple trigonometry to determine the distance to the fixated object; however, the evidence suggests that the human brain is not good at this geometric computation except for objects within arm's length (Viguier, Clement, & Trotter, 2001). The vergence sensing system appears capable of quite rapid recalibration in the presence of other spatial information (Fisher & Cuiffreda, 1990).

Stereoscopic Depth

Stereoscopic depth is information about distance provided by the slight differences in images on the retinas of animals with two forward-looking eyes. Stereoscopic displays simulate these differences by presenting different images to the left and right eyes of viewers. There is an often expressed opinion that stereoscopic displays allow "truly" 3D images. In advertising literature, potential buyers are urged to buy stereoscopic display equipment and "see it in 3D." As should be plain from this chapter, stereoscopic disparity is only one of many depth cues that the brain uses to analyze 3D space, and it is by no means the most useful one. If fact, as much as 20% of the population may be stereo blind, yet they function perfectly well and are often unaware that they have

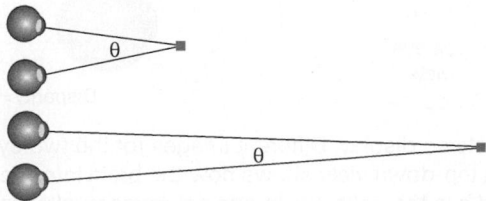

Figure 7.25 The vergence angle θ varies as the eyes fixate on near and far objects.

a disability. Nevertheless, stereoscopic displays can provide a particularly compelling sense of a 3D virtual space, and for a few tasks they can be extremely useful.

The basis of stereoscopic depth perception is forward-facing eyes with overlapping visual fields. On average, human eyes are separated by about 6.4 cm; this means that the brain receives slightly different images, which can be used to compute relative distances of pairs of objects. Stereoscopic depth is a technical subject, and we therefore begin by defining some of the terms.

Fig. 7.26 illustrates a simple stereo display. Both eyes are fixated on the vertical line (*a* for the right eye, *c* for the left eye). A second line, *d*, in the left eye's image is fused with *b* in the right eye's image. The brain resolves the discrepancy in line spacing by perceiving the lines as being at different depths, as shown.

Angular disparity is the difference between the angular separation of a pair of points imaged by the two eyes (disparity = α-β). *Screen disparity* is the distance between parts of an image on the screen (disparity = [*c*-*d*]-[*a*-*b*]).

If the disparity between the two images becomes too great, double vision (called *diplopia*) occurs. Diplopia is the appearance of the doubling of part of a stereo image when the visual system fails to fuse the images. The 3D area within which objects can be fused and seen without double images is called *Panum's fusional area*. In the worst case, Panum's fusional area has remarkably little depth. At the fovea, the maximum disparity before fusion breaks down is only 1/10 degree, whereas at 6 degrees of eccentricity

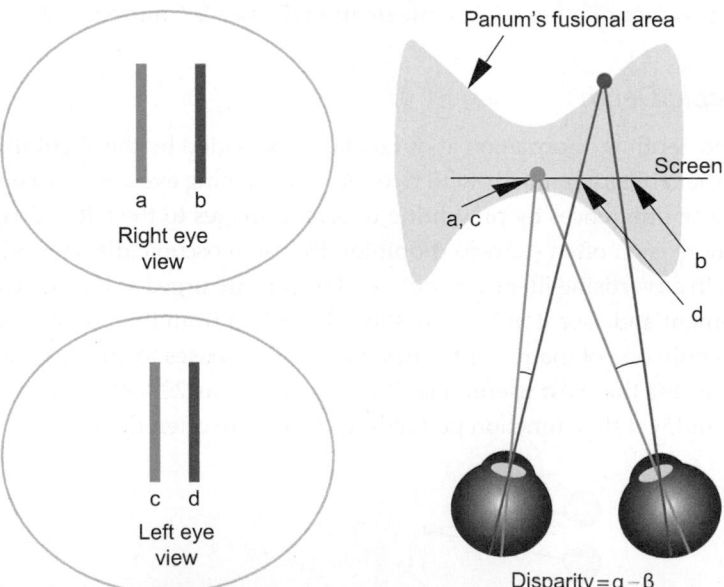

Figure 7.26 A simple stereo display. Different images for the two eyes are shown on the left. On the right, a top-down view shows how the brain interprets this display. The vertical lines a and b in the right-eye image are perceptually fused with c and d, respectively, in the left-eye image.

(of the retinal image from the fovea), the limit is 1/3 degree (Patterson & Martin, 1992). The reason why only small disparities can be handled is that disparity-detecting neurons in V1 are only capable of responding to small localized differences between the images from the two eyes (Qian & Zhu, 1997).

Stereopsis is a *superacuity*. We can resolve disparities of only 10 seconds of arc at better than chance. This means that under optimal viewing conditions we should be able to see a depth difference between an object at 1 km and an object at infinity.

It is worthwhile to consider what these numbers imply for monitor-based stereo displays. A screen with 30 pixels per centimeter, viewed at 57 cm, will have 30 pixels per degree of visual angle. The 1/10 degree limit on the visual angle before diplopia occurs translates into about 3 pixels of screen disparity. This means that we can only display 3 pixel-depth steps before diplopia occurs, either in front of or behind the screen, in the worst case. It also means it will only be possible to view a virtual image that extends in depth a fraction of a centimeter from the screen (assuming an object on the screen is fixated). However, some screens are now available that are much better, having 100 pixels per cm. These will allow more than three times the depth discrimination.

Also, it is important to emphasize that the diplopia thresholds given above represent a worst-case scenario. It is likely that antialiased images will allow better than pixel resolution, for exactly the same reason that vernier acuities can be achieved to better than pixel resolution (discussed in Chapter 2). In addition, the size of Panum's fusional area is highly dependent on a number of visual display parameters, such as the exposure duration of the images and the size of the targets. Moving targets, simulated depth of focus, and greater lateral separation of the image components all increase the size of the fusional area (Patterson & Martin, 1992). Depth judgments based on disparity can also be made outside the fusional area, although these are less accurate.

Problems with Stereoscopic Displays

It is common for users of 3D visualization systems with stereoscopic display capabilities to disable stereo viewing once the novelty has worn off. There are a number of reasons why stereoscopic displays are disliked. Double-imaging problems tend to be much worse in stereoscopic computer displays than in normal viewing of the 3D environment. One of the principal reasons for this is that in the real world objects farther away than the one fixated are out of focus on the retina. Because we can fuse blurred images more easily than sharply focused images diplopia problems in the real world are reduced. In addition, disparity and focus are complementary cues to depth (Held, Cooper, & Banks, 2012). Moreover, focus is linked to attention and foveal fixation, and in the real world double images of nonattended peripheral objects generally will not be noticed. Unfortunately, in present day computer graphics systems, particularly those that allow for real time interaction, depth of focus is rarely simulated. All parts of the computer graphics image are therefore equally in focus, even though some parts of the image may have large disparities. Thus, the double images that occur in stereoscopic computer graphics displays are very obtrusive unless depth of focus is simulated. These and many other factors are reviewed in Lambooij et al. (2009). Some are discussed in more detail below.

Frame Cancellation

Valyus (1966) coined the phrase *frame cancellation* to describe a common problem with stereoscopic displays. If the stereoscopic depth cues are such that a virtual image should appear in front of the screen, the edge of the screen appears to occlude the virtual object, as shown in Fig. 7.27. Occlusion overrides the stereo depth information, and the depth effect collapses. This is typically accompanied by a double image of the object that should appear in front.

> **[G7.7]** When creating stereoscopic images, avoid placing graphical objects so that they appear in front of the screen and are clipped by the edges of the screen. The simplest way of doing this is to ensure that no objects are in front of the screen in terms of their stereoscopic depth.

The Vergence-Focus Problem

When we change our fixation between objects placed at different distances, two things happen: The convergence of the eyes changes (vergence), and the focal lengths of the lenses in the eyes accommodate to bring the new object into focus (Hoffman, Girshick, Akeley, & Banks, 2008). The vergence and the focus mechanisms are coupled in the human visual system. If one eye is covered, the vergence and the focus of the covered eye change as the uncovered eye accommodates objects at different distances; this illustrates vergence being driven by focus. The converse also occurs—a change in vergence can drive a change in focus.

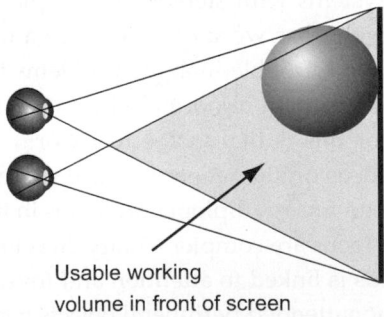 

Usable working
volume in front of screen

Figure 7.27 Frame cancellation occurs when stereoscopic disparity cues indicate that an object is in front of the monitor screen. Because the edge of the screen clips the object, this acts as an occlusion depth cue and the object appears to be behind the window, canceling the stereo depth effect. Because of this, the useable working volume of a stereoscopic display is restricted as shown.

In a stereoscopic display, all objects lie in the same focal plane, regardless of their apparent depth; however, accurate disparity and vergence information may fool the brain into perceiving them at different depths. Screen-based stereo displays provide disparity and vergence information, but no focus information. The failure to present focus information correctly, coupled with vergence, may cause a form of eyestrain (Wann et al., 1995; Mon-Williams & Wann, 1998; Lambooij et al. 2009).

This problem is present in both stereoscopic head-mounted systems and monitor-based stereo displays. Wann et al. (1995) concluded that vergence and focus cross-coupling "prevents large depth intervals of three-dimensional visual space being rendered with integrity through dual two-dimensional displays." This may account for the common reports of eyestrain occurring with dynamic stereoscopic displays. It is also worth noting that, because people lose the ability to refocus their eyes as they get older, this particular problem should decline with age.

> **[G7.8]** When rendering stereoscopic displays for 3D visualizations, add depth-of-focus information, if possible without blurring critical parts of the scene.

Distant Objects

The problems with stereoscopic viewing are not always related to disparities that are too large. Sometimes disparities may be too small. The stereoscopic depth cue is most useful at 30 m or less from the viewer. Beyond this, disparities tend to be too small to be resolved, except under optimal viewing conditions. For practical purposes, most useful stereoscopic depth is obtained within distances of less than 10 m from the viewer and may be optimal for objects held roughly at arm's length.

Making Effective Stereoscopic Displays

Because stereoscopic depth perception is a superacuity, the ideal stereoscopic display should have very high resolution, much higher than the typical desktop monitor. On current monitors, the fine detail is produced by pixels, and in a stereoscopic display the pixilation of features such as fine lines will generate false binocular correspondences. High-resolution displays enable the presentation of fine texture gradients and hence disparity gradients that are the basis for stereoscopic surface shape perception.

> **[G7.9]** When creating stereoscopic displays for 3D visualizations, use the highest possible screen resolution, especially in a horizontal direction, and aim to achieve excellent spatial and temporal antialiasing.

There are also ways of mitigating the diplopia, frame cancellation, and vergence-focus problems described previously, although they will not be fully solved until displays that can truly simulate depth become commercially viable. All the solutions involve reducing screen disparities by artificially bringing the computer graphics imagery into the fusional area. Valyus (1966) found that the diplopia problems were acceptable if no more than 1.6 degrees of disparity existed in the display. Based on this, he proposed that the screen disparity should be less than 0.03 times the distance to the screen; however, this provides only about ±1.5 cm of useful depth at normal viewing distances. Using a more relaxed criterion, Williams and Parrish (1990) concluded that a practical viewing volume falls between −25% and +60% of the viewer-to-screen distance. This provides a more usable working space.

One obvious solution to the problems involved in creating useful stereoscopic displays is simply to create small virtual scenes that do not extend much in front of or behind the screen. In many situations, though, this is not practical—for example, when we wish to make a stereoscopic view of extensive terrain. A more general solution is to compress the range of stereoscopic disparities so that they lie within a judiciously enlarged fusional area, such as that proposed by Williams and Parrish. A method for doing this is described in the next two sections.

Before going on, we must consider another potential problem. We should be aware that tampering with stereoscopic depth may cause us to misjudge distance. There is conflicting evidence as to whether this is likely. Some studies have shown stereoscopic disparity to be relatively unimportant in making *absolute* depth judgments. Using a special apparatus, Wallach and Karsh (1963) found that when they rotated a wire frame cube viewed in stereo, only half of the subjects were even aware of a doubling in their eye separation. Because increasing eye separation increases stereo disparities, this should have resulted in a grossly distorted cube. The fact that distortion was not perceived indicates that kinetic depth-effect information and rigidity assumptions are much stronger than stereo information. Ogle (1962) argued that stereopsis gives us information about the relative depths of objects that have small disparities especially when they are close together. When it comes to judging the overall layout of objects in space, other depth cues dominate. Also, many experiments show large individual differences in how we use the different kinds of depth information, so we will never have a simple one-size-fits-all account.

Overall, we can conclude that the brain is very flexible in weighing evidence from different depth cues and that disparity information can be scaled by the brain depending on other available information. Especially when the world is in motion relative to the observer, providing kinetic depth information, the brain prefers to see the world as solid and rigid and not warped (Glennerster, Tcheang, Gilson, Fitzgibbon, & Parker, 2006). Therefore, it should be possible to artificially manipulate the overall pattern of stereo disparities and enhance local 3D space perception without greatly distorting the overall sense of space, if other strong cues to depth, such as structure from motion and linear perspective, are provided. We (Ware, Gobrecht, & Paton, 1998) investigated dynamically changed disparities by smoothly varying the stereoscopic eye-separation parameter. We found that a participant's disparity range could be changed by about 30% over a two-second interval, without him or her even noticing, as long as the change was smooth.

[G7.10] When creating stereoscopic displays for 3D visualizations, adjust the virtual eye separation to optimize perceived stereoscopic depth while minimizing diplopia.

Cyclopean Scale

One simple method that we developed to deal with diplopia problems is called a *cyclopean scale* (Glennerster et al., 2006; Ware et al., 1998). As illustrated in Fig. 7.28, this manipulation involves scaling the virtual environment about the midpoint between the observer's estimated eye positions (where the Cyclops of mythology had his one eye). The scaling variable is chosen so that the nearest part of the scene comes to a point just behind the monitor screen. To understand the effects of this operation, consider first that scaling a virtual world about a *single* viewpoint does not result in any change in computer graphics imagery (assuming depth of focus is not taken into account). Thus, the cyclopean scale does not change the overall sizes of objects as they are represented on a computer screen. It does change disparities, though. The cyclopean scale has a number of benefits for stereo viewing: More distant objects, which would normally not benefit from stereo viewing because they are beyond the range where significant disparities exist, are brought into a position where usable disparities are present. The vergence-focus discrepancy is reduced. At least for the part of the virtual object that lies close to the screen, there is no vergence-focus conflict. Virtual objects that are closer to the observer than to the screen are also scaled so they lie behind the screen. This removes the possibility of frame cancellation.

Virtual Eye Separation

The cyclopean scale, although useful, does not remove the possibility of disparities that result in diplopia. In order to do so, it is necessary to compress or expand the disparity range. To understand how this can be accomplished, it is useful to consider a device called a *telestereoscope* (Fig. 7.29). A telestereoscope is generally used to increase disparities when distant objects are viewed, but the same principle can also be used to decrease the range of disparities by optically moving the eyes closer together. Fig. 7.30 illustrates the concept of virtual eye separation and demonstrates how the apparent

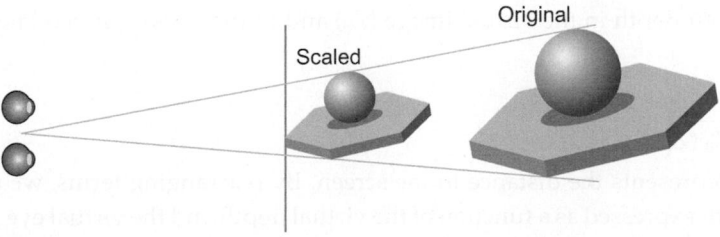

Figure 7.28 Cyclopean scale: A virtual environment is resized around a center point, midway between the left and right viewpoints.

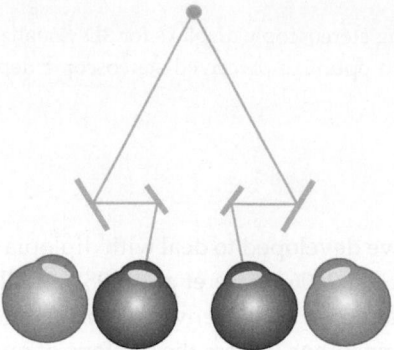

Figure 7.29 A telestereoscope is a device that uses mirrors or prisms to increase the effective eye separation, thereby increasing stereoscopic depth information (disparities).

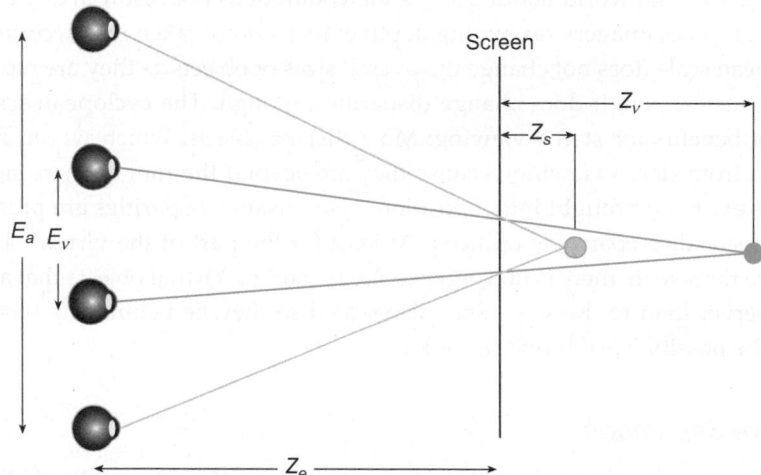

Figure 7.30 The geometry of virtual eye separation. In this example, the stereoscopic depth is decreased by computing an image with a virtual eye separation that is smaller than the actual eye separation.

depth of an object decreases if the virtual viewpoints have a wider eye separation than the actual viewpoint. We consider only a single point in the virtual space. If E_v is the virtual eye separation and E_a is the actual eye separation of an observer, the relationship between depth in the virtual image (Z_v) and in the viewed stereo image (Z_s) is a ratio:

$$\frac{E_v}{E_a} = \frac{Z_s (Z_y + Z_e)}{Z_v (Z_s + Z_e)}$$

(7.1)

where Z_e represents the distance to the screen. By rearranging terms, we can get the stereo depth expressed as a function of the virtual depth and the virtual eye separation:

$$Z_s = \frac{Z_e Z_v E_v}{E_a z_v + E_a Z_e - E_v Z_v}$$

(7.2)

Stereoscopic depth can just as easily be increased. If the virtual eye separation is smaller than the actual eye separation, stereo depth is decreased. If the virtual eye separation is larger than the actual eye separation, stereo depth is increased. $E_v = E_a$ for "correct" stereoscopic viewing of a virtual scene, although for the reasons stated this may not be useful in practice. When $E_v = 0.0$, both eyes get the same image, as in single viewpoint graphics. Note that stereo depth and perceived depth are not always equal. The brain is an imperfect processor of stereo information, and other depth cues may be much more important in determining the perceived depth. Experimental evidence shows that subjects given control of their eye-separation parameters have no idea what the "correct" setting should be (Ware et al., 1998). When asked to adjust the virtual eye-separation parameter, subjects tended to decrease the eye separation for scenes in which there was a lot of depth, but actually increased eye separation beyond the normal (enhancing the sensation of stereoscopic depth) when the scene was flat. This behavior can be mimicked by an algorithm designed to test automatically the depth range in a virtual environment and adjust the eye-separation parameters appropriately (after cyclopean scale). We have found the following function to work well for a large variety of digital terrain models. It uses the ratio of the nearest point to the farthest point in the scene to calculate the virtual eye separation in centimeters.

$$Eye\ Separation\ = 2.5 + 5.0 * (Near\ Point\ /Far\ Point)^2 \tag{7.3}$$

This function increases the eye separation to 7.5 cm for shallow scenes (as compared to a normal value of 6.4 cm) and reduces it to 2.5 cm for very deep scenes.

Artificial Spatial Cues

There are effective ways to provide information about space that are not based directly on the way information is provided in the normal environment, although the best methods are probably effective because they make use of existing perceptual mechanisms. One common technique used to enhance simple 3D scatterplots is illustrated in Fig. 7.31. A line is dropped from each data point to the ground plane. Without these lines, only a 2D judgment of spatial layout is possible. With the lines, it is possible to

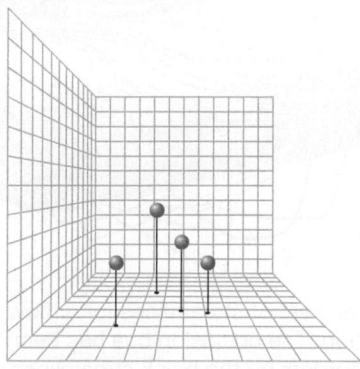

Figure 7.31 Dropping lines to a ground plane is an effective artificial spatial cue.

estimate 3D position. Kim, Tendick, and Stark (1991) showed that this artificial spatial cue can be at least as effective as stereopsis in providing 3D position information. It should be understood that, although the vertical line segments in Fig. 7.31 can be considered artificial additions to the plot, there is nothing artificial about the way they operate as depth cues. Gibson (1986) pointed out that one of the most effective ways to estimate the sizes of objects is with reference to the ground plane. Adding the vertical lines creates a link to the ground plane and the rich texture size and linear perspective cues embedded in it. In this respect, drop lines function in the same way as cast shadows, but they are generally easier to interpret and should result in more accurate judgments, given that cast shadows can be confusing with certain lighting directions.

[G7.11] In 3D data visualizations where a strong, preferably gridded, ground plane is available, consider using drop lines to add depth information for small numbers of discrete isolated objects.

Sometimes in computer graphics, foreground objects and objects behind them have the same color, causing them to visually fuse, which nullifies the occlusion cue. A technique has been developed that artificially enhances occlusion by putting a *halo* along the occluding edges of the foreground objects (see Fig. 7.32). Perception of occlusion relies on edge contrast and the continuity of an overlaying contour, and this depends on neural mechanisms for edge detection, but artificial enhancement can amplify these factors to a degree that rarely if ever occurs in nature.

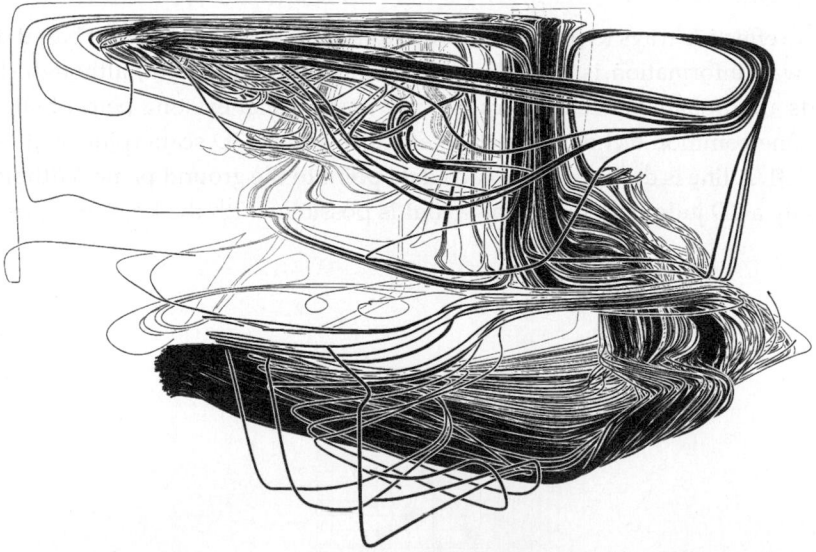

Figure 7.32 This figure shows a set of streamlines for airflow around a room. The principal depth cue is occlusion. The occlusion cue has been artificially enhanced by "halos" in the form of white borders on the black streamlines. (*From Everts, Bekker, Roerdink, and Isenberg (2009). Reproduced with permission.*)

[G7.12] In 3D data visualizations, consider using halos to enhance occlusion where this is an important depth cue and where overlapping objects have the same color or minimal luminance difference.

Computer graphics systems sometimes provide a function to implement what researchers call *proximity luminance covariance* (Dosher, Sperling, & Wurst, 1986). This function is confusingly called *depth cueing* in some computer graphics texts. Depth cueing in computer graphics is the ability to vary the color of an object depending on its distance from the viewpoint, as illustrated in Fig. 7.33. Normally, more distant objects are faded toward the background color, becoming darker if the background is dark and lighter if the background is light.

This cue is better named *proximity luminance contrast covariance*, because it is contrast, not luminance that produces the depth impression. Proximity contrast covariance simulates an environmental depth cue sometimes called *atmospheric depth*. This refers to the reduction in contrast of distant objects in the environment, especially under hazy viewing conditions. The depth cueing used in computer graphics is generally much more extreme than any atmospheric effects that occur in nature, and for this reason it can be considered an "artificial" cue. Dosher et al. (1986) showed that contrast covariance could function as an effective depth cue but was weaker than stereo for static displays. Evidence that this cue can be useful in visualizing blood vessels is provided by Kersten-Oertel, Chen, and Collins (2014).

Depth Cues in Combination

In designing a visualization, the designer has considerable freedom to choose which depth cues to include and which to leave out. One might think it best to simply include all the cues, just to be sure, but in fact this is not the best solution in most cases. There can be considerable costs associated with creating a stereoscopic display, for example,

Figure 7.33 Proximity luminance contrast covariance as a depth cue. The contrast with the background is reduced with distance. This simulates extreme atmospheric effects.

or with using real-time animation to take advantage of structure-from-motion cues. The hardware is more expensive, and a more complex user interface must be provided. Some cues, such as depth-of-focus information, are difficult or impossible to compute in the general case, because without knowing what object the observer is looking at, it is impossible to determine what should be shown in focus and what should be shown out of focus. A general theory of space perception should make it possible to determine which depth cues are likely to be most valuable. Such a theory would provide information about the relative values of different depth cues when they are used in combination.

Most of the early work on spatial information implicitly contains the notion that all spatial information is combined into a single cognitive model of the 3D environment and that this model is used as a resource in performing all spatial tasks (e.g., Bruno & Cutting, 1988). This theoretical position is illustrated in Fig. 7.34. Evidence is accumulating, however, that this unified model of cognitive space is fundamentally flawed.

The modern theory that is emerging is that depth cues are combined expeditiously, depending on task requirements (Jacobs & Fine 1999; Bradshaw, Parton, & Glennister, 2000); for example, Wanger et al. (1992) showed that cast shadows and motion parallax cues both helped in the task of orienting one virtual object to match another. Correct linear perspective (as opposed to parallel orthographic perspective) actually increased errors; it acted as a kind of negative depth cue for this particular task. With a different task, that of translating an object, linear perspective was found to be the most useful of the cues and motion parallax did not help at all. Further, Bradshaw et al. (2000) showed that stereopsis is critical in setting objects at the same distance from the observer, but motion parallax is more important for a layout task involving the creation of a triangle laid out in depth.

This alternative task-based model of depth perception is illustrated in Fig. 7.35. It does not assume an internal cognitive 3D model of the environment. Instead, depth cues are

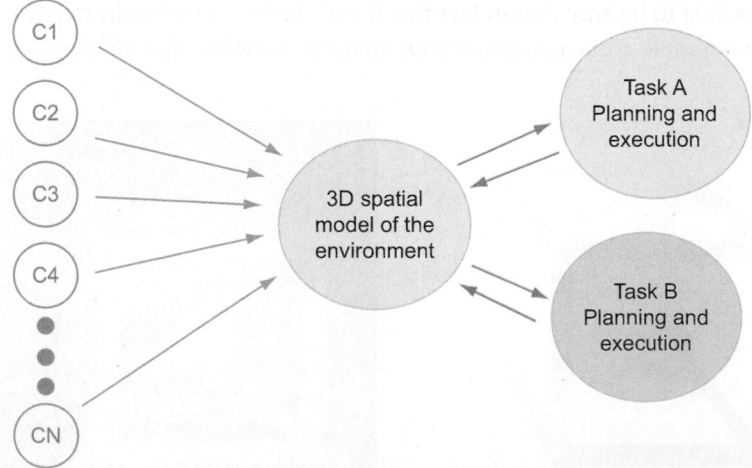

Figure 7.34 Most models of 3D space perception assume that depth cues (C1, …, CN) feed into a cognitive 3D model of the environment. This, in turn, is used as a resource in task planning and execution.

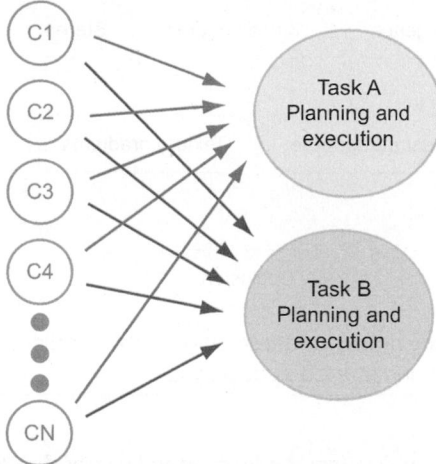

Figure 7.35 Experimental evidence suggests that depth cues (C1, …, CN) are weighted very differently for different tasks, suggesting that there is no unified cognitive spatial model.

combined in a Bayesian fashion; they are weighted according to both how much task information they provide and prior knowledge of the way the visual world is structured (Saunders & Chen, 2015). Cues are combined with different weightings depending on the task. Whatever the task, for example, threading a needle or running through a forest, certain depth cues are informative and other cues can be irrelevant. An application designer's choice is not whether to design a 3D or 2D interface, but rather which depth cues to use to best support a particular set of tasks. Depth cues can be applied somewhat independently. In a static picture, for example, we use all of the monocular pictorial depth cues, but not motion parallax or stereoscopic disparity. If we add structure-from-motion information, we get what we see at the movie theater. If we add stereo to a static picture, the result is the kind of stereoscopic viewer popular in Victorian times. We can also use far fewer depth cues. Modern desktop GUIs only use occlusion for windows, some minor shading information to make the menus and buttons stand out, and a cast shadow for the cursor.

There are some restrictions on our freedom to arbitrarily choose combinations of depth cues because some cues depend on the correct implementation of other cues. Fig. 7.36 shows a dependency graph for depth cues. An arrow means that a particular cue depends on another cue to appear correctly. This graph does not show absolute rules that cannot be broken, but it does imply that breaking the rules will have undesirable consequences; for example, the graph shows that kinetic depth depends on correct perspective. It is possible to break this rule and show kinetic depth with a parallel (orthographic) perspective but this has the undesirable consequence that a rotating object will appear to distort as it rotates. This graph is transitive; all of the depth cues depend on occlusion being shown properly because they all depend on something that in turn depends on occlusion. Occlusion is, in a sense, the most basic depth cue; it is difficult to break the occlusion dependency rule and have a perceptually coherent scene.

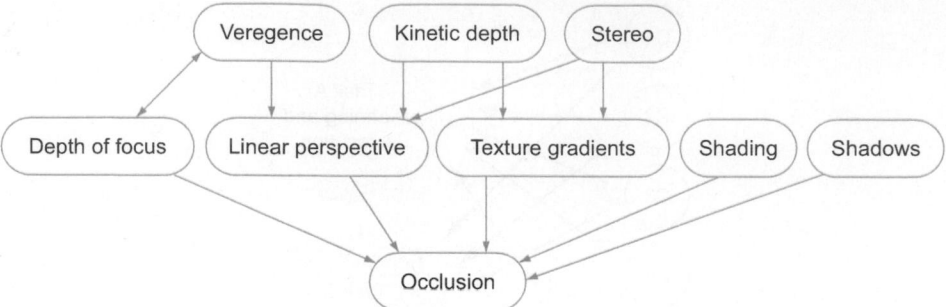

Figure 7.36 A dependency graph for depth cues. Arrows indicate how depth cues depend on each other for undistorted appearance.

> **[G7.13]** In 3D data visualizations, understand and use the depth cues that are most important for the critical tasks in an application. Implement other cues on which these critical cues depend.

Task-Based Space Perception

The obvious advantage of a task-based theory of space perception is that it can be directly applied to the design of interactive 3D information displays. The difficulty is that the number of tasks is potentially large, and many tasks that appear at first sight to be simple and unified are found, upon more detailed examination, to be multifaceted. Nevertheless, taking the task into account is essential; perception and action are intertwined. If we are to understand space perception, we must understand the purpose of perceiving.

The best hope for progress lies in identifying a small number of elementary tasks requiring depth perception that are as generic as possible. If the particular set of spatial cues associated with each task can be characterized, then the results can be used to construct design guidelines. The remainder of this chapter is devoted to analyzing the following tasks:

- Tracing paths in 3D graphs
- Judging the morphology of surfaces
- Finding patterns of points in 3D space
- Finding shapes of 3D trajectories
- Judging the relative positions of objects in space
- Judging the relative movements of self within the environment
- Reaching for objects
- Judging the "up" direction
- Feeling a sense of presence

This list of nine tasks is at best only a beginning; each has many variations, and none turns out to be particularly simple in perceptual terms.

Tracing Data Paths in 3D Graphs

Many kinds of information structures can be represented as networks of nodes and arcs, technically called *graphs*. Fig. 7.37 shows an example of object-oriented computer software represented using a 3D graph. Nodes in the graph stand for various kinds of entities, such as modules, classes, variables, and methods. The 3D spars that connect the entities represent various kinds of relationships characteristic of object-oriented software, such as inheritance, function calls, and variable usage. Information structures are becoming so complex that there has been considerable interest in the question of whether a 3D visualization will reveal more information than a 2D visualization. Is it a good idea?

One special kind of graph is a tree. Trees are a standard technique for representing hierarchical information, such as organizational charts or the structure of information in a computer directory. The cone tree is a graphical technique for representing tree-graph information in 3D (Robertson, Mackinlay, & Card, 1993). It shows the tree branches arranged around a series of circles, as illustrated in Fig. 7.38. The inventors of the cone tree claim that as many as 1000 nodes may be displayed without visual clutter using cone trees, clearly more than that could be contained in a 2D layout; however, with a cone tree, we do not see all 1000 nodes at a time, as some are hidden and parts of the tree must be rotated to reveal them. In addition, 3D cone trees require more complex and time-consuming user interactions to access nodes than are necessary for 2D layouts, so the task of tracing out a path will take longer to perform. Other 2D methods such as the hyperbolic tree (Lamping, Rao, & Pirolli, 1995) have proven to be more efficient.

Empirical evidence shows that the number of errors in detecting paths in 3D tree structures is substantially reduced if stereoscopic and motion depth cues are used. Sollenberger and Milgram (1993) investigated a task involving two 3D trees with intermeshed branches. The task was to discover to which of two tree roots a highlighted leaf was attached. Subjects carried out th task both with and without stereo depth, and with and without rotation to provide kinetic depth. Their results showed that both stereo and kinetic depth viewing reduced errors, but that kinetic depth was the more potent cue. However, an abstract tree structure is not necessarily a good candidate for 3D visualization, for the reason that a tree data structure can always be laid out on a 2D plane in such a way that none of the paths cross (path crossings are the main reason for errors in path-tracing tasks), so creating a 2D visualization is easy for trees.

Unlike trees, more general node–link structures, such as directed acyclic graphs, usually cannot be laid on a plane without some links crossing and these are a better test of whether 3D viewing allows more information to be seen. To study the effects of stereo and kinetic depth cues on 3D visualization of complex node-link structures, we

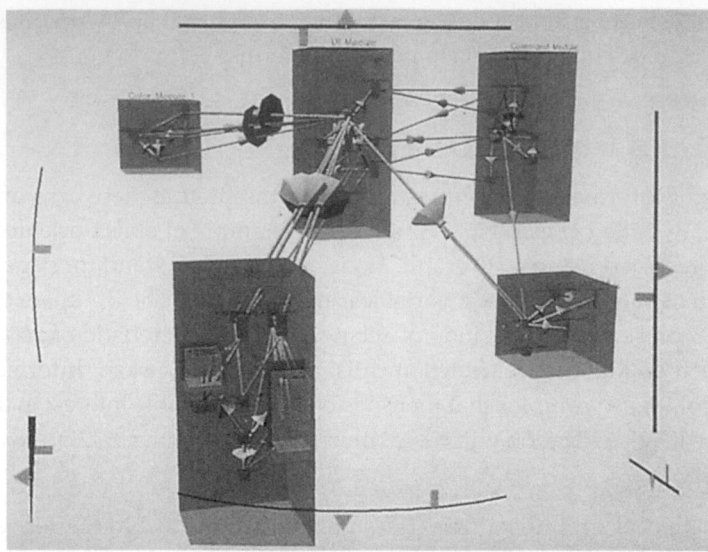

Figure 7.37 The structure of object-oriented software code is represented as a graph in 3D.

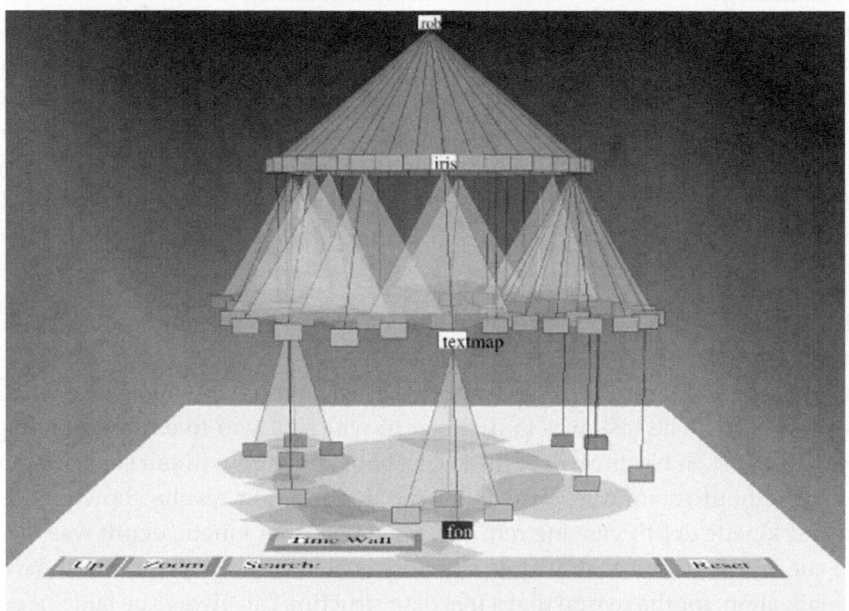

Figure 7.38 The cone tree invented by Robertson et al. (1993). *(Image courtesy of G. Robertson)*

systematically varied the size of a graph laid out in 3D and measured path-tracing ability with both stereoscopic and motion depth cues (Ware & Franck, 1996). Our results, illustrated in Fig. 7.39, showed a factor of 1.6 increase in the complexity that could be viewed when stereo was added to a static display, but a factor of 2.2 improvement

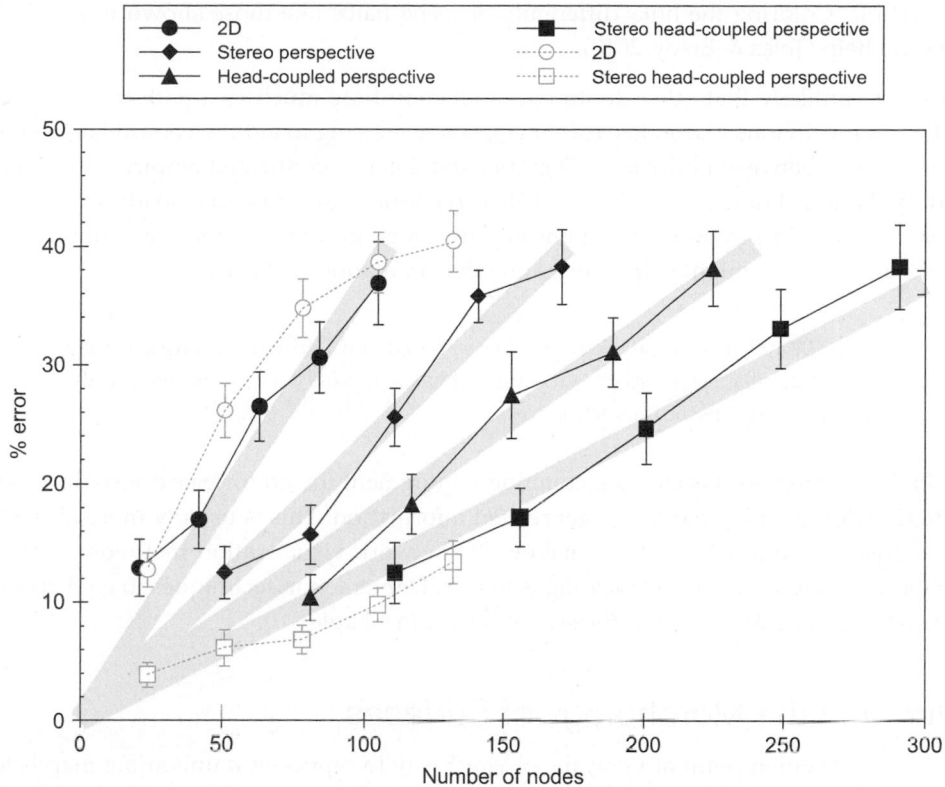

Figure 7.30 The plot shows that errors increased when the number of nodes increased, with and without stereo and/or motion parallax. The task involved tracing paths in a 3D graph (Ware & Franck, 1996).

when kinetic depth cues were added. A factor of 3.0 improvement occurred with both stereo and kinetic depth cues. These results held for a wide range of graph sizes. A subsequent experiment showed that the advantage of kinetic depth cues applied whether the motion was coupled to movements of the head or movements of the hand or consisted of automatic oscillatory rotation of the graph.

Having a higher resolution screen can increase the benefit of stereo and motion cues. We found an order of magnitude benefit to 3D viewing using an ultrahigh-resolution stereoscopic display and found that subjects were rapidly and accurately able to resolve paths in graphs with more than 300 nodes (Ware & Mitchell, 2008).

Although stereo viewing appears to be the most important cue for accuracy when tracing paths in 3D graphs, some studies have shown that stereo viewing speeds response times (Sollenberger & Milgram, 1993; Naepflin and Menozzi, 2001), so if time is critical, adding this cue confers an important benefit.

Occlusion is one additional depth cue that should make it easier to differentiate links in 3D graphs, but if all the links are uniformly colored the depth ordering will not be visible. Coloring the links differently or using halos like those shown in Fig. 7.32 should help (Telea & Ersoy, 2010).

It seems unlikely that other depth cues will contribute much to a path-tracing task. There is no obvious reason to expect perspective viewing to aid the comprehension of connections between nodes in a 3D graph, and this was confirmed empirically by our study (Ware & Franck, 1996). There is also no reason to suppose that shading and cast shadows would provide any significant advantage in a task involving connectivity, although shading might help in revealing the orientation of the arcs.

[G7.14] When it is critical to perceive large 3D node-link structures, consider using motion parallax, stereoscopic viewing and halos. But only use 3D viewing if the benefits outweigh the interaction costs.

Still, interacting with nodes is a common requirement for graph-based visualization; often nodes must be selected to get related information. This is usually more difficult and costly with a 3D interface, making 2D network visualization methods a better choice. An alternative to 3D viewing is to use 2D interaction techniques to gain access to larger graphs. We consider these alternatives in Chapter 10.

Judging the Morphology of Surfaces

From a Gibsonian point of view, the obvious way to represent a univariate map is to make it into a physical surface in the environment. Some researchers occasionally do just this; they construct plaster or foam models of data surfaces. But, the next best thing may be to use computer graphics techniques to shade the data surface with a simulated light source and give it a simulated color and texture to make it look like a real physical surface. Such a simulated surface can be viewed using a stereoscopic viewing apparatus, by creating different perspective images, one for each eye. These techniques have become so successful that the auto industry is using them to design car bodies in place of the full-size clay models that were once constructed by hand to show the curves of a design. The results have been huge cost savings and a considerably accelerated design process.

Four principal sets of visual cues for surface shape perception have been studied: shading models, surface texture, stereoscopic depth, and motion parallax. To determine which of these are the most effective, Norman et al. (1995) used computer graphics to render smoothly shaded rounded objects under various viewing conditions both with and without texture. They manipulated the entire list of variables given above—specular shading, Lambertian shading, texture, stereo, and motion parallax—in a multifactor experiment. Stereo and motion were studied only in combination with the other cues, because without shading or texture neither stereo nor motion cues can be effective.

Norman et al. (1995) found all of the cues they studied to be useful in perceiving surface orientation, but the relative importance of the cues differed from one subject to another. For some subjects, motion appeared to be the stronger cue; for others, stereo was stronger. A summary of their results with motion and stereo data combined is given in Fig. 7.40. Motion and stereo both reduced errors dramatically when used in combination with any of the surface representations. Overall, the combination of shading (either specular or Lambertian) with either stereo or motion was the best or nearly the best combination for all the subjects.

Random textures provide a weak clue to depth (Saunders & Chen, 2015) and when they are used judgments of slant are biased toward the plane orthogonal to the line of sight. More accurate judgments may be made with specific textures conforming to a surface in a particular way (Interrante et al., 1997). For these reasons, it is not meaningful to make general statements such as, "Lambertian shading is more useful than texture." The values of the different cues will also depend on the nature of the surface features that are important and the particular texture used.

Conformal Textures

The boundary contours of objects can interact with surface shading to change dramatically the perception of surface shape. Fig. 7.41 is adapted from Ramachandran (1988). It shows two shapes that have exactly the same shading but different silhouette contours. The combination of silhouette contour information with shading information is convincing in both cases, but the surface shapes that are perceived are very different. This tells us that shape-from-shading information is inherently ambiguous; it can be interpreted in different ways, depending on the contours.

Contours that are drawn on a shaded surface can also drastically alter the perceived shape of that surface. Fig. 7.42 has added shaded bands that provide internal contour information. As in Fig. 7.41, the actual pattern of shading within each of the two

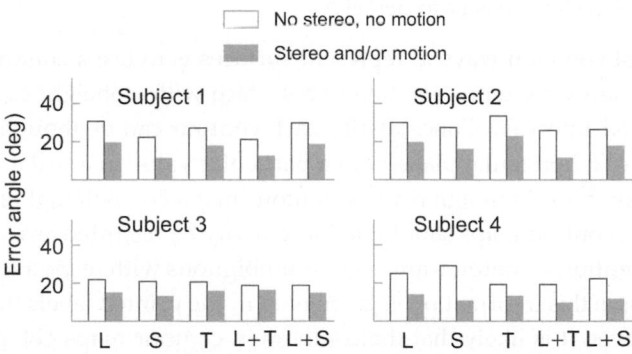

Figure 7.40 Results of the study of shape perception by Norman et al. (1995). The average errors in adjusted orientation are shown for five different surface representations. The different representations are labeled as follows: (L) Lambertian shading, (S) specular highlight shading, (T) texture with no shading, (L + T) Lambertian shading with texture, and (L + S) Lambertian shading with specular highlights. The four sets of histograms represent results from four different subjects.

Figure 7.41 When scanned from left to right, the sequences of gray values in these two patterns are identical. The external contour interacts with the shading information to produce the perception of two very differently shaped surfaces. *(Redrawn from Ramachandran (1988).)*

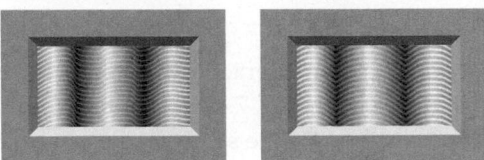

Figure 7.42 The left-to-right gray sequences in these patterns are identical. The internal contours interact with the shading information to produce the perception of two very differently shaped surfaces.

images is the same. It is the contour information that makes one surface shape appear so different from the other. This technique can be used directly in displaying shaded surfaces to make a shape easier to perceive.

One of the most common ways to represent surfaces is to use a contour map. A contour map is a plan view representation of a surface with isoheight contours, usually spaced at regular intervals. Conceptually, each contour can be thought of as the line of intersection of a horizontal plane with a particular value in a scalar height field, as illustrated in Fig. 7.43. Although reading contour maps is a skill that requires practice and experience, contour maps should not necessarily be regarded as entirely arbitrary graphical conventions. Contours are visually ambiguous with respect to such things as direction of slope; this information is given only in the printed labels that are attached to them. However, it is likely that the contours in contour maps get at least some of their expressive power because they provide perceptual shape and depth cues. As we have seen, both occluding (silhouette) contours and surface contours are effective in providing shape information. Contours provide a form of conformal texture, giving both shape and slope information. Contour maps are a good example of a hybrid code; they make use of a perceptual mechanism, and they are partly conventional. The combination of contours with shading can be especially effective (Fig. 7.44).

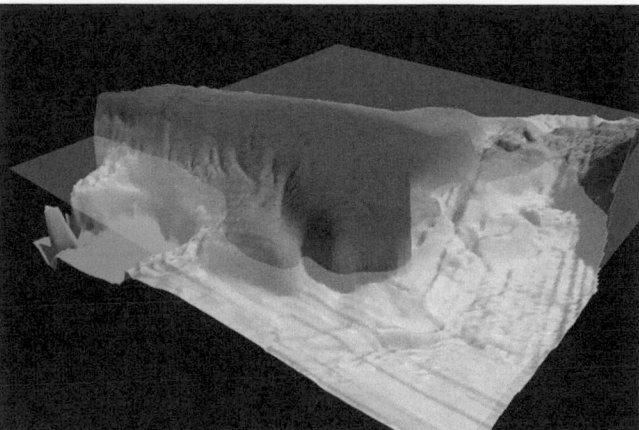

Figure 7.43 A contour is created by the intersection of a plane with a scalar field.

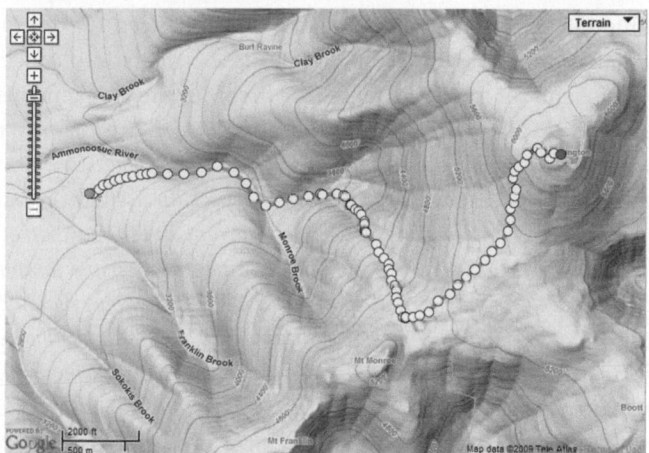

Figure 7.44 Shading provides the overall shape of the topography, but the contours provide both precise height information, supplementary shape, and gradient information. *(From Google, with permission.)*

Texturing surfaces is important when they are viewed stereoscopically. This becomes obvious if we consider that a uniform nontextured polygon contains no internal stereoscopic information about the surface it represents. Under uniform lighting conditions, such a surface also contains no orientation information. When a polygon is textured, every texture element provides stereoscopic depth information relative to neighboring points. Fig. 7.45 shows a stereoscopic pair of images representing a textured surface. Stereoscopic viewing also considerably enhances our ability to see one surface through another, semitransparent, one (Bair et al., 2009; Interrante et al., 1997).

Guidelines for Displaying Surfaces

Taken together, the evidence suggests that to represent a surface clearly it may be possible to do better than simply creating a photorealistic rendering of a scene using the most

Figure 7.45 Texture is important in stereo viewing because it provides high-resolution disparity gradients, which in turn provide essential information to the disparity-sensing mechanisms of the visual cortex.

sophisticated techniques of computer graphics. A simplified lighting model—for example, a single light source located at infinity—may be more effective than complex rendering using multiple light sources. The importance of contours and the easy recognizability of cartoon representation suggest that an image may be enhanced for display purposes by using techniques that are nonrealistic. Taking all these caveats into consideration, some guidelines may be useful for the typical case (the first four are restatements of G2.1, G2.2, G2.3, and G2.4 given in Chapter 2): *A simple lighting model, based on a single light source applied to a Lambertian surface, is a good default. The light source should be from above and to one side and infinitely distant. [G2.2] Specular reflection is especially useful in revealing fine surface detail. Because specular reflection depends on both the viewpoint and the position of the light source, the user should be given interactive control of both the lighting direction and the amount of specular reflection to specify where the highlights will appear. [G2.3] Cast shadows should be used, but only if the shadows do not interfere with other displayed information. The shadows should be computed to have blurred edges to make a clear distinction between shadow and surface pigment changes. [G2.4] Both Lambertian and moderate specular surface reflection should be modeled. More sophisticated lighting modeling, such as using the radiosity method, may help in the perception of occlusion and be useful in cases where other cues provide weak information.*

[G7.15] Consider using textures to help reveal surface shapes especially if they are to be viewed in stereo. This is only appropriate for relatively smooth surfaces and where texture is not needed for some other attribute. Ideally, texturing should be low contrast so as not to interfere with shading information. Textures that have linear components are more likely to reveal surface shape than textures with randomly stippled patterns. When one 3D surface is viewed over another, the top surface should have lacy, see-through textures.

[G7.16] Consider using both structure from motion (by rotating the surface) and stereoscopic viewing to enhance the user's understanding of 3D shape in a 3D visualization. These cues will be especially useful when one textured transparent surface overlays another.

There are also temporal factors to be considered if viewing times are brief. When we are viewing stereoscopic displays, it can take several seconds for the impression of depth to build up. However, stereoscopic depth and structure-from-motion information interact strongly. With moving stereoscopic displays, the time to fusion can be considerably shortened (Patterson & Martin, 1992). In determining the shape of surfaces made from random dot patterns, using both stereoscopic and motion depth cues, Uomori and Nishida (1994) found that kinetic depth information dominated the initial perception of surface shape, but after an interval of 4–6 seconds, stereoscopic depth came to dominate.

Bivariate Maps—Lighting and Surface Color

In many cases, it is desirable to represent more than one continuous variable over a plane. This representation is called a *bivariate* or *multivariate map*. From the ecological optics perspective discussed in Chapter 1, the obvious bivariate map solution is to represent one of the variables as a shaded surface and the other as color coding on that surface. A third variable might use variations in the surface texture. These are the patterns we have evolved to perceive. An example is given in Fig. 7.46, where one variable is a height map of the ocean floor and the surface color represents sonar backscatter strength. In this case, the thing being visualized is actually a physical 3D surface; however, the technique also works when both variables are abstract. A radiation field, for example, can be expressed as a shaded height map, and a temperature field can be represented by the surface color.

If this colored and shaded surface technique is used, some obvious tradeoffs must be observed. Because luminance is used to represent shape from shading by artificially illuminating the surface, we should minimally use luminance variation in coloring the surface. The surface coloring should be done mainly using the chromatic opponent channels discussed in Chapter 4. But, because of the inability of color to carry high spatial frequency information, only relatively gradual changes in color can be perceived; therefore, in designing a multivariate surface display, rapidly changing information

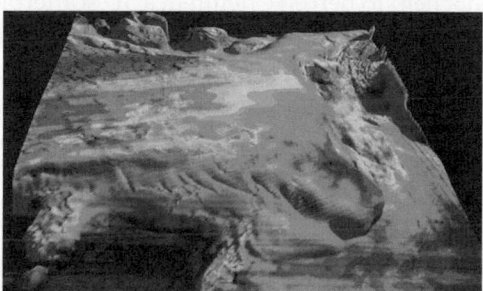

Figure 7.46 A bivariate map showing part of the Stellwagen Bank National Marine Sanctuary. One variable shows angular response of sonar backscatter, color coded and draped on the depth information given through shape from shading. *(From Mayer, Dijkstra, Hughes Clarke, Paton, and Ware (1997). Courtesy of Larry Mayer.)*

should always be mapped to luminance. For a more detailed discussion of these spatial tradeoffs, see Robertson and O'Callaghan (1988), Rogowitz and Treinish (1996), and Chapter 4 of this book.

A similar set of constraints applies to the use of visual texture. Normally, it is advisable to use luminance contrast in displaying texture, but this will also tend to interfere with shape from shading information. If we use texture to convey information, we have less available visual bandwidth to express surface shape and surface color. We can gain a relatively clear and easily interpreted trivariate map, but only so long as we do not need to express a great deal of detail. Using color, texture and shape from shading to display different continuous variables does not increase the total amount of information that can be displayed per unit area, but it does allow multiple map variables to be independently perceived.

> **[G7.17]** Consider the use of a shaded surface height field for one variable and color coding for the other as a method for displaying bivariate scalar field maps. This will work best if the shaded variable is relatively smooth. The colors should vary little in luminance, and should possibly be stepped.

Patterns of Points in 3D Space

The scatterplot is probably the most effective method for finding unknown patterns in 2D discrete data. When three attributes are given for each data point, one solution is to show it in 3D using depth cues. The attributes are mapped to positions on the x, y, and z axes, respectively. The resulting 3D scatterplot is usually rotated around a vertical axis, exploiting structure from motion to reveal its structure (Donoho, Donoho, & Gasko, 1988). This technique can be an alternative to the color and shape enhanced scatterplots discussed in Chapters 4 and 5. If needed, color and size can be added to the glyphs of a 3D scatterplot to show even more data attributes.

The problem of viewing 3D point clouds is similar to that of perceiving 3D networks. Perspective cues will not help to perceive depth in a 3D scatterplot, because a cloud of small, discrete points has no perspective information. If the points all have a constant and relatively large size, weak depth information will be produced by the size gradient. Similarly, with small points, occlusion will not provide useful depth information, but if the points are larger, some ordinal depth information will be perceivable. If there are a large number of points, cast shadows will not provide information, because it will be impossible to determine the association between a given point and its shadow. Shape-from-shading information will also be missing, because a point has no orientation information. Each point will reflect light equally, no matter where it is placed and no matter where the light source is placed.

It is likely then that the only depth cues in a 3D scatterplot are stereoscopic depth and structure from motion. Comparing these, a study by Aygar et al. (2017) showed kinetic depth to be a more powerful cue for identifying clusters of points in a 3D space than stereoscopic viewing, where the criterion was accuracy. Though having both cues was best. An additional benefit to stereoscopic viewing was that it resulted in more rapid responses, while using kinetic depth resulted in longer response times.

> **[G7.18]** To see structures in a 3D scatterplot, consider generating structure-from-motion cues by rotating or oscillating the point cloud around a vertical axis. Also use stereoscopic viewing, if possible, especially if response speed is important.

One of the problems with visualizing clouds of data points is that the overall shape of the cloud cannot easily be seen, even when stereo and motion cues are provided. One way to add extra shape information to a cloud of discrete points is to add shape-from-shading information artificially. It is possible to treat a cloud of data points as though each point were actually a small, flat, oriented object. These flat particles can be artificially oriented, if they lie near the boundary of the cloud, to reveal the shape of the cloud when shading is applied. In this way, perception of the cloud's shape can be considerably enhanced, and shape information can be perceived without additional stereo and motion cues. At the same time, the positions of individual points can be perceived. Fig. 7.47 illustrates this.

> **[G7.19]** If it is important to judge the morphology of the outer boundary of a 3D cloud of points, consider employing a statistical approximation method to estimate the local orientation of the cloud surface and use this to shade the individual points.

Perceiving Patterns in 3D Trajectories

A common problem in geospatial visualization is to understand the path of a particle, animal, or vehicle through space. A simple line rendering only provides 2D information and this is therefore unsuitable. Using motion parallax or stereoscopic viewing will help. Also, periodic drop lines to a ground plane can be used. In addition, rendering

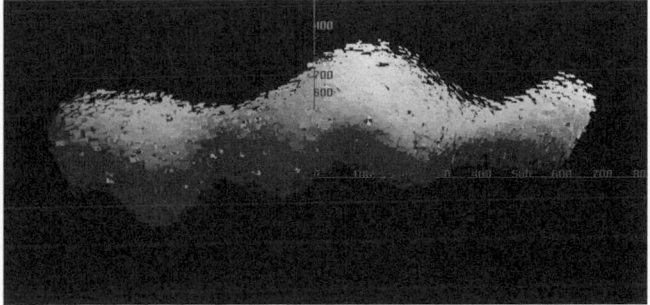

Figure 7.47 A cloud of discrete points is represented by oriented particles. An inverse square law of attraction has been used to determine the point normals. When the cloud is artificially shaded, its shape is revealed (Li, 1997).

the trajectory as a tube or box adds perspective and shape-from-shading cues, especially if rings are drawn around the tube at periodic intervals. An additional advantage of a box trajectory is that it can also convey roll information. Fig. 7.48 shows the trajectory of a humpback whale carrying out a bubble-net feeding maneuver (Ware, Arsenault, Plumlee, & Wiley, 2006).

> **[G7.20]** To represent 3D trajectories, consider using shaded tubes or box extrusions, with periodic bands to provide orientation cues. Apply motion parallax and stereoscopic viewing, if possible.

Computer simulations used in science and engineering can often produce 3D tensor fields. In a 3D vector field, each point in space is endowed with the attributes of direction and speed. In a tensor field each point can have many more attributes, representing phenomena such as shear or twist. The visualization of these fields is a specialized topic and we will not delve into it here. However, visualizing tensor fields can be done by adding attributes such as shape and color to extruded trajectories. A good starting place for work in this area is Delmarcelle and Hesselink (1993).

Judging Relative Positions of Objects in Space

Judging the relative positions of objects is a complex task, performed very differently depending on the overall scale and the context. When very fine depth judgments are made in the near vicinity of the viewer, such as are needed to thread a needle, stereopsis is the strongest single cue. Stereoscopic depth perception is a superacuity and is optimally useful for objects held at about arm's length. For these fine tasks, motion parallax is not very important, as evidenced by the fact that people hold their heads still when threading needles.

In larger environments, stereoscopic depth perception has a minimal role for objects at distances beyond 30m. Instead, when we are judging the overall layout of objects in a larger

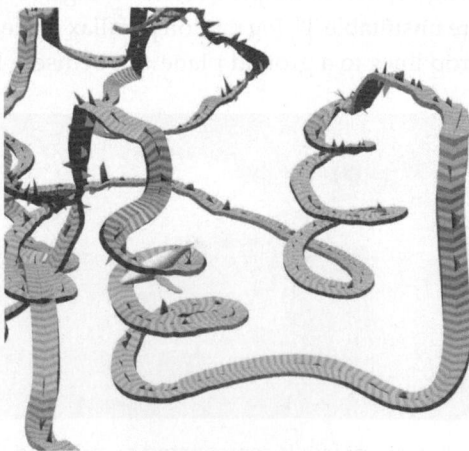

Figure 7.48 The trajectory of a humpback whale bubble-net feeding is shown using an extruded box.

environment, known object size, motion parallax, linear perspective, cast shadows, and texture gradients all contribute to our understanding, depending on the exact spatial arrangement.

Gibson (1986) noted that much of size constancy can be explained by a referencing operation with respect to a textured ground plane. The sizes of objects that rest on a uniformly textured ground plane can be obtained by reference to the texture element size. Objects slightly above the ground plane can be related to the ground plane through the shadows they cast. In artificial environments, a very strong artificial reference can be provided by dropping a vertical line to the ground plane.

Because 3D environments can be so diverse and used for so many different purposes, no specific additional guidelines are given here relating to judgments of object position in 3D. The optimal mix is a complex design problem, not something for simple guidelines. All of the depth cues we have been discussing can be applied and should be considered in a design solution.

Judging the Relative Movements of Self Within the Environment

When we are navigating through a virtual environment representing an information space, there are a number of frames of reference that may be adopted; for example, an observer may feel she is moving through the environment or that she is stationary and the environment is moving past. In virtual environment systems that are either helmet mounted or monitor based, the user rarely actually physically moves any great distance, because real-world obstacles lie in the way. If self-movement is perceived, it is generally an illusion. Note that this applies only to linear motion, not to rotations; users with helmet-mounted displays can usually turn their heads quite freely.

A sensation of self-movement can be strongly induced when the subject is not moving. This phenomenon, called *vection*, has been studied extensively. When observers are placed inside a large moving visual field—created either by a physical drum or by means of computer graphics within a virtual-reality helmet—they invariably feel that they are moving, even though they are not. A number of visual parameters, discussed below, influence the amount of vection that is perceived.

Field size—In general, the larger the area of the visual field that is moving, the stronger the experience of self-motion (Howard & Heckman, 1989).

Foreground/background—Much stronger vection is perceived if the moving part of the visual field is perceived as background and more distant from the observer than static foreground objects (Howard & Heckman, 1989). In fact, vection can be perceived even with a quite small moving field, if that field is perceived to be relatively distant. The classic example occurs when someone is sitting in a train stopped at a station and the movement of an adjacent train, seen through a window, causes that person to feel that he or she is moving, even though this is not the case.

Frame—Vection effects are considerably increased if there is a static foreground frame between the observer and the moving background (Howard & Childerson, 1994).

Stereo—Stereoscopic depth can determine whether a moving pattern is perceived as background or foreground, and thereby increase or decrease vection (Lowther & Ware, 1996).

In aircraft simulators and other vehicle simulators, the goal is for the user to experience a sense of self-motion, even though the simulator's actual physical motion is relatively small or nonexistent.

One of the unfortunate side effects of this perceived motion is simulator sickness. The symptoms of simulator sickness can appear within minutes of exposure to perceived extreme motion. Kennedy, Lilienthal, Berbaum, Baltzley, and McCauley (1989) reported that between 10% and 60% of users of immersive displays experienced some symptoms of simulator sickness. This high incidence may ultimately be a major barrier to the adoption of fully immersive display systems.

Simulator sickness is thought to be caused by conflicting cues from the visual system and the vestibular system of the inner ear. When most of the visual field moves, the brain usually interprets this as a result of self-motion. But, if the observer is in a simulator, no corresponding information comes from the vestibular system. According to this theory, the contradictory information results in nausea. There are ways to ensure that simulator sickness does occur and ways of reducing its effects. Turning the head repeatedly while moving in a simulated virtual vehicle is almost certain to induce nausea (DiZio & Lackner, 1992). This means that a virtual ride should never be designed in which the participant is expected to look from side to side while wearing a helmet-mounted display. Simulator sickness in immersive virtual environments can be mitigated by initially restricting the participant's experience to short periods of exposure, lasting only a few minutes each day. This allows the user to build up a tolerance to the environment, and the periods of exposure can gradually be lengthened (McCauley & Sharkey, 1992).

Selecting and Positioning Objects in 3D

In some interactive 3D visualization environments, users must be able to reach in and manipulate objects, and designers of 3D display systems must make choices about which depth cues to include. In a full-blown virtual-reality system, the usual goal is to include all of the depth cues at the highest fidelity possible, but in practical systems for molecular modeling or 3D computer-aided design, various tradeoffs must be made.

Two of the most important options are whether to use a stereoscopic display and whether to provide motion parallax through perspective coupled to head position. Both require an investment in technology not normally provided with computer workstations. The evidence suggests that, for accurate reaching, having a stereoscopic display is more important than the motion parallax that occurs through the motion of the user's head (and hence eyes) with respect to the objects being selected (Arsenault & Ware, 2004; Boritz & Booth, 1998). Stereoscopic viewing has become a critical component of robotic systems used in microsurgery, where the surgeon sees a magnified view of the surgical site and where the surgeon's hand motions are scaled down by robot manipulators to obtain greater precision.

One of the purposes of tracking head (and eye) position is to get a correct perspective view to support eye-hand coordination. A number of researchers have investigated how eye-hand coordination changes when there is a mismatch between feedback from the visual sense and the proprioceptive sense of body position. A typical experiment involves subjects pointing at targets while wearing prisms that displace the visual image relative to the proprioceptive information from their muscles and joints. Subjects adapt rapidly to the prism displacement and point accurately. Work by Rossetti et al. (1993) suggests that there may be two mechanisms at work: a long-term, slow-acting mechanism that is capable of spatially remapping misaligned systems, and a short-term mechanism that is designed to realign the visual and proprioceptive systems within a fraction of a second. These results have been confirmed in studies with fish-tank virtual-reality systems, showing that a large translational offset between the hand position and the object being manipulated with the hand has only a small effect on performance (Ware & Rose, 1999).

If they are large, rotational mismatches between what is seen and what is held may have a much greater negative impact on eye-hand coordination than translational mismatches. Experiments with prisms that invert the visual field have shown that it can take weeks to reach behavior approaching normal performance under this condition, and adaptation may never be complete (Harris, 1965).

In visually guided hand movement, what seems to be most important is feedback about the *relative* positions of the graphical object representing the user's hand (or a probe) and the object itself. The stereoscopic system is exquisitely tuned to depth differences but not to absolute depths. Indeed, one of the main reasons why humans have stereoscopic depth perception is to support visually guided reaching. Research has shown that as long as continuous visual feedback is provided, without excessive lag, people can adjust rapidly to simple changes in the eye-hand relationship (Held, Efstanthiou, and Green, 1966).

Getting perfect registration between a user's hand and a virtual object, as shown in Fig. 7.49, is very difficult. This suggests that it is better to show both the hand virtually or a virtual tool in the same space as a virtual object, rather than blend real-world and computer graphics imagery, because in this way it is easy to show the relative positions of the hand and object.

[G7.21] Use stereoscopic viewing when visually guided hand movements are critically important. If possible, use a graphical proxy for the user's hand and ensure accurate relative positioning between the hand proxy and the virtual objects to be manipulated.

[G7.22] In 3D environments that support one-to-one mapping between the user's hand and a virtual object, ensure that the relative positions of a hand proxy, such as a probe, and an object being reached for are correct. Also, minimize rotational mismatch (>30 degrees) between the virtual space and the actual space within which the user's hand is moving.

Actually providing a sense of physical contact with nearby objects is also important in calibrating the proprioceptive system, especially for grasping (Mackenzie & Iberall,

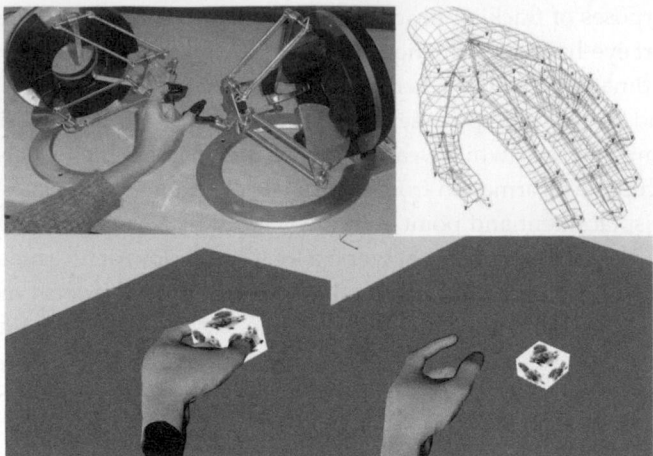

Figure 7.49 If both the hand proxy and the objects are virtual, it is easy to generate the correct relative positions of the hand and object. (*Courtesy of Siena Robotics and Systems Lab.* http://sirslab.dii.unisi.it/.)

1994). Unfortunately, this component of natural hand-object interaction is proving very difficult to simulate, and, although force feedback devices can provide a sense of contact, they currently have limited capabilities.

Judging the "up" Direction

In abstract 3D data spaces (for example, molecular models), there is often no sense of an "up" direction, and this can be confusing. In the natural environment, the "up" direction is defined by gravity and sensed by the vestibular system in the inner ear, by the presence of the ground on which we walk, and by oriented objects in our vicinity. Much of the research that has been done on perceived "up" and "down" directions has been done as part of space research, to help us understand how people can best orient themselves in a gravity-free environment. Nemire, Jacoby, and Ellis (1994) showed that linear perspective provides a strong cue in defining objects perceived at the same horizontal level. They showed that a linear grid pattern on the virtual floor and walls of a display strongly influenced what the participants perceived as horizontal; to some extent, this overrode the perception of gravity. Other studies have shown that placing recognizable objects in the scene very strongly influences a person's sense of self-orientation. The presence of recognizable objects with a known normal orientation with respect to gravity, such as a chair or a standing person, can strongly influence which direction is perceived as up (Howard & Childerson, 1994). Both of these findings can easily be adapted to virtual environments.

[G7.23] To define vertical polarity in a 3D data space, provide a clear reference ground plane and place recognizable objects on it that have a characteristic orientation with respect to gravity.

The Aesthetic Impression of 3D Space (Presence)

One of the most nebulous and ill-defined tasks related to 3D space perception is achieving a sense of *presence*. What is it that makes a virtual object or a whole environment seems vividly three dimensional? What is it that makes us feel that we are actually present in an environment? Much of presence has to do with a sense of engagement, and not necessarily with visual information. A reader of a powerfully descriptive novel may visualize (to use the word in its original cognitive sense) himself or herself in a world of the author's imagination—for example, vividly imagining Ahab on the back of the great white whale, *Moby-Dick*.

Presence might not seem to belong in a task-based classification of spatial information, being usually thought of as an ill-defined aesthetic quality, but in fact a number of practical applications require a sense of presence. For an architect designing a virtual building to present to a client, the feeling of spaciousness and the aesthetic quality of that space may be all-important. In virtual tourism, where the purpose is to give a potential traveler a sensation of what the Brazilian rain forest is really like, presence is also crucial.

A number of studies have used virtual-reality techniques for phobia desensitization. In one study by North, North, and Coble (1996), patients who had a fear of open spaces (agoraphobia) were exposed to progressively more challenging virtual open spaces. The technique of progressive desensitization involves taking people closer and closer to the situations that cause them fear. As they overcome their fears at one level of exposure, they can be taken to a slightly more stressful situation. In this way, they can overcome their phobias, one step at a time. The reason for using virtual-reality simulations in phobia desensitization is to provide control over the degree of presence and to reduce the stress level by enabling the patient to exit the stressful environment instantaneously. After treatment in a number of virtual environments, the experimental subjects of North et al. scored lower on a standardized Subjective Units of Discomfort test.

When developing a virtual-reality theme park attraction for Disneyland, Pausch et al. (1996) observed that high frame rate and high level of detail were especially important in creating a sense of presence for users "flying on a magic carpet." Presenting a stereoscopic display did not enhance the experience. Empirical studies have also shown that high-quality structure-from-motion information contributes more to a sense of presence than does stereoscopic display (Arthur et al., 1993). The sense of presence, however, is not a single unified perceptual dimension. Hendrix and Barfield (1996) found stereoscopic viewing to be very important when subjects were asked to rate the extent to which they felt they could reach for and grasp virtual objects, but it did not contribute at all to the sense of the overall realism of the virtual condition. Hendrix and Barfield did find that having a large field of view was important to creating a sense of presence.

[G7.24] To create a vivid sense of presence in a 3D data space, provide a large field of view, smooth motion, and a lot of visual detail.

Conclusion

High-quality, interactive stereoscopic displays are now inexpensive, although even mediocre-quality virtual-reality systems are still expensive. Creating a 3D visualization environment is considerably more difficult than creating a 2D system with similar capabilities. We still lack design rules for 3D environments, and many interaction techniques are competing for adoption. The strongest argument for the ultimate ascendancy of 3D visualization systems, and 3D user interfaces in general, must be that we live in a 3D world and our brains have evolved to recognize and interact within 3D. The 3D design space is richer than the 2D design space, because a 2D space is a part of 3D space. It is always possible to flatten out part of a 3D display and represent it in 2D.

Nevertheless, it also should be cautioned that going from 2D to 3D adds far less visual information than might be supposed. Consider the following simple argument. On a one-dimensional line of a computer display, we can perceive 1000 distinct pixels. On a 2D plane of the same display, we can display $1000 \times 1000 = 1,000,000$ pixels, but going to a 3D stereoscopic display only increases the number of pixels by a factor of 2, and this does not double the available information because the two images must be highly correlated for us to perceive stereoscopic depth. We may only be able to stereoscopically fuse images that differ by 10%, usually much less. This suggests a small increase in the amount of information through the use of stereo viewing.

Of all the depth cues, motion parallax is the one most likely to enable us to see more information, but only for certain cognitive tasks. In the case of networks, a network several times larger can be perceived with stereo and motion parallax cues, although even here, if interaction with nodes is critical, interactive 2D methods are likely to be superior. The other depth cues, such as occlusion and linear perspective, certainly help us perceive a *coherent* 3D space, but as the study of Cockburn and McKenzie (2001) suggests, we should not automatically assume that 3D provides more readily accessible information. Most of the pattern-perception machinery of the visual system operates in 2D, not in 3D, and for this fundamental reason even when a 3D view is being used it is critical to understand what pattern information appears on the 2D image plane.

Deciding whether or not to use a 3D display must involve deciding whether there are sufficient important subtasks for which 3D is clearly beneficial. The complexity and the consistency of the user interface for the whole application must be weighed in the decision. Even if 3D is better for one or two subtasks, the extra cost involved and the need for nonstandard interfaces for the 3D components may suggest that a 2D solution would be better overall. In terms of overall assessment, the cost of navigation is an essential component, and many 3D navigation methods are considerably slower than 2D alternatives. Even if we can show somewhat more information in 3D getting to the right viewpoint may be slow. In Chapter 10, we will resume the discussion of the value of 3D versus 2D displays by considering the various costs of interactively acquiring knowledge.

CHAPTER EIGHT

Visual Objects and Data Objects

The object metaphor is pervasive in the way we think about information, no matter how abstract. Object-oriented programming is one example; the body politic is another. Object-related concepts are also basic in modern systems design. A modular system is one that has easily understood and easily replaced components. Good modules are plug compatible with one another; they are discrete and separate parts of a system. The concept of a module has a lot in common with the perceptual and cognitive structures that define visual objects. This suggests that visual objects may be an excellent way to represent modular system components. A visual object provides a useful metaphor for encapsulation and cohesiveness, both important concepts in defining modular systems.

In an abstract sense, an object can be thought of as any identifiable, separate, and distinct part of the visual world. Information about visual objects is cognitively stored in a way that ties together critical features, such as oriented edges and patches of color and texture, so that they can be identified, visually tracked, and remembered. Because visual objects cognitively group both visual attributes, if we can represent data values as visual features and group these features into visual objects, we will have a very powerful tool for organizing related data. Familiar objects can also cognitively activate neural networks supporting interactions on those objects, and this further adds to their affordances.

Objects in the world are usually identifiable as meaningful entities, like chairs, mugs, automobiles, and other myriad things. In data visualization, when a data entity is represented as something object-like it is still relatively abstract, a cylinder or a box

Information Visualization. https://doi.org/10.1016/B978-0-12-812875-6.00008-6

shape. But if data is mapped into the shapes of a recognizable thing, then all the mental associations of that thing become activated. This is one reason why mapping data to features of human faces, for example, may be a problem. But in this chapter we will encounter the object display, this is a design concept wherein abstract, but still recognizable representations, e.g., of a human lung, are used in a data display.

Two radically different types of theory have been proposed to explain object recognition. The first is image based. It proposes that we recognize an object by matching the visual image with something roughly like a snapshot stored in memory. The second type is structure based. It proposes that objects are analyzed in terms of primitive three-dimensional (3D) forms and the structural interrelationships between them. Both of these models have much to recommend them, and it is entirely plausible that each is correct in some form. It is certainly clear that the brain has multiple ways of analyzing visual input. Both models provide interesting insights into how to display data effectively. We begin with the image-based theory of object recognition and examine some evidence supporting it.

Image-Based Object Recognition

The image-based theory is supported by the fact that people have a truly remarkable ability to recognize pictorial images they have seen before. In an arduous experiment, Standing, Conezio, and Haber (1970) presented subjects with 2560 pictures at a rate of one every 10 seconds. This was like the family slide show from hell; it took more than 7 hours spread over a 4-day period to show them all. Amazingly, when subsequently tested, subjects were able to distinguish pictures from others not previously seen with better than 90% accuracy.

It is important to make a distinction between *recognition* and *recall*. We have a great ability to recognize information that we have encountered before, as the picture memory experiment of Standing et al. shows. However, if we are asked to reconstruct visual scenes—for example, to recall what happened at a crime scene—our performance is much worse. Recognition is much better than recall. People did not really remember all of those pictures; they were only able to say, tentatively, that they might have seen them.

People can also recognize objects in images that are presented very rapidly. Suppose you asked a group of people "Is there a dog in one of the following pictures?" and then showed them a set of images, rapidly, all in the same place, at a rate of 10 per second. Remarkably, they will be able to detect the presence, or absence, of a dog, somewhere in the sequence of images most of the time. This experimental technique is called *rapid serial visual presentation* (RSVP). Experiments have shown that the maximum rate for the ability to detect common objects in images is about 10 images per second (Potter, 1976; Potter & Levy, 1969). We should interpret this result cautiously. Although interesting, it does not mean that people processed more than a small amount of information from each image.

A related phenomenon is *attentional blink*. If, in a series of images, a second dog were to appear in an image within 350 ms of the first, people do not notice it (or anything else). This moment of blindness is the attentional blink (Coltheart, 1999). It is conjectured that the brain is still processing the first dog, even though the image is gone, and this prohibits the identification of other objects in the sequence.

More support for image-based theories comes from studies showing that three-dimensional objects are recognized most readily if they are encountered from the same view direction as when they were initially seen. Johnson (2001) studied subjects' abilities to recognize bent pipe structures. Subjects performed well if the same viewing direction was used in the initial viewing and in the test phase. They performed poorly if a different view direction was used in the test phase, but they were also quite good at identification from exactly the opposite view direction. Johnson attributed this unexpected finding to the importance of silhouette information. Silhouettes would have been similar, although flipped left-to-right from the initial view.

Searching an Image Database

Presenting images rapidly in sequence (RSVP) may be a useful way to allow users to scan picture databases (De Bruijn, Spence, & Tong, 2000; Spence & Witkowski, 2013; Wittenburg, Ali-Ahmad, LaLiberte, & Lanning, 1998). The fact that people can search rapidly for an image in a sequence of up to 10 pictures per second suggests that presenting images using RSVP may be efficient. Contrast this with the usual method of presenting image collections in a regular grid of small thumbnail images. If it is necessary to make an eye movement to fixate each thumbnail image, it will not be possible to scan more than three to four images per second. Even though RSVP seems promising, there are a number of design problems that must be solved in building a practical interface. Once a likely candidate image is identified as being present in an RSVP sequence, the particular image must be extracted from the set. By the time a user responds with a mouse click several images will have passed, more if the user is not poised to press the stop button. Thus, either controls must be added for backing up through the sequence, or part of the sequence must be fanned out in a conventional thumbnail array to confirm that candidate's presence and study it further (Spence, 2002; Wittenburg et al., 1998).

The one place where RSVP has found actual application is in the rapid reviewing or fast forwarding of online movies. Rapid serial presentation may also provide a way of searching video content by viewing a quick sequence of selected frames (Tse, Marchionini, Ding, Slaughter, & Komlodi, 1998). Wildemuth et al. (2003) suggested that a speed up of 64× faster than the original video may be optimal in allowing viewers to get the gist of what is occurring. Video data compressed in this way might make it possible to review a day's worth of video in a few minutes. Currently, most fast forwarding is not "smart" in that it does not select particularly representative video frames; but if it were this, it would likely be an improvement over what is available at the time of writing.

Surveillance Videos and Life Logging

A form of RSVP can also have applications in the review of surveillance videos. In this case there are obvious gains to be had for intelligent preprocessing of the video material so that more interesting sequences are speeded up less (Huang, Chung, Yang, Chen, & Huang, 2014). Some gains are obvious and simple. Since much of surveillance video captures hours of empty corridors, these sections can be enormously condensed, and only sections where there is movement shown. More sophisticated methods will automatically distinguish human movement from the flickering shadows of a tree moving in the wind.

It is becoming possible to have a personal memory data bank containing video and audio data collected during every waking moment through the course of a person's lifetime. This can be achieved with an unobtrusive miniature camera, perhaps embedded in a pair of eyeglasses, and, assuming continuing progress in solid-state storage, the data can be stored in a device weighing a few ounces and costing a few hundred dollars (Gemmel et al., 2006). The implications of such *life logging* devices seem profound at first encounter; they appear to represent the ultimate memory aid—the user need never forget anything.

A key issue, though, is the interface to the stored data. If we want to recall a meeting we know happened sometime in 2004 we clearly cannot replay the entire year's worth of data to find the event, even very fast. But the most serious problem for the life logging concept is that seeing a video replay is not at all the same as remembering. A replay of some forgotten event, such as a meeting, will be more akin to a re-experience, one that occurs without the context of the goals of the person involved, even if it is oneself. When people review their own videos, they do not spontaneously remember what happened; instead, they must mentally reconstruct it (Sellen et al., 2007). A meaningful reconstruction of a particular meeting may require a review of videos of other activities for weeks prior to the event, together with relevant documents and e-mail communications between the participants. The result is that a reconstruction of a single meeting might take days of work if a well-designed interface to the data is available.

Such arguments have led researchers to suggest that the main value of life logging is to jog the memory of the participant rather than being a substitute for memory. Accordingly, a study by Sellen et al. (2007) investigated the value of video imagery in helping people recall personal events using their *SenseCam* system. They found that a few days later SenseCam imagery roughly doubled the number of events that could be recalled, from two to four, for a particular half-day interval.

Memorability of Visualizations

A pair of recent studies by Borkin et al. (2013, 2016) addressed the issue of what makes a visualization memorable after a brief exposure. The first had exposures of only 1 second and this showed that having identifiable images in a visualization leads to an increase in recognition scores. This is not surprising, and they did not determine if people actually remembered any meaningful information about the data being represented. The second experiment gave people a longer 10 seconds exposure and followed up with questions regarding both whether people recognized that they had seen a visualization before and the extent to which they recalled meaningful content. The recall test was done with study participants viewing a blurred image so that they could not read text, data axes and other detailed information. The results showed that having images in a visualization significantly increased the likelihood of recognition and the quality of recall. The paper also stressed the importance of textual information, especially titles.

Fig. 8.1 shows a comparison between the most recognizable visualization in and the least recognizable visualization in their study. The blurry overlays show where people fixated, in the encoding phase and in the recognition phase. Although this is only a single example, it is clear that people tend to fixated on the interesting images. Also, on recall they tended to place a fixation in each of the component panels, as well as directing fixations at the headings. They also stressed the importance of both data redundancy and message redundancy.

Object and Pattern Size for Optimal Identification

Although most objects can easily be recognized independently of the size of the image on the retina, image size does have some effect. Fig. 8.2 illustrates this. When the picture is seen from a distance, the image of the Mona Lisa face dominates; when it is viewed up close, smaller objects become dominant and a gremlin, a bird, and a claw emerge. Experimental work by Biederman and Cooper (1992) suggests that the optimal size for recognizing a visual object is about 4–6 degrees of visual angle. This gives

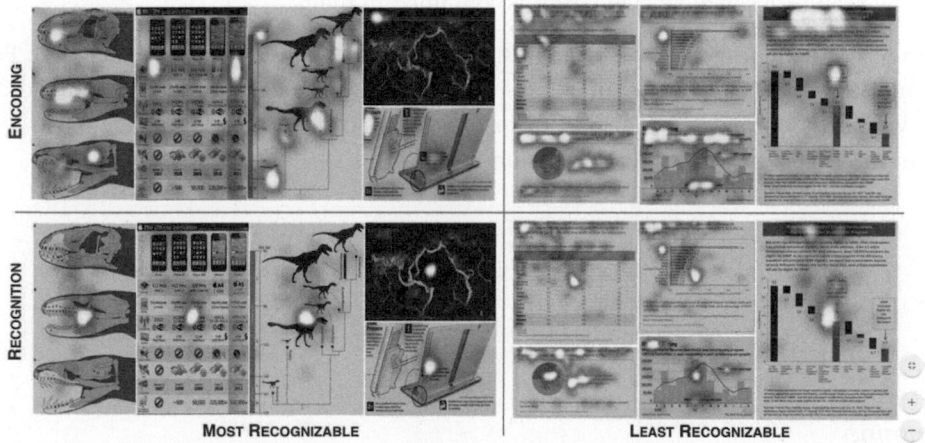

Figure 8.1 On the left is shown a highly memorable infographic whereas the one on the right is far less memorable. The overlaying colors show people directed their gaze during a brief inspection. (*From Borkin et al. (2016). Reprinted with permission.*)

Figure 8.2 When the image is viewed from a distance, the face dominates, but when looked at from 30 cm the gremlin hiding in the shadows of the mouth and nose emerges. At this distance, the gremlin has a visual angle of about 4 degrees, optimal for seeing a pattern. (*Adapted from the work of the Tel Aviv artist Victor Molev.*)

a useful rule of thumb for the optimal size for rapid presentation of visual images so that we can best see the visual patterns contained in them.

Other work suggests that the optimal size for single objects may be even smaller. For example, Fig. 8.3 shows a set of images of aircraft used in a rapid identification study by Watson and Ahumada (2015). The results suggested that the optimal size was less than 2 degrees for efficient identification.

> **[G8.1]** For optimal identification, make important patterns and complex objects have a size of approximately 4–6 degrees of visual angle. For optimal detection, simple objects should be smaller <2 degrees. This is not a rigid requirement because there is only a gradual fall off in skill as we depart from the optimal.

Priming

If you cognitively identify something, even if it is fleeting and irrelevant, you will identify it faster if you see it again in the near future (Bartram, 1974). This effect is called *priming*. Most studies of priming involve intervals between the two events of

Figure 8.3 Images of aircraft used in a rapid identification study by Watson and Ahumada (2015). *(From Watson and Andrew Watson (2015). Reprinted with permssion)*

minutes or hours, but Cave and Squire (1992) showed priming effects for picture naming that lasted for weeks.

Priming effects can occur even if information is not consciously perceived, and because of this priming is sometimes called *implicit memory*. Bar and Biederman (1998) exposed pictorial images to subjects so briefly that it was impossible for them to identify the objects. They followed the brief image exposure with what is called a *visual mask*, a random pattern shown immediately after the target stimulus to remove the target from the visual iconic store (a short-term buffer that holds the visual image for a fraction of a second), and they rigorously tested to show that subjects performed at chance levels when reporting what they had seen. Nevertheless, 15 minutes later, this unperceived exposure substantially increased the chance of recognition. Although the information was not consciously perceived, exposure to the particular combination of image features apparently primed the visual system to make subsequent recognition easier. They found that the priming effect decreased substantially if the imagery was displaced sideways. They concluded that the mechanism of priming is highly image dependent and not based on high-level semantic information.

Lawson, Humphreys, and Watson (1994) devised a series of experiments in which subjects were required to identify a specified object in a series of briefly presented pictures. Recognition was much easier if subjects had been primed by *visually similar* images that were not representations of semantically related objects. They argued that this should not be the case if objects are recognized on the basis of a high-level, 3D structural model of the kind that we will discuss later in this chapter; only image-based storage can account for their results. All of this adds support to the image-based theory of object recognition, because the effects are based on two-dimensional (2D) image information.

Structure-Based Object Recognition

Image-based theories of object recognition imply a rather superficial level of analysis of visual objects, but there is evidence that a much deeper kind of structural analysis must also occur. Fig. 8.4 shows two novel objects, probably never seen by the reader

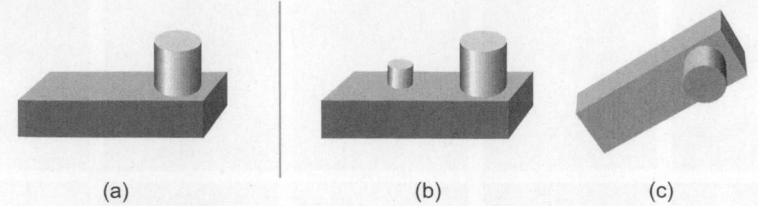

(a)   (b)   (c)

Figure 8.4 The object shown in (a) seems most similar to the object shown in (c), despite the fact that the *images* of (a) and (b) are most similar.

before. Yet, despite the fact that the images in Fig. 8.4(a) and (c) are very different from one another, they can be rapidly recognized as representations of the same object. No image-based theory can account for this result; it can only be based on a structural analysis of the relationships of the component parts.

Geon Theory

Fig. 8.5 provides a somewhat simplified overview of a neural network model of structural object perception, developed by Hummel and Biederman (1992). This theory proposes a hierarchical set of processing stages leading to object recognition. Visual information is decomposed first into edges, then into component axes, oriented blobs, and vertices. At the next layer, 3D primitives such as cones, cylinders, and boxes, called *geons*, are identified. A selection of geons is illustrated in Fig. 8.6(a). Next, the structure is extracted that specifies how the geon components interconnect; for example, in a human figure, the arm cylinder is attached near the top of the torso box. Finally, object recognition is achieved.

Silhouettes

Silhouettes appear to be especially important in determining how we perceive the structure of objects. The fact that simplified line drawings are often silhouettes may, in part, account for our ability to interpret them. At some level of perceptual processing, the silhouette boundaries of objects and the simplified line drawings of those objects excite the same neural contour extraction mechanisms. Halverston (1992) noted that modern children tend to draw objects on the basis of the most salient silhouettes, as did early cave artists. Many objects have particular silhouettes that are easily recognizable—think of a teapot, a shoe, a church, a person, or a violin. These canonical silhouettes are based on a particular view of an object, often from a point at right angles to a major plane of symmetry. Fig. 8.7 illustrates canonical views of a teapot and a person.

David Marr suggested ways in which the brain might use silhouette information to extract the structures of objects (Marr, 1982). He argued that "buried deep in our perceptual machinery" are mechanisms that contain constraints determining how silhouette information is interpreted.

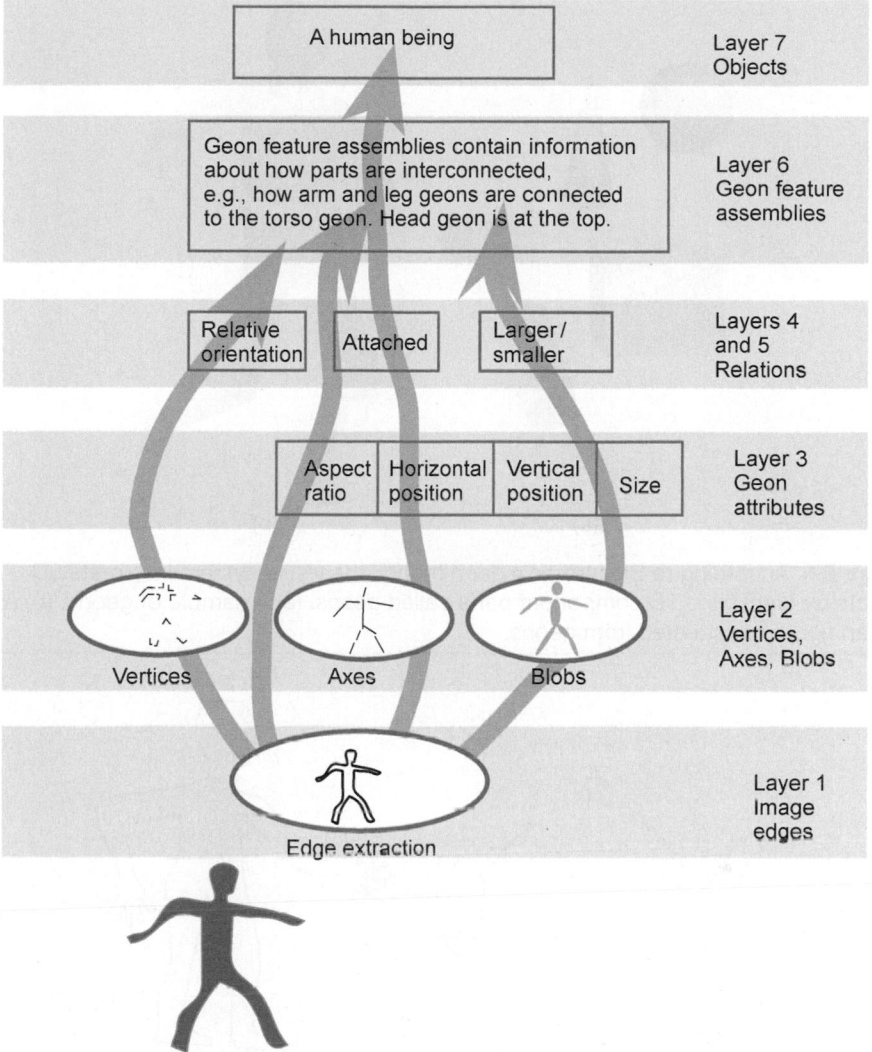

Figure 8.5 A simplified view of Hummel and Biederman's (1992) neural network model of form perception.

Three rules are embedded in this perceptual machinery:

1. Each line of sight making up a silhouette grazes the surface exactly once. The set of such points is the contour generator. The idea of the contour generator is illustrated in Fig. 8.8.

2. Nearby points on the contour of an image arise from nearby points on the contour generator of the viewed object.

3. All the points on the contour generator lie on a single plane.

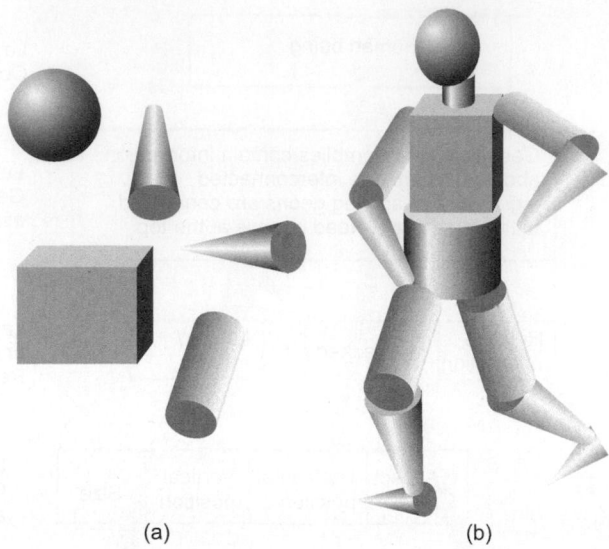

(a)   (b)

Figure 8.6 According to Biederman's geon theory, the visual system interprets 3D objects by identifying 3D component parts called *geons*. (a) A sample of geons. (b) A human figure constructed from geons.

Figure 8.7 Many objects have canonical silhouettes, defined by the viewpoints from which they are most easily recognized. In the case of the man, the overall posture is unnatural, but the component parts—hands, feet, head, etc.—are all given in canonical views.

Under Marr's default assumptions, contour information is used in segmenting an image into its component solids. Marr and Nishihara (1978) suggested that concave sections of the silhouette contour are critical in defining the ways in which different solid parts are perceptually defined. Fig. 8.9 illustrates a crudely drawn animal that we nevertheless readily segment into head, body, neck, legs, and so on. The most important features for this segmentation are concavities in the silhouette. Marr and Nishihara also proposed that the axes of the parts become cognitively connected to form a structural skeleton, so the object description consists of component parts and a description of how they are connected.

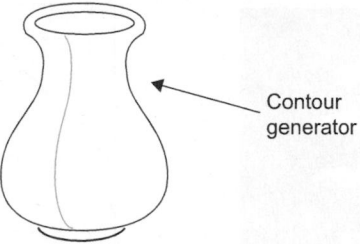

Contour
generator

Figure 8.8 According to Marr, the perceptual system makes assumptions that occluding contours are smoothly connected and lie in the same plane. *Adapted from Marr (1982).*

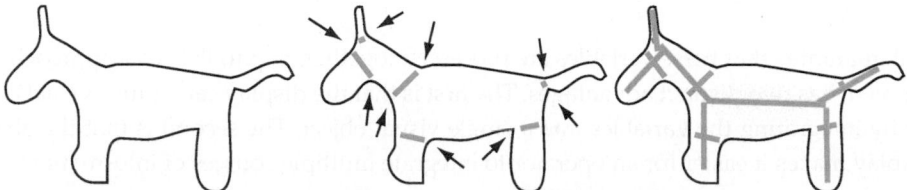

Figure 8.9 Concave sections of the silhouette define subparts of the object and are used in the construction of a structural skeleton. *(Redrawn from Marr and Nishihara (1978)).*

One of the consequences of structural theories of perception is that certain simplified views should be easier to read. There are practical advantages to this; for example, a clear diagram may sometimes be more effective than a photograph. This is exactly what Ryan and Schwartz (1956) showed when they found that a hand could be perceived more rapidly in the form of a simplified line drawing than in the form of a photograph (see Fig. 8.10), but this result should not be overgeneralized. Other studies have shown that time is required for detailed information to be perceived (Price & Humphreys, 1989; Venturino & Gagnon, 1992). Simplified line drawings may be most appropriate only when rapid responses are required.

Although image-based theories and structure-based theories of object recognition are usually presented as alternatives, it may be that both kinds of processes occur. If geons are extracted based on concavities in the silhouette, certain views of a complex object will be much easier to recognize. Further, it may well be that viewpoint-dependent aspects of the visual image are stored in addition to the 3D structure of the object. Indeed, it seems likely that the brain is capable of storing many kinds of information about an object or scene if they have some usefulness. The implication is that, even though 3D objects in a diagram may be more effective in some cases, care should be taken to provide a good 2D layout. Both image-based cues and structural cues should be clearly presented.

The Object Display and Object-Based Diagrams

Wickens (1992) is primarily responsible for the concept of an object display as a graphical device employing a "single contoured object" to integrate a large number of separate variables. Wickens theorized that mapping many data variables onto a single object

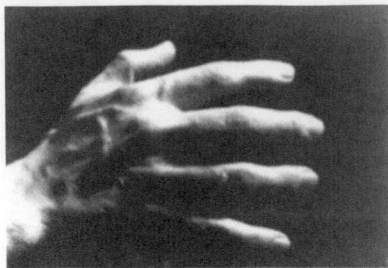 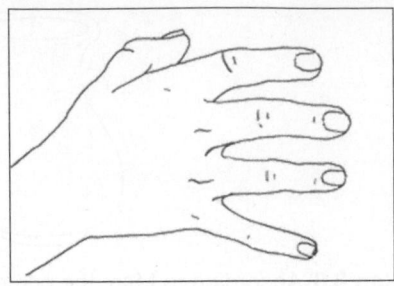

Figure 8.10 A photograph and a simplified line drawing of a hand. Ryan and Schwartz (1956) showed that a cartoon drawing was recognized more rapidly than a photograph.

will guarantee that these variables are processed together, in parallel. This approach, he claimed, has two distinct advantages. The first is that the display can reduce visual clutter by integrating the variables into a single visual object. The second is that the object display makes it easier for an operator to integrate multiple sources of information.

Generally, object displays will be most effective when the components of the objects have a natural or metaphorical relationship to the data being represented. Fig. 8.11 shows an object display developed for anesthesiologists working in operating theaters. It is the responsibility of anesthesiologists to monitor the output from a large number of sensors attached to a patient and from the reading to infer the state of the patient, especially relating to the delivery of oxygen to the brain through the cardiovascular system. George Blike and his coworkers developed a display that maps these instrument readings to a set of complex glyphs as illustrated in the figure (Blike, Surgenor, & Whalen, 1999). The central glyph represents the heart and this incorporates four different measurements. The height of the glyph represents the volume pumped by a single heart-beat, and its width represents the heart rate (number of beats per minute). The glyph size is an emergent property showing overall heart throughput. The bowing or bulging of the sides of the heart object is produced from two cleverly transformed measurements, the pulmonary wedge pressure (PWP) and the central venous pressure (CVP), representing the pressure in the left- and right-hand sides of the heart, respectively. These control the degree of convexity or concavity on each side of the glyph in such a way that a concave shape is the result of too low pressure and a convex shape is the result of too high pressure. This provides an intuitive visual metaphor for these variables. The display enables an anesthesiologist to rapidly diagnose problems such as an embolism (blockage) or hemorrhage, and the laterality of the bulge or concavity indicate where they are occurring. In an evaluation study comparing this display with a more conventional display, errors were reduced by 66%.

In the Blike design, the object display has a number of clear advantages. It can reduce accidental misreadings of data values. Mistakes are less likely because components act as their own descriptive icons. In addition, the structural architecture of the system and the connections between system components are always visible, and this may help in diagnosing the causes and effects of problems.

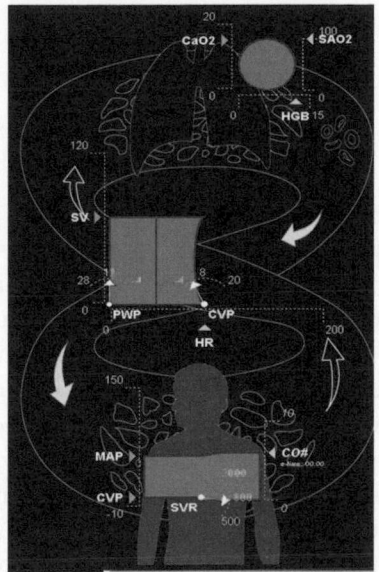

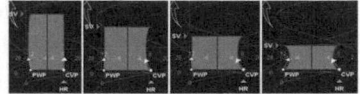

A hemorrhage in progress

Figure 8.11 An object display designed for use by anesthesiologists (Blike et al., 1999). *(© Draeger Medical Systems, Inc. All rights reserved. Not to be reproduced without written permission.)*

The disadvantage of object displays is that they lack generality; an object display must be custom designed for each specific application, which means that they are only appropriate when a great deal of effort can be devoted to a careful design. Object displays should be validated with a user population to ensure that the data representation is clear and properly interpreted. This requires far more effort than displaying data as a table of numbers or a simple bar chart.

[G8.2] Consider using an object display where standardized sets of data must be repeatedly analyzed and where the data can be mapped to semantically meaningful objects. This method is only suitable for customized applications.

The general properties of an effective object display are summarized in the following guidelines.

[G8.3] Design object displays in such a way that numbers are tied to recognizable visual objects representing system components.

[G8.4] Design object display layouts using connecting elements that clearly indicate the physical connections between components of a system.

[G8.5] Design object display glyphs to have emergent properties revealing the effect of important interactions between variables.

[G8.6] Design object display glyphs to become more salient when critical values are reached in the data.

The Geon Diagram

Biederman's geon theory, outlined earlier, can be applied directly to object display design. If cylinders and cones are indeed perceptual primitives, it makes sense to construct diagrams using these geon elements. This should make the diagrams easy to interpret if a good mapping can be found from the data to a geon structure. The geon diagram concept is illustrated in Fig. 8.12. Geons are used to represent the major components of a compound data object, whereas the architecture of the data object is represented by the structural skeleton linking the geons. The size of a geon becomes a natural metaphor for the relative importance of a data entity or its complexity or relative value. The strength of the connections between the components is given by the neck-like linking structures. Additional attributes of entities and relationships can be coded by coloring and texturing. Research suggests that such diagrams can be easier to interpret and remember (Irani, Tingley, & Ware, 2001).

In Biederman's theory, surface properties of geons, such as their colors and textures, are secondary characteristics. This makes it natural to use the surface color and texture of the geon to represent data attributes of a data object. Abstract semantics may be expressible, in a natural way, through the way geons are interconnected. In the everyday environment there is meaning to the relative positioning of objects that is understood at a deep, possibly innate level. Because of gravity, above is different from below.

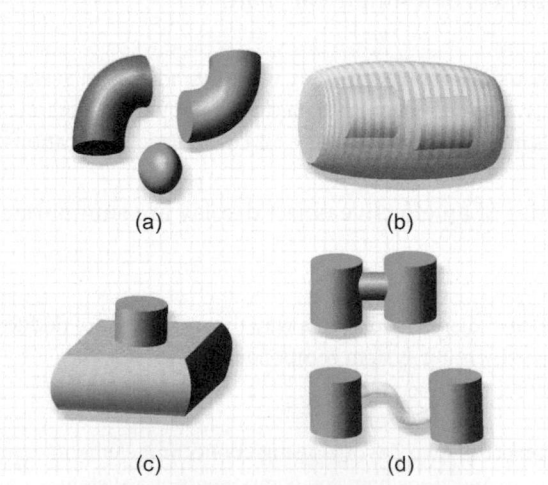

Figure 8.12 Certain spatial relationships between objects can readily represent abstract concepts. (a) That objects belong to the same class is better shown by shape than by color. (b) A part-of relationship. (c) A dependency relationship. (d) Strong and weak relationships.

If one object is inside another transparent object, it is perceived either as contained by that other object or as a part of it. Irani et al. (2001) suggested that the semantics inherent in the different kinds of relationships of real-world objects might be applied to diagramming abstract concepts. Based on this idea, the researchers developed a set of graphical representations of abstract concepts. Some of the more successful of these mappings are illustrated in Fig. 8.12 and listed as follows. However, only some of these are given formal status as guidelines.

- Sometimes we wish to show different instances of the same generic object. Geon theory predicts that having the same shape should be the best way of doing this. Geon shape is dominant over color, which is a secondary attribute. Thus, the elbow shapes in Fig. 8.12(a) are seen as two instances of the same object, whereas the two green objects are not.

- Having an object inside another transparent object is a natural representation of a part-of relationship. The inside objects seem part of the outside object, as seen in Fig. 8.12(b).

- One object above and touching another, as shown in Fig. 8.12(c), is easily understood as representing a dependency relationship.

- A thick bar between two objects is a natural representation of a strong relationship between two objects; a thinner, transparent bar represents a weak relationship. See Fig. 8.12(d). Although the geon diagram is a 3D representation, there are reasons to pay special attention to the way it is laid out in 2D in the x, y plane. As discussed earlier, some silhouettes are especially effective in allowing the visual system to extract object structure. A commonsense design rule is to lay out structural components principally on a single plane. A diagramming method resembling the bas-relief stone carvings common in classical Rome and Greece may be optimal. Such carvings contain careful 3D modeling of the component objects, combined with only limited depth and a mainly planar layout.

[G8.7] Consider representing system components using geons—simple 3D shaded objects such as spheres, cylinders, cones, and boxes.

[G8.8] Consider using the color and surface texture of geons to represent secondary attributes of represented entities.

[G8.9] Consider using a geon-based diagram in instances where the diagram is relatively simple, fewer than 30 components, and where entities and relationships must be shown.

[G8.10] Consider representing relationships between components by means of joints between objects. Tubes can be used to express certain types of relations. A small geon attached to a larger geon can show that it is a component part.

[G8.11] Consider using geon shapes to represent the primary attribute of represented entities.

[G8.12] Consider placing an object inside a second transparent object to express a part of relationship.

[G8.13] When creating 3D diagrams, lay out system components as much as possible in a 2D plane orthogonal to the line of sight. Be sure that connections between diagram components are clearly visible.

[G8.14] When creating diagrams showing entities and relationships, use properties such as size and thickness to represent the strength of the relationship between entities.

3D Glyphs

In scientific visualization, it is common that computed fields can have attributes beyond simple scalars and vectors. These may encode attributes such as twist and shear. We will not go into this technical subject here, except to observe that 3D glyphs have been developed to visualize these quantities. An example from Jankun–Kelly, Lanka, and Swan (2010) is illustrated in Fig. 8.13. These objects, called superellipsoid

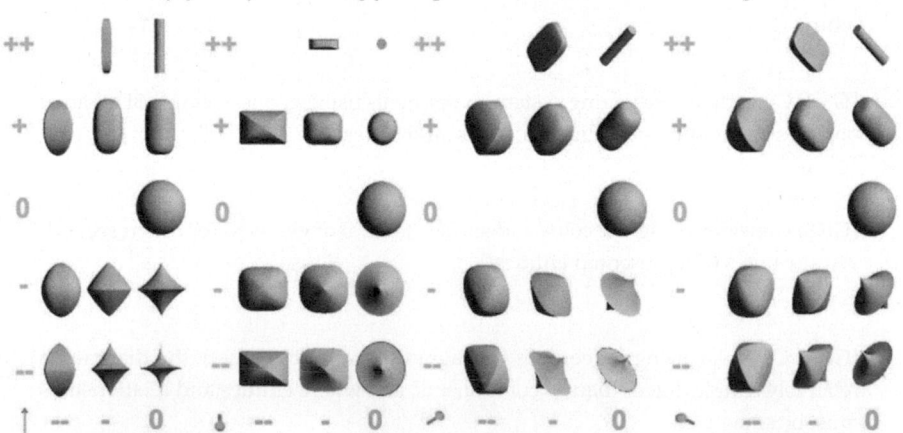

Figure 8.13 3D glyphs (on the right) developed by Jankun-Kelly et al. (2010) and evaluated against the alternatives shown to the left. (*From T.J. Jankun-Kelly (2010). Reproduced with permission.*)

glyphs, encode orientation as well as other properties important in the analysis of liquid crystals. An evaluation study was carried out showing that this particular coding scheme was superior to three others. Any interested reader should delve into this and related work (see also, Schultz & Kindlmann, 2010). It is also worth bearing in mind that the most effective pattern analysis capabilities of the visual system work in the 2D image plane, so the interpretation of 3D glyphs will be viewpoint dependent which may result in errors of interpretation.

Faces

Faces are special objects in human perception. Infants learn about faces faster than they learn about other objects. We are born with visual systems primed to learn to recognize important humans, especially our own mothers (Bruce & Young, 1998; Bushnell, Sai, & Mullin, 1989; Morton & Johnson, 1991). A specific area of our brains, the right middle fusiform gyrus, is critically important in face perception (Kanwisher, McDermott, & Chun, 1997; Kanwisher, Stanley, & Harris, 1999; Puce, Allison, Gore, & McCarthy, 1995). This area is also useful for recognizing other complex objects, such as automobiles. Faces have an obvious importance in communication; we use facial expressions to communicate our emotion and degree of interest. Cross-cultural studies by Paul Ekman and coworkers strongly suggest that certain human expressions are universal communication signals, correctly interpreted across cultures and social groups (Ekman, 2003; Ekman & Friesen, 1975). Ekman identified six universal expressions: anger, disgust, fear, happiness, sadness, and surprise. These are illustrated in Fig. 8.14, along with determination and elation (a variation on happiness).

The motion of facial features is also important in conveying emotion. Animated images are necessary to convey a full range of nuanced emotion; it is especially important to show motion of the eyebrows (Basilli, 1978; Sadr, Jarudi, & Sinha, 2003). Both static and dynamic facial expressions are produced by the contractions of facial muscles, and the

Figure 8.14 Happiness, elation, anger, sadness, disgust, determination, fear, and surprise.

facial action coding system (FACS) is a widely applied method of measuring and defining groups of facial muscles and their effect on facial expression (Ekman, Friesen, & O'Sullivan, 1988).

The eyebrows and mouth are particularly significant in signaling emotions, but the shape of the eyes is also important. There is evidence that false smiles can be distinguished from true smiles from the particular expression around the eyes that occurs with the contraction of a muscle that orbits the eye (Ekman, 2003; Ekman et al., 1988). This muscle contracts with true smiles but not with false ones. According to Ekman (2003) it is difficult, if not impossible, to control this voluntarily and thus fake a "true" smile.

The main application of FACS theory in computer displays has been in the creation of computer avatars that convey human emotion (Kalra, Gobbetti, Magnenat-Thalmann, & Thalmann, 1993; Ruttkay, Noot, & Hagen, 2003). Appropriate emotional expression may help make a virtual salesperson more convincing. In computer-aided instruction, the expression on a human face could reward or discourage. The little symbols called *emoticons*, such as Θ and Λ, commonly used in text messaging take advantage of the ease with which we recognize emotions even when expressed using the most rudimentary graphics.

> **[G8.15]** For perceptually efficient and compact expressions of human emotion, consider using small glyphs representing simplified faces. These are likely to be especially effective in conveying the basic emotions of anger, disgust, fear, happiness, sadness, and surprise.

Among the earlier examples of object displays are Chernoff faces, named after their inventor, Herman Chernoff (1973). In his technique, a simplified image of a human face is used as a display. Examples are shown in Fig. 8.15. To turn a face into a display, data variables are mapped to different facial features, such as the length of the nose, the curvature of the mouth, the size of the eye, the shape of the head, etc. Jacob, Egeth, and Bevon (1976) carried out a classification task using a series of displays that were progressively more object-like. The displays included Chernoff faces, tables, star plots, and the whisker plots described in Chapter 5. They found that more object-like displays, including Chernoff face plots, enabled faster, more accurate classification.

Despite their initial promise, Chernoff faces have not generally been adopted in practical visualization applications. The likely reason for this is the idiosyncratic nature of the method. When data is mapped to faces, many kinds of perceptual interactions can occur. Sometimes the combination of variables will result in a particular stereotypical face, perhaps a happy face or a sad face, and this will be identified more readily. In addition, there are undoubtedly great differences in our sensitivity to the different features. We may be more sensitive to the curvature of the mouth than to the height of the eyebrows, for example. This means that the perceptual space of Chernoff faces is likely to be extremely nonlinear. In addition, there are almost certainly many uncharted

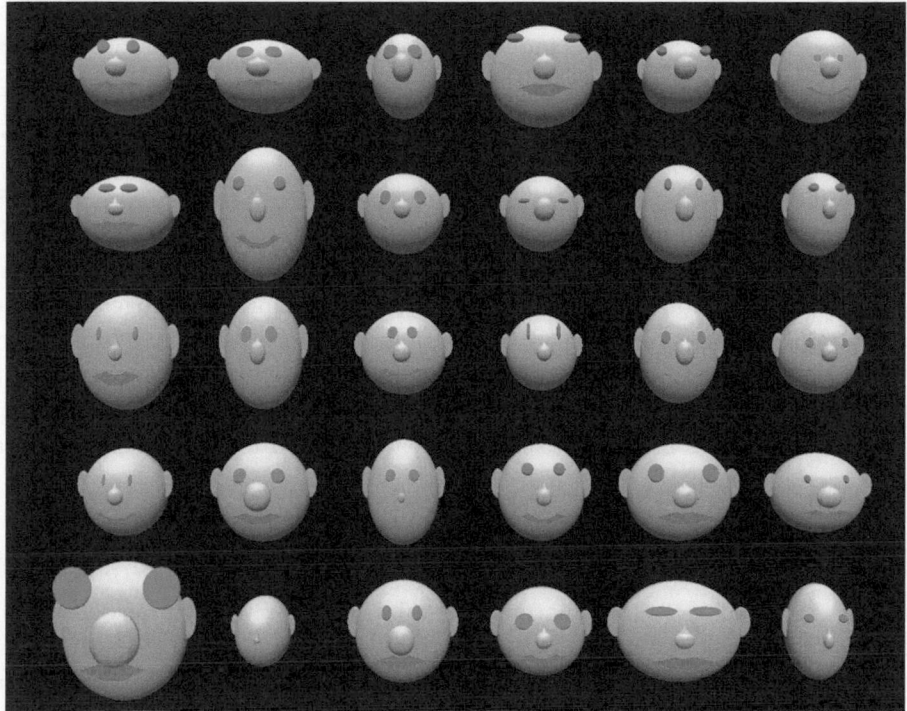

Figure 8.15 Chernoff faces. Different data variables are mapped to the sizes and shapes of different facial features—a bad idea because of unpredictable effects from emergent expressions. (*Courtesy Davide Heise, dhelse@andrews.edu.*)

interactions between facial features, and these are likely to vary from one viewer to another, leading to large distortions in the way the data is perceived.

Coding Words and Images

Bertin, in his seminal work, *Semiology of Graphics* (1983), distinguished two distinct sign systems. One cluster of sign systems is associated with auditory information processing and includes mathematical symbols, natural language, and music. The second cluster is based on visual information processing and includes graphics, together with abstract and figurative imagery. More recently, the dual coding of Paivio (1987) proposed that there are fundamentally two different types of information stored in distinct working memory and long-term memory systems; he called them *imagens* and *logogens*. Roughly speaking, imagens denote the mental representation of visual information, whereas logogens denote the mental representation of language information. This duality of systems is called *dual coding theory*.

Visual imagens consist of objects, natural groupings of objects, and whole parts of objects (for example, an arm), together with spatial information about the way they are laid out in a particular environment, such as a room. Logogens store basic information pertaining to language, although not the sounds of the words. Logogens are processed by a set of functional subsystems that provide support for reading and writing, understanding and producing speech, and logical thought. Logogens need not necessarily be tied to speech, but they are associated with nonvisual language. In the profoundly deaf the same language subsystems exist and are used in the reading and production of Braille and sign language.

The architecture of dual coding theory is sketched in Fig. 8.16. Visual-spatial information enters through the visual system and is fed into association structures in the nonverbal imagen system. Visual text is processed visually at first, but the information is rapidly transferred into the nonvisual association structures of logogens. Acoustic verbal stimuli are processed primarily through the auditory system and then fed into the logogen system. Logogens and imagens, although based on separate subsystems, can be strongly interlinked; for example, the word *cat* and language-based concepts related to cats will be linked to visual information related to the appearance of cats and their environment.

Mental Images

Much of dual coding theory is uncontroversial. It has been known for decades that there are different neural processing centers for verbal information and visual information. Examples of purely verbal processing brain regions are Broca's area, which is part of the frontal cortex that when damaged results in an inability to speak intelligibly, and Wernicke's area, which results in an inability to comprehend speech when damaged.

It is the idea that we can "think" visually that is relatively recent. One line of evidence comes from mental imaging. When people are asked to compare the size of a lightbulb with the size of a tennis ball, or the green of a pea with the green of a pine tree, most claim that they use *mental images* of these objects to carry out the task (Kosslyn,

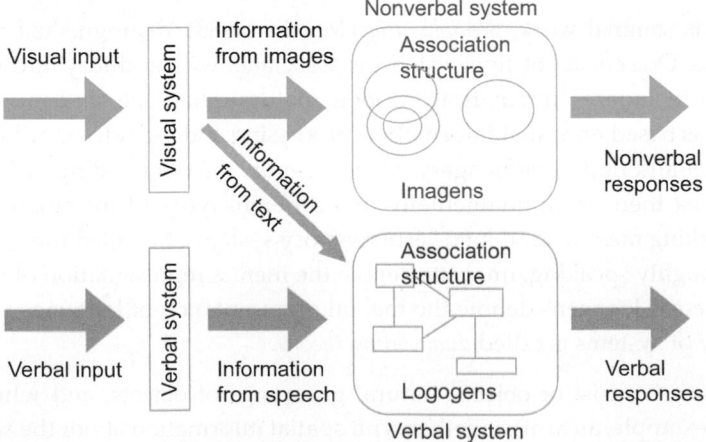

Figure 8.16 Dual coding theory.

1994). Other studies by Kosslyn and his coworkers show that people treat objects in mental images as if they have real sizes and locations in space. Recently, positron emission tomography (PET) has been used to reveal which parts of the brain are active during specific tasks. This shows that when people are asked to perform tasks involving mental imaging the visual processing centers in the brain are activated. When they mentally change the size and position of an imagined object, different visual areas of the brain are activated (Kosslyn et al., 1993). In addition, if visual processing centers in the brain are damaged, mental imaging ability is disrupted (Farah, Soso, & Dashieff, 1992). It would seem that when we see a cow and when we mentally visualize a cow, the same neural pathways are excited, at least in part. Indeed, modern visual memory theory takes the position that visual object processing and visual object recognition are part of the same process. To some extent, the visual memory traces of objects and scenes are stored as part of the processing mechanism; thus, it is not necessary for an object to be fully processed for recognition to take place (Beardsley, 1997). This can account for the great superiority of recognition over recall. We can easily recognize that we have seen something before, but reproducing it in a drawing or with a verbal description is much more difficult.

This implies that the simple dual coding theory illustrated in Fig. 8.16 is misleading in one important respect. The diagram implies that memories for visual inputs are stored *after* processing through the visual system; however, image memory is not a separate storage bin but an integral part of the perceptual system. Visual images are analyzed on their way through the system and visual memories are activated by the incoming information as they simultaneously shape it. There is no separate store; memory is distributed through the brain at every level of processing.

Labels and Concepts

Much of what we perceive when we "see" an object is not out there in the world, but stored in our memories. We perceive objects as tables, chairs, trees, flowers, cups, books, or as one of the thousands of other things we know about. As part of perception, objects are automatically labeled, and our knowledge of the characteristics, uses, and relationships to other objects is brought to a state of readiness in mind. Even an unknown amorphous blob is seen as *like* other objects of a similar size and smoothness—its material properties are automatically inferred from its texture and color, and its potential for manipulation is automatically assessed.

It takes learning and prior experience to develop high-level object concepts, and their characteristics are necessarily somewhat idiosyncratic. A musician will see a violin in a very different way than a nonmusician who hates classical music. In each case, the violin will be seen to have a very different set of affordances and what is perceived will be colored by this. Despite these differences, human communication depends on socially agreed-upon labels for objects, classes of objects, and concepts within a community, and the perception of the more basic characteristics of common objects will be similar for most individuals.

Object Categorization

Categorization is the abstraction of things and ideas into groups and most if not all categories have verbal labels. The words *cheese*, *tree*, *plant*, *company*, and *bacteria* are all category labels. Virtually all of the things we see and think of as objects are classified automatically in the brain within 100 ms of our seeing them. When we see a spoon, not just its shape is registered, but the verbal label also becomes activated. A large array of concepts relating to culinary activity and eating may become primed and brought to a state of readiness.

Objects that we know well combine clusters of attributes that are visual with clusters of attributes that are verbally related concepts. They may also have properties that awaken activities in our movement control systems, in the case of things that we may pick up and manipulate or use as tools. Kahneman, Treisman, and Gibbs (1992) named this collection of visual and nonvisual properties an *object file* (see Fig. 8.17).

Even objects that are unfamiliar can be categorized by their utility. A fist-sized chunk of any material may be used as a projectile, as potential building material, or, if it is hard, as a tool.

Our modern understanding of how the human brain categorizes ects began with the pioneering research of Eleanor Roschobj (1973, 1975). Prior to this, from the time of

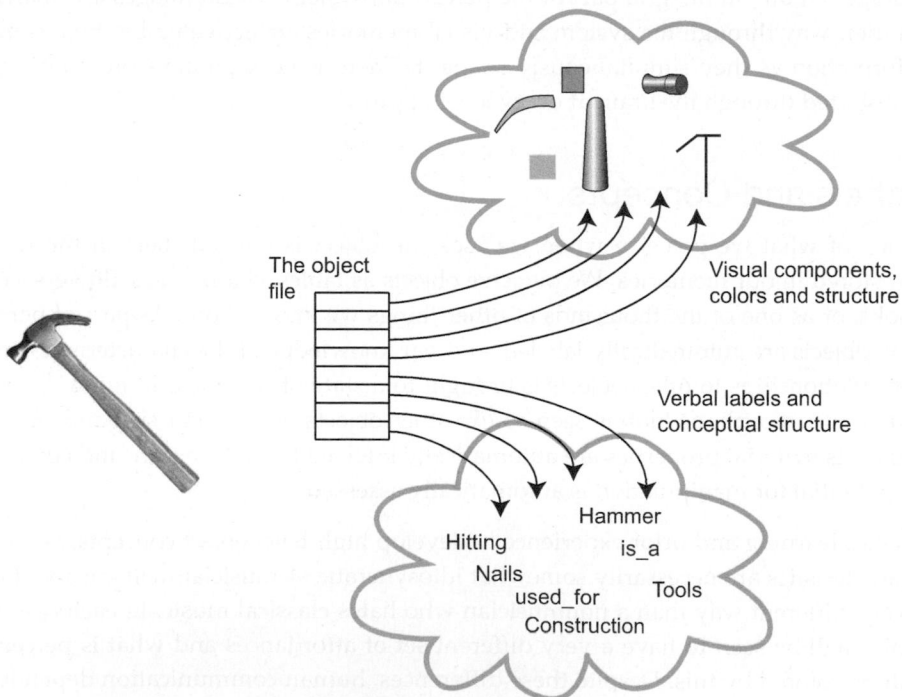

Figure 8.17 The object file is a proposed cognitive mechanism that links multiple attributes of an object. These attributes can be both visual and nonvisual.

Aristotle, object classification had been treated as if the brain did a formal logical analysis of sensory data. This approach leads to a world in which things belong to categories with sharp boundaries. Either something is a fruit, or it is not. Rosch's work showed that the way we actually perceive objects is much more flexible. People perceive apples and oranges to definitively be fruits, but they are much less certain about cucumbers and tomatoes.

Rosch discovered that there are certain categories she called *basic level*, with other categories above and below. The concept of *dog* is a basic-level category, with *animals* as a superordinate category and particular breeds as subordinate categories. Basic-level categories are the most commonly used broad categories and are learned first by infants. People are more likely to categorize a particular animal, such as pet canine, as a dog than as members of the higher level category of animal. Rosch defined basic-level categories in terms of three criteria: *They have similar shape*; this is obviously true of dogs, which are much more mutually similar than, say, the category of animals. *They have similar motor interactions*; that is, we tend to do the same things with members of a particular class. *They have similar nonvisual attributes*, which refers to all the nonvisual properties we learn to be associated with objects, including the materials they are made from and their likely associations with other objects. Because of the visual similarity of basic-level categories, Rosch observed that usually a single drawing can be used to represent the entire class. Such drawings are also classified with the shortest reaction times.

Later work by Jolicoeur et al. (1984) added refinements to Rosch's work. He and his coworkers found that certain category members are identified faster than others even though they are at the same level of the hierarchy. For example, a medium-sized canine with neither especially long nor short legs will be categorized as a dog faster than a dachshund.

The Enactive View

The object file metaphor discussed above encapsulates a somewhat static view of perception and memory, wherein object properties and their linked attributes are recovered from memory through the act of perception.

In the last decade or so more action-oriented theoretical approaches have arisen, which emphasize the links between perception and both past and future actions. One theory is called enactive perception (Hutto & Myin, 2012). Another, the sensory-motor account (O'Regan & Noë, 2001). Although there are differences between these, there are many similarities in that they both emphasize that perception is fundamentally an activity designed to support actions within the environment. Perception is based on the previous neural activations from exploratory activities that lead to observations of similar objects in similar environment. The perception of a particular kind of object naturally and inextricably involves activations of potentials for action relating to the perceived object. Perceiving a cup, a chair, or a stone, is based on prior sensory and exploratory activities involving cups, chairs, or stones and this prepares us for interacting with this particular cup, chair, or stone. Another common theme of the enactive theory is that the brain evolved to predict the consequences of potential actions (Barselou, 2008) and it is constantly making predictions regarding the environment and the consequences of actions within the environment.

Fig. 8.18 illustrates a cluster of activations that might arise in the brain as a result of object perception. It differs from the object file account (Fig. 8.17) in that the neural pathways activated are not merely a cluster of attributes recovered from storage; instead, they relate to potential activities, such as making use of an object, making an utterance relating to that object, or predicting how the object will change relative to its environment, both in the absence of action or as a result of some action. This action oriented view of perception and cognition will be a central theme of the final two chapters of this book. The main implication for data visualization is that visual objects representing data should, wherever possible, support activities to seek further information or take action related to the currently perceived information.

Canonical Views and Object Recognition

Palmer, Rosch, and Chase (1981) showed that not all views of an object are equally easy to recognize. They found that many different objects have something like a *canonical view* from which they are most easily identified. From this and other evidence, a theory of object recognition has been developed, proposing that we recognize objects by matching the visual information with internally stored viewpoint-specific exemplars, or *prototypes*; the brain stores a number of key views of each object (Edelman, 1995; Edelman & Buelthoff, 1992). This is the image-based object memory theory introduced at the start of this chapter. The views are not simple snapshots; however, they allow recognition despite simple geometric distortions of the image that occur in perspective transformation. This explains why object perception survives the kinds of geometric distortions that occur when a picture is viewed and tilted with respect to the observer.

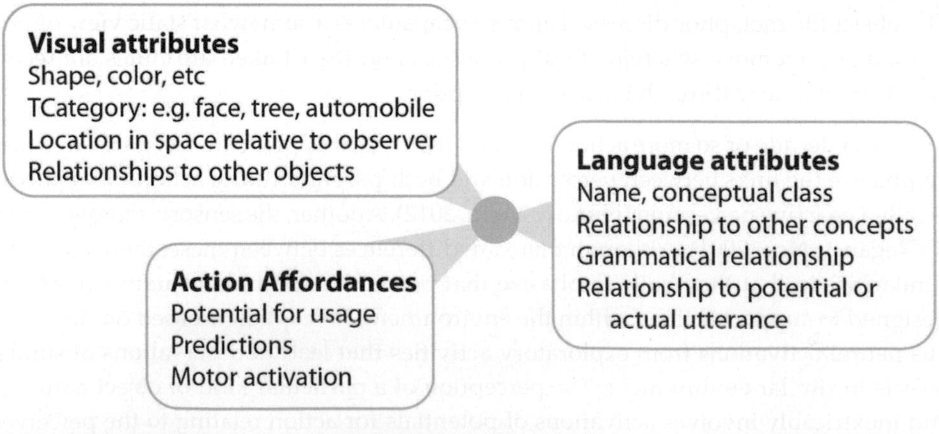

Visual attributes
Shape, color, etc
TCategory: e.g. face, tree, automobile
Location in space relative to observer
Relationships to other objects

Action Affordances
Potential for usage
Predictions
Motor activation

Language attributes
Name, conceptual class
Relationship to other concepts
Grammatical relationship
Relationship to potential or
    actual utterance

Figure 8.18 An illustration of the dynamic neural activations that may occur as a result of object perception according to the enactive view.

There are strict limits on the extent to which we can change an image before recognition problems occur. Palmer et al. (1981) had observers rate how well pictures taken from different perspectives resembled the object depicted. The results showed strongly that certain views were judged more typical than others (see Fig. 8.19). Moreover, this had a large effect on the amount of time it took subjects to name the object shown. Other studies have revealed that objects are named faster when they are upright (Jolicoer, 1985), but changing the size of the represented object has a relatively small effect. Also, numerous studies show impaired face recognition if the faces are shown upside down (Rhodes, 1995).

> **[G8.16]** To make a visual image that represents a class of things, use a canonical example in its normal orientation displayed from a typical viewpoint, but only if a suitable exemplar exists.

There are many cases where simple images cannot be used to represent categories of objects. One reason is that most things belong to many overlapping sets of categories, and many categories do not have canonical object representations. Consider the category of pet. A pet can be a goldfish, an insect, or a snake, as well as the more typical dogs and cats. No simple sketch can represent all of these, as they do not share a canonical set of visual features. Some abstract categories are even more difficult. The philosopher Wittgenstein (1953) used the example of games to argue that categories should be thought of as loosely associated bundles of properties, rather than concepts that can be defined by a few formal rules. Board games, sports such as soccer, and

Figure 8.19 Noncanonical and canonical views of a horse and a car.

games such as charades all belong to the game category. Such categories are very difficult to formally pin down, and, like pets, have no canonical representation.

Concept Mapping

Researchers in the field of information visualization have put considerable effort into creating visual representations of ideas and abstract concepts. These can be considered as potential visual thinking tools.

Concept Maps and Mind Maps

Mind mapping is technique that is promoted as a learning aid for students (Jonassen, Beissner, & Yacci, 1993). It consists of sketching out links between related ideas, concepts, and things, as illustrated in Fig. 8.20. Usually, such maps are constructed informally by sketching them on paper, but computer-based tools also exist. Essentially, a mind map is a type of node-link diagram in which the nodes represent concepts and the links represent relationships between concepts. The central idea to be explored is placed in the middle of the page and it is expanded out from there. Usually mind maps are drawn as tree structures with no cross links between branches, but this can be restrictive. In Fig. 8.20 almost all of the ideas have links to almost all of the other ideas. An individual can use a mind map as a tool for organizing his or her own personal concept structure, and it may reveal patterns of relationships between ideas that had not been evident when the concepts were stored internally. A mind map can also be constructed as a group exercise, in which case it becomes a tool for building a common understanding.

In a mind map any idea or object can be put down. Related visualizations are the *concept map* and the *argument map* (Davies, 2011). Both of these have more formal rules for

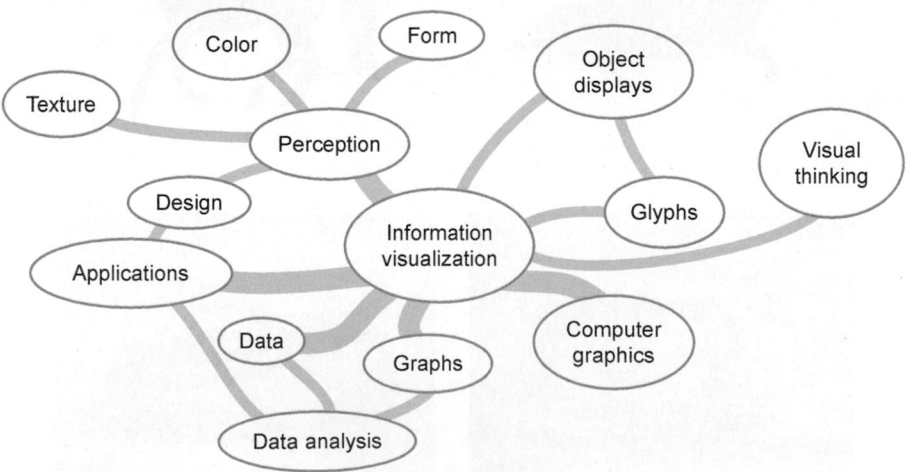

Figure 8.20 A mind map surrounding the concept "information visualization." Only a few of the possible links are shown.

their construction. There is also the *entity-relationship (ER) diagram*, which is a formal construct used in software and business modeling. Although an ER diagram has much in common with concept maps and mind maps, it is typically not used as a learning tool.

Most educational theory suggests that in order to learn concepts it is important that students actively work to integrate new ideas into the framework provided by their existing knowledge (Hay, Kinchin, & Lygo-Baker, 2008; Willis, 1995). This is the central theme of constructivist education theory that has its roots in the work of the Russian psychologist Lev Vygotsky (1978). Constructivism also emphasizes the social roots of knowledge and that much of our concept formation is shaped by social pressures (Karagiorgi & Symeou, 2005).

The educational use of mind maps and concept maps would seem to fit well with constructivist theory. To construct such a map, students must actively draw out links between various concepts as they understand them. The problem is that the cognitive engagement tends to be somewhat superficial for mind maps, since it does not require that students think deeply about the *nature of the links*. For example, simply knowing that there is a link between disease and urban living is of marginal value, but if we know something about how diseases are propagated then we can design better sanitation systems. Because concept maps and argument maps require more analytic skills they are likely to be more effective. There is some empirical evidence that concept maps can be aids to learning (e.g., Hay et al., 2008), but because the key activity is typically the deconstruction of some body of text to extract concepts or arguments, it may be that the visualization is not a critical component; simple lists of concepts or arguments might be as effective.

The best note-taking techniques appear to be hybrids combining concept organization techniques (using connecting lines and boxes) with more detailed textual information (Novak, 1981). Other structured note-taking methods can be effective, such as arranging ideas in a matrix (Kiewra, Kauffman, Robinson, DuBois, & Staley, 1999).

There are other reasons for mapping concepts into a visual space. Recently, sophisticated computer algorithms have been developed to parse large text databases in order to understand how ideas, as expressed in society at large, are related to one another and how they develop over time. For example, the SPIRE system creates a classification of documents with respect to a keyword query and can be applied to databases consisting of hundreds of thousands of documents (Wise et al., 1995). The result of the SPIRE algorithm is a set of vectors in an *n*-dimensional space. To help people understand the resulting clusters of documents, Wise et al. created a visualization called a *ThemeScape*, which shows the two most important dimensions as a kind of data landscape. This is illustrated in Fig. 8.21. Flags on top of hills label and identify the largest clusters of documents in this space. Essentially, a ThemeScape uses the two most significant dimensions of the abstract data space to create a smoothed 2D histogram. Spatial proximity and salience show the major concentrations of information and, to

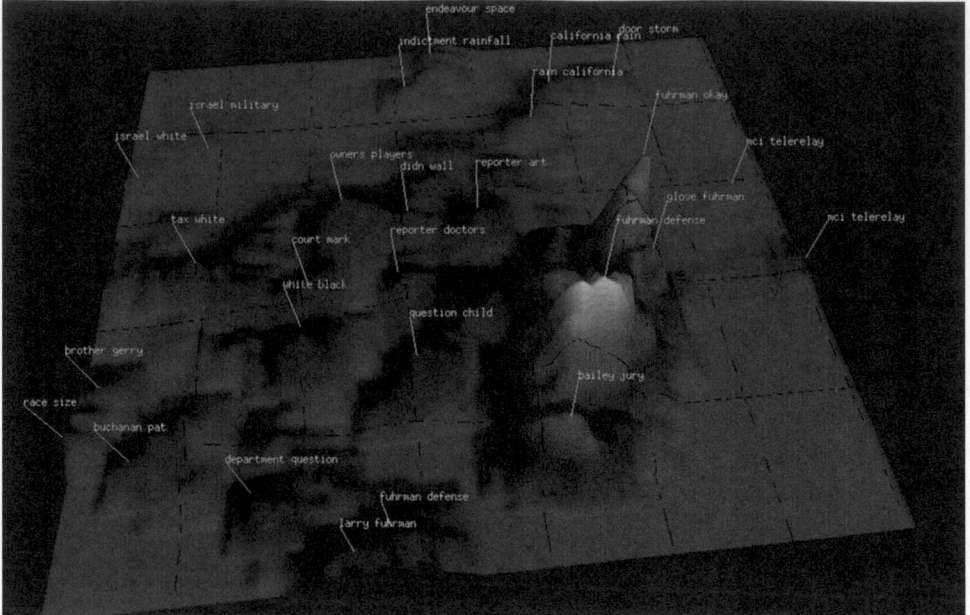

Figure 8.21 An entire week of CNN news stories is summarized in a ThemeScape. (*From Wise et al. (1995). Reproduced with permission.*)

some extent, their relationships. This kind of display will be useful when two dimensions really do capture most of the variability in the data.

Other visualizations have been designed to map out the temporal evolution of larger themes in text databases. ThemeRiver is an application developed by Havre, Hetzler, and Nowell (2000) designed to show how ideas become more prevalent over time, and then fade away. It has been used to show the temporal trajectory of major news stories.

Visualizations such as ThemeScape and ThemeRiver can perhaps be used to understand the *zeitgeist* of the time. Politicians want to know which issues are receiving the most press attention and these displays may help. But, like concept maps, both displays provide only the most superficial information about the relationships of ideas. In addition, because very high-dimensional data has been mapped into a low-dimensional space, proximities between concepts are only sometimes meaningful.

Other systems have been developed to map human knowledge into a node-link diagram. Bollen et al. (2009) used a very large university database derived from Internet searches carried out by university students and faculty. Their goal was to understand which areas of scholarly endeavor are most closely related. Their algorithm judged there to be a connection between disciplines when there were information selections (via mouse clicks) in different disciplines by the same person, close together in time. This is called *clickstream* data. The resulting map of knowledge is shown in Fig. 8.22. It shows the physical sciences to the right and social sciences and clinical areas to the left, with the arts in the center. This particular layout is arbitrary; an artifact of the

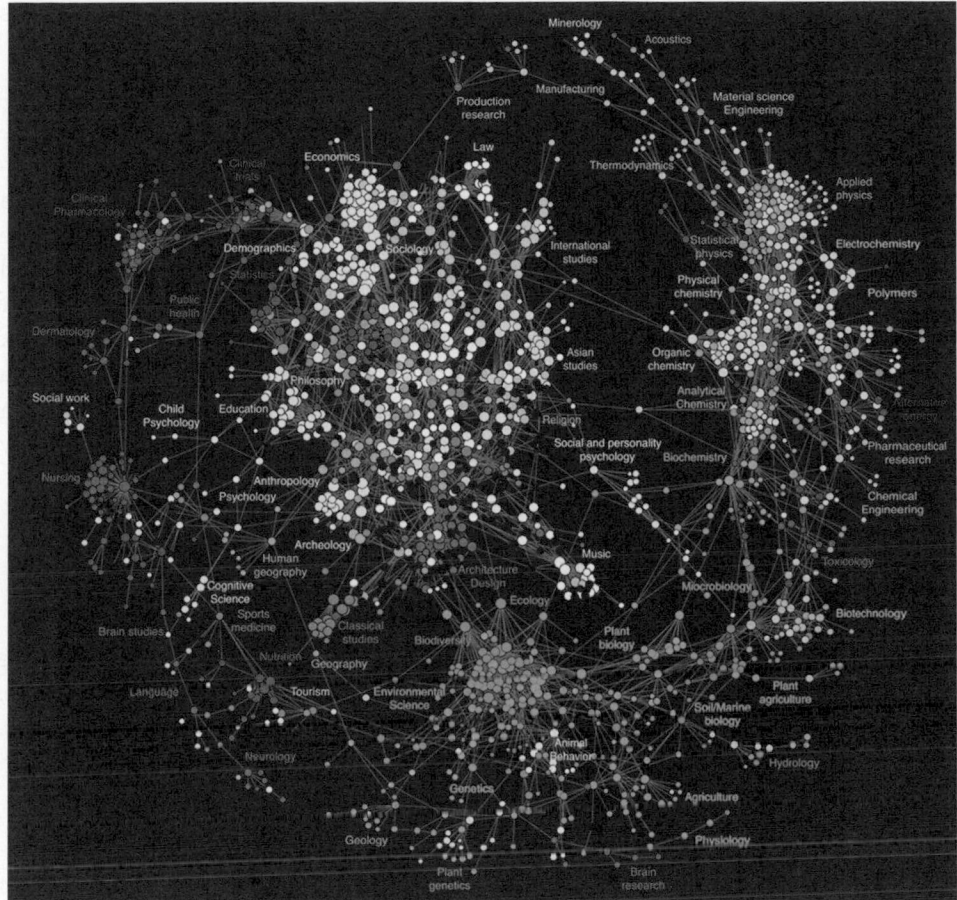

Figure 8.22 A diagram showing the links between academic disciplines using clickstream data. (*From Bollen et al. (2009). Reproduced with permission.*)

algorithm, but the connections between areas is meaningful. Highly interconnected areas mean that scholars were researching in both disciplines. Such a map might be used by university administrators thinking about the logical structure of faculties, or it might be used to organize government funding agencies according to the most closely linked scholarly areas.

Iconic Images versus Words versus Abstract Symbols

We have choices when creating a visualization that requires symbols. We can use abstract visual symbols such as triangles, squares, or circles; we can use pictorial icons, such as an image of broccoli to represent "vegetables"; or we can use words or phrases. The best solution depends on a number of factors—the purpose of the visualization, the number of data points and how dense they are, and the availability of canonical images. For example, if the quantity represented is something like the price/earnings ratio of a stock, then pictorial icons are not available.

In general, pictorial icons are best used when the purpose of a visualization is pedagogical, and they are not intended for the data analyst who usually insists on far more detailed information. The reason for using the pictorial icon in an infographic is cognitive efficiency, especially for the occasional user. Using an image to represent a data object means that it is not necessary to consult a key to get its category, ensuring one less step in the process of understanding. Infographics are often designed for rapid understanding by people who may have only a marginal interest in the content —for example, the readers of magazine or newspaper articles. A general audience may lack familiarity with more specialized (and abstract) charting conventions, so reducing a step can easily make the difference between something that is ignored and something that provides information. Also, in infographics the information content is usually quite low, so there is more space available for images.

> **[G8.17]** Consider using pictorial icons for pedagogical purposes in infographics. Use them only where a canonical or culturally defined image is available.

When using representative visual symbols as glyphs to display quantity we must be aware of the potential distortion inherent in varying size to display relative quantity; linear coding using multiples is generally preferable. Using the stacked hamburgers in the manner of Otto Neurath's Isotypes (1936), as shown in Fig. 8.23, is likely better than

Fast food and vegetable consumption

1980   2010

Figure 8.23 In infographics, repeated pictorial icons are often used to represent quantity.

using a single big hamburger and a single big broccoli, each sized to represent some quantity. As discussed in Chapter 5 (guideline G5.17), it is particularly disastrous to use the volume of an object to represent a numerical quantity. In many diagrams and charts it is common to use pictorial symbols to represent various kinds of categorical information. This is especially true of so-called infographics. Stacks of little house-shaped symbols and stacks of little car-shaped symbols may be used to represent the rates of home and car ownership in different countries. A hamburger is sometimes used to represent junk food in a chart. Broccoli has achieved similar status as a symbol for healthy food.

The choice of abstract symbols versus labeled points and regions should also be made on the basis of cognitive efficiency. Abstract symbols are effective when there are many data points belonging to a few different categories. Abstract symbols can be more compact than pictorial icons. Also, if visual clustering is important, the effective use of low-level visual features discussed in Chapters 5 and 6 becomes critical.

> [G8.18] When a large number of data points must be represented in a visualization, use symbols instead of words or pictorial icons.

Written and spoken language has orders of magnitude more category labels than there are standardized pictorial icons. This means that words must be chosen over pictorial icons in most cases, but diagrams densely populated with printed words can become unintelligible. Directly labeling objects in visualizations using words is most suitable when there is a single member for each category, or only a few, and where the category density is low.

> [G8.19] Use words directly on the chart where the number of symbolic objects in each category is relatively few and where space is available.

Static Links

When text is integrated into a static diagram, the Gestalt principles discussed in Chapter 6 apply, as Fig. 8.24 shows. Simple proximity is commonly used in labeling maps. A line drawn around the object and text creates a common region. A line or common region can also be used to associate groups of objects with a particular label. Arrows and speech balloons linking text and graphics also apply the principle of connectedness.

> [G8.20] Use Gestalt principles of proximity, connectedness, and common region to associate written labels with graphical elements.

Scenes and Scene Gist

Rapid categorization occurs with scenes as well as visual objects. If you flip channels on a TV, within 100 ms of the new image appearing your brain will have classified it as being a beach scene, a street scene, an interior, a store, a bar, an office, or any one

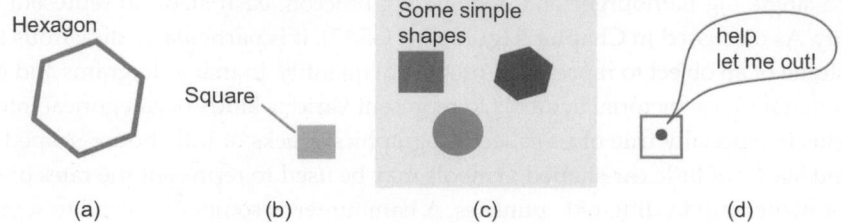

Figure 8.24 Gestalt principles used to guide the linking of text and graphics: (a) Proximity. (b) Continuity/connectedness. (c) Common region. (d) Common region combined with connectedness.

of many different types of scenes. Moreover, your brain will be primed for activities within that particular scene; in particular, the sequences of eye movements needed to find a certain detail in a specific scene will be facilitated (Oliva, 2005; Oliva, Torralba, Castelhano, & Henderson, 2003).

In the perception of gist, the broad spatial layout of a scene is identified in addition to the identification of its basic-level category (Potter, 1976). Also, a cognitive framework may be activated that includes priming the actions that may be useful for dealing with the new information.

Scene gist is important in data visualization because what we see depends enormously on the context. The gist of familiar visual displays will be processed just as fast as the gist of natural scenes, and it will have a similar effect on our response biases. The expectations and priming of the brain will have a huge effect, especially in cases where a rapid response is required. This provides another argument for consistency of representation for common types of visualization.

Priming, Categorization, and Trace Theory

We now return to the topic of priming and discuss how it affects categorization. Priming can have both positive and negative consequences with regard to categorization. In some ways, priming can be regarded as a biasing of perception. Ratcliff and McKoon (1996) made sketches of pairs of objects that were visually very similar but belonged to very different categories (Fig. 8.25). They found normal priming when an image was shown for a second time, a week later, in a rapid naming task; however, when the similar image (within a different category) was shown a week later, naming was actually slowed.

They argued that the result adds support to a trace theory of cognitive skill learning. According to this theory, whenever we successfully complete a cognitive activity, such as identifying an object, all the various neural pathways that were activated at the time become strengthened, so that the next time the same object is presented, processing is facilitated. But, strengthening a set of pathways inevitably means that alternative pathways are less likely to be activated in similar circumstances, introducing a

Figure 8.25 Pairs of sketches developed by Ratcliff and McKoon (1996). Each pair has visual similarity, but the objects represented have very different uses.

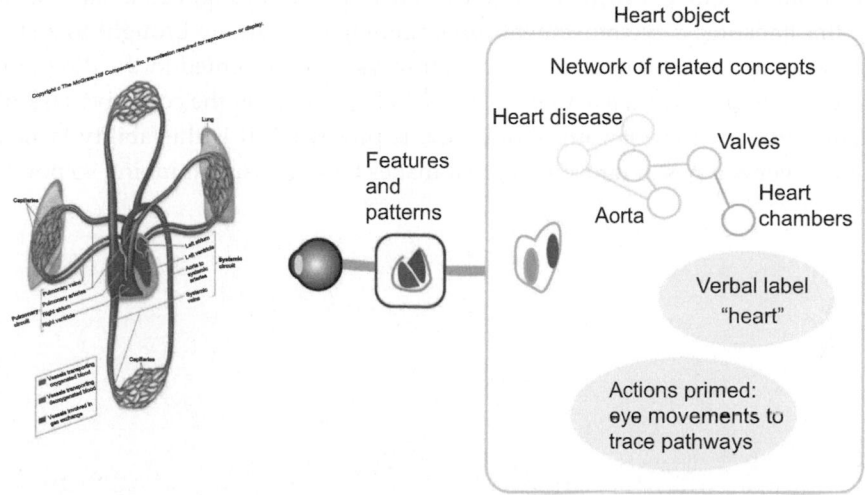

Figure 8.26 The percept of an object consists mostly of information stored in memory that has been activated by the visual information; this remains linked to a relatively small amount of information coming from the external world.

form of bias. One of the implications is that priming, and indeed all categorization, is a two-edged sword. Priming and categorization can lead to errors. Once we learn a particular interpretation of a pattern, we get faster at classifying it in a certain way, automatically classifying it at a glance, but this means that we are less likely to come up with alternative interpretations.

We shall return to the issue of priming, and sensory learning in general, in the following chapters as we begin to consider the process of visual thinking.

Conclusion

In this chapter, we have moved well beyond thinking of perception only as the extraction of information from what is imaged on the retina. Once an object is identified as *something*, as opposed to an abstract collection of features and colors, a range of associations is automatically activated in the brain, and these associations are what make up most of what we subjectively perceive. Some of these cognitive responses are in the visual system; others are in the language centers and in the regions that control actions. To illustrate this point, Fig. 8.26 shows the range of cognitive activities that might occur when someone looks at a diagram of the human blood circulation system. They are fixating on, and trying to understand, a part of the diagram that schematically depicts the heart. A small amount of information is held in visual working memory, consisting of visual patterns relating to the left and right chambers of the heart. The overall topology (chambers are part of heart) and shape have also been processed and held in working memory. As part of the mental act of identification, the verbal label "heart" becomes activated, as well as a network of related concepts. Concepts further from the current focus of cognitive attention are brought to a state of readiness. Simultaneously, eye-movement programming systems are brought to a state of readiness to do such things as trace the pathways, as represented in the diagram. All of this visual and nonvisual activity is exquisitely focused on the cognitive task of the moment. Little or no irrelevant information is processed. It is this ability to flexibly combine diverse types of information that makes human visual thinking so powerful.

CHAPTER NINE

Images, Narrative, and Gestures for Explanation

Most of this book, up to this point, has been about how to display data for the data analyst. It has been about data *exploration* and how to present data so that new things can be discovered. But there is another major use of visualization, and that is the *explanation* of patterns in data. Once something has been understood, the knowledge must often be passed on to other people, with the goal of convincing them that one interpretation or another is correct. The cognitive processes involved (i.e., interpreting data and explaining data) are very different.

One way of elucidating this difference is to think about who or what is in control of the cognitive sequence. The process of visual thinking can be thought of as a kind of collaborative dialog between a person and a visual representation, especially if the visualization is computer-based and interactive. In the case of data exploration, the cognitive processes of the data analyst are in control. Conversely, in the case of the presentation of results, it is the presenter, the author of an article, or the designer of a poster who is, or should be, in control of the cognitive thread (Ware, 2009). The audience takes in a series of visual patterns and words in a sequence that is controlled by the presenter. Multimedia material will occupy most of the capacity of both visual and verbal working memories in the brains of audience members, creating a narrative thread. As individuals construct meaning from the incoming material, they form or reform a series of ideas and concepts. In this chapter, we will explore the different ways that images and words can be used to create narrative structure.

We will address the problem of integrating visual and verbal materials in multimedia presentations. We will also address the particularly thorny but interesting problem of whether or not we should be using visual languages to program computers. Although

Information Visualization. https://doi.org/10.1016/B978-0-12-812875-6.00009-8

computers are rapidly becoming common in every household, very few people are programmers and it has been suggested that visual programming languages may make it easier for "nonprogrammers" to program computers.

The Nature of Language

Before going on to consider whether or not we can or should have such a thing as a visual language, we need to think about the nature of language. Noam Chomsky revolutionized the study of natural language because he showed that there are aspects of the syntactic structure of language that generalize across cultures (Chomsky, 1965). A central theme of his work is the concept that there are "deep structures" of language, representing innate cognitive abilities based on inherited neural structures. In many ways, this work forms the basis of modern linguistics. The fact that Chomsky's analysis of language is also a cornerstone of the theory of computer languages lends support to the idea that natural languages and computer languages have the same cognitive basis.

Other evidence supports the innateness theory. There is a critical period for normal language development that extends to about age 10; however, language is most easily acquired in the interval from birth to age 3 or 4. If we do not obtain fluency in some language in our early years, we will never become fluent in any language. Also, there are areas in the brain specialized for spoken language production (Broca's area) and language comprehension (Wernicke's area). These are distinct from the areas associated with visual processing, suggesting that language processing, whatever it is, is distinct from visual processing.

Sign Language

Despite the evidence for special brain areas, being verbal is not a defining characteristic of natural language capacity. Sign languages are interesting because they are examples of true visual languages. But, as with spoken language, if we do not acquire sign languages early in life, we will never become very adept at using them. Sign languages are not translations of spoken languages, but are independent, having their own grammars. Groups of deaf children spontaneously develop sign languages that have the same deep structures and grammatical patterns as spoken language. These languages are as syntactically rich and expressive as spoken language (Goldin-Meadow & Mylander, 1998).

Sign languages grew out of the communities of deaf children and adults that were established in the 19th century, arising spontaneously from the interactions of deaf children with one another. Sign languages are so robust that they thrived despite efforts of well-meaning teachers to suppress them in favor of lip reading—a far more limiting channel of communication. There are many sign languages; British sign language is a radically different language from American sign language, and the sign language of France is similarly different from the sign language of francophone Quebec (Armstrong, Stokoe, & Wilcox, 1994).

Although in spoken languages words do not resemble the things they reference (with a few rare exceptions), signs are partially based on similarity; for example, see the signs for a tree illustrated in Fig. 9.1. Sign languages have evolved rapidly. The pattern appears to be that a sign is originally created on the basis of a form of similarity in the shape and motion of the gesture, but over time, the sign becomes more abstract and similarity becomes less and less important (Deuchar, 1990). It is also the case that even signs apparently based on similarity are only recognized correctly about 10% of the time without instruction, and many signs are fully abstract.

Even though sign language is understood visually and produced through hand gestures, the same brain areas are involved in comprehension and production as are

Figure 9.1 Three different sign language representations of a tree. Note that they are all very different and all incorporate motion. (*From Bellugi and Klima (1976), Reproduced with permission.*)

involved in speech comprehension and production (Emmorey & McCullough, 2009). This tells us that the brain has distinct language subsystems that have the same function, no matter what the sensory input or means of production.

To summarize, language processing uses specialized areas of the brain, even when the information is presented visually by written words or hand gestures. These processing areas are distinct from those involved in visual pattern and object recognition.

Language is Dynamic and Distributed Over Time

We take in spoken, written, and sign language *serially*; it can take a few seconds to hear or see a short sentence. Armstrong et al. (1994) argued that, in important ways, spoken language is essentially dynamic. Verbal expression does not consist of a set of fixed, discrete sounds; it is more accurately described as a set of vocal gestures producing dynamically changing sound patterns. The hand gestures of sign language are also dynamic, even when denoting static objects, as Fig. 9.1 illustrates. There is a dynamic and inherently temporal phrasing at the syntactic level in the sequential structure of nouns and verbs. Also, written language, although it comes in initially through the visual channel, is transformed into a sequence of mentally recreated dynamic utterances when it is read. In contrast with the dynamic, temporally ordered nature of language, relatively large sections of static pictures and diagrams can be understood *in parallel*. We can comprehend the gist of a complex visual structure in a fraction of a second, based on a single glance.

Is Visual Programming a Good Idea?

The difficulty of writing and understanding computer programs has led to the development of a number of so-called visual languages in the hope that these can make the task easier; however, we must be very careful in discussing these as languages. Visual programming languages are mostly static diagramming systems, so different from spoken languages that using the term *language* for both can be more misleading than helpful. There is a case to be made that computer programming languages have more in common with natural language processing than with visual processing, and that for this reason, programming is better done using methods that relate more closely to natural language.

Consider the following instructions that might be given to a mailroom clerk:

Take a letter from the top of the In tray.

Put a stamp on it.

Put the letter in the Out tray.

Continue until all the letters have stamps on them.

This is very like the following short program, which beginning programmers are often asked to write:

Repeat

　　get a line of text from the input file

　　change all the lowercase letters to uppercase

　　write the line to the output file

Until (there is no more input)

This example program can also be expressed in the form of a diagram called a flow-chart (see Fig. 9.2).

Flowcharts provide a salutary lesson to those who design visual programming languages. Flowcharts were once part of every introductory programming text and it was often a contractual requirement that large bodies of software be documented with flowcharts describing the code structure. Once almost universally applied, flowcharts are now almost defunct. Why did flowcharts fail? It seems reasonable to attribute this to a lack of commonality with natural language.

Written and spoken languages, as well as sign languages, are packed with words such as *if*, *else*, *not*, *while*, *but*, *maybe*, *perhaps*, *probably*, and *unlikely*. These provide external manifestations of the logical structure of human thought (Pinker, 2007). We learn the skills of communication and refine our thinking skills early in life when we learn to talk. Using natural language-like pseudocode transfers these skills we already have gained in expressing logic through natural language.

A graphical flowchart representing the same program must be *translated* before it can be interpreted in the natural language processing centers. If, as infants, we learned to communicate by drawing diagrams on paper and if society had developed a structured language for this purpose, then visual programming would make sense, but this is not the case.

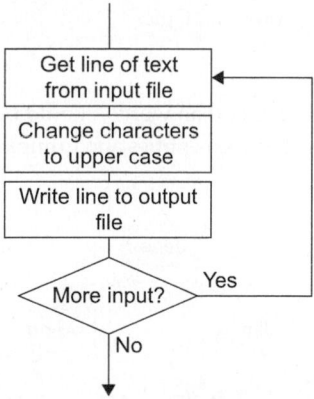

Figure 9.2 A flowchart is often a poor way to represent information that can be readily expressed in natural language-like pseudocode.

Nevertheless, some types of information are much better described in the form of diagrams. A second example illustrates this. Suppose that we wish to express a set of propositions about the management hierarchy of a small company.

Jane is Jim's boss.

Jim is Joe's boss.

Anne works for Jane.

Mark works for Jim.

Anne is Mary's boss.

Anne is Mike's boss.

This pattern of relationships is far more clearly expressed in a diagram, as shown in Fig. 9.3. These two examples suggest that visual language, in the form of static diagrams, has certain expressive capabilities that are very different from, and perhaps complementary to, natural language. Diagrams should be used to express structural relationships among program elements, whereas words should be used to express detailed procedural logic.

Throughout this book, it has been argued that the strength of visualization is that the perceptual representation of certain types of information can be easily understood. Logical constructs do not appear to constitute one of the types of information for which a natural visual representation exists. Also, although the existence of sign languages suggests that there *can* be visual analogs to natural language, the principle of arbitrariness still applies, so there is no advantage to this form or representation. On balance, the evidence suggests that the detailed logic of programming is best done using methods that rely on words more than graphical codes. Accordingly, we propose the following two broad principles:

[G9.1] Use methods based on natural language (as opposed to visual pattern perception) to express detailed program logic.

[G9.2] Graphical elements, rather than words, should be used to show structural relationships, such as links between entities and groups of entities.

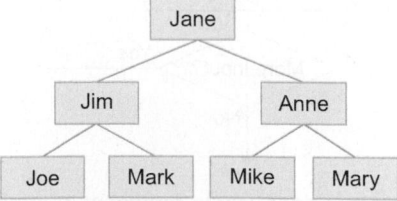

Figure 9.3 A simple organization chart showing the management structure.

None of the above should be taken as an attack on visual programming environments, such as Microsoft Visual Basic or Borland's Delphi, but it is worth noting that these are hybrids, as they are far from purely visual. They have many words in their user interfaces, and the way in which programming is done is mixed; some operations are done by connecting boxes, but others require text entry.

Visual Programming for Children

KidSim was a visual programming language based on animated characters (Cypher & Smyth, 1995). Rader, Brand, and Lewis (1997) carried out an extensive independent evaluation of KidSim in two classrooms over the course of a year. The system was deliberately introduced without explicit teaching of the underlying programming concepts. They found that children rapidly learned the interactions needed to draw animated pictures but failed to gain a deep understanding of the programs.

A more recent visual programming language for children, called *Scratch* (Maloney, Resnick, Rusk, Silverman, & Eastmond, 2010), has found widespread use in classrooms. It uses snap together blocks representing commands to control animated on-screen characters (Fig. 9.4). The program has special wraparound blocks to represent loops and conditional (if) statements. Both are illustrated in Fig. 9.4. It is notable that the language, although it has many visual components, uses words "if" and "forever" to represent more abstract programming concepts. The program is motivating for children because they can control animated characters in a small world environment. While this and similar languages may not be suitable for large complex programs, they may provide a good introduction to basic concepts of programming. A study by Franklin et al. (2016) suggests that concepts learned in Scratch can indeed be transferred to text-based programming languages. Another classroom evaluation claimed "significant improvement regarding learning programming concepts, logic, and computational practices" (Sáez-López, Román-González, & Vázquez-Cano, 2016).

Images versus Sentences and Paragraphs

The greatest advantage of words over images and diagrams, either static or dynamic is that spoken and written natural language is ubiquitous. It is by far the most elaborate, complete, and widely shared system of symbols that we have available. For this reason alone, it is only when there is a clear advantage that visual techniques are preferred. That said, images have clear advantages for certain kinds of information, and a combination of images and words will often be best. A visualization designer has the task of deciding whether to represent information visually, using words, or both. Other related choices involve the selection of static or moving images and spoken or written text. If both words and images are used, methods for linking them must be selected. Useful reviews of cognitive studies that bear on these issues have been summarized and applied to multimedia design by a number of authors, including Strothotte and Strothotte (1997), Najjar (1998), and Faraday (1998). What follows is a summary of

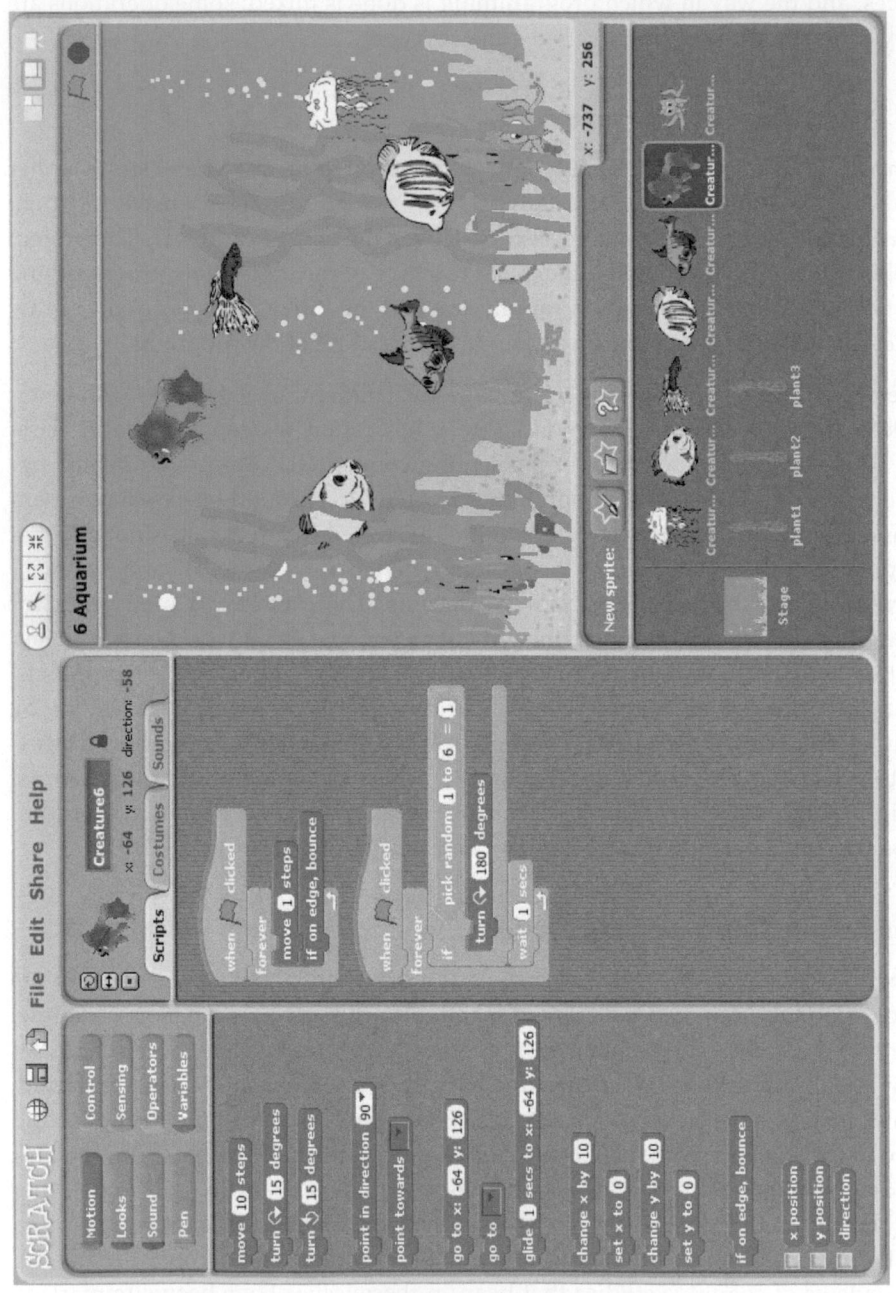

Figure 9.4 An example screen illustrating the Scratch user interface.

some of the key findings, beginning with the issue of when to use images or words separately and in combination.

We have been discussing the special case of programming languages, but the same principles apply in general to the question of whether to display information graphically or with text. Text is better than graphics for conveying abstract concepts (Najjar, 1998), and procedural information is best provided using text or spoken language, or sometimes text integrated with images (Chandler & Sweller, 1991).

We can begin by proposing a more general version of guideline G9.1.

> **[G9.3]** Use methods based on natural language (as opposed to visual pattern perception) to represent abstract concepts.

Of course, it is important that the information be *well* presented, no matter what the medium. Visual information must be meaningful and capable of incorporation into a cognitive framework for a visual advantage to be realized (Bower, Karlin, & Dueck, 1975).

There are also design considerations relating to the viewing time for images. It takes time to scan a complex diagram for its details. Only a little information is extracted in the first glance. A number of studies support the idea that we first comprehend the shape and overall structure of an object, and then we comprehend the details (Price & Humphreys, 1989; Venturino & Gagnon, 1992). Because of this, simple line drawings may be most effective for quick exposures.

Links Between Images and Words

The central claim of multimedia theory is that providing information in more than one medium of communication will lead to better understanding (Mousavi, Low, & Sweller, 1995). Mayer, Moreno, Boire, and Vagge (1999) and others have translated this into a theory based on dual coding. They suggest that if active processing of related material takes place in both visual and verbal cognitive subsystems, learning will be better. It is claimed that duplicate coding of information in more than one modality will be more effective than single-modality coding. The theory also holds that it is not sufficient for material to be simply presented and passively absorbed; it is critical that both visual and verbal representation be actively constructed, together with the connections between them.

Supporting multimedia theory, studies have shown that images and words in combination are often more effective than either in isolation (Faraday & Sutcliffe, 1997; Wadill & McDaniel, 1992). Faraday and Sutcliffe (1997) found that propositions given with a combination of imagery and speech were recalled better than propositions given only through images. Faraday and Sutcliffe (1999) showed that multimedia documents with frequent and explicit links between text and images can lead to better comprehension.

Fach and Strothotte (1994) theorized that using graphical connecting devices between text and imagery can explicitly form cross-links between visual and verbal associative memory structures. Care should be taken in linking words and images. For obvious reasons, it is important that words be associated with the appropriate images. These links between the two kinds of information can be static, as in the case of text and diagrams, or dynamic, as in the case of animations and spoken words. There can be a two-way synergy between text and images.

Despite these studies, there is little or no support for the claim that providing information in both images and words is better than providing information in either medium. None of the early studies actually presented the *same* information in both media (Mayer, Hegarty, Mayer, & Campbell, 2005). Showing a picture of a pile containing apples, oranges, and bananas is not the same as showing the word *fruit*. But, there is a considerable advantage in choosing the most appropriate kind of representation for elements of a data set, and often this will involve a mixed-media representation; some information is best represented using words, whereas other information is best represented using lines, textures, and colored regions. Of course, it is essential that different types of representation be clearly and effectively linked. A much better multimedia principle is the following:

[G9.4] To represent complex information, separate out components according to which medium is most efficient for each display—that is, *images*, moving or static, or *words*, written or spoken. Present each kind of information accordingly. Use the most cognitively efficient linking techniques to integrate the different kinds of information.

We now turn our attention to efficient linking methods.

Integrating Visual and Verbal and the Narrative Thread

In a textbook, written words must be linked with static diagrams, whereas in a lecture, written words, spoken words, static images, and moving images are all choices.

Linking Text with Graphical Elements of Diagrams

Beyond merely attaching text labels to parts of diagrams, there is the possibility of integrating more complex procedural information. Chandler and Sweller (1991) showed that instructional procedures for testing an electrical system were understood better if blocks of text were integrated with the diagram, as shown in Fig. 9.5. In this way, process steps could be read immediately adjacent to the relevant visual information. Sweller, Chandler, Tierner, and Cooper (1990) used the concept of limited-capacity working memory to explain these and similar results. They argued that when the information is integrated there is a reduced need to store information temporarily while switching back and forth between locations.

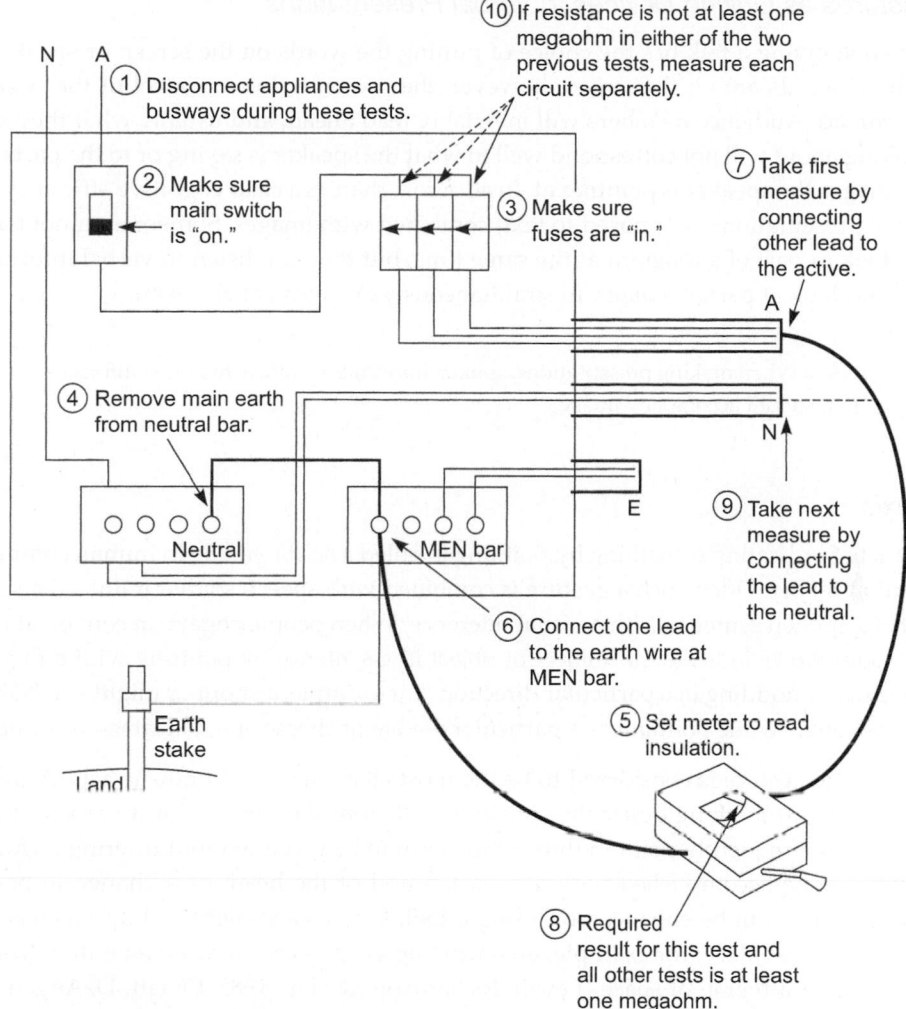

N A

① Disconnect appliances and busways during these tests.

② Make sure main switch is "on."

③ Make sure fuses are "in."

④ Remove main earth from neutral bar.

Neutral

MEN bar

⑥ Connect one lead to the earth wire at MEN bar.

Earth stake

L and

⑩ If resistance is not at least one megaohm in either of the two previous tests, measure each circuit separately.

⑦ Take first measure by connecting other lead to the active.

A

N

E

⑨ Take next measure by connecting the lead to the neutral.

⑤ Set meter to read insulation.

⑧ Required result for this test and all other tests is at least one megaohm.

Figure 9.5 An illustration used in a study by Chandler and Sweller (1991). A sequence of short paragraphs is integrated with the diagram to show how to conduct an electrical testing procedure. (*Chandler and Sweller (1991), Reprinted with permission.*)

[G9.5] Place explanatory text as close as possible to the related parts of a diagram, and use a graphical linking method.

At this point, it is worth commenting that the above guideline is not followed in most textbooks, and the one you are reading is no exception. This is because of the constraints of the publishing industry. Textbook layout is completely out of the hands of the author, making it extremely difficult to carefully integrate the words and graphics (Ware, 2008). As a result, text and figures are frequently separated by a few pages, leading to inevitable decline in cognitive efficiency.

Gestures as Linking Devices in Verbal Presentations

Someone giving a talk has the choice of putting the words on the screen or speaking them. If words are on the screen, however, the presenter loses control of the cognitive thread. Audience members will inevitably read ahead, and usually what they are thinking about will not correspond well to what the speaker is saying or to the parts of the images the speaker is pointing at. In addition, there is a clear cognitive efficiency to verbal presentation (as opposed to text) combined with images. Someone cannot read and look at part of a diagram at the same time, but they can listen to verbal information and look at part of a diagram simultaneously (Mousavi et al., 1995).

> [G9.6] When making presentations, spoken information, rather than text information, should accompany images.

Deixis

The act of indicating something by pointing is called a *deictic gesture* in human communication theory. Often such a gesture is combined with speech so that it links the subject of a spoken sentence with a visual reference. When people engage in conversation, they sometimes indicate the subject or object in a sentence by pointing with a finger, glancing, or nodding in a particular direction. For example, a shopper might say, "Give me that one," while pointing at a particular wedge of cheese at a delicatessen counter.

The deictic gesture is considered to be the most elementary of linguistic acts. A child can point to something desirable, usually long before she can ask for it verbally, and even adults frequently point to things they wish to be given without uttering a word. Deixis can be accomplished with a glance, a nod of the head, or a change in body orientation. It can be enhanced by using a tool, such as a straight rod. Deixis has its own rich vocabulary; for example, an encircling gesture can indicate an entire group of objects or a region of space (Levelt, Richardson, & Heu, 1985; Oviatt, DeAngeli, & Kuhn, 1997), and a flutter of the hand may add uncertainty to the bounded region.

To give a name to a visual object, we often point and speak its name. Teachers will talk through a diagram, making a series of linking deictic gestures. To explain a diagram of the respiratory system, a teacher might say, "This tube connecting the larynx to the bronchial pathways in the lungs is called the trachea," with a gesture toward each of the important parts.

Deictic techniques can be used to bridge the gap between visual imagery and spoken language. Some shared computer environments are designed to allow people at remote locations to work together while developing documents and drawings. Gutwin, Greenberg, and Roseman (1996) observed that, in these systems, voice communication and shared cursors are the critical components in maintaining dialog. Transmitting an image of the person speaking is usually much less valuable. Another major advantage of combining gestures with visual media is that this multimodal communication results in fewer misunderstandings (Oviatt, 1999; Oviatt et al., 1997), especially when English is not the speaker's native language.

> **[G9.7]** Use some form of deixis, such as pointing with a hand or an arrow, or timely highlighting to link spoken words and images.

Oviatt et al. (1997) showed that, given the opportunity, people like to point and talk at the same time when discussing maps. They studied the ordering of events in a multimodal interface to a mapping system in which a user could both point deictically and speak while instructing another person in a planning task using a shared map. The instructor might say something like "Add a park here" or "Erase this line" while pointing to regions of the map. One of their findings was that pointing generally preceded speech; the instructor would point to something and then talk about it.

> **[G9.8]** If spoken words are to be integrated with visual information, the relevant part of the visualization should be highlighted just before the start of the accompanying speech segment.

Web-based presentation enables a form of deixis with textual material. Links can be made by mouse clicks. In a study of eye movements, Faraday and Sutcliffe (1999) found that people would read a sentence and then look for the reference in an accompanying diagram. Based on this finding, they created a method for making it easy for users to make the appropriate connections. A button at the end of each sentence caused the relevant part of the image to be highlighted or animated in some way, thus enabling readers to switch attention rapidly to the correct part of the diagram. They showed that this did indeed result in greater understanding.

Symbolic Gestures

In everyday life, we use a variety of gestures that have symbolic meaning. A raised hand signals that someone should stop moving or talking. A wave of the hand signals farewell or hello. Some symbolic gestures can be descriptive of actions; for example, we might rotate a hand to communicate to someone that they should turn an object. McNeill (1992) called these gestures *kinetographics*. With input devices, such as the dataglove, that capture the shape of a user's hand, it is possible to program a computer to interpret a user's hand gestures. This idea has been incorporated into a number of experimental computer interfaces. In a notable study carried out at MIT, researchers explored the powerful combination of hand gestures and speech commands (Thorisson, Koons, & Bolt, 1992). A person facing the computer screen first asked the system to

Make a table.

This caused a table to appear on the floor in the computer visualization. The next command,

On the table, place a vase,

was combined with a gesture placing the fist of one hand on the palm of the other hand to show the relative location of the vase on the table. This caused a vase to appear on top of the table. Next, the command

Rotate it like this

was combined with a twisting motion of the hand, causing the vase to rotate as described by the hand movement.

Full-body sensing devices, such as the Microsoft Kinect, make this approach very affordable. Although the use of such devices outside of the realm of video games is still experimental, combining words with gestures may ultimately result in communication that is more effective and less prone to error (Mayer & Sims, 1994).

Expressive Gestures

Gestures can have an expressive dimension in addition to being deictic. Just as a line can be given a variety of qualities by being made thick, thin, jagged, or smooth, so can a gesture be made expressive (Amaya, Bruderlin, & Calvert, 1996; McNeill, 1992). A particular kind of hand gesture, called a *beat*, sometimes accompanies speech, emphasizing critical elements in a narrative. Bull (1990) studied the way political orators use gestures to add emphasis. Vigorous gestures usually occurred at the same time as vocal stress. Also, the presence of both vigorous gestures and vocal stress often resulted in applause from the audience. In the domain of multimedia, animated pointers sometimes accompany spoken narrative, but often quite mechanical movements are used to animate the pointer. Perhaps by making pointers more expressive, critical information can be brought out more effectively.

Animated versus Static Presentations

In the early days of multimedia research, extravagant claims were made for the superiority of animated presentations combined with written or spoke text, compared to static presentation of the information. These claims have not withstood careful analysis. A review of the studies carried out by Tversky, Morrison, and Betrancourt (2002) found that the majority failed to show advantages of animated over static presentations. Where they did find a difference, it could be attributed to the lack of equivalence of the information presented dynamically versus statically.

In one of the few studies where care was taken to ensure that the *same* information was available in both animated and static presentations, Mayer et al. (2005) found that the static version resulted in better retention of the information and better ability to generalize from the materials, indicating a deeper understanding. To present the static information, they used cartoon-like series of frames, with each frame illustrating a key concept. Fig. 9.6 shows one of the examples they used. In this case, the goal was to explain how a toilet flushing mechanism works.

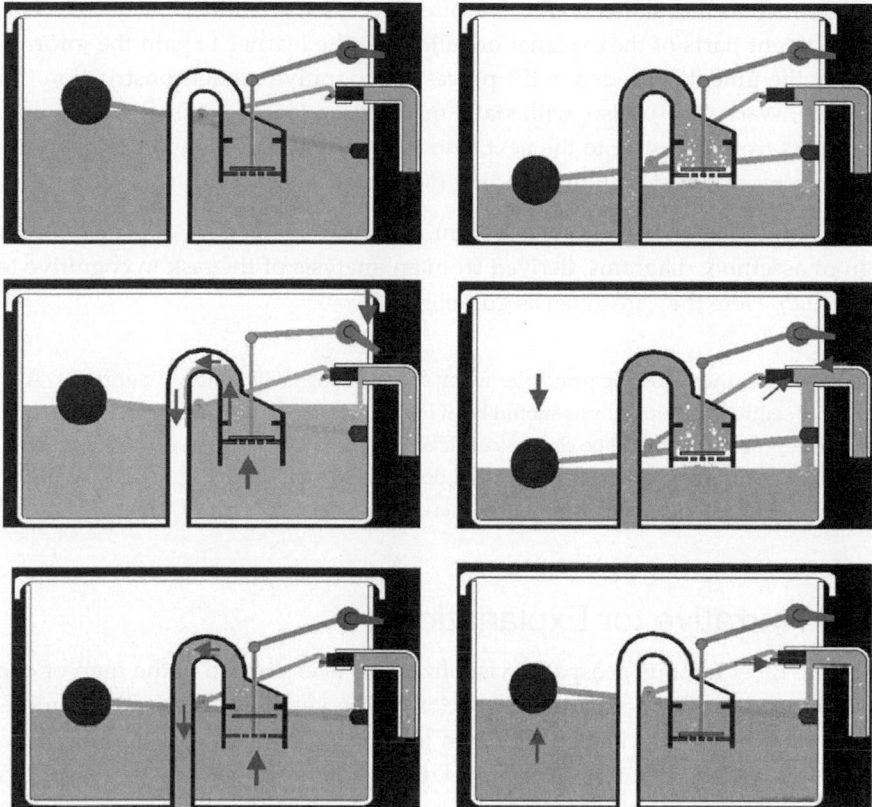

Figure 9.6 One of the explanatory diagrams used in a study by Mayer et al. (2005) to investigate animated versus static diagrams. (*From Mayer et al. (2005), Reproduced with permission.*)

A study by Palmiter, Elkerton, and Paggett (1991) provided two kinds of instructions for a procedural task; one was an animated demonstration, and the other was a written text. They found that immediately following instruction, the animated demonstration produced better performance, but a week later the results reversed, as those who received written instructions did better. They explained these results by suggesting that in the short term, subjects given animated instructions could simply mimic what they had recently seen. In the longer term, the effort of interpreting the written instructions produced a deeper symbolic coding of the information that was better retained over time.

An explanation for the failure to find an advantage for animations can be found in an analysis of the cognitive processes involved in constructing meaning. In order to construct a cognitive model explaining a series of events, it is necessary for the learner to construct hypotheses and then test them against the available information. The static diagram may provide better support for this than an animated sequence for a number of reasons. Usually, the key information relating to the hypotheses can be more clearly presented statically, although of course this depends on good design. A static diagram sequence, such as that shown in Fig. 9.6, offers access at any time, via eye movements, to the different parts of the explanation, allowing the learner to gain the information at exactly the time it is needed in the process of cognitive model construction (Mayer et al., 2005; Ware, 2009). Also, with static materials, a learner must mentally animate components from one state to the next, and it is precisely this kind of cognitive effort that can promote a deeper understanding (Mayer et al., 2005).

Heiser, Phan, Agrawala, Tversky, and Hanrahan (2004) offer a set of principles for the design of assembly diagrams, derived from an analysis of the task in cognitive terms (see Fig. 9.6). Here they are given as guidelines.

> **[G9.9]** Use the following principles when constructing an assembly diagram: (1) A clear sequence of operations should be evident to maintain the narrative sequence. (2) Components should be clearly visible and identifiable. (3) The spatial layout of components should be consistent from one frame to the next. (4) Actions should be illustrated, along with connections between components.

Visual Narrative for Explanation

One of the most famous geospatial visualizations ever created is the map of cholera cases surrounding a water pump in London in the year 1854. This was identified as the source of the disease by the physician John Snow and it was a landmark case in epidemiology. After the pump was closed, the epidemic ended. But the visualization was not instrumental in the discovery (Johnson, 2007), rather it was created after the pump closing as part of an explanatory narrative to convince others of the importance of a clean water supply.

The presentations of findings are one of the most important uses of visualizations. Often this is done with a narrative sequence of visualizations. Even where there is only a single visualization, the presenter is likely to impose a narrative, bringing attention to different aspects in a particular order designed to make it comprehensible.

A key variable in narrative visualizations is the extent to which they are author driven, or reader (audience) driven (Segel & Heer, 2010). In terms of cognition, it is useful to think of what is driving the cognitive thread. We can think of this as the sequence of content temporarily resident in the visual and verbal working memories of an audience member. Part of this is driven by external content, the images, and words of the presentation; part consists of activated memory traces from long-term memory and the cognitive operations linking the external material to what the audience already knows.

In an engaging lecture, the cognitive thread is largely driven by the presenter's words and the images shown. By contrast, in the case of a scientist using an interactive visualization to explore data, the cognitive thread is largely driven by the scientist (Ware, 2008). It is useful to consider different narrative forms involving visualization with respect to what is driving the cognitive thread. Below are brief descriptions of six common forms.

The formal presentation. In academia, engineering, and business, whenever a larger audience is involved, the most common form of presentation is a lecture with an accompanying slide deck. Up to a final question period, the narrative is entirely driven by the presenter, and if the presentation is successful, the thread of ideas in the minds of the audience will be driven by the presentation. An example is the movie "An Inconvenient Truth", by Al Gore.

The slide deck. Often slide decks are circulated following a lecture. These provide a more flexible narrative form because the user can skip parts that are already understood and cycle repeatedly through the sections of most interest. This is a kind of mixed mode; the cognitive thread is partly driven by the narrative sequence encapsulated in the slide deck by its designer, and partly driven by the specific interests and needs of the reader.

The cartoon sequence. Assembly instructions for furniture are often given in the form of a cartoon-like sequence of images (Fig. 9.7). These support a straightforward reading as a simple linear narrative, but the viewer can also scrutinize a single frame or a short subset of the frames.

Sequence of interactive visualizations. Through the availability of tools such as D3 it is becoming possible to intersperse interactive visualizations within a sequence of web pages (Segel & Heer, 2010). This enables a mixed mode, where the cognitive thread is sometimes strongly driven by the presenter and sometimes by the person interacting with an embedded visualization. Designing such presentations effectively is extraordinarily complex and anecdotal evidence suggests that participants typically carry out only the simplest interactions.

The conference poster. At some conferences, such as the American Geophysical Union (AGU), hundreds of posters are used to present science stories. The narrative thread

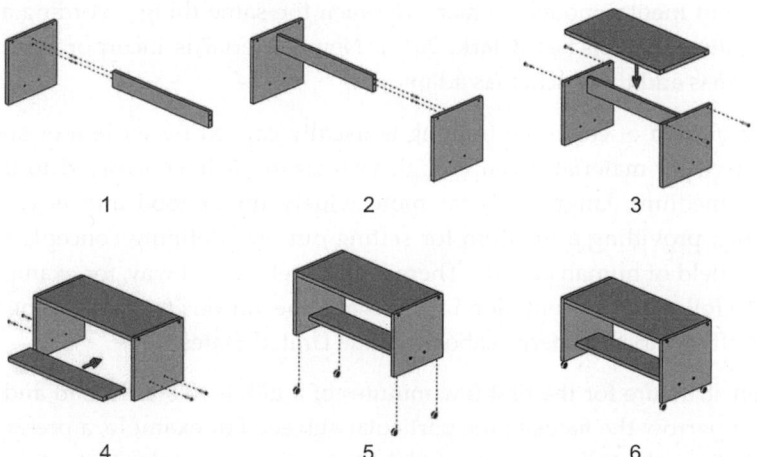

Figure 9.7 An example of an assembly diagram designed according to a set of cognitive best practices developed by Heiser et al. (2004). (*From J. Heiser,.*)

has a loose structure imposed by the layout of the poster, but the viewer is also free to jump from one part of the poster to another. Many viewers will look at visualizations first, prior to reading introductory material.

Cinematic narrative. A scientific presentation can take the form of cinematic documentary, using all of the cinematic devices to present some story about data. It has become common for these videos to be disseminated via YouTube. It is increasingly common for formal presentations to be recorded, showing both the speaker and the slides, to make a form of cinematic narrative, albeit one with poor production values. The main difference between this and a live presentation is the lack of social pressure to attend and the availability of distracting materials. In a controlled comparison between live lectures and recorded content, Schreiber, Fukuta, and Gordon (2010) found that audience members rated the quality of both the materials and the presentation to be higher in the case of live presentation. However, a test of comprehension showed no significant differences between the groups based on presentation mode. Other smaller studies (e.g., Ramlogan, Raman, & Sweet, 2014) have shown improved performance for live presentations.

All of the above forms use both visualizations and words in setting out the narrative. In the following sections we consider, in perceptual and cognitive terms, the common rhetorical devices that serve to structure narrative. In doing so we will compare and contrast the way verbal and visual materials serve various functions.

Introduction and Initial Framing

The goal of the beginning of any presentation, verbal or visual, is to set up a cognitive framework or schema in the minds of its audience. Learning always involves fitting new knowledge into existing cognitive frameworks (Paas, Renkl, & Sweller, 2003). A cognitive framework can be thought of as set of neural activations corresponding to memories and mental models (which are much the same thing according at modern active cognitive approaches (Clark, 2013). New material is incorporated into these active schemas and those schemas adapt to it.

The major burden of cognitive framing is usually carried by written or spoken language, not visual material. Even though visualizations have evolved to become an expressive medium, language is far more widely understood and is vastly richer semantically, providing a medium for setting out and defining concepts relating to almost any field of human activity. There is no purely visual way, for example, of saying, "In the following presentation I will discuss the various factors causing the death of whales off the north eastern seaboard of the United States".

A common structure for the first few minutes of a talk is to start broad and in a very short order narrow the focus to the particular subject. For example, a presenter might begin by talking about the impacts of global warming on coastal ecology. This will be narrowed down in the first minute or two, and on the first slide to a particular geographic region under consideration and a particular problem of interest, for example the likely disappearance of salt marshes. This will set the stage for a detailed presentation on the dynamics of salt marshes. Cognitively, the goal is for audience members to build a cognitive framework for the coming material, and to prime relevant concepts so that they are ready for activation.

Visual imagery can also help establish an initial cognitive schema. Usually these are not data visualizations; instead, photographic images are commonly used and they help establish and motivate the context for what is to follow. For example, pictures of salt marshes could help establish the issue and environment of concern.

A second goal of an introduction is to motivate the audience so that they care about the subject material. Ultimately, there has to be a cognitive reward for assimilating the new material. This can be as banal as the need to pass an exam, or at the other extreme, it may connect with the major personal goals of an individual. Images can help with this. An image of an entangled whale can help motivate dry statistics about the number of whales that are entangled and make people care more about a talk on whale mortality. A positive image of healthy babies can help motivate dry statistics relating to services for mothers.

Ongoing Reframing and Narrative Transitions

In a data intensive presentation, the introduction is typically followed by a series of slides mostly presenting data by means of visualizations. Each new visualization will usually require additional verbal framing to motivate the material and its implications. It also necessary to verbally explain the visual semantics and this is where many presentations fall short. Audience members cannot be expected to read legends without guidance and need to be told to pay attention to such things as which colored areas are important in a heat map and what they represent, what links represent in a node-link diagram, what axes represent in a chart, and so on.

A key consideration in the design of narratives should be the minimization of cognitive costs of transitions from one slide to the next (Hullman et al., 2013). Whenever a new visualization type appears, the user has the cognitive load of understanding its particular semantics. Even when the visualization consists of common types of charts, such as bar charts or time-series plots, there is a substantial cognitive cost to understand each of the axis variables. With every new chart the axis variables and scales may change, changing the meaning of the points, lines or bars, and this has a cost too. Hullman et al. (2011) suggest a strategy of minimizing the differences between successive visualizations to reduce these costs. Visualizations that follow each other should ideally be of the same general type (chart, node-link diagram, map), have consistent scales, and be consistent in the use of axes, color codings, and shape codings of variables.

> **[G9.10]** In designing a narrative that includes a sequence of visualizations, reduce the cognitive cost by grouping the same types of visualizations together. Also, be consistent in visual encodings, such as the use of color, texture, and shape to encode variables.

Presentation design is complicated because consistency between successive visualizations is far from the only consideration. For example, in the presentation of a series of case studies, it may make more sense to present all of the evidence relating to a particular case together, followed by all of the evidence for the next case, and so on even though this may require frequent changes of visualization type.

Controlling Attention in a Narrative Sequence

As already discussed, a successful presentation will, to a large extent, control the progression of ideas (images, phrases, as well as higher level concepts) in the minds of the audience. Part of this involves the cognitive framing and motivation of material discussed previously, but there is also the moment-to-moment control of attention.

Most of the time, the direction of attention is achieved by means of the deictic gestures discussed previously in this chapter. Words are used to explain the meaning of graphical elements, such as chart axes, while deictic gestures are used to indicate the ones being described. This pointing and explaining is needed so that viewers understand what the various shapes and colors represent. An audience cannot be relied on to read axis labels and keys. Most importantly, notable features of the data (as represented by the visualization) must be pointed out together with their implications.

There is another deictic form commonly used with digital slide presentations, namely *sequential highlighting* (Segel & Heer, 2010). This has the same function as a deictic gesture, but can be much richer than a simple act of indicating an object. Groups of elements can be highlighted at once, and many graphical devices can be used for the highlighting. Items may be circled, transient color coded borders can be added, or the background can be reduced in contrast. It is also possible to use animation in highlighting, a moving dot, like a karaoke prompt can lead attention from point to point.

Another common way to graphically provide a narrative sequence is by means of a sequence of cartoon-like frames, containing a progression of small visualizations. The convention of reading cartoons from left to right is enough to ensure that they will be viewed in that order.

Cinematic Devices for Directing Attention

In cinematography, attention is controlled by means of different kinds of camera shots and transitions between them. Establishing shots, zooms, close-ups, and dolly shots, as well as various kinds of transitions, are just a few of the common methods. These are, for the most part, beyond the scope of this book, only because most of them have not been formally studied by vision scientists; however, anyone wishing to make high-quality science videos would do well to study this craft. Here, we will restrict ourselves to work that has been done by psychologists and researchers working on effective educational visualizations.

Moving the viewpoint in a three-dimensional (3D) visualization can function as a form of narrative control. Obviously, we can only see what is in the camera frame, and large centrally placed objects are more likely to draw attention than small peripheral objects. A virtual camera can be moved from one part of a 3D data space to another, drawing attention to different features (Hochberg, 1986). In some complex 3D visualizations, a sequence of shots is spliced together to explain a complicated process.

Shot transitions are defined by an instantaneous movement of a camera in space and/ or time; the result can be confusion with respect to where and when the viewer feels he is situated. Hochberg and Brooks (1978) developed the concept of *visual momentum* in trying to understand how cinematographers link different camera shots together so the viewer can relate objects seen in one film clip with objects seen in the next. As a starting point, they argued that in normal perception people do not take more than a few glances at a simple static scene; following this, the scene "goes dead" visually. In cinematography, the device of the "cut" enables the director to create a kind of heightened visual awareness, because a new perspective can be provided every second or so. The problem faced by the director is that of maintaining perceptual continuity. If a car travels out of one side of the frame in one scene, it should arrive in the next scene traveling in the same direction; otherwise, the audience may lose track of it and pay attention to something else.

Hochberg (1986) showed that identification of image detail was better when an establishing shot preceded a detail shot than when the reverse ordering was used. This suggests that an overview map should be provided first when an extended spatial environment is being presented. An option that is available in data visualization is to always display a small overview map. The use of an overview map is common in many adventure video games and it has been adopted in many geospatial visualizations. Such maps are usually small insets that provide a larger spatial context, supplementing the more detailed local map. The general problem of providing focus and context is also discussed in Chapters 10 and 11.

> **[G9.11]** Use cinematic conventions, such as establishing shots and visual momentum to maintain continuity from one "scene" to the next in a presentation of a complex 3D data space.

A second device that can be used to allow viewers to cognitively link one view of a data space to the next is what Wickens (1992) called an *anchor*. Certain visual objects may act as visual reference points, tying one view of a data space to the next. An anchor is a constant, invariant feature of a displayed world. Anchors become reference landmarks in subsequent views. Ideally, when cuts are made from one view to another, several anchors should be visible from the previous frame. One common kind of anchor used in visualization are axis marks that show some kind of scale information. A third method for maintaining visual continuity is the idea of an overview map as discussed previously in this chapter and in Chapter 10.

> **[G9.12]** Use graphic devices, such as anchors and landmark objects, to help maintain visual continuity from one view of a data space to another.

Animated Images

Despite the evidence presented earlier that static representations are at least as good as animated representations, researchers have continued to investigate ways that dynamic representations can be made more effective. As we have noted, the problem with animations is that only a short segment is likely to be applicable to a viewer's cognitive modeling processes at any instant. If the sequence is long, much time is wasted replaying it just to get the bit that is currently relevant. One technique designed to help with this is to break explanatory animations into short segments. Each section can be viewed when the user is mentally prepared to engage with that particular aspect of the cognitive task. If it is short, it can easily be replayed multiple times.

In a study of an instructional animation explaining the causes of day and night (based on rotation of the Earth), Hasler, Kersten, and Sweller (2007) compared three modes of presentation. In the first, the animation was run straight through, although it could be replayed. In the second, stop and start buttons allowed the user to pause and resume play at any time. In the third, the animation was broken into a series of segments, each of which could be independently played. The results showed that both of the interactive modes produced higher test performance with lower cognitive load scores.

> **[G9.13]** Animated instructions should be broken into short meaningful segments. Users should be given a method for playing each segment independently.

> **[G9.14]** If a visualization consists of an extended animation, provide support for selecting a short segment and displaying it in a loop.

It also seems plausible that concepts having to do with causality can be represented in a way that is immediately understood though the use of animation. The work of researchers such as Michotte (1963), Heider and Simmel (1944), and Rimé, Boulanger, Laubin, Richants, and Stroobants (1985), discussed in Chapter 6, shows that people can perceive events such as hitting, pushing, and aggression when geometric shapes are moved in simple ways. With a static diagram, it is possible to use some device, such as an arrow, to denote a causal relationship between two entities; however, the arrowhead is a conventional learned symbol that perceptually shows only that there is *some* relationship, not necessarily causality. The work of Michotte showed that with appropriate animation and timing of events, a causal relationship will be directly and unequivocally perceived.

A final point about animation is that certain visualizations are intended to teach people to perform physical movements—for example, teaching someone a tennis stroke. There is increasing evidence that the brain contains *mirror neurons*. These are cells that respond directly to the actions of others, and they facilitate the perceiver in performing those exact same motions (Rizzolatti & Sinigaglia, 2008). This suggests that a clear advantage should be obtained in teaching movements using animation, as opposed to a series of static images. Based on a study of mechanical troubleshooting, Booher (1975) concluded that an animated description is the best way to convey perceptual motor tasks, but verbal instruction is useful to qualify the information.

> **[G9.15]** Use animation of human figures to teach people how to make specific body movements by imitation.

It is also likely that mirror neurons can be the medium for motivating learners. If our brains mirror an enthusiastic person, this may make us more enthusiastic (see Fig. 9.8). Certainly, energetic, exaggerated body gestures are common to many motivational speakers.

Visual Rhetorical Devices and the Representation of Uncertainty

The term *rhetorical device* is used in language exposition for something that makes an argument clear. It can also be used to discuss graphical devices that make visualization clear (Hullman & Diakopoulos, 2011). This is a short section only because this entire book is predominantly devoted to the topic. How graphical marks, color, contour, texture, and other visual variables can be used to effectively display data is the subject of preceding chapters.

Figure 9.8 Mirror neurons may be the medium, whereby one person motivates another. *(From http://www.honeysquad.com/index.php/tag/add-new-tag/. With permission.)*

There is also a more conceptual sense of visual rhetoric, relating to how well a visualization can be understood with minimal explanation. This is a difficult topic and has to do with the mappings between much more abstract concepts, which are usually represented verbally, and their graphical counterparts.

A good example is the representation of risk and uncertainty in data. At its most basic, uncertainty can be treated as a simple property of data. Each data point is represented by a mean and an estimate of the error of that mean. The error estimate is usually based on assumed random variation in the data. When political surveyors give their results, they provide both means (X% favor Republicans and Y% favor Democrats) and also a margin of error for the poll. This can also be done graphically, and the standard method for this kind of data is to provide a bar chart with standard error bars like that shown on the left in Fig. 9.9. If the error bars do not overlap this means that there is a statistically significant difference between the means.

Correll and Gleicher (2014) studied a number of alternative representations for uncertainty, all of which give more information than simple error bars. Fig. 9.9 illustrates them. The one on the right, for example, called a "violin plot" shows an actual normal distribution centered on each mean. In a study they asked people how confident people were about differences between means being "meaningful" (for example predicting the outcome of an election) using the different representations. People should be less confident when there is more overlap between error distributions. Their study participants were, appropriately, less certain with the alternative to the conventional standard error bar. They also noted that when provided with simple standard error bars people tend toward binary judgments; they are more confident than they should be for points just inside the boundaries and less confident than they should be for points just outside the boundaries.

[G9.16] Consider using rich representations of error distributions, such as the violin plot, or a plot with multiple bands of uncertainty represented.

Another effect noted by Correll and Gleicher is that the bar chart causes people to consider outcomes lying within the bars of a bar chart (just below the top) as more likely than those lying outside of the bars (just above the top), even though they are equally probable. Consequently, representations not consisting of solid bars may be preferred, like the three alternatives in Fig. 9.9. However, there may be other design considerations. A solid bar is almost certainly a more intuitive representation of quantity than a line hovering above the axis of a chart. A designer has to trade off understanding of uncertainty with intuitive understanding of quantity.

A more profound issue relating to the representation of uncertainty has to do with the real world implications of that uncertainty. This is called *risk*. For example, in business planning it is common to estimate the risk of a potential event negatively impacting a

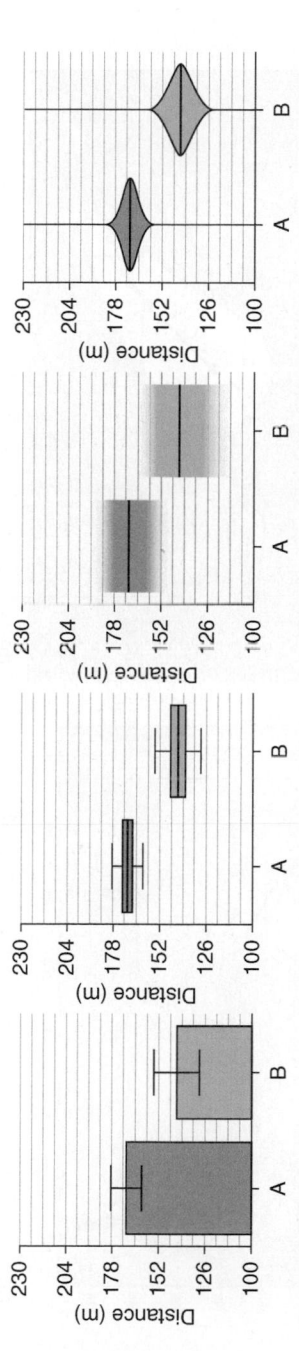

Figure 9.9 Different ways of representing the uncertainty in the same two data values. *(From Correll and Gleicher (2014). Reproduced with permission.)*

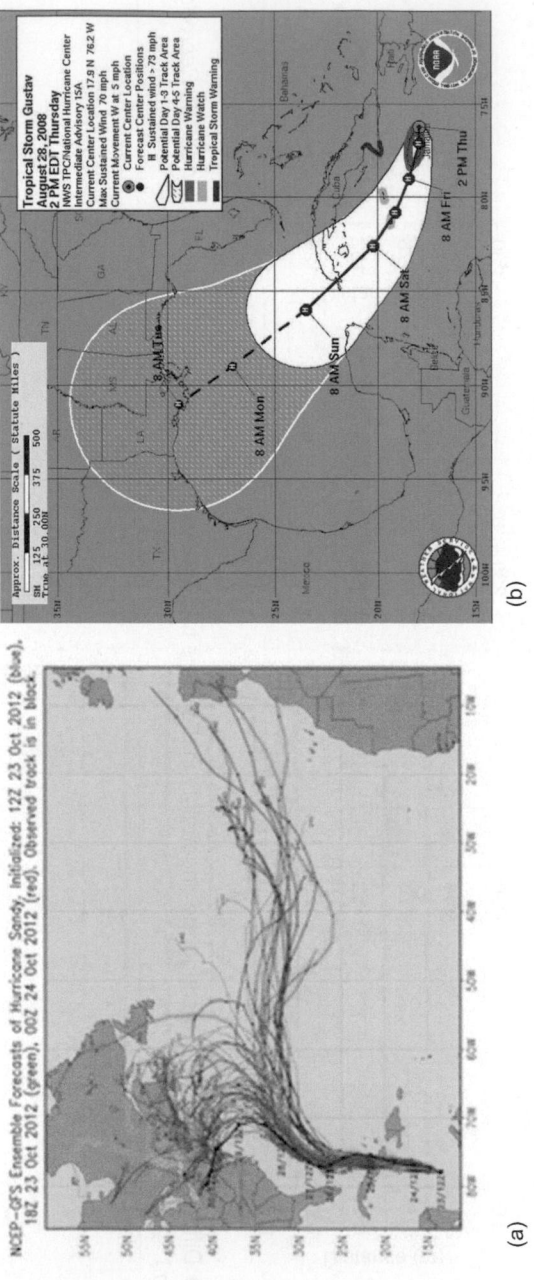

Figure 9.10 (A) The cone of uncertainty frequently used to show predictions of the path of a hurricane. (B) Multiple hurricane forecast tracks from an ensemble model. (*Courtesy of National Centers for Environmental Predictions, and NOAA.*)

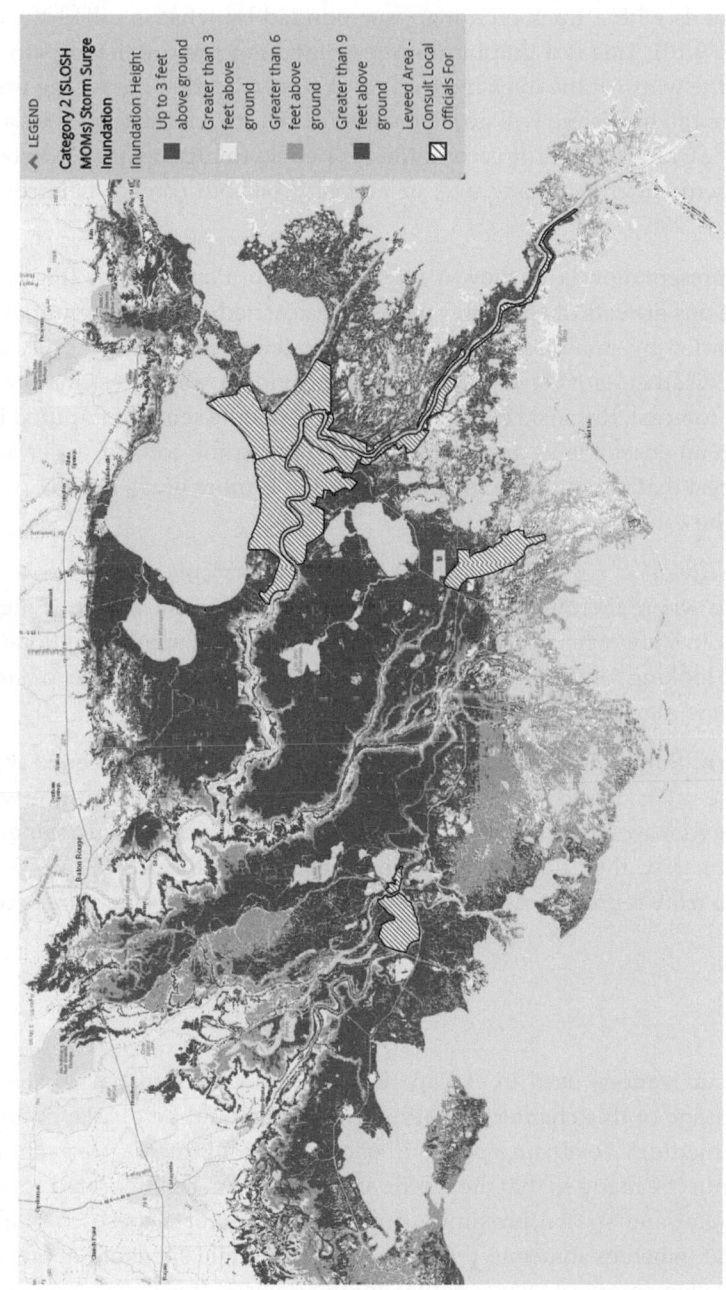

Figure 9.11 A storm surge hazard map representing a worst case scenario. (*Courtesy of National Centers for Environmental Predictions, and NOAA.*)

project and to place a monetary value on that risk. In many instances, what should be represented in a visualization is not uncertainty, but risk.

A good example is hurricane forecasts. A common method for showing the estimated path of a hurricane is with a track on a map, surrounded by what is called the *cone of uncertainty* (Fig. 9.10). This is a graphical representation of the predicted path of a hurricane, where the width of the track increases over time reflecting increasing uncertainty about where the hurricane will go. The width of the cone represents the "average forecast error". Unfortunately, it is common for people to misconstrue the size of the cone to represent either hurricane size, or intensity, or both (Broad, Leiserowitz, Weinkle, & Steketee, 2007).

An alternative representation is to show a set of tracks from an *ensemble* (Fig. 9.10). Ensemble simulations are sets of computer model runs carried out with input parameters randomly varied by small amounts to reflect modeling uncertainty. The variations in modeled weather as it develops over time provide a way of estimating the uncertainty in the forecast. Ruginski et al. (2008) showed people sets of computed hurricane tracks from an ensemble as an alternative to showing the cone of uncertainty. Their results suggest that the multiple track presentation is more likely to be correctly interpreted than the cone view.

Yet another alternative is to present explicit risk maps. For example, regions on a map can be highlighted where there is at least a 10% chance of 100 mph winds or higher. Additional maps can show where there is at least a 10% chance of significant flooding. If what people are looking for is guidance on how likely it is that they will be in harm's way, then such maps may be more useful in decision support.

The National Storm Surge Hazard maps produced by NOAA come closer to representing risk. These maps, based on many simulation runs, show the depth of water that could occur under worst-case scenarios for different categories of hurricane (see Fig. 9.11). Unfortunately, they do not show the probability of the worst case occurring so they fail to truly represent risk of flooding for someone deciding to ride out a hurricane.

Conclusion

Most complex visualizations used in explanations are hybrids of visual and verbal material. The message of this chapter is that information should be displayed in the most appropriate medium. To obtain a positive benefit from multimedia presentations, cross-references must be made so that the words and images can be integrated conceptually. Both temporal and spatial proximity can be used to create these cross-links. The deictic gesture, wherein someone points at an object while speaking about it, is probably the most elementary of visual–verbal linking devices. It is deeply embedded in human discourse and provides the cognitive foundation for other linking devices.

CHAPTER TEN

Interacting with Visualizations

The kinds of interactions we discuss in this chapter are what Kirsh and Maglio (1994) called *epistemic* actions. An epistemic action is an activity intended to uncover new information. A good visualization is not just a static picture or a three-dimensional (3D) virtual environment that we can walk through and inspect like a museum full of statues. A good visualization allows us to interact and find more data about any thing that seems important. Shneiderman (1998) developed a mantra to guide visual information-seeking behavior and the interfaces that support it: "Overview first, zoom and filter, then details on demand." In reality, however, we are just as likely to see an interesting detail, zoom out to get an overview, find some related information in a lateral segue, and then zoom in again to get the details of the original object of interest. The important point is that a good computer-based visualization is an interface that can support all of these activities. Ideally, every data object on a screen will be active and not just a blob of color. It will be capable of displaying more information as needed, disappearing when not needed, and accepting user commands to help with the thinking processes.

Interactive visualization is a process made up of a number of interlocking feedback loops that fall into three broad classes. At the lowest level is the data manipulation loop, through which objects are selected and moved using the basic skills of eye-hand coordination. Delays of even a fraction of a second in this interaction cycle can seriously disrupt the performance of higher level tasks. At the intermediate level is an exploration and navigation loop, through which an analyst finds his or her way in a large visual data space. As people explore a new town, they build a cognitive spatial

Information Visualization. https://doi.org/10.1016/B978-0-12-812875-6.00010-4

model using key landmarks and paths between them; something similar occurs when they explore data spaces. In the case of navigating data spaces, the time taken to get to a new vantage to find a particular piece of information is a direct *cost of knowledge*. Faster navigation means more efficient thinking. At the highest level is a problem-solving loop through which the analyst forms hypotheses about the data and refines them through an augmented visualization process. The process may be repeated through multiple visualization cycles as new data is added, the problem is reformulated, possible solutions are identified, and the visualization is revised or replaced. Sometimes the visualization may act as a critical externalization of the problem, forming a crucial extension of the cognitive process. This chapter deals with two of the three loops: low-level interaction and exploration. General problem solving is discussed in Chapter 11.

Data Selection and Manipulation Loop

A number of well established "laws" describe the simple, low-level control loops needed in tasks such as the visual control of hand position or the selection of an object on the screen.

Choice Reaction Time

Given an optimal state of readiness, with a finger poised over a button, a person can react to a simple visual signal in about 130 msec (Kohlberg, 1971). If the signals are very infrequent, the time can be considerably longer. Warrick, Kibler, Topmiller, and Bates (1964) found reaction times as long as 700 msec under conditions where there could be as much as two days between signals. The participants were engaged in routine typing, so they were at least positioned appropriately to respond. If people are not positioned at workstations, their responses will naturally take longer.

Sometimes, one must make a choice before reacting to a signal. A simple choice-reaction-time task might involve pressing one button if a red light goes on and another if a green light goes on. This kind of task has been studied extensively. It has been discovered that reaction times can be modeled by a simple rule called the *Hick-Hyman law* for choice reaction time (Hyman, 1953). According to this law,

$$\text{Reaction time} = a + b \, \log_2 (C) \tag{10.1}$$

where C is the number of choices, and a and b are empirically determined constants. The expression $\log_2(C)$ represents the amount of information processed by the human operator, expressed in bits of information.

Many factors have been found to affect choice reaction time—the distinctness of the signal, the amount of visual noise, stimulus-response compatibility, and so on—but under optimal conditions the response time per bit of information processed is about 160 msec, plus the time to set up the response. Thus, if there are eight choices (3 bits of information), the response time will typically be on the order of the simple reaction time plus approximately 480 msec. Another important factor is the degree of accuracy required. People respond faster if they are allowed to make mistakes occasionally, and this effect is called a *speed-accuracy tradeoff*. For a useful overview of factors involved in determining reaction time, see Card, Moran, and Newell (1983).

Two-Dimensional Positioning and Selection

In highly interactive visualization applications, it is useful to have graphical objects function not only as program output—a way of representing data—but also as program input—a way of finding out more about data. Selection using a mouse or similar input device (such as a joystick or trackball) is one of the most common interactive operations, and it has been extensively studied. A simple mathematical model provides a useful estimation of the time taken to select a target that has a particular position and size:

$$Selection\ time = a + b\ \log_2 (D/W + 1 : 0) \tag{10.2}$$

where D is the distance to the center of the target, W is the width of the target, and a and b are constants determined empirically; see Fig. 10.1(a). These are different for different devices.

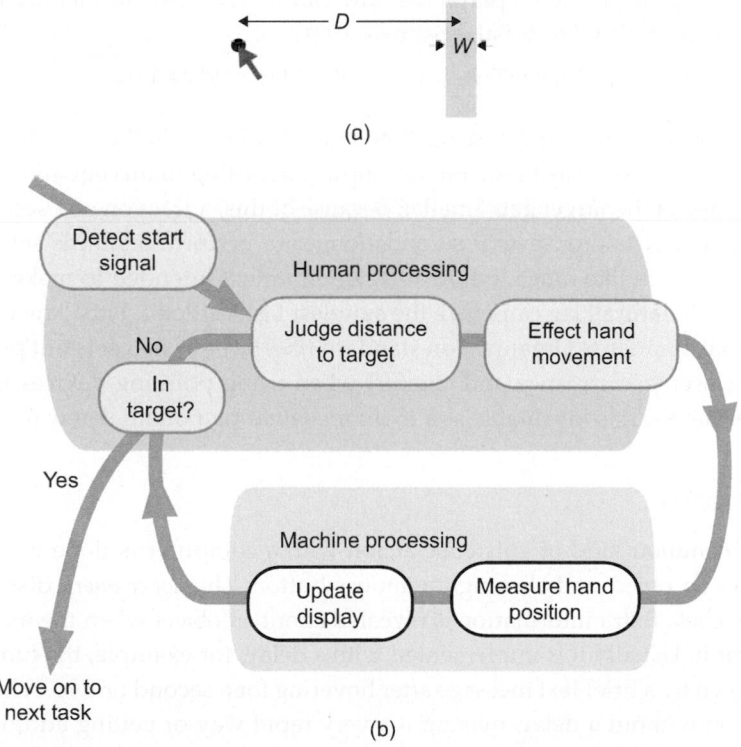

Figure 10.1 (a) A simplified reaching task, where the red cursor must be moved into the beige rectangle. (b) The visually guided reaching control loop, where the human processor makes adjustments based on visual feedback from the computer.

This formula is known as *Fitts' law*, after Fitts (1954). The term $\log_2(D/W+1.0)$ is known as the *index of difficulty* (ID). The value $1/b$ is the *index of performance* (IP) and is given in units of bits per second. There are a number of variations in the index-of-difficulty expression, but the one given here is the most robust (MacKenzie, 1992). Typical IP values for measured performance made with the fingertip, the wrist, and the forearm are all in the vicinity of 4 bits per second (Balakrishnan & MacKenzie, 1997). To put this into perspective, consider moving a cursor 16 cm across a screen to a 0.5-cm target. The index of difficulty will be about 5 bits. The selection will take more than a second longer than selecting a target that is already under the cursor.

Fitts' law can be thought of as describing an iterative process of eye-hand coordination, as illustrated in Fig. 10.1(b). The human starts by judging the distance to the target and initiates the hand movement. On successive iterations, a corrective adjustment is made to the hand movement based on visual feedback showing the cursor position. Greater distances and smaller targets both result in more iterations. The logarithmic nature of the relationship derives from the fact that, on each iteration, the task difficulty is reduced in proportion to the remaining distance.

In many of the more complex data visualization systems, especially those that are internet-based, there is a significant lag between a hand movement and the visual feedback provided on the display Fitts' law can be modified to include lag (Liang, Shaw, & Green, 1991; Ware & Balakrishnan, 1994):

$$\text{Mean time} = a + b\ (HumanTime + MachineLag)\ \log_2(D/W+1:0) \tag{10.3}$$

HumanTime is the human processing time and *MachineLag* is the time the computer takes to update the display based on user input. According to this equation, the effects of lag increase as the target gets smaller. Because of this, a fraction of a second lag can result in a subject taking several seconds longer to perform a simple selection task. This may not seem like much, but in a VR environment intended to make everything seem easy and natural, lag can make the simplest task difficult. Fitts' law is part of an International Standards Organization standard (ISO 9214-9) that sets out protocols for evaluating user performance and comfort when using pointing devices with visual display terminals. It is invaluable as a tool for evaluating potential new input devices.

Hover Queries

The most common kind of epistemic action with a computer is done by dragging a cursor over an object and clicking the mouse button. The *hover query* dispenses with the mouse click. Extra information is revealed about an object when the mouse cursor passes over it. Usually it is implemented with a delay; for example, the function of an icon is shown by a brief text message after hovering for a second or two. A hover query can function without a delay, making it a very rapid way of getting additional information. This enables the mouse cursor to be dragged over a set of data objects, quickly revealing the data contents and perhaps allowing an *interactive query rate* of several per second in special circumstances.

[G10.1] For the fastest epistemic actions, use hover queries, activated whenever the mouse cursor passes over an object. These are only suitable where the query targets are dense and inadvertent queries will not be overly distracting.

Path Tracing

Fitts' law deals with single, discrete actions, such as reaching for an object. Other tasks, such as tracing a curve or steering a car, involve continuous ongoing control. In such tasks, we are continually making a series of corrections based on visual feedback about the results of our recent actions. Accot and Zhai (1997) made a prediction, based on Fitts' law, that applies to continuous steering tasks. Their derivation revealed that the speed at which tracing could be done should be a simple function of the width of the path:

$$v = W/\tau \tag{10.4}$$

where v is the velocity, W is the path width, and τ is a constant that depends on the motor control system of the person doing the tracing. In a series of experiments, the researchers found an almost perfect linear relationship between the speed of path following and the path width, confirming their theory. The actual values of τ lay between 0.05 and 0.11 sec, depending on the specific task. To make this more concrete, consider the problem of tracing a pencil along a 2-mm-wide path. Their results suggest that this will be done at a rate of between 1.8 and 4 cm/s.

Two-Handed Interaction

In most computer interfaces, users select and move graphical objects around the screen with a mouse held in one hand, leaving the other hand unoccupied, but when interacting in the everyday world we frequently use both our hands. This leads us to the question of how we might improve the computer interface by taking advantage of both hands (Buxton & Myers, 1986).

The most important principle that has been discovered relating to the way tasks should be allocated to the two hands is Guiard's *kinematic chain theory* (Guiard, 1987). According to this theory, the left hand and the right hand form a kinematic chain, with the left hand providing a frame of reference for movements with the right, in right-handed individuals. For example, if we sculpt a small object out of modeling clay, we are likely to hold it in the left hand and do the detailed shaping with the right. The left hand reorients the piece and provides the best view, whereas the right pokes and prods within that frame of reference.

Interface designers have incorporated this principle into superior interfaces for various tasks (Bier, Stone, Pier, Buxton, & DeRose, 1993; Kabbash, Buxton, & Sellen, 1994). In an innovative computer-based drawing package, Kurtenbach, Fitzmaurice, Baudel, and Buxton (1997) showed how templates, such as the French curve, could be moved rapidly over a drawing by a designer using his left hand while using his right hand to paint around the shape.

364 Interacting with Visualizations

> **[G10.2]** When designing interfaces for two-handed data manipulations, the non-dominant hand (usually the left) should be used to control frame-of-reference information, while the dominant hand (usually the right) should be used to make detailed selections or manipulations of data.

Skill Learning

Over time, people become more skilled at any task, barring fatigue, sickness, or injury. A simple expression known as the *power law of practice* describes the way task performance speeds up over time (Card et al., 1983):

$$\log(T_n) = C - \alpha \log(n) \tag{10.5}$$

where $C = \log(T_n)$ is based on the time to perform the task on the first trial, T_n is the time required to perform the nth trial, and α is a constant that represents the steepness of the learning curve. The implication of the log function is that it may take thousands of trials for a skilled person to improve his performance by 10% because he is far along the learning curve. In contrast, a novice may see a 10% gain after only one or two trials.

One of the ways in which skilled performance is obtained is through the chunking of small subtasks into programmed motor procedures. The beginning typist must make a conscious effort to hit the letters *t*, *h*, and *e* when typing the word *the*, but the brains of experienced typists can execute preprogrammed bursts of motor commands so that the entire word can be typed with a single mental command to the motor cortex. Skill learning is characterized by more and more of the task becoming automated and encapsulated but rapid and clear feedback is essential (Newell, 1991).

> **[G10.3]** To encourage skill development, a computer system should provide rapid and clear feedback of the consequences of user actions.

Control Compatibility

Some control movements are easier to learn than others, and this depends heavily on prior experience. If you move a computer mouse to the right, causing an object on the screen to move to the right, this positioning method will be easy to learn. A skill is being applied that you gained very early in life when you first moved an object with your hand and that you have been refining ever since. But, if the system interface has been created such that a mouse movement to the right causes a graphical object to move to the left, this will be incompatible with everyday experience, and positioning the object will be difficult. In the behaviorist tradition of psychology, this factor is generally called *stimulus-response (S–R) compatibility*. In modern cognitive psychology, the effects of S-R compatibility are readily understood in terms of skill learning and skill transfer.

In general, it will be easier to execute tasks in computer interfaces if the interfaces are designed in such a way that they take advantage of previously learned ways of doing things. Nevertheless, some inconsistencies are easily tolerated, whereas others are not. For example, many user interfaces amplify the effect of a mouse movement so that a small hand movement results in a large cursor movement. Psychologists have conducted extensive experiments that involve changing the relationship between eye and hand. If a prism is used to laterally displace what is seen relative to what is felt, people can adapt in minutes or even seconds (Welch & Cohen, 1991). This is like using a mouse that is laterally displaced from the screen cursor being controlled. People are also able to adapt easily to relatively small inconsistencies between the angle of a hand movement and the angle of an object movement that results. For example, a 30-degree angular inconsistency is barely noticed (Ware & Arsenault, 2004).

On the other hand, if people are asked to view the world inverted with a mirror, it can take weeks of adaptation for them to learn to operate in an upside-down world (Harris, 1965). Snyder and Pronko (1952) had subjects wear inverting prisms continuously for a month. At the end of this period, reaching behaviors seemed error free, but the world still seemed upside down. This suggests that if we want to achieve good eye-hand coordination in an interface, we do not need to worry too much about matching hand translation with virtual object translation, but we should worry about large inconsistencies in the axis of rotation.

> [G10.4] When designing interfaces to move objects on the screen, be sure that object movement is in the same general direction as hand movement.

Some imaginative interfaces designed for virtual reality involve extreme mismatches between the position of the virtual hand and the proprioceptive feedback from the user's body. In the Go-Go Gadget technique (named after the cartoon character Inspector Gadget), the user's virtual hand is stretched out far beyond his or her actual hand position to allow for manipulation of objects at a distance (Poupyrev, Billinghurst, Weghorst, & Ichikawa, 1996).

Studies by Ramachandran (1999) provide interesting evidence that even under extreme distortions people may come to act as if a virtual hand is their own, particularly if touch is stimulated. In one of Ramachandran's experiments, he hid a subject's hand behind a barrier and showed the subject a grotesque rubber Halloween hand. Next, he stroked and patted the subject's actual hand and the Halloween hand in exact synchrony. Remarkably, in a very short time, the subject came to perceive that the Halloween hand was his or her own. The strength of this identification was demonstrated when the researcher hit the Halloween hand with a hammer. The subjects showed a strong spike in galvanic skin response (GSR), indicating a physical sense of shock. No shock was registered without the stroking. The important point from the perspective of VR interfaces is that even though the fake hand and the subject's real hand were in quite different places a strong sense of identification occurred (Slater, Pérez Marcos, Ehrsson, & Sanchez-Vives, 2009).

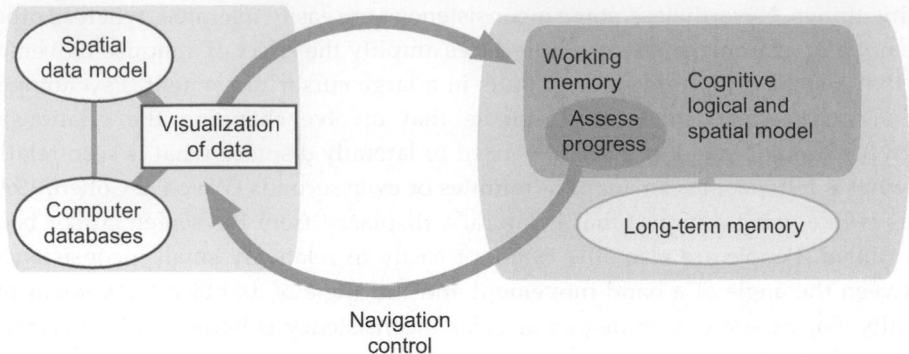

Figure 10.2 The navigation control loop.

Consistency with real-world actions is only one factor in skill learning. There are also the simple physical affordances of the task itself. It is easier for us to make certain body movements than others. Very often we can make computer-mediated tasks easier to perform than their real-world counterparts. When designing a house, we do not need to construct it virtually with bricks and concrete. The magic of computers is that a single button click can often accomplish as much as a prolonged series of actions in the real world. For this reason, it would be naive to conclude that computer interfaces should evolve toward VR simulations of real-world tasks.

Exploration and Navigation Loop

Viewpoint navigation is important in visualization when the data is displayed in an extended and detailed space. Viewpoint navigation is cognitively complex, encompassing theories of path finding and map use, cognitive spatial metaphors, and issues related to direct manipulation and visual feedback.

Fig. 10.2 sketches the basic navigation control loop. On the human side is a cognitive logical and spatial model whereby the user understands the data space and his or her progress through it. If the data space is maintained for an extended period, parts of its spatial model may become encoded in long-term memory. On the computer side, the view of the visualization is changed, based on user input. We start with the problem of 3D locomotion; next we consider the problem of path finding and finally move on to the more abstract problem of maintaining focus and context in abstract data spaces.

Locomotion and Viewpoint Control

Some data visualization environments show information in such a way that it looks like a 3D landscape, not just a flat map. This is achieved with remote sensing data from other planets, as well as maps of the ocean floor and other data related to the terrestrial environment. Increasingly common are laser scans of various environments, including the interiors of buildings and tree canopy maps. Other sources of data for visualization are computer models of various kinds such as models of storms in the atmosphere, atoms and molecules, flows occurring in combustion chambers, and so on. In all cases it is necessary to have an interface to navigate the data space to get to an optimal viewpoint.

One of the requirements for navigation is the correct perception of 3D space through the provision of depth cues presented in Chapter 7. All the perspective cues are important in providing a sense of scale and distance, although the stereoscopic cue is important only for close-up navigation in situations such as walking through a crowd. When we are navigating at higher speeds, in an automobile or a plane, stereoscopic depth is irrelevant, because the important parts of the landscape are beyond the range of stereoscopic discrimination. Under these conditions, structure-from-motion cues and information based on perceived objects of known size are critical.

> **[G10.5]** To support view navigation in 3D data spaces, a sufficient number of objects must be visible at any time to judge relative view position, and several objects must persist from one frame to the next to maintain continuity.

Ideally, frame rates should be at high and animation should be smooth. This is especially important in VR. Low frame rates cause lag in visual feedback and, as discussed previously, this can introduce serious performance problems.

Wayfinding, Cognitive Maps, and Real Maps

People use a variety of strategies for navigating through their environments (Ekstrom, Spiers, Bohbot, & Rosenbaum, 2018). The kinds of knowledge used are varied and include the following: *declarative knowledge*, which is nonspatial knowledge of places and landmarks, *procedural knowledge* about the sequence of turns and methods used to get from one place to another, *topological knowledge* about where the navigation pathways are and how they are interconnected, and *spatial knowledge* about the layout of places in space, as in a map view. In an early influential theory Seigel and White (1975) proposed that knowledge is acquired sequentially. First, declarative information about key landmarks is learned; second, procedural knowledge about routes from one location to another is developed; third, a cognitive spatial map is formed. But this view has been discredited (e.g, Zhang, Zherdeva, & Ekstrom, 2014) and it is now clear that all three kinds of information, as well at navigations heuristics and strategies operate from the beginning when infants first learn to navigate their surroundings.

The modern view is that both navigation and navigation planning are active dynamic processes that take advantages of all the kinds of knowledge that has been acquired, together with knowledge of strategies and methods for navigating. Increasingly, complex navigation used the external cognitive tools, such as GPS-linked maps and route-finding software. We use navigation strategies stored in our long-term memories—we can navigate somewhere because we have done it before, and increasingly our strategies incorporate the use of external interactive maps.

Cognitive maps can be acquired directly from an actual map more rapidly than by traversing the terrain (Zhang et al., 2014). In an early classic study Thorndyke and Hayes-Roth (1982) compared people's ability to judge distances between locations in a large building. Half of them had studied a map for half an hour or so, whereas the other half never saw a map but had worked in the building for many months. The results showed that maps function as powerful cognitive tools; for estimating the straight-line Euclidean distance between two points, a brief experience with a map was equivalent to working in the building for about a year.

People can most easily construct spatial mental maps of the objects they can see from a particular vantage point (Shelton & McNamara, 2001). Colle and Reid (1998) conducted an experimental study using a virtual building consisting of a number of rooms connected by corridors. The rooms contained various objects. In a memory task following the exploration of the building, subjects were found to be very poor at indicating the relative positions of objects located in different rooms, but they were good at indicating the relative positions of objects within the same room. This suggests that cognitive spatial maps form easily and rapidly in environments where the viewer can see everything at once, as is the case for objects within a single room. It is more likely that the paths from room to room were captured as procedural knowledge. The practical application of this is that overviews should be provided wherever possible in extended spatial information spaces.

[G10.6] Consider providing an overview map to speed up the acquisition of a mental map of a data space.

[G10.7] Consider providing a small overview map to support navigation through a large data space.

Perspective views are less effective in supporting the generation of mental maps. Darken, Allard, and Achille (1998) reported that Navy pilots typically fail to recognize landmark terrain features on a return path, even if these were identified correctly on the outgoing leg of a low-flying exercise. This suggests that terrain features are not encoded in memory as fully three-dimensional structures, but rather are remembered in some viewpoint-dependent fashion as predicted by the image-based theory of object recognition discussed in Chapter 8.

Frames of Reference

The ability to generate and use something cognitively analogous to a map can be thought of in terms of applying a different perspective or frame of reference to the world. A map is like a view from a viewpoint high in the sky. Cognitive frames of reference are often classified into *egocentric* and *allocentric*, where allocentric simply means external. According to this classification, a map is just one of many allocentric views.

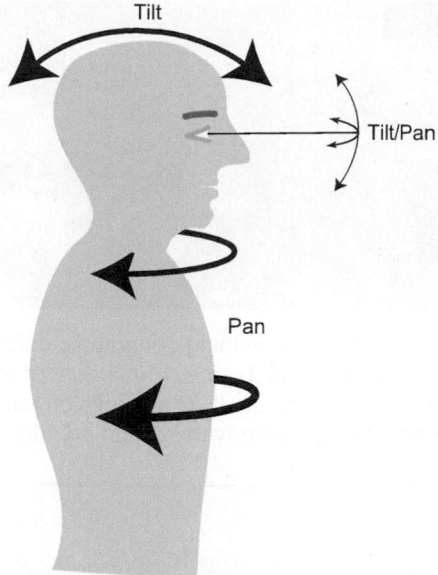

Figure 10.3 Most of the time we only rotate our viewpoint about two axes, corresponding to tilt and pan.

Egocentric Frame of Reference

The egocentric frame of reference is, roughly speaking, our subjective view of the world. It is anchored to the head or torso, not the direction of gaze (Bremmer, Schlack, Duhamel, Graf, & Fink, 2001). Our sense of what is ahead, left, and right does not change as we move our eyes around the scene, but it does change with body and head orientation. As we explore the world, we change our egocentric viewpoint primarily around two, not three, axes of rotation. As illustrated in Fig. 10.3 we turn our bodies mostly around a vertical axis (pan) to change heading, and swivel our heads on the neck (also pan) about a similar vertical axis for more rapid adjustments in view direction. We also tilt our heads forward and back but generally not to the side (roll). The same two axes are represented in eye movements; our eyeballs do not rotate about the axis of the line of sight. More concisely, human angle of view control normally has only two degrees of freedom (pan and tilt) and lacks roll.

A consequence of the fact that we are most familiar with only two of the three degrees of freedom of viewpoint rotation is that when viewing maps, either real or in a virtual environment, we are most comfortable with only two degrees of freedom of rotation. Fig. 10.4 illustrates an interface for rotating geographical information spaces constructed to have the same two degrees of freedom (Ware et al., 2001). The widgets allow rotation around the center point (equivalent to turning the body) and tilt from horizontal up into the plane of the screen (equivalent to forward and back head tilt), but they do not allow rotation around the line of site through the center of the screen (equivalent to the rarely used sideways head tilt).

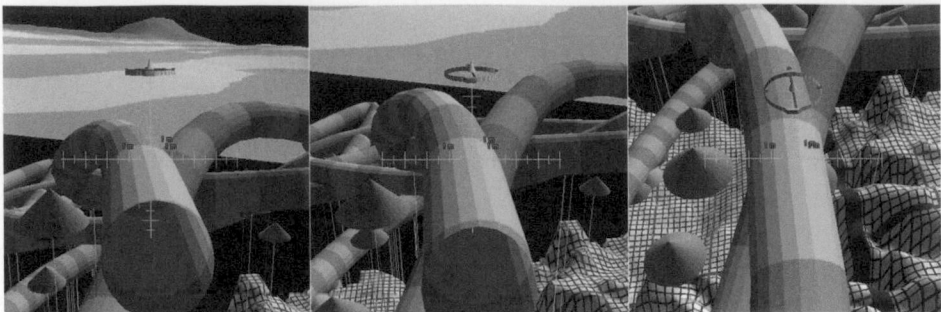

Figure 10.4 View control widgets for examining geographic data. Note that the rotational degrees of freedom match the rotational degrees of freedom of egocentric coordinates. The three views show different amounts of tilt. The handle on the top widgets can be dragged up and down to change tilt and moved left and right to rotate about the vertical axis.

[G10.8] In interfaces to view map data in 3D, the default controls should allow for tilt around a horizontal axis and rotation about a vertical axis, but not rotation around the line of sight.

Because we tend to move our bodies forward and only rarely sideways, a simple interface to simulate human navigation can be constructed with only three degrees of freedom, two for rotations (heading and tilt) and one to control forward motion in the direction of heading. If a fourth degree of freedom is added, it may be most useful to allow for something analogous to head turning. This allows for sideways glances while traveling forward.

Egocentric navigation is important when we navigate short distances on foot within buildings or through the environment. Part of this is dead reckoning especially when we travel unfamiliar terrain without landmarks, such an unknown woodlands. But, we are not good at judging how far we have walked or how much we have turned. Blindfolded people will start to walk in circles within 100 m (Souman, Frissen, Sreenivasa, & Ernst, 2009). People use various strategies to overcome this; landmarks, the grid layout of some cities and most building can be used to advantage. More skilled navigators can use sun direction or the direction of wind and waves on water to help (Ekstrom et al. 2018).

Recent work in neuroscience has uncovered a neural basis for egocentric navigation in processes operating in a mid-brain structure called the hippocampus, a region of the brain that has long been known to be important for our understanding of space. Three types of neurons have been identified: border cells signal impenetrable barriers, place cells signal specific locations (e.g., at the fridge, by the stove, on the sofa) (Solstad, Boccara, Kropff, Moser, & Moser, 2008), and grid cells contain an updated map of where we are currently, relative to our surroundings (Hafting, Fyhn, Molden,

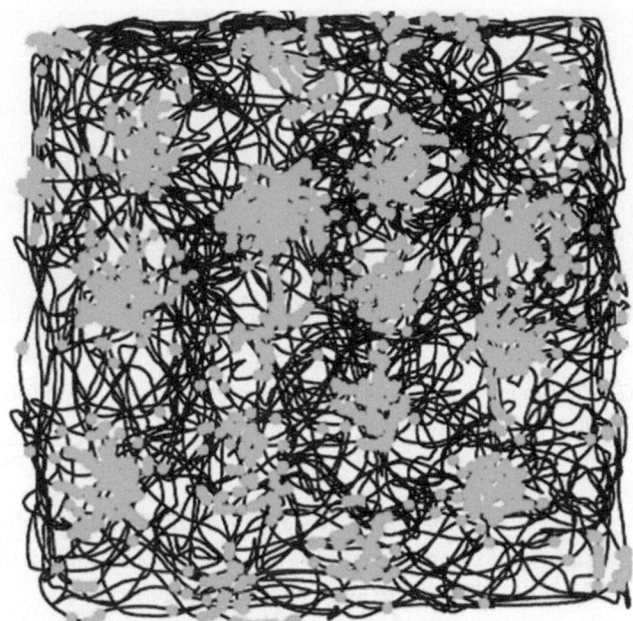

Figure 10.5 Grid cells in the Hippocampus of a rat encode a spatial map of the space occupied by the animal. (*Courtesy of Jonathan Whitlock.*)

Moser, & Moser, 2005). Grid cells contain links to place cell as well as to object cell information. A remarkable series of studies by Moser and Moser (summarized in 2016) show the hippocampus contains grid cells that mark a set of locations in a local environment. The studies were done with rats whose brains were instrumented with microelectrodes. As the rats moved in a square enclosure, neurons corresponding to different locations fired (see Fig. 10.5). The hippocampus is known to be critical for location information and memory formation in general and so it seems likely that all mammals (including humans) have similar structure helping to maintain orientation within local spaces.

Allocentric Frames of Reference

The term *allocentric* simply means external. In 3D computer graphics, external frames of reference are used for applications such as monitoring avatars in video games, controlling virtual cameras in cinematography, and monitoring the activities of remote or autonomous vehicles. Obviously, there is an infinite number of allocentric views. The following is a list of some of the more important and useful ones:

- *Another person's view.* For some tasks, it can be useful to take the egocentric view of someone else who is already present in our field of view. Depending on the angular disparity in the relative directions of gaze, this can be confusing, especially when the other person is facing us.

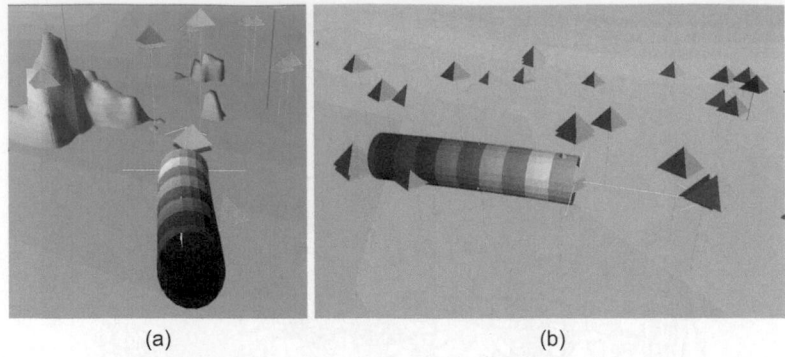

(a)   (b)

Figure 10.6 (a) God's-eye view of a moving vehicle represented by the tube object in the foreground. (b) Wingman's view of the same vehicle.

- *Over the shoulder view.* A view from just behind and to the side of the head of an individual. This view is commonly used in cinematography. This is close to an egocentric view.

- *God's-eye view.* Following a vehicle or avatar from above and behind, as shown in Fig. 10.6(a). This view is very common in video games. Because it provides a wider field of view, it can be better for steering a remote vehicle than the more obvious choice, an egocentric view from the vehicle itself (Wang & Milgram, 2001). It provides the stimulus response compatibility of an egocentric view.

- *Wingman's view.* Following a vehicle or avatar while looking at it from the side, as shown in Fig. 10.6(b). Allocentric views that follow a moving object, such as the God's-eye or wingman's views, are sometimes called *tethered* (Wang & Milgram, 2001).

Map Orientation

Three views are commonly available in electronic map and chart displays:

- *North-up plan view.* This is the classic orthographic map view, with north up, usually with the vehicle placed in the middle, oriented appropriately.

- *Track-up plan view.* Also an orthographic map view, but oriented so that the heading of the vehicle is in the vertical up direction on the map.

- *Track-up-perspective view.* This is another name for the God's-eye view already mentioned. In this case, the map is given a perspective view on the screen. The viewpoint is above and behind the vehicle.

The first two of these are illustrated in Fig. 10.7(a,b) and the third in Fig. 10.7(c).

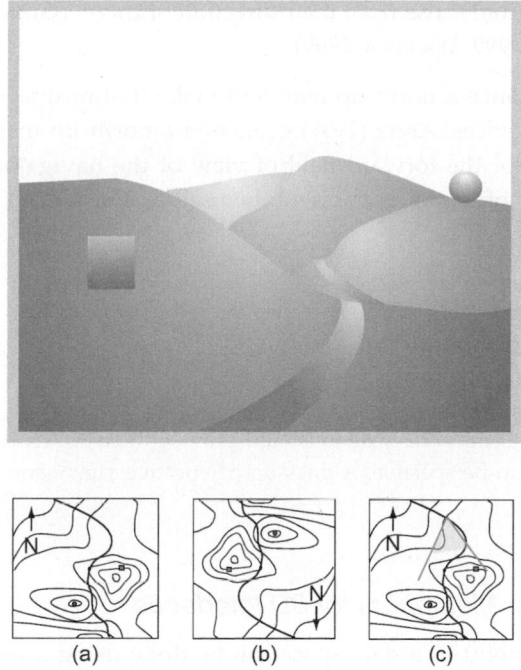

Figure 10.7 (a) North-up map. (b) Track-up map. (c) North-up map with user view explicitly displayed.

A number of studies have compared north-up plan views with track-up views and suggested that the track-up view is preferable in that it is easier to use and results in fewer errors (Levine, Marchon, & Hanley, 1984; Shepard & Hurwitz, 1984; Aretz, 1991). Nevertheless, experienced navigators often prefer the north-up over the track-up view because it gives them a consistent frame of reference for interpreting geographic data. This is especially important when two map interpreters are communicating over a phone or internet link—for example, in battlefield situations or when scientists are collaborating at a distance.

In visual cognitive terms, using a map involves comparing imagery on a display with objects in the world. This can be conceptualized as creating a cognitive binding between visual objects visible in two different spatial reference frames. In his work on displays for pilots, Aretz (1991) identified two different mental rotations necessary for successful map use. The first, azimuthal rotation, is used to align a map with the direction of travel. The track-up display executes this rotation in the display computer, eliminating the need for the task to be performed mentally. The second is vertical tilt. A map can be horizontal, in which case it directly matches the plane of the displayed information, or it can be oriented vertically, as is typical of the map displays used in car dashboards. Of these two transformations, azimuthal misalignment is the one that gives the most cognitive difficulty, and its difficulty increases in a nonlinear fashion. People take much longer and are less accurate when a map is misaligned more than 90 degrees in an azimuthal sense from their direction of travel (Gugerty & Brooks, 2001; Hickox & Wickens, 1999; Wickens, 1999).

It is possible to enhance a north-up map and make it almost as effective as a track-up map, even for novices. Aretz (1991) evaluated a north-up map with the addition of a clear indicator of the forward field of view of the navigator. This significantly enhanced the ability of the users to orient themselves. Fig. 10.7(c) illustrates this kind of enhanced map.

> **[G10.9]** When designing an overview map, provide a "you are here" indicator that shows location and orientation.

> **[G10.10]** Maps used in navigation should provide three views: north-up, track-up, and track-up-perspective. A track-up perspective view should normally be the default.

Spatial Navigation Metaphors for 3D Interfaces

Changing the viewpoint in a data space can be done using a navigation metaphor, such as walking or flying, or it can be done using a more abstract, nonmetaphoric style of interaction, such as zooming in to a selected point on a data object. Ultimately, the goal is to get to the most informative view of the data space efficiently. The use of metaphors may make learning the user interface easier, but a nonmetaphoric interaction method may ultimately be the best. Interaction metaphors are cognitive models for interaction that can profoundly influence the design of interfaces to data spaces. Here are two sets of instructions for different viewpoint control interfaces:

1. "Imagine that the model environment shown on the screen is like a real model mounted on a special turntable that you can grasp, rotate with your hand, move sideways, or pull toward you."

2. "Imagine that you are flying a helicopter and its controls enable you to move up and down, forward and back, left and right."

With the first interface metaphor, if the user wishes to look at the right side of the scene, she must rotate the scene to the left to get the correct view. With the second interface metaphor, the user must fly her vehicle forward and around to the right, while turning in toward the target. Although the underlying geometry in the two cases is the same, the user interface and the user's conception of the task are very different.

Navigation metaphors have two fundamentally different kinds of constraints on their usefulness. The first of these constraints is essentially cognitive. The metaphor provides the user with a model that enables the prediction of system behavior given different kinds of input actions. A good metaphor is one that is apt, matches the system well, and is easy to understand. The second constraint is more of a physical limitation. The implementation of a particular metaphor will naturally make some actions

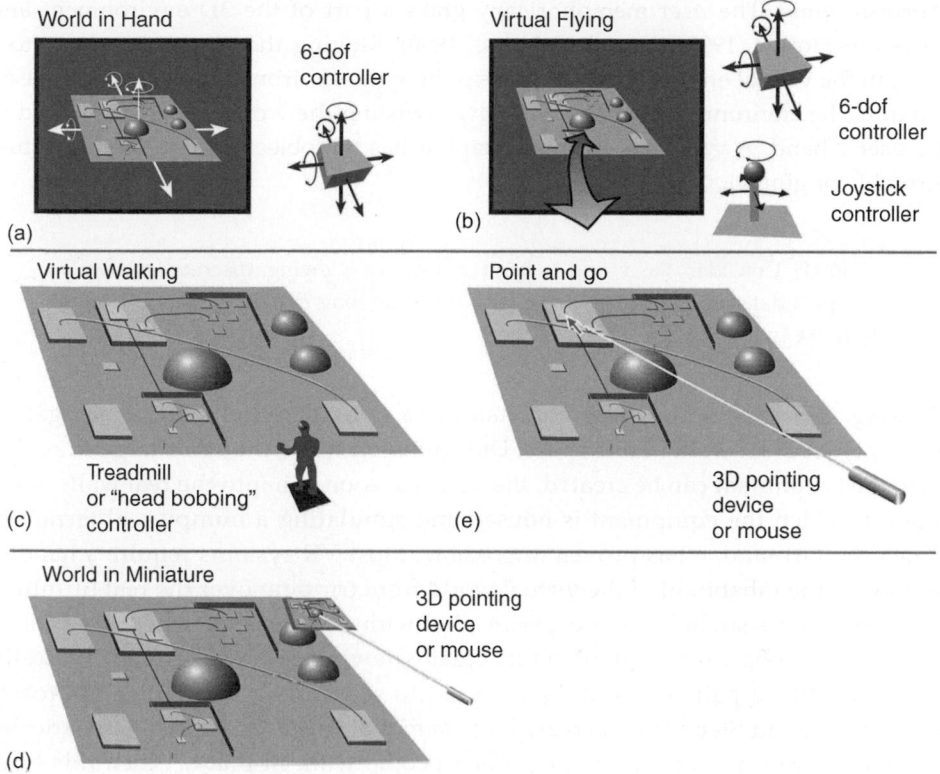

Figure 10.8 Five navigation metaphors: (a) World-in-hand. (b) Flying. (c) Walking (e) Point and go. (d) World in Miniature.

physically easy to carry out and others difficult to carry out; for example, a walking metaphor limits the viewpoint to a few feet above ground level and the speed to a few meters per second. Both kinds of constraints are related to Gibson's concept of affordances—a particular interface affords certain kinds of movement and not others, but it must also be perceived to embody those affordances.

Note that we are going beyond Gibson's view of affordances here. As discussed in Chapter 1, Gibsonian affordances are directly perceived properties of the physical environment. In computer interfaces interaction is indirect, mediated through the computer, and so is perception of data objects, so Gibson's concept as he framed it does not strictly apply. We must extend the notion of affordances to apply to both the physical constraints imposed by the user interface and cognitive constraints relating to the user's understanding of the data space. A more useful definition of an interface with good cognitive affordances is one that makes the possibility for action plain to the user and gives feedback that is easy to interpret.

Five main classes of metaphors have been employed in the problem of controlling the viewpoint in virtual 3D spaces. Fig. 10.8 provides an illustration and summary. Each metaphor has a different set of affordances.

World-in-hand. The user metaphorically grabs a part of the 3D environment and moves it (Houde, 1992; Ware & Osborne, 1990). Moving the viewpoint closer to a point in the virtual environment involves pulling the environment closer to the user. Rotating the environment similarly involves twisting the world as if it were held in the user's hand. A variation on this metaphor has the object mounted on a virtual turntable or gimbal.

[G10.11] Consider the world-in-hand model for viewing discrete, relatively compact data objects. Not suitable for navigating long distances over extended terrains.

Walking. One way of allowing inhabitants of a virtual environment to navigate is to simply let them walk in real space. Unfortunately, even though a large extended virtual environment can be created, the user will soon run into the real walls of the room in which the equipment is housed and simulating a bumpy real terrain to match the virtual one has proven impossible. Most VR systems require a handler to prevent the inhabitant of the virtual world from tripping over the real furniture. A number of researchers have experimented with devices such as exercise treadmills so that people can walk without actually moving over the ground. Typically, something like a pair of handlebars is used to steer. In an alternative approach, Slater, Usoh, and Steed (1995) created a system that captures the characteristic up-and-down head motion that occurs when people walk in place. When this head bobbing is detected, the system moves the virtual viewpoint forward in the direction of head orientation.

[G10.12] Consider some form of virtual walking on the spot interface for flat terrains.

Flying. Modern digital terrain visualization packages commonly have fly-through interfaces that enable users to smoothly create an animated sequence of views of the environment. Some of these are quite literal, having aircraft-like controls. Others use the flight metaphor only as a starting point. No attempt is made to model actual flight dynamics; rather, the goal is to make it easy for the user to get around in 3D space in a relatively unconstrained way. We (Ware & Osborne, 1990) developed a flying interface that used simple hand motions to control velocity. Unlike real aircraft, this interface makes it as easy to move up, down, or backward as it is to move forward. Subjects with actual flying experience had the most difficulty; because of their expectations about flight dynamics, pilots did unnecessary things such as banking on turns and were uncomfortable with stopping or moving backward. Subjects without flying experience were able to pick up the interface more quickly. Despite its lack of realism, this was rated as the most flexible and useful interface when compared to others based on the world-in-hand and eyeball-in-hand metaphors. It later became part of the user interface for Fledermaus, a 3D geospatial visualization package.

[G10.13] consider using the flying metaphor for viewing large data spaces. Do not simulate actual flying. If the space is very large consider the automatic adaptation of speed to the current location.

Point and Go. With a point and go interface, the user points at a location, using either a mouse, or some other pointing device, and the system moves the viewpoint to near that location. If virtual walking is being simulated, the user might point to a location, or a point on the floor, and the system "walks" them there, maintaining the viewpoint at a natural height (Janowski et al., 2014). Another variant is to draw out a path that the viewpoint follows (Igarashi, Kadobayashi, Mase, & Tanaka, 1998).

[G10.14] Consider that a point and go interface may be the most flexible navigation method for interfaces including full immersive virtual reality, and desktop 3D.

World in Miniature Navigation. It is common in 2D map interfaces to have an overview as a well as larger view showing a magnified subset. Clicking on a point in the overview map results in that area being shown enlarged. This is a form of navigation. Dragging in the enlarged view results in panning and scrolling to change the view locally (Ware & Lewis, 1995). It is possible to have a scale change of up to 20x between the overview and the magnified view.

The same idea has been generalized with the worlds in miniature (WIM) concept (LaViola et al., 2017; Stoakley, Conway, & Pausch, 1995) here the virtual 3D world contains a smaller 3D model of itself. Selecting a point in the 3D model results in teleportation to that location.

The optimal navigation method depends on the exact nature of the task. A virtual walking interface may be the best way to give a visitor a sense of presence in an architectural space, but a point and go interface is more flexible. Something loosely based on the flying metaphor may be a more useful way of navigating through fully 3D spaces such as, for example, the distribution of galaxies in space or the interconnected structure of the brain. The affordances of the virtual data space, the real physical space, and the input device all interact with the mental model of the task that the user has constructed.

All of the above metaphors can be adapted for use in both 3D desktop applications and VR Interfaces. However, VR has proven to be mostly useful for simulators, not data visualization. Simulators for boats planes cars and other technologies, have their own special interfaces which must be reproduced.

An important general point is that almost all the navigation metaphors reduce the number of degrees of freedom of a navigation task. Although general viewpoint movement is a six degrees of freedom (dof) task, most human locomotion involves simply turning and moving forward, reducing the problem to two degrees of freedom.

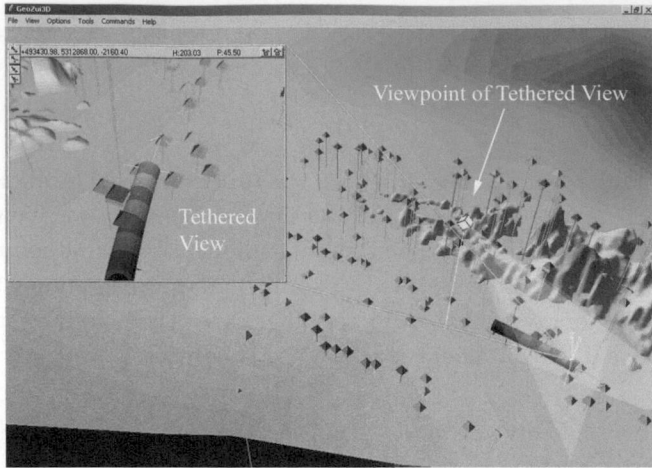

Figure 10.9 An attached window providing a different 3D perspective in GeoZui3D.

Point and go interfaces may also involve only two degrees of freedom; since rotating the wrist with a pointer ray involves only two angles of rotation (twist around the ray does not matter), moving a mouse is also two degrees of freedom. However, an additional degree of freedom may be needed for tilting the viewpoint. Reducing the degrees of freedom is a good strategy for most navigation tasks.

[G10.15] For navigation interfaces, reduce the number of degrees of freedom to the minimum needed to intuitively carry out the required set of navigation tasks.

Magnified Views

In visualization systems where large data spaces are represented, it is common to have one window that shows an overview and several others that show expanded details. The major perceptual problem with the use of multiple windows is that detailed information in one window is disconnected from the overview (context information) shown in another. The great advantage of the multiple window technique over others (covered later in this chapter) is that it does not distort and it is able to show focus and context simultaneously. Its main disadvantage is the cost of setting up and manipulating extra windows.

If we have multiple views simultaneously, then the links between views can be made visually explicit (Ware & Lewis, 1995). Fig. 10.9 shows an attached window used in a 3D zooming user interface. The method includes a viewpoint proxy, a transparent pyramid showing the direction and angle of the tethered view, and lines that visually link the secondary window with its source (Plumlee & Ware, 2003).

Evidence from usage suggests that the use of multiple windows with viewpoint proxies can be effective with scale differences of at least a factor of 30, meaning that this method is preferable to distortion methods where there is a larger difference between focus and context information.

[G10.16] For large 2D or 3D data spaces, consider providing one or more windows that show a magnified part of the larger data space. These can support a scale difference of up to 30 times. In the overview, provide a visual proxy for the locations and directions of the magnified views.

Interfaces with less Literal Metaphors

We have been dealing with the problem of how people navigate through 3D data spaces, under the assumption that the methods used should reflect the way we navigate in the real world. There are also navigation methods where the metaphors are less literal, some of which we have already touched on, such as overview maps. Also, there are many interactions used in data visualization, such as brushing and dynamic queries, which are even more abstract but extremely useful. In the remainder of this chapter, we will introduce these.

Interfaces for Nonmetaphoric Spatial Navigation

Several successful spatial navigation techniques do not use an explicit interaction metaphor but do involve visual spatial layout. These techniques make it easy to move quickly from one view to another at different scales; because of this, they are said to solve the *focus-context* problem. Think of the problem of wayfinding as one of discovering specific objects or detailed patterns (focus) in a larger data landscape (context). The focus-context problem is simply a generalization of this, the problem of finding detail in a larger context.

In a way, the terms *focus* and *context* are misleading. It implies that the small scale is the more important subject of attention, but in data analysis important patterns can occur at any spatial scale. The important thing is to be able to easily relate large-scale patterns to small-scale patterns. We will not abandon the focus and context terms, though, because they are too deeply entrenched.

The three kinds of focus-context problems are concerned with the spatial properties, structural properties, or temporal properties of a data set. Sometimes all three can be involved.

- *Spatial scale.* Spatial-scale problems are common to all mapping applications; for example, a marine biologist might want to understand the spatial behavior of individual codfish within a particular school off the Grand Banks of Newfoundland. This information is understood in the context of the shape of the continental shelf, as well as the boundary between cold Arctic water and the warm waters of the Gulf Stream.

- *Structural scale.* Complex systems can have structural components at many levels. A prime example is computer software. This has structure within a single line of code, structure within a subroutine or procedure (perhaps 50 lines of code), structure at the object level for object-oriented code (perhaps 1000 lines of code), and structure at the system level. Suppose that we want to visualize the structure of a large program, such as a digital telephone switch (comprising as many as 20 million lines of code); we may wish to understand its structure through as many as six levels of detail.

- *Temporal scale.* Many data visualization problems involve understanding the timing of events at very different scales. In understanding data communications, for example, it can be useful to know the overall traffic patterns in a network as they vary over the course of a day. It can also be useful to follow the path of an individual packet of information through a switch over the course of a few microseconds.

It is worth noting that the focus-context problem has already been spatially solved by the human visual system, at least for moderate changes in scale. The brain continuously integrates detailed information from successive fixations of the fovea with the less-detailed information that is available at the periphery. This is combined with data coming from the one or two prior fixations. For each new fixation, the brain must match key objects in the previous view with those same objects moved to new locations. Differing levels of detail are supported in normal perception because objects are seen at much lower resolution at the periphery of vision than in the fovea. The fact that we have no difficulty in recognizing objects at different distances means that scale-invariance operations are supported in normal perception. The best solutions to the problem of providing focus and context in a display are likely to take advantage of these perceptual capabilities.

The structural levels of detail in computer programs, the temporal scale of long time series from monitoring communications, and the spatial scale of maps are very different application domains, but they belong to a class of related visualization problems and they can all be *represented* by means of spatial layouts of data. The same interactive techniques can often be applied. In the following sections, we consider the perceptual properties of two other techniques for solving the focus-context problem: distortion and rapid zooming. These should be compared to the use of multiple windows, discussed previously.

Distortion Techniques

A number of techniques have been developed that spatially distort a data representation, giving more room to designated points of interest and decreasing the space given to regions away from those points. What is of immediate interest is spatially expanded at the expense of what is not, thus providing both focus and context. Some techniques have been designed to work with a single focus, such as the hyperbolic tree browser (Lamping, Rao, & Pirolli, 1995), as shown in Fig. 10.10.

An obvious perceptual issue related to the use of distorting focus-context methods is whether the distortion makes it difficult to identify important parts of the structure.

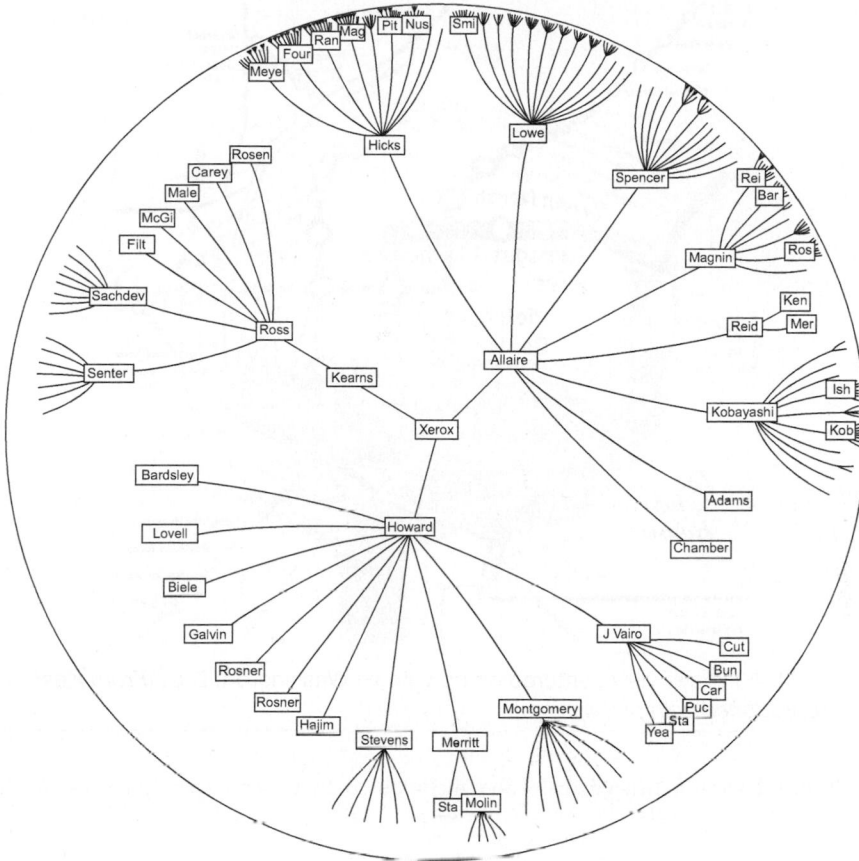

Figure 10.10 Hyperbolic tree browser from Lamping et al. (1995). The focus can be changed by dragging a node from the periphery to the center.

This problem can be especially acute when actual geographical maps are expanded. For example, Fig. 10.11, from Keahey (1998), shows a distorted map of the Washington, D.C., subway system. The center is clear as intended, but the labels on the stations surrounding the center have been rendered unintelligible. This leads to the next guideline.

[G10.17] When designing a visualization that uses geometric fisheye distortion methods, allow a maximum scale change factor of five.

Distorting layout algorithms will also sometimes move parts of an information structure to radically different locations in the display space. This, of course, entirely defeats the purpose of focus and context, which depends on memory of patterns to relate information represented at different spatial scales.

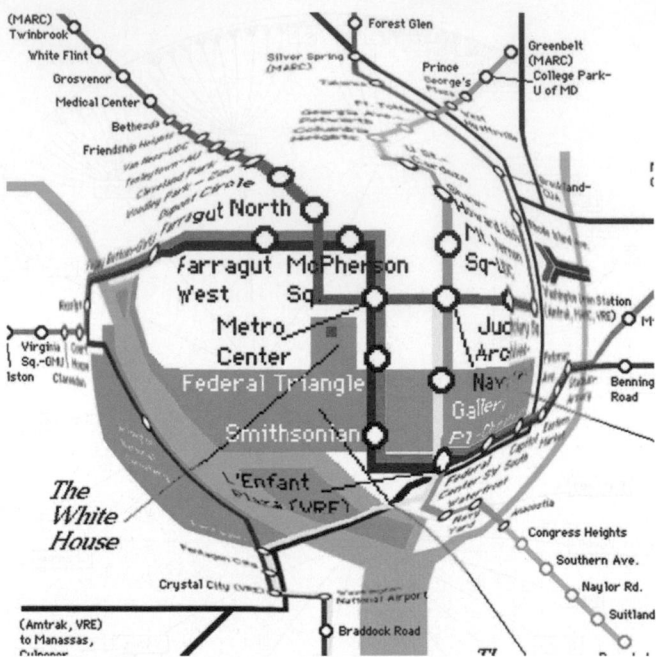

Figure 10.11 A fisheye view centered on downtown Washington, D.C. *(From Keahey (1998). Reproduced with permission.)*

[G10.18] Design fisheye distortion methods so that meaningful patterns are always recognizable.

Rapid Zooming Techniques

Another way of enabling people to comprehend focus and context is to use a single window but make it possible to transition quickly between spatial scales. Rapid zooming techniques do this. A large information landscape is provided, although only a part of it is visible in the viewing window at any instant. The user is given the ability to zoom rapidly into and out of points of interest, which means that, although focus and context are not simultaneously available, the user can move quickly and smoothly from focus to context and back. If smooth scaling is used, the viewer can perceptually integrate the information over time. This is commonly used for geospatial applications, such as Google Earth. The Pad and Pad++ systems (Bederson & Hollan, 1994) are based on this principle but are for nonspatial data. They provide a large planar data landscape, with an interface using a simple point-and-click technique to move quickly and smoothly in and out.

The proper rate of zoom has been a subject of study (Guo, Zhang, & Wu, 2000; Plumlee, 2004). Plumlee's (2004) results suggest that the rate of zoom should be independent of the number of objects displayed and the frame rate but individual preferences vary widely. Some people prefer a zoom rate as slow as 2× per second, while others prefer a rate as fast as 8× per second (a zoom rate of 8× per second means that the scale is

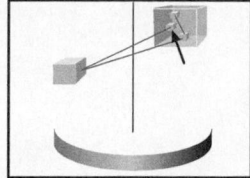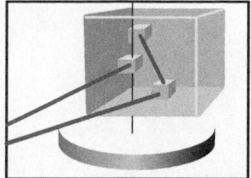

Figure 10.12 Center of workspace navigation. Clicking and dragging down on the box shown on the left causes it to move to the center of the workspace and expands the space around that center. Dragging up shrinks the space.

changing smoothly by a factor of eight every second). Both studies suggest a default zoom rate of 3 to 4× per second.

> **[G10.19]** When designing a zooming interface, set a default scaling rate of 3 to 4× (magnification or minification) per second. The rate should be user changeable so that experts can increase it.

Mackinlay, Card, and Robertson (1990) invented a rapid navigation technique for 3D scenes that they called *point of interest* navigation. This method moves the user's viewpoint rapidly, but smoothly, to a point of interest that has been selected on the surface of an object. At the same time, the view direction is smoothly adjusted to be perpendicular to the surface. A variant of this is to relate the navigation focus to an object. Parker, Franck, and Ware (1998) developed a similar technique that is object based rather than surface based; clicking on an object scales the entire 3D virtual environment about the center of that object while simultaneously bringing it to the *center of the workspace*. This method is illustrated in Fig. 10.12.

In all these systems, a key issue is the rapidity and ease with which the view can be changed from a focal one to an overview and back. Less than a second of transition time is probably a good rule of thumb, but the animation must be smooth to maintain the identity of objects in their contexts.

Magic Lenses

When using drawing packages, people spend a lot of time moving between the drawing and various menus positioned off to the side of the screen. The *toolglass* and *magic lens* approach, developed by Bier et al. (1993), got around this problem by allowing users to use the left hand to position tool palettes and the right hand to do normal drawing operations. This allowed for very quick changes in color or brush characteristics. As an additional design refinement, they also made some of the tools transparent (hence toolglasses).

In an application more relevant to information visualization, Stone, Fishkin, and Bier (1994) developed the magic lens idea as a set of interactive information filters implemented as transparent windows that the user can move over an information visualization with the left hand. The magic lens can be programmed to be a kind of data X-ray,

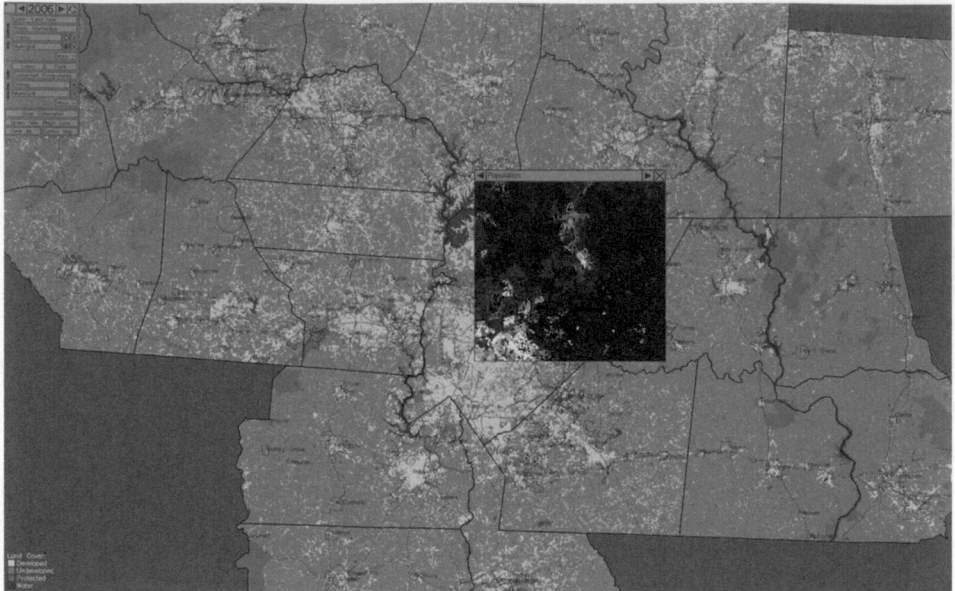

Figure 10.13 A magic lens showing population density with a background map showing land-use patterns. *(From Butkiewicz et al. (2010). Courtesy of Tom Butkiewicz.)*

revealing normally invisible aspects of the data. Fig. 10.13, for example, shows a map with land use patterns in the area around Charlotte, North Carolina (Butkiewicz et al., 2010). The magic lens reveals population density in the area it covers. A good interface for selections to be made based on population density would use the right hand, in a conventional way, to control a cursor to "click through" the magic lens, while the left hand would be used to position the lens. Sometimes magic lenses should be offset from the focus of interest so that they do not obscure it, with a frame shown to indicate the source region. For a survey of magic lens techniques see Tominski, Gladisch, Kister, Dachselt, and Schumann (2014).

Nonmetaphoric Interactions with Nonspatial Data

Up to this point most of this chapter has been concerned with interfaces for spatial navigation and interaction with spatial data. But in the field of information visualization most of the data is nonspatial, consisting of multi-dimensional discrete data or networks. Of course, all visualization is spatial, and an interaction, such as selecting a point, is a spatial act governed by Fitts' Law, as described earlier. However different kinds of interactions have proven to be useful for nonspatial data.

Drill Down

Any graphical mark in a data visualization can be a potential source of additional information. We click on a node in a node-link diagram to obtain more information about what that node represents. This is called *drilling down*.

In many interfaces graphical objects can be opened and expanded to reveal more information, or closed to hide it and conserve valuable screen space.

The act of closing an object has them own technical term—*elision*. In visual elision, parts of a structure are hidden until they are needed. Typically, this is achieved by collapsing a large graphical structure into a single graphical object.

A critical factor in the support of drill-down operations is called information scent (Pirolli & Card, 1995). If hundreds of nodes are visible on a screen, each of which can potentially lead to more information, information seeking is impossible unless there is some graphical or textual information to suggest where to go. Most often this is provided by a combination of text labels and graphical cues such as shape and color. The ability to provide information scent can provide a fundamental limit on the value of drill down hierarchical interfaces and we will revisit this issue in the final chapter.

> **[G10.20]** Where drill down operations have been implemented provide as much information scent as possible.

The Drill Down Epistemic Action Cost Hierarchy

A key design issue in supporting drill down is choosing the method for revealing additional information. The following is a sequence from low cognitive cost to high cognitive cost.

1) *Eye fixation:* The most natural way of obtaining more information about a visible entity is to fixate it. This causes the object to be imaged on the fovea where more detail may be seen, if it is available. Eye fixation is not normally considered a drill down operation; however, eye fixation is an epistemic action to obtain information just as much as clicking on an object. Eye fixations can allow for drill down operations executed at a rate of 3/sec.

2) *Hover:* With a hover query, simply moving a cursor over a symbol causes additional information to be revealed without significant lag. The information is displayed in a compact form as near as possible to the symbol. Typically, with a hover query, only a single set of drill down attributes is visible at a time. These queries can allow for drill operations executed at a rate of 1/sec.

3) *Click to open, Click to close*: Click to open causes an information panel to be revealed showing additional attributes of the entity. This can have the form of a small linked rectangle, embedded in the display, or it can be displayed in a side panel. Normally it takes an additional click to close the drill down panel which allows for multiple panels to be shown simultaneously. A newly opened panel may obscure the base visualization. If the panel is placed to the side, then a method should be provided for linking the drill down information to the selected symbol. Opening and closing extra panels is a cognitively costly operation which will only occur every few seconds.

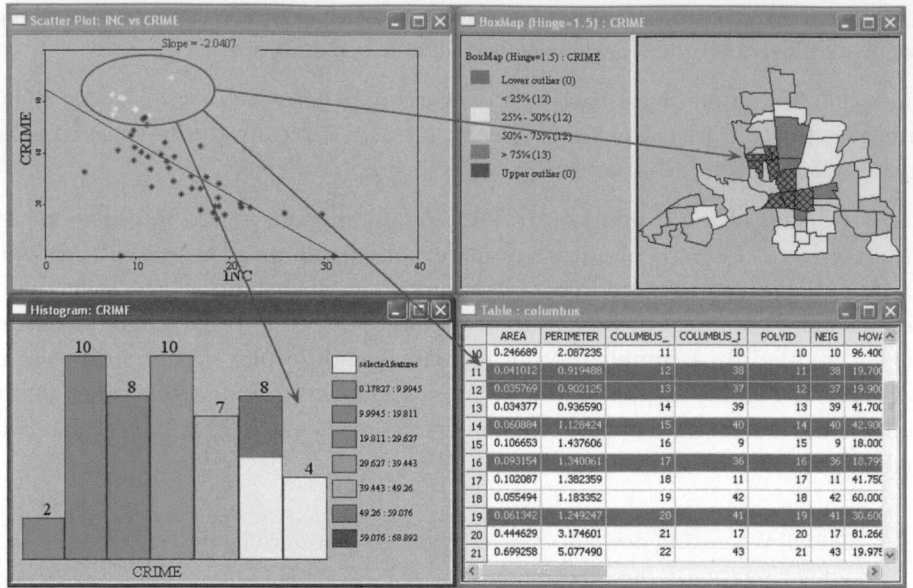

Figure 10.14 The same data is displayed in four different ways, using a scatterplot, a histogram, a map, and a table. Selecting points in one view causes them to be highlighted in all other views. This is called *brushing (*http://www.spatialanalysisonline.com/; *Courtesy of Dr. Mike de Smith.)*

4) *Click to open new display window, replacing previous window:* The most disruptive form of drill down is having a new screen containing the drill down information replace the original screen. Closing the new screen or using a back button restores the original display. Replacing the original screen with a new display window causes a loss of context and this places a burden on working memory if the new information must be related to what was previously seen. The problem will be worse if many drill down operations are carried out in sequence. Working memory limitations can make it necessary to redo drill down operations many times.

[G10.21] As a general principle, lower cost drill down epistemic actions are preferred over high-cost methods, but only if they reveal information adequate to the task.

Cross View Brushing

It is often useful to represent data in several different views simultaneously. Fig. 10.14 is a complex display showing a graph of crime plotted against income level, a map view of crime statistics, a table view of more detailed numbers, and a histogram. Each of these views provides a different way of looking at the same set of numbers and each has advantages, but what if we want to relate patterns revealed in the scatterplot to locations on the map? This is a problem that can be solved by a method called *brushing* (Becker & Cleaveland, 1987). In brushing, selecting a data object in any one of the views causes those same data objects to be highlighted wherever they appear in all of the other views. Brushing is one of the earliest and most essential methods developed for interactive visualization. In many cases linking views is impossible without it.

Designing the highlighting methods used in brushing can be challenging. Ideally the same highlighting method would be used in all views, but because each of the subsidiary views can have its own color coding and symbology, this may be impossible. See Chapter 5 for a detailed discussion of the issues involved in highlighting data.

Dynamic Queries

Ahlberg, Williamson, and Shneiderman (1992) developed an interface that enables a researcher to narrow down the set of points that is displayed using a set of sliders, one for each data dimension of a multi-dimensional data set. dynamic query is a method for interactively filtering data using range sliders. Each slider adjustment is an epistemic action, narrowing the range of what is displayed. They called the interactive hiding and revealing of data in this way *dynamic queries*, and they demonstrated it with a number of interactive multivariate scatterplot prototypes. It also became the basis for the Spotfire product. Fig. 10.15 shows an example of it in the form of the FilmFinder demonstration application. This provides the user with a slider to select on the basis of movie length, another to select on the basis of year of production, and more to select actor and director names.

Generalized Fisheye Views

The concept of a generalized fisheye view (Furnas, 1986) is that when the user touches a data object the computer reveals and hides other information according to a *degree of interest* function. In practice this is a function computing what is most likely to be relevant, since computers are presently poor at estimating the interest levels of their users. Entities most likely to be relevant are brought into visual prominence and less relevant entities are reduced in prominence or hidden. This is a very broad concept which underlies many of the following techniques.

Network Zooming

Earlier in this chapter, we discussed methods for zooming in and out in large spatial displays.

One application of generalized fisheye views is in the adaptive display of large node-link diagrams (Bartram et al., 1994; Schaffer et al., 1993). In their intelligent zoom system (illustrated in Fig. 10.16), a hierarchical network diagram is being examined. As parts of the network are expanded to see more detailed connections within components,

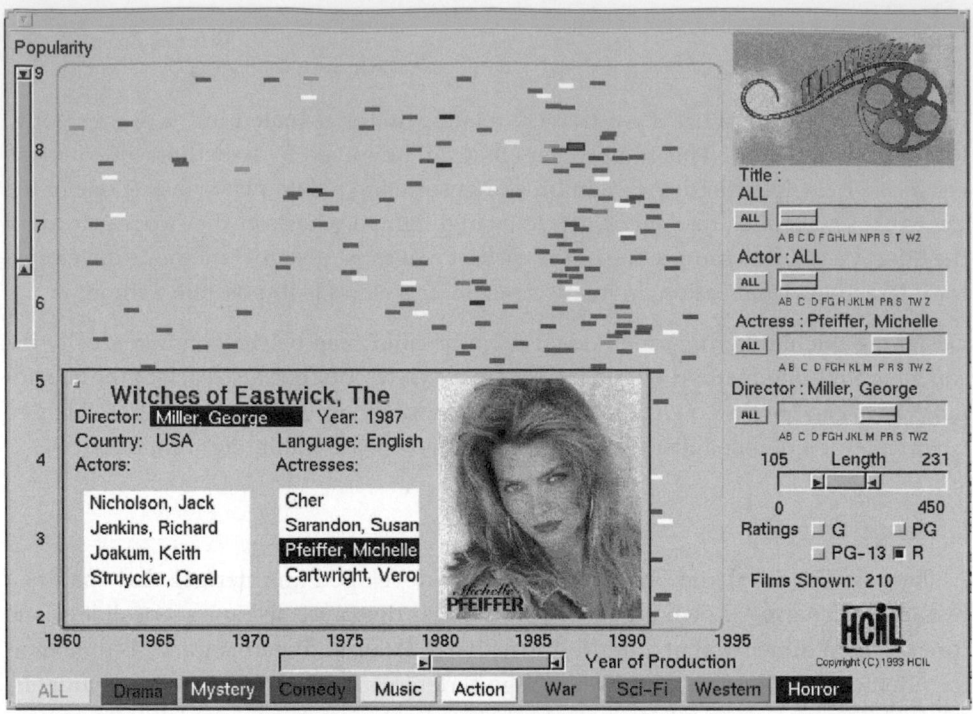

Figure 10.15 The FilmFinder application of Ahlberg and Shneiderman (1994) used dynamic queries to support rapid interactive updating of the set of data points mapped from the database to the scatterplot display in the main window. *(Ahlberg and Shneiderman (1994), Courtesy of Matthew Ward.)*

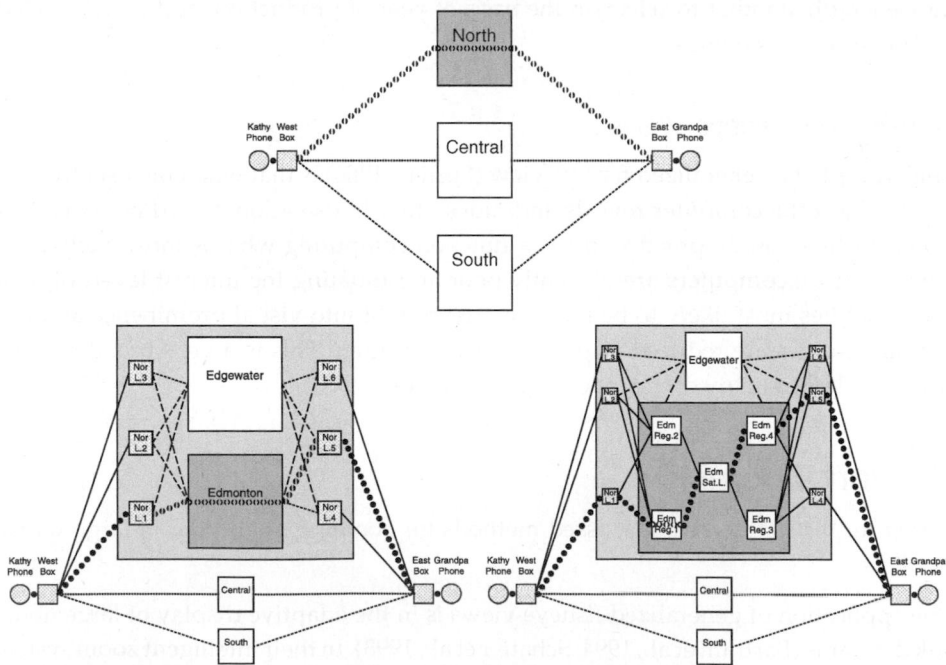

Figure 10.16 A series of frames showing the intelligent zoom interface. Areas of interest expand when selected; other objects shrink accordingly. *(Redrawn from Schaffer et al. (1993).)*

other parts become more compact. If the user starts to explore other parts of the network, some of the boxes that had previously been opened will be closed to make room, hiding their contents.

The cognitive issues, regarding working memory load, are the same as for any kind of zooming interface. It is critical that if different parts of a network are to be compared, they either are simple enough to be stored in working memory, or the system allows them to be displayed side-by-side, supporting eye-movement comparisons.

Near Neighbor Highlighting in Networks

Sometimes information objects in a display are interrelated in ways that are highly task relevant. If we inquire about a particular data object—say, a node representing a criminal suspect—then we also might want to know about his associates. Normally, the designer will group these related objects on the screen, but this is not always possible because of other design constraints, so related objects become distributed across the display. Also, there are many cases where the amount of information is such that a simplified representation of every data object can be placed on the screen but not with adequate clarity or detail.

In *degree of relevance highlighting*, we are interested in displaying all of the information on the screen at once, but because of its density it cannot all be made legible. A simple interaction solves the problem; touching an object causes both it and other task-relevant data objects to be highlighted, and the highlighted objects may also reveal additional details. Degree of relevance is calculated using a computer algorithm designed to rate the task relevance of other entities in the database, based on interaction history. The simplest version of this involves only the most recent selection.

One way that this approach has been employed is in network diagrams consisting of nodes and links. Most static diagrams contain fewer than 30 or so graphically represented entities and a similarly small number of lines linking or enclosing them. Having too many nodes and links makes it impossible to trace out the connections between them. Degree of relevance highlighting makes it possible to deal with much larger diagrams.

The *Constellation* system of Munzner, Guimbretire, and Robertson (1999) provides an example of how interactive degree-of-relevance highlighting can provide views into a very complex semantic network, far larger than can be displayed with static concept maps. Fig. 10.17 shows a screenshot, but this static image does not do justice to the system. Constellation used hover queries to allow for rapid highlighting of subsets of the graph. Links attached to a node become highlighted as the cursor passes over the node. In addition, when the user clicks on a particular node, closely related semantic concepts are allocated more screen space and larger fonts. In essence, the computer provides a *visual information scent*, to use Pirolli and Card's (1995) term, as a guide to the best place to search for more information. By using this technique, a large amount of semantic information can be accessed very quickly.

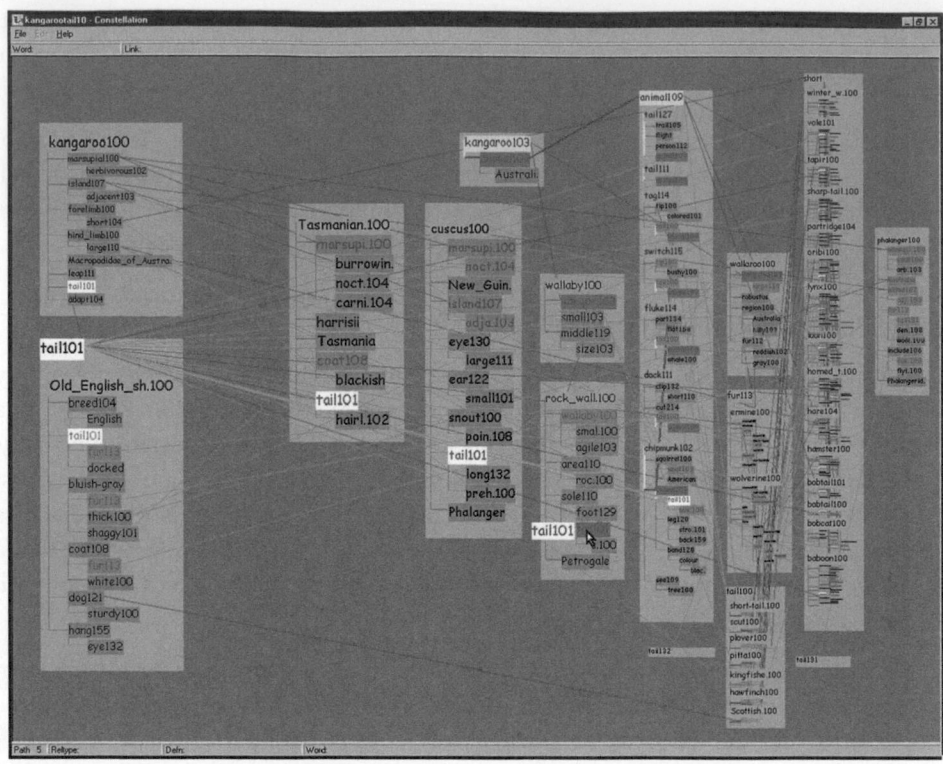

Figure 10.17 A screen image of the constellation system (Munzner et al., 1999) showing a view into the MindNet semantic network database. *(From Munzner et al. (1999), Reproduced with permission.)*

Note that the rapid query techniques get around the usual problems of graph layout. Most of the work in graph layout is aimed at producing aesthetically pleasing drawings of graph structures by paying particular attention to minimizing edge crossings of nodes (Di Battista, Eades, Tamassia, & Tollis, 1998). A clear static graph drawing of the information in Fig. 10.17 is probably impossible because there are simply too many links. In Constellation, Munzner abandoned the usual criteria, allowing edges to cross each other and to cross nodes, using interactive techniques to reveal information as needed and enabling visual access to much larger structures.

Table Manipulations

We have already seen forms of zooming applied to maps and to network diagrams. Now we consider a third application in table-based visualization. A table is not usually thought of as a visualization. But some methods allow multiple foci to be simultaneously expanded, such as the *table lens* (Rao & Card, 1994) illustrated in Fig. 10.18. In this case, instead of numbers filling in the cells of the table, bars representing numerical values are used. The result is that the table becomes a kind of interactive visualization. In the table lens of Rao and Card, common spreadsheet-like interactions were

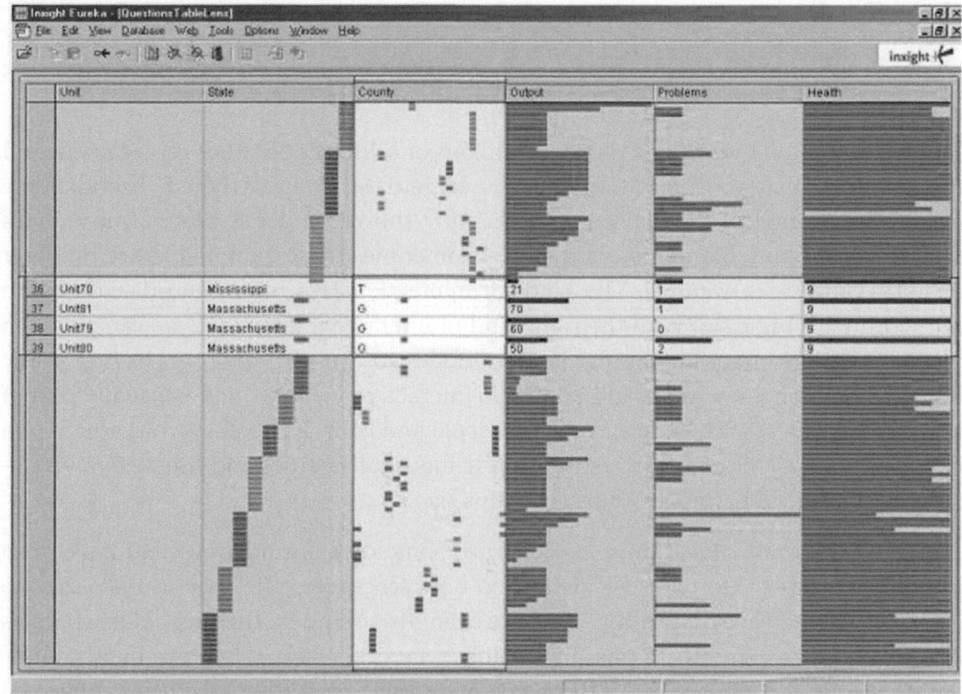

Figure 10.18 Table lens from Rao and Card (1994). Multiple row- and column-wise centers of focus can be created.

implemented, so that, for example, all the rows could be sorted according to the values in a particular column. This makes it possible to quickly visualize various kinds of relationships. For example, suppose that the table consists of the variable typically measured during hospital stays: blood pressure, heart rate, and various blood chemistry metrics, one row per patient. By sorting on blood pressure will bring high blood pressure patients to the top of the table and make it easy to see what other measured values these people have in common. This is a simple example, but it gives an idea of how an interactive table can be used in analysis.

Parallel Coordinates or Scatterplot Matrix

This set of techniques would not be complete without including the two major methods that have been developed for visualizing multidimensional discrete data. The methods are called *scatterplot matrix* and *parallel coordinates,* respectively. And, as discussed in Chapter 6 (see Fig. 6.54) which is better is still open for debate. In both cases a kind of interactive range query is essential to make these methods useful. With the scatterplot matrix, the user drags out a rectangle on one of the subplots and the same points are highlighted in all of the plots. With parallel coordinates, the user drags out the range on one of the vertical axes and the set of lines passing through that range are highlighted. The lines in a parallel coordinates plot are equivalent to points in a scatterplot matrix.

Conclusion

Often visualization is proposed as a way of dealing with the problem of interpreting "big data".

The fact is that real-world big data has millions or billions of entities represented, and it is very rare that a visualization of such a large data set as a whole is useful. Some early visualization of the entire internet simply showed a dense blob, of tiny nodes fine threads linking filamentous structures. Sometimes these qualified as art, but their analytic value was minimal. The kinds of interactions we have been discussing do not work with big data. With the right kind of interactive technique we can get from a static network diagram having 30 or so nodes to a useful diagram having a few hundred or even a few thousand nodes. So interactive visualization is usually part of a two-stage process. The first stage is not visual and consists of a keyword search or a database query. This can may result in a few thousand entities and interactive visualization can indeed help with data sets of this size.

Another important caveat must be added to some of the guidelines that have been provided. It has to do with the distinction between sheer efficiency in the access to information and ease of learning. We have been discussing navigating a data space as quickly and transparently as possible. Doing so involves supporting eye-hand coordination, using well-chosen interaction metaphors, and providing rapid and consistent feedback. The word *transparent* in user interface design is a metaphor for an interface that is so easy to use that it all but disappears from consciousness, but transparency can also come from practice and not just good initial design. A violin has an extraordinarily difficult user interface, and to reach virtuosity may take thousands of hours, but once virtuosity is achieved the instrument will have become a transparent medium of expression. This highlights a thorny problem in the development of novel interfaces. It is very easy for the designer to become focused on the problem of making an interface that can be used quickly by the novice, but it is much more difficult to research and develop designs for the expert. It is almost impossible to carry out experiments on expert use of radical new interfaces for the simple reason that no one will ever spend enough time on a research prototype to become truly skilled. Also, someone who has spent thousands of hours navigating using a set of buttons on a game controller will find that particular user interface easy to use and natural, even though novices find it very difficult. This means that even a poorly designed user interface may be best for a user population that is already highly skilled with it. A simple example is the use of hot keys. These encode some operation in a single keystroke. They are harder to learn but for frequent operations, such as cut and paste, they can provide significant productivity gains.

> **[G10.22]** Provide acceleration using hot keys and equivalents for frequent simple tasks so that expert users can increase their productivity.

CHAPTER ELEVEN

Thinking With Visualizations

Pirolli and Card (1995) drew the following analogy between the way animals seek food and the way people seek information. Animals minimize energy expenditure to get the required gain in sustenance; humans minimize effort to get the necessary gain in information. Foraging for food has much in common with seeking information because, like edible plants in the wild, morsels of information are often grouped but separated by long distances in an information wasteland. Pirolli and Card elaborated the idea to include information "scent"—like the scent of food, this is the information in the current environment that will assist us in finding more succulent information clusters.

Reducing the cost of knowledge requires that we optimize cognitive algorithms that run on a peculiar kind of hybrid computer; part of this computer is a human brain, including its visual system, and part is a digital computer with a graphical display. In Chapter 1 we discussed user costs and benefits, but now we take a more system-oriented view with the following overarching principle for this chapter:

> [G11.1] Design cognitive systems to maximize cognitive productivity.

Cognitive productivity is the amount of valuable cognitive work done per unit of time. Although it is only possible to put a value on this some of the time, maximizing productivity is nevertheless the (often implicit) goal of systems designed to support knowledge workers. In this chapter, we will be examining the characteristics of human-computer cognitive systems and the algorithms that run on them in order to better design systems that increase cognitive throughput.

Information Visualization. https://doi.org/10.1016/B978-0-12-812875-6.00011-6

The Cognitive System

An interactive visualization can be considered an internal interface between human and computer components in a problem-solving system. We are all becoming cognitive cyborgs in the sense that a person with a computer-aided design program, access to the Internet, and other software tools is capable of problem-solving strategies that would be impossible for that person acting unaided. A business consultant plotting projections based on a spreadsheet business model can combine business knowledge with the computational power of the spreadsheet to plot scenarios rapidly, interpret trends visually, and make better decisions.

Fig. 11.1 illustrates the key components of this kind of cognitive system. On the human side, a critical component is visual working memory; we will be concerned especially with the constraints imposed by its low capacity. At any given instant, visual working memory contains only a small amount of information relating to the visual display generated by a computer. It can also contain information about the *visual query* that is being executed by means of a visual pattern search.

For visual queries to be useful, a problem must first be cast in the form of a visual pattern that, if identified, helps solve part of the problem. Finding a number of big red circles in a geographic information system (GIS) display, for example, may indicate a problem with water pollution. Finding a long, red, fairly straight line on a map can show the best way to drive between two cities. Once the visual query is constructed, a visual pattern search provides answers.

Every part of the brain can be considered as holding long-term memory, but it is not a static store, rather it is a repository of the learned skills associated with thinking, both visual and nonvisual. These skills allow for execution, both of basic patterns searches and of much more complex mental models representing aspects of the world. As we shall see, long-term memory, like all memory, contains executable predictive processes.

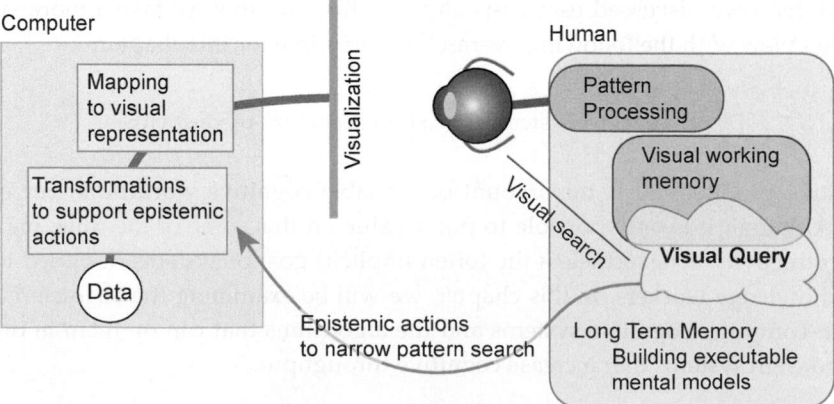

Figure 11.1 The cognitive system considered in this chapter.

Part of the thinking process consists of what Karsh (2009) calls *epistemic actions*. These can be eye movements to pick up more information. Or, in the case of an interactive visualization, these can be mouse movements, causing programs to execute in the computer, changing the nature of the information that is displayed. These computer-side operations, such as brushing to highlight related information or zooming in on some information, make it easier to process visual queries by finding task-relevant patterns. Alternatively, the selection of a visual object may trigger the highlighting of other objects that a computer algorithm suggests are relevant. This narrows the visual search, speeding the resolution of a visual query.

In the remainder of this chapter we will introduce the perceptual and cognitive machinery important in the visual thinking process before moving on, in the final chapter, to consider the design of visual thinking processes where both human and computer contribute to problem solving.

The Predicting Brain

We can only act if we can predict the outcomes of our actions, and many researchers now think that predicting the future is the fundamental principle guiding cognitive processing (Clark, 2013). This principle guides brain function from the most basic levels on up. As an example of basic level prediction, for the layout of the world to be understood, the outcome of an eye movement must be forecast so that the information received when our gaze lands at a new point of fixation can be used properly to guided hand and eye movements, and so that the brain knows where this new bit of high-resolution imagery lies in the context of the world at large. At a higher level, all planning involves predictive modeling of the consequences of a course of action.

According to current theory, the most important function of memory is not retrieving past events but predicting future ones (Clark, 2013). In *On Intelligence,* Hawkins and Blakeslee (2007) suggest that the functions of prediction and exception handling are the reason for the layered architecture of the visual cortex. The prediction hypothesis suggests that for most inputs the brain has already computed what is expected in the incoming imagery. It is only when a difference from what was predicted is found that a signal is sent to higher level processing. This makes it possible for higher level processes to be freed from routine work. In other words, it is only when exceptions (to the predictions) occur that tasks are kicked-up to a higher level in the neural hierarchy. Necessary for this to work, memory must be integral to the processing mechanisms for incoming information; it is also necessary for memory to be a kind of executable predictive model based on prior experience.

For example, experienced drivers are mostly in autopilot mode, the routine operations of staying within the white lines and maintaining distance from the car in front take little mental energy and so a driver can use cognitive resources to plan the day at work, or even do visual design thinking (where this involves constructing mental images).

It is only when the car begins to behave strangely or another driver moves erratically that higher cognitive functioning is interrupted.

This leads to an enormous savings in information processing. The brain does not need to reprocess and recompute everything from moment to moment. For the most part, only minor adjustments need to be made to the ongoing state-of-the-world representation. All attention can therefore be devoted either to the task at hand or to handling emergency exceptions. The allocation of attention is critical; it is useful to think of attention in a broad sense to mean the momentary allocation of available neural computing resources. In other words, attention pervades everything. Moreover, this predictive system is coupled tightly with interactive behaviors. As Hawkins and Blakeslee (2004, p. 158) put it

> As the cascading prediction unfolds, it generates the motor commands necessary to fulfil the prediction. Thinking, predicting, and doing are all part of the same unfolding of sequences moving down the cortical hierarchy.

Eye movements are determined by memory stored in the eye-movement control mechanisms of the brain. The neural signals sent to cause an eye movement are calibrated according to what happened when similar signals were sent previously—was there an overshoot or an undershoot? But eye movements are also a high-level skill; the fixation patterns of an experienced driver are guided by memories of where problems are likely to occur such as at intersections and where there are pedestrians. What is true for eye movement is also true for hand movements and by extension to all manipulations of controls in user interfaces. Zuanazzi and Noppeney (2018) suggest that the brain iteratively adjusts its predictions of the sensory inputs at multiple levels across the cortical hierarchy.

This integral linkage of neural coding, prediction, and action is completely compatible with the Bayesian view of neural processing. According to this theory, neurons encode prior information in order to predict (and effect) future actions (Knill & Pouget, 2004).

At a much higher cognitive level, predictive memory is important in sequencing of behavior, and at the highest level it is obviously critical in planning and problems solving. It is obvious that we cannot make actions if we cannot, to some extent, predict the probable outcome of those actions. So prediction is clearly fundamental to planning. Problem solving involves running a cognitive simulation of a solution under consideration. However, such cognitive simulations are not at all like the formally precise simulations we see that occur in engineering models. They mostly operate below the level of consciousness, manifested only as the feeling that a certain set of actions is the right course of action. Interestingly, Ritter, Sussman, Deacon, Cowan, and Vaughan (1999) uncovered evidence that in some cases two cognitive systems can simultaneously and unconsciously prepare for alternative conflicting developments in the state of the world.

One thing that is remarkable is how much of the brain is active at any given time. The brain is a powerful machine in which many areas, although specialized, are constantly being retuned to support the task at hand. But this also means that attention is a strictly limited resource. Any glitch in lower level operations impinges on our ability to perform higher level cognition. This leads us again to note that it is critical to make use of prior knowledge in designing interfaces. Easy to use usually means not something that has some inherent naturalness, but rather something already understood. Using prior learning for basic activities greatly reduces the number of exceptions that must be handled by high-level cognition.

Memory and Attention

The classic view of dealing with memory is in terms of capacity and it is still useful to think in these terms without losing sight of the new view of memory as being about prediction and action. So we will begin this section with a review of the basic capacities.

As a first approximation, there are three types of memory: iconic, working, and long term (see Fig. 11.2). There may also be a fourth intermediate store that determines which information from working memory finds its way into long-term memory.

Iconic memory is a very short-term image store, holding what is on the retina until it is replaced by something else or until several hundred milliseconds have passed (Sperling, 1960). This is image-related information, lacking semantic content. Iconic memory functions as a temporary buffer, storing information from a single fixation. During the next fraction of a second, attentional processes can pull out a few simple patterns from the iconic store.

Visual working memory holds the visual objects of immediate attention. The contents of working memory can be drawn from either long-term memory (in the case of mental images) or input from the iconic store, but most of the time information in working memory is a combination of external visual information made meaningful through the experiences stored in long-term memory and mental imagery.

Long-term memory is the information that we retain from everyday experience, perhaps for a lifetime, but it should not be considered as separate from working memory. Instead, working memory can be better conceived of as information activated within long-term memory. As already discussed, executable long-term memory is part of every component of the brain.

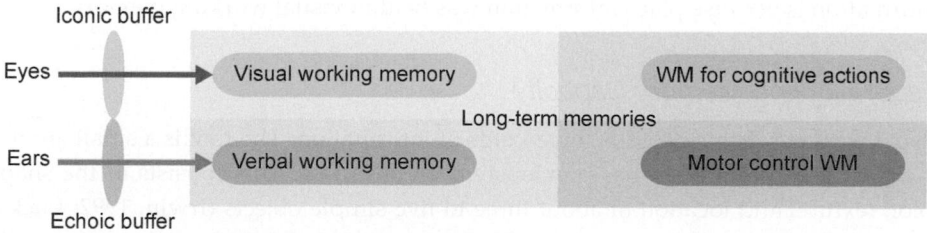

Figure 11.2 Three types of memories are iconic stores, working memory stores, and long-term memory stores.

Working Memories

There are separate working memory subsystems for processing auditory and visual information, as well as subsystems for body movements and verbal output (Thomas et al., 1999). There may be additional working memory stores for sequences of cognitive instructions and for motor control of the body. Kieras and Meyer (1997), for example, proposed an amodal control memory containing the operations required to accomplish current goals and a general purpose working memory containing other miscellaneous information. There is no central processor; instead, different potential activation loops compete with a winner-take-all mechanism, causing only one to become active, determining what we will do next (Carter, Botvinick, & Cohen, 2011). This loop itself has a strictly limited capacity which is why cognitive support tools (like a pencil and paper) are so useful.

Visual thinking is only partly executed using the uniquely visual centers of the brain. In fact, it emerges from the interplay of visual and nonvisual systems, but because our subject is visual thinking we will hereafter refer to most nonvisual processes generically as *verbal-propositional processing* (see Chapter 9 for a discussion of the issues relating to representations based on words and images). It is functionally quite easy to separate visual and verbal-propositional processing. Verbal-propositional subsystems are occupied when we speak, whereas visual subsystems are not. This allows for simple experiments to separate the two processes. Postma and De Haan (1996) provided a good example. They asked subjects to remember the locations of a set of easily recognizable objects—small pictures of cats, horses, cups, chairs, tables, etc.—laid out in two dimensions on a screen. The objects were then placed in a line at the top of the display and the subjects were asked to reposition them in their original locations, a task the subjects performed quite well. In another condition, subjects were asked to repeat a nonsense syllable, such as "blah," while in the learning phase. This time, they did much worse. Saying "blah" did not disrupt memory for the locations themselves; instead, it only disrupted memory for what was at the locations. This was demonstrated by having subjects place a set of disks at the positions of the original objects, which they could do with relative accuracy. In other words, when "blah" was said in the learning phase, subjects learned a set of locations but not the objects at those locations. This technique is called *articulatory suppression*. The reason why saying "blah" disrupted working memory for the objects is that task-relevant object information was stored using a verbal-propositional coding. The reason it did not disrupt location information is because place information was held in visual working memory.

Visual Working Memory Capacity

Visual working memory holds three kinds of information. The first is a small amount of information from what has previously been observed. This consists of the shape, color, texture, and location of about three to five simple objects (Irwin, 1992; Luck & Vogel, 1997; Melcher, 2001; Xu, 2002). The exact number depends on the task and the kind of pattern, and the amount of shape information is strictly limited to the very basic structure. The second kind of information is mental imagery that is imagined

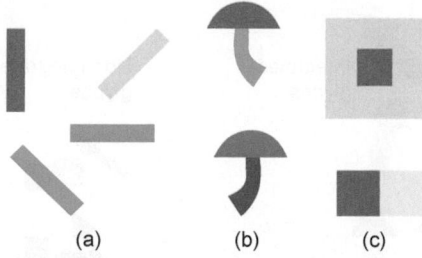

(a)   (b)   (c)

Figure 11.3 Patterns used in studies of the capacity of visual working memory. *((a, c) From Vogel et al. (2001). (b) From Xu (2002). Reproduced with permission.).)*

objects and their layouts in space (Kosslyn, 1994), which is also is limited to a very small number of items. The third kind of information is the contents of a visual query. If you are looking for something specific you will be much less likely to notice changes in other visual information. Information in visual working memory is held only for 1 or 2 seconds. Most if the time it lasts only for a fraction of a second as it replaced by new information from the current fixation.

Fig. 11.3(a) illustrates the kinds of patterns used in a series of experiments by Vogel, Woodman, and Luck (2001) to study the capacity of visual working memory. In these experiments, one set of objects was shown for a fraction of a second (e.g., 0.4 second), followed by a blank of more than 0.5 second. After the blank, the same pattern was shown, but with one attribute of an object altered—for example, its color or shape. The results from this and a large number of similar studies have shown that about three objects can be retained without error, but these objects can have color, shape, and texture. If the same amount of color, shape, and texture information is distributed across more objects, memory declines for each of the attributes.

Only quite simple shapes can be stored in this way. Each of the mushroom shapes shown in Fig. 11.3(b) uses up two visual memory slots (Xu, 2002). Subjects do no better if the stem and the cap are combined than if they are separated. Intriguingly, Vogel et al. (2001) found that if colors were combined with concentric squares, as shown in Fig. 11.3(c), then six colors could be held in visual working memory, but if they were put in side-by-side squares, then only three colors could be retained. Melcher (2001) found that more information could be retained if longer viewing was permitted, up to five objects after a 4-sec presentation.

There are implications for data glyph design. (A glyph, as discussed in Chapter 5, is a visual object that displays one or more data variables.) If it is important that a data glyph be held in visual working memory, then it is important that its shape allows it to be encoded according to visual working memory capacity. Fig. 11.4 shows two ways of representing the same data. One consists of an integrated glyph containing a colored arrow showing orientation by arrow direction, temperature by arrow color, and pressure by arrow width. A second representation distributes the three quantities among three separate visual objects: orientation by an arrow, temperature by the color

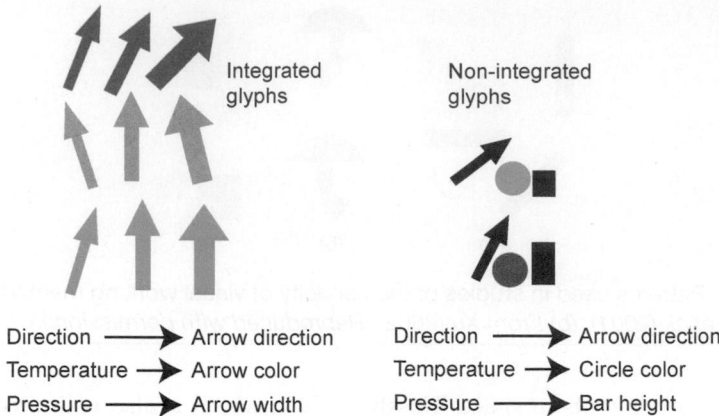

Integrated glyphs

Non-integrated glyphs

Direction ⟶	Arrow direction
Temperature ⟶	Arrow color
Pressure ⟶	Arrow width

Direction ⟶	Arrow direction
Temperature ⟶	Circle color
Pressure ⟶	Bar height

Figure 11.4 If multiple data attributes are integrated into a single glyph, more information can be held in visual working memory.

of a circle, and air pressure by the height of a rectangle. The theory of visual working memory and the results of Vogel et al. (2001) suggest that three of the integrated glyphs could be held in visual working memory, but only one of the nonintegrated glyphs.

Visual Working Memory for Visual Comparisons

Visual pattern comparisons are a common cognitive subtask in data visualization. For example, cells may be compared on a microscope slide, or patterns of connections may be compared in different regions of a large network diagram. Often the positions of the features in a larger context are also important.

To support both visual comparisons of details and help with the focus and context problem, many systems afford epistemic actions that provide the user with a method for moving attention easily between detail and context views. These techniques (introduced in Chapter 10) include methods such as zooming or adding extra linked windows, and some may be faster than others. In most cases, though, the important constraint on cognitive performance is imposed by visual working memory capacity.

To help analyze the problem of which focus and context interface is likely to be best we will take as a model the task of comparing patterns that are isolated small islands of information in a large geographical space. This is illustrated in Fig. 11.5. The figure shows extra linked windows, placed so as to show two areas of detail.

A simpler alternative to having extra windows is a straightforward zooming interface. With a zooming interface, comparisons are made through rapid scale changes. The user must zoom in and look at one area of detail, hold the pattern (or part of it) in visual working memory, zoom out to get an overview and seek another pattern, and then zoom in again to make a comparison. The pattern in visual working memory is compared to new patterns found during the search process. If a possible match is found, it may be necessary to zoom in and out and back and forth to confirm details.

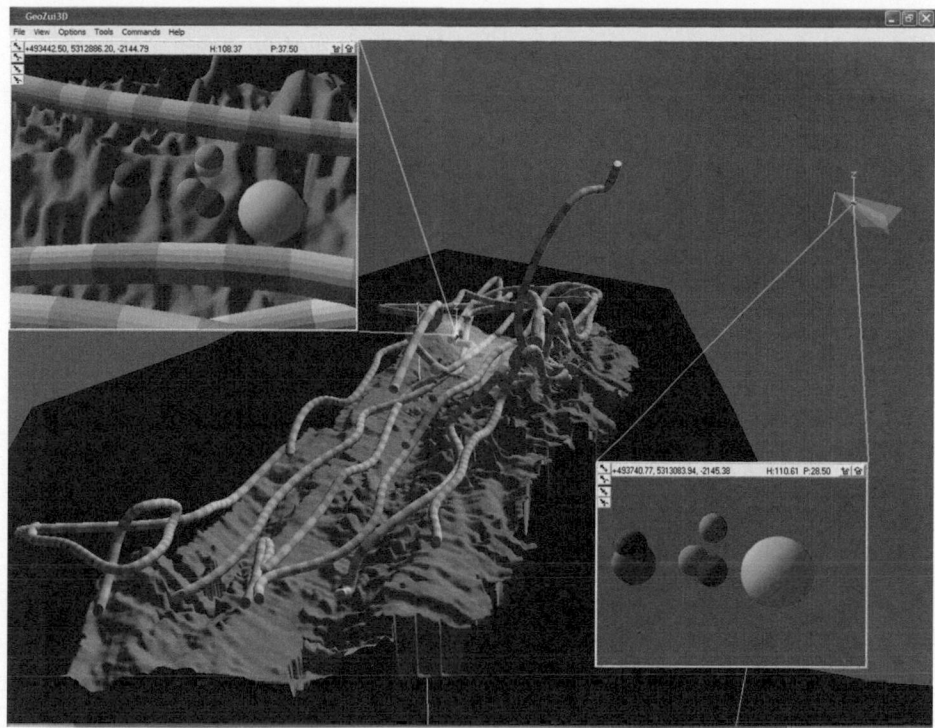

Figure 11.5 Linked subwindows allow details to be compared while the overall context can also be seen (GeoZui3D interface).

With the use of extra windows, as shown in Fig. 11.5, parts of the main display are magnified. When two such windows are in position, it is possible simply to make eye movements between them to assess the relationship more rapidly.

The general procedure for this task is given in Box 11.1. It involves moving back and forth between patterns to make comparisons. This movement is an epistemic action that depends on the interface that has been provided. One way of implementing the epistemic action is through an interface that makes zooming rapid and easy. Another way is to provide support for extra magnifying windows. If two extra magnifying windows are used, they must be set up over pairs of patterns to make the comparison, but when the windows are in place the visual comparison can be made with much more rapid eye movements (Plumlee & Ware, 2002).

The critical resource here is visual working memory capacity, because this determines how many visits, back and forth, are required to make a comparison between a pair of patterns. If the master pattern is simple enough to be held in visual working memory, then zooming will often be more efficient, because it avoids the overhead of setting up multiple windows. If more than three visual working memory–sized chunks are in the master pattern, then it will be necessary to zoom back and forth between them, and the multiwindow solution will be faster.

Box 11.1   *Small pattern comparisons in a large information space*

Display Environment: A Large Data Space with Small Isolated Patterns that Must be Compared in Some way.

1. *Execute an epistemic action by navigating to the location of the first pattern.*

2. *Retain a subset of the first pattern in visual working memory.*

3. *Execute an epistemic action by navigating to the candidate location of a comparison pattern.*

4. *Compare the working memory pattern with part of the pattern at the candidate location.*

    4.1 *If a suitable match is found, terminate the search.*

    4.2 *If a partial match is found, navigate back and forth between the candidate location and master pattern location, loading additional subsets of candidate pattern into visual working memory and making comparisons until a suitable match or a mismatch is found.*

5. *If a mismatch is found repeat from 1, cognitively marking candidate locations that have already been evaluated.*

In its simplest form, the time taken to perform this task is given by:

$$Time = setup\ cost + number\ of\ comparison\ queries \qquad (11.1)$$

The number of comparison queries depends on the complexity of the patterns to be compared and visual working memory capacity; for example, if there are seven simple components in the patterns to be compared, the number of comparison queries will be approximately three, because only two to five components can be stored in visual working memory to make a single comparison. The actual number depends on the individuals working memory capacity and the exact configuration of the patterns.

Plumlee and Ware (2002) modeled and predicted user performance on this task with the two interfaces we have been discussing—simple zooming versus multiple windows. The number of zooms versus window movements necessary to complete the task of finding identical clusters of simple shapes widely separated in a geographical space was estimated. Visual working memory was considered as a critical resource. The predictions of the model are shown in Fig. 11.6 (left), modeled for capacities of visual working memory at two, three, and four items, leading to a range of predictions as shown by the broad colored wedges. When there are fewer visual chunks in the patterns to be compared, the zooming interface is best. As the number of chunks increases, the extra window interface is better. The crossover should be at about three chunks. The measured results, shown Fig. 11.6 (right), closely matched the prediction.

The model we have been describing here is greatly simplified. In fact, because eye movements have such a low cost, when people make side-by-side comparisons with

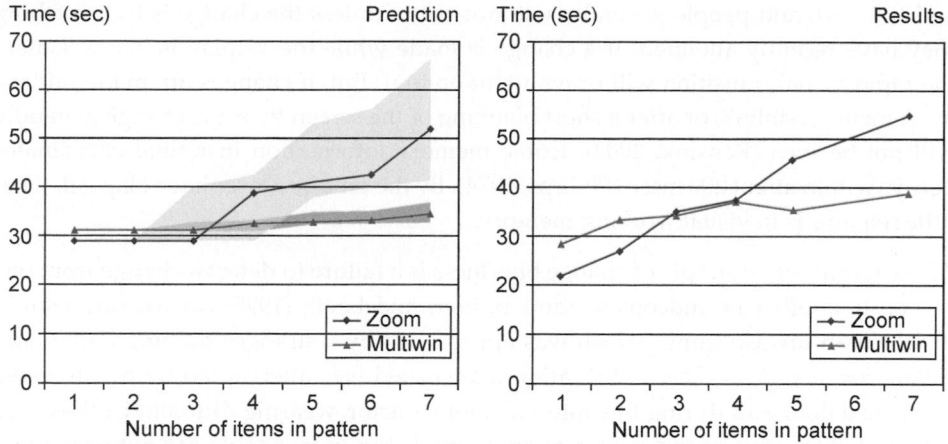

Figure 11.6 Model predictions are shown on the left. Measured task performance is shown on the right. Multiple windows speed performance relative to the use of a zooming interface when the number of objects to be compared is five or more.

the multiple windows interface they act as if they are only comparing one object at a time (instead of three). They make many more eye movement than necessary and they also make far fewer errors than with zooming (Plumlee & Ware, 2006). So the multi-window solution is more reliable as well as faster.

Still, in many cases, detailed modeling is not required to decide if a user interface should support extra windows for detailed pattern comparisons. We can give the following rule of thumb:

> [G11.2] In large data spaces containing small islands of critical information, consider enabling the user to add extra windows showing magnified areas of the larger space. This is especially useful for tasks that require frequent queries to compare patterns having more than three visual working memory chunks.

In Chapter 12 we consider other solutions for the provision of support for pattern comparisons.

Change Blindness

The finding that visual working memory has a very low capacity has extraordinary implications for how much we perceive and how we interpret visualizations. Among other things it suggests that our impression that we see the world in all its complexity and detail is illusory. In this section, we review some of the evidence showing that this is in fact the case.

One of the consequences of the very small amount of information held in visual working memory is a phenomenon known as *change blindness* (Rensink, 2000). Because we remember so little, it is possible to make large changes in a display between one view and the next, and people generally will not notice unless the change is to something they have recently attended. If a change is made while the display is being fixated, the rapid visual transition will draw attention to it. But, if changes are made mideye movement, midblink, or after a short blanking of the screen then the change generally will not be seen (Rensink, 2002). Iconic memory information in retinal coordinates decays within about 200 msec (Phillips, 1974). By the time 400 msec have elapsed, what little remains is in visual working memory.

An extraordinary example of change blindness is a failure to detect a change from one person to another in midconversation. Simons and Levin (1998) carried out a study in which an unsuspecting person was approached by a stranger holding a map and asking for directions. The conversation that ensued was interrupted by two workers carrying a door and during this interval another actor, wearing different clothes, was substituted to carry on the conversation. Remarkably, most people did not notice that they were talking to a different person!

To many people, the extreme limitation on the capacity of visual working memory seems quite incredible. How can we experience a rich and detailed world, given such a shallow internal representation? Part of the answer to this dilemma is that the world "is its own memory" (O'Regan, 1992). We perceive the world to be rich and detailed, not because we have an internal detailed model, but simply because whenever we wish to see detail we can get it, either by focusing attention on some aspect of the visual image at the current fixation or by moving our eyes to see the detail in some other part of the visual field. We are unaware of the jerky eye movements by which we explore the world and only aware of the complexity of the environment through detail being brought into working memory on a need-to-know, just-in-time fashion (O'Regan, 1992; Rensink, O'Reagan, & Clark, 1997; Rensink, 2002).

A second part of the explanation of how we sustain the illusion of seeing a rich and detailed word is *gist*. Gist is the activated general knowledge we have about particular kinds of environments. Much of the information we think we are perceiving externally is not external at all, but is contained in the gist already stored in our long-term memories. So, in an instant what we actually perceive consists of a little bit of external information and a lot of internal information activated from long-term memory. We are seeing, mostly, what we already know about the world. To this is added the implicit, unconscious knowledge that we can rapidly query the external world for more information by means of a rapid eye movement. No sooner do we think of some information that we need than we have it at the point of fixation. This gives rise to the illusion that we see the whole world in detail.

Spatial Information

For objects acquired in one fixation to be reidentified in the next fixation requires some kind of buffer that holds locations in egocentric coordinates as opposed to retinocentric coordinates (Hochberg, 1968). This also allows for a very limited synthesis of information obtained from successive fixations. In addition, the lateral interparietal area

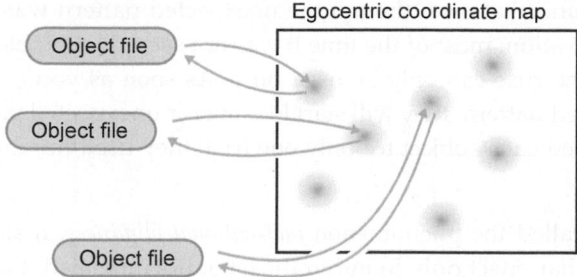

Figure 11.7 A spatial map of a small number of objects recently held by attention in working memory.

appears to play a crucial role in linking retinocentric coordinate maps in the brain with "action oriented" egocentric coordinate maps (Colby, 1998). Egocentric-spatial location memory also holds remarkably little information, although probably a bit more than the three objects that Vogel et al. (2001) suggested. It may be possible to remember some information about approximately nine locations (Postma, Izendoorn, & De Haan, 1998). Three of these may contain links to object files (introduced in Chapter 8), whereas the remaining ones specify only that there is something at a particular region in space, but very little more. Fig. 11.7 illustrates the concept. The neurophysiological mechanism for this is the hippocampal grid cells discussed in the previous chapter.

An interesting question is how many *moving* targets can be tracked continuously. The answer seems to be about four or five. Pylyshyn and Storm (1988) carried out experiments in which visual objects moved around on a display in a pseudorandom fashion. A subset of the objects was visually marked by changing color, but then the marking was turned off. If there were five or fewer marked objects, subjects could continue to keep track of them, even though they were now all an identical black. Pylyshyn coined the term *FINST, for fingers of instantiation*, to describe the set of pointers in a cognitive spatial map that would be necessary to support this task. The number of individual objects that can be tracked appears to be slightly larger than the capacity of visual working memory, perhaps because some of the moving objects may be grouped perceptually into fewer chunks (Yantis, 1992).

Attention

Experiments showing that we can hold three or four objects in visual working memory required intense concentration on the part of the participants. But, most of the time, when we interact with displays or just go about our business in the everyday world, we will not be attending that closely. In a remarkable series of studies, Mack and Rock (1998) tricked subjects into not paying attention to the subject of the experiment, although they wanted to make sure that subjects were at least looking in the right direction. They told subjects to attend to an X-shaped pattern for changes in the length of one of the arms; perfect scores on this task indicated they had to be attending. Then the researchers presented a pattern that the subject had not been asked to look for. They found that even though the unexpected pattern was close to, or even on, the point of fixation, most of the time it was not seen. The problem with this kind of study is that the ruse can only be used once. As soon as you ask subjects if they saw the unexpected pattern, they will start looking for unexpected patterns. Mack and Rock therefore used each subject for only one trial; they used hundreds of subjects in a series of studies.

Mack and Rock called the phenomenon *inattentional blindness*. It should not be considered as a peculiar effect only found in the laboratory. Instead, this result probably reflects everyday reality much more accurately than the typical psychological experiment in which subjects are paid to closely attend. The implication is that most of the time we simply do not register what is going on in our environment unless we are looking for it and this reinforces the view that attention is central to most perception.

Although we are blind to many changes in our environment, some visual events are more likely to cause us to change attention than others. Mack and Rock found that although subjects were blind to small patterns that appeared and disappeared, they still noticed larger visual events, such as patterns larger than one degree of visual angle appearing near the point of fixation.

Visual attention is not strictly tied to eye movements. Although attending to some particular part of a display often does involve an eye movement, there are also attention processes operating within each fixation. The studies of Treisman and Gormican (1988) and others (discussed in Chapter 5) showed that we process simple visual objects serially at a rate of about one every 40–50 msec. Because each fixation typically will last for 100–300 msec, this means that our visual systems process between two and six simple objects or shapes within each fixation before we move our eyes to attend visually to some other region.

Attention is also not limited to specific locations on a screen. We can, for example, choose to attend to a particular pattern that is a component of another pattern, even though the patterns overlap spatially (Rock & Gutman, 1981). These query-driven tuning mechanisms are based on the channels—color, size, orientation, motion—discussed in Chapter 5. As discussed, the possibility of choosing to attend to a particular attribute depends on whether or not it is preattentively distinct (Treisman, 1985); for example, if a page of black text has some sections highlighted in red, we can choose to attend only to the red sections, easily ignoring the rest. Having whole groups of objects that move is especially useful in helping us to attend selectively (Bartram & Ware, 2002). We can attend to the moving group or the static group, with relatively little interference between them.

The selectivity of attention is by no means perfect. Even though we may wish to focus on one aspect of a display, other information is also processed, apparently to quite a high level. The well-known *Stroop effect* illustrates this (Stroop, 1935). In general, words, which are tied to verbal information, and visual features represent very separate channels of information but the Stroop effect demonstrates interference between these channels. In a set of words printed in different colors, as illustrated in Fig. 11.8,

RED GREEN YELLOW **BLUE BLACK** GREEN **PURPLE BLUE BLACK**
ORANGE GREEN **RED** GREEN YELLOW **BLUE BLACK** GREEN
PURPLE BLUE BLACK ORANGE **BLACK GREEN RED**

GREEN RED BLUE **YELLOW PURPLE** RED **BLACK BLUE BLACK**
GREEN ORANGE **BLUE** RED PURPLE **YELLOW RED** BLACK
YELLOW GREEN ORANGE BLACK **GREEN RED GREEN**

Figure 11.8 As quickly as you can, try to name the colors in the set of words at the top, and then try to name the colors in the set of words below. Even though they are asked to ignore the meaning of the words, people are slowed down by the mismatch in the second set. This is referred to as the *Stroop effect*, which shows that some processing is automatic.

if the words themselves are color names that *do not match* the ink colors, subjects name the ink colors more slowly than if the colors match the words. This means that the words are processed automatically; we cannot entirely ignore them even when we want to. More generally, it is an indication that all highly learned symbols will automatically invoke verbal-propositional information that has become associated with them. But, still, these crossover effects are relatively minor. The main point is that the focus of attention largely determines what we will see, and this focus is set by the task we are undertaking.

Jonides (1981) studied ways of moving a subject's attention from one part of a display to another. He looked at two different ways, which are sometimes called *pull cues* and *push cues*. In a pull cue, a new object appearing in the scene pulls attention toward it. In a push cue, a symbol in the display, such as an arrow, tells someone where a new pattern is to appear. Pull cues are faster; it takes only about 100 msec to shift attention based on a pull cue but can take between 200 and 400 msec to shift attention based on a push cue. Because motion is readily directed in the periphery of vision, it is probably the best pull cue to use.

> [G11.3] Use pull cues preferentially over push cues to redirect attention in an interactive display.

Vigilance

Sometimes people must search for faint and rarely occurring targets in complex backgrounds. The invention of radar during World War II created a need for radar operators to monitor noise-filled screens for long hours, searching for visual signals representing incoming enemy aircraft. This led to research aimed at understanding how people can maintain vigilance while performing monotonous tasks. This kind of task is common to airport baggage X-ray screeners, industrial quality-control inspectors, and the operators of large power grids. Vigilance tasks commonly involve visual targets, although they can be auditory. There is extensive literature concerning vigilance (for reviews, see Davies & Parasuraman, 1980; Wickens, 1992). Here is an overview of some of the more general findings.

1. Vigilance performance falls substantially over the first hour.

2. Fatigue has a large negative influence on vigilance.

3. To perform a difficult vigilance task effectively requires a high level of sustained attention, using significant cognitive resources. This means that dual tasking is not an option during an important vigilance task. It is not possible for operators to perform some useful task in their "spare time" while simultaneously monitoring for some signal that is difficult to perceive.

4. Irrelevant signals reduce performance. The more irrelevant visual information presented to a person performing a vigilance task, the more difficult the task becomes.

5. The difficulty of seeing targets varies inversely with target frequency. People are more than twice as likely to see frequent targets than rare ones (Wolfe et al., 2007).

Overall, people perform poorly on vigilance tasks, but there are a number of techniques that can improve performance. One method is to provide reminders at frequent intervals about what the targets will look like. This is especially important if there are many different kinds of targets. Another is to take advantage of the visual system's sensitivity to motion. A difficult target for a radar operator might be a slowly moving ship embedded in a great many irrelevant noise signals. Scanlan (1975) showed that if a number of radar images are stored up and rapidly replayed, the image of the moving ship can easily be differentiated from the visual noise. Generally, anything that can transfer the visual signal into the optimal spatial or temporal range of the visual system should help detection. If the signal can be made perceptually different or distinct from irrelevant information, this will also help. The various factors that make color, motion, and texture distinct can all be applied.

Wolfe et al. (2007) found a method for counteracting the infrequent target effect. In a task that closely approximated airport screening, they showed that inserting retraining sessions into the work schedule improved detection rates considerably. These retraining sessions contained bursts of artificially *frequent* targets with *feedback* regarding correctness of detection. It is also possible to introduce artificial targets during normal work so long as the operator is informed that they are false as soon as they are selected.

> [G11.4] In search tasks for infrequent targets, insert retraining sessions during which targets are frequent and feedback is given regarding success or failure. Alternatively, introduce false targets into the work flow with immediate feedback.

Attention Switching and Interruptions

One of the goals of cognitive systems design is to tighten the loop between human and computer, making it easier for the human to obtain important information from the computer via the display. Simply shortening the amount of time it takes to acquire a piece of information may seem like a small thing, but human visual and verbal working memories are very limited in capacity and the information stored is easily lost; even a few seconds of delay or an increase in the cognitive load can drastically reduce the rate of information uptake by the user. When a user must stop thinking about the task at hand and switch attention to the computer interface itself, the effect can be devastating to the thought process. The result can be the loss of all or most of the cognitive context that has been set up to solve the real task. After such an interruption, the train of thought must be reconstructed. Research on the effect of interruptions tells us that this can greatly reduce cognitive productivity (Cutrell, Czerwinski, & Horvitz, 2000; Field & Spence, 1994).

Visualizations and Mental Images

People can, to some extent, build diagrams in their heads without the aid of external inputs. These mental images are important because the mental operations involved in reasoning with visualizations very often involve combinations of mental imagery and external imagery.

The following are key properties of mental images:

- Mental images are transitory, maintained only by cognitive effort and rapidly fading without it (Kosslyn, 1990).

- Only relatively simple images can be held in mind, at least for most people. Kosslyn (1990) had subjects add more and more imaginary bricks to a mental image. What they found was that people were able to imagine four to eight bricks and no more. Because the bricks were all identical, however, it is almost certain that the limit he found would have been smaller for more complex objects—for example, a red triangle, a green square, a blue circle.

- People are able to form mental images of aggregations, such as a pile of bricks. This partially gets around the problem of the small number of items that can be imagined.

- Operations can be performed on mental images. Individual parts can be translated, scaled or rotated, and added, deleted, or otherwise altered (Shepard & Cooper, 1982).

- People sometimes use visual imagery when asked to perform logical problems (Johnson-Laird, 1983). For example, a person given the statement, "Some swans are black", might construct a mental image containing an aggregation of white dots (as a chunk representing swans) and a mental image of one or two black dots.

- Visual imagery uses the same neural machinery as normal seeing, at least to some extent. Studies using functional magnetic resonance imaging (fMRI) of the brain and conducted while subjects carried out various mental imaging operations have shown that parts of the visual system are activated. This includes activations of the primary visual cortex (Kosslyn & Thompson, 2003).

Because no one doubts that mental imagery originates at higher level visual centers, this suggests top-down activation, with the lower levels providing a kind of canvas on which mental images are formed.

- Mental imagery can be combined with external imagery as part of the visual thinking process. This capability includes mental additions and deletions of parts of a diagram (Massironi, 2004; Shimojima & Katagiri, 2008). It also includes the mental labeling of diagram parts. Indeed, the mental attribution of meaning to parts of diagrams is fundamental to the perception of diagrams; this is how a network of dots and lines can be understood as communications links between computers. Cognitive relabeling can also occur, however. When thinking about the robustness of a network, for example, a communications engineer might imagine a state where a particular link in a diagram becomes broken.

Object Files, Coherence Fields, and Gist

In Chapter 8, we introduced the term *object file* from Kahneman, Treisman, and Gibbs (1992) to describe the grouping of visual and verbal attributes into a single entity held in working memory. Now we shall consider the needs of cognition in action and argue that considerably richer bundles of information come into being and are held briefly, tying together both perception and action.

Providing context for an object that is perceived is the gist of a scene. Gist is used mainly to refer to the properties that are pulled from long-term memory as the image is recognized. Visual images can activate both visual and verbal-propositional gist in as little as 100 msec (Potter, 1976). Gist consists of both visual information about the typical structure of objects and their environment, including predictions of the likely behaviors of objects. The gist of a scene contains a wealth of general information that can help guide our actions, so that when we see a familiar scene, for example, a densely populated shopping place, a visual framework of the typical locations of things will be activated, as well as the likely behaviors of the people and things in our field of view.

Rensink (2002) developed a model that ties together many of the components we have been discussing. This is illustrated in Fig. 11.9. At the lowest level are the elementary visual features that are processed in parallel and automatically. These correspond to elements of color, edges, motion, and stereoscopic depth. From these elements, prior to focused attention, low-level precursors of objects, called protoobjects, exist in a continual state of flux. At the top level, the mechanism of attention forms different visual objects from the protoobject flux. Note that Rensink's protoobjects are located at the top of his "low-level vision system." He is not very specific on the nature of protoobjects, but it seems reasonable to suppose that they have characteristics similar to the midlevel pattern perception processes in the three-stage model laid out earlier in this book. Also, they are highly influenced by top-down gist information from the environment.

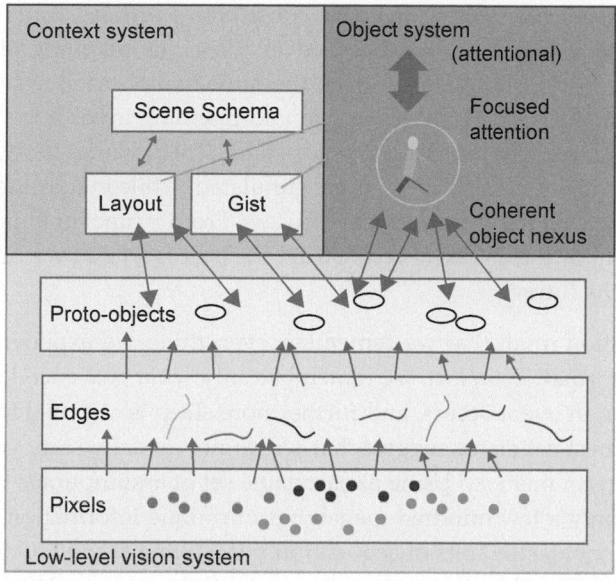

Figure 11.9 A summary of the components of Rensink's (2002) model of visual attention.

We can extend Rensink's model according to the theory of predictive cognition introduced earlier in this chapter. Protoobjects necessarily have links to executable predictive memory traces so task-specific information needed to support actions relating to visual objects is bound together with the objects themselves (Wheeler & Treisman, 2002). This broadens the concept of the object file still further by linking perception to action.

The notion of proto-objects in a continuous state of flux also suggests how visual displays can provide a basis for creative thinking, because they allow multiple visual interpretations to be drawn from the same visualization. Another way to think about this is that different patterns in the display become cognitively highlighted, as we consider different aspects of a problem.

Long-Term Episodic Memory and World Modeling

Long-term memory, like working memory, is distributed and specialized into subsystems dealing with every part of cognition, from low-level motor skills, such the control of finger movements, to the parts of the brain involved in high-level reasoning. In this section we are concerned with the kind of long-term memory supporting conscious recall of events—called *episodic memory* (Tulving, 1983). The newer view of episodic memory is that it is an active reconstruction of past events, and not at all like the playback of a movie. From the few hints that we can actually recall our brains construct a plausible story based on our accumulated knowledge of how the world works. Memory connections can easily become corrupted or misdirected; as a result, people often misremember events with a strong feeling of subjective certainty (Loftus & Hoffman, 1989). This leads to the notorious unreliability of eyewitness testimony.

The fact that episodic memory is an active constructive process, leads to the idea that the same cognitive machinery can be used in conscious planning of future actions (Schacter, Addis, & Buckner, 2007). Indeed the same neural machinery underlies each process (Buzsáki, 2015). Both episodic recall and planning involve the construction of scenarios starting from some basis of memory and a lot of world knowledge. The only difference is that in one case past events are simulated, while in the other, future events are simulated by a similarly constructive process. From a functional point of view the biological reason for the ability to reconstruct the past is so that we can operate more successfully in the future.

There is a common myth that we remember everything we experience but we lose the indexing information; in fact, we remember only what gets encoded in the first 24 hours or so after an event occurs, and furthermore sleep is essential for memory consolidation. The best estimates suggest that we do not actually store very much information in long-term memory. Using a reasonable set of assumptions, Landauer (1986) estimated that only a few hundred megabytes of unique information are stored over a lifetime. This equates to 2 bits of acquisition per waking second. Other much larger estimates are based on the number of synapses in the brain (e.g., 240×10^{12} for the cortex, Koch 1999) and evidence that they can each encode four levels of information (2 bits). But the larger estimates assume that every connection is devoted to lossless storage. The actual number is likely to be orders of magnitude smaller because thousands of synaptic connections are channeled into the firing of a single neuron. In any case, the amount is small in relation to modern computer capacity which leads to the obvious conclusion that computers and the internet should be viewed as enormous cognitive prostheses augmenting human memory.

Concepts

Human long-term memory can be usefully characterized as a network of linked concepts (Collins & Loftus, 1975; Yufic & Sheridan, 1996). Once a concept is activated and brought to the level of working memory, other related concepts become partially activated; they are primed and ready to be used in ongoing cognition. Our intuition supports this model. If we think of a particular concept—for example, data visualization—we can easily bring to mind a set of related concepts: computer graphics, perception, data analysis, potential applications. Each of these concepts is linked to many others.

The network model makes it clear why some ideas are more difficult to recall than others. Concepts and ideas that are distantly related naturally take longer to find; it can be difficult to trace a path to them and easy to take wrong turns in traversing the concept net, because no map exists. For this reason, it can take minutes, hours, or even days to retrieve some ideas. A study by Williams and Hollan (1981) investigated how people recalled names of classmates from their high school graduating class, 7 years later. They continued to recall names for at least 10 hours, although the number of falsely remembered names also increased over time. What about purely visual long-term memory? It does not appear to contain the same kind of network of abstract concepts that characterizes verbal long-term memory; however, there may be some rather specialized structures in visual scene memory. Evidence for this comes from studies showing that we identify objects more rapidly in the right context, such as bread in a kitchen (Palmer, 1975). The power of images is that they rapidly evoke verbal-propositional memory traces; we see a cat and a whole host of concepts associated with cats become activated. Images provide rapid evocation of the semantic network, and predictive behaviors (Intraub & Hoffman, 1992; Hobeika, Diard–Detoeuf, Garcin, Levy, & Volle, 2016).

Information in memory is highly structured in overlapping and interconnected ways. The term *chunk* and the term *concept* are both used in cognitive psychology to denote important units of stored information. The two terms are used interchangeably here. The process of grouping simple concepts into more complex ones is called *chunking*. A chunk can be almost anything: a mental representation of an object, a plan, a group of objects, or a method for achieving some goal. The process of becoming an expert in a particular domain is largely one of creating effective high-level concepts or chunks. Chunks of information are continuously being prioritized, and to some extent reorganized, based on the current cognitive requirements (Anderson & Milson, 1989).

Knowledge Formation

It has long been recognized that consolidation of information into long-term memory only occurs when active processing is done to integrate the new information with existing knowledge (Craik & Lockhart, 1972). Although there are different kinds of long-term memory stored in different areas of the brain, there is a specialized structure in the midbrain called the hippocampus (Small et al., 2001) that is critical to all episodic memory consolidation. If people have damage in this area they lose the ability to form new long-term memories, although they retain ones they had from before the damage. It has been shown that sleep is important in the longer term retention of information (Chambers, 2017). During sleep, information is reorganized, into more efficient cognitive chunks, and less useful information is lost. This is the case for both visual and nonvisual information.

The dominant theory about how long-term memories are physically stored is that they are traces—neural pathways made up of strengthened synaptic connections between the hippocampus and areas of the cortex specialized for different kinds of information. Recall consists of the activation of a particular pathway (Dudai, 2014). So, working memory consists of activated circuits that are embodiments of long-term memories. This explains the phenomenon that visual recognition is far superior to recall. As visual information is processed through the visual system, it activates the long-term memory traces of visual objects that have previously been processed by the same system. In recognition, a visual memory trace is being reawakened. In recall, it is necessary for us to actually describe some pattern, by drawing it or using words, but we only have very limited access to the memory trace. In any case, the memory trace will not generally contain sufficient information for reconstructing an object. Recognition only requires enough information that an object can be differentiated from other objects.

The memory trace theory also explains priming effects; if a particular neural circuit has recently been activated, it becomes easier to activate again, hence it is primed for reactivation. It is much easier to recall something that we have recently had in working memory. Seeing an image will prime subsequent recognition so we identify it more rapidly the next time (Bichot & Schall, 1999).

> **[G11.5]** Consider using thumbnail images in use user interfaces to take advantage of the efficiency of recognition memory.

One theory of the way concepts are formed and consolidated into long-term memories is through repeated associations between events in the world, establishing or strengthening neural pathways. This is called the *Bayesian* approach, after the famous originator of this essentially statistical theory. Bayes' law describes the probabilities of events based on prior known probabilities. Applying this to brain processing (Clark, 2013), the brain encodes prior knowledge (as probabilities) in neurons, which in turn make predictions about future events. As more information is received neural connections are modified, accordingly. This theory can account for much of the low-level pattern learning that occurs in the brain.

The majority of high-level concept learning, however, occurs on a single exposure, ruling out a statistical theory that relies on many repeated cooccurrences to build connections. An alternative to the Bayesian theory is the idea that new concepts are built on existing concepts, and ultimately all are derived from models gleaned from our early interactions with the physical world. This theory allows for single event learning of new concepts, something that should not happen according to Bayesian theory, but which is commonly observed in studies of infants. According to this view, concepts are tied to the sensory modality of the formative experiences. In particular, causal concepts are generally based on a kind of approximate modeling based on everyday physics. Wolff (2007) calls this the *physicalist* theory. A basic assumption of physicalist theories is that physical causation is cognitively more basic than non-physical causation, such as social or psychological causal factors. Supporting this is evidence that our ability to perceive physical causation first develops in infants at around three to 4 months, earlier than the ability to perceive social causation, which occurs around six to 8 months (Cohen et al., 1998). In addition, Wolff (2007) showed that a dynamics model is accepted as a representation of social causation. Also, linguists such as Pinker (2007) and Lakoff and Johnson (1980) point to the enormous richness of concrete spatial and temporal metaphors in thought, as revealed by language, showing that highly abstract concepts are often based on concepts that have a basis in the spatial and temporal physics of everyday life. Visual spatial metaphors are embodied in many conceptualizations of time. Mechanistic spatial metaphors are also important in very abstract conceptualization. For example, one argument is said to *rest on*, or be *supported* by another.

Knowledge Generalization

Once we take the position that novel concepts are based on a scaffolding of existing concepts, the critical question becomes how and under what circumstances does this occur? A study by Goldstone and Sakamoto (2003) applied the physicalist theory to show how even a very abstract concept can be generalized. They studied the problem of teaching a powerful class of computer algorithms called *simulated annealing*. These borrow a metaphor from the field of metallurgy and make use of controlled randomness to solve problems. These methods are also based on another metaphoric idea called *hill climbing*, which we need to understand first. In hill climbing a problem space is imagined metaphorically as a terrain with hills and valleys. The best solution is the top of the highest peak. Goldstone actually inverted the metaphor and considered the best solution to be the bottom of the deepest hollow, the lowest point on the terrain. The hill climbing method involves starting at some random point in the problem space and moving upward. The valley descending counterpart involves finding a random point and moving downward—think of a marble rolling down small hill. In either case, a problem with this algorithm is that the marble can get stuck in a small local valley—not the best solution.

To help students understand how simulated annealing can help with hill climbing, Goldstone and Sakamoto gave students the interface shown in Fig. 11.10. Red dots rained downward and when they hit the green hills they slid down into the valleys. The result, as shown, is that most of the dots find the best solution at the bottom of the deepest valley, but some get stuck in a smaller valley that is less than optimal. Students could improve the success rate with a slider that caused a controlled amount of randomness to be injected. In this case, the red dots bounced when they hit the terrain, in a random direction, with the amount of scattering being determined by the slider. Students were able to learn through this interactive interface how the best solutions came about by starting with a lot of randomness (the dots bounced a lot) and then decreasing it over time. This is how simulated annealing works.

But, could they generalize the knowledge and apply it to a different task? In order to measure knowledge transfer, they had students try to solve a very different problem, finding the best path between two points in a space filled with obstacles. This second problem is illustrated in Fig. 11.11. In this example, the students were told that the random points were connected in an underlying (not visible) linked list and spring forces pulled adjacent points together. Simply pulling the points would not result in a solution because they could get stuck on the obstacles that fill the space. The addition of randomness, through simulated annealing, can solve this problem, too.

One of the student participants said:

> *Sometimes the balls get stuck in a bad configuration. The only way to get them unstuck is to add randomness to their movements. The randomness jostles them out of their bad solution and gives them a chance to find a real path.*

Goldstone and Sakamoto showed that students were able to transfer knowledge from one problem to another thereby gaining a deeper understanding. They also found

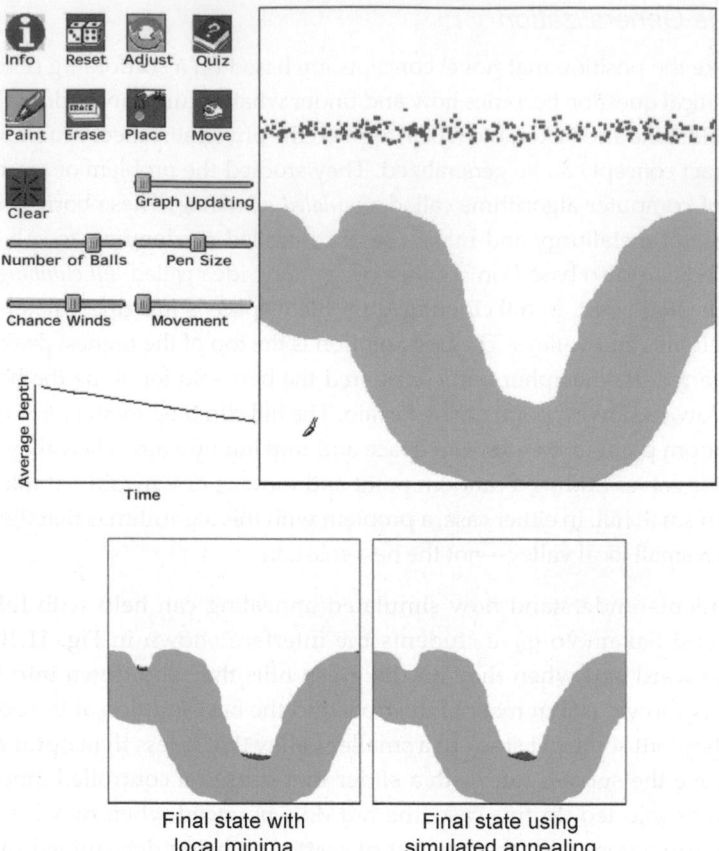

Figure 11.10 Screens from a user interface designed to teach students the concept of simulated annealing. (*From Goldstone and Sakamoto (2003). Reproduced with permission.*)

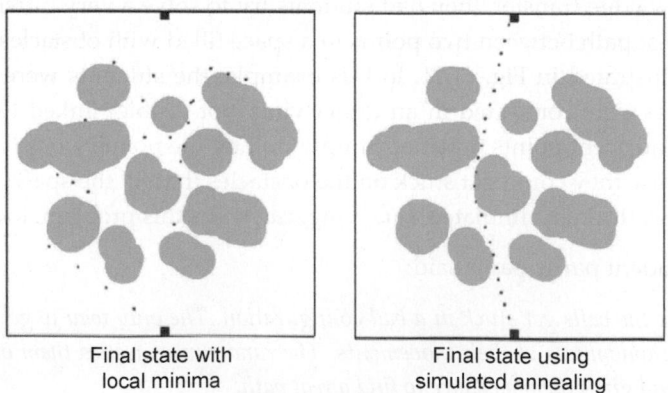

Figure 11.11 Finding a path through a set of obstacles can also be done through simulated annealing. (*From Goldstone and Sakamoto (2003). Reproduced with permission.*)

other interesting things. For the students with weaker understanding, greater transfer was obtained if there were more superficial differences between the two simulations (to achieve this, color similarities were removed). Another experiment showed that a certain degree of abstraction helped. If soccer balls were used instead of abstract points, knowledge transfer was reduced.

> **[G11.6]** Consider using visual analogies based on simple mechanistic physics to teach abstract concepts.

Cognitive Biases and Automatic Processing

Kahneman and Egan (2011) argue that we have two different systems of cognition: a quick response system and a slower more analytic system. The quick response system uses strong learned pathways in the brain, whereas the slow system is based on the episodic memory-bases scenario testing mechanisms introduced earlier.

We need the fast system for many situations where decision-making must be rapid. But the fast system is prone to biases. One of these is *confirmation bias*. We tend to only perceive evidence in support of strongly held beliefs. Another common bias effect is *anchoring*. We tend to overweight the most recent evidence available. For example, if people are first asked, "Are there more or less than 25 countries in Africa?", when they are subsequently asked "How many countries in Africa are there?", they are likely to guess in the vicinity of 25. If they are first asked "Are there more or less than 50 countries in Africa?" they are likely to guess in the vicinity of 50, a much more accurate answer.

A related bias is the *overestimation of the importance of small samples*. Part of this is a lack of information, part is a *recency* effect. For example, most people think that assault weapons brought into schools are a bigger hazard to children than handguns everywhere, but 1300 children are killed by (mostly) handguns each year in the US, while fewer than 10 are killed each year in school shootings, which get all the publicity. People are not optimal statisticians and so even though it is useful to think of the brain as a Bayesian operator it is one which is heavily biased in that it over weights both small samples and recent information.

Another cognitive bias is *loss aversion*. People avoid games where they are equally likely to lose 10 dollars or win 15 dollars, even though over many games they will come out ahead. The amygdala, a midbrain structure involved in processing of rewards and emotions in general, seems to be involved in this (De Martino, 2010). People who have damage to their amygdalas showed unbiased responding.

Sensemaking with Cognitive Tools

To this point this chapter has been aimed mostly at developing a general overview of human cognitive processes. We now consider how cognition occurs with visualizations being employed as cognitive tools beginning in this chapter with the overall process of discovering meaning and continuing in the final chapter with more detailed processes.

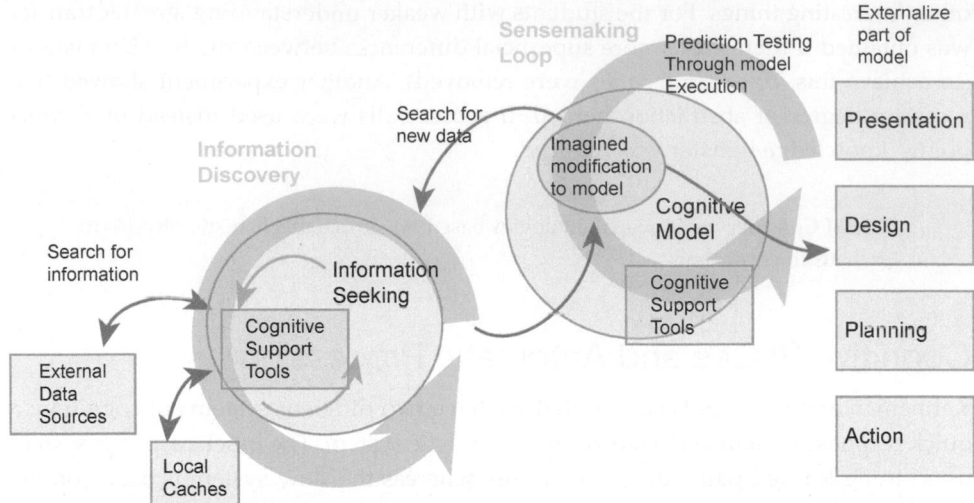

Figure 11.12 The overall goal of exploratory visualization is sensemaking. The purpose is improvements in the executable mental models we develop to understand the world.

Sensemaking is a term applied to the process whereby meaning is constructed through data analysis. Sensemaking provides a broad process framework in which many of the more specialized analytic tasks reside (Pirolli & Card, 2005).

Our brains construct mental models enabling us to perform different kinds of simulation tasks and these models can be made much more powerful if linked to computer-based tools and their embedded algorithms. For example, our model of route planning is likely linked to the use of Google maps as a tool. Our model of business planning is linked to the use of spreadsheet projections with embedded graphs, or some more sophisticated business intelligence software. Our model of engineering design is linked to CAD software. Our model of shopping is linked to the use of e-commerce web sites. Tellingly, all of these include visualization as a core component of the interface between the human and the computer components. Such distributed cognitive systems models enable users to predict both the consequences of their own actions and the consequences of the actions of others and thereby to act effectively in the world.

The process of sensemaking is illustrated in Fig. 11.12. It has two broad categories of cognitive processes, information discovery and sensemaking itself. These are highly interlinked and each has many cognitive subprocesses. The first stage is information discovery, sometimes called *foraging*. This involves "processes aimed at seeking information, searching and filtering it, and reading and extracting information" (Pirolli & Card, 2005).

In large-scale data analytics a key part of information discovery is called *data wrangling* or *data marshalling*. This involves getting data which is often messy, incomplete, or which is stored in a variety of formats into a mode where the data can be ingested into the tools used in the sensemaking loop.

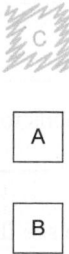

Figure 11.13 Blocks A and B are drawn on the paper. The yellow irregular line represents an imagined block, C.

The second big loop in Fig. 11.12 is sensemaking itself which has the goal of developing a mental model in the mind of the analyst that accounts for the evidence and can be applied to some analytic problem. This sounds quite formal and technical, but the same processes apply to both large-scale analytics carried out in business and government decision making and shopping online for a gas barbeque.

Finally, the purpose of sensemaking, like all cognition, is action in the world, and the outputs have many forms, including the presentation of results to others, a new engineering design put into production, a plan of action to be executed later, or a direct action of some kind, such as a purchase or a directive to some other agent.

Reasoning with a Hybrid of Visual and Mental Imagery

Almost all visual thinking is a process of reasoning where external imagery is combined with mental imagery. We see a visual representation of data and we mentally project meaning onto it. For example, a line on a social network diagram is "seen as" a communication channel. We may also imagine additions to what is represented. Mental imagery is used to represent alternative interpretations or possible additions to an external visualization. Visual queries are executed on the combined external/internal image.

Sometimes mental images can be combined with an external diagram, which enables visual queries to be executed on the combined external/internal image. An experiment by Shimojima and Katagiri (2008) illustrates this. They showed subjects a simple block diagram containing blocks labeled A and B, with block A above block B, as shown in Fig. 11.13. Next, they told the subjects to consider the case of another block, C, that was above block A. Finally, they asked them the question, "Is block C above or below block B?"

This reasoning task could be carried out using logic and the rule of transitivity which applies to relative height. If (A>B) and (C>A) it follows that (C>B). But, in fact, people solve the problem perceptually. The experiment was carried out using equipment to monitor subjects' eye movements, and it was found that when subjects were asked to perform this task they looked up into the blank space above block B as if they were imagining a block there. They were acting as if they could "see" block C above block

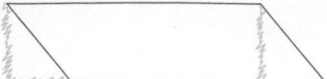

Figure 11.14 The imagined (yellow) additions to the parallelogram suggest a method for calculating the area of a parallelogram.

A. In their imaginations they could also see that block C was above block B. In other words, they solved the problem using a percept that was a hybrid of external information from the display with a visually imagined addition.

Another example comes from Wertheimer (1959), who studied children solving geometric problems. The children were asked to find a formula that could be used to calculate the area of a parallelogram. They already knew that the area of a rectangle is given by the width multiplied by the height, and they were given the drawing shown in Fig. 11.14. To solve this problem some of the students mentally imagined extra construction lines and were (according to Wertheimer) able to perceive a solution by examining the combined mental and actual image. They noticed that the parallelogram could be converted to a rectangle if a triangle were cut off from the right and placed on the left. This gave them the answer—the area of a parallelogram is also given by the width of its base times its height.

To generalize, all reasoning with diagrams involves perceiving task-relevant patterns in the display and mentally adding semantic attributes. Sometimes mental additions are made to the diagram, such as possible links that are not externally represented, and in these cases visual queries can be executed on the combined internal/external image to solve a problem.

The addition of mental imagery to external imagery has a great many variations. One of its limitations is our ability to mentally imagine additions to visualizations, and this is extremely restricted, at least for most people (Kosslyn, 1990). Because of this, much of the most flexible and creative visual thinking involves externalizing tentative solutions. This is called creative sketching, and we deal with it next.

Design Sketching

An excellent example of the visual thinking process is design sketching using pencil and paper as cognitive tools. Sketching on paper, a blackboard or a tablet computer is fundamental to the creative process of most artists, designers, and engineers. There is a huge difference between creative sketching and the production of a finished drawing. Creative sketches are thinking tools primarily composed of rapidly drawn lines that are mere suggestions of meaning (Kennedy, 1974; Massironi, 2004), whereas finished drawings are polished recordings of fully developed ideas.

Sketches can be considered as externalizations of mental imagery. Someone who begins a sketch is literally trying to represent on paper something he has imagined. Because of the limitations of visual imaging (Kosslyn, 1990), what can be mentally imaged is

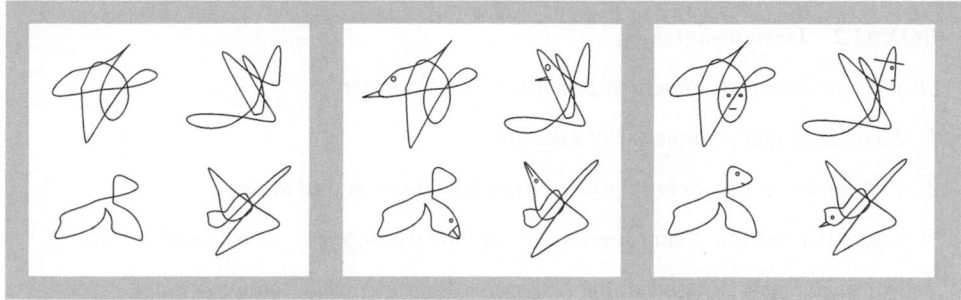

Figure 11.15 The metamorphosis of scribbles. (*From Ware (2009), based on a concept by Massironi (2004). Reproduced with permission.*)

quite simple. If something, however crude, that represents a mental image can be put down as a sketch, then further elements can be mentally imaged as additions to what is already on the paper.

Sketches benefit from the abstract nature of lines. A line can represent an edge, a corner, or the boundary of a color region, as well as something quite abstract, such as the flow of people in a large store. Lines on the paper can be reinterpreted to have different meanings. A scribbled area on the sketch of a garden layout can be changed from lawn to patio to vegetable garden, simply by an act of imagination. The psychologist Massironi (2004) invented an exercise that dramatically illustrates the ease with which the brain can interpret lines in different ways. First draw a scribble on a piece of paper—a single line with three or four large loops should be sufficient. Next, try to turn the scribble into a bird simply by adding a "<" and an "o." In a surprising number of instances, the meaningless loops will become resolved into heads and wings and the result will be very satisfactory birds (see Fig. 11.15).

The creative sketching algorithm is set out in Box 11.2. It involves a cycle in which concepts are externalized through marks on paper and then interpreted through analytic visual queries. Additions or deletions are mentally imaged so as to provide a low-cost way of testing new concepts in the context of those already set down. Those that pass the test will result in new externalizations. Sketches themselves are disposable; starting over is always an option.

Architects are known to be prolific sketchers; Suwa and Tversky (1997) studied how they used sketches in the early stages of design. They found that a kind of analytic seeing was important and that there were often unintended consequences resulting from the placement of sketch lines. Sometimes these resulted in constructive solutions that had not been previously noticed.

An example of how sketching might be used in an architectural design project is given in Fig. 11.16. The site constrains the basic footprint of the building to the two rectangles that have been roughly scribbled, as shown in Fig. 11.16(a). The architect next imagines the main entrance in the center of the large rectangle, shown in Fig. 11.16(b), but immediately realizes that the space needed for an entrance hall and its associated ticket

---

BOX 11.2   *Design sketching*

Display environment: Paper and pencil or tablet computer.

1. *Mentally image some aspect of a design.*

2. *Put marks on display to externalize aspects of the imagined design.*

3. *Construct analytic visual queries to determine if design meets task requirements.*

4. *If a major flaw is found in the design as represented that cannot be easily fixed (by erasure or other graphical correction), discard sketch.*

5. *Mentally image design additions to the sketch and/or mentally reattribute the meaning of particular lines and other marks.*

6. *Execute visual queries to critically assess the value of mentally imaged additions in the context of existing sketch.*

7. *If mental additions are perceived as valuable, externalize by adding marks or by erasures.*

8. *Repeat from 5, revising the sketch, or discard the sketch and begin from 1.*

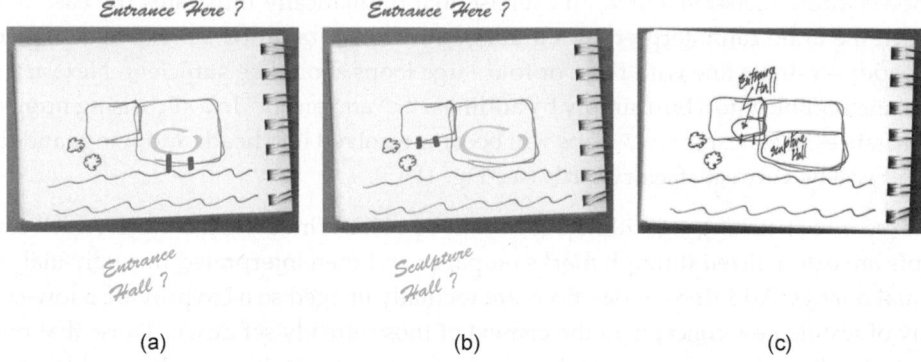

(a)   (b)   (c)

Figure 11.16 (a) The entrance is imagined on the right. (b) An alternative is imagined with an entrance on left. (c) The solution is externalized.

---

offices will conflict with the client's wish to have a great sculpture hall with windows looking out in that direction. The architect next imagines the entrance and entrance hall in the smaller rectangle and, because this works better, adds lines to externalize the concept.

For creativity to be supported, the medium used for design must afford tentative interactions. The lack of precision in quick, loose sketches actually allows for multiple interpretations. The sketches that people construct as part of the creative process are rapid, not refined, and readily discarded. Giving a child high-quality watercolor paper and paints is likely to inhibit creativity if the child is made aware of the expense and cautioned not to "waste" the materials. Schumann, Strotthotte, Raab, and Laser (1996) carried out an empirical study of architectural perspective drawings executed in three different styles: a precise line drawing, a realistically shaded image, and a sketch. All of the drawings contained the same features and level of detail. The sketch version was rated substantially higher on measures of ability to stimulate creativity, changes in design, and discussions.

Review of Visual Cognitive System Components

We conclude this chapter with a brief review of the components of the cognitive system to be considered in the construction of the efficient visual thinking tools and techniques discussed in the next chapter.

General Cognition

General cognition is carried out by a hierarchical system of predictors, operating from low-level pattern finding to high-level episodic model building. At the highest level visual thinking with visualization is distributed among in-the-head activities in the various centers of the brain. Important components of this system are the visual cortex for pattern identification, the forebrain for higher level thinking and concept formation, the midbrain structures of the hippocampus and amygdala for spatial planning, memory and motivation, and the motor cortex and cerebellum for movement planning and execution.

In functional terms, this the human brain operates with two distinct memory systems, working memory and long-term memory. Information in working memory is only transferred to long-term memory if it is cognitively acted on and this depends on its perceived importance. Sleep is also critical in rearrangement, grouping, and forgetting of long-term memory components.

Low-level pattern information is acquired by Bayesian processes, where large numbers of examples reinforce efficient sets of feature processes for common patterns in the world. At a higher level, other mechanisms support predictive scenario building and allow us to acquire information and concepts, sometimes in a single trial.

Working Memories

Working memories hold information briefly as a part of ongoing cognition and are a key bottleneck in cognition. Visual working memory can hold only a few simple patterns. Verbal working memory holds about 2 seconds of verbal or other acoustic information. Ongoing short-term cognitive plans also have a very limited capacity and may be said to constitute an additional form of memory.

Long-term Memory

The entire brain can be considered as a repository of executable long-term memory, since every neuron learns. Long-term episodic memory allows us to partially reconstruct past events and simulate future events.

Table 11.1 *Approximate Time to Execute Various Epistemic Actions.*

Epistemic Action	Approximate Time	Cognitive Effort
Attentional switch within a fixation	50 msec	Minimal
Saccadic eye movement	150 msec	Minimal
Hover queries	1 second	Medium
Selection	2 second	Medium
Hypertext jump	3 second	Medium
Zooming	2 second + log scale change	Medium
Virtual flying	30 second or more	High
Virtual walking	30 second or more	High

Visual Queries

A visual query is the formulation of a hypothesis pertaining to a cognitive task that can be resolved by means of the discovery, or failure to fine, of a visual pattern. The execution of visual queries involves eye movements planned using a task-weighted spatial map of protopatterns. Those patterns most likely to be relevant to the current task are scheduled for attention, beginning with the one weighted most significant. As part of this process, partial solutions are marked in visual working memory by setting placeholders in the egocentric spatial map. When our eyes alight on a region of potential interest, the information located there is processed serially. If we are looking for a simple visual shape among a set of similar shapes, the rate of processing is about 40 msec per item.

Epistemic Actions

Epistemic actions are actions intended to help in the discovery of information, such as mouse selections or zooming in on a target. The lowest cost epistemic action is eye movement. Eye movements allow us to acquire a new set of informative visual objects in 100–200 msec. Information acquired in this way will be integrated readily with other information that we have recently acquired from the same space. Thus, the ideal visualization is one in which all the information for visualization is available on a single high-resolution screen. The cost of navigating is only a single eye movement or, for large screens, an eye movement plus a head movement. Hover queries may be the lowest cost epistemic action. Hover queries cause extra information to pop up rapidly as the cursor moves over a series of data objects. No click is necessary. Table 11.1 provides a set of approximate values for the temporal cost of various types of epistemic actions. As a general principle, an interface design should aim for epistemic actions with low temporal and cognitive costs.

CHAPTER TWELVE

Designing Cognitively Efficient Visualizations

In this final chapter we outline a methodology for arriving at perceptually and cognitively efficient visualizations. We must acknowledge that this addresses only part of the design problem. It leaves out critical parts of the process, such as requirements discovery, discussed above, and how to use the many software tools designed for actually building visualizations. The reader is referred to other excellent texts for help with these practical problems of design—a list is given at the end of this chapter. What is offered here is an abstract view of design as a kind of universal process, while acknowledging that this process must be tempered by real world constraints. The whole purpose of this book has been to provide reasons, grounded in perception and cognition for making design choices. Here we present a basic high-level process for arriving at design solutions.

The Process

There are seven basic steps that are almost always part of any visualization design process. In most cases these steps should be part of a spiral design methodology, with multiple iterations. The steps are: 1) a high-level cognitive task description, 2) a data inventory, 3) cognitive task requirements analysis, 4) the identification of visualization types, 5) the identification and choice of cognitively efficient interaction methods, 6) prototyping and application, and 7) evaluation.

Information Visualization. https://doi.org/10.1016/B978-0-12-812875-6.00012-8

Step 1: High-Level Cognitive Task Description

At the start of the design process, team members must establish, in a general way, the problem to be solved by the final product. Initially, the description should not specify the implementation method so as not to prejudge the solution. Refinement and details will come later. The purpose of this step is to set out the broad goals for the new product. Examples of broad problem statements are "we need an interface to monitor Twitter to pull out information relevant to our business", "we need an improved way of showing wave and wind forecast information as an overlay on an electronic nautical chart", "we need to let people see the different ways they consume energy in their homes".

At this stage, the kind of cognitive tool being envisioned must be defined. For example, is it intended to support sensemaking, monitoring, design, or planning? Many applications involve several of these broad categories, but is it useful to understand which is the broad target.

Step 2: Data Inventory

The sooner a designer can become familiar with the data available for a planned application the better. Understanding data is basic to understanding what questions can be asked of it, and there is little point in designing a visualization for data that does not exist. Both the structure of the data and the semantics will be important in determining which type of visualization should be used. Data can be enormously varied in these properties but the following list contains some of the attributes that are likely to appear in any inventory.

Quantity. Very big data requires different approaches to medium or small data. In general, visualization cannot help directly with big data which must be filtered down to a manageable size. It is important, nevertheless, to understand the size of the overall problem.

Structure. The structure of the data should be described. For example, does it consist of hierarchically organized entities, map layers, a network, or multidimensional discreet records? Usually several of these types of data are present. Chapter 1 introduces the kinds of structures that may be used in visualization.

The semantics of interrelationships and interdependencies. This is distinct from structure. For example, we might have a social network data set describing the relationships between individuals. We might also have a georeferenced map data set describing how these individuals move about on a minute-by-minute basis. In this case the linkage between these data sets is through the individuals who are common to both.

Time to access. Sometimes real-time or near real-time access to data is critical to cognitive performance. In many cases, a major part of the value of a new visualization project will be decreasing the time to view.

Ease of access. We do not refer here to ease of access in the user interface sense, rather at this stage we need to know something about the technical difficulties that may be encountered in getting data. It is common for data to require new infrastructure to support visualization. There may be monetary costs involved in accessing third party data. Sometimes issues relating to security or confidentiality can be stumbling blocks.

Quality and reliability. It is often the case that data are messy and this may be for many reasons. Sometimes it is only collected intermittently. Sometimes different people or systems annotated it in different ways. Some data is inherently noisy because it is near the limits of the resolution of an instrument. The cost of collecting better data may be prohibitive. Clean standardized data is far easier to deal with, but we must know what we are actually faced with and design to cope where necessary.

Delivery infrastructure. Systems and online databases may exist for the delivery of data for a new visualization application or the project may require new infrastructure. Also, many visualizations rely on prior analytics and the tools that are available must be understood.

Available back-end processing tools. Tools for visualizing small data sets may stand alone, directly accessing the relevant data. Big data inevitably requires a suite of back end analytic tools with which the visualization software must interface.

Step 3: Cognitive Task Refinement

Once the data is understood, the set of tasks can be refined. As a general strategy it is useful to work top down, breaking down the overarching goal into more and more focused analytic questions. At this stage, it is also worth thinking hard about which parts of the analytic problem are likely to be amenable to solutions using visualization. Visualization is not the solution to every problem; for example, an automatic computer pattern search may be more appropriate for a task that is repetitive and standardized.

A good starting point for analytic tasks is to apply the "Who, What, Where, When, Why, and How" mantra of the investigative journalist. We can use these terms to break down the analytic goals into meaningful components, and as we shall see they can also help determine the kind of visualization that is appropriate.

Who, What

"Who" and "What" questions refer to the entities we are concerned with and the relationships between them. The important entities are determined by the problem and the data. Entities can be individuals or organizations, places such as buildings, or things such as vehicles. For some applications, the most important entities may be routers in a communications network. Entities can have attributes; for example, if people are the entities, attributes could their heights, weights, workplaces, and so on.

Frequently, visualization queries have to do with understanding complex systems of relationships. This is what we usually mean when we talk about discovering a pattern in a data set. There are an almost infinite number of possible relationships between entities and their various attributes. Some are structural relationships—a door is part of a house. Some are communications—Jane sent a message to Jack on the 30th of April. They can be abstract or very specific. Sometimes it is a matter of choice whether a piece of information is conceptualized as an attribute of an entity or a relationship between entities. For example, a home address can be an attribute of a person, or it can be a relationship between a person (an entity) and a building (another entity).

Where

"Where" relates to queries about location, or patterns of locations. The reason why we need to set geospatial queries into their own category is because maps are both the earliest visualizations and one of the most highly evolved. Most people have at least some understanding of how to read a map, unlike many other types of visualization.

When

"When" is similar to "Where" in that it is a particular kind of attribute of an entity. Questions of interest can involve single events in time or a series of events occurring over time—"Is the rate of gun violence increasing or decreasing?" Sometimes we may wish to know about a time interval—"How long did it take for the tank to empty?" Many entities can have both start and end times. Some kinds of data are continuous in time, for example, the temperature at a particular location. Often some kind of feature analysis is used to extract discrete events from the time series. As with spatial patterns, it is essential to determine where perceiving temporal patterns is important to our analytic task. In these cases, visualization is likely to be helpful.

How: Combinations of Who, What, Where, and When

Often, the value of visualization comes from the way it supports queries that require the integration "Who," "What," "Where," and "When" questions. This usually involves investigating relationships between entities. In some cases, we may need to discover how the patterns of events occur over time and space. For example, visualizations have been constructed to show the migration patterns of marine birds revealing how they aggregate in dense colonies for breeding then disperse around the world to feed. Or we may wish to understand the transportation patterns for business and recreational travelers. This will involve integrating both spatial and temporal information.

Broadly speaking, "How" questions relate to *relationships* between *entities*. How did information get from person to person? How are events linked to people and places? How did a certain set of events develop over time?

Why

The "Why" of visual thinking is about identifying the broad analytic objectives of a visualization. In the science domain, one broad goal is the facilitation of serendipitous discoveries, which often occur when a scientist notices a new pattern in a visual representation of data. More common goals are the clear presentation of results of experiments, or the monitoring of an experiment apparatus.

In the case of business analytics, the objective may be to understand overall trends in the marketplace, the distribution of sales by product group, or the ongoing needs of customers.

Understanding broad objectives leads to establishing overall design goals. For example, is the planned visualization tool intended to help with system monitoring, scientific discovery, or educating students?

Step 4: Identification of Appropriate Visualization Types

In step 4 we are finally ready to start thinking about design, how to take the data we have and the problems we want to solve and come up with an interactive visualization interface. For now, we are setting aside the discussion of the interaction methods and will get to them in Step 5.

Fortunately, most visualizations belong to only a few basic types: *charts, maps, node-link diagrams,* and *composites* of these, although there are many variants of each. Also, given the data inventory and the answers to the Who, What, Where, When, and How questions, the choice of one or more of types is usually clear. Table 12.1 summarizes how the common types of questions together with the type of data available, determine the visualization type. Following is a brief description to each type, with references back to the relevant chapters where more detail is provided.

Charts

Charts the most common types of visualization used in data analysis. They are always available in statistical packages and spreadsheets, or in more modern tools such as Tableau. Charts generally require table data as inputs; that is, data usually represented with an entity for each row and some number of columns for the attributes. Standard charts include time series plots, x-y scatterplots, frequency histograms, and various kinds of bar charts. Three basic types are illustrated here together with some of the common visual queries they are designed to support.

Bar Charts are used to illustrate the distribution of data in different categories. Two bar chart configurations are shown in Fig. 12.1. They provide examples of data values distributed according to two category sets and each has strengths and weaknesses. Both of the bar charts support reasoning about the cost of transportation, broken down into components for different income categories. The version in 1(a) is better

Table 12.1 *Common Questions for Data Visualization.*

Questions	Data Available	Visualization Type
Who, what type entity queries	Entities and their attributes	Glyphs representing attributes, either on a char or map.
Who, what statistical relationships between sets of entities	Entities and their scalar attributes	Chart such as a bar chart, scatterplot or enhanced scatterplot. Scatterplot matrix or parallel coordinates may be useful if data has many dimensions
Who what, network relationship queries	Network of relationships	Node-link diagram
Where	Spatial data	Map display
When	Time series data	Chart: Time series plot
How connectivity queries	Network data	Node-link diagram
How	Multiple data type: E.g. network and spatial	Composite visualization

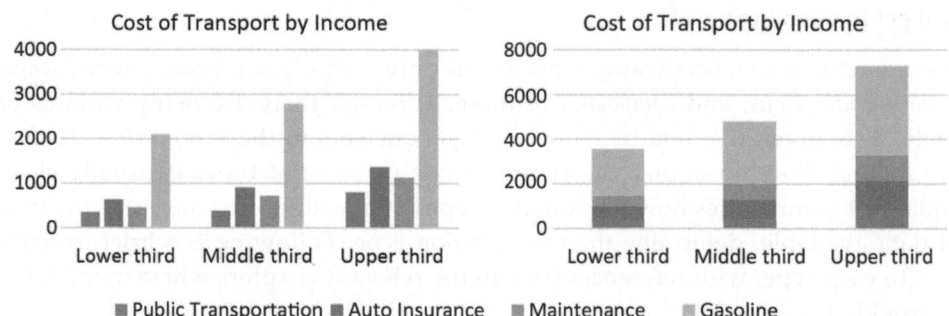

Figure 12.1 (a) The side by side bar chart is grouped by categories. It supports queries regarding the relative values within and across categories. (b) The stacked version supports queries about the sum of category values. It is less accurate for reading individual amounts.

for judging the actual quantities in the subcategories. The version in 1(b) is better for judging proportions; for example, we can see that gasoline consumption is about half the cost in each income group.

See Chapters 5 and 6 for an in-depth discussion of methods for representing quantities.

Scatter plots. Conventional 2D scatter plots provide a powerful method for examining the relationship between two variables. Two of the most common relationships of interests are correlations and clustering. Correlation indicates a relationship between variables, whereas clusters reveal groups. Both can lead to important insights. However, there are also a great range of other patterns that may be discovered.

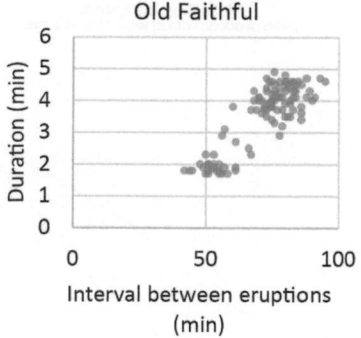

Figure 12.2 An example of a scatter plot.

The example shown in Fig. 12.2 shows the relationship between the duration of eruptions of the Old Faithful geyser in Yellowstone Park and the interval between them. It shows both a correlation and clustering. This is exactly the kind of visualization that would cause a scientist to build a theoretical model of the underground hydraulics which could lead to such a pattern.

While 2D scatter plots work well for comparisons between two variables, when there are more variables involved it is necessary to resort to other devices, including varying the color, size, or even motion of the points (Chapter 6). For five or more variables, methods include the generalized draftsman's plot and parallel coordinates (also Chapter 6).

Time series and other continuous variable plots. Time series plots are the most common way of supporting "When" queries. Usually time is represented by distance on the x-axis progressing from left to right. The y-axis provides the range of values of a variable of interest and continuous lines show how these values change through time. There are many variations some of which are discussed in Chapters 5 and 6. Fig. 12.3 is a sophisticated example illustrating the record low arctic sea ice seen in the fall of 2016. This curve represented in blue can be compared to the mean and the standard deviation over the years 1981–2010.

A tricky design problem occurs when many series must be compared. One solution to this problem is to use many small plots as illustrated in Fig. 12.4.

The reason for using time series graphs is to answer visual queries relating to temporal patterns. A common query is to compare trends: Is stock *A* doing better than stock *B*?

Another common task requirement is support for the discovery of anomalies or exceptional cases. Sometimes anomalies represent bad data, but in other cases, the anomaly is of critical importance as is the case in Fig. 12.3 where the anomaly is the greatly reduced amount of ice in the Arctic compared to the mean and standard deviation for previous years.

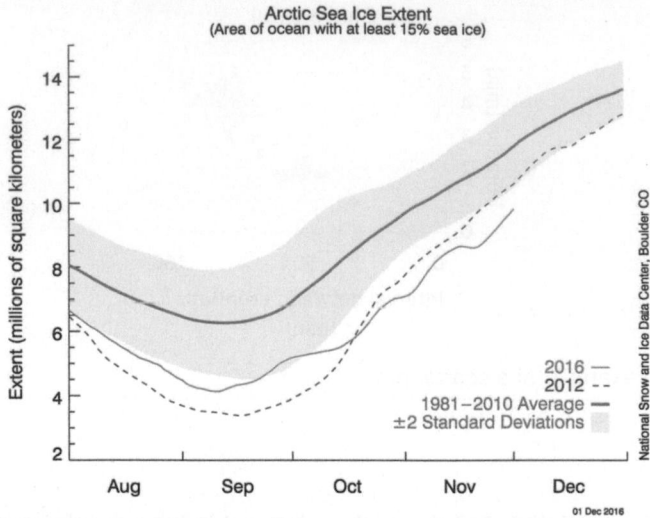

Figure 12.3 Arctic Ice Data. *(From National Snow and Ice Data Center* http://nsidc.org/arcticseaicenews/.)

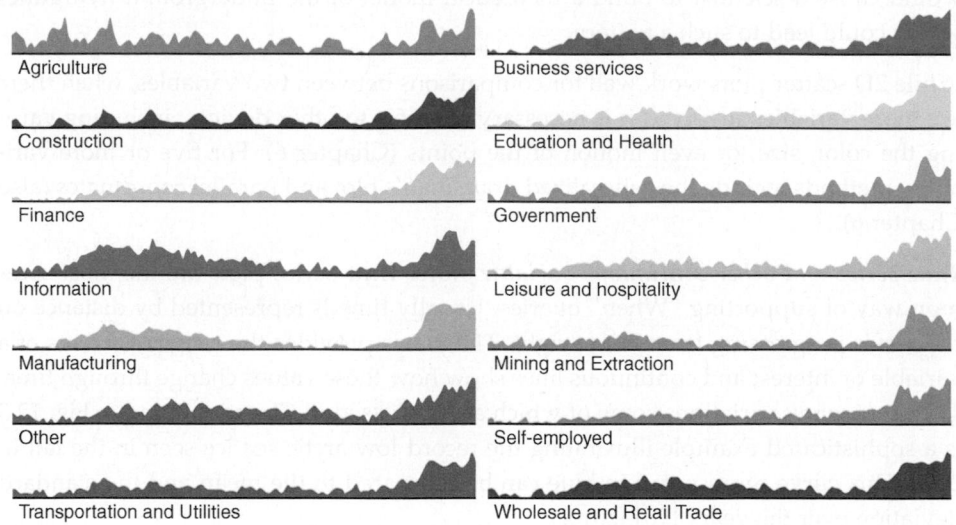

Figure 12.4 Time series plots can sometimes be useful even when very small. *(Courtesy of Jeff Heer.)*

Maps

A map is a display in which there is a spatial correspondence between layout of the original data and the way it is displayed. Three examples are given in Fig. 12.5 each from a very different application domain. We tend to take maps for granted, but they are far from being images of data. Most maps use symbol sets carefully designed to meet the requirements of spatial layout. The difficulty in map design comes from the inherent conflict between using symbols which have a size and shape, not related to

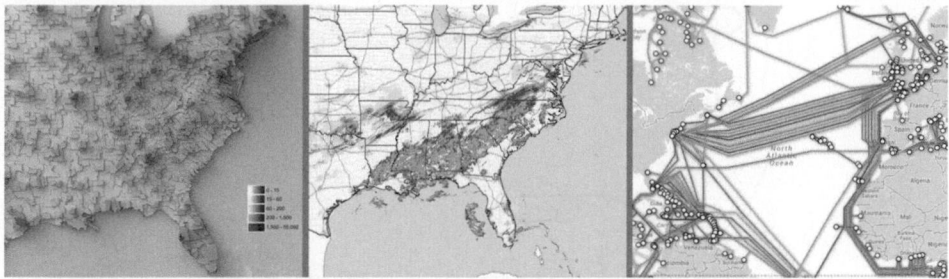

Figure 12.5 Three very different maps. Left Population Density map with raised prisms and soft shadows. *(From Stewart & Kennelly (2010). Used with permission.)*

the spatial context (for example, a line representing a road where the line thickness does not represent the road width, and the line color represents the class of road) and aspects of the map that are spatial. Most maps are 2D, but in scientific visualization, examples of 3D data maps are common; for example, a model of a 3D hurricane may be displayed in 3D using techniques such as volume rendering.

Many maps are hybrids of purely spatial information and other kinds of information contained in overlaid symbols. For example, the map on the right in Fig. 12.5 combines spatial layout with a network diagram.

Geospatial data is important for many applications, from transportation, to mining, to climate and weather. In many cases the designer must contend with established conventions for symbols, textures, and colors. This results in the usual tradeoffs between the advantages of using symbols which some of the users are already familiar with and what may be a more optimal design for a particular application.

The key indicator for the use of a map in a visualization is the need to support spatial pattern queries, although not all geospatial data requires the use of a map. If, for example, we only need to know certain statistics for a list of a few well-known major cities, a map may not be needed and a list may suffice. Many climate scientists are concerned about the south to north transport of heat by deep and shallow ocean currents, but they do not ask for a map of these currents. They only need to know the numerical value as predicted by different climate models.

Perceptual and cognitive issues relating to 2D map design are covered mostly in Chapters 4, 5 and 6 and 7 addresses 3D map design.

Network Diagrams

In a typical network diagram, entities are displayed as nodes and relationships are displayed as links (usually lines) connecting the nodes. Network diagrams are obvious choices for the visualization of many kinds of data, including social networks, communication networks, and biological networks, such as the metabolic pathways in cells. One point which is often underappreciated is that in many cases there is a choice between representing relationships as a network diagram or a Euler diagram.

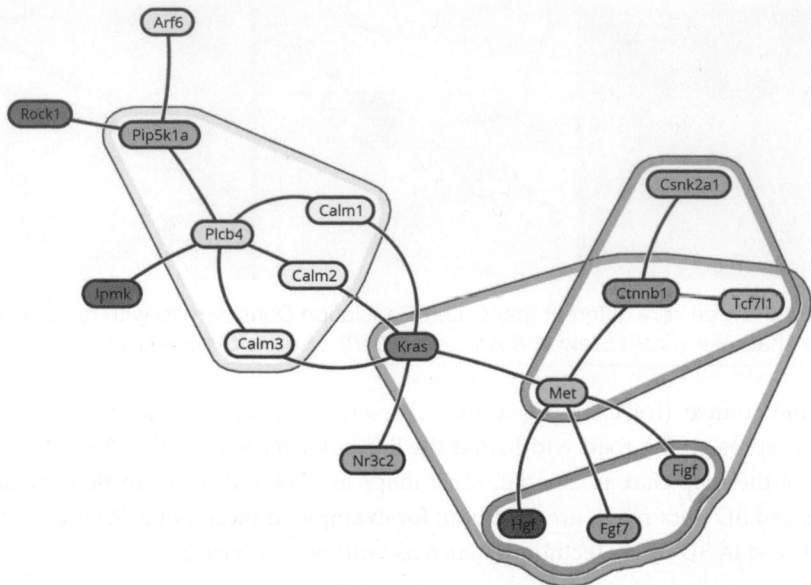

Figure 12.6 A hybrid of a Network diagram, and an Euler diagram. *(Courtesy of Alexander Pico.)*

Euler diagrams can often be clearest if the nodes can be classified into a small number of overlapping sets. Network diagrams are best when the node degree (number of connected neighbors) is small. In some cases, Euler and network diagrams can be combined, with some relationships denoted by lines surrounding sets of nodes, as in a Euler diagram and other relationships defined by explicit links. Fig. 12.6 shows an example. A useful review covering the visualization of diagrams representing sets is provided by Alsallakh et al. (2014, pp. 1–21).

Issues relating to perception of both network and Euler diagrams are discussed mainly in Chapter 6. Chapters 4 and 5 contain information relevant to creating visually distinctive nodes and links.

Composites

Many visualization problems require multiple types of diagram. Sometimes they are constructed so that they fill the same space. For example, a road map is a hybrid between a map and network diagram, with the map providing spatial layout and the roads defining a network topology. A particular kind of composite is a "Dashboard" this is a display constructed to monitor critical information relating to a business, or engineering plant. In chemical plant, the dashboard might show the rate of flow through critical valves, temperatures in reaction chambers, as well as plant output.

Many visualizations are composites in a less-integrated sense. They contain different frames including, for example, a map, a scatterplot, and a time series plot. What makes them a single visualization is that they are linked through one or more of the interactive methods that we discuss in the final part of this chapter.

To summarize the main point of this section, even though the number of visualization designs is enormous, most visual query requirements can be satisfied by one or more of the basic types: charts, maps, network diagrams, tables, or combinations of these. Of course, there are many flavors of each type and in the cases of charts and maps there are whole subfields devoted to their design. At the end of this chapter some pointers to this extensive literature are provided.

Step 5. Applying Visual Thinking Design Patterns for Cognitive Efficiency

Each of the basic types of visualization described above can show only a small amount of data. By adding interaction, the amount of data that can be usefully visualized can be greatly increased, sometimes by a few orders of magnitude. The remainder of this chapter covers the most common interactive techniques, highlighting the perceptual and cognitive issues associated with each one.

In the previous chapter we covered the process of visual thinking in distributed cognitive systems, wherein humans and computers form a cognitive unit with a visualization as the interface. In the following sections we cover much of the same material in a more practical, design-oriented fashion. What follows are descriptions of some of the more common interactive methods applicable to data visualization. These are presented as a set of *Visual Thinking Design Patterns* (Ware, Wright, & Pioch, 2013). Visual thinking design patterns (VTDPs) take their inspiration from Alexander's design patterns (Alexander, Ishikawa, & Silverstein, 1977) intended for architects as well as designed patterns used by software engineers (Gamma et al., 1995). Design patterns are intended to provide an accessible and structured method for combining knowledge about interaction methods and visualization designs together with cognitive and perceptual principles. Like their precedents, they are intended to describe best practice examples of solutions to design problems where interactive visualization a necessary component.

VTDPs provide a method for taking into account perceptual and cognitive issues especially key bottlenecks in the visual thinking process, such as limited visual working memory capacity. They also provide a way of reasoning about semiotic issues in perceptual terms via the concept of the visual query. The set of design patterns presented in the remainder of this chapter is by no means complete. Others, such as the kinds of interactive plotting of data from spreadsheets and other analytic tools such as Tableau, Qlikview, or MS Power BI, are too diverse and varied to be captured in a short treatment.

It would also be remiss not to point out that there are other methodologies for incorporating cognitive principles into design. About 3 decades ago the GOMS (goals, operators, methods, and selection rules) model (Card, Moran, & Newell, 1983) was introduced and more sophisticated approaches have followed in the form of the ACT-R (Anderson, 2007; Anderson, Matessa, & Lebiere, 1997) model and EPIC (Kieras & Meyer, 1997) cognitive modeling systems. These systems provide executable cognitive models, containing timings for cognitive computations and as well as for common interactions such as mouse movements. However, in order to use these models as part of a design process a proposed interface must be designed in detail and executed in a simulation that includes both cognitive operations and how the behavior or the computer application. This is beyond the capabilities of all but a few specialized centers. Set against this is the need for agile design based on rapid prototyping, possibly the most common design methodology. Visual thinking patterns provide the basic knowledge needed for the agile approach.

A visual thinking design pattern typically contains the following components. Not all patterns will contain all of the components:

1) *Problem Statement.* A statement of the problem to be solved, together with one or more examples of use cases.

2) *General Cognitive Operations.* Visual thinking usually involves combining mental imagery and perceived external symbols in working memory. A key bottleneck in cognitive processing is the capacity of visual working memory, which is usually a maximum of four simple patterns or shapes if the patterns are previously unknown. If patterns are well known, a skilled analyst can hold more complex patterns in working memory as coded chunks.

3) *Visual Queries.* A visual query is one of the most critical cognitive operations in visual thinking. It involves the transformation of some aspect of a problem into visual pattern search. Understanding visual queries is the key to detailed display design. A good design is one that supports efficient visual query execution.

4) *Visual Pattern Processing. A* visual pattern is the target of a visual query. The goal of efficient graphic design is to ensure that data is mapped into graphical form in such a way that all probable visual queries can be efficiently executed.

5) *Epistemic Actions.* Epistemic actions are any actions designed to seek information. Interactive visualization works via specialized computer support for epistemic actions, such as zooming, or clicking on an object to obtain more information.

6) *Interaction Computation.* This includes all parts of a visual thinking algorithm that are executed in a computer. Of particular relevance to VTDPs are computations involved in rapidly changing how information is displayed such as zooming or changing the range of the data that is displayed with a time-slider.

7) *Externalizing.* These are instances where the user saves some knowledge gained by putting it out into the world. Examples are adding annotations to a visualization or checking boxes to indicate that certain information is deemed important or irrelevant.

8) *Data budget.* A data budget is the size of the data which can be usefully reasoned with by means of an interactive visualization.

The remainder of this chapter is devoted to some of the most common and effective design patterns used in interactive visualization. There are many variations on this basic set as well as refinements for particular application domains. Anyone using these patterns should use them as a starting point for reasoning about a design solution rather than as templates. Many of the design patterns can be part of a broader pattern of sensemaking discussed in the previous chapter.

Visual Monitoring

The term monitoring is used when an operator is responsible for maintaining a level of awareness of some system or situation. Monitoring has been studied extensively for the design of control room displays used with power distribution networks, factory processes, and controls for complex vehicles such as aircraft. Monitoring panels, called information dashboards, are increasingly used in business. The use of monitoring in visual analytics may require a more flexible, dynamic approach since what is being monitored will change more frequently than for these other applications.

> *Example 1:* A business executive uses a dashboard to display check recent sales figures by region and aspects of the supply pipeline.

> *Example 2:* A technician in a chemical factory is required to monitor the ongoing state of flow through pipes, pressure levels and various other processes to ensure that the plant is performing within defined parameters and that there are no warning signs.

> *Example 3:* An analyst responsible for monitoring the impact of Hollywood productions using Twitter is expected to report on adverse publicity memes, as well as total volumes and global trends.

Characteristics of Monitoring

Dual task and multitask. Typically, monitoring is only one of the responsibilities of a system operator, business executive, or analyst. In their monitoring activity, analysts are expected to be alert to new developments, or critical situations, but they usually have an additional workload of other tasks. Because of this monitoring is intermittent and cognitive costs are incurred during task switching (Trafton, Altmann, Brock, & Mintz, 2003).

Exceptions handling. Changes to the status quo are often especially important in monitoring. Sometimes there are designated threshold values that if exceeded require specific actions. For example, a significant drop in pulse rate or blood pressure in a patient being monitored may require actions by medical staff.

Trends and emerging patterns. Operators and analysts are expected to be cognizant of general trends and emergent patterns in a number of variables.

Links to actions. The goal of monitoring is to enable people to take appropriate actions as a result of exceptions, trends, and emerging patterns. Taking action is another form of task switching with attendant cognitive costs.

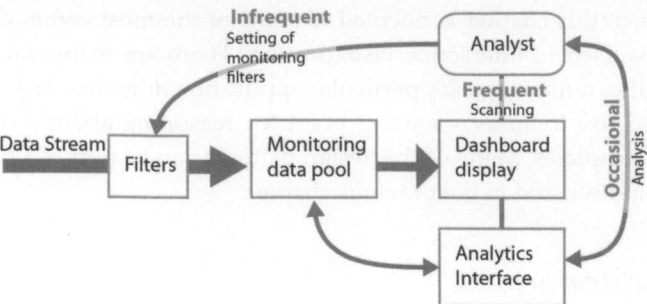

Figure 12.7 Analytics monitoring involves cognitive activities occurring on three distinct time scales.

Vigilance. Certain kinds of monitoring constitute what are called vigilance tasks. These are prolonged, monotonous, visual search tasks where a rare and often weak signal may have disastrous consequences if missed. As discussed in the previous chapter, one way of countering vigilance and maintaining attention is to add artificial targets which, when selected, reveal their falsehood.

Cognitive Work Flow

A typical monitoring application involves cognitive activities occurring on three distinct time scales (see Fig. 12.7). Typically, analytics is based on a set of customized filters to pull out information of interest. These filters are *infrequently* adjusted by the analyst. As analytics tasks evolve these filters must be changed to meet new requirements, although the changes must be infrequent enough to allow a time series to be accumulated so that normative trends exist against which exceptions can be tested. For example, an incoming Twitter feed might be filtered for memes relating to a particular person, product, or event. The *most frequent* task in monitoring is the visual scanning of the display to detect new events emerging risks, or other changes in the domain of interest, which can occur at intervals from a few second to a few hours. If a strict monitoring schedule is needed, computer-based reminders should be implemented. Of *intermediate frequency* is a switch to analysis. Supporting this in a fluid way is essential in analytics because only minimal hints of emergent trends will be available on the screen, requiring drill down operations on many pieces of information for everything that is potentially of interest.

Interaction Guideline. Support rapid transitions to analytics mode. Ideally, this should not result in key monitoring elements being hidden. Provide a second screen for more intense analytics if possible.

In a discussion of the requirements for business information dashboards, Few (2013) argues strongly that they should be single screens, with critical information visible to facilitate the monitoring task. In other words, interaction should not be required to access monitored variables.

Display Guideline. Provide a single unobscured screen to support essential monitoring tasks. Interaction should not be required to get at key information.

Visual Query Guideline. Optimize graphical displays for visual queries regarding change and trends in underlying data. Time series representations are often important, but they must be carefully designed to show critical threshold variables.

User Interrupt Guideline. Research shows that people are more sensitive to movement in the periphery of vision than to, for example, color. This means that using motion or blinking for alerts is usually a good solution.

Design Guideline: Where a vigilance task is involved, implement methods to maintain attention such as adding relatively frequent false targets.

Drill Down

In data visualization, *drilling down* is the name given to the epistemic action whereby more information is obtained about a symbolically displayed entity. Shneiderman (1996) called this "details on demand."

> *Example 1.* A real estate map with symbols representing houses for sale. The user clicks on a symbol to get details of the listing.

> *Example 2.* A hierarchically organized file system. Clicking on a folder opens it to reveal its contents. The contents can include subfolders.

Drill down is useful in almost all visualizations wherever a symbol might be queried to provide additional information. The epistemic action for a drill down is usually a mouse click on a symbol, or sometimes a hover query. The results can range from a small amount of information in a pop-up information box or a large amount of information taking over the whole screen. Chapter 10 discusses some of the issues involved in making these design decisions.

Applicability Guideline. Some form of drill down operation should be implemented wherever a system has addition of task relevant information relating to a symbol.

In cases where there are many symbols on a screen, it is important that symbols represent as much information scent as possible otherwise the analyst may have to drill down and view a great deal of irrelevant material. Scent consists of a set of graphical attributes or words that represent a summary of the information referenced by the symbol.

Visual Query Guideline. Accurate information scent is critical to support drill down operations. This should, in a compact way, provide hints about what additional information is available. Consider a combination of words and graphical cues to provide scent.

In a complex display, it can be easy to lose track of which symbols have already been queried with a drill down operation. The marking of previously visited symbols can be done either mentally or by using a cognitive externalization, such as checking off symbols that failed to yield useful information.

Interaction Guideline. Consider providing history feedback concerning which symbols have already been investigated.

Limits on Drilling Down on Hierarchical Structures

Searching for information by drilling down has a fundamental limitation that is set out formally in *information foraging theory* (Pirolli, 2009). In cases where data are structured as a strict hierarchy, a drill down search involves following information scent down a multiway branching tree. Information scent is almost always less than perfect. Pirolli shows that even with high probability that the information scent is accurate, the search cost rises exponentially with the depth of the search tree. The branching factor is also a critical variable.

The equations of foraging theory are complex, but the implications are straightforward. Finding information via hierarchical drill down will be extremely inefficient for high-depth searches with high branching factors. For example, in the case where there is a 70% chance that information scent is an accurate predictor of information being reached from a particular symbol leading down a branch of the hierarchical tree, a five-level tree will only result in the required information being found 16% of the time. When information is not found by taking the most obvious choices, searches will be much longer. For deep hierarchies, drilling down is not an efficient search mechanism, because of the impossibility of providing accurate information scent. This is why keyword searches are preferred over drill down for large amounts of data.

Data Guideline. If data are structured as a deep hierarchy do not rely solely on drilling down to find information. Implement keyword search or some other method of finding information.

There is also the problem of providing visual scent for semantically complex information. Usually, the best way of succinctly describing the contents of a file is by carefully chosen keywords, not by elaborately structured visual symbols, although the keywords can be supplemented by graphically displayed category information using color or shape, for example.

Find Local Patterns in Small to Medium-Sized Networks

Small- to medium-sized node-link diagrams can help find solutions to many problems.

> *Example 1.* Who knows who in a social network? What are the relationships between them? How do they communicate?

> *Example 2.* In a software diagram, what modules depend on a particular node? What modules does it depend on?

> *Example 3.* In a map display, what is the best route between two locations?

A noninteractive node-link diagram is the most common solution for supporting this task, with attributes of entities graphically encoded in the nodes and the attributes of relationships encoded using graphical properties of the links. However, this only works for quite small network, typically with fewer than 30 nodes and a similar number of links.

Data Guideline. Use a fixed layout diagram where the number of nodes is < 30 and a maximum node degree is < 4.

If there are more than 30 nodes, an interactive technique called *degree-of-relevance highlighting* can make it possible to have a usable diagram where all the nodes are visible. In degree-of-relevance highlighting, we are interested in displaying all of the information on the screen at once, but because of its density it cannot all be made legible. An epistemic interaction solves the problem; touching a node causes both it and other closely linked nodes to be highlighted. The highlighted nodes may also reveal additional detail. Degree-of-relevance is calculated using a computer algorithm designed to rate the task relevance of other entities in the database based on a currently selected node.

In degree-of-relevance highlighting touching a node causes near neighbors and their links to become highlighted (Munzner, Guimbretire, & Robertson, 1999; Ware, Gilman, & Bobrow, 2008). A path radius of two or three links is used for highlighting obtained through a breadth first search beginning with the selected node. The advantage of this method is that it enables substantially larger graphs to be rapidly explored. The method can greatly expand the kind of network that can be reasoned with, but it is still limited by the number of nodes that can be clearly displayed on a screen. Usually this is less than 1000. Also, there can be no high-degree nodes. The problem with high-degree nodes is that selecting one of them can cause too much of the graph to be highlighted yielding little useable information.

The Constellation system of Munzner et al. (1999) discussed in Chapter 10 pioneered this kind of interaction. The MEgraph system is another example of degree-of-relevance highlighting (Ware & Bobrow, 2005; Ware et al., 2008). MEgraph used Fortune 500 companies as a test example, illustrated in Fig. 12.8. This graph is a kind of social network, showing links between companies (colored dots) via members of the boards of directors (gray dots) for those companies. When board members are on the boards of more than one company, they form a high-level social link between the companies. In MEgraph, touching a node causes motion highlighting of the social links between nodes and the labels of the companies to appear. A history mode makes it possible for prior subnetworks to remain highlighted.

Data Guideline. Consider using interactive degree-of-relevance highlighting for a network diagram having between 20 and 1000 nodes. Degree-of-relevance highlighting will not be effective where there are high degree nodes; for example, individual nodes with large numbers of links.

An additional constraint is the information scent supporting interaction. A thousand nodes is still a lot if the diagram fails to provide useful information about which to query.

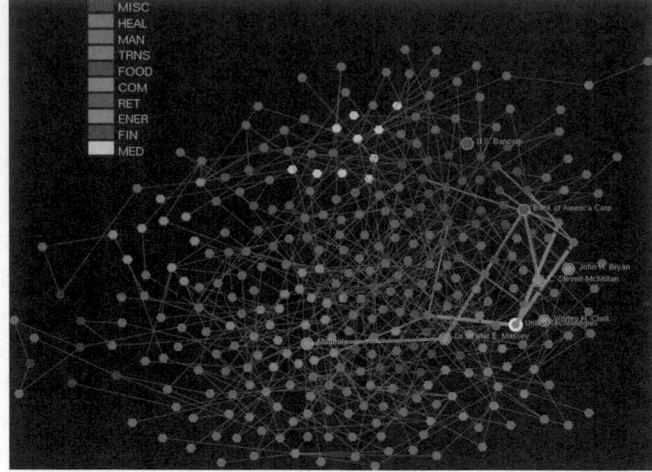

Figure 12.8 The MEgraph system uses motion as additional highlighting on the green lines and their attached nodes. This makes the two highlighted subnetworks independently searchable.

Visual Query Guideline. Take care to provide adequate information scent to support epistemic actions. Being able to determine the information values of nodes is critical so that the user knows where to start.

Degree-of-relevance highlighting can also be used to support pathfinding on a map or node-link diagram. Its use is especially common in map displays where the user selects two locations and the computer computes and highlights a route between them. Sometimes multiple alternative routes are found. The same can be done in a network diagram and it is especially commonly used to support reasoning about channels of communication between nodes.

Seed-then-Grow

Often a data analyst starts with a particular seed of information and then begins to gather related information. Each additional information nugget may lead to further expansion in a network of data. This has been called "Start with what you know, then grow" (Heer & Boyd, 2005).

> *Example 1.* Scholars searching for information related to what they have already discovered on a particular subject, frequently consult the reference list of a paper. For any paper they thereby discover they repeat the process.

> *Example 2.* In law enforcement, criminal organizations can be discovered by starting with one or two individuals and determining their associates. The associates of those associates may also be found, and so on.

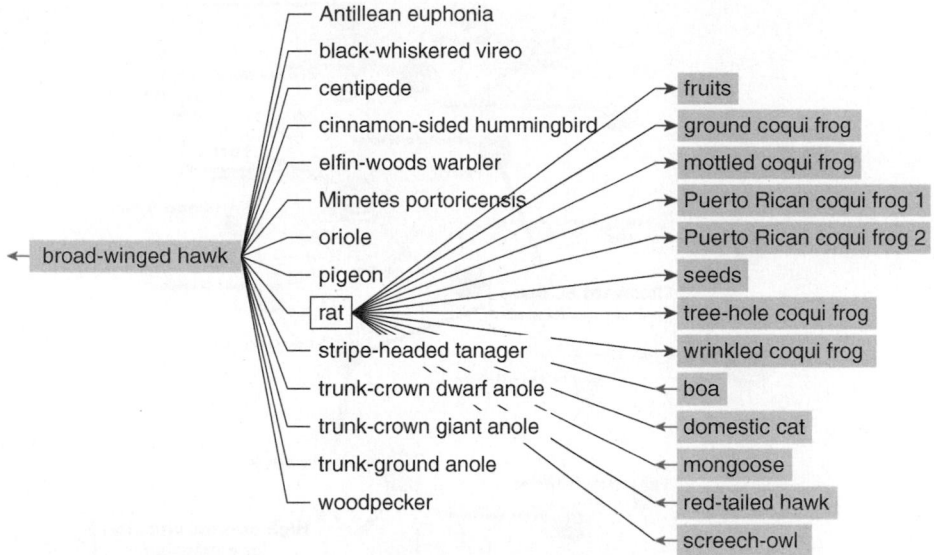

Figure 12.9 Interacting with a network representing a food web. *(From Lee, Parr, Plaisant, & Bederson, n.d. Used with permission.)*

Fig. 12.9 illustrates a *seed-then-grow* interface to a food web. Selecting the broad tailed hawk shows us all of the animals it eats. One of them is the rat and selecting the rat reveals both what it eats, highlighted in mauve, and what eats it, heighted in red.

Although seed-then-grow is quite different conceptually from drilling down on hierarchies, the constraints are the same. Searching a very large network by going from node to node is not effective. In the very early days of the internet users would navigate from information node to information node by following hyperlinks. As the internet grew, this method was largely abandoned in favor of Google type searches. But seed-then-grow can still be effective for small-constrained networks. Adequate information scent is critical to help show which links should be extended in a network. Fig. 12.10 shows an experimental system by Van Ham and Perer (2009) that provided a visual recommendation for links to be followed. These are shown in red.

Technically speaking, high-degree nodes are the bane of seed-then-grow interactions. A high-degree node is one which connects to a very large number of other nodes. For example, in searching a network of Twitter users, one is likely to find some tweeters who have thousands of followers. Opening all of these nodes individually by hand would be extremely time consuming.

Visual Query Guideline. Accurate information scent is critical to support seed-then-grow operations. Ideally, this should reveal something about the nodes that may be selected as well as the numbers of outgoing and incoming links and their types.

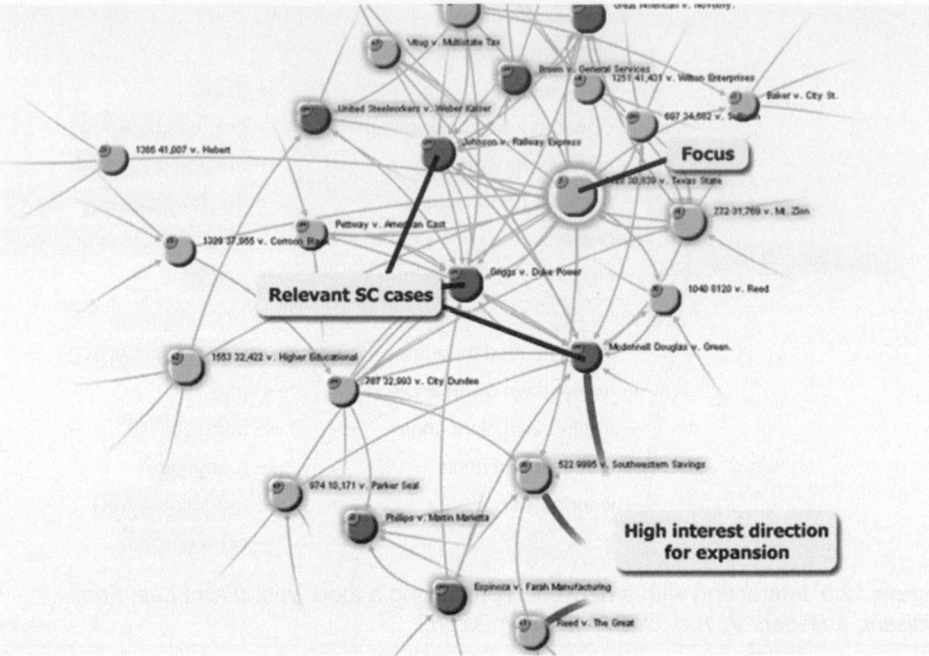

Figure 12.10 An Interactive seed-then-grow interface from Van Ham and Perer (2009). (*From Van Ham and Perer (2009)*.)

Data Guideline. If the data consists of a very large network do not rely solely on seed-then-grow to find information. Implement a keyword search or some other method of finding information.

Data Guideline. Consider that seed-then-grow may not be suitable for exploring with high-degree nodes. If there are high-degree nodes, use some method other than direct interaction for searching the links.

Pattern Comparisons in a Large Information Space

Sometimes we need to compare details in a large information space such as a high-resolution image or a large and complex network. The cognitive tasks are to find similarities and differences between small-scale patterns. Often it is also important to maintain contextual information relating to both of the patterns.

Example 1. A map display where we need to compare small-scale geological features on one part of a map with small-scale features in another part of the map.

Example 2. An X-ray image where we need to compare widely separated small patterns possible representing cancerous nodules.

Example 3. A network diagram showing metabolic pathways in a cell. We need to compare small subsystems of metabolic pathways across species.

Any visual pattern comparison involves loading some aspect of one pattern into visual working memory, to be later compared to some other pattern. Pattern comparisons are far more efficient if the transfer of attention between one pattern and another can be made using eye movements, because in this case the information only needs to be held for a fraction of a second. The particular constraint is that only three simple novel shapes can be held in working memory at a time. Chapter 11 covered this issue in some detail.

Cognitive Guideline. If pattern comparisons involve comparing more than three simple shapes or patterns, ensure that they can be displayed simultaneously so that the visual comparison can be made with a set of eye movements.

This visual pattern comparison problem posed by limited capacity visual working memory has a number of solutions and each of them has advantages and disadvantages. We consider four distinct design pattern solutions: zooming, extra magnifying windows, snapshot galleries and intelligent network zooming. The first two have already been discussed in Chapter 11.

Zooming

The most common solution to the Pattern Comparisons problem is to allow for rapid zooming (scale change) of the data display (Bederson & Hollan, 1994). Comparisons are made by zooming in on one detail, zooming out and then zooming in on another. However, since it can take several seconds to transition from one area of detail to another using this method it can be cognitively inefficient and place a burden on working memory.

Cognitive Guideline. Implement rapid zooming for comparisons if patterns are simple enough to be held in visual working memory.

Interaction Guideline. The optimal zoom rate is around a scale change of 4x/sec.

Magnifying Windows

Interactive magnifying windows can be attached by the user to focal points on an overview display. The focus of a window can be controlled dragging at the focal point or clicking on a new location. In some interfaces fine scale movement can be carried out by dragging in the magnifying window itself (Ware & Lewis, 1995). Fig. 11.5 shows multiple windows in a 3D environment. The problem with this solution can be the overhead involved in setting up the extra windows. If they are frequently needed they should always be present. There are also design tradeoffs relating the amount of screen space devoted to magnifying windows and the overview and the best solution will depend on the specific application.

Cognitive Guideline. Consider using magnifying windows when the patterns to be compared are more complex—more than three simple shapes or shape components.

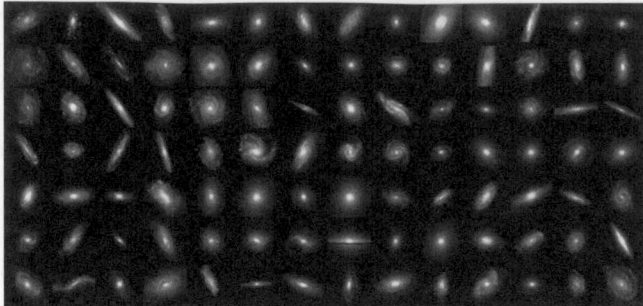

Figure 12.11 Views of 98 different galaxies are laid out in a matrix for ease of visual comparison. (*Courtesy of Zzolt Frei*.)

Snapshot Gallery

Small snapshots saved to a gallery support side-by-side comparisons of many complex patterns using eye movements. For example, Fig. 12.11 shows a selection of 98 different galaxies laid out so that they can be readily compared. Links back to locations in an overview map can provide context.

There can be a significant cognitive cost to saving individual snapshots to a gallery. The user interface for adding and organizing snapshots must be learned and there are costs to saving, labeling, and organizing snapshots. Because of this extra cognitive cost, the method is only useful when larger number of patterns must be compared. The point at which it is worth providing this support is highly application dependent, but any time more than five items must be visually compared, implementing a snapshot gallery should be considered.

Cognitive guideline. Use snapshot comparison to support eye movement–based comparisons when more than five patterns at a time must be compared.

Interaction guideline. Optimize the interface supporting of adding to and organizing snapshot galleries.

Nested Graph with Intelligent Zooming

If the patterns to be compared are parts of a largish node-link diagram, a form of fisheye view can be implemented based on the nested structure of the graph. Several different subnetworks can be expanded and thereby compared. In the intelligent zoom method (Schaffer et al., 1993) regions not expanded are contracted to save space. This is illustrated in Fig. 12.12. There are limitations on the complexity of the subgraphs that will inevitably restrict comparisons. At the time of this writing these limitations have not been quantified.

Cross-View Brushing

Many visualizations are composites, containing a combination of charts, maps, and network diagrams laid out on the screen. In some cases the underlying data are represented in more than one of these views and the cognitive task of relating the different

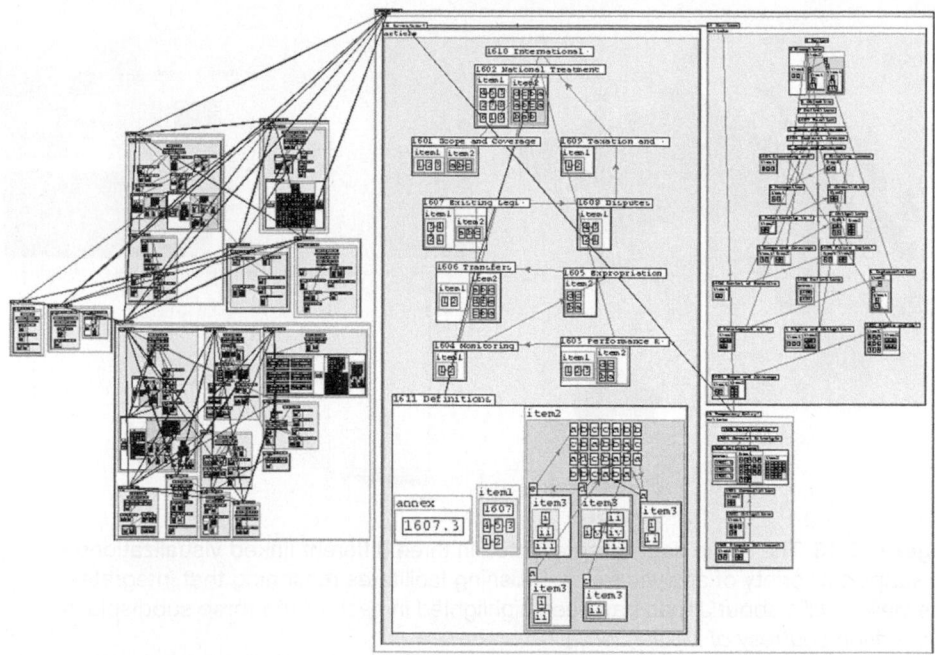

Figure 12.12 The intelligent zoom allows different subnetworks of a larger network to be selectively enlarged and thereby compared. (*From Schaffer et al. (1993).*)

views can be extremely challenging. An interactive method called brushing is very often the most effective solution to the problem of linking data across multiple views. Brushing is the name given to the technique whereby a subset of the data selected in one view is highlighted in that view and simultaneously highlighted in one or more additional views (Becker & Cleaveland, 1987). Fig. 12.13 shows an example where the same data are used in three different visualizations, a map view, a treemap view and a parallel coordinates view. The country of Japan has been selected in the treemap view and its location is thereby highlighted on the map view and the parallel coordinates view.

Example. The location of a company's retail outlets are shown on a map view. A scatter plot shows revenues plotted against operating costs with a symbol for each outlet. The analyst wishes to answer questions about where the most profitable stores are located.

The key interaction in brushing is selecting data points or data ranges. Once this is done, the system highlights them. The user constructs visual queries to reason about the patterns appearing in different views. Brushing enables the display of more attributes of a data set than would be otherwise possible so that network views, temporal views, geospatial views and chart views can all be effectively combined.

The reason why brushing is cognitively efficient is that it support the rapid comparisons of patterns in separated charts, maps and diagrams by means of eye movements and this greatly reduces working memory load. But this requires the use of effective

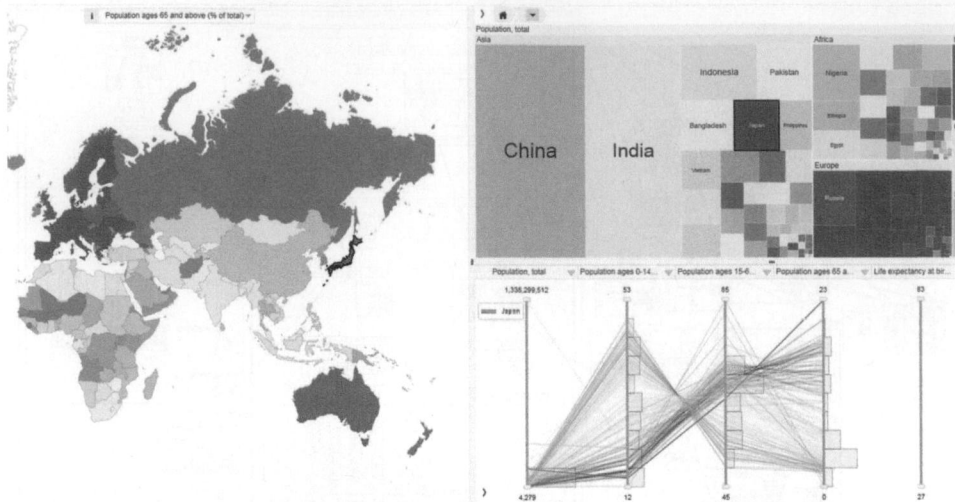

Figure 12.13 The same data is represented in three different linked visualizations to support a variety of analytic tasks. Brushing facilitates reasoning that integrates the views. Data about Japan has been highlighted in each of the three subdisplays. (*Illustration courtesy of Mikael Jern.*)

highlighting methods and ideally the highlighting method will be consistent across the different data views. This presents a design challenge because each of the views may have its own design requirements and color-coding conventions. For example, in Fig. 12.13, data about Japan is highlighted using a black outline in both the map and the treemap view. But in the parallel coordinate view Japan is inconsistently highlighted as a dark blue line, making the connection less obvious. There is a good design reason for this, using a black line would affect the color-coding used in this chart; the line would no longer appear blue. Surrounding the blue line with black lines would overly thicken it and this would be a major problem if multiple lines were brushed in the parallel coordinates plot. See Chapter 5 for a discussion of the perceptual issues involved in designing highlighting schemes.

Interaction Guideline. Rapid visual feedback is necessary to support interactive brushing. Ideally highlighting should occur in less than a 10th of a second.

Visual Query Design Guideline. Use strong highlighting methods for brushing. Possibilities include reducing the visual contrast of nonbrushed objects while increasing the vividness and luminance contrast of brushed entities. Another possibility is to use motion or blinking to draw attention to the brushed entities.

Dynamic Queries

Dynamic queries are a method for restricting what is shown on the screen according to one or more data attributes (Ahlberg, Williamson, & Shneiderman, 1992). Dynamic queries are designed to work with multidimensional discrete data. That is, data where

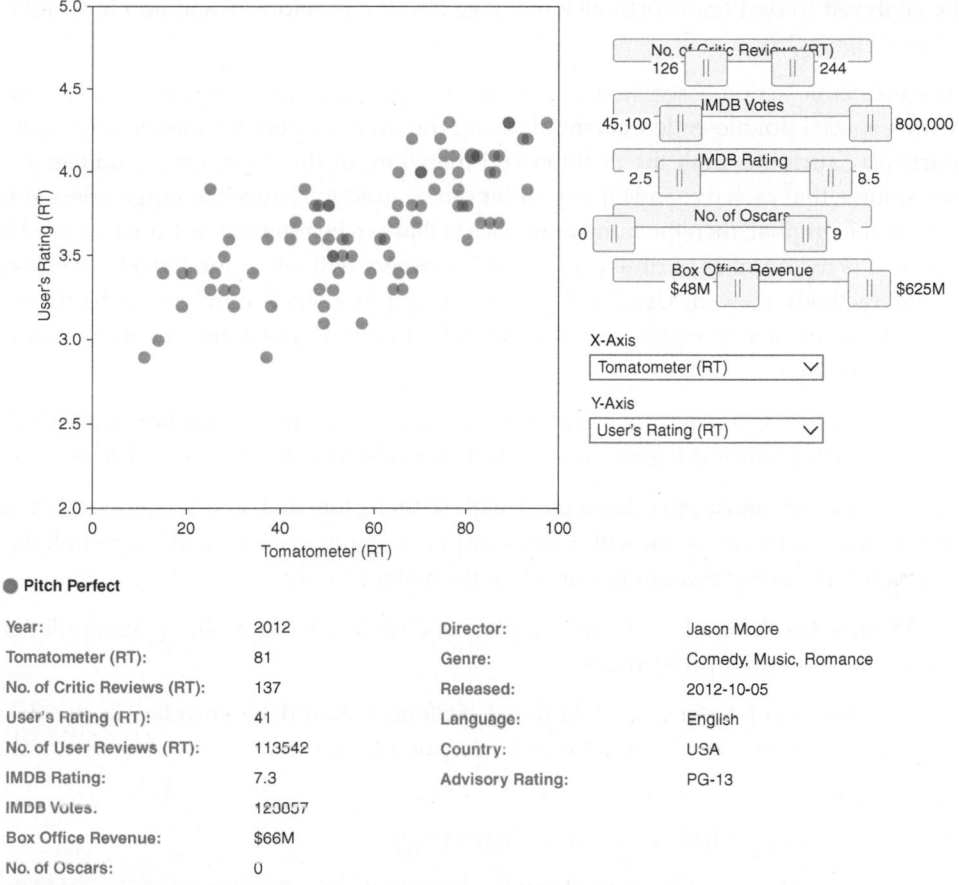

Figure 12.14 Aperture JS example implementation of dynamic queries for a movie database. (*Image courtesy of Uncharted.*)

each entity has a number of attributes. The method uses custom sliders, each restricting the range of data points displayed according to a particular attribute value.

Example 1. Interface to select movies according to criteria from multiple review sites. Criteria to include ratings from different review sites, number of Oscars and other factors.

Example 2. Stats are available from thousands of heart disease patients. They include blood pressure, heart rate, lipids and other blood chemistry as well as other variables such as income, exercise, and education. A researcher needs to quickly explore relationships between the variables.

The dynamic query solution is to have a set of sliders, one for each attribute of a database. Each double-ended slider restricts the range of what is being displayed. The application illustrated in Fig. 12.14 allows for information from both Rotten Tomatoes and the Internet Movie Database to be combined for hundreds of movies to be analyzed to find one worth viewing. (See also the previous discussion in Chapter 10 and Fig. 10.15).

The epistemic action associated with dynamic queries is the adjustment of a slider with a special double-ended cursor allowing the user to select a range of values on a particular attribute. Both the position and the width of the slider can be adjusted. If we assume that each dynamic query slider can be used to reduce the range selected to 10% of the original, then the number of objects that can be interactively queried is $> 10^d$ where d is the number of dimensions. So five sliders will allow for 100,000 objects to be interactively viewed. Usually the goal is to get to a small number of objects displayed on the screen which can then be individually queried further using a drill down operation.

Data Guideline. Consider the use of dynamic queries where the number of entities is less than 10^d, where d is the number of attributes selectable by means of sliders.

The method has most often been used with scatter plots and to a lesser extent time series plots, but it can work with ranges displayed on maps, and with node-link diagrams where restrictions can be placed on the nodes or links.

Interaction Guideline. Ideally, the display update following a slider manipulation should be very rapid (<100 msec).

Information Scent Guideline. Additional attributes should be encoded in the data glyphs to facilitate visual search for task relevant information.

Model-Based Interactive Planning

For an increasing number of applications human decision-making is supported by a computer simulation of a system. The model forecasts the behavior of a system by starting with a set of initial conditions and running it forward in time for a period which may range from hours to many years. The user operates in an interactive loop, adjusting model parameters and examining the predicted outcome. In this way the flexibility and subtlety of human understanding can be combined with computation power in a distributed cognitive system.

> *Example 1.* A business spreadsheet is used to forecast profit margins based on assumptions about such variables as materials costs, labor costs, cost of transportation, etc. The output is a time series of forecast revenues and profits.
>
> *Example 2.* A traffic behavior model is used to simulate the effect of alternative intersection designs on congestion patterns.
>
> *Example 3.* A model of interactions between a set of commercial fish species is used to forecast the effects of changing the allowable catch.

Fig. 12.15 shows an interface to the MSPROD fisheries model (St Jean, Ware, & Gamble, 2016). The analyst can change the fishing effort on different species categories and

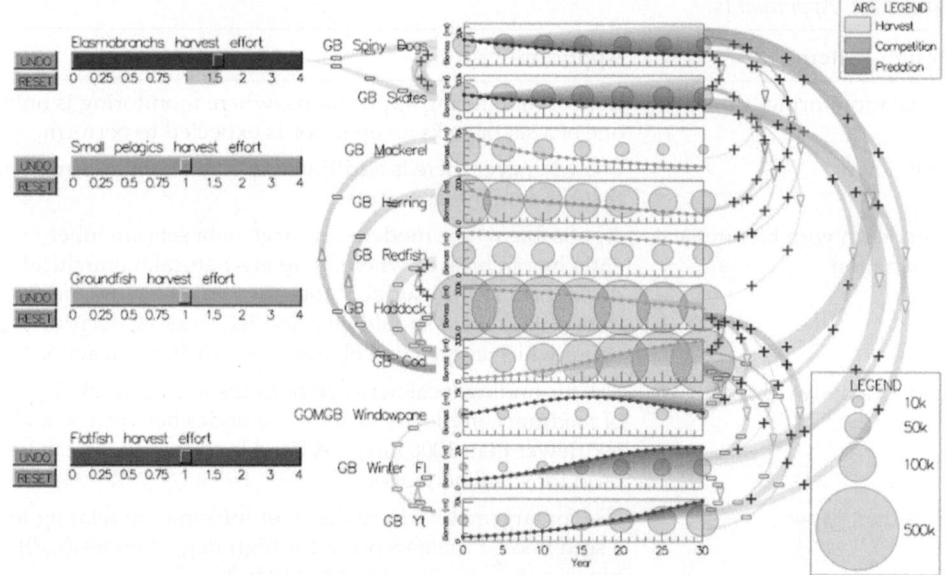

Figure 12.15 A visualization linked to a model of interactions of fish species.

immediately see the resulting change in a 30-year forecast of the fish populations. The shaded portion of each time series plot shows the change from a previous forecast. The model is based on known predation of one species on another, for example, dogfish each lots of cod, as well as on competition between species; for example, haddock and cod are both groundfish competing for the same underlying food resources. A user such as a fisheries administrator can change the amount of allowable catch on a particular fish species and see the forecast effects of this change for all ten species.

One of the problems with computer-based modeling is that most systems only show results and the inner workings of the model are invisible. The system shown in Fig. 12.15 is an attempt to counter this problem by showing the chain of cause and effect from one species to another. The arcs to the left and right show interactions between fish species representing competition and predation. An increase in the catch of elasmobranchs (dogfish and skates) results in a decrease in the populations of those species and a considerable increase in cod and winter flounder. The latter benefit because they are a favorite food of elasmobranchs. But windowpane stocks decrease because they compete with cod. The dynamically sized links reveal the inner workings of the model and allow for an analyst to not only see that a forecast has changed, but also to understand the reason for the change.

Design Guideline. As far as possible, make the underlying workings of the model visible to the user so that results can be explained.

In many cases, computer models of systems include uncertainties in the predictions. The problem of displaying these uncertainties has already been discussed in Chapter 9 for hurricane simulations. In generally it is always important to display model

Table 12.2 *Applicability.*

Design Pattern	Applicability
Visual monitoring	Use for monitoring applications, where monitoring is only one of a set of tasks an operator is expected to perform.
Drill down	Use whenever there is additional task relevant information that the symbol represents.
Drill down with hierarchical aggregation	Applicable where moderately large data sets are inherently hierarchical or where there is a natural hierarchical decomposition. To support cognitive efficiency, adequate information scent should be provided to assist decisions about which aggregated objects merit drill down actions.
Find local network patterns	Use for finding local network patterns in a network that is of medium complexity (number of nodes between 30 and 500, fewer than 1000 links). A fixed layout diagram can be used for small networks.
Seed-then-grow	Use for large networks to discover information relating to a seed node. Problems occur for high-degree nodes (>10) because the network expands too fast.
Pattern comparisons	Use to compare localized patterns in a large information space. Solutions include zooming, extra windows, a snapshot gallery, and intelligent network zooming.
Cross-view brushing	Use to link multiple data views in composite displays.
Dynamic queries	Use for multidimensional discrete data the maximum data set size is approximately 2^d where d is the number of selectable dimensions.
Model-based planning	Applicable whenever a computer model is available to support forecasting. Limited by the level of uncertainty in the forecast.

uncertainties, especially in the case the area large. The system shown in Fig. 12.13 had an alternative view in which uncertainties where shown—in the case of the fisheries model, the uncertainties were very large.

Cognitive Guideline. Make model uncertainties visible, so that decision makers can take these into account.

Choosing Which Interaction Design Pattern(s) to Implement

Given a problem, a set of cognitive tasks and a source of applicable data, the visualization designer's task is to choose from a set of visualization types (charts, maps, network diagrams and tables) together with the most effective interaction methods. As an aid to this, Table 12.2 provides a summary of the applicability of the different VTDPs.

Step 6 Prototype Development

In order to test the cognitive affordances of design alternatives, it is usually necessary to have some form of prototype. This can be as simple as a set of design sketches of key screens, or as elaborate as a working prototype application, demonstrating key design ideas but lacking full functionality. The purpose is to provide a basis for reasoning about cognitive efficiency when the visualization is applied to the cognitive tasks identified in Step 3. Rapid prototyping is a large and diverse topic and it is beyond the scope of this book. The reader should consult a text such as Preece, Rogers, and Sharp (2015) or Snyder (2003) for prototyping methods.

Step 7: Evaluation and Design Refinement

Given a prototype system, the final design steps involve evaluating how well it meets the task requirements, discovering usability bugs and so on. One easy to use method is called a cognitive walkthrough. This involves having a potential user go through the steps needed to carry out a set of tasks while talking aloud. Places where they become confused about the information being displayed or fail to use the system properly will become immediately apparent. This method can also help to identify cognitive bottlenecks, such as unreasonable memory load, or instances where repetitive work can be offloaded to the computer.

Usually, an early stage prototype is only a starting point, especially for a complex system. The prototype will continue to be refined and functionality increased through multiple design iterations. Evaluation is also a large and diverse topic that is beyond the scope of this book. Useful resources for user interface evaluation include Wilson (2013) and Krug (2013).

Conclusion

This chapter has outlined the basics of a cognitive engineering approach to the design of interactive visualizations; but it is necessarily incomplete, missing some important aspects of the design process. Good design requires many skills. For a start, interview skills are essential to understand the needs of targeted users. Discovering requirements is difficult because many users cannot articulate their needs and also because there may be solutions to their problems they have never imagined. Also, some users do not wish to be bothered talking to designers about new products because they have spent decades developing expertise with tools they already use and have little incentive to change. Users can lack perspective, not understanding how their part of a work flow fits into a bigger picture of data analytics. As a result, part of the skill of a good designer is to understand the essence of a task, abstracting it from what is current practice. Another skill is to draw on a wealth of experience with other software tools and see which can be adapted to a particular problem area. A good designer must also be skilled in the art of the possible. New software must work in the context of existing software tools. Budgets are limited and available developers are usually only familiar with certain development environments. The designer also needs the skill of persuasion to be able to present design ideas to customers and the skill of listening to understand the feedback they receive. What has been presented in this book has been a set of perceptual and cognitive principles. These can provide important and useful guidance, but they are only a part of what comprised good design.

Useful Textbook References

There are ways of approaching the problems of visualization design which differ from the first principles approach based on human perception set out in this book. This final section provides a brief annotated bibliography of a few of the many textbooks in the field of data visualization and related fields which offer alternative visions. Visualization design is an eclectic discipline and so introductions to human perception and cognition are recommended as well as books on human-computer interaction and programming.

General Books on Visualization

Visualization Analysis and Design. Tamara Munzner (2014). AK Peters/CRC Press. Munzner's excellent book on Information Visualization provides a hierarchical nested model ranging from problem characterization as the outer shell to algorithm design as the inner shell.

Graphical Methods for Data Analysis: John M. Chambers (2017). Chapman and Hall/CRC Press. This is a true classic first published in 1983. Not for the beginner, but an excellent resource for those who want an in depth understanding of how to display statistical data.

Design for Information: an Introduction to the Histories, Theories, and Best Practices Behind Effective Information Visualizations. Isabelle Meirelles, (2013). Rockport Publishers. This book takes a designer's perspective. Lots of thought-provoking examples.

The Functional Art: An introduction to information graphics and visualization. Aberto Cairo, (2012). New Riders. Presenting data to the public is an important part of information visualization and many news outlets, such at the New York Times, present elaborate visualizations to complement news stories. Design principles for this medium are presented in Cairo's book.

The Visual Display of Quantitative Information. Edward Tufte, (2001). Graphics Press, Cheshire, USA. This is one of the several books by Tufte written from a design perspective. The idea of minimal and clear expression is paramount. Excellent advice for the printed representation of data.

User Interface Design

Interactive visualization can be considered a subdiscipline of human-computer interaction. Visualizations are usually only a part of an interactive application. A broad understanding of what makes a good user interface is therefore essential.

Designing the User Interface: Strategies for Effective Human-Computer Interaction. Edition V. Ben Shneiderman, Plaisant, C., and Cohen, M.S. (2009). Pearson Education. An authoritative and comprehensive introduction to user interface design and evaluation. It has undergone decades of revision beginning life as Software Psychology, published in 1980.

Interaction Design: Beyond Human-Computer Interaction. Jenny Preece, Rogers, Y., & Sharp, H. (2015). John Wiley & Sons. An excellent introduction to interactive methods and methods for evaluating user interfaces.

Human Perception

Anyone interested in broadening their understanding of how human perception works would do well to begin with a general introductory textbook.

Sensation and Perception, Fifth Edition, Jeremy M. Wolfe, Keith R. Kluender, Dennis M. Levi (2017) Sinauer. This is a comprehensive textbook by a group of authors who are all top researchers in their respective subfields of human perception.

Cognitive Neuroscience. Marie T. Banich & Compton, R. J. (2018). Cambridge University Press. New tools such as functional MRI are revealing the brain mechanisms responsible for perception and cognition. This is an overview of this rapidly developing field.

Human Cognition

The following books have changed our thinking about how thinking works. The first two are about distributed cognition and the way cognition comes about through the interplay of neural processes in the brain and cognitive tools, other people and things in the external world.

Cognition in the Wild. Hutchins (1995). The MIT Press. A landmark study of how big ship navigation is done. It establishes how complex cognition is not carried out solely in the brain of the individual but is a complex interaction among many individuals as well as things in the environment and instruments that function as cognitive tools.

Natural-born Cyborgs: Minds, Technologies, and the Future of Human Intelligence. Andy Clark, (2003). Oxford University Press. Clark is a contemporary philosopher who argues that cognitive technologies are "deep and integral parts of the problem-solving systems that constitute human intelligence. They are best seen as proper parts of the computational apparatus that constitutes our minds." In other words, we are cognitive cyborgs who are increasingly coupled to computer-based thinking tools.

Thinking, Fast and Slow (Vol. 1). Daniel Kahneman, & Egan, P. (2011). Farrar, Straus and Giroux. An exploration of the implications of humans having two cognitive systems, a fast system based on highly learned patterns that allows us to make quick decisions which are often biased, and a slow system that employs deliberative reasoning. An excellent introduction to some of the ways people are biased in decision making.

Programming Visualizations from Scratch

For the greatest flexibility visualizations must be programmed from scratch, in which case skill with both a programming language and a graphics language will be needed. There are a huge variety of languages available. The following are introductions to three of the most common programming environments.

OpenGL SuperBible: Comprehensive Tutorial and Reference (seventh Edition). Graham Sellers, Richard Wright and Nicholas Haemel, (2015). Addison-Wesley Professional. OpenGL evolved from Silicon Graphics Graphical Language and, coupled with C++, has for decades been the preferred environment for programming computer graphics in general and data visualizations in particular. In recent years, this has been supplanted by Shader graphics for demanding applications, but beginning with OpenGL is still best way to acquire a general understanding of computer graphics.

IPython Interactive Computing and Visualization Cookbook. Cyrille Rossant. (2018). Packt Publishing. Python has emerged as the dominant scripting language for analyzing data and constructing visualizations.

Data visualization with D3. js cookbook. Zhu, N. Q. (2013). Packt Publishing Ltd. D3 is a widely used JavaScript library for producing, interactive data visualizations in web browsers.

Most visualizations are not programmed from scratch but instead are developed using specialized software applications specific to a field of science or data analytics. There are packages for flow visualization, GIS, genomics, molecular modeling, business intelligence, seismology, oceanography, network analysis, and hundreds of other application areas. Unfortunately, there are far too many of these areas of application for specific recommendations to be provided here. Standard search tools should quickly reveal what is available.

Changing Primaries

This appendix describes the operation of transforming one set of primaries into another. The mathematical name for this operation is a *change of basis*.

To convert a color from one set of primary lights to another, it is first necessary to define a conversion between the primaries themselves. We can think of this as matching each of the new primary lights using the old primary system. Suppose we designate our original set of primaries P_1, P_2, and P_3 and the new set of primaries Q_1, Q_2, and Q_3. We now use our original primaries to create matches with each of the new primaries in turn. Let us call the amount of each of the P primaries c_{ij}.

Thus,

$$Q_1 \equiv c_{11}P_1 + c_{12}P_2 + c_{13}P_3$$
$$Q_2 \equiv c_{21}P_1 + c_{22}P_2 + c_{23}P_3$$
$$Q_3 \equiv c_{31}P_1 + c_{32}P_2 + c_{33}P_3 \tag{A.1}$$

If we denote the matrix of c_{ij} values C, then

$$P = CQ \tag{A.2}$$

To reverse the transformation, invert the matrix:

$$P \equiv C^{-1}Q \tag{A.3}$$

This same matrix can now be used to convert any set of values expressed in one set of primaries to the other set of primaries. Thus, the values p_1, p_2, and p_3 represent the amounts of the lights in primary system P needed to make a match.

$$Sample \equiv p_1 P_1 + p_2 P_2 + p_3 P_3 \qquad (A.4)$$

Then we can calculate the values q in primary system Q simply by solving

$$q = Cp \qquad (A.5)$$

CIE Color Measurement System

To determine a standard observer, a set of red, green, and blue lamps is used by a number of representative subjects to match all the pure colors of the spectrum. The result is called a set of *color-matching functions*. The set of color-matching functions for the Commission Internationale de l'Eclairage (CIE) standard observer is illustrated in Fig. B.1. They were obtained with red, green, and blue pure spectral hues at 700, 546, and 436 nanometers, respectively, using a number of trained observers. Notice that there are negative values in these functions. These exist for the reasons discussed in Chapter 4. It is not possible to match directly all spectral lights with these, or any other, primaries.

For a number of reasons, the CIE chose not to use the standard-observer color-matching functions directly as the color standard, although it would have been perfectly legitimate to do so. Instead, they chose a set of abstract primaries called the *XYZ tristimulus values* and transformed the original color-matching functions into this new coordinate system. The process is the transformation from one coordinate system to another, as described in Appendix A. The transformed color-matching functions are illustrated in Fig. B.2.

The CIE *XYZ* tristimulus values have the following properties:

1. All tristimulus values are positive for all colors. To achieve this, it was necessary to create primaries that do not correspond to any real lights. The *XYZ* primary axes are purely abstract concepts. However, this model has the advantage that all perceivable colors fall within the CIE gamut. They are, in effect, a set of virtual primaries.

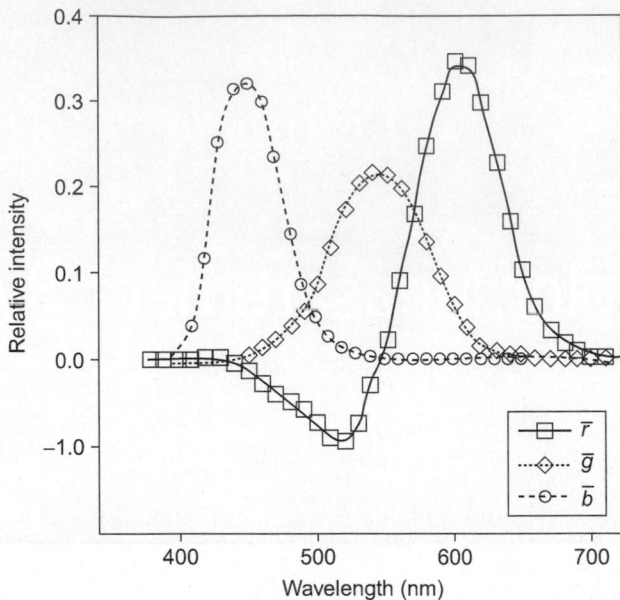

Figure B.1 The color-matching functions that define the CIE 1931 standard observer. To obtain these, each pure spectral wavelength was matched by a mixture of three primary lights.

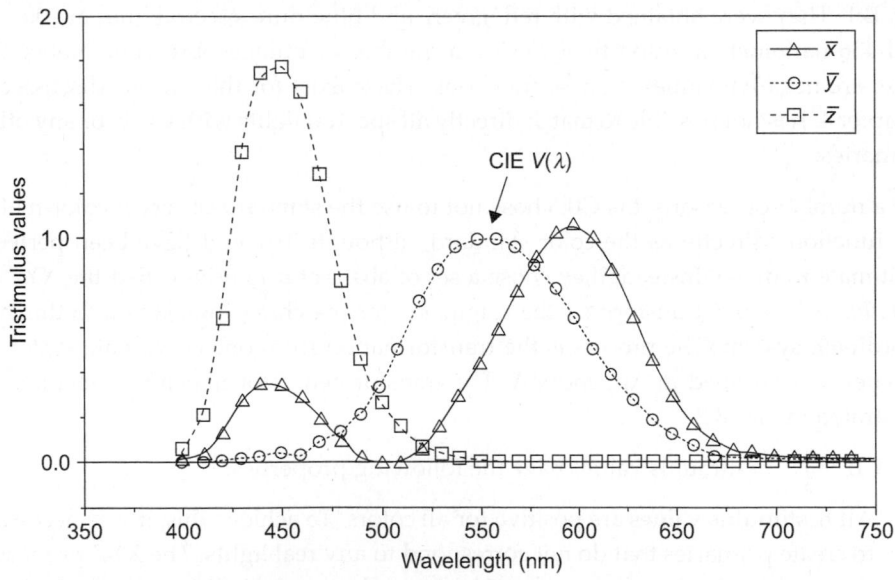

Figure B.2 The CIE tristimulus functions used to define the color of a light in *XYZ* tristimulus coordinates.

2. The X and Z tristimulus values have zero luminance. Only the Y tristimulus value contains luminance information, and the color-matching function ($\bar{y}$) is the same as the $V(\lambda)$ function, discussed in Chapter 3.

To determine the XYZ tristimulus values for a given patch of light, we integrate the energy distribution with the three ($\bar{x}$, $\bar{y}$, $\bar{z}$) color-matching functions that define the CIE standard. Note that this is a generalization of the process of obtaining luminance described in Chapter 3 only here, we obtain three values to fully specify a color:

$$X = K_m \int_\lambda E(\lambda)\, \bar{x}_\gamma d\lambda$$
$$Y = K_m \int_\lambda E(\lambda)\, \bar{y}_\gamma d\lambda \qquad (B.1)$$
$$Z = K_m \int_\lambda E(\lambda)\, \bar{z}_\gamma d\lambda$$

If $K_m = 680$ lumens/watt and $E(\lambda)$ is measured in watts per unit area solid angle (steradians), then Y gives luminance.

This appendix provides only a very brief introduction to the complex and technical subject of colorimetry. Many important issues have been neglected that must be taken into account in serious color measurement. One issue is whether the light to be measured is an extended source, such as a monitor, in which case we measure in light emitted per unit area (candelas per square meter), or a lamp, in which case we measure total light output in all directions.

The subject becomes still more complex when we consider the measurement of surface colors; the color of the illuminating source must be taken into account, and we can no longer use a trichromatic system. Fortunately, computer monitors, because they emit light, do allow us to use a trichromatic system. The reader who intends to get involved in serious color measurement should obtain one of the standard textbooks, such as Wyszecki and Stiles (1982) or Judd and Wyszecki (1975).

818 Color Measurement Science

2. The X and Z tristimulus values have zero luminance. Only the Y tristimulus value contains luminance information, and the color-matching function $\bar{y}(\lambda)$ is the same as the $V(\lambda)$ function we used in Chapter 4.

To determine the XYZ tristimulus values for a given patch of light, we integrate the energy distribution with the three $\bar{x}$, $\bar{y}$, $\bar{z}$ color-matching functions that define the CIE standard. Note that this is a generalization of the process of obtaining luminance described in Chapter 5 only now we obtain three values to fully specify a color:

$$X = K_m \int P(\lambda) \bar{x}(\lambda) d\lambda$$

$$Y = K_m \int P(\lambda) \bar{y}(\lambda) d\lambda \qquad (8.1)$$

$$Z = K_m \int P(\lambda) \bar{z}(\lambda) d\lambda$$

If $K_m = 680$ lumens/watt and $P(\lambda)$ is measured in watts per unit area-solid angle (steradians), then Y gives luminance.

This appendix provides only a very basic introduction to the complex and technical subject of colorimetry. Many important issues have been neglected that must be taken into account in serious color measurement. One issue is whether the light to be measured is an extended source, such as a monitor, in which case we measure the light emitted per unit area (candelas per square meter), or a lamp, in which case we measure the total light output in all directions.

The subject becomes still more complex when we consider the measurement of surface color. When the color of the illuminating light source must be taken into account, and we can no longer use a mathematical system. Fortunately, crosshatch monitors, because they emit light, do allow us to use a tristimulus system. The reader who intends to get involved in serious color measurement should obtain one of the standard textbooks, such as Wyszecki and Stiles (1982) or Judd and Wyszecki (1975).

Guidelines

Chapter 1

Chapter 2

Chapter 3

Chapter 4

Chapter 5

Chapter 6

Chapter 7

	Page number

Chapter 8

Chapter 9

Chapter 10

Chapter 11

Chapter 12

No short guidelines

Bibliography

Accot, J., & Zhai, S. (1997). Beyond Fitts' law: Models for trajectory-based HCI tasks. In *Proceedings of CHI* (Vol. 97) (pp. 295–302).

Ahlberg, C., & Shneiderman, B. N. (1994). Visual information seeking using the film-finder. In *Proceedings of CHI* (Vol. 94) (pp. 433).

Ahlberg, C., Williamson, C., & Shneiderman, B. (1992). Dynamic queries for information exploration. In *Proceedings of CHI* (Vol. 92) (pp. 619–626).

Alexander, C. (1964). *Notes on the synthesis of form.* Cambridge, MA: Harvard University Press.

Alexander, C., Ishikawa, S., & Silverstein, M. (1977). *A pattern language.* Oxford University Press.

Alsallakh, B., Micallef, L., Aigner, W., Hauser, H., Miksch, S., & Rodgers, P. (2014). *Visualizing sets and set-typed data: State-of-the-art and future challenges.* EuroVis–State of The Art Reports. The Eurographics Association, 1–21.

Amaya, K., Bruderlin, A., & Calvert, T. (1996). Emotion from motion. In *Proceedings of graphics interface* (Vol. 96) (pp. 222–229).

Anderson, J. R. (2007). *How can the human mind occur in the physical universe?* Oxford, UK: Oxford University Press.

Anderson, J. R., Matessa, M., & Lebiere, C. (1997). Act-r: A theory of higher-level cognition and its relation to visual attention. *Human–Computer Interaction, 12,* 439–462.

Anderson, J. R., & Milson, R. (1989). Human memory: An adaptive perspective. *Psychological Review, 96*(4), 703–719.

Anderson, S. J., Mullen, K. T., & Hess, R. E. (1991). Human peripheral spatial resolution for achromatic and chromatic stimuli: Limits imposed by optical and retinal factors. *Journal of Physiology, 442,* 47–64.

Anstis, S. M. (1974). A chart demonstrating variations in acuity with retinal position. *Vision Research, 14,* 589–592.

Anstis, S. M., & Cavanaugh, P. (1983). A minimum motion technique for judging equiluminance in color vision. In J. D. Mollon, & L. T. Sharpe (Eds.), *Physiology and psychophysics* (pp. 156–166). London: Academic Press.

Arditi, A. (1987). Binocular vision. In K. R. Boff, L. Kaufman, & J. P. Thomas (Eds.), *Handbook of perception and human performance* (pp. 23–41). New York: Wiley.

Aretz, A. J. (1991). The design of electronic map displays. *Human Factors, 33*(1), 85–101.

Armstrong, D. E., Stokoe, W. C., & Wilcox, S. E. (1994). Signs of the origin of syntax. *Current Anthropology, 35*(4), 349–368.

Arsenault, R., & Ware, C. (2004). The importance of stereo, eye coupled perspective and touch for eye–hand coordination. In M. Slater, et al. (Ed.), *Presence: Teleoperators and virtual environments* (pp. 549–559). Cambridge, MA: MIT Press.

Arthur, K. W., Booth, K. S., & Ware, C. (1993). Evaluating task performance for fish-tank virtual worlds. *ACM Transactions on Information Systems*, *11*(3), 239–265.

Aygar, E., Ware, C., & Rogers, D. (2018). The contribution of stereoscopic and motion depth cues to the perception of structures in 3D point clouds. *ACM Transactions on Applied Perception*, *15*(2), 9–15.

Bach, B., Riche, N. H., Hurter, C., Marriott, K., & Dwyer, T. (2017). Towards unambiguous edge bundling: Investigating confluent drawings for network visualization. *IEEE Transactions on Visualization and Computer Graphics*, *23*(1), 541–550.

Baddeley, A. D., & Hitch, G. J. (1974). Working memory. In G. H. Bower (Ed.), *The psychology of learning and motivation: Advances in research and theory* (pp. 647–667). Hillsdale, NJ: Erlbaum.

Baddeley, A. D., & Logie, R. H. (1999). Working memory: The multiple-component model. In A. Miyake, & P. Shah (Eds.), *Models of working memory* (pp. 28–61). Cambridge, UK: Cambridge University Press.

Badler, N. I., Manoochehri, K. H., & Baraff, D. (1986). Multi-dimensional interface techniques and articulated figure positioning by multiple constraints. In *Proceedings of workshop on interactive 3D graphics* (pp. 151–169).

Baecker, R. M. (1981). *Sorting out sorting, presented at ACM SIGGRAPH Conference.* Dallas, TX: Film and Video Versions Available from Morgan Kaufmann, San Francisco.

Baecker, R. M., & Small, I. (1990). Animation at the interface. In B. Laurel (Ed.), *The art of human–computer interface design* (pp. 251–267). Reading, MA: Addison-Wesley.

Baecker, R. M., Small, I., & Mander, R. (1991). Bringing icons to life. In *Proceedings of CHI* (Vol. 91) (pp. 1–12).

Baird, J. C., Romer, D., & Stein, T. (1970). Test of a cognitive theory of psychophysics: Size discrimination. *Perceptual and Motor Skills*, *30*(2), 495–501.

Bair, A. S., House, D. H., & Ware, C. (2009). Factors influencing the choice of projection textures for displaying layered surfaces. In *Proceedings of ACM symposium on applied perception in graphics and visualization* (pp. 101–108).

Balakrishnan, R., & MacKenzie, I. S. (1997). Performance differences in the fingers, wrist and forearm in computer input control. In *Proceedings of CHI* (Vol. 97) (pp. 303–310).

Ballesteros, S. (1989). Some determinants of perceived structure: Effects of stimulus and tasks. In B. E. Shepp, & S. Ballesteros (Eds.), *Object perception: Structure and process* (pp. 235–266). Hillsdale, NJ: Erlbaum.

Banks, M. S., Cooper, E. A., & Piazza, E. A. (2014). Camera focal length and the perception of pictures. *Ecological Psychology*, *26*(1–2), 30–46.

Bar, M., & Biederman, I. (1998). Subliminal visual priming. *Psychological Science*, *9*, 464–469.

Barfield, W., Hendrix, C., Bjorneseth, O., Kaczmarek, K. A., & Lotens, W. (1995). Comparison of human sensory capabilities with technical specifications of virtual environment equipment. *Presence, 4*(4), 329–356.

Barlow, H. (1972). Single units and sensation: A neuron doctrine for perceptual psychology? *Perception, 1*, 371–394.

Barsalou, L. W. (2008). Grounded cognition. *Annual Review of Psychology, 59*, 617–645.

Bartram, L. (1998). Perceptual and interpretative properties of motion for information visualization. In *Proceedings of the workshop on new paradigms in information visualization and manipulation* (pp. 3–7).

Bartram, L., Ho, A., Dill, J., & Henigman, E. (1995). The continuous zoom: A constrained fisheye technique for viewing and navigating large information spaces. In *Proceedings of UIST* (Vol. 95) (pp. 207–215).

Bartram, L., Ovans, R., Dill, J., Dyck, M., Ho, A., & Harens, W. S. (1994). Contextual assistance in user interfaces to complex, time-critical systems: The intelligent zoom. In *Proceedings of graphics interface* (Vol. 94) (pp. 216–224).

Bartram, L., Patra, A., & Stone, M. (2017). Affective color in visualization. In *Proceedings of the CHI conference on human factors in computing systems* (pp. 1364–1374). ACM.

Bartram, L., & Ware, C. (2002). Filtering and brushing with motion. *Information Visualization, 1*(1), 66–79.

Bartram, L., Ware, C., & Calvert, T. (2003). Moticons: Detection, distraction and task. *International Journal of Human–Computer Studies, 58*(5), 515–545.

Bassili, J. N. (1978). Facial motion in the perception of faces and of emotional expressions. *Journal of Experimental Psychology: Human Perception and Performance, 4*, 373–379.

Bassili, J. N. (1979). Emotion recognition. *Journal of Personality and Social Psychology, 37*, 2049–2058.

Baudisch, P., Good, N., & Stewart, P. (2001). Focus plus context screens: Combining display technology with visualization techniques. In *Proceedings of UIST* (Vol. 01) (pp. 31–34).

Bauer, B., Jolicoeur, P., & Cowan, W. B. (1996). Distractor heterogeneity versus linear separability in colour visual search. *Perception, 25*, 1281–1294.

Beardsley, T. (1997). The machinery of thought. *Scientific American, 277*, 78–83.

Beck, J. (1966). Effect of orientation and of shape similarity on perceptual grouping. *Perception and Psychophysics, 1*, 300–302.

Becker, R. A., & Cleaveland, W. S. (1987). Brushing scatterplots. *Technometrics, 29*(2), 127–142.

Beck, J., & Ivry, R. (1988). On the role of figural organization in perceptual transparency. *Perception and Psychophysics, 44*, 585–594.

Beck, D. M., Pinsk, M. A., & Kastner, S. (2005). Symmetry perception in humans and macaques. *Trends in Cognitive Sciences, 9*(9), 405–406.

Beckwith, M., & Restle, F. (1966). Process of enumeration. *Psychological Review, 73*(5), 437.

Bederson, B., & Hollan, J. (1994). Pad++: A zooming graphical interface for exploring alternate interface physics. In *Proceedings of UIST* (Vol. 94) (pp. 17–36).

Bellugi, U., & Klima, E. S. (1976). Two faces of sign: Iconic and abstract. *Annals of the New York Academy of Sciences, 280,* 514–538.

Benedikt, M. (1991). Cyberspace: Some proposals. In M. Benedikt (Ed.), *Cyberspace: First steps* (pp. 119–224). Cambridge, MA: MIT Press.

Bennett, A., & Rabbetts, R. B. (1989). *Clinical visual optics* (2nd ed.). Oxford: Butterworth Heinemann, 31.

Berlin, B., & Kay, P. (1969). *Basic color terms: Their universality and evolution.* Berkeley: University of California Press.

Berry, R. N. (1948). Quantitative relations among vernier, real depth and stereoscopic depth acuities. *Journal of Experimental Psychology, 38,* 708–721.

Berry, E., Kapur, N., Williams, L., Hodges, S., Watson, P., Smyth, G., et al. (2006). The use of a wearable camera, SenseCam, as a pictorial diary to improve autobiographic memory in a patient with limbic encephalitis. *Neuropsychological Rehabilitation, 17*(4/5), 582–601.

Bertin, J. (1977). *Graphics and graphic information processing.* Berlin: de Gruyter Press.

Bertin, J. (1983). In W. J. Berg, trans (Ed.), *Semiology of graphics.* Madison: University of Wisconsin Press.

Bhatt, R., Carpenter, G., & Grossberg, S. (2007). Texture segregation by visual cortex: Perceptual grouping, attention, and learning. *Vision Research, 47,* 3173–3211.

Bichot, N. P., & Schall, J. D. (1999). Effects of similarity and history on neural mechanisms of visual selection. *Nature Neuroscience, 2*(6), 549–554.

Bickerton, D. (1990). *Language and species.* Chicago: University of Chicago Press.

Biederman, I. (1987). Recognition-by-components: A theory of human image understanding. *Psychological Review, 94*(2), 115–117.

Biederman, I., & Cooper, E. (1992). Size invariance in visual object priming. *Journal of Experimental Psychology: Human Perception and Performance, 18,* 121–133.

Bier, E. A., Stone, M. C., Pier, K., Buxton, W., & DeRose, T. D. (1993). Tool glasses and magic lenses: The see-through interface. In *Proceedings SIGGRAPH* (Vol. 93) (pp. 73–80).

Bieusheuvel, S. (1947). Psychological tests and their application to non-European peoples. In G. B. Jeffrey (Ed.), *Yearbook of education* (pp. 185–207). London: University of London Press.

Bingham, G. P., Bradley, A., Bailey, M., & Vinner, R. (2001). Accommodation, occlusion, and disparity matching are used to guide reaching: A comparison of actual versus virtual environments. *Journal of Experimental Psychology: Human Perception and Performance, 27*(6), 1314–1334.

Bishop, C. M., & Tipping, M. E. (1998). A hierarchical latent variable model of data visualization. *IEEE Trans on Pattern Analysis and Machine Intelligence, 20*(3), 281–293.

Blake, R., & Holopigan, K. (1985). Orientation selectivity in cats and humans assessed by masking. *Vision Research, 23*(1), 1459–1467.

Blike, G. T., Surgenor, S. D., & Whalen, K. (1999). A graphical object display improves anesthesiologists' performance on a simulated diagnostic task. *Journal of Clinical Monitoring and Computing, 13*, 37–44.

Bollen, J., Van de Sompel, H., Hagberg, A., Bettencourt, L., Chute, R., Rodriguez, M. A., et al. (2009). Clickstream data yields high-resolution maps of science. *PLoS One, 4*, e4803.

Booher, H. R. (1975). Comprehensibility of pictorial information and printed word in proceduralized instructions. *Human Factors, 17*(3), 266–277.

Boritz, J., & Booth, K. S. (1998). A study of interactive 6 DOF docking in a computerised virtual environment. In *Proceedings of the IEEE virtual reality annual international symposium* (pp. 139–146).

Borkin, M. A., Bylinskii, Z., Kim, N. W., Bainbridge, C. M., Yeh, C. S., Borkin, D., et al. (2016). Beyond memorability: Visualization recognition and recall. *IEEE Transactions on Visualization and Computer Graphics, 22*(1), 519–528.

Borkin, M. A., Vo, A. A., Bylinskii, Z., Isola, P., Sunkavalli, S., Oliva, A., et al. (2013). What makes a visualization memorable? *IEEE Transactions on Visualization and Computer Graphics, 19*(12), 2306–2315.

Borland, D., & Taylor, R. M. (2007). Rainbow color map (still) considered harmful. *IEEE Computer Graphics and Applications, 27*(2), 14–17.

Boroditsky, L. (2000). Metaphoric structuring: Understanding time through spatial metaphors. *Cognition, 75*(1), 1–28.

Bovik, A. C., Clark, M., & Geisler, W. S. (1990). Multichannel texture analysis using localized spatial filters. *IEEE Transactions on Pattern Analysis and Machine Intelligence, 12*, 55–73.

Bower, G. H., Karlin, M. B., & Dueck, A. (1975). Comprehension and memory for pictures. *Memory and Cognition, 3*(2), 216–220.

Bowman, D. A., Koller, D., & Hodges, L. F. (1997). Travel in immersive virtual environments: An evaluation of viewpoint motion control techniques. In Proc. *Virtual reality annual international symposium, 1997., IEEE 1997* (pp. 45–52). IEEE.

Bradshaw, M. E., Parton, A. D., & Glennister, A. (2000). The task-dependent use of binocular disparity and motion parallax information. *Vision Research, 4*, 3725–3734.

Bray, T. (1996). Measuring the web. *Computer Networks and ISDN Systems, 28*, 993–1005.

Bremmer, E., Schlack, A., Duhamel, J. R., Graf, W., & Fink, G. R. (2001). Spaced coding in primate posterior parietal cortex. *Neuroimage, 14*, S46–S51.

Brewer, C. A. (1996a). Guidelines for selecting colors for diverging schemes on maps. *Cartographic Journal, 33*(2), 79–86.

Brewer, C. A. (1996). Prediction of simultaneous contrast between map colors with Hunt's model of color appearance. *Color Research and Application, 21*(3), 221–235.

Bridgeman, B. (1991). Separate visual representations for perception and visually guided behavior. In S. R. Ellis (Ed.), *Pictorial communications in virtual and real environments* (pp. 316–327). London: Taylor & Francis.

Broad, K., Leiserowitz, A., Weinkle, J., & Steketee, M. (2007). Misinterpretations of the "cone of uncertainty" in Florida during the 2004 hurricane season. *Bulletin of the American Meteorological Society, 88*(5), 651–667.

Brooks, E. E. (1988). Grasping reality through illusion: Interactive graphics serving science. In *Proceedings of CHI* (Vol. 88) (pp. 1–11).

Bruce, V., & Morgan, M. J. (1975). Violations of symmetry and repetition in visual principles. *Perception, 4,* 239–249.

Bruce, V., & Young, A. (1986). Understanding face recognition. *British Journal of Psychology, 77,* 305–327.

Bruce, V., & Young, A. (1998). *In the eye of the beholder: The science of face perception.* Oxford: Oxford University Press.

Bruckner, S., & Gröller, E. (2007). Enhancing depth-perception with flexible volumetric halos. *IEEE Transactions on Visualization and Computer Graphics, 13*(6), 1344–1351.

Bruno, N., & Cutting, J. E. (1988). Minimodality and the perception of layout. *Journal of Experimental Psychology: General, 117,* 161–170.

Bull, P. (1990). What does gesture add to the spoken word? In H. Barlow, C. Blakemore, & M. Weston-Smith (Eds.), *Images and understanding* (pp. 108–121). Cambridge, UK: Cambridge University Press.

Burke, R., & Brickson, L. (2013). Focus cue enabled head-mounted display via microlens array. ACM Transactions on Graphics, 32, 220.

Burr, D. C., & Ross, J. (1982). Contrast sensitivity at high velocities. *Vision Research, 22*(4), 479–558.

Bushnell, I. W. R., Sai, E., & Mullin, J. T. (1989). Neonatal recognition of the mother's face. *British Journal of Developmental Psychology, 7,* 3–15.

Butkiewicz, T., Meentemeyer, R. K., Shoemaker, D. A., Chang, R., Wartell, Z., & Ribarsky, W. (2010). Alleviating the modifiable areal unit problem within probebased geospatial analyses. *Computer Graphics Forum, 29*(3), 923–932.

Buxton, W., & Myers, B. (1986). A study in two-handed input. In *Proceedings of CHI* (Vol. 86) (pp. 321–326).

Buzsáki, G. (2015). Hippocampal sharp wave–ripple: A cognitive biomarker for episodic memory and planning. *Hippocampus, 25*(10), 1073–1188.

Cabral, B., & Leedom, L. C. (1993). Imaging vector fields using line integral convolution. In *Proceedings of SIGGRAPH* (Vol. 93) (pp. 263–272).

Caelli, T., & Bevan, P. (1983). Probing the spatial frequency spectrum for orientation sensitivity with stochastic textures. *Vision Research, 23*(1), 39–45.

Caelli, T., Manning, M., & Finlay, D. (1993). A general correspondence approach to apparent motion. *Perception, 22,* 185–192.

Caelli, T., & Moraglia, G. (1985). On the detection of Gabor signals and discrimination of Gabor textures. *Vision Research, 25*(5), 671–684.

Callaghan, T. C. (1989). Interference and dominance in texture segmentation: Hue, geometric form and line orientation. *Perception and Psychophysics, 46*(4), 299–311.

Campbell, E. W., & Green, D. G. (1965). Monocular versus binocular visual acuity. *Nature, 208,* 191–192.

Card, S. K., Moran, T. P., & Newell, A. (1983). *The psychology of human–computer interaction.* Hillsdale, NJ: Erlbaum.

Card, S. K., & Nation, D. (2002). Degree-of-interest trees: A component of an attentionreactive user interface. In *Proceedings of advanced visual interfaces* (pp. 231–245).

Card, S. K., Pirolli, P., & Mackinlay, J. D. (1994). The cost-of-knowledge characteristic function: Display evaluation of direct-walk dynamic information visualizations. In *Proceedings of CHI* (Vol. 94) (pp. 238–244).

Card, S. K., Robertson, G. G., & York, W. (1996). The WebBook and the web Forager: An information workspace for the world wide web. In *Proceedings of SIGCHI* (Vol. 96) (pp. 111–117).

Carroll, J. M., & Kellogg, W. A. (1989). Artifact as theory-nexus: Hermeneutics meets theory-based design. In *Proceedings of SIGCHI* (Vol. 89) (pp. 7–14).

Carter, C. S., Botvinick, M. M., & Cohen, J. D. (2011). The contribution of the anterior cingulate cortex to executive processes in cognition. *Reviews in the Neurosciences, 10*(1), 49–58.

Casey, S. (1993). *Set phasers on stun and other true tales of design, technology and human error.* Santa Barbara, CA: Aegean Publishing.

Cataliotti, J., & Gilchrist, A. L. (1995). Local and global processes in lightness perception. *Perception and Psychophysics, 57*(2), 125–135.

Cave, C. B., & Squire, L. R. (1992). Intact and long-lasting repetition priming in amnesia. *Journal of Experimental Psychology: Learning, Memory, and Cognition, 18,* 509–520.

Chambers, A. M. (2017). The role of sleep in cognitive processing: Focusing on memory consolidation. *Wiley Interdisciplinary Reviews: Cognitive Science, 8*(3), e1433.

Chambers, J. M., Cleveland, W. S., Kleiner, B., & Tukey, R. A. (1983). *Graphical methods for data analysis.* Belmont, CA: Wadsworth.

Chandler, R., & Sweller, J. (1991). Cognitive load theory and the format of instruction. *Cognition and Instruction, 8,* 293–332.

Charbonnell, J. R., Ware, J. L., & Senders, J. W. (1968). A queuing model of visual sampling: Experimental validation. *IEEE Transactions on Man–Machine Systems, MMS-9,* 82–87.

Chau, A. W., & Yeh, Y. Y. (1995). Segregation by color and stereoscopic depth in three-dimensional visual space. *Perception and Psychophysics, 57*(7), 1032–1044.

Chen, R. R. S. (1976). The entity-relationship model—toward a unified view of data. *ACM Transactions on Database Systems, 1,* 1–22.

Chernoff, H. (1973). Using faces to represent points in k-dimensional space. *Journal of the American Statistical Association, 68,* 361–368.

Chomsky, N. (1965). *Aspects of the theory of syntax.* Cambridge, MA: MIT Press.

Chuang, J., Stone, M., & Hanrahan, P. (2008). A probabilistic model of the categorical association between colors. In *Color and imaging conference, v. 2008* (pp. 6–11) (1).

CIE Subcommittee E-1.3.1. (1971). *Recommendations on uniform color spaces.* Paris: Commission Internationale de l'Eclariage (CIE). Supplement #2 to CIE Publication #15.

Clark, A. (2001). Natural-born cyborgs? In *Cognitive technology: Instruments of mind* (pp. 17–24). Berlin, Heidelberg: Springer.

Clark, A. (2013). Whatever next? Predictive brains, situated agents, and the future of cognitive science. *Behavioral and Brain Sciences, 36*(3), 181–204.

Cleveland, W. S., & McGill, R. (1983). A color-caused optical illusion on a statistical graph. *American Statistician, 37*(2), 101–105.

Cleveland, W. S., & McGill, R. (1984). Graphical perception, experimentation, and application to the development of graphical methods. *Journal of the American Statistical Association, 79*(387), 531–554.

Cockburn, A., & McKenzie, B. (2001). 3D or not 3D? Evaluating the effect of the third dimension in a document management system. In *Proceedings of SIGCHI* (Vol. 99) (pp. 434–441).

Cohen, M. E., & Greenberg, D. R. (1985). The hemi-cube: A radiosity solution for complex environments. In *Proceedings SIGGRAPH* (Vol. 85) (pp. 31–40).

Colby, C. L. (1998). Action-oriented spatial reference frames in cortex. *Neuron, 20,* 15–24.

Cole, J. (1995). *Pride and a daily marathon.* Cambridge, MA: MIT Press.

Colle, H. A., & Reid, G. B. (1998). The room effect: Metric spatial knowledge of local and separated regions. *Presence, 7*(2), 116–128.

Collins, A. M., & Loftus, E. E. (1975). A spreading activation theory of semantic processing. *Psychological Review, 82,* 407–428.

Coltheart, V. (1999). *Fleeting memories: Cognition of brief visual stimuli.* Cambridge, MA: MIT Press.

Coren, S., & Ward, L. M. (1989). *Sensation and perception* (3rd ed.). New York: Harcourt Brace Jovanovich.

Cornsweet, T. N. (1970). *Visual perception.* New York: Academic Press.

Correll, M., & Gleicher, M. (2014). Error bars considered harmful: Exploring alternate encodings for mean and error. *IEEE Transactions on Visualization and Computer Graphics, 20*(12), 2142–2151.

Craik, E., & Lockhart, R. (1972). Levels of processing: A framework for memory research. *Journal of Verbal Learning and Behavior, 11,* 671–684.

Cross, A. R., Armstrong, R. L., Gobrecht, C., Paton, M., & Ware, C. (1997). Three-dimensional imaging of the Belousov–Zhabotinsky reaction using magnetic resonance. *Magnetic Resonance Imaging, 15*(6), 719–728.

Cruz-Neira, C., Sandin, D. J., DeFanti, T. A., Kenyon, R. V., & Hart, J. C. (1992). The CAVE: Audio visual experience automatic virtual environment. *Communications of the ACM, 35*(6), 65–72.

Cutrell, E. B., Czerwinski, M., & Horvitz, E. (2000). Effects of instant messaging interruptions on computing tasks. In *Proceedings of CHI* (Vol. 2000) (pp. 99–100).

Cutting, J. E. (1986). *Perception with an eye for motion*. Cambridge, MA: MIT Press.

Cutting, J. E. (1991). On the efficacy of cinema, or what the visual systems did not evolve to do: Visual enhancements in pick-and-place tasks. In S. R. Ellis (Ed.), *Pictorial communication in virtual and real environments* (pp. 486–495). London: Taylor & Francis.

Cutting, J. E., Springer, K., Braren, P. A., & Johnson, S. H. (1992). Wayfinding on foot from information in retinal, not optical flow. *Journal of Experimental Psychology: General, 121*, 41–72.

Cypher, A., & Smyth, D. (1995). KidSim: End user programming of simulations. In *Proceedings of CHI* (Vol. 95) (pp. 27–34).

Czerwinski, M., van Dantzich, M., Robertson, G. G., & Hoffman, H. (1999). The contribution of thumbnail image, mouse-over text and spatial location memory to Web page retrieval in 3D. In *Proceedings of interact* (Vol. 99) (pp. 163–170).

Dakin, S. C., & Herbert, A. M. (1998). The spatial region of integration for visual symmetry detection. In *Proceedings of the royal society of London, series B* (Vol. 265) (pp. 659–664).

Darken, R. P., Allard, T., & Achille, L. B. (1998). Spatial orientation and wayfinding in large-scale virtual spaces: An introduction. *Presence, 7*(2), 101–107.

Darken, R. P., & Banker, W. P. (1998). Navigating in natural environments: A virtual environment training transfer study. In *Proceedings of VRAIS* (Vol. 98) (pp. 12–19).

Darken, R. P., & Sibert, J. L. (1996). Wayfinding strategies and behaviors in large virtual worlds. In *Proceedings of CHI* (Vol. 96) (pp. 142–149).

Daugman, J. G. (1984). Spatial visual channels in the Fourier plane. *Vision Research, 24*, 891–910.

Daugman, J. G. (1985). Uncertainty relation for resolution in space, spatial frequency, and orientation optimized by two-dimensional visual cortical filters. *Journal of the Optical Society of America, A, 2*, 1160–1169.

Davies, D. R., & Parasuraman, R. (1980). *The psychology of vigilance*. London: Academic Press.

Davies, M. (2011). Concept mapping, mind mapping and argument mapping: what are the differences and do they matter? *Higher education, 62*(3), 279–301.

De Bruijn, O., Spence, R., & Tong, C. H. (2000). Rapid serial visual presentation: A space–time trade-off in information presentation. In *Proceedings of advance visual interfaces (AVI 2000)* (pp. 189–192).

De Martino, B., Camerer, C. F., & Adolphs, R. (2010). Amygdala damage eliminates monetary loss aversion. *Proceedings of the National Academy of Sciences, 107*(8), 3788–3792.

Deering, M. (1992). High-resolution virtual reality. *ACM SIGGRAPH Computer Graphics, 26*(2), 195–202.

DeFanti, T. A., Dawea, G., Sandin, D. J., Schulze, J. P., Otto, P., Girado, J., et al. (2009). The StarCAVE, a third-generation CAVE and virtual reality OptIPortal. *Future Generation Computer Systems, 25*, 169–178.

Dehaene, S. (1997). *The number sense: How the mind creates mathematics*. Oxford: Oxford University Press.

Delmarcelle, T., & Hesselink, L. (1993). Visualizing second-order tensor fields with hyperstreamlines. *IEEE Computer Graphics and Applications*, *13*(4), 25–33.

Deregowski, J. B. (1968). Picture recognition in subjects from a relatively picture-less environment. *African Social Research*, *5*, 356–364.

Deuchar, M. (1990). Are the signs of language arbitrary? In H. Barlow, C. Blakemore, & M. Weston Smith (Eds.), *Images and understanding* (pp. 168–179). Cambridge, UK: Cambridge University Press.

Di Battista, G., Eades, P., Tamassia, R., & Tollis, I. G. (1998). *Graph drawing: Algorithms for the visualization of graphs*. Upper Saddle River, NJ: Prentice Hall.

Díaz, J., Ropinski, T., Navazo, I., Gobbetti, E., & Vázquez, P. P. (2017). An experimental study on the effects of shading in 3D perception of volumetric models. *The Visual Computer*, *33*(1), 47–61.

Dickinson, S., Christensen, H., Tsotsos, J., & Olofsson, G. (1997). Active object recognition integrating attention and viewpoint control. *Computer Vision and Image Understanding*, *6*(3), 239–260.

Dimara, E., Manganari, E., & Skuras, D. (2017). Survey data on factors influencing participation in towel reuse programs. *Data in brief*, *10*, 26–29.

Dimara, E., Bezerianos, A., & Dragicevic, P. (2018). Conceptual and methodological issues in evaluating multidimensional visualizations for decision support. *IEEE Transactions on Visualization and Computer Graphics*, *24*(1), 749–759.

Distler, C., Boussaoud, D., Desmone, R., & Ungerleider, L. G. (1993). Cortical connections of inferior temporal area REO in Macaque monkeys. *Journal of Comparative Neurology*, *334*, 125–150.

DiZio, P., & Lackner, J. R. (1992). Spatial orientation, adaptation and motion sickness in real and virtual environments. *Presence*, *1*(3), 319–328.

Doeller, C. F., Barry, C., & Burgess, N. (2010). Evidence for grid cells in a human memory network. *Nature*, *463*(7281), 657.

Donoho, A. W., Donoho, D. L., & Gasko, M. (1988). MacSpin: Dynamic graphics on a desktop computer. *IEEE Computer Graphics and Applications*, *8*(4), 51–58.

Dosher, B. A., Sperling, G., & Wurst, S. A. (1986). Trade-offs between stereopsis and proximity luminance covariance as determinants of perceived 3D structure. *Vision Research*, *26*(6), 973–990.

Douglas, S., & Kirkpatrick, T. (1996). Do color models really make a difference? In *Proceedings of CHI* (Vol. 96) (pp. 399–405).

Drascic, D., & Milgram, P. (1991). Positioning accuracy of a virtual stereoscopic pointer in a real stereoscopic video world. In *Proceedings of SPIE* (Vol. 1457) (pp. 58–69).

Drasdo, N. (1977). The neural representation of visual space. *Nature*, *266*, 554–556.

Driver, J., McLeod, P., & Dienes, Z. (1992). Motion coherence and conjunction search. *Perception and Psychophysics*, *51*(1), 79–85.

Drucker, S. M., & Zeltzer, D. (1995). CamDroid: A system for implementing intelligent camera control. In *Proceedings of symposium on interactive 3D graphics* (pp. 139–144).

Drury, C. G., & Clement, N. R. (1978). The effect of area, density, and number of background characters on visual search. *Human Factors, 20*, 597–603.

Duda, R., & Hart, P. E. (1973). *Pattern classification and scene analysis*. New York: Wiley.

Dudai, Y. (2004). The neurobiology of consolidations, or, how stable is the engram? *Annual Reviews of Psychology, 55*, 51–86.

Dudai, Y., & Evers, K. (2014). To simulate or not to simulate: What are the questions? *Neuron, 84*(2), 254–261.

Duncan, J., & Humphreys, G. (1989). Visual search and stimulus similarity. *Psychological Review, 96*, 433–458.

Durgin, E. H., Proffitt, D. R., Olson, T. J., & Reinke, K. S. (1995). Comparing depth from motion with depth from binocular disparity. *Journal of Experimental Psychology: Human Perception and Performance, 21*(3), 679–699.

Dwyer, E. M. (1967). The effect of varying the amount of realistic detail in visual illustrations. *Journal of Experimental Education, 36*, 34–42.

Dzhafarov, E. N., Sekuler, R., & Allik, J. (1993). Detection of changes in speed and direction of motion: Reaction time analysis. *Perception & Psychophysics, 54*, 733–750.

D'Zmura, M., Lennie, P., & Tiana, C. (1997). Color search and visual field segregation. *Perception and Psychophysics, 59*(3), 381–388.

Eckstein, M. P., Beutter, B. R., Pham, B. T., Shimozaki, S. S., & Stone, L. S. (2007). Similar neural representations of the target for saccades and perception during search. *Neuron, 27*, 1266–1270.

Edelman, S. (1995). Representation of similarity in 3D object discrimination. *Neural Computation, 7*, 407–422.

Edelman, S., & Buelthoff, H. H. (1992). Orientation dependence in the recognition of familiar and novel views of 3D objects. *Vision Research, 32*, 2385–2400.

Edwards, B. (1979). *Drawing on the right side of the brain*. Los Angeles, CA: J.E. Tarcher.

Egeth, H., & Pachella, R. (1969). Multidimensional stimulus identification. *Perception and Psychophysics, 5*, 341–346.

Ekman, P. (2003). *Emotions revealed: Recognizing faces and feelings to improve communication and emotional life*. New York: Times Books.

Ekman, P., & Friesen, W. (1975). *Unmasking the face: A guide to recognizing emotions from facial expressions*. Upper Saddle River, NJ: Prentice Hall.

Ekman, P., & Friesen, W. (1978). *The facial action coding system*. Palo Alto, CA: Consulting Psychologists Press.

Ekman, P., Friesen, W., & O'Sullivan, M. (1988). Smiles when lying. *Journal of Personality and Social Psychology, 54*, 414–420.

Ekman, G., & Junge, K. (1961). Psychophysical relations in visual perception of length, area and volume. *Scandinavian Journal of Psychology, 2*(1), 1–10.

Ekstrom, A. D., Spiers, H. J., Bohbot, V. D., & Rosenbaum, R. S. (2018). *Human spatial navigation*. Princeton University Press.

Eley, M. G. (1988). Determining the shapes of land surfaces from topographical maps. *Ergonomics, 31*, 355–376.

Elmes, D., Kantowitz, B. H., & Roedinger, H. L. (1999). *Research methods in psychology* (6th ed.). Pacific Grove, CA: Brooks/Cole.

Elvins, T. T., Nadeau, D. R., & Kirsh, D. (1997). Worldlets: 3D thumbnails for wayfinding in virtual environments. In *Proceedings of UIST* (Vol. 97) (pp. 21–30).

Elvins, T. T., Nadeau, D. R., Schul, R., & Kirsh, D. (1998). Worldlets: 3D thumbnails for 3D browsing. *Proceedings of CHI, 98*, 163–170.

Emmorey, K., & McCullough, S. (2009). The bimodal bilingual brain: Effects of sign language experience. *Brain & Language, 109*, 124–132.

Englehardt, Y., de Bruin, J., Janssen, T., & Scha, R. (1996). The visual grammar of information graphics. In *Proceedings of workshop on visual representation, reasoning, and interaction in design* (pp. 1–11).

Enns, J. T., Austin, E. L., Di Lollo, V., Rauchenberger, R., & Yantis, S. (2001). New objects dominate luminance transients in setting attentional priority. *Journal of Experimental Psychology: Human Perception and Performance, 27*(6), 1287–1302.

Eriksen, C. W., & Hake, H. N. (1955). Absolute judgements as a function of stimulus range and number of stimulus and response categories. *Journal of Experimental Psychology, 49*, 323–332.

Everts, M. H., Bekker, H., Roerdink, J. B. T. M., & Isenberg, T. (2009). Depth-dependent halos: Illustrative rendering of dense line data. *IEEE Transactions on Visualization and Computer Graphics, 15*(6), 1299–1306.

Fach, P. W., & Strothotte, T. (1994). Cognitive maps: A basis for designing user manuals for direct manipulation interfaces. In M. J. Tauber, D. E. Mahling, & E. Arefi (Eds.), *Cognitive aspects of visual languages and visual interfaces* (pp. 89–117). New York: Elsevier.

Faraday, P. (1998). *Theory-Based design and evaluation of multimedia presentation interfaces* Ph.D. thesis. London: City University.

Faraday, P., & Sutcliffe, A. (1997). Designing effective multimedia presentations. In *Proceedings of CHI* (Vol. 97) (pp. 272–279).

Faraday, P., & Sutcliffe, A. (1999). Authoring animated Web pages using "contact points.". In *Proceedings of CHI* (Vol. 99) (pp. 458–465).

Farah, M. J., Soso, M. J., & Dashieff, R. M. (1992). Visual angle of the mind's eye before and after unilateral occipital lobectomy. *Journal of Experimental Psychology: Human Perception and Performance, 18*, 214–246.

Feiner, S., MacIntyre, B., Haupt, M., & Solomon, E. (1993). Windows on the world, 2D windows for 3D augmented reality. In *Proceedings of UIST* (Vol. 93) (pp. 145–155).

Feldman, J. A. (1985). Four frames suffice: A provisional model of vision and space. *Behavioural and Brain Sciences, 8*, 265–289.

Few, S. (2012). *Show me the numbers: Designing tables and graphs to enlighten.* Analytics Press.

Field, D. J., Hayes, A., & Hess, R. E. (1993). Contour integration by the human visual system: Evidence for a local "association field." *Vision Research, 33*(2), 173–193.

Field, G., & Spence, R. (1994). Now, where was I? *New Zealand Journal of Computing*, *5*(1), 35–43.

Findlay, J. M., & Gilchrist, I. D. (2005). Eye guidance and visual search. In G. Underwood (Ed.), *Cognitive processes in eye guidance* (pp. 259–281). Oxford: Oxford University Press.

Fine, I., & Jacobs, R. A. (2000). Perceptual learning for a pattern discrimination task. *Vision Research*, *41*, 449–461.

Fine, I., & Jacobs, R. A. (2002). Comparing perceptual learning across tasks: A review. *Journal of Vision*, *2*, 190–203.

Fisher, S. K., & Cuiffreda, K. J. (1990). Adaptation to optically increased interocular separation under naturalistic viewing conditions. *Perception*, *19*, 171–180.

Fitts, P. M. (1954). The information capacity of the human motor system in controlling the amplitude of movements. *Journal of Experimental Psychology*, *47*, 381–391.

Fleet, D. (1998). *Visualization of communications in 3D* Master's thesis. Canada: University of New Brunswick.

Foley, J. D., van Dam, A., Feiner, S. K., & Hughes, J. E. (1990). *Computer graphics: Principles and practice* (2nd ed.). Reading, MA: Addison-Wesley.

Fowler, R. H., & Dearholt, D. W. (1990). Information retrieval using pathfinder networks. In R. W. Schvaneveldt (Ed.), *Pathfinder associative networks: Studies in knowledge organization* (pp. 165–178). Norwood, NJ: Ablex.

Fowler, D., & Ware, C. (1989). Strokes for representing univariate vector field maps. In *Proceedings of graphics interface* (Vol. 89) (pp. 249–253).

Franklin, D., Hill, C., Dwyer, H. A., Hansen, A. K., Iveland, A., & Harlow, D. B. (2016). Initialization in scratch: Seeking knowledge transfer. In *Proceedings of the 47th ACM technical symposium on computing science education ACM* (pp. 217–222).

Frisby, J. P. (1979). *Seeing, illusion, brain and mind*. Oxford: Oxford University Press.

Frisby, J. P., Buckley, D., & Duke, P. A. (1996). Evidence for good recovery of lengths of real objects seen with natural stereo viewing. *Perception*, *25*, 129–154.

Fuchs, J., Isenberg, P., Bezerianos, A., Fischer, F., & Bertini, E. (2014). The influence of contour on similarity perception of star glyphs. *IEEE Transactions on Visualization and Computer Graphics*, *20*(12), 2251–2260.

Fuchs, J., Isenberg, P., Bezerianos, A., & Keim, D. (2017). A systematic review of experimental studies on data glyphs. *IEEE Transactions on Visualization and Computer Graphics*, *23*(7), 1863–1879.

Furnas, G. W. (1986). Generalized fisheye views. In *Proceedings of CHI* (Vol. 86) (pp. 17–26).

Furnas, G. W. (1991). New graphical reasoning models for understanding graphical interfaces. In *Proceedings of CHI* (Vol. 91) (pp. 71–78).

Gallistel, C. R., & Gelman, R. (1992). Preverbal and verbal counting and computation. *Cognition*, *44*(1), 43–74.

Gamma, Helm, R., Johnson, R., & Vlissides, J. (1995). *Design patterns: Elements of reusable object-oriented software*. Addison-Wesley.

492 *Bibliography*

Garner, W. R. (1974). *The processing of information and structure*. Hillsdale, NJ: Erlbaum.

Geertz, C. (1973). *The interpretation of cultures*. New York: Basic Books.

Gemmell, J., Bell, G., & Lueder, R. (2006). MyLifeBits: A personal database for everything. *Communications of the ACM, 49*(1), 88–95.

Gibson, J. J. (1979). *The ecological approach to visual perception*. Boston: Houghton Mifflin.

Gibson, J. J. (1986). *The ecological approach to visual perception*. Hillsdale, NJ: Erlbaum.

Gilbert, S. A. (1997). *Mapping mental spaces: How we organize perceptual and cognitive information*. Ph.D. thesis. Cambridge: Massachusetts Institute of Technology.

Gilchrist, A. L. (1979). The perception of surface blacks and whites. *Scientific American, 240*, 88–96.

Gilchrist, A. L. (1980). When does perceived lightness depend on perceived spatial arrangement? *Perception and Psychophysics, 28*, 527–538.

Gilhooly, K. J. (1988). *Thinking: Directed, undirected and creative*. London: Academic Press.

Ginsburg, A. P., Evans, D. W., Sekuler, R., & Harp, S. A. (1982). Contrast sensitivity predicts pilots' performance in aircraft simulators. *American Journal of Optometry and Physiological Optics, 59*, 105–108.

Glennerster, A., Tcheang, L., Gilson, S. J., Fitzgibbon, A. W., & Parker, A. J. (2006). Humans ignore motion and stereo cues in favor of a fictional stable world. *Current Biology, 16*(4), 428–432.

Goldin-Meadow, S., & Mylander, C. (1998). Spontaneous sign systems created by deaf children in two cultures. *Nature, 391*, 279–281.

Goldschmidt, G. (1991). The dialectics of sketching. *Creativity Research Journal, 4*(2), 23–143.

Goldstein, D. A., & Lamb, J. C. (1967). Visual coding using flashing lights. *Human Factors, 9*, 405–408.

Goldstone, R. L., & Sakamoto, Y. (2003). The transfer of abstract principles governing complex adaptive systems. *Cognitive Psychology, 46*, 414–466.

Goldstone, R. L., & Son, J. Y. (2003). The transfer of abstract principles using concrete and idealized simulations. *The Journal of the Learning Sciences, 14*, 69–110.

Gonzalez, R. C., & Woods, P. (1993). *Digital image processing* (2nd ed.). Reading, MA: Addison-Wesley.

Goodman, N. (1968). *Language of art*. New York: Bobbs-Merrill.

Goodwin, C. J. (2001). *Research in psychology: Methods and design*. New York: Wiley.

Gray, C. M., Konig, P., Engel, A. K., & Singer, W. (1989). Oscillatory responses in cat visual cortex exhibit intercolumnar synchronisation which reflects global stimulus properties. *Nature, 388*, 334–337.

Gray, W. G. D., Mayer, L. A., & Hughes Clarke, J. E. (1997). *Geomorphological applications of multibeam sonar and high-resolution DEM data from Passamaquoddy Bay*. Ottawa: Geological Association of Canada. '97 Proceedings Abstracts 57.

Gray, W. D., Simms, C. R., Fu, W. T., & Schoelles, M. J. (2006). The soft constraints hypothesis: A rational analysis approach to resource allocation for interactive behavior. *Psychological Review, 113*(3), 461–482.

Gregory, R. L. (1977). Vision with isoluminance color contrast: A projection technique and observations. *Perception, 6*(1), 113–119.

Grimson, W. E. L., Ettinger, G. J., Kapur, T., Leventon, M. E., Wells, W. M., III, & Kikinis, R. (1997). Utilizing segmented MRI data in image-guided surgery. *International Journal of Pattern Recognition and Artificial Intelligence, 11*(8), 1367–1397.

Grossberg, S., & Williamson, J. (2001). A neural model of how horizontal and interlaminar connections of visual cortex develop into adult circuits that carry out perceptual grouping and learning. *Cerebral Cortex, 11*(1), 37–58.

Gugerty, L., & Brooks, J. (2001). Seeing where you are heading: Integrating environmental and egocentric reference frames in cardinal direction judgments. *Journal of Experimental Psychology: Applied, 7*(3), 251–266.

Guiard, Y. (1987). Asymmetric division of labor in skilled bimanual action: The kinematic chain as a model. *Journal of Motor Behavior, 19,* 486–517.

Guitard, R., & Ware, C. (1990). A color sequence editor. *ACM Transactions on Graphics, 9*(3), 338–341.

Guo, H., Zhang, V., & Wu, J. (2000). *The effect of zooming speed in a zoomable user interface.* Student CHI Online Research Experiments (SHORE). Retrieved from http://otal.umd.edu/SHORE2000/zoom/.

Gutwin, C., Greenberg, S., & Roseman, M. (1996). Workspace awareness support with radar views. In *Proceedings of CHI* (Vol. 96) (pp. 210–211).

Hafting, T., Fyhn, M., Molden, S., Moser, M.-B., & Moser, E. I. (2005). Microstructure of a spatial map in the entorhinal cortex. *Nature, 436*(7052), 801.

Hagen, M. A. (1974). Picture perception: Toward a theoretical model. *Psychology Bulletin, 81,* 471–497.

Hagen, M. A., & Elliott, H. B. (1976). An investigation of the relationship between viewing conditions and preference for true and modified perspective with adults. *Journal of Experimental Psychology: Human Perception and Performance, 5,* 479–490.

Hallett, P. E. (1986). Eye movements. In K. R. Boff, L. Kaufman, & J. P. Thomas (Eds.), *Handbook of perception and human performance* (Vol. 1) (pp. 25–28). New York: Wiley.

Halverston, J. (1992). The first pictures: Perceptual foundations of paleolithic art. *Perception, 21,* 389–404.

Haring, M. J., & Fry, M. A. (1979). Effect of pictures on children's comprehension of written text. *Educational Communication and Technology Journal, 27*(3), 185–190.

Harris, C. S. (1965). Perceptual adaptation to inverted, reversed and displaced vision. *Psychological Review, 72*(6), 419–444.

Harrison, B., & Vincente, K. J. (1996). An experimental evaluation of transparent menu usage. In *Proceedings of CHI* (Vol. 96) (pp. 391–398).

Hasler, B. S., Kersten, B., & Sweller, J. (2007). Learner control, cognitive load and instructional animation. *Applied Cognitive Psychology, 21,* 713–729.

Havre, S., Hetzler, B., & Nowell, L. (2000). ThemeRiver: Visualizing theme changes over time. In *Proceedings of IEEE information visualization conference* (pp. 115–123).

Hawkins, J., & Blakeslee, S. (2004). *On Intelligence.* Times Books, New York.

Hawkins, J., & Blakeslee, S. (2007). *On intelligence: How a new understanding of the brain will lead to the creation of truly intelligent machines.* Macmillan.

Hay, D., Kinchin, I., & Lygo-Baker, S. (2008). Making learning visible: The role of concept mapping in higher education. *Studies in Higher Education, 33*(3), 295–311.

Healey, C. G. (1996). Choosing effective colors for data visualization. In *Proceedings of IEEE visualization conference* (pp. 263–270).

Healey, C. G., Booth, K. S., & Enns, J. T. (1998). High-speed visual estimation using pre-attentive processing. *ACM Transactions on Human–Computer Interaction, 3*(2), 107–135.

Healey, C. G., Kocherlakota, S., Rao, V., Mehta, R., & St Amant, R. (2008). Visual perception and mixed-initiative interaction for assisted visualization design. *IEEE Transactions on Visualization and Computer Graphics, 14*(2), 396–411.

Heer, J., & Agrawala, M. (2006). Multi-scale banking to 45 degrees. *IEEE Transactions on Visualization and Computer Graphics, 12*(5), 701–708.

Heer, J., & Boyd, D. (2005). Vizster: Visualizating online social networks. In *Proc. IEEE information visualization* (pp. 32–39).

Heider, B., Meskanaite, V., & Peterhaus, E. (2000). Anatomy and physiology of a neural mechanism defining depth order and contrast polarity at illusory contours. *European Journal of Neuroscience, 12*(11), 4117–4130.

Heider, E., & Simmel, M. (1944). An experimental study of apparent behavior. *American Journal of Psychology, 57*, 243–259.

Heiser, J., Phan, D., Agrawala, D., Tversky, B., & Hanrahan, P. (2004). Identification and validation of cognitive design principles for automatic generation of assembly instructions. In *Proceedings of advanced visual interfaces* (Vol. 04) (pp. 311–319).

Held, R. T., Cooper, E. A., & Banks, M. S. (2012). Blur and disparity are complementary cues to depth. *Current Biology, 22*, 1–6.

Held, R., Efstanthiou, A., & Green, M. (1966). Adaptation to displaced and delayed visual feedback from the hand. *Journal of Experimental Psychology, 72*, 887–891.

Hendrix, C., & Barfield, W. (1996). Presence within virtual environments as a function of visual display parameters. *Presence, 5*(3), 272–289.

Hering, E. (1920/1964). *Grundzuge der Lehr vom Lichtsinn.* Berlin: Springer-Verlag. Outlines of a theory of light sense (L. M. Hurvich & D. Jameson, trans.). Cambridge, MA: Harvard University Press.

Herndon, K. P., Zelenik, R. C., Robbins, D. C., Conner, D. B., Snibbe, S. S., & van Dam, A. (1992). Interactive shadows. In *Proceedings of UIST* (Vol. 92) (pp. 1–6).

Herskovits, M. J. (1948). *Man and his works.* New York: Knopf.

Hickox, J. C., & Wickens, C. D. (1999). Effect of elevation angle disparity, complexity and feature type on relating out-of-cockpit field of view to an electronic cartographic map. *Journal of Experimental Psychology: Applied, 5*(3), 284–301.

Hill, B., Roger, T., & Vorhagen, E. W. (1997). Comparative analysis of the quantization of color spaces on the basis of the CIELAB color-difference formula. *ACM Transactions on Graphics, 16*(2), 109–154.

Hillstrom, A. P., & Yantis, S. (1994). Visual attention and motion capture. *Perception and Psychophysics, 55*(4), 399–411.

Hobeika, L., Diard–Detoeuf, C., Garcin, B., Levy, R., & Volle, E. (2016). General and specialized brain correlates for analogical reasoning: A meta–analysis of functional imaging studies. *Human Brain Mapping, 37*(5), 1953–1969.

Hochberg, J. (1968). In the mind's eye. In R. N. Haber (Ed.), *Contemporary theory and research in visual perception* (pp. 309–331). New York: Holt, Rinehart and Winston.

Hochberg, J. (1971). Perception: Space and movement. In J. W. Klink, & L. A. Riggs (Eds.), *Experimental psychology* (pp. 475–550). New York: Holt, Rinehart and Winston.

Hochberg, J. (1986). Representation of motion and space in video and cinematic display. In K. R. Boff, L. Kaufman, & J. P. Thomas (Eds.), *Handbook of perception and human performance* (pp. 1–64). New York: Wiley.

Hochberg, J. E., & Brooks, V. (1962). Pictorial recognition as an unlearned ability. *American Journal of Psychology, 75*, 624–628.

Hochberg, J., & Brooks, V. (1978). Film cutting and visual momentum. In J. W. Senders, D. E. Fisher, & R. A. Mony (Eds.), *Eye movements and the higher psychological functions* (pp. 293–313). Hillsdale, NJ: Erlbaum.

Hoffman, D. M., Girshick, A. R., Akeley, K., & Banks, M. S. (2008). Vergence–accommodation conflicts hinder visual performance and cause visual fatigue. *Journal of Vision, 8*(3), 33.

Hollingworth, A., & Henderson, J. M. (2002). Accurate visual memory for previously attended objects in natural scenes. *Journal of Experimental Psychology: Human Perception and Performance, 28*(1), 113–136.

Holten, D., & van Wijk, J. J. (2009). A user study on visualizing directed edges in graphs. In *Proceedings of SIGCHI* (Vol. 2009) (pp. 2299–2308).

Holten, D., & van Wijk, J. J. (2010). Evaluation of cluster identification performance for different PCP variants. *Computer Graphics Forum, 29*(3), 793–802.

Horgan, J. (1997). *The end of science: Facing the limits of knowledge in the twilight of the scientific age.* Reading, MA: Helix Books.

Horwitz, B., Amunts, K., Bhattacharyya, R., Patkin, D., Jeffries, K., Zilles, K., et al. (2003). Activation of Boca's area during the production of spoken and signed language: A combined cytoarchitectonic mapping and PET analysis. *Neuropsychologia, 41*(14), 1868–1876.

Hotelling, H. (1933). Analysis of a complex of statistical variables into principal components. *Journal of Educational Psychology, 24*, 498–520.

Houde, S. (1992). Iterative design of an interface for easy 3-D direct manipulation. In *Proceedings of CHI* (Vol. 92) (pp. 135–142).

Houtkamp, R., Spekreijse, H., & Roelfsema, P. R. (2003). A gradual spreading of attention during mental curved tracing. *Perception and Psychophysics, 65*(7), 1136–1144.

Howard, I. P. (1991). Spatial vision within egocentric and exocentric frames of reference. In S. R. Ellis, M. K. Kaiser, & A. J. Grunwald (Eds.), *Pictorial communication in virtual and real environments* (pp. 338–358). London: Taylor & Francis.

Howard, I. P., & Childerson, L. (1994). The contributions of motion, the visual frame, and visual polarity to sensations of body tilt. *Perception, 23,* 753–762.

Howard, I. P., & Heckman, T. (1989). Circular vection as a function of the relative sizes, distances and positions of two competing visual displays. *Perception, 18*(5), 657–667.

Howard, J. H., & Kerst, S. M. (1981). Memory and perception of cartographic information for familiar and unfamiliar environments. *Human Factors, 23*(4), 495–504.

Huang, F. C., Chen, K., & Wetzstein, G. (2015). The light field stereoscope: Immersive computer graphics via factored near-eye light field displays with focus cues. *ACM Transactions on Graphics (TOG), 34*(4).

Huang, C. R., Chung, P. C. J., Yang, D. K., Chen, H. C., & Huang, G. J. (2014). Maximum a posteriori probability estimation for online surveillance video synopsis. *IEEE Transactions on Circuits and Systems for Video Technology, 24*(8), 1417–1429.

Huber, D. E., & O'Reilly, R. C. (2003). Persistence and accommodation in short-term priming and other perceptual paradigms: Temporal segregation through synaptic depression. *Cognitive Science, 27,* 403–430.

Hullman, J., & Diakopoulos, N. (2011). Visualization rhetoric: Framing effects in narrative visualization. *IEEE Transactions on Visualization and Computer Graphics, 17*(12), 2231–2240.

Hullman, J., Drucker, S., Riche, N. H., Lee, B., Fisher, D., & Adar, E. (2013). A deeper understanding of sequence in narrative visualization. *IEEE Transactions on visualization and computer graphics, 19*(12), 2406–2415.

Hummel, J. E., & Biederman, I. (1992). Dynamic binding in a neural network for shape recognition. *Psychological Review, 99*(3), 480–517.

Humphreys, G. W., & Bruce, V. (1989). *Visual cognition: Computational, experimental and neurological perspectives.* Hillsdale, NJ: Erlbaum.

Hurvich, L. M. (1981). *Color vision.* Sunderland, MA: Sinauer Associates.

Hutchins, E. (1995). *Distributed cognition.* Cambridge, MA: MIT Press.

Hutto, D. D., & Myin, E. (2012). *Radicalizing enactivism: Basic minds without content.* Mit Press.

Hyman, R. (1953). Stimulus information as a determinant of reaction time. *Journal of Experimental Psychology, 45,* 423–432.

Iavecchia, J. H., Iavecchia, H. P., & Roscoe, S. N. (1988). Eye accommodation to headup virtual images. *Human Factors, 30*(6), 689–702.

Igarashi, T., Kadobayashi, R., Mase, K., & Tanaka, H. (1998). Path drawing for 3D walkthrough. In *Proceedings ACM symposium on user interface software and technology* (pp. 173–174).

Immel, D. S., & Brock, P. J. (1986). An efficient radiosity approach for realistic image synthesis. *IEEE Computer Graphics and Applications, 6*(2), 26–35.

InsKelberg, A., & Dimsdale, B. (1990). Parallel coordinates: A tool for visualizing multidimensional geometry. In *Proceedings of IEEE visualization conference* (pp. 361–378).

Interrante, V., Fuchs, H., & Pizer, S. M. (1997). Conveying 3D shape of smoothly curving transparent surfaces via texture. *IEEE Transactions on Visualization and Computer Graphics, 3*(2), 98–117.

Intraub, H., & Hoffman, J. E. (1992). Reading and visual memory: Remembering scenes that were never seen. *American Journal of Psychology, 105,* 101–114.

Irani, P., Tingley, M., & Ware, C. (2001). Using perceptual syntax to enhance semantic content in diagrams. *IEEE Computer Graphics and Applications, 21*(5), 76–84.

Irani, P., & Ware, C. (2003). Diagramming information structures using 3D perceptual primitives. *ACM Transactions on Computer–Human Interaction, 10*(1), 1–19.

Irwin, D. E. (1992). Memory for position or identity across eye movements. *Journal of Experimental Psychology: Learning, Memory and Cognition, 18,* 307–317.

Irwin, R. J., & McCarthy, D. (1998). Psychophysics: Methods and analyses of signal detection. In K. A. Lattal, M. Perone, et al. (Eds.), *Handbook of research methods in human operant behavior* (pp. 291–321). New York: Plenum Press.

Ishii, H., & Kobayashi, M. (1992). ClearBoard: A seamless medium of shared drawing and conversation with eye contact. In *Proceedings of CHI* (Vol. 92) (pp. 525–532).

Ishikawa, T., Fujiwara, H., Imai, O., & Okabe, A. (2008). Wayfinding with a GPS-based mobile navigation system: A comparison with maps and direct experience. *Journal of Environmental Psychology, 28*(1), 74–82.

Jackson, R., MacDonald, L., & Freeman, K. (1994). *Computer-generated color: A practical guide to presentation and display.* New York: Wiley.

Jackson, R., MacDonald, L., & Freeman, K. (1998). *Computer-generated color.* Chichester, UK: Wiley Professional Computing.

Jacob, R. J. K. (1991). The use of eye movements in human-computer interaction techniques: What you look at is what you get. *ACM Transactions on Information Systems, 9*(3), 152–169.

Jacob, R. J. K., Egeth, H. E., & Bevon, W. (1976). The face as a data display. *Human Factors, 18,* 189–200.

Jankowski, J., & Hachet, M. (2015). Advances in interaction with 3D environments. *Computer Graphics Forum, 34*(1), 152–190.

Jankun–Kelly, T. J., Lanka, Y. S., & Swan, J. E. (2010). An evaluation of glyph perception for real symmetric traceless tensor properties. *Computer Graphics Forum Blackwell Publishing Ltd, 29*(3), 1133–1142.

Jern, M., Thygesen, L., & Brezzi, M. (2009). A web-enabled Geovisual analytics tool applied to OECD regional data. In *Proceedings Eurographics* (pp. 137–144).

Jobard, B., & Lefer, W. (1997). Creating evenly spaced streamlines of arbitrary density. In *Visualization in scientific computing Proceedings of the 8th Eurographics workshop* (Vol. 97) (pp. 43–56).

Johansson, G. (1973). Visual perception of biological motion and a model for its analysis. *Perception and Psychophysics, 14*(2), 201–211.

Johnson, S. H. (2001). Seeing two sides at once: Effects of viewpoint and object structure on recognizing three-dimensional objects. *Journal of Experimental Psychology: Human Perception and Performance, 27*(6), 1468–1484.

Johansson, G. (1975). Visual motion perception. *Scientific American, 232,* 76–98.

Johnson, S. (2007). *The Ghost Map.* Riverhead Trade, Johnson, S. H. (2001). Seeing two sides at once: Effects of viewpoint and object structure on recognizing three-dimensional objects. *Journal of Experimental Psychology: Human Perception and Performance, 27*(6), 1468–1484.

Johnson-Laird, P. N. (1983). *Mental models*. Cambridge, MA: Harvard University Press.

Johnson, B., & Shneiderman, B. (1991). Treemaps: A space-filling approach to the visualization of hierarchical information structures. In *Proceedings of IEEE information visualization conference* (pp. 43–50).

Jolicoeur, P., Gluck, M. A., & Kosslyn, S. M. (1984). Pictures and names: Making the connection. *Cognitive psychology*, *16*(2), 243–275.

Jolicoeur, P. (1985). The time to name disoriented natural objects. *Memory & cognition*, *13*(4), 289–303.

Jonassen, D. H., Beissner, K., & Yacci, M. A. (1993). *Structural knowledge: Techniques for conveying, assessing, and acquiring structural knowledge*. Hillsdale, NJ: Erlbaum.

Jonides, J. (1981). Voluntary versus automatic control over the mind's eye. In J. Long, & A. D. Baddeley (Eds.), *Attention and performance* (Vol. 9) (pp. 187–203). Hillsdale, NJ: Erlbaum.

Jordan, G., Deeb, S. S., Bosten, J. M., & Mollon, J. D. (2010). The dimensionality of color vision in carriers of anomalous trichromacy. *Journal of Vision*, *10*(8), 12.

Jorg, S., & Hormann, H. (1978). The influence of general and specific labels on the recognition of labelled and unlabelled parts of pictures. *Journal of Verbal Learning and Verbal Behaviour*, *17*, 445–454.

Judd, D. B., & Wyszecki, G. W. (1975). *Color in business, science and industry* (3rd ed.). New York: Wiley.

Kabbash, P., Buxton, W., & Sellen, A. (1994). Two-handed input in a compound task. In *Proceedings of CHI* (Vol. 94) (pp. 417–423).

Kahn, K. (1996a). Drawings on napkins, video-game animation and other ways to program computers. *Communications of the ACM*, *39*(8), 49–59.

Kahn, K. (1996). ToonTalk—an animated programming environment for children. *Journal of Visual Languages and Computing*, *7*(2), 197–217.

Kahneman, D., & Egan, P. (2011). *Thinking, fast and slow* (Vol. 1). New York: Farrar, Straus and Giroux.

Kahneman, D., & Henik, A. (1981). Perceptual organization and attention. In M. Kubovy, & J. R. Pomerantz (Eds.), *Perceptual organization* (pp. 181–209). Hillsdale, NJ: Erlbaum.

Kahneman, D., Treisman, A., & Gibbs, B. J. (1992). The reviewing of object files: Object-specific integration of information. *Cognitive Psychology*, *24*, 175–219.

Kaiser, M., Proffitt, D., Whelan, S., & Hecht, H. (1992). Influence of animation on dynamic judgments. *Journal of Experimental Psychology: Human Perception and Performance*, *18*(34), 669–690.

Kalaugher, P. G. (1985). Visual effects with a miniature Leonardo's window: Photographs and real scenes fused stereoscopically. *Perception*, *14*, 553–561.

Kalra, P., Gobbetti, E., Magnenat-Thalmann, N., & Thalmann, D. (1993). A multimedia testbed for facial animation control. In T. S. Chua, & T. L. Kunii (Eds.), (*Multi-Media modeling Proceedings of MMM 93*). (pp. 59–72). Singapore: World Scientific.

Kanizsa, G. (1976). Subjective contours. *Scientific American*, *234*, 48–64.

Kanwisher, N., McDermott, J., & Chun, M. (1997). The fusiform face area: A module in human extrastriate cortex specialized for the perception of faces. *Journal of Neuroscience*, *17*, 4302–4311.

Kanwisher, N., Stanley, D., & Harris, A. (1999). The fusiform face area is selective for faces, not animals. *NeuroReport, 10*(1), 183–187.

Karagiorgi, Y., & Symeou, L. (2005). Translating constructivism into instructional design: Potential and limitations. *Educational Technology & Society, 8*(1), 17–27.

Karsh, D. (2009). Problem solving and situated cognition. In P. Robbins, & M. Aydede (Eds.), *The cambridge handbook of situated cognition* (pp. 264–306). Cambridge, UK: Cambridge University Press.

Kawai, M., Uchikawa, K., & Ujike, H. (1995). Influence of color category on visual search. In *Annual meeting of the association for research in vision and ophthalmology* Paper #2991, Tampa Bay.

Keahey, A. T. (1998). The generalized detail-in-context problem. In *Proceedings of IEEE information visualization conference* (pp. 44–51).

Kelly, D. H. (1979). Motion and vision II: Stabilized spatio-temporal threshold surface. *Journal of the Optical Society of America, 69*, 1340–1349.

Kennedy, J. M. (1974). *A psychology of picture perception*. San Francisco: Jossey-Bass.

Kennedy, R. S., Lilienthal, M. G., Berbaum, K. S., Baltzley, D. R., & McCauley, M. E. (1989). Simulator sickness in U.S. Navy flight simulators. *Aviation, Space and Environmental Medicine, 15*, 10–16.

Kersten-Oertel, M., Chen, S. J. S., & Collins, D. L. (2014). An evaluation of depth enhancing perceptual cues for vascular volume visualization in neurosurgery. *IEEE Transactions on Visualization and Computer Graphics, 20*(3), 391–403.

Kersten, D., Mamassian, P., & Knill, D. C. (1997). Moving cast shadows induce apparent motion in depth. *Perception, 26*, 171–192.

Kersten, D., Mamassian, P., Knill, D. C., & Bulthoff, I. (1996). Illusory motion from shadows. *Nature, 351*, 228–230.

Kieras, D. E., & Meyer, D. E. (1997). An overview of the EPIC architecture for cognition and performance with application to human–computer interaction. *Human–Computer Interaction, 12*, 391–438.

Kiewra, K. A., Kauffman, D. F., Robinson, D., DuBois, N., & Staley, R. K. (1999). Supplementing floundering text with adjunct displays. *Journal of Instructional Science, 27*, 373–401.

Kim, S., Hagh-Shenas, H., & Interrante, V. (2003). Showing shape with texture: Two directions are better than one. In *Proceedings of SPIE* (Vol. 5007) (pp. 332–339).

Kim, W. S., Tendick, F., & Stark, L. (1991). Visual enhancements in pick-and-place tasks. In S. R. Ellis (Ed.), *Pictorial communication in virtual and real environments* (pp. 265–282). London: Taylor & Francis.

Kindlmann, G., Reinhard, E., & Creem, S. (2004). Face-based luminance matching for perceptual colormap generation. In *Proceedings of IEEE visualization conference* (pp. 299–306).

Kindlmann, G., & Westin, F. F. (2006). Diffusion tensor visualization with glyph packing. *IEEE Transactions of Visualization and Computer Graphics, 12*(5), 1329–1335.

Kirby, R. M., Marmanis, H., & Laidlaw, D. H. (1999). Visualizing multivalued data from 2D incompressible flows using concepts from painting. In *Proceedings of IEEE visualization conference* (pp. 333–340).

Kirsh, D., & Maglio, P. (1994). On distinguishing epistemic from pragmatic action. *Cognitive Science, 18*, 513–549.

Knill, D. C., & Pouget, A. (2004). The Bayesian brain: The role of uncertainty in neural coding and computation. *TRENDS in Neurosciences, 27*(12), 712–719.

Koch, C. (2004). *Biophysics of computation: Information processing in single neurons.* Oxford University Press.

Koffka, K. (1935). *Principles of Gestalt psychology.* New York: Harcourt-Brace.

Kohlberg, D. L. (1971). Simple reaction time as a function of stimulus intensity in decibels of light and sound. *Journal of Experimental Psychology, 54*, 757–764.

Kolers, P. A. (1975). Memorial consequences of automatized encoding. *Journal of Experimental Psychology: Human Learning and Memory, 1*, 689–701.

Komerska, R., & Ware, C. (2003). Haptic task constraints for 3D interaction. In *Proceedings of IEEE haptic interfaces for virtual environments and teleoperator systems symposium* (pp. 270–277).

Kosara, R., Miksch, S., & Hauser, H. (2002). Focus + context taken literally. *IEEE Computer Graphics and Applications, 22*(1), 22–29.

Kosslyn, S. M. (1987). Seeing and imagining in the cerebral hemispheres: A computational approach. *Psychological Review, 94*, 148–175.

Kosslyn, S. M. (1990). Thinking visually. *Mind and Language, 5*(4), 324–341.

Kosslyn, S. M. (1994). *Image and brain: The resolution of the imagery debate.* Cambridge, MA: MIT Press.

Kosslyn, S. M., Alpert, N. M., Thompson, W. L., Maljkovic, S. B., Weise, C. E., Chabreis, S., et al. (1993). Visual mental imagery activates topographically organized visual context: PET investigations. *Journal of Cognitive Neuroscience, 5*, 263–287.

Kosslyn, S. M., & Thompson, W. L. (2003). When is early visual cortex activated during mental imagery? *Psychological Bulletin, 129*(5), 723–746.

Kroll, J. E., & Potter, M. C. (1984). Recognizing words, pictures and concepts: A comparison of lexical, object and reality decisions. *Journal of Verbal Learning and Verbal Behaviour, 23*, 39–66.

Krug, S. (2013). *Don't make me think revisited: A common sense approach to Web usability.* Pearson Education India.

Kubovy, M. (1986). *The psychology of linear perspective and Renaissance art.* Cambridge, UK: Cambridge University Press.

Kurtenbach, G., Fitzmaurice, G., Baudel, T., & Buxton, B. (1997). The design and evaluation of a GUI paradigm based on two-hands, tablets and transparency. In *Proceedings of CHI* (Vol. 97) (pp. 35–42).

Laidlaw, D. H., Ahrens, E. T., Kramers, D., Avalos, M. J., Readhead, C., & Jacobs, R. E. (1998). Visualizing diffusion tensor images of the mouse spinal cord. In *Proceedings of IEEE visualization conference* (pp. 127–134).

Laidlaw, D. H., Kirby, R. M., Davidson, J. S., Miller, T. S., da Silva, M., Warren, W. H., et al. (2001). Quantitative comparative evaluation of 2D vector field visualization methods. In *Proceedings of IEEE visualization conference* (pp. 143–150).

Lakoff, G., & Johnson, M. (1980). *Metaphors we live by*. University of Chicago Press.

Lamping, J., Rao, R., & Pirolli, P. (1995). A focus + content technique based on hyperbolic geometry for viewing large hierarchies. In *Proceedings of CHI* (Vol. 95) (pp. 401–408).

Landauer, T. K. (1986). How much do people remember? Some estimates of the quantity of learned information in long-term memory. *Cognitive Science*, *10*, 477–493.

Land, M. K., & Tatler, B. (2009). *Looking and acting: Vision and eye movements in natural behavior*. Oxford: Oxford University Press.

Laramee, R. S., & Ware, C. (2002). Rivalry and interference with a head-mounted display. *ACM Transactions on Human–Computer Interaction*, *9*(3), 1–14.

Larkin, J. H., & Simon, H. A. (1987). Why a diagram is (sometimes) worth ten thousand words. *Cognitive Science*, *11*, 65–99.

LaViola Jr, J. J., Kruijff, E., McMahan, R. P., Bowman, D., & Poupyrev, I. P. (2017). 3D user interfaces: theory and practice. Addison-Wesley Professional.

Lawson, R., Humphreys, G. W., & Watson, D. (1994). Object recognition under sequential viewing conditions: Evidence for viewpoint-specific recognition procedures. *Perception*, *23*, 595–614.

Lee, D. N., & Young, D. S. (1985). Visual timing of interceptive action. In D. Ingle, M. Jeannerod, & D. N. Lee (Eds.), *Brain mechanisms of spatial vision* (pp. 1–30). Leiden, The Netherlands: Martinus Nijhoff.

Lennie, P. (1998). Single units and cortical organization. *Perception*, *27*, 889–935.

Leslie, A. M., & Keeble, S. (1987). Do six-month-old infants perceive causality? *Cognition*, *25*, 265–288.

Levelt, W., Richardson, G., & Heu, W. (1985). Pointing and voicing in deictic expressions. *Journal of Memory and Language*, *24*, 133–164.

Levine, M. (1975). *A cognitive theory of learning*. Hillsdale, NJ: Erlbaum.

Levine, M., Marchon, I., & Hanley, G. (1984). The placement and misplacement of you are here maps. *Environment and Behavior*, *16*(2), 139–157.

Levkowitz, H., & Herman, G. T. (1992). The design and evaluation of color scales for image data. *IEEE Computer Graphics and Applications*, *12*(1), 72–80.

Levoy, M., & Whitaker, R. (1990). Gaze-directed volume rendering. *Computer Graphics*, *24*(2), 217–224.

Li, Y. (1997). *Oriented particles for scientific visualization*. Canada: Master's thesis, University of New Brunswick.

Li, Z. (1998). A neural model of contour integration in the primary visual cortex. *Neural Computing*, *10*(4), 903–940.

Liang, J., Shaw, C., & Green, M. (1991). On temporal–spatial realism in the virtual reality environment. In *Proceedings of UIST* (Vol. 91) (pp. 19–25).

Li, J., Martens, J.-B., & van Wijk, J. J. (2010). Judging correlation from scatterplots and parallel coordinate plots. *Information Visualization*, *9*(1), 13–29.

Limoges, S., Ware, C., & Knight, W. (1989). Displaying correlation using position, motion, point size, or point color. In *Proceedings of graphics interface* (Vol. 89) (pp. 262–265).

Linos, P. K., Aubet, P., Dumas, L., Helleboid, Y., Lejeune, D., & Tulula, P. (1994). Visualizing program dependencies: An experimental study. *Software Practice and Experience*, 24(4), 387–403.

Linstrom, C. J., Silverman, C. A., & Susman, W. M. (2000). Facial motion analysis with a video and computer system: A preliminary report. *American Journal of Otology*, 21, 123–129.

Little, W., Fowler, H. W., & Coulson, J. (Eds.). (1972). *Shorter oxford english dictionary* (3rd ed.) (Vol. 2) (p. 2364). Oxford: Oxford University Press.

Liu, S., & Hua, H. (2009). Time multiplexed dual-focal plane head-mounted display with liquid lens. *Optics Letters*, 34(11), 1642–1644.

Liu, E., & Picard, R. W. (1994). Periodicity, directionality, and randomness: World features for perceptual pattern recognition. In *Proceedings of the 12th international conference on pattern recognition* (pp. 184–189).

Livingston, M. S., & Hubel, D. H. (1988). Segregation of form, movement and depth: Anatomy, physiology and perception. *Science*, 240, 740–749.

Lloyd, R. (1997). Visual search processes used in map reading. *Cartographica*, 34(1), 11–32.

Loftus, E. E., & Hoffman, H. G. (1989). Misinformation and memory: The creation of new memories. *Journal of Experimental Psychology: General*, 118, 100–104.

Logan, G. D. (1994). Spatial attention and the apprehension of spatial relations. *Journal of Experimental Psychology: Human Perception and Performance*, 20, 1015–1036.

Lokuge, I., Glibert, S. A., & Richards, W. (1996). Structuring information with mental models: A tour of Boston. In *Proceedings of CHI* (Vol. 96) (pp. 413–419).

Lowther, K., & Ware, C. (1996). Vection with large-screen 3D imagery. In *Proceedings of CHI* (Vol. 96) (pp. 233–234).

Luck, S. J., & Vogel, E. K. (1997). The capacity of visual working memory for features and conjunctions. *Nature*, 390, 279–280.

Lu, C., & Fender, D. H. (1972). The interaction of color and luminance in stereoscopic vision. *Investigative Ophthalmology*, 11, 482–490.

Luo, M. R., Cui, G., & Rigg, B. (2001). The development of the CIE 2000 colour–difference formula: CIEDE2000. *Color Research & Application*, 26(5), 340–350.

Macdonald-Ross, M. (1977). How numbers are shown. *Educational Technology Research and Development*, 25(4), 359–409.

MacKenzie, I. S. (1992). Fitts' law as a research and design tool in human–computer interaction. *Human–Computer Interaction*, 7, 91–139.

Mackenzie, C. L., & Iberall, T. (1994). The grasping hand. In *Advances in psychology series* (Vol. 104). Amsterdam: North-Holland.

Mackinlay, J. D., Card, S. K., & Robertson, G. G. (1990). Rapid controlled movement through a virtual 3D workspace. In *Proceedings SIGGRAPH '90* (Vol. 24) (pp. 171–176).

Mack, A., & Rock, I. (1998). *Inattentional blindness*. Cambridge, MA: MIT Press.

Mackworth, N. H. (1976). Ways of recording line of sight. In R. A. Monty, & J. W. Senders (Eds.), *Eye movements and psychological processing* (pp. 173–178). Hillsdale, NJ: Erlbaum.

MacLeod, C. M. (1991). Half a century of research on the Stroop effect: An integrative review. *Psychological Bulletin, 109*(2), 163–203.

Madison, C., Thompson, W., Kersen, D., Shirley, P., & Smits, B. (2001). Use of interreflection and shadow for surface contact. *Perception and Psychophysics, 63,* 187–193.

Mahny, M., Vaneyecken, L., & Oosterlinka, A. (1994). Evaluation of uniform color spaces after the adoption of CIElab and CIEluv. *Color Research and Application, 19*(2), 105–121.

Malik, J., & Perona, P. (1990). Preattentive texture discrimination with early vision mechanisms. *Journal of the Optical Society of America, A7*(5), 923–932.

Maloney, J., Resnick, M., Rusk, N., Silverman, B., & Eastmond, E. (2010). The scratch programming language and environment. *ACM Transactions on Computing Education (TOCE), 10*(4), 16.

Mark, D. M., & Franck, A. U. (1996). Experiential and formal models of geographical space. *Environment and Planning B: Planning and Design, 23*(1), 3–24.

Marr, D. (1982). *Vision.* New York: W.H. Freeeman.

Marr, D., & Nishihara, H. K. (1978). Representation and recognition of the spatial organization of three-dimensional shapes. In *Proceedings of the royal society of London series B* (Vol. 207) (pp. 269–294).

Masin, S. C. (1997). The luminance conditions of transparency. *Perception, 26,* 39–50.

Massie, T. H., & Salisbury, J. K. (1994). The PHANToM haptic interface: A device for probing virtual objects. *Dynamic Systems and Control, 55*(1), 295–301.

Massironi, M. (2004). *The psychology of graphic images.* Hillsdale, NJ: Erlbaum.

Matlin, M. W. (1994). *Cognition* (3rd ed.). Fort Worth, TX: Harcourt Brace.

Mayer, L. A., Dijkstra, S., Hughes Clarke, J., Paton, M., & Ware, C. (1997). Interactive tools for the exploration and analysis of multibeam and other seafloor acoustic data. In N. G. Pace, E. Pouliquen, O. Bergem, & A. P. Lyons (Eds.), *High-Frequency acoustics in shallow water* (pp. 355–362). Office of Naval Research, U.S. National Liaison Officer to the SACLANTCEN.

Mayer, R. E., Hegarty, M., Mayer, S., & Campbell, J. (2005). When static media promote active learning: Annotated illustrations versus narrated animations in multimedia instruction. *Journal of Experimental Psychology: Applied, 11*(4), 256–265.

Mayer, R. E., Moreno, R., Boire, M., & Vagge, S. (1999). Maximizing constructivist learning from multimedia communications by minimizing cognitive load. *Journal of Educational Psychology, 91*(4), 638–643.

Mayer, R. E., & Sims, V. K. (1994). For whom is a picture worth a thousand words? Extensions of a dual-coding theory of multimedia learning. *Journal of Educational Psychology, 86,* 389–401.

McCauley, M. E., & Sharkey, T. J. (1992). Cybersickness: Perception of self-motion in virtual environments. *Presence, 1*(3), 311–318.

McCormick, E., Wickens, C. D., Banks, R., & Yeh, M. (1998). Frame of reference effects on scientific visualization subtasks. *Human Factors, 40,* 443–451.

McGreevy, M. W. (1992). The presence of field geologists in Mars-like terrain. *Presence, 1*(4), 375–403.

McManus, I. C. (1977). Note: Half a million basic color words: Berlin and Kay and the usage of color words in literature and science. *Perception, 26,* 367–370.

McNeill, D. (1992). *Hand and mind: What gestures reveal about thought.* Chicago: University of Chicago Press.

Megaw, E. D., & Richardson, J. (1979). Target uncertainty and visual scanning strategies. *Human Factors, 21*(3), 303–316.

Melcher, D. (2001). Persistence of visual memory for scenes: A medium-term memory may help us keep track of objects during visual tasks. *Nature, 412,* 401.

Metelli, E. (1974). The perception of transparency. *Scientific American, 230,* 91–98.

Meyer, G. W., & Greenberg, D. R. (1988). Color-defective vision and computer graphics displays. *IEEE Computer Graphics and Applications, 8*(5), 28–40.

Michotte, A. (1963). *The perception of causality* (T. Miles & E. Miles, trans.). London: Methuen.

Mihtsentu, M. T., & Ware, C. (2015). Discrete versus solid: Representing quantity using linear, area, and volume glyphs. *ACM Transactions on Applied Perception (TAP), 12*(3), 12.

Milner, A. D., & Goodale, M. A. (1995). The visual brain in action. *Oxford Psychology Series* (Vol. 27). Oxford: Oxford University Press.

Mitchell, P., Ware, C., & Kelley, J. (2009). Designing flow visualizations for oceanography and meteorology using interactive design space hill climbing. In *Proceedings of SMC* (Vol. 2009) (pp. 355–361).

Miyake, A., & Shah, P. (1999). Toward unified theories of working memory: Emerging general consensus, unresolved theoretical issues, and future research directions. In A. Miyake, & P. Shah (Eds.), *Models of working memory* (pp. 442–481). Cambridge, UK: Cambridge University Press.

Mon-Williams, M., & Wann, J. P. (1998). Binocular virtual reality displays: When problems do and don't occur. *Human Factors, 40*(1), 42–49.

Montemurro, M. A., Rasch, M. J., Murayama, Y., Logothetis, N. K., & Panzeri, S. (2008). Phase-of-firing coding of natural visual stimuli in primary visual cortex. *Current Biology, 18*(5), 375–380.

Moray, N. (1981). Monitoring behavior and supervising control. In K. R. Boff, L. Kaufman, & J. P. Thomas (Eds.), *Handbook of perception and human performance 2* (pp. 40–46). New York: Wiley.

Moray, N., & Rotenberg, I. (1989). Fault management in process control: Eye movements and action. *Ergonomics, 32*(11), 1319–1342.

Moroney, N., Fairchild, M. D., Hunt, R. W., Li, C., Luo, M. R., & Newman, T. (January 2002). The CIECAM02 color appearance model. In *Proceedings Color and Imaging Conference. Society for Imaging Science and Technology* (2002(1)) (pp. 23–27).

Morovi, J. (2008). *Color gamut mapping.* New York: Wiley.

Morton, J., & Johnson, M. H. (1991). CONSPEC and CONLEARN: A two-process theory of infant face recognition. *Psychological Review, 98,* 164–181.

Mousavi, S. Y., Low, R., & Sweller, J. (1995). Reducing cognitive load by mixing auditory and visual presentation modes. *Journal of Educational Psychology, 87,* 319–334.

Mullen, K. Y. (1985). The contrast sensitivity of human color vision to red–green and blue–yellow chromatic gratings. *American Journal of Optometry and Physiological Optics, 359,* 381–400.

Munzner, T., Guimbretire, E., & Robertson, G. (1999). Constellation: A visualization tool for linguistic queries from MindNet. In *Proceedings of IEEE information visualization conference* (pp. 132–135).

Najjar, L. J. (1998). Principles of educational multimedia user interface design. *Human Factors, 40*(2), 311–323.

Nakayama, K., Shimono, S., & Silverman, G. H. (1989). Stereoscopic depth: Its relation to image segmentation, grouping and the recognition of occluding objects. *Perception, 18,* 55–68.

Nakayama, K., & Silverman, G. H. (1986). Serial and parallel processing of visual feature conjunctions. *Nature, 320,* 264–265.

Nemire, K., Jacoby, R. H., & Ellis, S. R. (1994). Simulation fidelity of a virtual environment display. *Human Factors, 36*(1), 79–93.

Neurath, O. (1936). International picture language. In *The first rules of isotype.* With isotype pictures. Kegan Paul & Company.

Neveau, C. E., & Stark, L. W. (1998). The virtual lens. *Presence, 7*(4), 370–381.

Newell, A. (1990). *Unified theories of cognition.* Cambridge, MA: Harvard University Press.

Newell, K. M. (1991). Motor skill acquisition. *Annual Review of Psychology, 42*(1), 213–237.

Newell, A., & Rosenbloom, P. (1981). Mechanisms of skill acquisition and the law of practice. In J. R. Anderson (Ed.), *Cognitive skills and their acquisition* (pp. 1–55). Hillsdale, NJ: Erlbaum.

Norman, D. A. (1988). *The psychology of everyday things.* New York: Basic Books.

Norman, J. E., Todd, J. T., & Phillips, E. (1995). The perception of surface orientation from multiple sources of optical information. *Perception and Psychophysics, 57*(5), 629–636.

Noro, K. (1993). Industrial application of virtual reality and possible health problems. *Japanese Journal of Ergonomica, 29,* 126–129.

North, M. N., North, S. M., & Coble, J. R. (1996). Effectiveness of virtual environment desensitization in the treatment of agoraphobia. *Presence, 5*(3), 346–352.

Novak, J. D. (1981). Applying learning psychology and philosophy of science to biology teaching. *The American Biology Teacher, 43*(1), 12–20.

Novak, J. D. (1991). Clarify with concept maps: A tool for students and teachers alike. *The Science Teacher, 58*(7), 45–49.

O'Regan, J. K., & Noë, A. (2001). A sensorimotor account of vision and visual consciousness. *Behavioral and Brain Sciences, 24*(5), 939–973.

Oakes, L. M. (1994). Development of infants' use of continuity cues in their perception of causality. *Developmental Psychology, 30,* 869–879.

Ogle, K. N. (1962). The visual space sense. *Science, 135,* 763–771.

Oliva, A. (2005). Gist of the scene. In L. Itti, & G. Rees (Eds.), *Neurobiology of attention* (pp. 251–256). San Diego, CA: Academic Press.

Oliva, A., & Schyns, P. (1997). Coarse blobs or fine edges? Evidence that information diagnosticity changes the perception of complex visual stimuli. *Cognitive Psychology, 34,* 72–107.

Oliva, A., Torralba, S., Castelhano, M. S., & Henderson, J. M. (2003). Top-down control of visual attention in object detection. In *Proceedings of IEEE international conference on image processing* (pp. 253–256).

Oviatt, S. (1999). Mutual disambiguation of recognition errors in a multimodal architecture. In *Proceedings of CHI* (Vol. 99) (pp. 576–583).

Oviatt, S., DeAngeli, A., & Kuhn, K. (1997). Integration and synchronization of input modes during multimodal human computer interaction. In *Proceedings of CHI* (Vol. 97) (pp. 415–422).

Owlsley, C. J., Sekuler, R., & Siemensne, D. (1983). Contrast sensitivity through adulthood. *Vision Research, 23,* 689–699.

O'Regan, J. K. (1992). Solving the "real" mysteries of visual perception: The world as an outside memory. *Canadian Journal of Psychology, 46,* 461–488.

Paas, F., Renkl, A., & Sweller, J. (2003). Cognitive load theory and instructional design: Recent developments. *Educational Psychologist, 38*(1), 1–4.

Paivio, A. (1987). *Mental representations: A dual coding approach.* Oxford Psychology Series. Oxford: Oxford University Press.

Paivio, A., & Csapo, K. (1969). Concrete image and verbal memory codes. *Journal of Experimental Psychology, 80,* 279–285.

Palmer, S. E. (1975). The effect of contextual scenes on the identification of objects. *Memory and Cognition, 3*(5), 519–526.

Palmer, S. E. (1992). Common region: A new principle of perceptual grouping. *Cognitive Psychology, 24,* 436–447.

Palmer, S. E. (1999). Vision science: Photons to phenomenology. MIT press.

Palmer, S. E., & Rock, I. (1994). Rethinking perceptual organization: The role of uniform connectedness. *Psychonomic Bulletin and Review, 1*(1), 29–55.

Palmer, S. E., Rosch, E., & Chase, P. (1981). Canonical perspective and perception of objects. In J. Long, & A. Baddeley (Eds.), *Attention and performance* (Vol. 9). Hillsdale, NJ: Erlbaum.

Palmiter, S., Elkerton, J., & Paggett, P. (1991). Animated demonstrations vs. written instructions for learning procedural tasks: A preliminary investigation. *International Journal of Man–Machine Studies, 34,* 687–701.

Parker, G., Franck, G., & Ware, C. (1998). Visualizing of large nested graphs in 3D: Navigation and interaction. *Journal of Visual Languages, 9,* 299–317.

Pashler, H. (1995). Attention and visual perception: Analyzing divided attention. In S. Kosslyn, & D. Osherson (Eds.), *An invitation to cognitive science: Visual cognition* (Vol. 2) (pp. 71–100). Cambridge, MA: MIT Press.

Patterson, R., & Martin, W. L. (1992). Human stereopsis. *Human Factors, 34*(6), 669–692.

Pausch, R., Snoddy, J., Taylor, R., Watson, S., & Haseltine, E. (1996). Disney's Aladdin: First steps towards storytelling in virtual reality. In *Proceedings SIGGRAPH* (Vol. 96) (pp. 193–203).

Pearson, D., Hanna, E., & Martinez, K. (1990). Computer-generated cartoons. In H. Barlow, C. Blakemore, & M. Weston Smith (Eds.), *Images and understanding* (pp. 46–60). Cambridge, UK: Cambridge University Press.

Peli, E. (1999). Optometric and perceptual issues with head-mounted display (HMD). In P. Mouroulis (Ed.), *Optical design for visual instrumentation* (pp. 205–276). New York: McGraw-Hill.

Perrett, D. I., Oram, M. W., Harries, M. H., Bevan, R., Hietanen, J. K., Benson, P. J., et al. (1991). Viewer-centered and object-centered coding of heads in the Macaque temporal cortex. *Experimental Brain Research, 86,* 159–173.

Perry, M. (2003). Distributed cognition. In J. M. Carroll (Ed.), *HCI models, theories, and frameworks: Toward a multidisciplinary science* (pp. 193–223). San Francisco: Morgan Kaufmann.

Peterson, H. E., & Dugas, D. J. (1972). The relative importance of contrast and motion in visual detection. *Human Factors, 14,* 207–216.

Phillips, W. A. (1974). On the distinction between sensory storage and short-term visual memory. *Perception and Psychophysics, 16,* 283–290.

Pickett, R. M., & Grinstein, G. G. (1988). Iconograhic displays for visualizing multidimensional data. In *Proceedings of IEEE conference on systems, man, and cybernetics* (pp. 514–519).

Pickett, R. M., Grinstein, G. G., Levkowitz, H., & Smith, S. (1995). Harnessing pre-attentive perceptual processes in visualization. In G. Grinstein, & H. Levkowitz (Eds.), *Perceptual issues in visualization* (pp. 33–45). New York: Springer.

Pilar, D. H., & Ware, C. (2013). Representing flow patterns by using streamlines with glyphs. *IEEE Transactions on Visualization and Computer Graphics, 19*(8), 1331–1341.

Pineo, D., & Ware, C. (2010). A neural modeling of flow rendering effectiveness. *ACM Transactions on Applied Perception, 7*(3), 1–15.

Pinker, S. (2007). *The stuff of thought: Language as a window into human nature.* New York: Viking Press.

Pirolli, P. (2003). Exploring and finding information. In J. M. Caroll (Ed.), *HCI models, theories and frameworks: Toward a multidisciplinary science* (pp. 157–191). San Francisco: Morgan Kaufmann.

Pirolli, P., & Card, S. K. (1995). Information foraging in information access environments. In *Proceedings of CHI* (Vol. 95) (pp. 51–58).

Pirolli, P., & Card, S. (May 2005). The sensemaking process and leverage points for analyst technology as identified through cognitive task analysis. In *Proc. International Conference on Intelligence Analysis* (5) (pp. 2–4).

Plumlee, M. (2004). *Linking focus and context in 3D multiscale environments, doctoral dissertation.* Durham: University of New Hampshire.

Plumlee, M., & Ware, C. (2002). Modeling performance for zooming vs. multi-window interfaces based on visual working memory. In *Proceedings of advanced visual interfaces* (pp. 59–68).

Plumlee, M., & Ware, C. (2003). An evaluation of methods for linking 3D views. In *Proceedings SIGGRAPH* (Vol. 2003) (pp. 193–201).

Plumlee, M., & Ware, C. (2006). Cognitive costs of zooming versus using multiple windows. *ACM Transactions on Applied Perception, 13*(2), 1–31.

Poirson, A. B., & Wandell, B. A. (1996). Pattern-color separable pathways predict sensitivity to simple colored patterns. *Vision Research, 36*(4), 515–526.

Posner, M. I., & Keele, S. (1968). On the generation of abstract ideas. *Journal of Experimental Psychology, 77*, 353–363.

Post, D. L., & Greene, E. A. (1986). Color name boundaries for equally bright stimuli on a CRT: Phase I. *Society for Information Display, Digest of Technical Papers, 86*, 70–73.

Post, D., Han, B., & Ifju, P. (1997). *High sensitivity Moiré: Experimental analysis for mechanics and materials.* New York: Springer.

Postma, A., & De Haan, E. H. E. (1996). What was where? Memory for object locations. *Quarterly Journal of Experimental Psychology, 49A*(1), 178–199.

Postma, A., Izendoorn, R., & De Haan, E. H. E. (1998). Sex differences in object location memory. *Brain and Cognition, 36*, 334–345.

Potter, M. C. (1976). Short-term conceptual memory for pictures. *Journal of Experimental Psychology: Human Learning and Memory, 2*, 509–522.

Potter, M. C. (2002). Recognition memory for briefly presented pictures: The time course of rapidly forgetting. *Journal of Experimental Psychology: Human Perception and Performance, 28*(5), 1163–1175.

Potter, M. C., & Levy, E. I. (1969). Recognition memory for a rapid sequence of pictures. *Journal of Experimental Psychology, 81*, 10–15.

Poupyrev, I., Billinghurst, M., Weghorst, S., & Ichikawa, T. (1996). The Go-Go interaction technique: Non-linear mapping for direct manipulation in VR. In *Proceedings of UIST* (Vol. 96) (pp. 79–80).

Preece, J., Rogers, Y., & Sharp, H. (2015). *Interaction design: Beyond human-computer interaction.* John Wiley & Sons.

Price, C. J., & Humphreys, G. W. (1989). The effects of surface detail on object categorization and naming. *Quarterly Journal of Experimental Psychology, 41A*, 797–828.

Puce, A., Allison, T., Gore, J. C., & McCarthy, G. (1995). Face-sensitive regions in human extra-striated cortex studied by functional MRI. *Journal of Neurophysiology, 74*, 1192–1199.

Pylyshyn, Z. W., & Storm, R. W. (1988). Tracking multiple independent targets: Evidence for a parallel tracking mechanism. *Spatial Vision, 3*, 179–197.

Qian, N., & Zhu, Y. (1997). Physiological computation of binocular disparity. *Vision Research, 37*, 1811–1827.

Quinlan, P., & Humphreys, G. (1987). Visual search for targets defined by combinations of color, shape and size: An examination of task constraints on feature and conjunction searches. *Perception and Psychophysics, 41*(5), 455–472.

Rader, C., Brand, C., & Lewis, C. (1997). Degrees of comprehension: Children's understanding of a visual programming environment. In *Proceedings of CHI* (Vol. 97) (pp. 351–358).

Ramachandran, V. S. (1988). Perception of shape from shading. *Nature, 331,* 163–166.

Ramachandran, V. S. (1999). *Phantoms in the Brain: Probing the mysteries of the human mind.* New York: Quill Press.

Ramlogan, S., Raman, V., & Sweet, J. (2014). A comparison of two forms of teaching instruction: Video vs. live lecture for education in clinical periodontology. *European Journal of Dental Education, 18*(1), 31–38.

Rao, R., & Card, S. K. (1994). The table lens: Merging graphical and symbolic representations in an interactive focus + context visualization for tabular information. In *Proceedings of CHI* ('94) (pp. 318–322).

Ratcliff, R., & McKoon, G. (1996). Bias effects in implicit memory tasks. *Journal of Experimental Psychology, 125*(4), 403–421.

Raymond, J. E., Shapiro, K. L., & Arnell, K. M. (1992). Temporary suppression of visual processing in an RSVP task: An attentional blink? *Journal of Experimental Psychology: Human Perception and Performance, 18,* 849–860.

Regan, D. (1989). Orientation discrimination for objects defined by relative motion and objects defined by luminance contrasts. *Vision Research, 18,* 1389–1400.

Regan, D., & Hamstra, S. (1991). Shape discrimination for motion and contrast defined contours: Squareness is special. *Perception, 20,* 315–336.

Rensink, R. A. (2000). The dynamic representation of scenes. *Visual Cognition, 7,* 17–42.

Rensink, R. A. (2002). Change detection. *Annual Review of Psychology, 53,* 245–277.

Rensink, R. A., & Baldridge, G. (2010). The perception of correlation in scatterplots. *Computer Graphics Forum, 29,* 1203–1210.

Rensink, R. A., O'Regan, J. K., & Clark, J. J. (1997). To see or not to see: The need for attention to perceive changes in scenes. *Psychological Science, 8*(5), 368–373.

Rheingans, P. (1999). Task-based color scale design: 3D visualization for data exploration and decision making. In *Proceedings of applied image and pattern recognition* (pp. 35–43). Bellingham, WA: SPIE Press.

Rhodes, G. (1995). Face recognition and configurational coding. In T. Valentine (Ed.), *Cognitive and computational aspects of face recognition* (pp. 47–68). New York: Routledge.

Rhodes, P. A., & Luo, M. R. (1996). A system of WYSIWYG colour communication. *Displays, 16*(4), 213–221.

Richards, W. (1967). Differences among color normals: Classes I and II. *Journal of the Optical Society of America, 57,* 1047–1055.

Richards, W., & Koenderink, J. J. (1995). Trajectory mapping: A new non-metric scaling technique. *Perception, 24,* 1315–1331.

Riggs, L. A., Merton, P. A., & Mortion, H. B. (1974). Suppression of visual phosphenes during saccadic eye movements. *Vision Research, 14,* 997–1010.

Rimé, B., Boulanger, B., Laubin, P., Richants, M., & Stroobants, K. (1985). The perception of interpersonal emotions originated by patterns of movements. *Motivation and Emotion, 9,* 241–260.

Ritter, W., Sussman, E., Deacon, D., Cowan, N., & Vaughan, H. G. (1999). Two cognitive systems simultaneously prepared for opposite events. *Psychophysiology, 36*(6), 835–838.

Rizzolatti, G., & Sinigaglia, C. (2008). *Mirrors in the Brain: How we share our actions and emotions*. Oxford: Oxford University Press.

Robertson, G., Czerwinski, M., Larson, K., Robbins, D., Thiel, D., & van Dantzich, M. (1998). Data Mountain: Using spatial memory for document management. In *Proceedings of UIST* (Vol. 89) (pp. 153–162).

Robertson, G., Mackinlay, J. D., & Card, S. W. (1993). Information visualization using 3D interactive animation. *Communications of the ACM, 36*(4), 57–71.

Robertson, P. K., & O'Callaghan, J. E. (1986). The generation of color sequences for univariate and bivariate mapping. *IEEE Computer Graphics and Applications, 6*(2), 24–32.

Robertson, P. K., & O'Callaghan, J. E. (1988). The application of perceptual colour spaces to the display of remotely sensed data. *IEEE Transactions on Geoscience and Remote Sensing, 26*(1), 49–59.

Rock, I., & Gutman, D. (1981). The effect of inattention on form perception. *Journal of Experimental Psychology: Human Perception and Performance, 7*(2), 275–285.

Rogers, E. (1995). A cognitive theory of visual interaction. In J. Glasgos, N. H. Narayanan, & B. Chandraseekaran (Eds.), *Diagrammatic reasoning: Cognitive and computational perspectives* (pp. 481–500). Cambridge, MA: AAAI Press/MIT Press.

Rogers, B., & Cagnello, R. (1989). Disparity curvature and the perception of three-dimensional surfaces. *Nature, 339*, 137–139.

Rogers, B., & Graham, M. (1979). Similarities between motion parallax and stereopsis in human depth perception. *Vision Research, 22*, 261–270.

Rogowitz, B. E., & Treinish, L. A. (1996). How not to lie with visualization. *Computers in Physics, 10*(3), 268–273.

Romesburg, C. H. (1984). *Cluster analysis for researchers*. Belmont, CA: Lifetime Learning Publications.

Rood, O. N. (1897). *Modern chromatics*. Reprinted in facsimile in 1973. New York: Van Nostrand Reinhold.

Rosch, E. (1973). On the internal structure of perceptual and semantic categories. In T. E. Moore (Ed.), *Cognitive development and the acquisition of language* (pp. 111–144). New York: Academic Press.

Rosch, E. (1975). Cognitive representation of semantic categories. *Journal of Experimental Psychology: General, 104*(3), 192–233.

Roscoe, S. R. (1991). The eyes prefer real images. In S. R. Ellis, M. Kaiser, & A. J. Grunwald (Eds.), *Pictorial communication in virtual and real environments* (pp. 577–585). London: Taylor & Francis.

Rosenthal, N. E. (1993). Diagnosis and treatment of seasonal affective disorder. *Journal of the American Medical Association, 270*, 2717–2720.

Rosetti, Y., Koga, K., & Mano, T. (1993). Prismatic displacement of vision induces transient changes in the timing of eye-hand coordination. *Perception and Psychophysics, 54*(3), 355–364.

Ruginski, I. T., Boone, A. P., Padilla, L. M., Liu, L., Heydari, N., Kramer, H. S., et al. (2016). Non-expert interpretations of hurricane forecast uncertainty visualizations. *Spatial Cognition & Computation*, *16*(2), 154–172.

Rumbaugh, J., Booch, G., & Jacobson, I. (1999). *Unified modeling language reference manual*. Reading, MA: Addison-Wesley Object Technology Series.

Russo, J. E., & Rosen, L. D. (1975). An eye fixation analysis of multi-alternative choice. *Memory and Cognition*, *3*, 267–276.

Rutkowski, C. (1982). An introduction to the human applications standard computer interface, Part 1: Theory and principles. *Byte*, *7*(11), 291–310.

Ruttkay, Z., Noot, H., & Hagen, P. (2003). Emotion disc and emotion squares: Tools to explore the facial expression space. *Computer Graphics Forum*, *22*(1), 49–53.

Ryan, T. A., & Schwartz, C. B. (1956). Speed of perception as a function of mode of representation. *American Journal of Psychology*, *69*, 60–69.

Sadr, J., Jarudi, F., & Sinha, P. (2003). The role of the eyebrows in face recognition. *Perception*, *32*(3), 285–293.

Sáez-López, J. M., Román-González, M., & Vázquez-Cano, E. (2016). Visual programming languages integrated across the curriculum in elementary school: A two year case study using "scratch" in five schools. *Computers & Education*, *97*, 129–141.

Saito, T., & Takahashi, T. (1990). Comprehensible rendering of 3-D shapes. *ACM SIGGRAPH Computer Graphics*, *24*(4), 197–206.

Sarkar, M., & Brown, M. H. (1994). Graphical fisheye views. *Communications of the ACM*, *37*(12), 73–83.

Saunders, J. A., & Chen, Z. (2015). Perceptual biases and cue weighting in perception of 3D slant from texture and stereo information. *Journal of Vision*, *15*(2), 14.

Saussure, F. de (1959). *Course in general linguistics*. New York: Reprinted by Fontana/Collins (Published posthumously based on lectures given at the University of Geneva between 1906 and 1911.).

Sayim, B., Jameson, K. A., Alvarado, N., & Szeszel, M. K. (2005). Semantic and perceptual representations of color: Evidence of a shared color-naming function. *Journal of Cognition and Culture*, *5*(3), 427–486.

Scanlan, L. A. (1975). Visual time compression: Spatial and temporal cues. *Human Factors*, *17*, 337–345.

Schacter, D. L., Addis, D. R., & Buckner, R. L. (2007). The prospective brain: Remembering the past to imagine the future. *Nature Reviews. Neuroscience*, *8*, 657–661.

Schaffer, D., Zuo, Z., Bartram, L., Dill, D., Dubs, S., Greenberg, S., et al. (1993). Comparing fisheye and full-zoom techniques for navigation of hierarchically clustered networks. In *Proceedings of graphics interface* (Vol. 93) (pp. 87–96).

Schreiber, B. E., Fukuta, J., & Gordon, F. (2010). Live lecture versus video podcast in undergraduate medical education: A randomised controlled trial. *BMC Medical Education*, *10*(1), 68.

Schreiber, B., Wickens, C. D., Alton, J., Renner, G., & Hickox, J. C. (1998). Navigational checking using 3D maps: The influence of elevation angle, azimuth and foreshortening. *Human Factors*, *40*, 209–223.

Schroeder, W., Martin, K., & Lorenson, B. (1997). *The visualization toolkit*. Upper Saddle River, NJ: Prentice Hall.

Schultz, T., & Kindlmann, G. L. (2010). Superquadric glyphs for symmetric second-order tensors. *IEEE Transactions on Visualization and Computer Graphics*, *16*(6), 1595–1604.

Schumann, J., Strotthotte, T., Raab, A., & Laser, S. (1996). Assessing the effect of non-photorealistic rendered images in CAD. In *Proceedings of CHI* (Vol. 96) (pp. 35–41).

Schwarz, M., Cowan, W., & Beatty, J. (1987). An experimental comparison of RGB, YIQ, LAB, HSV and opponent color models. *ACM Transactions on Graphics*, *6*(2), 123–158.

Segel, E., & Heer, J. (2010). Narrative visualization: Telling stories with data. *IEEE Transactions on Visualization and Computer Graphics*, *16*(6), 1139–1148.

Seigel, A. W., & White, S. H. (1975). The development of spatial representations of large-scale environments. In H. W. Reese (Ed.), *Advances in child development and behaviour* (pp. 9–55). London: Academic Press.

Sekuler, R., & Blake, R. (1990). *Perception* (2nd ed.). New York: McGraw-Hill.

Selker, T., & Koved, L. (1988). Elements of visual language. In *Proceedings of IEEE symposium on visual languages* (pp. 38–44).

Sellen, A., Buxton, B., & Arnott, J. (1992). Using spatial cues to improve videoconferencing. In *Proceedings of CHI* (Vol. 92) (pp. 651–652).

Sellen, A., Fogg, A., Aitken, M., Hodges, S., Rother, C., & Wood, K. (2007). Do life-logging technologies support memory for the past? An experimental study using SenseCam. In *Proceedings of CHI* (Vol. 07) (pp. 81–90).

Serra, L., Hern, N., Choon, C. B., & Poston, T. (1997). Interactive vessel tracing in volume data. In *Proceedings of symposium on interactive 3D graphics* (pp. 131–137).

Shelton, A. L., & McNamara, T. P. (2001). Systems of spatial reference in human memory. *Cognitive Psychology*, *43*, 274–310.

Shenker, M. (1987). Optical design criteria for binocular helmet-mounted display. *Proceedings of SPIE*, *778*, 173–185.

Shepard, R. N. (1962). The analysis of proximities: Multidimensional scaling with unknown distance function, Part I. *Psychometrika*, *27*(2), 125–140.

Shepard, R. N., & Cooper, L. A. (1982). *Mental images and their transformations*. Cambridge, MA: MIT Press.

Shepard, R. N., & Hurwitz, S. (1984). Upward direction mental rotation and discrimination of left and right. *Cognition*, *18*, 161–193.

Sheridan, T. (1972). On how often the supervisor should sample. *IEEE Transactions on Systems Man and Cybernetics*, *6*, 140–145.

Shimojima, A., & Katagiri, Y. (2008). An eye-tracking study of exploitations of spatial constraints in diagrammatic reasoning. In *Proceedings of the 5th International conference on diagrammatic representation and inference* (pp. 74–88).

Shirley, P., & Marschner, P. (2009). *Fundamentals of computer graphics* (3rd ed.). Natick, MA: A.K. Peters.

Shneiderman, B. (1996). The eyes have it: A task by data type taxonomy for information visualizations. In *Proc. IEEE symposium on visual languages* (pp. 336–343). Washington: IEEE Computer Society Press.

Shneiderman, B. (1998). *Designing the user interface* (3rd ed.). Reading, MA: Addison-Wesley.

Sigman, M., & Gilbert, C. D. (2000). Learning to find a shape. *Nature Neuroscience, 3*, 264–269.

Simons, D. J., & Levin, D. T. (1998). Failure to detect changes to people during a realworld interaction. *Psychonomic Bulletin and Review, 5*, 644–669.

Singer, W., & Gray, C. M. (1995). Visual feature integration and the temporal correlation hypothesis. *Annual Review of Neuroscience, 18*, 555–586.

Slater, A., & Kirby, R. (1998). Innate and learned perceptual abilities in the newborn infant. *Experimental Brain Research, 123*, 90–94.

Slater, M., Pérez Marcos, D., Ehrsson, H., & Sanchez-Vives, M. V. (2009). Inducing illusory ownership of a virtual body. *Frontiers in Neuroscience, 3*, 29.

Slater, M., Usoh, M., & Steed, A. (1995). Taking steps, the influence of walking technique on presence in virtual reality. *ACM Transactions on CHI, 2*(3), 201–219.

Slocum, T. S. (1983). Predicting visual clusters on graduated circle maps. *American Cartographer, 10*(1), 59–72.

Small, S. A., Nava, A. S., Perera, G. M., DeLaPaz, R., Mayeux, R., & Stern, Y. (2001). Circuit mechanisms underlying memory encoding and retrieval in the long axis of the hippocampal formation. *Nature Neuroscience, 4*, 442–449.

Smith, A. R. (1978). Color gamut transform pairs. *Computer Graphics, 12*, 12–19.

Smith, G., & Atchison, D. A. (1997). *The eye and visual optical instruments*. Cambridge, UK: Cambridge University Press.

Snyder, E. W., & Pronko, N. H. (1952). *Vision with spatial inversion*. Wichita, KS: University of Wichita Press.

Sollenberger, R. L., & Milgram, P. (1993). The effects of stereoscopic and rotational displays in the three-dimensional path tracing task. *Human Factors, 35*(3), 483–500.

Solomon, J. A., & Pelli, D. (1994). The visual filter mediating letter identification. *Nature, 369*, 395–397.

Solstad, T., Boccara, C. N., Kropff, E., Moser, M. B., & Moser, E. I. (2008). Representation of geometric borders in the entorhinal cortex. *Science, 322*(5909), 1865–1868.

Souman, J. L., Frissen, I., Sreenivasa, M. N., & Ernst, M. O. (2009). Walking straight into circles. *Current Biology, 19*(18), 1538–1542.

Spangenberg, R. W. (1973). The motion variable in procedural learning. *AV Communication Review, 21*(4), 419–436.

Spence, R. (2002). Rapid, serial and visual: A presentation technique with potential. *Information Visualization, 1*, 13–19.

Spence, I., & Efendov, A. (2001). Target detection in scientific visualization. *Journal of Experimental Psychology: Applied, 7*(1), 13–26.

Spence, I., Kutlesa, N., & Rose, D. L. (1999). Using color to code quantity in spatial displays. *Journal of Experimental Psychology: Applied, 5*(4), 393–412.

Spence, R., & Witkowski, M. (2013). *Rapid serial visual presentation: Design for cognition.* Heidelberg: Springer.

Sperling, G. (1960). The information available in brief visual presentations. *Psychological Monographs: General and Applied, 74*(11).

St Jean, C., Ware, C., & Gamble, R. (June 2016). Dynamic change arcs to explore model forecasts. *Computer Graphics Forum, 35*(3), 311–320.

Standing, L., Conezio, I., & Haber, R. N. (1970). Perception and memory for pictures: Single trial learning of 2560 visual stimuli. *Psychonomic Science, 19,* 73–74.

Stankiewicz, B. J., Hummerl, J. E., & Cooper, E. E. (1998). The role of attention in priming for left–right reflections of object images: Evidence for a dual representation of object shape. *Journal of Experimental Psychology: Human Perception and Performance, 24,* 732–744.

Stasko, J. T. (1990). Tango: A framework and system for algorithm animation. *IEEE Computer, 23*(9), 27–39.

State, A., Livingston, M. A., Garrett, W. E., Hirotal, G., Whitton, M. C., & Pisano, E. D. (1996). Technologies for augmented reality systems: Realizing ultrasound-guided needle biopsies. In *Proceedings SIGGRAPH* (Vol. 96) (pp. 439–446).

Stenning, K., & Oberlander, J. (1994). A cognitive theory of graphical and linguistic reasoning: Logic and implementation. *Cognitive Science, 19,* 97–140.

Stevens, S. S. (1946). On the theory of scales of measurement. *Science, 103,* 677–680.

Stevens, S. S. (1961). The psychophysics of sensory function. In W. A. Rosenblith (Ed.), *Sensory communication* (pp. 1–33). Cambridge, MA: MIT Press.

Stewart, J., & Kennelly, P. J. (2010). Illuminated choropleth maps. *Annals of the Association of American Geographers, 100*(3), 513–534.

Stoakley, R., Conway, M. J., & Pausch, R. (1995). Virtual reality on a WIM: Interactive worlds in miniature. In *Proc.SIGCHI conference on human factors in computing systems* (pp. 265–272). ACM Press/Addison-Wesley Publishing Co.

Stone, M. C., Cowan, W. B., & Beatty, J. C. (1988). Color gamut mapping and the printing of digital color images. *ACM Transactions on Graphics, 7*(4), 249–292.

Stone, M. C., Fishkin, K., & Bier, E. A. (1994). The movable filter as a user interface tool. In *Proceedings of CHI* (Vol. 94) (pp. 306–312).

Stone, M., Szafir, D. A., & Setlur, V. (2014). An engineering model for color difference as a function of size. In *Color and Imaging Conference* (Vol. 2014, No. 2014, pp. 253–258). Society for Imaging Science and Technology.

Stroop, J. R. (1935). Studies of interference in serial verbal reactions. *Journal of Experimental Psychology, 18,* 643–662.

Strothotte, C., & Strothotte, T. (1997). *Seeing between the pixels.* Berlin: Springer-Verlag.

Sun, E., Staerk, L., Nguyen, A., Wong, J., Lakshminarayanan, V., & Mueller, E. (1988). Changes in accommodation with age: Static and dynamic. *American Journal of Optometry and Physiological Optics, 65*(6), 492–498.

Suwa, M., & Tversky, B. (1997). What do architects perceive in their design sketches? A protocol analysis. *Design Studies, 18,* 385–403.

Suwa, M., & Tversky, B. (2002). External representations contribute to the dynamic construction of ideas. In *Diagrams '02: Proceedings of the second International conference on diagrammatic representation and inference* (pp. 341–343).

Sweet, G., & Ware, C. (2004). View direction, surface orientation and texture orientation for perception of surface shape. In *Proceedings of graphics interface* (Vol. 2004) (pp. 97–106).

Sweller, J., Chandler, P., Tierner, P., & Cooper, G. (1990). Cognitive load as a factor in the structuring of technical material. *Journal of Experimental Psychology, 119*(2), 176–192.

Swets, J. A. (1996). *Signal detection theory and ROC analysis in psychology and diagnostics: Collected papers*. Mahwah, NJ: Erlbaum.

Tabachnick, B. G., & Fidell, L. S. (2001). *Using multivariate statistics* (4th ed.). New York: HarperCollins.

Tarini, M., Cignoni, P., & Claudio Montani, C. (2006). Ambient occlusion and edge cueing to enhance real time molecular visualization. *IEEE Transactions on Visualization and Computer Graphics, 12*(5), 1237–1244.

Telea, A., & Ersoy, O. (2010). Image-based edge bundles: Simplified visualization of large graphs. *Computer Graphics Forum, 29*(3), 843–852.

Theeuwes, J., & Kooi, F. L. (1994). Parallel search for a conjunction of contrast polarity and shape. *Vision Research, 34*(22), 3013–3016.

Thomas, K. M., King, S. W., Franzen, E. L., Welsh, T. E., Berkowitz, A. L., Noll, D. C., et al. (1999). A developmental functional MRI study of spatial working memory. *NeuroImage, 10*, 327–338.

Thorisson, K., Koons, D., & Bolt, R. (1992). Multi-modal natural dialogue. In *Proceedings of CHI* (Vol. 92) (p. 653).

Thorndyke, P. W., & Hayes Roth, B. (1982). Differences in spatial knowledge acquired from maps and navigation. *Cognitive Psychology, 14*, 560–589.

Tittle, J. S., Todd, J. T., Perotti, V. J., & Norman, J. F. (1995). Systematic distortion of perceived three-dimensional structure from motion and binocular stereopsis. *Journal of Experimental Psychology: Human Perception and Performance, 21*(3), 663–687.

Todd, J. T., & Mingolla, E. (1983). Perception of surface curvature and direction of illumination from patterns of shading. *Journal of Experimental Psychology: Human Perception and Performance, 9*(4), 583–595.

Tominski, C., Gladisch, S., Kister, U., Dachselt, R., & Schumann, H. (2014). A survey on interactive lenses in visualization. *EuroVis State-Of-The-Art Reports, 3*(2).

Trafton, J. G., Altmann, E. M., Brock, D. P., & Mintz, F. E. (2003). Preparing to resume an interrupted task: Effects of prospective goal encoding and retrospective rehearsal. *International Journal of Human-Computer Studies, 58*(5), 583–603.

Treisman, A. (1985). Preattentive processing in vision. *Computer Vision, Graphics and Image Processing, 31*, 156–177.

Treisman, A., & Gelade, G. (1980). A feature integration theory of attention. *Cognitive Psychology, 12*, 97–136.

Treisman, A., & Gormican, S. (1988). Feature analysis in early vision: Evidence from search asymmetries. *Psychological Review, 95*(1), 15–48.

Treisman, A., Vieira, A., & Hayes, A. (1992). Automaticity and preattentive processing. *American Journal of Psychology, 105*, 341–362.

Trumbo, B. E. (1981). A theory for coloring bivariate statistical maps. *American Statistician, 35*, 220–226.

Tse, T., Marchionini, G., Ding, W., Slaughter, L., & Komlodi, A. (1998). Dynamic key frame presentation techniques for augmenting video browsing. In *Proceedings of advanced visual interfaces* (pp. 185–194).

Tufte, E. R. (1983). *The visual display of quantitative information.* Cheshire, CT: Graphics Press.

Tufte, E. R. (1990). *Envisioning information.* Cheshire, CT: Graphics Press.

Tulving, E. (1983). *Elements of episodic memory.* Oxford: Oxford University Press.

Tulving, E., & Madigan, S. A. (1970). Memory and verbal learning. *Annual Review of Psychology, 21*, 437–484.

Turk, G., & Banks, D. (1996). Image-guided streamline placement. In *Proceedings SIGGRAPH* (Vol. 96) (pp. 453–460).

Turner, M. R. (1986). Texture discrimination by Gabor functions. *Biological Cybernetics, 55*, 71–82.

Tversky, B., Morrison, J. B., & Betrancourt, M. (2002). Animation: Can it facilitate? *International Journal of Human–Computer Studies, 57*, 247–262.

Tweedie, L. (1997). Characterizing interactive externalizations. In *Proceedings of CHI* (Vol. 97) (pp. 375–382).

Tweedie, L., Spence, R., Dawkes, H., & Su, H. (1996). Externalizing abstract mathematical models. In *Proceedings of CHI* (Vol. 96) (pp. 406–412).

Ullman, S. (1984). Visual routines. *Cognition, 18*, 97–159.

Uomori, K., & Nishida, S. (1994). The dynamics of the visual system in combining conflicting KDE and binocular stereopsis cues. *Perception and Psychophysics, 55*(5), 526–536.

Urness, T., Interrante, V., Longmire, E., Marusic, I., O'Neill, S., & Jones, T. W. (2006). Strategies for the visualization of multiple 2D vector fields. *IEEE Computer Graphics and Applications, 26*(4), 74–82.

de Valois, R. L., & de Valois, K. K. (1975). Neural coding of color. In E. C. Carterette, & M. P. Friedman (Eds.), *Handbook of perception Vol. 5 seeing* (pp. 117–166). New York: Academic Press.

Valyus, N. A. (1966). *Stereoscopy.* (translated from the original). London: Focal Press.

Van Ham, F., & Perer, A. (2009). Search, show context, expand on demand": Supporting large graph exploration with degree-of-interest. *IEEE Transactions on Visualization and Computer Graphics, 15*(6), 953–960.

Venturino, M., & Gagnon, D. (1992). Information trade-offs in complex stimulus structures: Local and global levels in naturalistic scenes. *Perception and Psychophysics, 52*(4), 425–436.

Veron, H., Southard, D. A., Leger, J. R., & Conway, J. L. (1990). Stereoscopic displays of terrain database visualization. In *Proceedings of symposium on interactive 3D graphics* (pp. 39–42).

Viguier, A., Clement, G., & Trotter, Y. (2001). Distance perception within near visual space. *Perception, 30*, 115–124.

Vinson, N. G. (1999). Design guidelines for landmarks to support navigation in virtual environments. In *Proceedings of CHI* (Vol. 99) (pp. 278–285).

Vogel, E. K., Woodman, G. F., & Luck, S. J. (2001). Storage of features, conjunctions and objects in visual working memory. *Journal of Experimental Psychology: Human Perception and Performance, 27*(1), 92–114.

Vygotsky, L. S. (1978). *Mind in society: The development of higher psychological processes.* Cambridge, MA: Harvard University Press.

Wade, N. J., & Swanston, M. T. (1966). A general model for the perception of space and motion. *Perception, 25,* 187–194.

Wadill, P., & McDaniel, M. (1992). Pictorial enhancement of text memory: Limitations imposed by picture type and comprehension skill. *Memory and Cognition, 20*(5), 472–482.

Wainer, H., & Francolini, C. M. (1980). An empirical enquiry concerning human understanding of two variable maps. *American Statistician, 34*(2), 81–93.

Wallach, H. (1959). The perception of motion. *Scientific American, 201,* 56–60.

Wallach, H., & Floor, L. (1971). The use of size matching to demonstrate the effectiveness of accommodation and convergence as cues for distance. *Perception and Psychophysics, 10,* 423–428.

Wallach, H., & Karsh, E. (1963). The modification of stereoscopic depth perception based on oculomotor cues. *Perception and Psychophysics, 11,* 110–116.

Wallach, H., & O'Connell, D. N. (1953). The kinetic depth effect. *Journal of Experimental Psychology, 45,* 205–217.

Wanger, L. (1992). The effect of shadow quality on the perception of spatial relationships in computer-generated images. In *Proceedings of symposium on interactive 3D graphics* (pp. 39–42).

Wanger, L. R., Ferwander, J. A., & Greenberg, D. A. (1992). Perceiving spatial relationships in computer-generated images. *IEEE Computer Graphics and Applications, 12*(3), 44–58.

Wang, Y., & Frost, B. J. (1992). Time to collision is signaled by neurons in the nucleus rotundus of pigeons. *Nature, 356,* 236–238.

Wang, Y., & MacKenzie, C. L. (1999). Object manipulation in virtual environments: Relative size matters. In *Proceedings of CHI* (Vol. 99) (pp. 48–55).

Wang, W., & Milgram, P. (2001). Dynamic viewpoint tethering for navigation in large-scale virtual environments. In *Proceedings of the human factor and ergonomics society* (pp. 1862–1866).

Wann, J. P., Rushton, S. K., & Lee, D. N. (1995). Can you control where you are heading when you are looking at where you want to go? In B. G. Bardy, R. J. Bootsmal, & Y. Guiard (Eds.), *Studies in perception and action III* (pp. 201–210). Hillsdale, NJ: Erlbaum.

Wann, J. P., Rushton, S., & Mon-Williams, M. (1995). Natural problems for stereoscopic depth perception in virtual environments. *Vision Research, 35*(19), 2731–2736.

Ware, C. (1988). Color sequences for univariate maps: Theory, experiments, and principles. *IEEE Computer Graphics and Applications, 8*(5), 41–49.

Ware, C. (1989). Fast hill shading with specular reflection and cast shadows. *Computers and Geosciences, 15,* 1327–1334.

Ware, C. (2008). Towards a perceptual theory of flow visualization. *IEEE Computer Graphics and Applications, 28*(2), 6–11.

Ware, C. (2010). *Visual thinking: For design.* Elsevier.

Ware, C., & Arsenault, R. (2004). Frames of reference in virtual object rotation. In *Proceedings of ACM symposium on applied perception in graphics and visualization* (pp. 135–141).

Ware, C., Arsenault, R., Plumlee, M., & Wiley, D. (2006). Visualizing the underwater behavior of humpback whales. *IEEE Computer Graphics and Applications, 26*(4), 14–18.

Ware, C., Arthur, K. W., & Booth, K. S. (1993). Fish tank virtual reality. In *Proceedings of INTERCHI* (Vol. 93) (pp. 37–42).

Ware, C., & Balakrishnan, R. (1994). Object acquisition in VR displays: Lag and frame rate. *ACM Transactions on Computer Human Interaction, 1*(4), 331–357.

Ware, C., & Beatty, J. C. (1988). Using color dimensions to display data dimensions. *Human Factors, 30*(2), 127–142.

Ware, C., & Bobrow, R. (2004). Motion to support rapid interactive queries on Node-Link diagrams. *ACM Transactions on Applied Perception, 1,* 1–15.

Ware, C., & Bobrow, R. (2005). Supporting visual queries on medium sized node-link diagrams. *Information Visualization, 4*(1), 49–58.

Ware, C., Bolan, D., Miller, R., Rogers, D. H., & Ahrens, J. P. (2016). Animated versus static views of steady flow patterns. In *Proceedings of the ACM symposium on applied perception.* (pp. 77–84). ACM.

Ware, C., Bonner, J., Knight, W., & Cater, R. (1992). Moving icons as a human interrupt. *International Journal of Human–Computer Interaction, 4*(4), 341–348.

Ware, C., & Cowan, W. B. (1982). Changes in perceived color due to chromatic interactions. *Vision Research, 22,* 1353–1362.

Ware, C., & Cowan, W. B. (1987). Chromatic mach bands: Behavioral evidence of lateral inhibition in color vision. *Perception and Psychophysics, 41,* 173–178.

Ware, C., & Cowan, W. B. (1990). The RGYB color geometry. *ACM Transactions on Graphics, 9*(2), 226–232.

Ware, C., & Franck, G. (1996). Evaluating stereo and motion cues for visualizing information nets in three dimensions. *ACM Transactions on Graphics, 15*(2), 121–140.

Ware, C., Gilman, A. T., & Bobrow, R. J. (2008). Visual thinking with an interactive diagram. *Lecture Notes in Artificial Intelligence, 5223,* 118–126.

Ware, C., Gobrecht, C., & Paton, M. (1998). Dynamic adjustment of stereo display parameters. *IEEE Transactions on Systems, Man and Cybernetics, 28*(1), 56–65.

Ware, C., Kelley, J. G., & Pilar, D. (2014). Improving the display of wind patterns and ocean currents. *Bulletin of the American Meteorological Society, 95*(10), 1573–1581.

Ware, C., & Knight, W. (1995). Using visual texture for information display. *ACM Transactions on Graphics, 14*(1), 3–20.

Ware, C., & Lewis, M. (1995). The DragMag image magnifier. In *Proceedings of CHI* (Vol. 95) (pp. 407–408).

Ware, C., & Mikaelian, H. (1987). An evaluation of an eye tracker as a device for computer input. In *Proceedings of CHI* (Vol. 87) (pp. 183–188).

Ware, C., & Mitchell, P. (2008). Visualizing graphs in three dimensions. *ACM Transactions on Applied Perception*, 5(1), 1–15.

Ware, C. (2009). Quantitative texton sequences for legible bivariate maps. *IEEE Transactions on Visualization and Computer Graphics*, 15(6), 1523–1530.

Ware, C., & Osborne, S. (1990). Explorations and virtual camera control in virtual three-dimensional environments. *Computer Graphics*, 24(2), 175–183.

Ware, C., Plumlee, M., Arsenault, R., Mayer, L. A., Smith, S., & House, D. (2001). Geo-Zui3D: Data fusion for interpreting oceanographic data. In *Proceedings of oceans* (Vol. 2001) (pp. 1960–1964).

Ware, C., Purchase, H., Colpoys, L., & McGill, M. (2002). Cognitive measurements of graph aesthetics. *Information Visualization*, 1, 103–110.

Ware, C., & Rose, J. (1999). Rotating virtual objects with real handles. *ACM Transactions on CHI*, 6(2), 162–180.

Ware, C., TurtonK, T. L., Bujack, R., Samsel, F., Shrivastava, P., & Rogers, D. H. (2018). Measuring and modeling the feature detection threshold functions of colormaps. *IEEE Transactions on Visualization and Computer Graphics*.

Ware, C., Wright, W., & Pioch, N. J. (2013). Visual thinking design patterns. *In DMS*, 150–155.

Warren, W. H. (1984). Perceiving affordances: Visual guidance of stair climbing. *Journal of Experimental Psychology: Human Perception and Performance*, 10, 683–703.

Warrick, M. S., Kibler, A., Topmiller, D. H., & Bates, C. (1964). Response time to unexpected stimuli. *American Psychologist*, 19, 528.

Watanabe, T., & Cavanaugh, P. (1996). Texture laciness: The texture equivalent of transparency. *Perception*, 25, 293–303.

Watson, A. B., & Ahumada, A. J. (2015). Letter identification and the neural image classifier. *Journal of Vision*, 15(2), 15.

Weigle, C., Emigh, W., Liu, G., Taylor, R., Enns, J., & Healey, C. (2000). Oriented texture slivers: A technique for local value estimation of multiple scalar fields. In *Proceedings of graphics interface 2000* (pp. 163–170).

Welch, R. B. (1978). *Perceptual modification: Adapting to altered sensory environments*. New York: Academic Press.

Welch, R. B., & Cohen, M. M. (1991). Adaptation to variable prismatic displacement. In S. R. Ellis (Ed.), *Pictorial communication in virtual and real environments* (pp. 295–304). London: Taylor & Francis.

Wenderoth, P. (1994). The salience of vertical symmetry. *Perception*, 23, 221–236.

Wertheimer, M. (1959). *Productive thinking*. New York: Harper Torchbooks.

Wetherill, G. B., & Levitt, H. (1965). Sequential estimation of points on a psychometric function. *British Journal of Mathematical and Statistical Psychology*, 18, 1–10.

Wheeler, M. E., & Treisman, A. (2002). Binding in short-term visual memory. *Journal of Experimental Psychology: General*, 131, 48–64.

Wickens, C. D. (1992). *Engineering psychology and human performance* (2nd ed.). New York: HarperCollins.

Wickens, C. D. (1999). Frames of reference for navigation. In D. Gopher, & A. Koriat (Eds.), *Attention and performance* (pp. 113–144). Cambridge, MA: MIT Press.

Wickens, C. D., Haskell, I., & Harte, K. (1989). Ergonomic design for perspective flight path displays. *IEEE Control Systems Magazine, 9*(4), 3–8.

van Wijk, J. J., & Telea, A. (2001). Enridged contour maps. In *Proceedings of IEEE visualization conference* (pp. 69–74).

van Wijk, J. J., & van de Wetering, H. (1999). Cushion treemaps. In *Proceedings of IEEE information visualization conference* (pp. 73–78).

Wildemuth, B. M., Marchionini, G., Yang, M., Geisler, G., Wilkens, T., Hughes, A., et al. (2003). How fast is too fast? Evaluating fast forward surrogates for digital video. In *Proceedings of the 3rd ACM/IEEE-CS joint conference on digital libraries* (pp. 185–194).

Wilkins, A. (1995). *Visual stress*. Oxford: Oxford University Press.

Williams, L. J. (1985). Tunnel vision induced by a foveal load manipulation. *Human Factors, 27*(2), 221–227.

Williams, A. J., & Harris, R. L. (1985). *Factors affecting dwell times on digital displays*. Technical Memorandum 86406. Langley, VA: NASA.

Williams, M. D., & Hollan, J. D. (1981). The process of retrieval from very long-term memory. *Cognitive Science, 5*, 87–119.

Williams, S. P., & Parrish, R. V. (1990). New computational control techniques and increased understanding for stereo 3-D displays. In *Proceedings of SPIE* (Vol. 1256) (pp. 73–82).

Willis, J. (1995). A recursive, reflective instruction design model based on constructivist–interpretivist theory. *Educational Technology, 35*(6), 5–23.

Wilson, C. (2013). *User interface inspection methods: A user-centered design method*. Newnes.

Wilson, H. R., & Bergen, J. R. (1979). A four mechanism model for threshold spatial vision. *Vision Research, 19*, 19–32.

Wise, J. A., Thomas, J. J., Pennock, K., Lantrip, D., Pottier, M., Schur, A., et al. (1995). Visualizing the non-visual: Spatial analysis and interaction with information and text documents. In *Proceedings of IEEE information visualization conference* (pp. 51–58).

Witkin, A., & Kass, M. (1991). Reaction diffusion textures. In *Proceedings of the 18th annual conference on computer graphics and interactive techniques* (pp. 299–308).

Wittenburg, K., Ali-Ahmad, W., LaLiberte, D., & Lanning, T. (1998). Rapid-fire image previews for information navigation. In *Proceedings of advanced visual interfaces* (pp. 76–82).

Wittgenstein, L. (1953). *Philosophical Investigations*. Oxford, UK: Blackwell.

Wolfe, J. M., & Gancarz, G. G. (1996). Guided search 3.0: A model of visual search catches up with Jay enoch 40 years later. In V. Lakshminarayanan (Ed.), *Basic and clinical application of visual science* (pp. 189–192). Dordrecht: Kluwer Academic.

Wolfe, J. M., & Horowitz, T. S. (2004). Opinion: What attributes guide the deployment of visual attention and how do they do it? *Nature Reviews. Neuroscience, 5*(6), 495.

Wolfe, J. M., Horowitz, T. S., Van Wert, M. J., Kenner, N. M., Place, S. S., & Kibbi, N. (2007). Low target prevalence is a stubborn source of errors in visual search tasks. *Journal of Experimental Psychology: General, 136*(4), 623–638.

Wong, P. C., & Bergeron, R. D. (1997). Multivariate visualization using metric scaling. In *Proceedings of IEEE visualization conference* (pp. 111–118).

Wyszecki, G., & Stiles, W. S. (1982). *Color science concepts and methods, quantitative data and formulae* (2nd ed.). New York: Wiley Interscience.

Xu, Y. (2002). Limitations of object-based features encoding in visual short-term memory. *Journal of Experimental Psychology: Human Perception and Performance, 28*(2), 458–468.

Yantis, S. (1992). Multielement visual tracking: Attention and perceptual organization. *Cognitive Psychology, 24*, 295–340.

Yates, E. A. (1966). *The art of memory*. Chicago: University of Chicago Press.

Yeh, Y., & Silverstein, L. D. (1990). Limits of fusion and depth judgment in stereoscopic color displays. *Human Factors, 32*(1), 45–60.

Yoshimura, T., Nakamura, Y., & Sugiura, M. (1994). 3D direct manipulation interface: Development of the Zashiki–Warashi system. *Computers and Graphics, 18*(2), 201–207.

Young, M. J., Landy, M. S., & Maloney, L. T. (1993). A perturbation analysis of depth perception from combinations of texture and motion cues. *Vision Research, 33*, 2685–2696.

Young, E. W., Takane, Y., & de Leeuw, J. (1978). The principal components of mixed measurement level multivariate data: An alternating least squares method with optimal scaling features. *Psychometrika, 43*, 279–281.

Yufic, Y. M., & Sheridan, T. B. (1996). Virtual networks: New framework for operator modeling and interface optimization in complex supervisory control systems. *Annual Review of Control, 20*, 179–195.

Zeiler, M. D., & Fergus, R. (2014). Visualizing and understanding convolutional networks. In *European conference on computer vision* (pp. 818–833). Springer.

Zeki, S. (1992). The visual image in mind and brain. *Scientific American, 267*(3), 69–76.

Zeki, S. (1993). *A vision of the brain*. Oxford: Blackwell.

Zhai, S., Buxton, W., & Milgram, P. (1994). The "silk cursor": Investigating transparency for 3D target acquisition. In *Proceedings of CHI* (Vol. 94) (pp. 459–464).

Zhang, J. (1997). The nature of external representations in problem solving. *Cognitive Science, 21*(2), 179–217.

Zhang, H., Zherdeva, K., & Ekstrom, A. D. (2014). Different "routes" to a cognitive map: Dissociable forms of spatial knowledge derived from route and cartographic map learning. *Memory & Cognition, 42*(7), 1106–1117.

Zuanazzi, A., & Noppeney, U. (2018). Additive and interactive effects of spatial attention and expectation on perceptual decisions. *Scientific Reports, 8*.

Author Index

Note: Page numbers followed by "f" indicates figures, "t" indicates tables.

Subject Index

Note: Page numbers followed by "f" indicates figures, "t" indicates tables, and "b" indicates boxes.